Communities Directory

A Guide to Cooperative Living

WITHDRAWN

Communities Directory

A Guide to Cooperative Living

1995 Edition
(revised for 1996)

Published by
Fellowship for Intentional Community
Rutledge, Missouri

With financial support from the following sources:
Federation of Egalitarian Communities
Community Catalyst Project
Sandhill Farm

Printed on 100% recycled unbleached paper

ISBN 0-9602714-4-9

Second Edition, Second Printing, June 1996

Printed by Cushing-Malloy, Ann Arbor, Michigan, U.S.A.

The following articles are reprinted here, after appearing in the first edition of this directory:
How to Visit an Intentional Community
Consensus Ingredients
Legal Options for Intentional Communities

The following articles are reprinted with permission:
A Word about Cults
Copyright © 1985 by Corinne McLaughlin and Gordon Davidson.
The Tyranny of Structurelessness
Copyright © 1975 by The Second Wave. All rights reserved.
Community as Crucible first appeared in *Circles of Strength*, copyright © 1993 by Helen Forsey.
Movers of Mountains, Shapers of Worlds first appeared in *Communities* magazine, issue number 84, 1994.
Intentional Communities as Laboratories for Learning about Direct Democracy first appeared in *Communities* magazine, issue number 80/81, 1993.

Cover Design and Layout: Rick Bickhart
Cover Photos
    Front: 100 Mile Lodge (all)
    Back: 100 Mile Lodge (left)
        Jonathan Roth of Twin Oaks (right)
Layout Design: Geoph Kozeny, Jillian Downey, and Elph Morgan
    based on previous work by Geoph Kozeny

How to Use This Directory to Find an Intentional Community

YOUR APPROPRIATE PATHS in using this directory will depend on
- what you already know about (or seek in) a community,
- whether you're looking for a specific group (one you already know something about), or
- if you're interested in any group that satisfies a number of characteristics.

Do You Know the Name?

Look for a description in the Listings, which begin on page 211, and the cross-reference Chart (sorted alphabetically by community name), which begins on page 189. If you don't find it there, try the list of communities that are "Renamed, Regrouped, Dead, Disbanded, Lost, & No Replies," which begins on page 327. If the community is outside North America, check the International Listings, which begin on page 341, and the international cross-reference Chart (sorted alphabetically), which begins on page 342.

Do You Know the Geographic Region?

Look at the Maps beginning on page 177 to locate the North American groups in this directory, or the Key to Communities by State/Province (sorted by country, and alphabetically within state or province), which begins on page 187. If the community is outside North America, go to the list on page 344, which sorts communities by country, arranged alphabetically. After you know the name, use the instructions above.

Do You Know Some Defining Characteristics?

Examine the cross-reference Chart beginning on page 189. Hopefully, the specific characteristics you're seeking are among those reviewed in the Chart. If the community is outside North America, study the international cross-reference Chart, which begins on page 341. If a desired characteristic does not appear in the Chart, try locating relevant keywords in the Index, starting on page 417.

Still Can't Find It?

If you followed the steps outlined above and didn't get to a pot of gold, there are still other possibilities.

Some groups have chosen to downplay their living situation in deference to their "work." Check through the Resources section for groups that are doing things in line with your interests but may not put themselves forward as a community.

If you still can't find it, we suggest you write us or call with your specific request. We've gathered file cabinets full of information—far more than we could possibly include in this directory—and it's possible that at our office we still have something for you. There are, for example, over 150 groups that reported that they "still exist as a community, but don't wish to be listed at this time." Instructions on how to place a request for information and/or referrals are outlined on page 438.

In addition to the *Directory*, we publish *Communities* magazine. A regular feature of this quarterly is a Directory Update section, where we include all the new and revised listings that we collect over the three months between issues. If you subscribe to *Communities* you'll be getting all the latest information, just as soon as it comes into print. See page 440 for subscription information.

Another choice is to purchase annual supplements to the *Directory*. For a one-time fee of $5, we'll send you annual compilations of all the new and revised community listings, for as long as this edition lasts. See the card at the back of the book or page 438 for details about this offer.

Finally—you may have information about a group that we don't know about. If so, please let us know! We'd like to invite their participation in future listings. Please use the appropriate card bound at the back of the book to share any new leads you have. Thanks!

Table of Contents

THE LISTINGS
North American Intentional Communities

International Intentional Communities

Resources

APPENDIX

Welcome...

...TO THE SECOND EDITION of the Fellowship's *Communities Directory*, and the twelfth directory published in a series started by *Communities* magazine in 1972. It's been four years and 18,000 copies since we released the last one, and here we are again.

For those of you acquainted with the Fellowship's first effort, there will be a lot that's familiar. Once again, we've completed work later than intended; once again we were able to draw together more listings than expected; once again we've overworked our production staff; and once again we think we've produced the best directory ever created.

The basic layout is the same as last time, with some notable improvements. In particular, we've expanded the information in the cross-reference Chart, and added breathing space to the Chart layout, hopefully making it more useful and more usable. We're also initiating a *Directory Update* option for everyone who wants to stay current with the latest listings and address changes. See page 438 for details about this.

State of the Movement

Four years is how long U.S. Presidents are given before undergoing a major review (it's called voting), and this seems an appropriate interval to reflect on developments in the communities movement. The first point to make is that interest in community—in all its forms—is growing tremendously.

Witness—

- We are in the midst of the biggest wave of inquiries about community and announcements of new starts in 20 years (we know because many of these come our way, and *somebody* is buying all these *Directories*).
- When the Fellowship hosted the Celebration of Community in August 1993, over 800 people attended, making it the largest intentional community gathering ever held.
- Cohousing has burst onto the scene, introducing large segments of the population to the advantages of resource sharing, the tools to design thriving neighborhoods, and the flexibility to combine private space for individuals with public space for group dynamics—in short, the promise of community.
- M. Scott Peck's books remain bestsellers years after their release, and one of his main messages is the important link between community building and peacemaking, starting at home and working up to the global.
- Getting back to Presidents, when Bill Clinton was elected in 1992, he used the "c"-word (that's "community" if you're keeping score at home) at least three times in his acceptance speech.

Now that you're convinced that community is hot, what, you may ask, is different? I've already mentioned cohousing. A big media splash has accompanied the arrival of this Danish import, and the number of operating groups has mushroomed. While we had an article on this phenomenon in the last edition, we didn't list a single cohousing community; this time we're listing 15 established and 20 forming, plus five cohousing resource groups. From the movement perspective, the most exciting aspect of this surge is that lots of people are getting a first taste of community, and the amazing array of options available in cooperative living.

While most groups listing in the *Directory* are open to new members, many have struggled to absorb all the seekers that have materialized in recent years, and new construction has lagged behind the demand for space. Many communities have reported lighting the "no vacancy" sign for the first time in years, if ever. This has spurred many seekers to become do-it-yourselfers and form new communities. It has also inspired a few established groups to spin off sister communities.

- Twin Oaks accumulated a waiting list of over 30, and chose to underwrite a new community rather than create temporary housing for all the new people. Acorn started in late 1992, a mere bike ride away.

- Short Mountain couldn't handle all those seeking residency in recent years, and during one of their fall festivals, some of those on the waiting list coalesced a new group. IDA sprang up in October 1993, just down the road from the older group—farther than a holler away, yet close enough to come by regularly for saunas and potlucks.
- Space limitations at Shannon Farm inspired some there to join with ex-Twin Oakers and others to create Deer Rock in 1994—just a few miles over a nearby ridge line.

The Movement's Growing Edge

While no region is reporting a cooling off in community interest, some places have clearly heated up. The western halves of Virginia and North Carolina, the southern portions of Minnesota and Wisconsin, southern Arizona around Tucson, and all parts of Colorado have pushed the needle on our community Richter scale.

From a network perspective, one of the most exciting shifts in the movement has been the increased willingness of groups in struggle—whether new or established—to ask for outside help. There used to be a stubborn "by golly we can solve all our own problems" attitude, or even an "it doesn't really count unless we do it alone" mind-set. Groups today though, are looking around for additional thinking. Especially on topics like consensus and other forms of inclusive decision making, group conflict, organizational structure, and community building.

Wonderfully enough, there is a matching rise in the number of people putting themselves forward with these skills. Last edition of the *Directory* we had no one advertising these services, and now we have nearly a dozen. Many communities report asking for help for the first time. At the same time, it's easier than ever to find out what others are doing, given this new *Directory*, the revival of *Communities* magazine, and a variety of new books about the connection between community and the quality of life. Networking is so self-reinforcing that it's hard to tell if the demand was always there or not. Fortunately, it doesn't matter.

With all the increased flow of information about and among communities, established groups are making a substantial difference for newer ones in the areas of land tenure, financing, and legal structure. Tax codes, zoning restrictions, corporation laws, and bank loan requirements were all created without communities in mind, and in consequence, groups often struggle to figure out how they can best get their financial and legal needs met. Movement connections are helping in two ways:

First, older groups are making available the creative and sometimes hard-earned solutions they've evolved to meet these challenges. This gives new groups something to start with, often saving them the trouble of being their own wheelwrights. You'll find articles in this directory that touch on some of this.

Second, some groups and networks are now making surplus funds available to others in the movement, recognizing the value of extending to each other something more substantial than moral support and technical advice. And it's more than just doing unto others—loaning funds to other communities can be good business! After all, who is in a better position to fully assess the complex social and financial factors in a community loan application than people from successful communities? The Fellowship, for example, is developing its own Community Loan Fund to take advantage of this expertise (see page 103 for more details on this). We expect this trend toward inter-movement cooperation to continue, and look for increased sophistication in identifying needs and matching them with pre-invented wheels, already in stock.

On the near horizon, there are two poorly met needs within the movement that are gaining attention: people with multiple chemical sensitivities (known to some as environmental illness) and those needing assistance for mental and/or emotional disabilities. Sometimes it's a seeker who cannot find a suitable home, and sometimes it's a community trying to get help for a struggling member.

In either case, there have been only isolated attempts to develop responses and organize resources to meet these challenges. It seems likely that awareness of these two issues will continue to grow, and it remains to be seen how well the movement will respond. You can keep abreast of new developments by reading *Communities* magazine—we'll let you know as the story unfolds.

That's an overview of what we're seeing on the movement level, and where we think it's headed. On the personal level, it's our hope that the *Directory* will help *you* get from where you are to where you want to go.

Acknowledgments:
A Tip of the Hard Hat to the Intrepid Crew That Crafted This Labor of Love
[*Communities Directory*, erected A.D. MCMXCV]

Now THAT the ribbon's been cut, we can all smile and admire the overall effect. In the true tradition of major construction projects, there have been delays, cost overruns, and occasional misunderstandings about who was doing what—but all those fade into the background now that the finished product is ready for use. Before moving in your furniture I ask you to take a moment and acknowledge the long, unglamorous hours that underlay the construction of this handsome directory. Here's to the team that put this thing together!

Knowing the importance of a high-quality finished product, we relied heavily on our experience from building the last *Directory*. It helped enormously that we could start with serviceable blueprints from that effort (sure we tinkered with the design, but we didn't have to go back to scribbling on napkins, like we did in '88). Since we were using many of the same crew, we benefited from having already worked through some major challenges in labor relations (not to mention the intricacies of long-distance electronic editing).

The foundation upon which the *Directory* rests is the Community Listings. Given the volatile and shifting nature of the information, it's a tricky problem engineering a strong and stable base. Geoph Kozeny, our master mason, has worked long and hard to develop and maintain the most comprehensive and accurate database possible. And since he was collecting bricks and mixing mortar anyway, he also organized the Resource section of this edifice.

Naturally, Geoph had a lot of help hauling in the new materials, and we hereby present a framed certificate of appreciation to the members of our telephone survey crew: Valerie Edra, John Arkin, Loren Schein, SYD Fredrickson, Delia Davila, Ella Peregrine, Rob Sandelin, Tim Miller, Lois Arkin, Craig Green, Bonnie Fish, and a host of Twin Oakers—Valerie, Nexus, Christie, Marione, Rneé, Joan, Helen, Spoon, Lee Ann, Alex, and Karen. SYD has also earned an engraved wall plaque for having singlehandedly organized the initial solicitation mailing, back in the spring of 1992.

In this line of work, most listings are delivered one at a time, and the ones we got often needed cleaning up before we could set them in place. Several people had a hand in massaging the data into clarity and consistency, and Tyler Kemp did yeoperson duty in this regard.

While Geoph's foundation work was demanding, he also dabbled in other phases of construction. He framed and did the finish work for the Listings section, the Resources section, and for the Index, and, at the end, walked around with a nail set, putting the final touches on the camera-ready copy.

Alex McGee took a week out of her life to travel to Ann Arbor and hand craft the Maps.

The elegant Feature Article wing was framed by master editor Dan Questenberry, operating out of Shannon Farm. His crew included Julie Mazo, Virgil Cater, and Harvey Baker.

The camera-ready boards were sheetrocked by the dedicated and talented Ann Arbor team of Jillian Downey and Elph Morgan, headquartered at Hei Wa House. They got last-minute Appendix help from layout specialist Paul DeLapa, who gave the back porch some clean lines and coherence. Elph also finished the most intricate room in the building, the cross-reference Charts. No one in the crew has a finer eye for detail, so it was an easy choice to assign him there. The Chart data arrived in waves, over many months, and all of it was hand set into its allotted place in Elph's computer. Those data entry hands belonged to Christine Chumbler, Lorna Koestner, Laura Silver, Heather Abramson, Irit Kleiman, Melissa Chiu, and Jill Reinstein.

Interior design was handled again by Jenny Upton, also out of Shannon Farm. She went from room to room with her color chips, cheerfully and tastefully matching graphics with text.

The facade was ably handled by Rick Bickhart. It's the second time we've used him for the cover design and you'll probably recognize his "look" from last time.

Financing was easier this time, as we were substantially able to pay for the printing with money made from sales of the first edition. It also helped that we had Diana Christian renting out space in the new building before it was complete. Her advertising sales helped the cash flow considerably.

10

As you know, it's hard to live in a house before it's built, and we gratefully acknowledge the shelter provided our itinerant workers. In particular, Geoph, who has been on the road since 1988 and adds new dimension to the term "journeyman," was made welcome at several sites during the course of construction. For providing at least a work week's worth of office space, plus all else that they did for him, we extend a special pat on the back to Deborah Altus, Allen Butcher, Nancy Derthick, Chris Paine, Bob Poeschl, Ginny and Don Aldrich, Sandhill Farm, Shannon Farm, Purple Rose, East Wind, Twin Oaks, Alpha Farm, Hei Wa House, and Hearthaven.

Finally, thanks again to Steve Kehoe, our printer liaison in Ann Arbor, for indefatigable good humor in the face of our shifting deadlines. Our imprecision never seemed to wreck Steve's day.

I am proud of the high morale of the crew and the solid quality of the work turned in. We tried to get everything just right, but I'm sure you'll have ideas for how we could have made it better (the customer always does!). There's a Feedback Survey on page 411, and we encourage you to use it. We're always trying to build better, and we need your ideas.

Meanwhile, we've been able to keep the cost of ownership down to 20 dollars; that's 25 percent more than last time, but there are 44 percent more listings and 34 percent more pages. It's still a solid value. You'll find the key to the front door on page 5. Hopefully this purchase will play an important part in your search for the good life—it may not be Utopia, but maybe you can see it from here.

Laird Sandhill, Foreperson
(...and believe me, there were several days when it would have helped to have been four persons)

How You Can Help

Communities magazine invites you to help us help each other.

Reader Involvement: Feedback enables us to take your opinions and preferences into consideration as we continue to refine and improve our publications and services. We encourage you to send letters to the editor on any topic related to the *Directory*, community, or cooperative living. We will print your contribution as space allows in future issues of *Communities*.

Editorial Support: In addition to letters, we invite your participation and editorial input on future issues of the magazine. For the ambitious, we have opportunities for guest editors of future issues, organizing articles around a certain theme. For those who have an intriguing idea, experience, or story about some aspect of community, please consider submitting an article for consideration.

If you have photos or drawings which accompany your writing, so much the better. If you have compelling community graphics which are unattached to any writing, we're interested in those as well—perhaps we can match them up with submissions that are graphically impaired.

Advertising Support: If you have a product or service that would be of interest to our readers, please consider placing an ad with us. See page 436 for a copy of our advertising rate sheet.

Subscription/Distribution: We need the help of communities, cooperative organizations, and communitarians everywhere. If you are not a subscriber, please take a moment to fill out the subscription form on page 440 right now. You can also help us by distributing flyers and by suggesting that the bookstores, libraries, and health food stores in your area carry *Communities*. If you publish a newsletter or magazine, you could help by running a promotional blurb about us. If you have a community center or storefront where you could sell copies or display flyers, we would be happy to pay you a commission for every sale and subscription you generate. Another way you can help us and a friend is to give a gift subscription to *Communities*. Or you can make a tax-deductible donation to help *Communities* continue to grow and prosper. We promise to make each dollar count. For details about any or all of the opportunities above, please contact:

Communities magazine, Rt 1 Box 155-D, Rutledge, MO 63563
Phone: 816-883-5545

What This Directory Is...and Isn't

THE EDITORIAL STAFF of the *Directory* worked long and hard to include information about as many intentional communities as possible. We believe it to be the most comprehensive directory ever produced. And yet we know that there are many, many communities that are not listed, despite our best efforts.

The fact is, many communities are not looking for contact with others, or prefer that referrals come only by word of mouth. Some groups worry that exposure in the *Directory* will generate too much attention, and too many visitors. In other cases, a community has been created to meet the specific needs of its members who are more or less happy with what they have. All in all, we've been in touch with about 150 existing groups that prefer to remain unlisted.

The communities we've included are those which (within limits) do want contact with others. They may be looking for more members, they may be curious to find other groups doing similar things, or they may simply be willing to talk about what works for them.

What Is an "Intentional Community"?

We've been wrestling with this question since forever, as you can see by reading "Who We Are: An Exploration of What 'Intentional Community' Means," on page 33. Given that there is no uniformly accepted definition and that we have no staff for verifying claims, we chose to let communities define themselves. Basically, any group of two or more adults that chose to call itself a community was welcome to participate.

We didn't want to be in the role of passing judgment on others, or deciding which styles of community were more worthy than others. Since the criteria for such comparisons vary from one person to the next, the responsibility for evaluating the information and determining which leads to pursue has been left to you, the reader.

We asked communities to submit listings only if they did not advocate violent practices or interfere with members' freedom to leave the group at any time—but we left it to each community to determine, in its own view, whether they were in compliance.

To the best of our knowledge, we have included no community that has standards contrary to either of these two basic principles. At the same time, it is important to note that very little of the information in the *Directory* has been confirmed by first-hand observation of our staff. We have included only information that has been recently verified (as of the date at the end of each listing) by someone representing the community or organization—*we have made no attempt to independently assess the accuracy of their statements and representations.*

If you find community descriptions or contact information to be inaccurate or misleading, please let us know. There is a Directory Additions & Corrections card bound at the back of the book and we depend on reader responses to help us keep our information as up-to-date as possible. If the problem is a factual error and there is no dispute, we simply make the correction in our master file and notify readers in print at the next opportunity. However, if there is disagreement about what is going on, and the community doesn't agree with the complaint, then we open a Feedback File on that community that includes statements from all parties. For a fee of $1 per community, we'll provide summaries of what's in the file for any given group. Keep in mind, though, that we seldom get complaints of this nature, and for the overwhelming number of listed communities there will be nothing in the file. If you want to make a request for feedback about a given community, please see the instructions on page 438.

"Forming" Communities

As agents of change and voices for lifestyle options, intentional communities are a particularly volatile component of society. They change a lot—especially communities that are not yet settled. Given our interest in having up-to-date information, we struggled with the question of whether to include forming communities at all...since much of their information will have changed by the time you read their listing. The rate of change (and disbandments) for forming groups is typically much higher than that of more established groups.

Despite this concern, we have decided to include forming communities because (1) it is important to illustrate as fully as possible the breadth of the alternatives available (or being attempted); and (2) many new communities fail for lack of energy provided by prospective members, or insufficient support from established groups with similar goals and approaches. We hope that the *Directory* will play an important role in fulfilling both of these needs.

Having decided to include them, we still had to define them. Again we were faced with the dilemma of having subjective terminology; what some consider stable may appear unsettled to others. For this directory we have labeled as "forming" any community describing itself as such, any community with fewer than four adult members, and any group that has not lived together for at least a year.

In many cases, forming communities have only recently coalesced and are looking to grow—but that is not always the case. Sometimes a group has been around quite a while, yet is still working to settle one or more key questions about how to develop. Other groups with this classification were once well established, but have now shrunk and may be wavering between continuing and disbanding.

We have designated forming communities by the ingenious method of printing "(Forming)" after their names in the Listings section, and by labeling them with an "[F]" in the Index and in the Chart.

Reader Beware...

It can't be overemphasized that the groups depicted in this directory are not Utopias realized. Many of them are quite wonderful places to live and work, places where the residents share a common vision or purpose. Most are ripe with good intentions and dedication, and are fertile environments for personal growth and work toward the greater good. Most also suffer occasional bouts of such human failings as egocentric behavior, power struggles, miscommunication, and unrealistic expectations.

The *Directory* is a forum that allows each group to share its vision, and it's natural that most groups want to put their best foot forward. It's up to each reader to assess the information that describes each group—and try to identify what statements are part of the "grand plan," and which ones reflect the day-to-day reality. May your search be interesting and fruitful.

Full-Spectrum Articles

In the pages immediately following, we are pleased to present 31 feature articles about various aspects of community living, grouped by subject area. We've included nine reprints all together—five from the last *Directory* edition, two that appeared first in *Communities* magazine, and two from other sources—the rest of the articles are original works.

In soliciting articles, we indicated our openness to the full range of community choices and viewpoints. We specified only that "community" be the unifying theme, and that articles be more informative and engaging than promotional and laudatory.

We feel that this collection gives a valuable overview of community living, yet we are aware that all views and topics worthy of attention are not represented. Even though everyone was invited, not everyone was inspired. And in the end we could only choose from among what was submitted.

We invite you to turn the page and sample what we've collected. Our intent is to be more stimulating than definitive. So we ask you to see these articles not as a final word, but as a point of departure. Community is a full participation activity, and we want you to be part of the process.

How to Do a Communities Directory

(Or the Story behind Some of the Things We've Done Differently This Time Around)

IN PRODUCING this second edition of the *Directory*, we took substantial advantage of the successful format we created for the first one. For all the similarities though, we did tinker with some of the features, and we thought you might enjoy a glimpse at what we took into account in making those changes. Below is a selection of some of the more interesting wrinkles we faced with this edition, and the story behind our creative attempts to iron them out.

Should we charge communities and resources for listings? We didn't. We wanted participation as full as we could get, and were afraid that many smaller groups—who make up the vast majority—would not pay to be included. At the same time, we had trouble during compilation of the previous edition, editing listings down to a reasonable length (it was amazing how many words people thought would fit into a 200-word limit). We neatly solved that problem this time—and helped finance production costs into the bargain—by offering a basic listing free (36 lines for communities and 28 lines for resources) and charging $3/line beyond that.

What price should we set for the Directory? This is a bone we worried over quite a lot. On the one hand, we're concerned about accessibility and getting as wide a distribution as possible. On the other hand, the profits from this book underwrite everything else the Fellowship does, like paying staff salaries, publishing *Communities* magazine, subsidizing board-member travel to network meetings, etc.—we have no trouble thinking up worthy ways to spend the money.

We sold the later printings of the last edition at $16, and met with little price resistance—people found it a bargain. Because this edition has 44 percent more listings and more than 100 additional pages, we've decided to bump the price to $20 for individuals. While we think this book is readily worth $30, we are holding in view that each dollar can mean a lot for some of the folks whom this directory might help the most. For institutions we are charging the full $30, figuring they'll get wider circulation out of it and can generally better afford it.

This is an unusual way to price a book. Magazines do it all the time (set a different price for individuals and institutions), but books generally go with one price. We thought split pricing fit our circumstances better, so we did it.

How do we handle complaints about listed communities? Now here we have a hornets' nest. Based on our experience with the first edition, we know that users were overwhelmingly pleased with what they got. Sure, there were inaccuracies, yet most of these—misprints, changes of address and phone number, even groups disbanding—were innocent enough and to be expected. More troubling were the small number of complaints we got about communities coming across as substantially different than their listings promised.

Occasionally we got reports that a community had misrepresented themselves in their listing, and people felt confused and angry about it. Often they had invested precious time and money in getting to a place, only to find it was quite different than expected. They were upset and wanted to warn others away from a similar disappointment. Beyond seeing to it that the criticism got back to the community—in as constructive a form as we could manage—what should we have done?

Our basic approach to all networking is to assume that people are telling the truth, as they know it. As experienced communitarians, we know that the same event can produce amazingly different experiences for different people. What is sacred to one can be profane to another; it's not a matter of being perverse or malicious. We take the view that it is not the Fellowship's role to arbitrate reality, or decide where the "truth" lies in such disputes. Where, after all, would we start?

We don't have the staff to verify the accuracy of community self-descriptions (leaving aside the interesting question of why people should place more stock in our version of the "truth," even if we had one). Even so, does that absolve us from responsibility for printing a listing that some people find misleading or distorted? If we establish a policy of indicating in print that we've received critical feedback about a community, that could be devastating to its reputation—even if we didn't print what the criticism was. Thinking this through, we realized that the communities would likely ask us to question just as carefully the accuracy of the complaint, if not the motivation of the complainer. Quickly, the whole deal got to be a colossal headache.

So we chose another path: we will welcome complaints, and try to promote constructive dialog between the complainer and the community, with the goal of reducing disagreement to the extent possible. If everything gets resolved in a mutually satisfactory manner, fine. If not, all views of the residual disagreement will go into a Feedback File on that community, the contents of which we'll summarize for inquirers upon request. To cut down on casual requests, and make some attempt to compensate for the time it takes to process them, we are charging $1 per community. See page 438 for information on where to send feedback or how to request what exists in the Feedback File for particular communities.

Stay tuned to see if we can stay upright on the feedback tightrope.

Guidelines for Contacting and Visiting Communities

WE'RE CONFIDENT this directory will stimulate inquiries and visits to intentional communities—a development that most communities will welcome. Based on our collective experience with seekers and communities, we offer the following guidance on how to make contacts and visits work well for everyone.

Correspondence

When writing, it's usually a good practice to include a self-addressed, stamped envelope (SASE) and a small donation. These are invariably appreciated, and in some cases they're expected (if we know this to be the case, we have included a note at the end of the group's description).

Unfortunately, not all communities answer all inquiries promptly. There are a variety of reasons for this—sometimes groups are swamped with inquiries; sometimes groups are not currently interested in additional members; sometimes other events have completely overshadowed answering the mail (financial crisis, medical emergency, tension within the group); sometimes letters simply get misplaced or lost. We asked communities, "Can you commit to answering correspondence promptly?" For the groups which answered negatively we have included the code "[cc]" at the end of their listings. So please take note.

The letters most likely to be answered promptly are those which are personable, short to medium in length, and pose interesting and/or thought-provoking questions. Most communities are full of busy people, and many will never get around to reading an initial letter longer than about two pages.

Tell something about yourself: your background, your interests, your needs, your endearing quirks, and what you're looking for in a community. Experience in group living and working situations is not typically required, but it can be a major "plus" when a community is screening for prospective members. Try to be up front about your interest in contact…are you looking for a home, just curious about community, or something in between?

Try to be as specific as possible when asking questions, focusing on what is important to you. Note that you're not likely to get a very revealing response to a general question such as "Please tell me about your community." If that's what you write, often a standard flyer (if one exists) is all you'll get in return. Most communities report that simple one-line inquiries like this rarely lead to secondary contact, much less to visits or new members, and so are given less serious attention. The other extreme—also to be avoided—is a long series of in-depth questions which reads like a university entrance exam. The more time and effort it will take to answer your letter, the less likely it is that someone will get around to doing it.

Visiting

Do not assume that a community is open to visits just because it's listed in the *Directory*. Our questionnaire asked, "Are you open to visitors who make arrangements in advance?" You'll find the communities' answers in the cross-reference Chart. If a community you're interested in has answered "Yes"or "Maybe," check their description in the Listings section to see if they have any specific restrictions about visiting.

If a visit seems appropriate, the next step is to contact the community to discuss visiting guidelines, mutual expectations, length of stay, and prospective dates. Keep in mind that while a community may usually be open to visits, there may be particular times that are not good for the community. The more flexibility you show, the more likely you'll be able to schedule a visit that suits everyone.

If the community suggests guidelines for visiting, try to respect them. Some communities have developed highly structured visitor programs, while others are very loose. In any event, dropping in on a community without prior arrangements is strongly discouraged. Most communities consider this disrespectful, and some will flatly refuse to let you stay.

It may happen that you set up a visit, and then find it necessary to change your plans. Whether you need to alter dates or wish to cancel the visit altogether, it's a courtesy to inform the community. Sometimes communities decide to turn away prospective visitors because others are already scheduled for the dates under consideration. If they are holding a space in their schedule for you, others may be needlessly inconvenienced if you don't report your change in plans.

If you are traveling by public transportation and need to be picked up, try to arrange a convenient time and place of arrival. With some planning, the connection can often be worked into an already scheduled trip. If a special trip is required, it is appropriate to reimburse the community for travel costs.

Communities have varying policies about giving visitors access to community resources, and it is wise to be clear at the outset. Ask about charges for room and board, and compensation for use of the telephone, postage, vehicles, etc. There may be restrictions on using some tools or machines, or eating some food supplies. You may need to bring your own towels, shampoo, bedding, etc., so ask in advance.

Remember, the community is home to the members, and you are a guest. Try to learn and respect the community's norms. Starting off well is often the key to getting the most out of your visit.

[For further perspectives on visiting communities, see the articles on "Finding Your Community" beginning page 39.]

Feedback

If a community is particularly responsive to your requests, we'd appreciate hearing about it...we want to know who's doing a stellar job. Naturally, we hope to hear a lot of stories about people's needs getting met and their expectations exceeded.

However, we know that won't always be the case; sometimes things won't work out as hoped for. If information in this directory appears to be incorrect, or if you believe you've been ignored or mistreated by one of the communities we've listed...please tell us about that, too. On page 409 we've included information on where to write us about your experience.

Happy Hunting!

An Evolving Culture

Michael McIntyre

Intentional Communities: Lifestyles Based on Ideals

18 Drawing on information from his visits to hundreds of communities across the continent, Geoph Kozeny gives an overview of the communities movement—not only its current state, but also how it has evolved and its prospects for the future. He points out the common bonds that link communities in spite of their diversity.

Community Building for the Long Term

25 Harvey Baker, Barbara Lee, and Jeanne Quinn offer suggestions from their years of experience about ways to build lasting community, including thoughts about decision making, conflict resolution, and common meals.

Community as Crucible

27 An interview of Laird Sandhill by Helen Forsey, discussing the inherent intensity of community living—the personal difficulties this can create, and the rich possibilities for rapid growth and change.

Seeking Group Renewal

31 Simon Poulter (Redfield, United Kingdom) describes "mid-life crisis" in his community, as an example of vexing issues common to established groups. He looks at the attempt to reestablish group cohesion after drifting away from the original purpose, and the importance of being clear on what commitment the group can and will give to resolving conflicts among members. Simon is hopeful that increased contact with other communities will help Redfield make progress on its issues.

Who We Are: An Exploration of What "Intentional Community" Means

33 Dan Questenberry has compiled responses from communitarians everywhere on the nature and description of intentional community. By describing ourselves, we clarify our group objectives—at home and as a movement. Twenty-six communitarians express visions, observations, distinctions, confusions, longings. Some descriptions were fashioned out of long debate. Most of them were submitted along with the Community Listings published in the *Directory*.

Intentional Communities: Lifestyles Based on Ideals

by Geoph Kozeny of Community Catalyst Project, San Francisco, California

Today many people are questioning our society's values, and asking what gives meaning to life. They bemoan the "loss of community," and are looking for ways to reintroduce community values into their lives.

There are several options now available to the average person that satisfy at least the basic cravings: many folks get involved with various civic or social change groups; others get more deeply involved in the activities of their church; still others create friendships and support networks in their neighborhoods. Those with strong motivation to live their values "full time" often seek to join or create intentional communities.

An "intentional community" is a group of people who have chosen to live together with a common purpose, working cooperatively to create a lifestyle that reflects their shared core values. The people may live together on a piece of rural land, in a suburban home, or in an urban neighborhood, and they may share a single residence or live in a cluster of dwellings.

This definition spans a wide variety of groups, including (but not limited to) communes, student cooperatives, land co-ops, cohousing groups, monasteries and ashrams, and farming collectives. Although quite diverse in philosophy and lifestyle, each of these groups places a high priority on fostering a sense of community—a feeling of belonging and mutual support that is increasingly hard to find in mainstream Western society.

Intentional communities are like people—you can categorize them based on certain distinguishing characteristics, but no two are ever identical. Differences among them, whether obvious or subtle, can be attributed to variations in philosophy, in mission or project emphasis, in behavioral norms, or in the personality and style of the leaders (if the group has identified leaders), and the individual members. Each group is somehow unique.

A Time-Honored Idea

Mainstream media typically promote the popular myth that shared living began with the "hippie crash pads" of the '60s—and died with the arrival of "yuppies" in the late '70s and early '80s.

The truth, however, is quite different. Today there are literally thousands of groups, with hundreds of thousands of members, that live in intentional communities and extended families based on something other than blood ties. This type of living has been around for thousands of years, not just decades.

It is well documented that early followers of Jesus banded together to live in a "community of goods," simplifying their lives and sharing all that they owned. That tradition continues to this day, particularly through many inner-city Christian groups that

Geoph Kozeny has been "on the road" since New Year's Day 1988, visiting over 250 intentional communities scattered across North America. He is himself a seasoned veteran of cooperative living—having lived in communities of one kind or another for over 20 years. Geoph is coordinator for the FIC communities database, serves on the Fellowship board, and is a regular columnist for *Communities* magazine. He volunteers full-time for the Community Catalyst Project, a nonprofit organization he created to (1) help communities get in touch with each other, (2) provide technical assistance and support, (3) offer referrals for seekers, and (4) promote public awareness of community living as a viable lifestyle option. Geoph's primary educational tool is a slide show he compiled (and regularly updates) to provide a representative overview of the backgrounds, philosophies, and lifestyles currently available in shared living communities. Another version of this overview of intentional communities has been published in Claude Whitmyer's book, *In the Company of Others* (Jeremy Tarcher, San Francisco, 1993).

live communally. These groups often pool resources and efforts in their ministry to the homeless, the poor, orphans, single parents, battered women, and otherwise neglected and oppressed minorities.

Yet shared living goes back much farther than that, predating the development of agriculture many thousands of years ago. Early hunter-gatherers banded together in tribes, not just blood-related families, and depended on cooperation for their very survival.

The advent of the isolated nuclear family is, in fact, a fairly recent phenomenon, having evolved primarily with the rise of industrialization, particularly the development of high-speed transportation. As transportation has become cheaper and faster, we've also witnessed an increase in transience, and the demise of the traditional neighborhood.

Roots and Realities

Although many contemporary community visions emphasize the creation of neighborhood and/or extended family ties, their philosophic roots are amazingly diverse. The range includes Christians, Quakers, and followers of Eastern religions, to '60s dropouts, anarchists, psychologists, artists, back-to-the-land survivalists—and the list goes on.

The scope of their primary values is equally broad, including ecology, equality, appropriate technology, self-sufficiency, right livelihood, humanist psychology, creativity, spirituality, meditation, yoga, and the pursuit of global peace. However, even among groups that base their philosophy on "achieving a holistic view of the world," it would be quite surprising to discover a community that has achieved "perfection" amidst the fast-paced chaos of modern life. Communities draw their membership from society at large, and those members bring with them generations of social conditioning. The attitudes, behaviors, and institutions prevalent in the broader society—including the very things we seek alternatives to—are a significant part of our upbringing. Merely identifying a problem and expressing a desire to overcome it does not mean that we presently have the perspective or skills needed to transcend it. The problems we see "out there" in the mainstream—greed, dishonesty, excessive ego, lack of self-esteem, factionalism, inadequate resources, poor communication skills, you

> "And all that believed were together, and had all things common; And sold their possessions and goods, and parted them to all men, as every man had need."—Holy Bible, King James Version, Acts 2:44–45.

name it—all manage to find a significant role in alternative cultures as well.

What is encouraging about many intentional communities is their tendency to be open to new ideas, their willingness to be tolerant of other approaches, and their commitment to live in a way that reflects their idealism. Although communities exist that are closed-minded and bigoted, they're the exception, not the rule. More often than not, people who consciously choose to live in an intentional community also have parallel interests in ecology, personal growth, cooperation, and peaceful social transformation—pursuing the work necessary to change destructive attitudes and behaviors often taken for granted in the prevailing culture.

Some Common Threads

Spirituality or religion, regardless of the specific sect or form, is probably the most common inspiration for launching a new community. Such groups bear a striking resemblance to their centuries-old predecessors—in spite of current developments in technology, education, psychology, and theology. Many of North America's leading centers for the study of meditation and yoga have been established by intentional communities based on the teachings of spiritual masters from the Far East. (Such centers include Kripalu in Massachusetts, Ananda Village in California, Satchidananda Ashram in Virginia, Ananda Marga in New York, and Maharishi University in Iowa. Each of these intentional communities serves a widely dispersed

Green Pastures Estate

Creating an extended family environment broadens the experience of every child in community.

Most members of intentional communities share a deep-felt concern about home, family, and neighborhood. Beyond the obvious purpose of creating an extended-family environment for raising a family, communities create an environment of familiarity and trust sufficiently strong that doors can safely be left unlocked. In today's world of escalating crime, merely having that kind of security may be reason enough to join.

Dozens of intentional communities, alarmed by rising student/teacher ratios and falling literacy rates in public schools, have opted to establish alternative schools and to form communities as a base of support for that type of education. Intentional communities comprise a sizeable chunk of the membership of the National Coalition of Alternative Community Schools, an organization of private schools, families, and individuals who share a commitment to create a new and empowering structure for education. Coalition members publish a quarterly newsletter and organize an annual spring conference for sharing resources and skills for social change.

Other communities, usually smaller, have created rural homesteads where they can pursue homeschooling without fear of legal pressure from local school officials. State laws favorable to schooling at home have been promoted, and in some cases initiated, by members of intentional communities. Many communities that homeschool are active in national associations organized specifically to support parents' rights, promote topical networking, and to increase the nation's awareness of homeschooling as a viable educational option.

Another popular issue these days is ecology. Over 90 percent of contemporary communities I've visited, including those located in urban areas, practice recycling and composting. Many serve as model environments or teaching centers for sustainable agriculture and appropriate technology, and feature such concepts as permaculture, organic gardening, grey water systems, solar and wind power, and passive solar home design. Eco-Home, a small shared household in Los Angeles, is an inspiring model of how to live ecologically in an urban environment. "The Farm," a large cooperative community in rural Tennessee, has launched a wide range of environmentally focused projects, including the development of advanced radiation detection equipment; a solar electronics company; a

group of practitioners, including those who live in "sister" communities, and many who live "out there" in the wider society.)

Among secular communities, the inspiration is typically based on bold visions of creating a new social and economic order—establishing replicable models that will lead to the peaceful and ecological salvation of the planet. In some cases, however, secular groups may opt for isolation, seeking to escape the problems of the rest of the world by creating instead a life of self-sufficiency, simplicity, and serenity.

solar car company; the Natural Rights Center (an environmental law project); and a publishing company that specializes in books about environmental issues, vegetarian cooking, natural health care, midwifery, Native Americans, children's stories, and pesticide-free gardening.

In the late 1960s, a wave of new communities influenced by the antiwar movement, the "sexual revolution," rock music, more permissive attitudes about drugs, and the popularization of Eastern religions sprung up to create cooperative lifestyles based on sexual liberation, born-again Christianity, and everything in between. In effect, these often naively idealistic utopian experiments functioned as a pressure cooker for personal and collective growth. Although many of the '60s groups folded during the creative but turbulent decade that followed, hundreds have survived into the '90s and are now thriving—having reevaluated, restructured, and matured over the years.

B.F. Skinner's book, *Walden Two* (a futurist novel based on his theories of behavioral psychology), inspired the creation of at least a dozen communal experiments. Los Horcones, one such community near Sonora, Mexico, is today one of the world's foremost experiments in behaviorist theory.

The Franchise Approach

Some communities hit upon a combination of philosophy and lifestyle that enables them to thrive. Occasionally one will embark on a program of systematic colonization to spread its message and its influence.

> **What is encouraging about many intentional communities is their tendency to be open to new ideas, their willingness to be tolerant of other approaches, and their commitment to live in a way that reflects their idealism.**

During the Reformation, a group of German Anabaptists decided to pool their goods and unite in Christian brotherhood. Jakob Hutter emerged as a primary leader five years later, in 1533. The community prospered, and subsequently formed many new colonies. Today there are nearly 400 colonies of the Hutterian Brethren in Canada and the United States, and a few more in South America and Europe. When a Hutterian community reaches its optimum capacity (100–150 members), the group acquires a new piece of land, builds a new set of structures (homes, barns, schools, etc.) acquires more agricultural equipment, and outfits an entire

"Commune"

Since the 1960s, the term "commune" has been used primarily as a pejorative to describe collections of young folks who have "dropped out" of mainstream culture to create an extended family with their peers. The implication, although inaccurate, is that all such groups emphasize sexual promiscuity, drug use (particularly marijuana), and lack of a work ethic. In fact, there are many communities (including most residential Christian groups) that expressly prohibit all three of these behaviors. The term is most commonly used today to designate an income-sharing community.

The feeling of belonging and mutual support helps foster a sense of community.

Leslie Goldman, Enchanted Gardener

new facility. Then the population divides into two groups—one group staying at the original site, and one moving on to the new one. Neighboring colonies support each other with backup labor and various resources, an approach that yields a very high ratio of success for the new colonies.

Each colony has common work and a common purpose, and most have an economic base of large-scale, machine-powered agriculture within an organizational structure resembling that of a producer cooperative. They have been so successful in their endeavors that in the '80s some of their neighbors on the Canadian plains initiated lawsuits to prevent Hutterites from acquiring more land, claiming that their modernized agricultural base and communal economy amounted to "unfair competition." Because the Hutterites have retained many of their original customs—including dress, family structure, a simple lifestyle, and the German language—many outsiders find the Hutterites to be quite out of place when compared to their contemporary neighbors.

In contrast, members of Emissaries of Divine Light, another spiritually based association, manage to fit right in with the mainstream culture. The Emissaries, founded in the early '30s, have a network of 12 major communities plus a number of urban centers that span the globe. Their overall focus is directed toward achieving a more effective and creative life experience, developing spiritual awareness without rules or a specific belief system. Their lifestyle would be described by many as "upper middle class," and business oriented. Nuclear family units, though not mandated, are the norm. Emissaries pride themselves on being on good terms with their neighbors. One long-standing resi-

dent of an Emissary community at the edge of a small Canadian town was elected mayor of the town for 15 consecutive years. The Emissary business staff is well respected—so much so that government tax officials in British Columbia regularly consult Emissary personnel before deciding on strategies for implementing new tax laws and regulations concerning nonprofit corporations.

The connections between and among the various Emissary communities worldwide are maintained in many ways: inspirational talks and special events are always recorded, and transcripts are kept on file at each Emissary center; some events are recorded on video, with copies distributed by mail; on a weekly basis, several centers link up via satellite for instantaneous transmission of related presentations originating from multiple locations. Most active members receive regular Emissary publications, some of which provide a network overview, and others which document the work of special interest subgroups. For example, many of the major Emissary centers have agricultural operations, which grow much of the food consumed by residents and guests. Known as "stewardship farms," these separate operations are managed and staffed by members who regularly share ideas and information about long-term sustainable agriculture. This special interest group publishes a regular newsletter and organizes periodic conferences, planning meetings, and exchange visits.

Network Alliances

The popular myth that the intentional communities movement died in the early '80s has been discouraging to many of the intentional communities that survived and thrived on their own. Many contemporary groups have suffered a lack of contact and support due to their mistaken impression that they were among the few survivors of a bygone era. Fortunately, there is growing interest shared by many independent communities for contact with like-minded groups, both nearby and around the world. Regional, continental, and even intercontinental networks—alliances for the sharing of ideas, resources, and social interests—are gaining support and visibility, thus enabling groups to learn from each others' failures and long-term successes.

One network of more than 50 Catholic Worker houses publishes a periodic newspaper and organizes occasional gatherings for the sharing of ideas, skills, rituals, friendship, and solidarity. Another values-based network is the Fellowship for Intentional Community (FIC), a North American network created to promote shared living in whatever forms it may take. The Fellowship handles thousands of inquiries yearly from seekers hoping to find a community to join, from communities looking for new members, from academics doing research, and from media people gathering material for stories. A third organization of note is the Federation of Egalitarian Communities (FEC), established to promote and develop democratically run communities based on equality, income sharing, nonviolence, cooperation, ecology, and sustainability. FEC encourages the identification and elimination of the "isms" (racism, sexism, classism, ageism, etc.), and emphasizes the importance of ongoing contact among member groups.

FEC communities tax themselves $200 per year plus one percent of net revenues, using this fund to finance joint recruitment campaigns, fundraising, and travel to meetings and between communities. They have also created a voluntary joint security fund for protection against the economic strain of large medical bills. This fund has now grown to more than $100,000 and is used in part as a revolving loan fund that provides low-interest loans to projects and community businesses compatible with FEC values. Member communities also participate in a labor exchange program that allows residents of one community to visit another and receive labor credit at home for work done away. This is especially handy when one community's peak workload occurs during another's off season, and the labor flows back and forth when most appreciated. The

"Cohousing"

Cohousing is a North American adaptation of a style of cooperative living that originated in Denmark in the 1960s. Cohousing communities combine the autonomy of private dwellings with many of the resource advantages of community living. Initial residents participate in the planning and design of the community so that it directly responds to their needs. Each household has a private residence, but also shares common facilities with the larger group (such as a dining hall, children's playrooms, workshops, guest rooms, and laundry facilities). Although individual dwellings are designed to be self-sufficient and each has its own kitchen, the common facilities—particularly the common dinners—are an important aspect of community life for both social and practical reasons. For more information on cohousing options in North America, contact The CoHousing Company, 1250 Addison Street #113, Berkeley, CA 94702, 510-549-9980.

Many contemporary groups are exploring ways to achieve a true sense of community while maintaining a balance between privacy and cooperation...

exchange of personnel also offers an opportunity to take a mini-vacation, learn a new skill, make new friends, maintain old ones, and share insights about common experiences.

The Federation also aspires to document collectively acquired wisdom, making it available to the public for the cost of copying and postage. They have created a "Systems & Structures Package"—a compilation of written documents on bylaws, membership agreements, property codes, behavior norms, labor and governance systems, visitor policies, and ideas about what to do when you have too many dogs. The point of sharing this information is to help new (and even some not-so-new) communities ease through the struggles of creating appropriate structures, offering models for what to do when good will and best intentions are not enough.

A Contemporary Wave

Historically, participation in shared living communities has come in cycles. One major wave just ahead of the U.S. Civil War included Brook Farm, an educational experiment that attracted the likes of Henry David Thoreau, Nathaniel Hawthorne, and Ralph Waldo Emerson. Other notable waves followed—one at the end of the last century including some still existing "Single Tax Colonies" (based on the economic philosophy of Henry George), one immediately preceding World War I, and another during the Great Depression. The last wave came out of the counterculture in the '60s, and now a new wave is beginning. This 1995 edition of the *Communities Directory* documents more than 50 new communities started during

the past five years, and that's merely the tip of the iceberg. Also listed are more than 160 that have survived at least a decade, and 80 others that have been in existence for more than two decades.

It is apparent that people—dissatisfied with the gap between their ideals and reality—will keep trying out new approaches until they find lifestyles that solve most of the problems they see in the dominant culture. History suggests that the process is endless. To paraphrase Karl Marx: today's solutions to yesterday's problems introduce new dynamics that become tomorrow's problems. An exciting feature of today's intentional communities movement is that its members are actively seeking to identify problems, working to find solutions, and trying to implement new insights in their daily lives.

Many contemporary groups are exploring ways to achieve a true sense of community while maintaining a balance between privacy and cooperation, a concept quite compatible with values prevalent in mainstream society today. Perhaps by emphasizing common concerns rather than differences in our lifestyle choices, innovations will find their way more quickly across cultural lines.

Although shared living does not appeal to everyone, history confirms again and again that ongoing social experiments inevitably lead to a variety of new social and technical innovations—developments that will eventually find many useful applications in other segments of society. It's hard to predict just when an intentional community will come up with something new that will be assimilated by mainstream culture. However, if social experimenting results in a product, a process, or a philosophy that makes life a little easier or a bit more fulfilling, then we'd be well advised to keep an open mind as we monitor the progress. ⚉

Community Building for the Long Term

by Harvey Baker and Barbara Lee of Dunmire Hollow, Waynesboro, Tennessee, and Jeanne Quinn

Living or working with people does not guarantee community; it takes intentionality and developed skills to build and maintain ongoing community. Even if the group is well established, the sense of community has a periodic ebb and flow, characteristic of the best of long-term personal relationships.

Years of experience with residential situations indicate that certain structural and subtle, non-structural elements help to maintain the community over time. Processes and agreements for membership help create group identity and commitment. They introduce the skills, attitudes, and behaviors necessary to maintain the group and provide guidelines for exclusion if necessary to protect the group. Clear expectations and agreements are absolutely necessary for long-term harmony and clarity of purpose.

For best results, these guidelines are created by consensus. Consensus decision making, though not the only possible method for community meetings, inherently encourages community. Consensus requires integration, listening, flexibility, and patience. Although reaching consensus can be slow, a well-built consensus usually reflects a more thorough consideration of the issues. It avoids the tyranny of the majority and the disenfranchisement of the minority, both of which are destructive of community spirit. Because everyone owns the final decision, it is more likely to succeed, with less griping and sabotage.

Clear meeting process and good facilitation are extremely valuable. Both help bring out the widest perspectives, enabling each person to feel heard. There is a tendency for the facilitator to be seen as a leader or chair of the group; however, the facilitator is ideally the servant of the group and the meeting process, creating an atmosphere in which everyone can think and communicate well. The role of facilitator is best shared among several people, both to reduce the leader image and to provide alternates when one facilitator is personally involved in a controversial issue. As the group gains meeting experience, members understand more deeply their responsibility to think clearly, stay focused, and make relevant contributions to the discussions. As individuals repeatedly contribute to group solutions, they feel increasingly empowered as members of the community and more able to take on additional responsibility.

Agreement to try to resolve conflict as it arises is another important element for long-term community health. Conflict is inevitable in any group and can be viewed as a major opportunity for personal and community growth. Unresolved conflict is destructive of community, whereas successfully resolved conflict builds community. As with consen-

Harvey Baker helped found Dunmire Hollow in 1974 and continues a deep involvement in his home community and custom woodworking business. He has been active with the administrative committee of the FIC board of directors for several years, and has worked with the FIC since before the 1986 reorganization. Harvey is a committed gardener, plays soccer, and enjoys cross-country trips on his bicycle, or his vintage BMW motorcycle. He has reported on community building in the *Foundation for Community Encouragement* newsletter, and this article is derived from that report.

Barbara Lee is a nature educator, gardener, and peace and ecology activist. She has lived in Dunmire Hollow for ten years, and is a member of a community-building church in Nashville.

Jeanne Quinn is a ceramic artist, and lives in a group house in Seattle. She is a past president of the Oberlin Student Cooperative Association, and has been active in NASCO. She lived with Harvey and Barbara in Dunmire Hollow for five months while building a reproduction of a Greek temple.

This article was first published in the Spring 1990 issue of *Communique*, the newsletter of the Foundation for Community Encouragement.

Clear meeting process enables each person to feel heard.

sus decision making, an agreement to work toward a mutual solution, rather than an imposed judgment or political victory, requires effort to see both sides, understand more fully the basis of the problem, and (sometimes reluctantly and painfully) to work together to find a mutually agreeable solution. Successes with small conflicts build confidence in the process and prepare people both emotionally and experientially for dealing with larger issues. The community is strengthened as members improve their skills in conflict resolution, mediation, facilitation, and other community-building activities.

In other areas of shared responsibilities (i.e., energy, money, attention, expertise), the methods used to provide and distribute community resources will build community if chosen wisely. Neither legislating numerical equality nor allowing the burden to fall on a small fraction of the group will build responsiveness to the community's needs, or a willingness in each member to freely contribute his or her share.

There are also more subtle factors to consider, almost universal in human culture because of their powerful combination of practical and symbolic values. One is "place"—a locale, preferably identified with the group rather than any one individual. Place can be very important in community identity and spirit.

Another is working together. Work demands cooperation, decision making, and trust. Working together reveals different facets of people's characters, personalities, and abilities that talking alone cannot. By giving the group a common goal, work gives meaning and expression to membership in the group. As goals are met, the group identifies with the success.

One of the most binding of human activities seems to be eating together. From the Last Supper to the PTA potluck, preparing and sharing the essentials for life provide opportunities for both a profound giving of ourselves and a pleasant social occasion. As we share space, time, energy, and food, community becomes associated with the fulfilling of our most basic human needs.

Finally, any community benefits from periodic boosts. Examples include assessment and reevaluation of purpose, common agreements to read and discuss informational or inspirational materials, workshops to build community skills, and planned activities specifically designed to bring members closer to each other and to the ideals they are trying to live out together. ⚉

Community as Crucible

Helen Forsey of Lothlorien Farm in Ontario's Ottawa Valley talks with Laird of Sandhill Farm, Rutledge, Missouri (Based on a 1992 interview for the book Circles of Strength - Community Alternatives to Alienation. *Reprinted here with permission. See bottom of page 302 for more information.)*

Helen Forsey: The community I live in now used to be a lot more collective and close-knit 15 or 20 years ago, but people found they had to have more distance in order to get along better with each other. They started doing less together, and now the group is very stable and friendly and mutually supportive, but loose-knit. There's a lot more distance and independence, a kind of balance we found was necessary.

A lot of people who've previously lived in very close-knit communities have found that the degree of intensity, of integration with everybody else, was not sustainable for them, that they needed to get away from it. Not in order to fragment their lives or their commitment, but to have a space where they weren't actively doing everything so closely with other people all the time.

Laird Sandhill: One of the fundamental choices that groups must make is how close they want to be; what level of engagement is desired. Is there a commitment to examining the feelings that come up around interactions in the group? Is the community willing to make this work a priority and allow time for it? I know of no more exciting product of community than the power of high-level communication and well-made decisions.

Many people would like the benefits of this work without the intensive struggle to get it. Of course, the problem is made worse by the fact that our dominant culture is hierarchic and competitive, so few of us have been raised to communicate and make decisions as equals, cooperating for mutual gain. Progress in this work is thus typically slow and hard earned. In fact, so slow that in some instances people can't get away from it fast enough. And they're perfectly willing, after years of honest trying, to go ahead and engage in more housework, more commuting, more of all those generally unpleasant aspects of everyday living, in exchange for not having to go to meetings! Communities have been pioneers in this work and the progress has come in fits and starts. Many good people have left community in frustration because the progress didn't come fast enough for them. After 15 years in this work, I am sobered by the losses: the road to dynamic group process is littered with the burned-out shells of the well-intentioned, whose community spirit was broken by the "40 years in the wilderness" they perceived to be standing between their reality and the utopian dream of deep bonding and honest, heartfelt communication.

Helen: If it's so difficult, why bother? What are the rewards of that kind of intensity, that unrelenting hard emotional and intellectual work?

Helen Forsey was a long-time member of Dandelion in Ontario, until it reformed as Stonehedge in 1991. While there, Helen was active in the Federation of Egalitarian Communities (FEC) and has known and worked with Laird since 1985. Helen now lives at Lothlorien Farm and is a freelance writer and activist.. She edited *Circles of Strength – Community Alternatives to Alienation* (New Society Publishers, 1993) from which this interview was drawn. See p. 302.

Laird, a cofounder of Sandhill Farm in 1974, continues to live and work on that organic farm. After years as Secretary of both the FEC and the Fellowship for Intentional Community, he has reduced his FEC load to focus on Fellowship work, including serving as Managing Editor of this directory and, until 1994, of *Communities* magazine. Laird is a consensus facilitation trainer, and appreciates the challenge of facilitating consensus groups in conflict. He's a jogger and an experienced networker who runs around visiting communities all over North America.

Gathering logs for house building.

Doug Jones, Birdsfoot Farm

Laird: I know of no better environment than intentional community for making progress on knowing yourself and knowing others. We engage in political issues through actually trying to create something—not just talking about it, but offering models of how things could be different. We're trying to bring these issues into every aspect of our lives and to weave a whole from it all. It's very exciting and very challenging, and it leads to a tremendous sense of aliveness—there's nothing dull about it!

It's like a crucible: the heat of it, the intensity. Community allows for a greater concentration of breakthroughs, and faster progress, surer progress. And yet it can also be dangerous; the hurt can be greater, the sense of being overwhelmed or betrayed. There can be this real wild swing, from joyous "Ah-hah" moments when groups surge past difficult barriers, to deep despair when the obstacles seem insurmountable and unbudgeable.

Helen: It can be sheer hell! There are dynamics that can develop, and precisely because it's all so intense and you can't easily get away from it, it can be as bad as anything that happens in traditional families, and that's saying a mouthful.

Laird: Yes, it can be destructive; it's possible to have abuses. People can get into things that they're not capable of finding a healthy way to resolve. Sometimes people don't belong together in a group, yet they struggle on as if the common values and agreements necessary for resolution were present. In such cases it can get nasty, especially where people are engaging in practices that they don't know how to control and there's no place to get away. It can be abusive and dangerous.

At times like that, a group needs to work for clarity in their common bonds, making sure that the opportunities are always there for people to grow and change. I've found it works best if a group moves forward only after fully considering every member's input.

For example, I once worked with a community of seven that was considering—for the third time—a proposal to alter how group finances were handled. After 15 minutes it became clear that six members favored the proposal, with one member ambivalent—not opposed, just uncertain. Unfortunately, that one person was the financial manager, and his active cooperation was essential to resolving the issue. So, while we might have papered over the ambivalence and called it a decision after 15 minutes, instead we labored for an hour-and-a-half to get at the underlying reservations. It took that long before the person could express what was worrying him *and* feel heard by everyone else. After that, all seven supported the proposal and the issue was settled. Looked at one way, exploring the underlying feelings took six times longer to get to the same conclusion that we were already at after 15 minutes. For some, this is the nightmare of consensus: tortuous examination of issues, that seems to plod along inefficiently. Yet this analysis overlooks some important benefits. For one thing, implementation. The reason the issue kept resurfacing in the group was that prior decisions were weak and they were carried out halfheartedly. Think of all the time spent in grumbling about this and the meeting time to consider the same issue three times. Now that's inefficient! For another thing, consider the effect on group morale. When an issue keeps popping up and doesn't get resolved, people develop a defeatist attitude about it and expect poor results from further deliberations. They start to dread meetings and don't expect their views to be heard by those holding different ones. In light of all this, those extra minutes spent dealing with the issue thoroughly can be seen for the bargain they really are.

Now don't get me wrong; it's hard work to do this well, and it's an ideal where we often fall short. It's part of our struggle as a movement, even as a culture.

Helen: So the work that some of you have been researching and developing in the crucible of our communities—this group facilitation and consensus process and mediation work—is an essential part of creating workable models for social change?

Laird: Absolutely. In particular, the aspect of how to work, not just with the ideas and the architecture of meetings, but also with the emotive input that people bring to the meetings. You must work with all of it. I've experienced many insights in my life, where the light bulb popped on over my head, but probably no realization has been more illuminating than the power and necessity of embracing people's feelings when doing group work. As a male traditionally raised, it has been especially difficult for me to learn to open up to emotions—both mine and others'. Yet I'm convinced that welcoming emotional expression is a necessary starting point for groups doing their best work, for people being truly present with each other and thinking clearly.

I wonder how many people have had the experience of good meetings. I run into people at some of these networking meetings who say, "I can't believe the meeting went like that! It was so caring, so productive!" To me that's normal now, but some people feel like it's a dream that they've never experienced before. It's great fun shattering their preconceptions, and expanding their horizons of what's possible.

Intentional communities are in a position to contribute to the wider society far out of proportion to our numbers, because the skills we're learning in cooperative decision making have application throughout the culture. Having gone through the crucible, we're tempered and often able to share our experiences effectively with a wide range of others.

Helen: What do you think the future holds for intentional communities?

Laird: Our future depends on how well we work with the upcoming generations. When we get through this pioneering stage, what are our children going to do? Places like Twin Oaks, East Wind, and many other communities have very few kids actually completing their growing up experiences in community. Children may spend a few years in a cooperative lifestyle, and then issues emerge between parents and nonparents that cause the families to relocate.

Doug Jones, Birdsfoot Farm

Knowing yourself and others creates a tremendous sense of aliveness.

• •

Intentional communities are in a position to contribute to the wider society far out of proportion to our numbers, because the skills we're learning in cooperative decision making have application throughout the culture.

• • • • • • • • • • • • • • • • • • • •

It's hard to tell how much children identify with the common bonds or values of their home communities, or even the wider movement. We have much to do in defining our relevance to the next generation.

Helen: Although it sometimes feels like a failure when our kids don't stay, there is still that very important formative year or so in community. That time can be pretty amazing for children, a total change from what they've had before, and that's going to be there for the rest of their lives.

Laird: Yes, the impact can be there—the influence, even if the exposure is brief relative to a person's whole childhood. What that will actually add up to in terms of contributions, impact on the society, who knows yet? But soon, we'll know. Many of the kids who were born and grew up in community are young adults out in the wider society now—some forming new intentional communities. You know, my childhood wasn't like theirs; and in very dramatic ways! I have a son who is 11 and a daughter who is four. They have spent their entire lives in community, and as they grow up, I think, "What are they going to be like? What are they going to do with their community experiences?"

As far as trends in community, there are encouraging signs. Unlike a lot of us ten or 20 years ago,

new groups seem more ready to ask for help right at the outset. Many in these groups don't feel they have to do community building all on their own, and they are transcending the rugged individualism that many bring into cooperative lifestyles from the mainstream.

In the sixties and seventies, some of us got far enough out of the mainstream to try group living, but not far enough to think, "We don't have to make this all up on our own. We can talk openly about our struggles, ask for help, and learn quicker." That's something my community wasn't smart enough to do back when we started. In our supreme naiveté, the four of us didn't even think about joining an existing community. We were sure that the way to get what we wanted was to start our own intentional community. And, oh my stars! We knew so little about what we were doing! Looking back on it, I just can't imagine how we survived. There was no end to what we didn't know.

I see a lot of young groups now advancing much faster and more surely because they don't fall into that individualist trap. Of course, there's also greater access to resources today. Years ago we didn't know where to turn for help, and now there are many useful directories, catalogs, tapes, and books. That's exciting! The prospects are very encouraging for the development of more and more intentional communities, each serving as a crucible for the tempering of different possibilities for social evolution. ⚏

Seeking Group Renewal

by Simon Poulter of Redfield, Winslow, Buckinghamshire, United Kingdom

Many intentional communities created in the 1970s are now well over a decade old and in some cases approaching their twentieth birthdays. Since that period, when a lot of communities took off with high ideologies and aims to change society, political thinking has moved on. The ecological agenda has been pushed to the forefront as it becomes increasingly evident that we cannot continue to exploit our planet in unsustainable ways.

Communitarians, in their pursuit of sustainable, cooperative lifestyles, have set out to demonstrate alternatives for the larger society. Yet, it has been argued that communities are "safe havens" for a few, and that our continued existence is dependent upon mainstream society.

But this is not an overview of the communities movement—rather it's a report of my personal impressions of the community reassessment that has taken place at the Redfield housing co-op in Buckinghamshire, England. Established in 1978, Redfield reached a point in the early nineties where community size and future growth dominated discussion.

Consultations with other communitarians confirmed that the problems and identity crises that Redfield was experiencing were not unique to us. Other communities were waking up to the necessity of creating structures for the next wave of communitarians—either expanding existing communities or, more likely, providing close support to groups setting up the new generation of communities.

With our future as a species at risk, Redfield seeks to participate in national and international movements for change. So, earlier in this decade, our community considered a membership growth campaign. But we soon realized that first we had to define our group sense of purpose more clearly. A common remark among our members was that we had plenty of ideas and projects but no direction.

Three months of debate did not bring us to a position where we could say in a collective voice, "Our direction is...." But community discussions helped us move toward a clearer understanding of individual perspectives and the different ideas of what Redfield might become.

Looking back on our search for consensus, it seems we were shaken by the limits of our structure and unable to grasp the need for healing and cleansing in the group. When we embarked upon our reassessment, there were underlying stresses, fears, and disaffection among Redfield members. As our search for direction continued, it seemed some members needed the community more than the community needed them. Emotional support appeared to be inadequate except for those who appeared resolute in accepting their pain.

The reassessment needed to be both individually and collectively focused if the effort was to be productive. Our intention as a group was to lay out guidelines for revitalizing the community in order to allow prospective members to be aware of our

---

Simon Poulter is a multimedia artist, including oil paintings and computer art. Since establishing the Exhibition Gallery at Redfield in 1990, he and his family have left Redfield to work with an artists collective.

Reassessment of an intentional community is really only feasible when it is "safe" for all to put themselves, their visions, and their troubles into the collective arena.

community purpose, what the community is all about. The investment is heavy on both sides and clarity would be mutually helpful. After all, we seek long-term members interested in our projects and sharing life at Redfield.

Communities may survive the loss of individual members if enough committed people remain who are able to uphold the aims and objectives of the community. But a smaller community can be brought to a standstill if several people leave simultaneously. The result of our reassessment at Redfield was that a small group stayed, embarking yet again on a membership campaign—a very consuming project.

Still, the search for common direction attracted us. Community direction can be a set of values commonly recognized and agreed upon by all members, or it can be a manifesto of creative thinking. The first option can lead to boiled down and indistinct values, which can hardly be called a direction. But group attempts at creative thinking have brought us to armadas of opposed ideologies, though we do share common convictions about ecological sustainability.

Some members would like to see a community of 40 people living on this site and another 40 living locally as part of an extended community. Others would like to see seven members facilitating a vast visitor center in the main house. Yet, as members resigned, the pressure to recruit new people caused us to all but abandon the idea of direction. Presently we accept that we have multiple directions, partly lamenting our disunity, yet optimistically thankful for our diversity.

Reassessment of an intentional community is really only feasible when it is "safe" for all to put themselves, their visions, and their troubles into the collective arena. It wasn't safe for everyone to do that at Redfield when we embarked on our search for direction. Consequently, we were stalled by divisions, grievances, and obvious incompatibilities— and we lost several members. New people coming here will in many ways unwittingly participate in our unresolved debate.

The group remaining at Redfield agreed to recruit new members based on their ability to complement the practical and interpersonal skills of current members. We seek to make room for enthusiasm and individual flair among both new and old members, while also emphasizing personal and collective responsibility.

Now we find direction and group identity through increased participation in networking with other groups, lobbying for the green political agenda, and providing support for the next generation of intentional communities.

Postscript
by Jonathan How of Redfield

Many communities exist for the benefit of their members—whoever they happen to be. Some members will have personal ambitions; some will have ambitions for the community; some will have lots of connections in the wider world; and some are looking for a place where they can live closely with a small group of people. Although all of these states of being can be individually fulfilling for the members themselves, it can be difficult for the community, as an organism, to become a learning and developing organization amidst competing priorities.

Members with ambitions for wider group development sometimes feel disappointed in Redfield; yet every organization must have a "core" business, and here that has always been the business of cooperative living together. Any organization that focuses on wider development without nurturing its core business is treading on dangerous ground, and it is just the same here. Of course, some day we may have "40 people on site and another 40 living locally," at which point our core business might be radically different. But it will still be about intentional cooperative living. ⏣

Who We Are: An Exploration of What "Intentional Community" Means

Edited by Dan Questenberry of Shannon Farm and Deer Rock, Afton, Virginia

More than 8,000 people, including over 2,000 children, live in 186 of the more established North American intentional communities and extended family groups listing in the previous edition of the *Directory of Intentional Communities* (1990). One hundred forty-two of those groups are rural, or have both urban and rural sites; 113 (80 percent) of the rural groups reported common holdings totaling more than 34,000 acres. Forty-four urban communities and extended families listed common holdings of 98 apartments and 46 group houses, plus additional group houses containing 113 more bedrooms. Of course, these 186 communities represent just a small fraction of the North American communities movement.

Eighty-four more communities of three or more members were listed in the *Directory* and provided some data, but didn't provide complete demographics. Over 150 communities in the FIC database have declined to be listed in the *Directory,* and another 550 did not respond to our mailings. There are thousands more residing in traditional monastic enclaves or service groups, tens of thousands living in Hutterite colonies, and millions of indigenous Americans living communally. So the information in this directory describes just a small portion of the cooperative lifestyles practiced in North America.

With any discussion of community demographics, a common description of intentional community is assumed—an assumption that prompts the question:

"What is—how do we describe—an intentional community?"

Join us in an expanding continent-wide brainstorm about the meanings of intentional community. Please send your thoughts on this word puzzle to the FIC. Aim for an inclusive description that *uniquely* defines the inspiring diversity of the communities movement. Test your description in discussions with other community members, and provide a copy of your tested description to the Fellowship as a contribution to this challenging dialogue.

Some of the following descriptions of intentional community may stimulate your creativity. The first descriptions were published in the *Fellowship for Intentional Community Newsletter*, Fall '91, Winter '93. Other descriptions were sent in by communitarians from across the continent along with their listings for this directory. Many of these descriptions illustrate the challenges of drawing a distinct boundary around a concept so inclusive as intentional community.

Harvey Baker, of Dunmire Hollow, has lived in his Tennessee community since 1974. Harvey described intentional community quite soulfully:

An "intentional community" is a group of people dedicated with intent, purpose, and commitment to a mutual concern. Generally the group shares land or housing, or is otherwise close enough geographically to be in continu-

---

Dan Questenberry has been the *FIC Newsletter* Editor and *Directory* Articles Editor. One of the incorporators of the Fellowship for Intentional Community in 1986, he's an FIC administrative committee member, as well as a former treasurer of School of Living Land Trust and Deer Rock, a new community near Shannon Farm. His interest in other intentional communities and movement demographics started simply, with visitor work at Shannon Farm beginning when he first joined in 1976. Dan is the owner-operator of an independent insurance agency, and enjoys participating in Fellowship volunteer work, meetings, and other alternative culture gatherings.

ous active fellowship so that it can effectively carry out the purposes to which it is dedicated.

Geoph Kozeny, a ten-year resident of Stardance in San Francisco (since renamed Purple Rose), has been traveling among and photographing North American intentional communities since 1988. A full-time networker, he has worked and presented slide show/lectures in hundreds of communities and worker cooperatives over the years. Geoph describes intentional community in another feature article here in this directory:

An "intentional community" is a group of people who have chosen to live together with a common purpose, working cooperatively to create a lifestyle that reflects their shared core values. The people may live together on a piece of rural land, in a suburban home, or in an urban neighborhood, and they may share a single residence or live in a cluster of dwellings.

Lisa Paulson, *Windwatch* newsletter editor at High Wind in Wisconsin, has lived in that community for over 14 years. She reports how their ecovillage has described intentional community:

…a group of people who come together deliberately in a residential situation around a specific vision, agenda or shared values. Certainly there are communities that adhere to the latter criteria whose members do not live together; however, when we think of intentional communities, it seems to imply being residential.

Within the term intentional community, we make two distinctions: "public" or "homesteading." Public intentional communities are dedicated to public service, outreach, educational programs, events, and networking. Such groups are broad, even global, in scope. Because interfacing with mainstream society is an essential counterpoint to experimenting with a more ideal way to live, at least some members of public communities must be in dialogue with visitors, researchers, and media representatives.

Building foundations for a new society from the ground up.

Eco-Village Staff, L.A. Eco-Village

"Homesteading" communities coalesce with perhaps the same vision of living together with real caring for each other as in the public groups. However, homesteaders are not so open to visitors and have no public programs. They want, perhaps, to create a small Utopia, protected and isolated from mainstream society.

Kat Kinkade, a founding member of Twin Oaks (Virginia), East Wind (Missouri), and Acorn (Virginia), just wrote a new book about her community experiences. *Is It Utopia Yet?* (published by Twin Oaks) begins with a definition:

"Intentional community"…(has) its own clear borders and membership. Some people call it a "utopian" community. The essential element in any intentional community, ours included, is that people who want to live in it will have to join, be accepted by those who already live there, and go by its rules and norms, which may in some ways differ from those in society at large.

Allen Butcher, a former member of East Wind and Twin Oaks, is a long-time student of intentional community economics. He defines community as follows:

Intentional community is an association displaying two primary characteristics. First, the members of the group maintain some level of common agreements, such as choosing a name for themselves and a system of governance. Second, the group carries on some collective actions, for example sharing a common residential property and usually other material assets. Essentially, any association may call itself an "intentional community" by common agreement. The lack of such an agreement results in an association being termed a "circumstantial community," which is similar to nations, cities, towns, or neighborhoods where individuals live in proximity by chance, and may or may not actively choose to be a part of the association imposed upon them. Both intentional and circumstantial communities can at times function as the other, depending upon their degree of common agreement and community action. (A. Allen Butcher, Community Tools: A "Virtual Library" of Community Development Resources, 1994, Fourth World Services, P.O. Box 1666, Denver, CO 80201-1666.)

I like a description that distinguishes intentional communities from other social, religious, or business organizations—a description useful for demographic studies of the communities movement:

An "intentional community" is a group of people living cooperatively, dedicated by intent and commitment to specific communal values and goals. Life inside each community is managed using established decision-making processes. Generally, intentional communities place high value on the shared ownership or lease of common

Making the Transition from "Definition" to "Description"

Beginning with discussions at the fall 1989 Fellowship board meeting, Allen Butcher and Dan Questenberry have been active in publicly promoting the development of a common definition of intentional community. At that meeting, participants were surprised to experience the depth of feelings precipitated by searching for a common definition. After continuing discussions in semi-annual Fellowship meetings over the next three years, participants realized a breakthrough in fall '92. At that meeting the Fellowship agreed to redirect the search for a common definition when we discovered that discussion of comparative descriptions could produce much more fruitful work. Definitions can be limiting and judging, whereas descriptions are inclusive, expansive, and illuminating.

This article is designed to elicit more comparative descriptions. Hopefully, reviewing this collection of descriptions will stimulate readers to look at communities even more closely, and consider what we share as a wider movement. By describing ourselves, in comparison with other communities, we can realize more clarity in our mission objectives at home and as a movement.

"...a group of people dedicated with intent, purpose, and commitment to a mutual concern."

facilities—housing, land, commercial buildings—which often serves to demonstrate communal values and goals to the wider society.

A "group house," or "extended family," is a smaller intentional community with members residing in a single-family dwelling, and often using casual decision-making processes, especially in the smallest groups.

David Spangler, one of the early members of Findhorn, has written and lectured about intentional community for decades. He describes community in these words:

Stephen C. Rasah, Camphill Village

When this was a small gathering of people it was very easy for us to experience community here; everyone worked with everybody else, we knew everyone's first name, we were together through the day and we had sanctuary all together. As the community grew, jobs became more specialized and people worked further afield, and being together became more difficult. Then the quality that makes community had to arise from something more than just physical proximity and daily encounter.

...Community is not something that is created when people come together and live together, rather it is something that is preexistent and we can awaken to it. There is never a time when we are not in community, and our practice is to awaken to that experience of communion.

Communities Define Community

The following descriptions were among the many submitted by groups with their listing information for creating this directory.

Matt Bojanovich, Adirondack Herbs
Broadalbin, New York

...a group of cooperating nonrelated humans, living by their own choice on one piece of land or in one house, for reasons which go beyond mere convenience—for at least some of the members. 10/30/92

Linda Woodrow, Black Horse Creek
Kyogle, Australia

This may seem like a frivolous answer, but I think it works as a definition. When I try to think what all "communities"—intentional, traditional, tribal, neighborhood...have in common, the only one I can put a finger on is gossip—in a positive sense....Communities are groups of people who care enough about each other to constantly monitor each other's lives, find them interesting, want to know and help and support. 10/1/93

R.G. Faithfull,
Braziers Park School of Integrative Social Research
Oxon, England

We define a community as a group of people who live

together and eat together and plan their future together. 2/5/93

Rodolfo Rosase, Comunidad Arcoiris
Mexico D.F., Mexico

Implicit in the term is an area or territory, a certain ideological, racial, economic, and/or political characteristic that separates it from other neighboring groups; and a higher degree of interpersonal contact and relationship between members. A community is a distinct social, economic, and political organism. 7/16/92

Forest, Earth Re-Leaf
Naalehu, Hawaii

A small group of close friends living close together with common agreements and goals. 11/25/92

Suresvara Dasa, Gita Nagari Village
Port Royal, Pennsylvania

A community is a group of people who cooperate to serve God with work, worship, and love. At Gita Nagari, we try to show the natural sweet relationship between the land, the animals, humanity, and God. We milk cows, work oxen, school our children, and try to live life in the spirit of Krishna's Bhagavad Gita, India's Song of God. 5/9/92

Tony Nenninger, Goodwater Community
Bourbon, Missouri

Community is a shared intention. We are a community because we share our intentions to nurture and protect water with others of like intent. The core of our community is defined by the ethos we choose to achieve our goals. 1/1/93

Bob Brown, Kidstown
Middletown, California

Community isn't a place. It is a feeling among people of wanting to be together. 7/27/92

Dieter Bensmann, Kommune Niederkaufungen
Kaufungen, Germany

Living and working together cooperatively, making decisions by consensus, common economy. 4/9/92

Jeff Moore, L'Arche—Homefires
Wolfville, Nova Scotia, Canada

People who have commitment to live and work together for larger social purpose. (Generally we do—but with a lot of transient people.) 7/10/93

• • • • • • • • • • • • • • • • • • • •

There is never a time when we are not in community, and our practice is to awaken to that experience of communion.

• • • • • • • • • • • • • • • • • • •

Kathy Moody, Laurel Hill Plantation
Natchez, Mississippi

Communities are replacements for extended families for people who have lost touch with their biological extended families or whose families cannot offer a loving environment. 12/11/92

Patrick Kimmons, Moonshadow
Whitwell, Tennessee

Any group of animals that interact toward a specific or nonspecific goal—similar orientation in time and space—communication—deliberate social survival ethics. 3/7/93

Niche (a common definition by the group)
Tucson, Arizona

Community, like love, is so craved, adored, and overused, it seems to have lost meaning, except as a kind of political/new-age slogan. We're becoming interested in more specific words, such as cooperative business, support group, neighborhood, and even commune 12/14/92

Mariah Wentworth, Rainbow Hearth Sanctuary
Burnet, Texas

An interdependent, cooperative grouping of aligned humans, animals, plants, earth energies, and benevolent multidimensional beings who together comprise a sensitive, sustainable ecosystem. (We're working on it!) 10/5/93

Marein Whitman, ReJenneration
Jenner, California

A group of people who share values, goals, commitments, and hopefully living space and food. A group of mutual respect and support. 5/5/92

John Burke, S.E.A.D.S. of Truth
Harrington, Maine

A group of people working together for a shared goal—housing, employment, food, energy, etc.—on a common land area. 8/17/92

Sky Jasper, The Sky Jahnna
Idyllwild, California

A true community, in my view, has many of the elements of the archetypal community—the family. Thus a community has clear relationships, commitment, physical proximity, common values, and a goal or goals that unite them. At least. The first three are basic. 7/17/93

Deborah Altus, Sunflower House
Lawrence, Kansas

We don't have a working definition of community. 4/21/92

John H. Affolter, Teramanto
Renton, Washington

"Intentional community" means a group of people of similar or like attitudes, goals, outlook, and worldview that is comprehensive in its functions, including residential or housing provision and work opportunities actually utilized by members for subsistence production of at least some of their necessities. The group's decision-making process is considered as important as its goals and is open to all members. 7/20/92

Intentional Community:
The Origin of the Name

Amazingly, the term "intentional community" can be traced directly to a point of origin. Al Andersen, President of the Fellowship of Intentional Communities in 1960 (The Fellowship was reincorporated in its present form in 1986, with a name change to the more expansive Fellowship for Intentional Community.) wrote this in 1993, as part of a eulogy for Griscom Morgan:

...in his book, The Small Community*...Arthur Morgan explains that he considered the small community to be the "seedbed of society," a seedbed that has been permitted largely to go into decay because of neglect and lack of appreciation for its value....It is clear that both Griscom and his father were not only interested in reviv-ing and energizing "community" in more conventional society, but also in the experimental frontiers represented by the various intentional communities which sprang up during and immediately after World War II, though they were initially called "cooperative communities."*

In order to promote interest in (small) community, Arthur Morgan founded Community Service, Inc., in 1940. By the mid-'40s...(he founded) the annual Small Community Conference. It was in the course of working at Community Service that I became aware of...Celo (North Carolina) and other cooperative communities (Macedonia–Georgia, Bruderhof–New York, Bryn Gweled–Pennsylvania, Tanguy–Pennsylvania)....I immediately approached Griscom with the idea of inviting members of these various cooperative communities to a gathering of their own, perhaps immediately following the next Small Community Conference. That must have been about 1948, or possibly 1949...

Individuals did come, from Celo, Macedonia, and other groups. Art Wiser from Macedonia (now a leader in the Rifton, New York, Bruderhof Community) showed exceptional interest. So much so that he assumed leadership of the new organization of cooperative communities initiated at that time.

...the cooperative community movement had...(a pioneering) role in the larger society....It was the role of establishing...a new global society, from the ground up. Accordingly, the new organization was initially called the Inter-Community Exchange. It soon became apparent, however, that the thing that the various cooperative communities had to exchange, and that others needed, was primarily fellowship. Almost simultaneously, the concept of "intentionality" came into play. Thus, the name of these groups was changed from "cooperative communities" to "intentional communities." The combination of these two changes led to the name change to Fellowship of Intentional Communities. As far as we know, that is the first appearance of the term. ⬩

Bibliography

Morgan, Arthur, *The Small Community, Foundation of Democratic Life*, Community Service Incorporated, P.O. Box 243, Yellow Springs, OH 45387, phone 513-767-2161 or -1461, 336 pages, $10. Catalog of intentional community books available upon request.

Finding Your Community

Jonathan Roth of Twin Oaks

How to Visit an Intentional Community

Seeking a Spiritual Community Home

Mainstreamer's Search for Community

Cohousing: A New Type of Housing for the Way We Live

Finding a Home: Urban Community

A Tale of Two Communes: A Scholar and His Errors

A Word about Cults

How to Visit an Intentional Community

by Kat Kinkade of Twin Oaks, Louisa, Virginia

The mechanics of visiting a community aren't very difficult. One writes a letter, waits for a response, follows directions, and that's that. But assuring oneself of a fruitful and satisfying visit is another matter. Most communities spend considerable time and energy talking about and worrying about optimizing visitors' experiences. Yet there are still shortcomings and miscommunication from time to time. Visitors can help by doing some thinking ahead of time to set themselves up for a good visit. This article is full of advice to the prospective visitor. Read it with your own plans in mind. Maybe it will give you some ideas.

It is useful to consider the question: Why is this particular community open to visitors at all? What do they want or need from them? I think it's safe to say that most communities that advertise in a directory are keeping an eye out for people who might join them. They may be openly seeking members, or they may be only selectively open, watching for someone with a high degree of compatibility.

There are other reasons for having visitors, and they will vary from group to group. Some may simply need help with their work. Others may welcome stimulation from outsiders. A number of groups make their living from welcoming visitors at various conferences and seminars. Some organizations are interested in spreading their philosophy or religion. What you can be sure of, however, is that a group opens itself to receive strangers for its own reasons and its own needs. It isn't just exercising neighborly hospitality.

On your side, you have your reasons for wanting to visit. So, it makes sense to seek visits with groups that not only have something to offer you, but also have something to gain from your stay.

No matter what a visitor's personal agenda may be, helping the community with daily work is quite likely to make the visit worthwhile on both sides. Work is appreciated, and good work is appreciated a lot! This is true on the smallest commune or the biggest cooperative. Shared work opens doors to friendship and mutual confidence that no amount of conversation can open. Most people know this intuitively.

Over the years my home communities have hosted thousands of visitors, a large percentage have pitched in willingly with our work—everything from collating newsletters to bucking hay—and they don't begrudge the time. They have helped us build what we have today, and I am personally grateful. It's one of the reasons we will probably continue to be open to thousands more. The visitor who feels touchy about being exploited during the few days or weeks of a visit just doesn't understand the trade-offs from the community point of view, and is unlikely to get much satisfaction from the visit.

Sometimes a visitor is perfectly willing to work, and repeatedly volunteers, but the community members don't seem to take the time or make the effort to find an appropriate job. If this happens and you aren't the sort who can just intuitively find ways to help out, just make sure your offer is clear. Then, enjoy yourself doing something else. Some groups

---

Kat Kinkade is a founding member of Twin Oaks (1967), East Wind (1974), and Acorn (1993). She has written, and Twin Oaks has published, two books about that community, *A Walden Two Experiment* and *Is It Utopia Yet?* At Twin Oaks Kat is active in various administrative and clerical functions, as well as choral singing, barbershop quartets, and community musical productions.

Helping the community with daily work enhances the visit on both sides.

Mary Ann Kenny, Glen Ivy

are not organized well enough to use visitor resources, and there's no point in bugging them about it.

A mistake to be avoided is treating communities like a sort of Disney World, put there for the interest of the public. For the most part, intentional communities are not showcases, are not kept up to impress outsiders, and are not particularly interested in being looked at by casual tourists. Resident communitarians may put up with a certain amount of tourism for income, or for outreach; but residents live their personal lives in community, and generally they don't enjoy uninvolved spectators.

Occasionally a visitor is not content with a guided tour, and causes exasperation by insisting on "talking to the residents to get a real feel for the place." The resident members in any community are generally friendly enough, but they may see too many strangers. The only way to get a feel for the place is to stay awhile; and the best way to do that is to invest yourself in a visit that is useful to both yourself and the host community.

Let us assume, then, that you are prepared to establish your welcome in a community by one means or another, and get on to other issues. One of the other main issues is expectations.

It's a good idea to read the printed material that

a community provides. While no substitute for a visit, it at least gives you an idea of the self image of the community. Of course this material will contribute to your expectations, as it should. This can be upsetting when your actual on-site experiences don't seem to have much to do with the lofty sentiments expressed on paper. Just the same, there are connections between stated group beliefs and their behavior norms. It is a mistake to ignore these connections, especially if you think of joining.

Years ago I knew a couple who read the philosophical material of a certain community and were appalled by it. They didn't agree with the published community tenets and didn't like the tone of the material either. However, they happened to meet someone from the group who was highly personable. So, they visited and found the entire group to be friendly, charming, and warm. My friends figured actions speak louder than words. They decided to ignore the declared goals of the community, believing instead the day-to-day behavior of the people they were getting to know and enjoy. They joined up.

But as the months of their membership progressed, my friends found themselves more and more at odds with the founding members of the community. Everybody was warm and courteous, but their goals weren't compatible. Serious internal dissension grew, which saw my friends in conflict with the original leaders over issues of community direction. Eventually the new couple left, and so did some other members, who were disillusioned by the bad feelings generated by the philosophical struggle.

This left the group weak, angry, and exhausted. It was a community tragedy, and not an uncommon one. I say, before joining an intentional community,

• • • • • • • • • • • • • • • • • • • •

Many visitors set themselves up for disappointment by expecting their visit to be blessed with a love affair or a relationship. Now, who am I to say this won't happen? In fact, it has happened to hundreds of people in hundreds of communities....But don't count on it.

. . . .

read and believe the community documents. The chances are good that the published goals and values of every community are deeply respected by many community members, even though the behavior of some members may give consistent impressions to the contrary.

Of course a visitor will have expectations of some sort, but it's useful to keep them to a modest level. I can think of several common expectations that frequently meet with disappointment.

There's the wealthy commune vision. At Twin Oaks we sometimes hear, "But I expected a rural group to have horses." Some people don't understand why the community isn't bursting with artistic work, or doesn't have its own school, or isn't generating its own power, or creating more original architecture. Such visitors haven't considered the wealth that must be allocated to realize such visions. Alternatively, visitors who look more closely can always find visions beyond financial survival that are attracting the energy of community members.

For instance, at my community we maintain a wide assortment of musical instruments and drums, and provide work credits for dramatic productions and a wide range of apprentice training. We have indexed an extensive library of books and tapes. The community maintains an intimate retreat cottage, mud pit, sweat lodge, swimming hole, gardens, pastures, and woodlands. We provide attractive transportation opportunities for political and cultural events, and a wide variety of conferences. The visions realized will vary in each community, according to the interests and skills of the members as they come and go.

Another more common expectation is the vision of a sense of community. Those with this vision expect to be included and loved fairly soon after arrival, because of an idea that all the people in a true community love one another. It is a serious disappointment when they realize that this kind of love grows only after time and mutual commitment, and cannot be grasped quickly.

Many people expect all communities to be wholehearted in their dedication to food self-sufficiency or healthful eating habits. I have seen some visitors to my community seriously shocked by our casual laissez-faire attitude toward diet. Some of us eat meat and frequently serve desserts, as well as indulge in a small amount of junk food. To many of us this seems moderate and reasonable, considering our abundance of whole grains, soy foods, and vegetables. To some visitors it seems like heresy and backsliding.

A viable community adapts to the needs and desires of its own members much more than it conforms to abstract ideals. The probability is high that it will not, if successful, be very fanatical in its ideals. There will be some determined core idealism, but otherwise compromises will prevail. Doubtless some communities don't compromise. Some don't last either. I suspect a connection.

Many visitors set themselves up for disappointment by expecting their visit to be blessed with a love affair or relationship. Now, who am I to say this won't happen? In fact, it has happened to hundreds of people in hundreds of communities, and maybe you will be blessed also. But don't count on it. If you join, that's another matter. The chances of a long-term community member finding, at one time or another, a loving relationship within or through the community are quite high if not absolutely guaranteed.

But the visitor? My advice is to set that hope firmly aside and seek enjoyment elsewhere. Trying too hard will just make it even less likely. As to the

The "sky hammock" at Twin Oaks.

notion of finding readily available casual sex in the commune, forget it.

The most interesting community visitor is a person who wants to join the community. Let's say you have read the community visitor materials, and you're ready for a change in your life. You've come with modest expectations, and the community looks pretty good to you. Even at this point, there are still considerations that may enhance the chances of a good connection to your chosen group.

Take this question: Shall I be on my best behavior while I visit, or shall I let them know what I am really like? By all means put your best foot forward! The experienced community makes allowances. We know that in a year or two you're not going to be jumping up and volunteering to wash the dishes, the way you did when you were visiting. But the eagerness to make a good impression makes a good impression. We'll like you wanting to please. It says something good about your social skills. We know that the real you is somewhat more of a mixed bag. So is the real us for that matter.

That's not the same thing as hiding vital information. If you have a serious medical problem or a sticky child custody situation or a history of drug abuse, you cannot expect a community to become involved in such major personal problems without prior knowledge and agreement.

Then there's the question: Shall I let them know my real opinions, or shall I just go along with their assumptions? The answer depends on the nature of the group. Are you joining a group with a religion that all members must accept? If so, it seems questionable ethically to join such a group without embracing that religion. On the other hand, a group that is essentially secular should not concern itself with your private opinions. It is your behavior that matters.

• •

This doesn't mean "Visitors should be seen and not heard," but there is value in listening a lot and reserving your opinions for later.

• •

Nothing is more obnoxious than the visitor who defies the important traditions of a community. Imagine, for example, a visitor passing out candy bars to children in a commune that accepts only healthy foods, using the argument that children should be free to choose their own diets. Joining any community entails giving up certain personal freedoms, even as you gain new ones (different ones in different communities). It is unmannerly in the extreme, to say nothing of ineffective, to insist on taking for yourself freedoms that the community members have voluntarily given up. A certain amount of "When in Rome do as the Romans do," is certainly appropriate.

On the other hand, if you are thinking of joining, and your happiness depends on something that you don't think the community has, don't give up too easily. Make it a point to ask, without being judgmental. It might be that the community is more flexible than it looks. There are many things that can be done, within my own community agreements, that aren't done very often for various reasons. If a prospective member who looks good to us wonders aloud if certain personal hobbies or practices would be supported at my community, we are happy to discuss possibilities. Certainly it's worth bringing up the subject and checking it out.

The community you see during any one visit is not the whole community. It is almost impossible for visitors to understand this, but it is profoundly true. A little slice of time cannot give a deep understanding of the nature of an intentional community. Your visit is influenced by many factors that are trivial in relation to the entire membership experience. The seasons have a great impact on community activity,

as does filling a big order for community products, participating in an emergency, or being there during a birth or a death. An influential member may be absent when you visit. Or, there may be other visitors at the same time who by their presence skew your impressions.

The particular issue being discussed avidly when you visit is probably only one of many. Your visit will not give you an accurate impression of either the long-term importance of the issue or the outcome. If you visit when somebody is angrily leaving the group, you will pick up on a different feeling from the one you'd get if you visit when things are going well and membership is solid.

Your impressions of the community will also be influenced by the group you hang out with. I strongly advise all visitors to be cautious of information from a member who is angry with the community and wants to air grievances. Negatively loaded information can give a sense of getting the lowdown on the community, but the value of such insights is questionable.

At a minimum, a visitor who hears about significant community grievances should make a point of bringing up the same issues with a member who is happy with the place. A disillusioned member on the way out is certainly not an objective informant. No place is perfect, but it's probably not as bad as it can be made to sound.

Regarding community controversy, there's not much point in a visitor getting involved. At Twin Oaks, public discussions are carried on in writing, on a bulletin board. The comments of visitors on controversies are not usually welcome. Other communities argue in meetings, and the same thing is true of visitor comments there. It may seem to the visitor that there is something quite relevant that hasn't been said, and somebody needs to say it. But this is virtually never true. No outsider can really understand these issues after a brief stay.

Even after joining, new members will still blunder. Only after time spent living with longer-term members can new people gain an effective understanding of controversial community issues. All this doesn't mean "Visitors should be seen and not heard," but there is value in listening a lot and reserving your opinions for later.

It can be valuable for the visitor to listen to the controversial discussion and then later ask questions of individuals, outside of meeting time. Be aware of framing your questions in a neutral form, "Why is it so important that…" or "What would happen if this approach were taken?" This personal approach will give you a chance to participate without being resented, and to learn more about community issues at the personal level. Be prepared to hear answers to your questions, and don't be hurt if your input isn't taken very seriously.

Every once in a while a visitor really does have knowledge that is immediately useful, and help offered in such cases is appreciated. Generally, this is technical help. For example, the community is having legal difficulties with a child custody case, and you are a retired lawyer from a firm that did a lot of custody work. Or the community is building a house, and you are an experienced builder. Or as a doctor, you notice that certain community norms are likely to lead to a particular disease. Note that the useful knowledge is not philosophical, but practical, the direct result of specialized training and experience.

In between solid technical expertise and personal opinion lie many visitor skill areas that may or may not be useful to share with a host community. The one I notice most often is massage. A lot of people are trained masseurs these days. Good. Offering to give massages is a courteous and friendly thing to do. You may or may not get any takers. The same is true for various schools of conflict resolution, facilitation, and therapy, and for artistic accomplishments that you can teach. If you have such a skill, your best tactic is to offer but not push it. If your guitar playing draws a happy crowd, good; you've added something to the group's happiness. On the other hand, if nobody wants to listen, oh well, try something else.

Any community's favorite visitor is the cheerful, helpful one who is genuinely impressed with the community and not very critical of shortcomings. Even if they don't join, leaving the community with a positive feeling is a nice thing to do. Of course it's always possible that some group at a particular time doesn't really need congratulations; it needs a kick in the pants. Even so, be very careful before you elect yourself to the job.

A word about doing the community circuit. People often set out to visit many different communities, but few ever finish their trek. They find out what they need to know after being at two or three

> **Any community's favorite visitor is the cheerful, helpful one, who is genuinely impressed with the community and not very critical of shortcomings….Of course it's always possible that some group at a particular time doesn't really need congratulations; it needs a kick in the pants.**

places. This being the case, it makes sense to look at the list of groups that sound interesting, and visit the most likely looking communities first. Directories get outdated, so write letters to more communities than you plan to visit. Some of your letters may not be answered.

When my fellow communitarians learned I was writing this article about how to visit a community, they asked me to pass along several messages. "Tell them this is our home." "Tell them not to drop in without being invited." "Tell them they sometimes have to take no for an answer." While I'm at it, I should explain that 19 out of every 20 visitors are a help and a pleasure to us. The growls and groans all come because of the exceptional twentieth.

Virtually all of those who publish the names and whereabouts of their groups do want and need a certain number and kind of visitors. So don't be discouraged. If you really want to live in an intentional community, you'll find one. ⚓

Seeking a Spiritual Community Home

by Victoria Adams of Still Water Sabbatical, Plains, Montana

For some of us, there comes a time in our lives when our spiritual development requires us to be in the company of like-minded folks, or in an atmosphere of genuine and sincere inquiry. When you are seeking a spiritually oriented community, there are a few questions that should be considered carefully.

Your first duty to yourself, and those you wish to share your time with, is to define your purpose for seeking such a community. Are you prepared to approach differences with an open mind, to learn from others as well as share your own feelings and needs?

What is the prospective community's position regarding each member's personal needs? Without going to the extreme of "looking out for number one," our personal health (mental, spiritual, and physical) needs to be nourished for us to function well. A community should offer a balanced lifestyle with the understanding that not everyone thrives with the same diet, physical regimen, or level of spiritual discipline.

Is there time provided for recreation and solitude? Are members allowed to wander off and let the breeze blow through the belfry and ring a bell or two? Or, are they kept in a constant tizzy of activity with little time to think? If you are sincerely seeking to develop your own spirituality, and not someone else's version of it, you must have time to digest what you learn. Your mind, as well as your body, requires rest, quietude, and time alone. It is at these

Sharing a celebration of spring.

Doug Jones, Birdsfoot Farm

Victoria Adams, together with her husband Jonathon, is one of the founding members of Still Water Sabbatical, a small but growing community of nondenominational believers located in northwest Montana. Their main goal was to develop a self-sufficient atmosphere where honest inquiry into the Christian faith, and its relationship to current world affairs, could occur. It is also their hope to make the results of that inquiry available by mail and bulletin board.

Victoria has taught adults and children in varied subject areas. In recent years, writing has taken the place of some of the classroom and general fellowship participation.

Mark Ivins, Institute for Social Ecology

Learning from others and from our deeper selves.

tude of compassion and mutual understanding, not arrogance or dissention.

Most religions and philosophies include the axiom that what is not shared will die; so we must share what we believe. However strong the desire to share is, though, in no event do you have the right to force others to believe as you do. In Christianity (as it is practiced at Still Water Sabbatical) God Himself does not override human free will; why then should we?

What is the relationship of the community to the natural world? Do lifestyle choices exhibit a caring attitude toward the earth? Whatever you believe about how this earth appeared, we are all very dependent on what the planet provides us. Make sure the group seriously considers the benefits from community activities versus the price—not just in dollars, but in social and environmental costs as well.

Are the principles being advocated for others carried out at home? Avoid those groups with a double standard—one set of rules for "us" and a different set for "them." A healthy attitude includes a sense of personal responsibility for what "we" are doing, as well as the desire to correct whatever "they" are doing.

It is also important to find a group that seeks creative alternatives when differences arise, and mutually beneficial solutions when there are conflicting interests. Seek a community that accepts the differences among its members within prestated parameters. Most important is the ability to leave amicably should you decide that a community is just not the place for you.

An intentional community that encourages your spiritual growth can be a rewarding place to live. From those of us at Still Water Sabbatical, good hunting, and may your journey be fruitful! ⚶

times that you learn *how* to think, to determine your own thoughts, rather than *what* to think, or what someone has told you to think. Keep in mind that development of our spiritual selves comes, for the most part, through interaction with those that we agree with, as well as the challenge of working with those we differ with.

What is the relationship of the community with society in general, or nonmembers living near it? Be very careful of groups who look at the rest of the world with an "us against them" attitude. It is best to find a group that devotes some energy to a wider community service; the kind that says "we care," not "we are superior." Sharing should come from an atti-

Mainstreamer's Search for Community

by Vivian Taylor of the Fresno Bee, *Fresno, California*

When I announced to friends and coworkers that I was taking a leave of absence from my job to tour the country, they all thought it was a great idea. But when I said I was going to investigate something called "intentional communities," the reaction was a mixture of curiosity ("What on earth *are* they?"), polite disinterest ("Oh? That's nice."), and incredulity. ("You mean you want to join one of those religious cults? You can't be serious!")

I wasn't surprised at the responses. After all, I was a typical mainstreamer: divorced, independent, a loner, at the peak of a career in journalism and, by the usual standards, successful and happy. I was also about to turn 60.

I'd been thinking for several years that in my quest for identity as an individual, I'd lost something valuable. Something I associated with the small towns of my childhood and the old circle of friends who over the years had become just a line of Christmas cards on the mantel in December.

I wanted to "belong" again—to more than my monthly book club and professional associations. I found what I'd been looking for in the 1990 *Directory of Intentional Communities*. But, was it too late for me to join a community? Could I just walk away from the security of a good job with good benefits? Could I move far away from my kids and grandkids? Could I fit in?

There was just one way to find out—see for myself! I chose six rural, secular communities, active in environmental and social issues, open to visitors, diverse and not exclusive, and at least 15 years old with 25 members or more. I also wanted to write about intentional communities to get the message out to other people, especially in the mainstream, who might be interested. The groups I chose were located primarily on the east and west coasts. I set out on my eight-week odyssey in April 1992.

Alpha Farm

My first destination was a 20-year-old community in the Coastal Range of western Oregon, about 50 miles east of Eugene, the most communal of the groups on my list. I drove up the California and Oregon coast on a sunny spring day. I stopped in Mapleton, as I had been instructed, at Alpha-Bit, the store owned and operated by Alpha members. One of the group's several enterprises, the store was started by the original members as a conscious effort to reach out to people in the towns near the farm. Alpha-Bit sells a wide range of books and crafts and has a food bar. I got directions to Deadwood, where the farm is located and drove 20 miles through one of the most breathtakingly beautiful little valleys I'd ever seen. When I arrived at Alpha Farm, I felt like I'd been transported to another world.

At first glance, I saw a typical farm—a charming old farmhouse, a big barn, and several other buildings, including a newer house built by the members.

Vivian Taylor is features copy editor/writer with the *Fresno Bee*. In 1992 she set out to look for an intentional community compatible with her own lifestyle visions. In her travels, Vivian attended a gathering of the Fellowship for Intentional Community which was meeting at Celo Land Trust in 1992. In that meeting, she spoke of her plans to report on intentional communities for the daily newspaper in her region. This story is from her news reports. Vivian has a son and a daughter, and enjoys painting, sculpture, and theater.

But, after two nights and a day participating in the life of the community, I saw much more. About 24 adults and six children lived at Alpha when I visited. Eleven adults were full members, seven were "residents" and the others were visitors.

At 6:30, the breakfast cook rings a gong in the yard, the collective alarm clock, and between 7:00 and 8:00 the kitchen and dining room of the main house are filled with chatter and laughter as everyone talks about the day ahead and enjoys a sumptuous breakfast. They all gather again at dinnertime for the evening meal.

They were a busy bunch. A chart on the wall indicated who was assigned to what task for the week. Many jobs rotate, others are assigned according to special talents and interests. For example, child care rotates among the parents, and building-design work is done by the resident architect. A more eclectic group would be hard to find. Ages ranged from two months to 70 years, including singles, couples with and without children, elderly parents, and grandparents. Backgrounds and spiritual beliefs were just as diverse.

Alpha Farm is a cooperative corporation, and each member is a director in return for shares. After they join, members' personal assets are held cooperatively, and if they leave, their assets can be withdrawn; all income is shared. The adult members head seven committees, rotating yearly. Alpha Coop manages overall business, finance, and planning; Alpha Growers supervises fields, orchards, and forests; Alpha-Bit manages the store; Alpha Enterprises looks after miscellaneous income-producing activities; Alpha Institute organizes consensus and facilitation workshops; Alpha Mail oversees a 300-household postal route; Alpha Household oversees the grounds, housekeeping and maintenance, and the cooking. Then there are several subcommittees, like the auto maintenance team and the shopping team. A very efficient operation. There are monthly business meetings, and spontaneous conferences are going on constantly.

But living at Alpha Farm involves a lot more than meetings. There is much camaraderie among the members as they work together, sharing good times, listening to each other's problems, and solving disputes. Beyond the farm, the group helps organize local ecology projects and continental intentional communities gatherings; Alpha mem-

> **As I helped in the kitchen and greenhouse, shared meals, toured the farm, and listened to their stories, I also realized that building a community takes real commitment and selflessness.**

bers serve on the board of the Fellowship for Intentional Community—which publishes this directory and provides many other network services.

The children seemed happy, carefree, and secure, and why not? They have each other and parents close by, and lots of "aunts and uncles and grandparents," in a safe environment with plenty of space to run. There are horses, cows, goats, chickens, dogs, and cats—a complete farm.

Caroline and Jim Estes remain from the eight Philadelphians who founded the community in 1972. Caroline leads workshops on consensus decision making, a group process used by many intentional communities. Jim, a retired newspaper editor, has started a local newspaper, which he publishes himself.

Visitors are welcome by prearrangement, and they put in a day's work like everyone else. Trial membership of a year is required before making a full commitment as a member.

In my brief stay at Alpha Farm, I was impressed with their industry and their care for each other and for the world beyond. As I helped in the kitchen and greenhouse, shared meals, toured the farm, and listened to their stories, I also realized that building a community takes real commitment and selflessness. While needs were satisfied and comforts were provided, material goods were not the highest priority at Alpha. I began to wonder about my own priorities. Could I give up my autonomy and my dependence on "things"?

● ● ● ● ● ● ● ● ● ● ● ● ● ● ● ● ● ●

I would discover, as I went along, that none of the communities grew and prospered without seams and flaws in the fabric they've woven.

● ● ● ● ● ● ● ● ● ● ● ● ● ● ● ● ●

Cerro Gordo Community

My next stop was just a couple of hours away. Cerro Gordo is located on about 1,150 acres of densely forested land that borders Lake Dorena, six miles south of Cottage Grove, Oregon.

Cerro Gordo's description in the *Directory* sounded ideal for a quasi-new-age mainstreamer like me: "an ecologically sound, human-scaled village for 2,500 people with homes, small businesses, and common facilities clustered in and around a pedestrian village. Bicycles or horses instead of cars. Homes privately owned, a community diverse and mutually supportive."

I had made arrangements to stay the night at a Cerro Gordo bed and breakfast owned by a member of the community. It was a delightful place. A sign instructed me to leave my car on the main road. I parked and walked back through the moist woods on a well-worn path to the house. Owner Suzanne Huedner, who works in Cottage Grove, had arranged for me to let myself in that morning and meet Chris Canfield there for an interview. I was surprised to learn that Cerro Gordo had started 16 years ago. I saw only a few homes as I drove up the gravel road into the forested hills.

Chris explained briefly that soon after the land was purchased by the Cerro Gordo group, they encountered difficulties with Oregon's land use laws. In short, everything pretty much stalled for about ten years. Inevitably, there has been controversy during the long wait. I would discover, as I went along, that none of the communities grew and prospered without seams and flaws in the fabric they've woven. Each had faced at least one major crisis of survival. But those individuals who carried on

against the odds had forged the strong bonds of friendship that I was looking for. It appeared that Cerro Gordo was weathering the storm. Chris said that permits have finally come through, and plans can now move ahead. I spent the day driving and walking along the road, enjoying the pristine beauty of the landscape, and visiting with the newest resident, a woman from San Diego who just retired at 62. Her excitement and pride in her home, built in partnership with a couple who will share it with her later, was contagious. And hearing more of the Cerro Gordo story from Suzanne at the B&B later that evening brought it all to life.

Homes are built in small groups with names like Homestead Hamlet, Wellspring, and Equestrian Cluster. Cerro Gordo had over 30 residents when I was there, but about 600 people are in various stages of involvement, Chris said. Gatherings in the summer and at Thanksgiving give seekers a chance to visit and meet each other and learn more about the community. The Cerro Gordo Town Forum publishes a newsletter, "a journal of symbiotic community," in which members and supporters share ideas and news. It is a community being designed and built by its members even before they live there. A sizeable financial investment is required to make Cerro Gordo your home, but shared units are encouraged. Homes are privately owned, but the land and all common facilities are co-owned in a complex financial arrangement, which is currently being reorganized.

The Farm

I had put many miles on my new van by the time I pulled up to the Gatehouse at The Farm near Summertown in southern Tennessee. The Gatehouse appeared to be a visitor's center, but it was locked and deserted. (I learned later that it would be opening soon for the summer season.) I had a letter with a name and phone number to call when I arrived. I drove on down the dusty road, passing houses and barns, and finally came to what appeared to be the center of the community. I peered in the open door of a low, wooden building where I heard voices and caught a whiff of the most delicious aroma known to humankind—fresh-baked bread. It was The Farm's bakery.

Near the bakery was the store, where community teenagers hang out after school. I called Marti from

Farm News Service

Lunch time at The Farm's day-care center.

the phone at the store and she took me to Dale's home, where I was to stay. Dale lived in a large mobile home with a greenhouse attached to the south side. She raised bedding plants for commercial nurseries. But her primary job was type and cover designer at the Book Publishing Company, one of The Farm's many enterprises.

Of all the communities I visited, The Farm was the only one I remembered hearing about back in the '70s. My daughter had known one of the young hippies who joined Stephen Gaskin's Caravan. Before founding The Farm, Gaskin, a former English professor at San Francisco State University, and 250 followers had toured the country looking for land.

They made the trip in 60 converted school buses, ending up in Tennessee on wooded farmland they bought collectively (now 1,750 acres). They lived in

the buses and in tents while they cleared land and built houses, planted gardens and orchards and vineyards, and had babies. Nearly all in their twenties, some with children already, they were ready to save the world, Dale said. Harsh reality soon set in. As Ina Mae Gaskin, Stephen's wife, related to me while we pulled weeds in her garden, all notions of "free love" quickly gave way to strict rules about marriage and responsibility.

I walked alone through the community the next day. Near most of the rustic, not particularly well-built houses, were the old, long-abandoned buses—partially hidden by trees and underbrush, ghostly reminders of those early days.

I found the clinic, a neat, modest frame building, and talked with the midwives while they ministered to pregnant women, most from outside the commu-

51

The Twin Oaks Communities Conference is a gathering for seekers and communards.

nity. I heard about those heady years when the group of 250 swelled to nearly 1,500, 700 of them children. With the help of a local doctor, the midwife program expanded and gained respect nationwide.

Later, Dale told me about the idealistic passion that had inspired a food distribution program for poor countries called Plenty USA (now based in Davis, California), an ambulance service in the South Bronx, a team sent to provide earthquake relief and education in Guatemala, and satellite farms in other states. These young, city-bred pioneers learned how to grow their own food and preserve and can fruits and vegetables. Their innovative ways with soy products (and the recipe books they've published) have entered the mainstream and made tofu as American as apple pie. They built a solar school and became leaders in the alternative school movement.

But hard times came. Too many mouths to feed and too many hands in the till with too little control, The Farm women said, brought them to near starvation and bankruptcy. In 1983, the group reluctantly abandoned the communal structure and formed a cooperative corporation with a board of directors, requiring members to support themselves and pay monthly dues to continue common ownership of the land and houses. Many left heartbroken or bitter. But The Farm survived and grew strong again, with some of the members who left returning over the years. Today there are about 250 members—about the same size as in 1971 when The Farm was established, but with many grown children scattered around the country, some in their own communal groups.

Just before I left, Ina Mae showed me the site of Stephen's newest project, a future community where those with special medical needs can live together and minister to each other. I left The Farm feeling richer for having shared briefly the lives of these remarkable communitarians.

Celo Land Trust

Celo, located near Burnsville, North Carolina, on about 1,100 acres, looked much like the other rural mountain communities in the southern Blue Ridge, which is to say, breathtakingly beautiful. There was a different feeling, though, probably related to Celo's age as an intentional community. It began in 1937.

I met Ernest Morgan, son of the community founder, Arthur Morgan. At 89, Ernest is still active in the business and life of the community and the boarding school. And he is full of stories.

Celo is one of the oldest land trust communities in the country, he said. About 30 families live on the land, not in clusters, but far apart with an emphasis on privacy for each home. The members call their housing investments "holdings" (leaseholds). At monthly meetings, an elected board makes decisions about the land and its upkeep. Some members are employed at the school, the Celo Health Center, and the summer camp for children. All members are economically self-sufficient and diverse in every way.

However, this individualistic bent is offset by a number of cooperative activities: food co-op, crafts co-op, Celo Press, Quaker Meeting, and Rural Southern Voice for Peace (RSVP—grassroots organizing for social justice). While these organizations were all created by Celo members, many participants are from outside the community.

It's difficult to join Celo as a member nowadays. The holdings have been filled for many years. There are 17 families on a waiting list, according to Ernest. But Celo members offer their knowledge and encouragement to the communities movement in other ways. Like Alpha Farm, Celo supports the networking activities of the Fellowship for Intentional Community.

My visit to Celo was planned to coincide with one of the semiannual board meetings of the Fellowship for Intentional Community (FIC), a gathering that Celo was hosting. The FIC meeting was the high point of the trip. I met about 20 people from communities of all kinds from around the country. Hearing about groups I wouldn't be able to visit personally expanded my experience greatly. Among them were Twin Oaks, a communal group in Virginia that has been a leader in the movement for many years; Green Pastures Estate, an Emissary community in New Hampshire; Sandhill Farm, an organic farm in Missouri; new communities in North Carolina and the Virginia mountains; Harbin Hot Springs, a retreat center in California; and Dunmire Hollow, an activist community in Tennessee.

The FIC meeting gave me a chance to observe consensus decision making, which I'd been hearing so much about, in actual practice. During the three days of business meetings and late-night planning sessions, I became aware of key projects the FIC has taken on in addition to compiling and publishing the *Communities Directory*. The Fellowship organized a nationwide gathering of communitarians and seekers in August 1993 in Olympia, Washington. The group also publishes a membership newsletter and a quarterly magazine called *Communities Journal of Cooperative Living*, operates a Speakers Bureau, makes referrals for consensus training and facilitation, and answers thousands of questions a year—from those seeking a home in intentional community, or information for a newspaper story, or technical data for academic research.

• • • • • • • • • • • • • • • • • • •

...I was reminded that it is people, not houses, that make up the community—though the houses are certainly tangible symbols of commitment to place.

• • • • • • • • • • • • • • • • • • •

Shannon Farm

I left Celo feeling high on community and drove north for six or seven hours, up through the Shenandoah Valley. Crossing over the crest of the Blue Ridge Mountains in a heavy rain, I arrived at Shannon Farm on the eastern slope of the mountains near Charlottesville, Virginia.

I settled in at the community group house, called Monacan, looking out to the river at the front of the property. Monacan is a central spot with a mail room and bulletin boards where Shannon folks do a lot of communicating. Reading the messages and comments gave me a vivid picture of the people who made Shannon their home. It was clear that their fierce eclecticism, expressed with vigor, also included respect and affection for each other.

The next day dawned clear and sunny. I strolled up the road past the new calf in the barn, and watched a horseback rider in the meadow near the little lake—beautiful against the mountain backdrop. Following a footpath through tall hardwoods and across a mountain pasture, I came upon a group of modern houses where my luncheon host lived. Corinne, 75, made a tasty meal for us, and showed me her solar home and the other homes in Mt. Ararat, her housing cluster. Then we toured each of the other housing clusters, with names like Another World, Honeycomb, Catbriar, and Wildwood. As she told stories of the people at Shannon, including her own, I was reminded that it is people, not houses, that make up the community—though the houses are certainly tangible symbols of commitment to place.

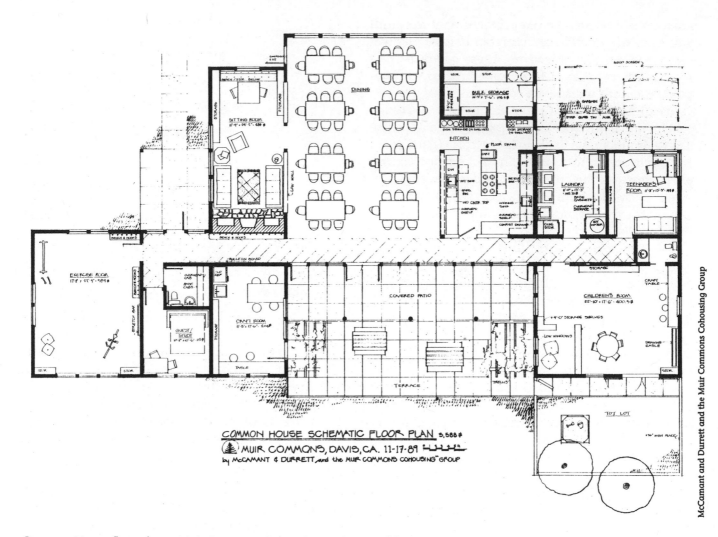

COMMON HOUSE SCHEMATIC FLOOR PLAN 5,588#
MUIR COMMONS, DAVIS, CA. 11-17-89
by McCAMANT & DURRETT, and the MUIR COMMONS COHOUSING GROUP

Common House floor plan at Muir Commons Cohousing in Davis, California.

Corinne chose Shannon as her home when she retired from her job in Washington, D.C., at 62. I found that her life had followed a pattern similar to my own. And there were others, like Julie, her husband Bob, and Maxine, all from California, who sought and found community in mid-life.

Shannon's spectacular 520 acres in the Rockfish River Valley are over 70 percent wooded with spring-fed streams crisscrossing the property. The community was started by a group of social activists drawn together from the Northeastern region in 1974, but new members were recruited from across the continent. Now there are about 60 adults ranging in age from 18 to 75 and about 20 children (who, like the kids at Alpha, enjoy the benefits of country life and playmates) who occupy about 26 family homes and several cabins. There are also three group houses, and farm and woodshop buildings. Most of the houses were built by Shannon labor.

Land, houses, and other buildings are owned by Shannon Farm Association, which is operated by a board of directors made up of full members. Business meetings are held monthly (the best time for visitors to come). Decisions are made by consensus. House-holders finance their houses, on which they hold long-term leases, which may be sold (without speculative gain) to other members or, at a discount, to Shannon Farm Association.

Shannon, unlike Celo, still has some limited room to grow. Provisional membership lasts at least six months to a year or more. Provisional members pay monthly dues of five percent of income after taxes ($30 minimum). Full members pay seven percent ($45 minimum). Most people have jobs off the land, but some work on the farm, at home, at various construction sites, or at Heartwood Design, a custom woodworking and cabinet shop with solar wood-drying kilns.

After a lively monthly meeting Saturday afternoon, many of the members gathered in one of the lovely backyards for a potluck supper. When I left Shannon early Sunday morning, I felt I was leaving friends, after only two-and-a-half days.

Arden Village

My last stop on the East Coast was the oldest community on my list. Arden—actually three adjoining settlements including Arden Town and Ardencroft—was established in 1900 when Frank Stephens, sculptor, and Will Price, architect, both of Philadelphia, bought 162 acres near Wilmington, Delaware, with the help of Joseph Fels, a wealthy soap manufacturer. All were disciples of Henry George, an economist whose "single tax" theory was popular at the time. The community demonstrates how a town can be operated successfully with George's system of land taxation (structural improvements are not taxed). The people of Arden have always been devoted to art and the theater—especially Shakespeare—and to English architecture. As the community grew and prospered, it attracted many artists, writers, and political radicals, but curiously, not that many Georgists.

Today, Arden is still a charming collection of mostly English Tudor-style cottages (Price's designs) ringing the "greens." Carefully preserved woods and a sparkling stream insulate the community from the encroaching urban sprawl. Today, as throughout Arden's history, about 60 artists and craftspeople live and work in the community. The theatrical tradition continues with productions at two rustic theaters. Arden has also kept alive its tradition of freethinking, outspoken people. Now, as then, Arden leaseholders are not questioned about beliefs, origins, or religion.

Cy and Pat Liberman were my gracious guides in the three days I spent at Arden. They moved to Arden when they married in 1936. Cy retired as a newspaper reporter in 1975. Since then they have

...when Paul began to show us through the common house and tell us about the other residents, we quickly realized that Muir Commons was indeed an intentional community, albeit in an urban setting.

coauthored books on cooking crabs and sailing, and published a new edition of *The Arden Book* for new residents, which is delightful reading for anyone interested in utopian communities.

As I met and talked with the villagers, I found that nearly a century had not dimmed the community spirit in this enchanting place. Their newsletter and bulletin boards were loaded with announcements of activities of all sorts, such as the Ardensingers, the Library "Gild," the Dinner Gild, the Gardeners Gild, the Music Gild—even the Table Tennis Gild. And on tap the following Saturday, Annual Woods Cleanup.

At the edge of Arden, the old stile still marks the entrance. Carved at the top in Old English are the words, "You Are Welcome Thither." I had felt most welcome in Arden, and took my leave very reluctantly.

Muir Commons Cohousing

Back home in Fresno, California, I wanted to see Muir Commons in Davis, the first U.S. cohousing project to be completed. I was aware of the concept—a sort of condo-turned-community approach to multihousing, designed and built by the people who will live in it. My criteria had specified rural communities, but I kept hearing about cohousing everywhere I visited.

A friend, an urban planner, drove up with me to Davis. I had arranged to meet one of the Muir

• •

Cohousing provides a compact way to build the spirit of community in our blighted cities, and a way to design housing to enable closer communication and sharing whether in the city or the country.

• • • • • • • • • • • • • • • • • • •

Commons residents, Paul Seif, at the common house. We found the street address, and felt a bit let down when we saw a double row of new housing units that looked no different than any other planned unit development in Fresno or Sacramento. But, when Paul began to show us through the common house and tell us about the other residents, we quickly realized that Muir Commons was indeed an intentional community, albeit in an urban setting.

Paul took us into the large dining room where Brian Dempsey was cooking dinner. The community shares 20 meals a month with the cooking rotated among the members—44 adults and 23 children. They also share laundry equipment, tools, and a large garden in the common area between the two rows of housing units. In the common house are an exercise room, a teen room, a playroom and yard for young children, a leisure room with a fireplace, and a guest bedroom. A walkway connects the 26 units and central areas. All of this is designed to encourage gathering and socializing, quite the opposite of most contemporary multihousing, which protects privacy.

Paul described the two years of often-frustrating meetings as the cohousing group learned how to work together, planning and building their community. Like many other intentional communities, Muir Commons uses consensus in their monthly meetings. Paul said that group experiences with consensus have built trust and fostered an other-oriented emphasis, making community meetings more productive over time.

Later I talked to Kathryn McCamant. She and her husband Charles Durrett, both Berkeley architects, introduced the cohousing concept with their 1988 book *Cohousing: A Contemporary Approach to Housing Ourselves*. The book was based on studies of such "living communities" in Denmark. A 1994 second edition has seven new chapters on North American cohousing.

Currently, Kathryn said, there are well over 100 cohousing groups in various stages of development in the United States, though most are still at the talking level. It seems to be an answer for baby boomers who yearn for community and some financial relief, but who need to be near urban centers to pursue their careers.

The cohousing contagion is evident even in the rural communities I visited. People at Cerro Gordo and Shannon were talking about a "cohousing cluster" within their communities.

This trend could be a new path for intentional community in the '90s. Rural land is much more expensive and harder to find now, especially on the two coasts. Cohousing provides a compact way to build the spirit of community in our blighted cities, and a way to design housing to enable closer communication and sharing whether in the city or the country.

As for me, I've just begun to explore the meaning and reality of community. I found reassuring answers to the questions that prompted my journey. And while I continue to look for "my community," I'll be working harder to be a communitarian right where I am today. ⑭

Cohousing: A New Type of Housing for the Way We Live

by Ellen Hertzman of The CoHousing Company, Berkeley, California

*I*t's 6:45 p.m, and people are beginning to congregate in the common sitting room and dining room. Jean pulls into the parking lot and ducks into her house to change from her office clothes. Jack has been outside playing a version of basketball with Tim and Gina's two-year-old. Martin glances up from his magazine from time to time. Sally's 11-year-old daughter comes in, proudly carrying the chocolate cake she baked for her mother's birthday. Norm is trying out the paper he'll deliver at a Seattle conference on a small group of listeners in the corner. His wife Gerda (who's already heard it a dozen times) is still up in their home, wrapping presents for their granddaughter whom they'll visit in the city. The tables are set and Elizabeth and Tim, the evening's cooks, put finishing touches on the meal. In the Emeryville CoHousing Community, dinner is about to start.

This dinner has been two years in the making. It evolved as a direct response to the common needs felt by a varied group of individuals: the need for responsive housing that provides privacy while at the same time facilitating community interaction and cooperation. Traditional housing was not adequately addressing their needs, so these individuals came together, engaged The CoHousing Company plus other housing professionals, and, working by consensus, designed housing that was planned according to their personal needs.

Dramatic demographic and economic changes are taking place in our society, and most of us are feeling the effects of those trends on our own lives. Common values that people once took for granted—family, community, and a sense of belonging—must now be actively sought out. Contemporary households are characterized by smaller families, women working outside the home, single parents, elderly, and singles living alone. These smaller households face a child-care crisis, social isolation, and a chronic time crunch, in part because their housing no longer suits them.

At the same time, increasing mobility has distanced many Americans from the extended families that have traditionally provided close social and economic support. Many people find themselves mis-housed, ill-housed, or even unhoused because of the lack of appropriate options.

To compound matters, the toll on the environment from current housing options is becoming more evident. The apparently unstoppable demand for more single-family housing is reducing the remaining green space around cities. Resources are devoured in the name of housing, and yet some of the key issues of ecological efficiency have not even been addressed.

The cohousing approach addresses such questions, with solutions that appeal to a wide variety of individuals. Pioneered 20 years ago, primarily in Denmark, over 200 such communities now exist there. In North America, the cohousing concept has

Ellen Hertzman has worked as Project Coordinator with The CoHousing Company for the past four years. The CoHousing Company was founded by architects Kathryn McCamant and Charles Durrett, who brought cohousing from Denmark to North America with their book, *CoHousing*. The Company offers architectural design services and consultation on all aspects of cohousing development. Ellen is coauthor of the second edition of *CoHousing*, and her articles on cohousing, community building, and group process have appeared in a variety of places. She has been facilitating groups and teaching consensus and group-process skills for over ten years.

Row houses line a pedestrian street where children play and neighbors stop to chat.

Trudeslund Cohousing, Denmark

experienced a groundswell of popular enthusiasm. People are looking for new answers to the realities of late-twentieth-century life.

Cohousing communities differ from typical housing developments on several levels. They are designed by the future residents, in conjunction with architects, developers, and other professionals, to address the needs of the residents, most specifically the desire for community. Residents come together frustrated at the isolation they feel in current housing designs, or because they wish to create for themselves a neighborhood in the old-fashioned sense, with a mix of generations and family types who interact and depend on each other. Cohousing communities are designed to have a neighborhood layout. There are self-sufficient individual dwellings, complete with kitchens, but the community focus is a common house with kitchen and dining room, children's room, workshop, guest room, laundry, and perhaps other facilities that the group may desire—

teen room, office space, crafts room, exercise room. The common house is designed to be used daily, as an extension of the private homes. Interaction there can be planned or spontaneous, and the possibilities for making life simpler and more enjoyable are delightfully endless!

Cohousing communities have evolved as a grassroots movement of people taking responsibility for their housing options. They draw on the best aspects of both traditional housing and community-oriented housing. Cohousing communities are distinctive in that each family or household has a separate dwelling and chooses how much they want to participate in community activities. A minimum level of participation is encouraged at the least. That participation might include cooking in the common house one night a month and serving on one committee. Cohousing developments are strengthened by accommodating a variety of ages and family types. Residents represent a cross section of old and young, families and singles—the variety adds depth to community life.

In many respects, cohousing communities are not a new idea. In the past, most people lived in villages or tightly knit urban neighborhoods. Even today, people in less-industrialized regions typically live in small communities. Members of such communities know one another's families and histories, talents and weaknesses. Traditional community relationships demand accountability, but in return provide security and a sense of belonging. Cohousing aims to provide the small household of today with a community designed to foster such values.

> In many respects, cohousing communities are not a new idea. In the past, most people lived in villages or tightly knit urban neighborhoods.

Cohousing Communities in the United States

Since the book *CoHousing: A Contemporary Approach to Housing Ourselves* was first published in the fall of 1988 (and revised and expanded in 1994), there has been a tremendous interest in this type of shared housing from a wide variety of individuals and groups. People of all ages, incomes, and lifestyles are attracted to the social and practical aspects of cohousing communities, as well as to the potential for shared resources and services. By 1994 more than 150 groups all across the continent were meeting to plan cohousing communities. Residents have occupied nine communities, several more are under construction, and many others are in some stage of the planning process.

Though cohousing groups can do much of the development work themselves, most hire professionals—attorneys, architects, developers—somewhere along the line. The CoHousing Company provides services in group organizing and facilitation, site search and acquisition, land development, architectural design, project management, and finance. The CoHousing Company works with groups through the entire development process, from the "Getting It Built" workshop that we have offered all over the country, through predevelopment basics, design, construction, and even the ongoing management of the community. Within the bounds of commercial development, the firm assists groups in creating housing that stretches the limits, believing that everyone should have a choice among many types of housing to find the type that suits them best.

Cohousing communities take many forms. Completed in 1991, the first American project is in suburban Davis, California, where a community of 26 town houses and a 3,600-square-foot common house stands on three acres. In contrast, the Emeryville community renovated an existing warehouse near the San Francisco Bay Area. In Benicia, California, 27 homes plus communal facilities will be built in a traditional small-town setting. In Colorado, 42 semirural acres are the site of a beautiful community. Whether urban, suburban, or rural, the key to the cohousing concept is the blend of privacy and community, and the involvement of future residents in the planning, design, and management of the community.

Thoughtful Housing Consumers

A group of future residents actively involved in the development process can address many issues not generally undertaken in conventional development. Areas that can be strongly affected before construction by a united group of consumers include energy efficiency, nontoxic building materials, and pedestrian orientation. Continuing resident participation in the development process encourages more thoughtful construction and waste management.

In Emeryville, an existing warehouse building was renovated, bringing new residential life to land that was already developed. At a density of 42 units per acre, the project makes particularly good use of the land. This density is five to ten times greater than many of the residents of the project had been used to. Yet it feels right, because residents consciously seek both to respect the privacy of others

• •

People of all ages, incomes, and lifestyles are attracted to the social and practical aspects of cohousing communities, as well as to the potential for shared resources and services.

• • • • • • • • • • • • • • • • • • • •

and to interact as a community. Residents will probably drive less than their conventionally housed counterparts, because the community they seek is just outside their door. Cohousing communities promise a way of breaking old patterns and creating new, more thoughtful neighborhoods.

As a warehouse conversion, the Emeryville project adds to the diversity of life in the neighborhood. The location in a transitional neighborhood of residences and light industry provides around the clock activity that is a deterrent to crime. Also, by creating a community in which the residents can feel secure, the Emeryville project helps answer the pressing question of how to create a comfortable and safe urban home for those who have much to fear in the city, especially women, children, and seniors. The innovative approaches of the Emeryville group provide an attractive model for revitalizing our cities and slowing down the urban sprawl.

The Benicia community has also had a positive impact on its surroundings, though as of this writing, construction has not yet begun. In seeking planning approvals from the city of Benicia—a small California town concerned with preserving its comfortable, people-oriented atmosphere—the cohousing planning group developed a careful presentation. They wished to demonstrate that the city requirement of two on-site parking spaces per town house was excessive. The project developer surveyed existing condominiums and determined that none of them made full use of all the allotted pavement. As a result of this survey, the city subsequently lowered

its parking space requirement, not only for the Benicia cohousing project but for all future projects, too. This decision will benefit the entire town by lessening the hold that cars have on it.

In Sacramento, The CoHousing Company worked with the Southside Park Cohousing Community, which is built on a downtown site bought from the Redevelopment Agency. This community provides a mixture of low, moderate, and market-rate housing.

Municipalities nationwide are in the process of defining and addressing the specific needs of the people who live there. Ultimately, like all communities, cohousing groups are about people and creating housing that seeks to meet people's needs: for community, for autonomy, for security, for simplicity, for efficiency, for cooperation, for fun.

It's 9:30, and in the Emeryville common house, dinner has been over for some time. Tim and Elizabeth are finishing up the dishes. They won't have to cook and clean again for another month. A few people are still drinking coffee and chatting in the dining room. Martin is back at his magazine; he could take it home to read but he prefers the swirl of life in the common house. Carrie dashed in to grab dinner, then headed home for a late night of desk work. The little ones have reluctantly been persuaded away from the children's room and home to bed. These people, who didn't know each other two years ago, have become a community. (♠)

Finding a Home: Urban Community

by Lisa Cigliana of Bright Morning Star, Seattle, Washington

My leap into communal living in 1993 opened my life to new ways of being. It also created more adjustments than I could have imagined. All sorts of questions emerged about my definition of intentional community, my role in community, and how to transition into community.

As a single woman living 2,000 miles from any blood relatives, I had spent my adult years living in the city, either alone or with one or two roommates. With roommates, the unspoken rule was that we each had our own independent life somewhere outside the living unit. While we jointly paid utilities and cleaned the house, we rarely ate together. Connections were tangential. We lived together out of convenience, not conviction.

In my outside social life, I attended meetings about community, but then went back to my own private apartment. Community was something separate, apart from my home; it was a hobby that I would set aside when it interfered with my independence.

Yet, this modern living left holes in my soul. I knew that my spirit was not being fed. After finding a copy of the *Directory of Intentional Communities*, I began to yearn for more community connections in my home life. I imagined living at Twin Oaks or some other rural, self-contained community, but I

The Love Israel Family

"...having a communal meal guarantees a semblance of family life."

Lisa Cigliana recently transitioned out of Bright Morning Star and into an independent shared home in Seattle. With her first journey into communal living behind her, she feels the need to ask some elemental questions all over again: What do I want out of intentional community? What can I offer to others? What kind of situation meets my needs? For now, these questions seem best asked while residing more or less on her own, but before you know it she'll probably be living communally again. Lisa believes that you are what you eat (not counting an occasional Diet Coke), and she participates in urban community by serving on the board of a local food bank and volunteering her time at a Seattle food cooperative. Lisa has a vision of someday taking a tour of selected intentional communities across the United States and the world.

I've been able to keep my job, my friends, and my city pleasures, such as first-run movies and live theater and music, and live in community, too.... If I end up moving to a rural community, Bright Morning Star is a perfect first step for trying out cooperative living.

knew that was a very big leap. Surely there were other options! I wanted to retain my single, urban lifestyle and still live cooperatively. So when I found a notice on a café bulletin board about a cooperative home, I called that day and did not look back. That's how I found Bright Morning Star, a group home in Seattle.

Moving to an intentional community was a big jump! But now, looking back after a few months, I heartily recommend the same process to all city dwellers who seek broader personal connections, more community, in their home life. I've been able to keep my job, my friends, and my city pleasures, such as first-run movies and live theater and music, and live in community, too. If I ever choose to live singly again, I can easily find another apartment situation. If I end up moving to a rural community, Bright Morning Star is a perfect first step for trying out cooperative living.

In my transition to residential community, I've learned about cooperative values. In today's urban environment, it is more and more common for people to see the home as a place to retreat, relax, and tune out the world. Folks recover from the stresses of work and congested city life by "vegging out" and watching TV. While I have lived this way, too, I've been disturbed by it. Can't home be a place of activity and nurture as well? As a child, I remember eagerly waiting for my dad to come home from work so that the whole family could be together—that was when family life happened!

Living Relationships

When I first moved to Bright Morning Star, the numbers seemed overwhelming to me—three adults and two teenagers, a house full of people who wanted to get to know me! I wanted to reciprocate but was so busy adapting to the new house and the group agreements that I did not have the time, energy, or frankly the desire to share conversations that first week or month. My home, once a bastion of solitude, was suddenly overpopulated.

However, over time, the communal meals provided a semblance of family life, other daily activities, chores, and meetings created a kind of knowingness and synergy that goes beyond verbal sharing. As each week goes by, other group members and I are increasingly involved in each others' lives. I still have my friends outside of Bright Morning Star, but now I have supportive relationships at home, too.

Privacy and Community

Privacy can be more ambiguous in community. Since all of my house members have lived together for eight years, they seem to have worked through territorial issues. My own territorial limits were tested when other house members initially felt freer than I liked about entering "my" room. The situation came to a head when I was out of town for a few days and my room was entered to check the window locks. They were indeed unlocked, but I still felt somewhat invaded.

Where was the compromise between security and individual privacy? When I lived in an apartment, people did not enter my room without permission. But other house members had a right to security despite my need for boundaries. I wanted a place in the house where I could keep materials such as journals and know that they were seen only by permission. In the end, I told my housemates that my bedroom was off-limits unless there was a legitimate need—such as checking the windows.

Simple Living Values

People have different ideas and priorities about how to live consciously and simplify their lives. For instance, I do not eat meat and I use public transportation rather than own a car, but until I moved into Bright Morning Star I enjoyed taking long showers and regularly tossed leftovers into the garbage. Now, some of my housemates own cars and some eat meat, but we also recycle water and save food for the compost pile and worm bin. How do our different values affect the community? Am I obstructionist if I don't save water? Do I judge house members who own cars for burning fossil fuels? Do I feel guilty if I take a long shower once in a while? These questions about priorities are present in many ecologically minded communities, including mine. However, it takes very little energy to recycle bath water for toilet flushing, or to put food scraps in containers for the worm bin. If ecological systems are put in place, the work of sustainability is certainly made easier, but the value decisions about long, hot showers and fossil fuels will not be resolved easily.

Community Responsibilities

At Bright Morning Star, we rotate cooking chores for a nightly communal meal. Since movies and community meetings often begin at 7 p.m., I have had to make choices between missing dinner or arriving at events late. We also have to schedule a weekly house meeting (finding a common day and time that all can attend is an interesting process). At times, it's simply inconvenient; other times, I resent the imposition of community on my life as a single woman. Yet home-cooked meals and gatherings with housemates are nurturing and satisfying experiences. Ultimately, it's worth the bother to have connections with domestic partners.

A final thought about starting the journey toward cooperative living: start where you are. Undoubtedly there are people in your town looking for cooperative lifestyles, seeking to share social energy as well as material expenses. I was acquainted with a member of Bright Morning Star for a year, through three different community groups. Yet, I didn't explore common interests with him or discuss dreams of cooperative living until I saw a notice for his community on a bulletin board. Who knows how many other opportunities I missed

• •

A final thought about starting the journey toward cooperative living: start where you are.

• •

by not talking with people about my dreams?

I look back a year ago to when I fantasized about living in some of the communities listed in the *Directory*. My imagination was not big enough to even guess that I would be living in a cooperative home by now. Perhaps I have more transitions ahead of me: creating urban work that is nurturing and sustainable, or maybe moving to a rural community. I am hopeful that my housemates will support my search for the ideal living arrangement wherever that takes me. But for now Bright Morning Star is for me. 🜨

A Tale of Two Communes: A Scholar and His Errors

by Michael S. Cummings, University of Colorado, Denver, Colorado

How could a conscientious communal scholar end up dead wrong on a vital aspect of a community he has been studying for years? How could he do it twice, making the opposite mistake the second time? How might he make amends by helping others avoid these errors? He might write this article.

Sunrise Ranch (1945–present) is a large, beautiful, stable, and conventional-appearing community at the foot of the Rocky Mountains about an hour's drive from Denver.[1]

Kerista (1971–1991) was an exciting, fluctuating, urban, group-marriage community in the Haight-Ashbury district of San Francisco that voted unanimously to disband at the beginning of 1992.

Sunrise Ranch initially inspired me in 1979 because of its attractiveness and practical achievements. Kerista attracted me in 1985, as it had attracted *Psychology Today* and the Phil Donahue Show in 1980, because of its single most innovative achievement, the "responsibly hedonistic" marital system of "polyfidelity."[2]

Emissaries Claim Spirit Is the Key to Their Success

My misconceptions about Sunrise Ranch related to whether its impressive accomplishments stemmed from its spirituality (as residents claimed) or from its political and economic structures (which most academic visitors suspected). My misconceptions about Kerista related to whether its members were independent self-actualizers (as members claimed) or self-deluding cultists (as my coresearchers suspected).

Sunrise Ranch is the oldest community of Emissaries of Divine Light, a nonsectarian spiritual movement that originated in the vision of founder Lloyd Meeker in 1932.[3] Worldwide, The Emissaries number several thousand supporters, a dozen full-fledged communities, and some 200 centers on seven continents. Sunrise Ranch came to my attention in 1979 when I asked a graduate student to find "the most impressive commune in Colorado." I wanted to arrange an attractive field trip for scholars attending the annual Utopian Studies Conference. The residents of Sunrise Ranch consist of four generations of friends and relatives who look, dress, and act like especially friendly "normal Americans," except they have relocated from city or suburb to a 400-acre organic farming village on the edge of a national forest.

This Emissary village includes grain and hay fields; fruit orchards, a five-acre vegetable garden, a large hydroponic greenhouse, canning and freezing facilities; beef, dairy, poultry, and egg production; a geodesic dome chapel; a beautiful new dining room pavilion and conference center; and a wide variety of single-family, multi-family, and apartment dwellings. There are skilled management, building construction, and maintenance teams; an extensive group of health-care professionals; state-

Mike Cummings is Chairman of the Political Science Department at the University of Colorado, an active member of the Communal Studies Association specializing in research concerning contemporary communities, and the owner of a long-time group house in Denver. Mike is coeditor of *Utopian Studies III* (University Press of America, Lanham, Maryland, 1991). Interests of his include learning Czech with his one-year-old, Anthony, from Anthony's mother, Petra, backpacking, fishing, motorcycling, dancing, and tennis.

of-the-art audio-visual facilities and a publishing company; programs in education, recreation, and the arts; a fire engine, laundry, sewage treatment, and power-generating plants. In short, everything necessary for the functioning of a small town.

The other utopian scholars and I went to Sunrise Ranch full of hard questions and skepticism, but after a day's visit we floated away on a Rocky Mountain high. There was no doubt that Sunrise Ranch was a communal success story. Our main skepticism had to do with The Emissaries' insistence that it was their shared spiritual awareness that had made all of this possible. As a social scientist, I was intent on discovering what political and economic institutions had produced such a communal feat.[4]

The Emissaries at Sunrise Ranch seemed to be living the very principles of cooperation and self-actualization that I had been teaching about in political-philosophy classes. The young people were lively and well behaved. The senior citizens remained active as long and as much as they wanted (the community treasurer was in her nineties). The incidence of illness was much lower than in the surrounding society, and life expectancy correspondingly higher. Pollution, unemployment, addiction, poverty, crime, and violence were virtually nonexistent. Was I, the social scientist, to believe that all of this had been created by "spirit?"

The Emissary Spiritual Philosophy

What is the Emissary spiritual philosophy, anyway? Simply put, Emissary spirituality consists of our seeking to harmonize with life's inherent creative design, which implies acting with integrity and love toward one another and serving as responsible stewards of the earth. Said negatively, The Emissaries resist the natural human tendencies toward egotism, blaming and manipulation of others, exploitation of nature, dogmatic beliefs, and the twin dangers of acting on mere impulse or adhering to rigid rules.

While I wanted to know who was running the show, who had funded it, and who owned the assets, my Emissary interviewees patiently replied with some version of "It's not this or that person or structure but Emissary spirituality that makes all of this possible." For many years, my basic response to this claim was some form of "Yes, but..." for my professional training was to seek out the key decision mak-

The Emissaries at Sunrise Ranch seemed to be living the very principles of cooperation and self-actualization that I had been teaching about in political-philosophy classes.

ers, the critical power holders, and the economic string pullers within an intentional community.

Most of the students and scholars I took to Sunrise Ranch, being similarly oriented, shared my concerns and my skepticism about the Emissaries' spiritual explanations. We felt that the Emissaries tended to avoid or deflect our nonspiritual questions about finances, governance, and family life. It was easy to sympathize with a Denver reporter's characterization that trying to pin down Emissary beliefs was like trying "to nail Jell-O to a wall." When we did get answers, they seemed to differ according to which Emissary we were talking to. For instance: "Who has the final say on important decisions if everyone doesn't agree?" Replies ranged all the way from the mystical-sounding "We don't really make decisions; the right one eventually emerges" to the no-nonsense "The foreman decides."

To our skepticism, The Emissaries responded that the only way to understand Emissary life was to experience it directly. The people at Sunrise Ranch appeared sincere, and I liked them personally, but I couldn't help feeling that their spiritual posture was, to some extent, a cop-out, or even a cover-up.

What Changed My View?

As I visited eight other Emissary communities in the United States, Canada, England, and France, I saw that the quality of life and the notable achievements of Sunrise Ranch characterized other Emissary communities as well. Yet the political, economic, and

● ● ● ● ● ● ● ● ● ● ● ● ● ● ● ● ● ● ● ●

Flexibility and informality work well for The Emissaries. Some situations call for a consensual or democratic approach, others are considered by a committee, and some are handled by one individual with particular knowledge or skill.

● ● ● ● ● ● ● ● ● ● ● ● ● ● ● ● ● ● ● ●

social structures varied greatly from one Emissary community to another. Experiencing these variations personally caused me to realize that structures, rules, or institutions could not adequately account for the success of Sunrise Ranch or any other Emissary community.

This realization prompted me to refocus my "research" away from interviewing members about Emissary structures. Instead I started participating more fully in Emissary life. I did less interviewing and more of whatever the residents were doing, working along with them in teams. At King View in Ontario, we chopped wood; while at Green Pastures, New Hampshire, we slaughtered and dressed turkeys. At Sunrise Ranch, we picked and shucked corn; at the San Francisco center, we rewired a bedroom. After painting at La Vigne in France, I nailed drywall at Mickleton, England.

People shared their concerns, openly expressed problems, and confronted conflicts. The 20 residents of the Vancouver center included me in their regular house meeting even though we had just met. The gathering started in a relaxed manner, and the general coordinator soon launched into a complaint about collections of items that had been left around the premises, a fine old mansion on a tree-lined street. Those involved explained themselves and a compromise emerged that balanced individual and community needs.

At Mickleton, the construction coordinator asked a worker to cancel the latter's "attunement" (spiritual therapy) session so the day's drywalling schedule could be maintained. The worker noted that this cancellation would be the second in two days. The coordinator explained the urgency of keeping the drywalling project on schedule. Within a minute or two, they reached an amicable resolution that honored the inconvenienced worker's sacrifice but met the immediate needs of the construction team.

Emissary Coordinators

The Emissaries have used various terms, including "focalizer" and, more recently, "coordinator" to denote a leader, or person in a position of responsibility. All residents of Emissary communities undergo several days of seminar training in leadership, and all residents are expected to accept leadership responsibilities in one or more spheres of community life.

Occasionally, an Emissary coordinator becomes ineffective over time, and a leadership change is needed. The Emissaries have no fixed procedure for recruiting or terminating their leaders. Rather, the groups allow a process of communication and understanding to occur by which change eventually emerges. Most Emissaries whose actions are creating problems willingly change their behavior or shift their sphere of activity. When an individual does not get the signals, or ignores them, he or she is eventually persuaded to try some other area or level of responsibility.

Emissaries resist fixed rules, whether about leadership, economic production, resident participation, religious practices, sexuality, or family life—which includes singles, cohabiting adults, and one- or two-parent nuclear and extended families. As to living arrangements, most Emissaries live singly or in nuclear families, although many have had group living experience. No stigma is attached to either lifestyle choice. Nor is there a set of commitment mechanisms among the Emissaries—such as those identified by Rosabeth Kanter[4]—to formalize the bond between the residents and the community.

Likewise, no single approach to economics seems key to Emissary productivity and growth. Sometimes private ownership works best, while at other times community ownership, or a mixture of the two, seems appropriate. For instance, while Sunrise Ranch has been fully communal, 100 Mile House, in British Columbia, and Green Pastures have always operated more cooperatively—with financially self-sufficient members.

Flexibility and informality work well for The Emissaries. Some situations call for a consensual or democratic approach, others are considered by a committee, and some are handled by one individual with particular knowledge or skill. By contrast, many intentional communities spend a great deal of time trying to design the right structures or rules to use in guiding community life. Kerista, for instance, had several dozen explicit rules of social dos and don'ts as part of a complex social contract.

What Unites Emissaries?

What, then, unites residents of Emissary communities in a common purpose with such a flexible, efficient community life? Ten years of observation and experience finally forced a change in thinking upon me. The Emissaries' own explanation for their practical success is the shared spiritual experience of seeking the natural design in life itself. This now seems to be a better explanation than any alternative I have been able to observe.

True, all Emissary communities have until recently been governed by a "coordinator" system in which those persons generally regarded as most able in a specific area of community life "gave focus" to those involved in that area. But even this shared system of leadership is flexibly adapted to local conditions, and it has proved only as strong as the spiritual commitment of those involved in it. In the last two years, many Emissary communities have been moving toward democratically elected councils—the subject of a future article.

After 13 years of visiting Emissary communities, I have come to wonder whether the life process itself may indeed provide us with a natural way to get along with one another and to thrive, if only we can attune ourselves to that process. In situations of uncertainty or disagreement, Emissaries seek to look within themselves, to attain what they call an inner stillness, and be guided by the movement of a natural design contained within life itself. We may question whether such a natural design actually exists, as opposed to all life plans being imposed by humans. Or, we may question whether Emissaries do so well together simply because they are agreed in thinking that there is a design for life. What seems beyond reasonable doubt, however, is that Emissary spirituality works in practice.

This answer may sound vague or even meaningless to many, but it is the most likely explanation I have been able to develop. I should be cautious and note that living in a tight-knit intentional community is not everyone's cup of tea, and it has not been my own choice. Indeed, only about one fourth of Emissaries worldwide live in an Emissary community; most limit their participation to service on Sundays and, possibly, a weekday attunement, group meeting, or project.

Critics of the Sunrise Ranch lifestyle include a small number of ex-residents who regard the Emissaries as a cult, a judgment that most ex-residents do not share. I have argued the pros and cons of Sunrise Ranch myself,[5] for it has been difficult for me to accept a spiritual explanation for the practical success of a modern, nondenominational community like Sunrise Ranch. But my shift from an interview format to brief periods of participation (cultural immersion) made the dynamics of daily life at Emissary communities more accessible and understandable to me. Also, by placing my original, single case study of Sunrise Ranch in the broader perspective of other Emissary communities, I came to see beyond the limitations of my initial, nonspiritual hypotheses.

It now appears that the spiritual explanation originally offered by Sunrise Ranch residents, though inherently subjective and biased, may be closer to the truth than the political and economic alternatives to which I'd been "objectively" committed. Ironically, the second case study, Kerista, reflects the opposite error—accepting communitarians' accounts of their experiences at face value.

Kerista Commune: Ideals Overshadow Doubts

Regarding my scholarly study of Kerista, I need to state my central bias up front. From the very beginning, I shared the major Keristan ideals and was profoundly impressed by each and every Keristan I met in that initial period. In retrospect, I believe it was this enthusiasm that made it difficult for me to view Kerista as a leader-dominated group with some "cult" behaviors, even in the face of increasingly troubling signs dating from before my first visit to Kerista in August of 1987.

Many communities besides Kerista have experimented with direct democracy, economic communism, equal rights for women, and mutual and self criticism. Few, however, have attempted the dramatic departure from monogamous marriage that Kerista called polyfidelity, meaning long-term sexual faithfulness to not one but several partners. The goal of polyfidelity is to maximize intimate friendship and sexual pleasure while eliminating jealousy and possessiveness.

Polyfidelity at Kerista

As polyfidelity was practiced at Kerista, individual members belonged to one of several families, called B-FICs, or Best Friend Identity Clusters. Each member was expected to be nonpreferential, but not necessarily equally "in love," with all family members of the opposite sex. Members slept with these heterosexual lovers equally and exclusively, one after the other, on a nightly, rotating schedule. B-FIC members of the same sex became one's best friends, called "starling sisters" or "starling brothers."

To prevent pregnancy and alleviate world overpopulation, Kerista required male members to have vasectomies, an indicator that after the required, presexual courting period, a commitment to the commune was viewed as long term and was taken seriously. By the mid-1980s, each prospective new member was required to take a series of three AIDS tests and to test negative for all three.

It was polyfidelity that got Kerista on such programs as the Phil Donahue Show in the 1970s, and it was primarily an interest in studying polyfidelity that drew me and my utopian studies colleagues Lyman Sargent and Lise Leibacher to Kerista for a four-day visit in 1987. Had the Keristans really been able to eliminate jealousy? Did multiple partners reduce the strength of individual relationships? How stable were the polyfidelitous families? Were the hedonistic Keristans productive in other spheres as well, or did they spend so much time and energy on sex and related issues that they had little left over for income-earning work? Wasn't there a downside to a schedule that automatically prevented two

lovers from sleeping with each other several nights in a row? What rules governed daytime behavior and overnight trips away from the commune?

In short, how well did polyfidelity actually work, and what costs did it entail? If it worked as well as the Keristans claimed, might it not have something to offer the larger society, beset by high levels of sexual frustration and neurosis, jealousy-motivated violence, and high divorce rates?

Getting to Know the Keristans

Prior to our on-site visit, my two colleagues and I had become familiar with half a dozen Keristans at Communal Studies Association conferences; Keristans traveling through Denver had visited with me several times; and all three of us had sampled the voluminous Keristan literature. Perhaps the ambitious visions expressed in their publications exceeded their likely grasp. But we had been uniformly impressed with the Keristans we had interacted with in terms of their intellect, their articulation, their openness, and their sense of commitment. Kerista was surely one of the more controversial communes in the United States, and we looked forward to our trip to San Francisco with considerable anticipation.

Our visit to Kerista turned out to be intense, fascinating, eye-opening—and disconcerting. As we toured the several neighboring Victorian flats that housed Kerista, our first impressions confirmed the commune's Haight-Ashbury, hippie origins: bright colors, hip clothes, energetic and sensual men and women, performance art and rock-music dances, motley living quarters in creative disarray, a highly interactive and verbal culture, universal computer literacy—and Brother Jud, the forceful, sixtyish, long-haired founder of Kerista.

By the second day of our visit, Jud[6] and those closest to him were becoming impatient with our "objective" scholarly stance. Weren't we sufficiently impressed with Kerista to be enthusiastic advocates, if not future members? We explained that the purpose of our first visit was to understand Kerista, not to praise or criticize it. While most of the Keristans continued to impress us with their enthusiasm, intelligence, and friendliness, we felt a growing estrangement from some of our hosts.

Jonathan Roth of Twin Oaks

Nevertheless, my colleagues became intensely uncomfortable during the remainder of their stay. Though I also felt uncomfortable with Jud and a few other Keristans, I continued to enjoy my interactions with most of our hosts and felt more curious than threatened.

Polyfidelity Assessed

Interestingly, our conclusions about polyfidelity in the narrow sense were perhaps our least controversial. Put briefly, polyfidelity seemed to be working well in the sense that sleeping rotations were maintained, members expressed sexual satisfaction with the system, we sensed little jealousy, and friendships seemed strong among long-time members.

Moreover, the regularity and variety of sexual activity seemed to have resulted in a high level of personal gratification and freedom from sexual tension without undermining the necessary work ethic. Kerista's computer company, Abacus, was well under way by 1987, and by 1991 had experienced spectacular growth into a profitable, $30-million-a-year firm that employed most of Kerista's two-dozen-plus adults.

We did question the strength and longevity of the romantic love relationships. There had been frequent B-FIC changes over the years, and the wording of the marital vow was not for life but "a *current intention* of lifetime involvement" (my emphasis). "Romance" had a spotted history at Kerista—viewed negatively less than two years earlier, romance had come to be viewed as both positive and possible within polyfidelity.

Gestalt-O-Rama as Hot Seat

About halfway through our visit, we participated in the Keristan mutual criticism process, called Gestalt-o-Rama. Indeed, we became the focus of some heated criticism, initiated by Jud. During this process, Jud called Lyman a "schmuck" for asking about Kerista's policy on drugs; I was taken to task for disagreeing with critical comments Jud had made about Sunrise Ranch; and Jud warned us that if we didn't shape up, our visit would be terminated. Apparently, we shaped up enough, since we were permitted to stay.

• • • • • • • • • • • • • • • • • • • •

...we had no reason to believe that polyfidelity was any more unworkable than conventional monogamy with its more than 50 percent divorce rate.

• • • • • • • • • • • • • • • • • • • •

We also found it hard to believe that Keristans were equally attracted to all of their sexual partners. We learned that during the day, as well as on trips, B-FIC members could in fact engage in more sex with some partners than with others.

On the other hand, we had no reason to believe that polyfidelity was any more unworkable than conventional monogamy with its more than 50 percent divorce rate. The fact that over the years we had heard occasional reports of Keristan infidelity did not negate the general viability of polyfidelity, any more than the much higher rate of infidelity among married Americans negates monogamy as a workable system.

Keristan Values Questioned

Far more controversial—among the three of us, as well as between the Keristans and us—were questions about (1) how well Kerista practiced what it preached about equality, democracy, feminism, and philanthropy, and (2) how the group reconciled the apparent contradiction between its highly idealistic internal practices and its patriotic enthusiasm for the oppressive external status quo, including U.S. big business and politics. In a draft article we sent the Keristans, the three of us raised the following questions.

(1) Though all Keristans were said to be equal, weren't some, especially Jud, "more equal" than others? Jud's authoritarian personality stood out like a sore thumb at Kerista. We had observed him try to dominate and, we thought, seriously abuse the Gestalt-o-Rama process of mutual criticism. We had heard him simply announce a policy change, and we got the impression that he expected his position to be rubber-stamped during the required voting process. Also, we had not seen Jud sharing in domestic chores, but had often seen him being served by others, especially women. Our uncertainty about Keristan equality made us uncertain about Keristan democracy as well.

(2) Wasn't there an unadmitted status hierarchy among the commune's several families, or B-FICs? It seemed to us that the Purple Submarine B-FIC, by far the largest at 16 members, also contained the most active, most long-standing, and most highly respected members.

(3) How truly feminist was Kerista? While proclaiming feminism, Keristans seemed to know little about the feminist movement itself. Also, they had resisted the argument advanced by Lyman and me (whom they knew) that we wanted to add Lise (whom they didn't know) to our research team in order to get a woman's point of view. "We think a man can understand the situation of women at Kerista just as well as a woman can," said Way, at the time a hard-core Jud supporter and one of Kerista's most zealous ideologues. At least half a dozen members, especially four or five women, seemed to us clearly superior to Jud as thinkers and leaders. Yet we sensed that Jud exercised far more influence than these more talented followers. We failed to uncover any special qualities that might justify Jud's revered status. Lyman and Lise became convinced outright that Kerista's feminism and egalitarianism were either a delusion or a sham.

(4) How much of the proclaimed one-third of net income earmarked for philanthropy did Kerista actually give to philanthropy? Kerista's very bright young accountant, Luv, had given us an impressively detailed explanation of Keristan finances. Communal income relied heavily on contributions from a few individuals (like Luv himself and female banking executive Zia), who had high paying outside jobs. While Kerista financed a number of free publications, we could never get beyond the officially crafted expression—"x" percent of net income is "made available for philanthropy"—to a concrete figure for actual dollars given. The only actual charity we learned of was a few hundred dollars given to a poor Jamaican household.

(5) Did the Keristans see any contradiction between their radically democratic, egalitarian, feminist, communal, philanthropic, and polyfidelitous model, on the one hand, and their patriotic identification with the U.S. government and corporate America, on the other? Critics of U.S. institutions have included not only "radical academics" (our self-description) like Lise, Lyman, and me, but some of the Keristans themselves in their pre-Reagan, pre-Abacus, radical-hippie days. Part of this change in thinking may be accounted for by the growth of Abacus. By 1987 this Keristan business already numbered among its customers several large corporations and the state of California.

The Keristans were not pleased with the questions in our draft article. We-the-researchers and they-the-subjects seemed to become somewhat disillusioned with each other. In the five years after our visit, we stayed in sporadic contact with the Keristans. But they became increasingly busy with their burgeoning computer business, and had less and less time to reply to our requests for updates.

A friendlier division also developed within our three-person research team. Lyman and Lise viewed Kerista as flouting its espoused values and verging on being an unadmitted Jud-cult. Though sharing my colleagues' concerns, I took the position that without conclusive evidence to the contrary, we should accept the Keristans' beliefs as true, or at least sincere and plausible.

Thus I adhered to my original confidence and belief in such Keristans as Lee, Jaz, Eve, Way, Luv, Zia, and Sym. They simply had too much on the ball as individuals to let a self-chosen leader control their choices. I pointed out to Lise and Lyman that the most influential Keristans were predominantly women, including the four who jointly owned Abacus on behalf of the community as a whole. If these women insisted that they were not being exploited by Jud or anyone else at Kerista, and indeed were thoroughly enjoying themselves, who were we to tell them their true feelings or correct their "false consciousness?"

My own view of the situation was that Jud, far from controlling anyone, was being benevolently tolerated and indulged, as a kind of elder statesman. I believed that Kerista would not only survive his passing, but would thrive even more.

Kerista Breaks Up; New Commune Forms in Hawaii

I was wrong. Between November 1991 and January 1992, Purple Submarine expelled Jud from the B-FIC; Jud left Kerista; and Kerista fell apart. With Jud gone, the members of the commune voted unanimously to terminate Kerista. I happened to visit just as the process of dissolution was starting. Later I received follow-up reports from a communal electronic bulletin board. These reports included Jud's charges against those who had expelled him—whom he dubbed the Gang of Five—as well as the official Keristan explanation of events. In July 1992, I visited the latest version of Purple Submarine (now a new ten-person polyfidelitous commune relocated in Hawaii), whose members had weathered Kerista's demise "without missing a single sleeping rotation," according to Lee. I spoke at least briefly with all eight adult members (they have Kerista's two children as well). Though pressed for cash—Abacus having fallen on hard times—these post-Keristans spoke confidently of the new, pared-down commune's future life together as polyfidelitous lovers.

Kerista Analyzed by Insiders

How do such long-time Keristans as Eve, Lee, Tye, Jaz, and Daniel look at Kerista in retrospect? "In many ways, it was your basic cult," says Eve, who cofounded Kerista with Jud in 1972. "Jud was a master salesman," says Lee. He sold the younger Keristans on himself and his utopian visions, using Gestalt-o-Rama as a control mechanism over others, but avoiding mutual criticism himself. Over the years, Jud seemed to become increasingly negative, intolerant, and defensive toward dissenters and outsiders whom he saw as threats to his authority.

But the time came when the mutual criticism process was finally focused on Jud, and he wouldn't take it. Relationships had been getting worse for many years, but individual Keristans were afraid to voice basic criticisms of Jud—or even Kerista in general—for fear they would be isolated, punished, or expelled. With years of growing dissatisfaction as a backdrop, the catalyst for expelling Jud was the unhappiness of the women in his B-FIC, Purple Submarine. Each time they tried to bring a new man into the B-FIC, Jud either prevented his joining or made his life so miserable that he eventually left.

Ex-Purple Submariners now say that their B-FIC was indeed a kind of upper class of Kerista that, under Jud's sway, dominated commune life. Jud's most avid female supporter prior to the breakup, Way, is reportedly also on the outs with most of the ex-Keristans. They see her as having psychologically manipulated members in many of the same ways as Jud did.

Why for five years did I accept the denials and rationalizations of a group that now calls itself an ex-cult? Why, on the other hand, had I been insufficiently open to the Emissaries' self-assessment, which I now substantially accept?[7] Part of the explanation probably rests in my own desire to believe in the workability of the Keristan ideals, and my own misweighing of the information available to me. My colleagues, Lise and Lyman, seemed to have been more accurate in their perceptions.

Polyfidelity, which reportedly continues to work well for the new group, was not what was wrong with Kerista. The hard lesson of the Keristan "cult," as former members now sometimes call it, seems to be that even strong individuals can fall prey to a community dynamic that encourages defense mechanisms like denial, rationalization, and compartmentalization.

Yet, even though polyfidelity can be a satisfying lifestyle, and the business was booming, Kerista failed. Could it be that personal empowerment and freedom of expression are more compelling, over the long term, than sex and money?

Conclusion

Hopefully, readers will not interpret this report as a glorification of Emissary communities and a debunking of Kerista. Emissary life is not for everyone, and some ex-Emissaries are critical of their experiences in community. On the other hand, the ex-Keristans I have talked with do not regret their years at Kerista, which they enjoyed in many ways and which they regard as a vital stage in their personal growth.

As the saying goes, different strokes for different folks. Living in any small community, like living in a close family, will always involve both the blessings and the pitfalls of intimacy.

A final warning. Readers will have to decide for themselves how much confidence to place in the born-again wisdom of a twice-mistaken scholar who

has seen the error of his ways. Surely I couldn't be wrong again. Or could I? I remain in contact with the Emissaries and the ex-Keristans. Let's hope further apologies are not called for in a later edition of this directory.

Endnotes

1. See Emissaries of Divine Light, *About Sunrise Ranch* (Loveland, CO: Eden Valley Press, 1982), and *A Statement of Purpose* (1977).

2. Kerista Commune, *Polyfidelity: Sex in the Kerista Commune and Other Related Theories on How to Solve the World's Problems* (San Francisco: Performing Arts Social Society, 1984).

3. Exeter, Martin Cecil, *On Eagle's Wings* (London: Mitre Press, 1977); Emissaries of Divine Light, *Opening Series* (Loveland, CO: Eden Valley Press, n.d.), and *A Statement of Purpose* (1977).

4. Kanter, Rosabeth Moss, *Commitment and Community: Communes and Utopias in Sociological Perspective* (Cambridge, MA: Harvard University Press, 1972). Indeed, at first glance, Emissary communities and Kerista alike provide more evidence for Donald Pitzer's view of communalism as a developmental aspect of social or spiritual movements, than for Kanter's success-or-failure model. See also Donald Pitzer, "The Theory of Developmental Communalism," a paper given at the Third Triennial Conference of the International Communal Studies Association, Elizabethtown College, Elizabethtown, PA, July 28, 1991.

5. Cummings, Michael S., "Sunrise Ranch as a Utopian Community," in Michael S. Cummings and Nicholas D. Smith, editors, *Utopian Studies III* (Lanham, MD: Society for Utopian Studies and University Press of America, 1991), pp. 59–65.

6. The three-letter Keristan names were all acronyms standing for important ideals or qualities. "Jud," for instance, stood for "Justice under democracy."

7. Preliminary evidence on the recent democratization movement in Emissary communities indicates that some of my early concerns may not have been entirely mistaken. ⓦ

A Word about Cults

by Corinne McLaughlin and Gordon Davidson of Sirius, Shutesbury, Massachusetts

At the same time that the hippie communes were attracting major attention in the '60s and early '70s, the so-called "cults"—manipulative, authoritarian mass movements—began growing in popularity and attracting many young people who were generally confused and lost, or burned out on drugs. Today, the cults are still recruiting large numbers of people, and are still sensationalized in the media.

Many people are desperate to change themselves and to change the world. Some are so lonely and alienated from family, religion, or friendships that any group that looks loving and supportive is very magnetic, even if the price is one's personal freedom. The very legitimate search for truth, personal and spiritual values, and transcendence is easily exploited by power-driven "cult" leaders.

There is a problem, though, in defining exactly what a cult is. The point at which a group actually crosses the line between what is acceptable and what is not depends a great deal on a person's values. As Ken Keyes, author of *The Handbook to Higher Consciousness*, expressed it:

A "cult" is a term you would use to apply to that which you don't like...so I don't really have much use for that term. I could tell you [about] the groups that I feel are sincerely trying to do something good for the world and that I like...I don't consider them "cults."

It may be hard to define exactly what a cult is since it is such a subjective, emotionally laden label.

However, we would warn people about a group that manifests many of the following traits:

- encourages the violation of personal ethics or encourages deception to prove loyalty to the group;
- encourages relinquishment of personal responsibility for actions;
- restricts access to outside people or information;
- inhibits critical thinking so that "group think" predominates, and many subjects are taboo for discussion;
- restricts the ability to leave the group;
- restricts privacy;
- uses intense indoctrination;
- demands absolute obedience;
- applies intense pressure toward group conformity;
- demands stereotyped behavior;
- physically or psychologically encourages overdependency;
- manipulates feelings in a conscious way;
- appeals to fear of not being saved or enlightened;
- appeals to greed;
- appeals to power;
- appeals to the glamour of being one of the elect;
- appeals to vanity and flattery;
- uses guilt or humiliation to control behavior;
- employs intimidation or threats;

Corinne McLaughlin and Gordon Davidson are cofounders of Sirius, an educational center and ecological village, and are both Fellows of the Findhorn Foundation in Scotland. Corinne has taught Transformational Politics at American University in Washington, D.C., and worked for the President's Council on Sustainable Development. Gordon formerly served as Executive Director of the Social Investment Forum where he coauthored the *CERES Principles*, a pledge of ecological responsibility for corporations seeking recognition as socially responsible investments. Gordon and Corinne's latest book is *Spiritual Politics: Changing the World from the Inside Out* published by Ballentine Books, 1994. Their discussion of cults is adapted from the fourth chapter of their basic reference work on intentional community, *Builders of the Dawn: Community Lifestyles in a Changing World* by Sirius Publishing, 1985 (reprinted with permission).

• •

A common element that distinguishes a cult from a healthy, participative community is interference with a person's free will rather than the nurturing of its use.

• • • • • • • • • • • • • • • • • • • •

- plays on low self-esteem or feelings of inadequacy;
- encourages sexual relationships with group leaders;
- uses high-pressure sales pitches and plays on loyalty of friends to attract members;
- evidences extreme paranoia, as in stockpiling of firearms for "protection."

A common element that distinguishes a cult from a healthy, participative community is interference with a person's free will rather than the nurturing of its use. Free will is the most basic and inviolate spiritual principle on earth. A benevolent community or spiritual teacher will respect a person's free will and encourage members to freely make their own choices, to take responsibility for any mistakes made, and to learn from them.

Bibliography

Deikman, Arthur J., "The Evaluation of Spiritual and Utopian Groups," *Journal of Humanistic Psychology* (Summer 1983), and *The Wrong Way Home: Uncovering the Patterns of Cult Behavior in American Society* (Boston: Beacon Press, 1990), $19.95.

McLaughlin, Corinne, and Gordon Davidson, *Builders of the Dawn: Community Lifestyles in a Changing World* (Shutesbury, MA: Sirius Publishing, 1985), $17.95 plus $1.50 postage.

Vaughn, Frances, "A Question of Balance: Health and Pathology in New Religious Movements," *Journal of Humanistic Psychology* (Summer 1983).

[Editor's note: Inclusiveness was a guiding value in creating the *Directory*; so information on a wide array of choices is offered. As editors we have relied primarily on information provided by local community sources, and are not in a position to judge the quality of some of this information. Still, there are "cult" communities—so the above guidelines may be helpful in distinguishing them from the vast majority of benevolent and self-affirming intentional communities.] ⚭

Personal Growth

Jillian Downey

Enabled and Disabled in Community: Sharing Life's Challenges

76 Long-term community member Daniel Bartsch has suffered deteriorating use of his legs during his tenure at Magic Community in Stanford, California. While the diagnosis of his condition has been unclear, he is now relying on a wheelchair to get around. We present here a transcription of discussions at Magic about the challenges and opportunities of fully integrating a differently abled member.

Padanaram Village School

83 Head teacher Steve Fuson discusses the intriguing blend of structure and flexibility at Padanaram's community school. Started with five students in 1972, it has now grown to engage eight teachers and about 60 students.

Movers of Mountains, Shapers of Worlds

86 Kirsten Johnsen, now 26, reflects on her childhood at Greenfield Ranch (Ukiah, California), revealing the joy and awkwardness of growing up in community. Having now reached the age that many of the original members were when Greenfield Ranch was founded, she has vital insights into the consequences and hopeful art of creating community.

Raising and Educating Children in Community

92 Diana Leafe Christian looks at what is known about raising children in community, drawing on surveys, panel discussions, lectures, and personal reports. She gives an overview of the pros and cons, comparing the differences one is likely to find in larger and smaller communities, new and established ones, homeschool versus private school options. She ends with key questions that parents might ask in evaluating a prospective community home.

Enabled and Disabled in Community: Sharing Life's Challenges

by Daniel Bartsch of Magic, Stanford, California

Magic is an intentional community founded to demonstrate how people can apply the methods and principles of ecology to better care for ourselves, each other, and the earth. Human attempts to dominate nature and each other are increasingly damaging. Like people in many other intentional communities, we at Magic are determined to live "with" rather than "over." Our degree of success will be measured in the quality of our own lives and the quality of our contributions to others.

When I came to Magic in 1981 the community was only a few years old. David was 35. I was 31. The four other Magicians were twenty-somethings. They'd all gone to Stanford and to Ivy League schools, but they were skeptical of the Establishment. They were idealistic, enthusiastic, affectionate, and ambitious. You might call them hippie/yuppie hybrids. I was a college dropout working as a machinist. I loved to learn but I hated school. In some ways I felt I was in over my head with these people. But I liked them and they liked me, and we shared basic values. So we gave it a whirl.

Between my thirtieth and fortieth birthdays, I lost some everyday abilities that most people take for granted—like walking and standing, and enduring small changes in temperature. In the process, I've become less worthy in terms of the values often acknowledged in our wider society. At the same time, I've become more worthy in ways fundamental to the values underpinning Magic.

To share how we Magicians are adapting to my changing condition, I've pieced together bits of several conversations. My story raises issues common to all human relationships, and to all individual lives: How much shall we give to or ask from each other? To what extent do we find satisfaction in separateness, and to what extent do we find it in unity?

Daniel: What do you recall about my arrival at Magic, Jeffrey?

Jeffrey: You'd been volunteering on the tree projects, and you'd taken care of the garden when the rest of us went away one weekend. I thought you were really sincere, and knew what you wanted. I also thought you'd had some experience in the world, and knew how to work.

Daniel: Did you worry that I wasn't on a fast track like the rest of you?

Jeffrey: I felt great about it. I was trying to get off the fast track. You remember I was working to stop Diablo Canyon (a nuclear power plant). I had no desire to "succeed" in the ways of most Stanford alumni.

I think all of us sensed a "class" issue—that you weren't in line for the same deal in society that the rest of us were, that you didn't have the same choices. People don't like to talk about pecking order, but you see it everywhere. I admired you for

---

Daniel Bartsch grew up in Ohio and California with one older and two younger sisters. He relished exploring the out-of-doors alone and with friends, and enjoyed learning practical skills from an engineer father and a homemaker mother. Sensitized to ecological issues by a favorite teacher while still in grade school, he dreamed utopian dreams from an early age. In his twenties he bounced between college and "straight" jobs, and life as a freewheeling vagabond artisan. Since 1980 he has been making Magic. His current interests include singing, drawing, herbology, and propagation of perennial edible plants.

Daniel at work.

Ellen Steiner

I'd been through the multiple sclerosis scare with Corinne during the prior seven years. I'd thought a lot about "blues" lines—"Nobody knows you when you're down and out." I realized that I wanted to be a reliable friend, but I was so ambitious. Jeffrey's right about wanting to build friendships on shared values. But I'd had a lot of experience in getting—and very little in giving.

Jeffrey: None of us understood the differences you brought to our group. We were convinced that with some combination of care and exercise you were going to be able to "get better." We were children of privilege. None of us had any experience with persistent disability. I thought of my own eyesight, correctable to 20/20 with lenses, as a terrible "flaw."

Daniel: I tried a thousand things: jogging in sand, hatha yoga, swimming, massage, weight lifting, different diets, special shoes of every description, electrical stimulation, drugs, crutches, half-leg braces, full-leg braces....

In spite of everything I did, each time I tried to walk the pain just grew until I became exhausted fighting it and got sick. Then I'd be in bed for a few days or weeks before I started the cycle again. I finally gave up in 1990 after I caught pneumonia and spent five days in the hospital, near death. The wheelchair seemed like such a stigma, but I'd run out of alternatives.

Kristi: When I lived at Magic, I couldn't figure you out. You had all these strange ideas about your feet. You did everything in your own way—rolling around the kitchen in an oversized office chair, wiring work boots with electric heaters. I didn't know what was "just" in your head—crazy maybe—and what was "real."

your idealism. I thought you were gutsy to hang onto it into your thirties, despite the hassles you endured in the corporate environment and the rest of the larger society.

I think all of us wanted to build our friendships around sharing ourselves, rather than forming alliances that enabled us to become more powerful and dominant. But I don't remember your saying anything about health problems.

Daniel: I knew I had "weak feet"; I'd been flat on my back a couple of times during my twenties, unable to walk because of foot pain. I had no idea what that meant. I always thought that if I were careful, and exercised to become stronger, then I'd be all right.

My mom and dad and older sister are all tall and skinny like me (I'm 6'5" and 165 pounds). We'd always been a pretty healthy family. When I joined Magic, I'd never heard of Marfan's syndrome, an inherited degenerative disease of the connective tissue that often affects really lanky people. Then doctors started asking me about it. Even now my diagnosis is uncertain. They say I'm "marginal" Marfan's.

David: When you first collapsed and weren't able to walk, I thought, "After he gets well, I hope he'll be more careful. Everybody here needs to stay in good shape if we're going to succeed in such a wildly idealistic venture."

••••••••••••••••••••••

I was amazed at how different I felt in that wheelchair; I wanted to scream at everyone, "I'm just doing this to see how it feels. I can walk. I can run. I'm OK."

. . . .

On top of it all, I was dealing with my own life issues. Being taken away from my mom before I was even old enough to go to school. Then moving out from my husband and into Magic. Knowing I didn't want to be a research scientist for the rest of my life, but wondering what else to do....

David: I admired you for your inventiveness, but I was wary that you might just be running down blind alleys. So often I felt that you were a "law unto yourself" with your fixes and accommodations.

I saw you working your heart out for Magic, and really giving to the rest of us, even though we had more than you in many ways. I really admired your heart. I remember telling several people that by your actions you had redefined the word "gentleman" for me.

But your style of taking care of yourself and your belongings was different from any of the rest of us. And then there were things like handwriting and spelling—I mean I'd been told since childhood how important those skills were.

Daniel: Yeah, I remember being a preschooler with my dad screaming at me about how math was everything, and unless I was good at math, I was doomed. The poor guy had a pretty hard time growing up as a tenement kid. My older sister and I took a lot of abuse. For most of my life I hated math, spelling, grammar, anything rigid and ordered that reminded me of my dad's "lessons."

David: About 1985 I was feeling that there was a lot more to you than met the eye. When I taught at Armstrong, a school for kids with learning disabilities, I saw others who reminded me of you. Some of them were really bright, but often they had really forced handwriting and ordered their thoughts in ways I found unusual. Some were insightful and smart in certain respects, but they were missing other skills I'd always associated with intelligence.

Daniel: I'm uncomfortable with the term "learning disability." I think my situation is more a reflection of my experience than some short circuit in my brain. I was really intimidated by my dad, and felt panic, hysteria, depression in the face of his belittling. I think I've shaped much of my life to this point around some of those early experiences. Only since Dad's death two years ago have the rest of the family members started working through this stuff.

David: Well, whatever the nature of our differences, I became afraid that you were going to be an impediment to my living well. Again and again I reminded myself that we shared a common view of the human condition and a common vision. Consciously I wanted to be your partner. Subconsciously I was scared that I was giving up too many other things I wanted.

Jeffrey: You were a catalyst for change at Magic, Daniel. You were always pushing for us to live our ideals. We had a meeting to discuss what to do with my paycheck, and you, Erica, David, and I agreed that we wanted to be communal—income sharing.

David: I was elated when we did that. I'd dreamed for years of "being in the same boat" with people who wanted to combine the strengths of science and loving. We were actually doing it, after all those years of talking and searching!

But I'll admit that I felt pretty dejected a few years later, when Erica and Jeffrey and everyone else but you and I had left. (Jeffrey returned five years later.) You were increasingly preoccupied with pain, and I was having a lot less fun.

Daniel: We talked about folding up and going in search of an established community. I'm glad we hung together. I think Magic is a unique experiment, a worthwhile bit of diversity in the communities movement.

David: In my heart I wanted to stay communal and live the principles we shared; but in my gut, I still felt afraid. I used to put it in terms of "not serving as effectively as I might"; but I suspected then, and still do now, that I was just trying to rationalize cutting and running.

In 1989 when I met the "perfect woman" at that Stanford conference, I was shaken. I imagined the life she and I might lead together, and doubted my commitment to you, to Magic, to community, to simple living....

Robin: This was about when I appeared at Magic. I volunteered on Planting for the Second Hundred Years (a Magic project to reforest grazed lands) while I was still at Stanford. You and David seemed a lot different from anyone I'd ever known. You were serious about living your values. I dropped out of school and you offered a month of temporary housing while I sorted out my life. That was six years ago!

When you and I talked, sometimes I felt that you wanted me to credit you in ways I didn't think you deserved.

I saw you wanting to be valued in Magic, which was visible to the world mostly in terms of David's public service activities. I don't blame you if you feel weird around him. Lots of people do! He's really smart and fit and principled, and says things that ruffle people.

Daniel: I've gone from biking, walking, and standing to sitting in my wheelchair or lying in bed during the time you've been here. Accepting that wheelchair was one of the hardest things I've ever done.

Remember when you took a spin in it to the California Avenue shopping district and came back shaking your head?

Robin: The word "invalid" is right on. People "invalidate" someone who is obviously limited. I was amazed at how different I felt in that wheelchair, I wanted to scream at everyone, "I'm just doing this to see how it feels. I can walk. I can run. I'm OK."

Daniel: Yeah, I can get beyond the initial blocks with people sometimes, but almost every relationship begins with my having to disprove someone's stereotype. When I'm at my best, I think of this as an opportunity to serve. Sometimes, though, it gets old.

> Seeing you laughing with all your wires and equipment and your wheelchair, I often think, "If you can laugh, I can laugh."

Robin: What I first liked about Magic was you and David, so different in many ways, but really taking care of each other and doing public service work I respected. I saw all that you were doing behind the scenes. I said to myself, "You didn't have to be anything more for me to value you." But, then I took over a lot of your work, and I felt resentful sometimes.

When I was growing up, our maid, Margarita, cleaned the house. I was studying to be an engineer, not to clean a bathroom or process salvaged food donated by the local grocery. We are still so tied to money values!

Daniel: When my dad was dying a year ago and I went home to help my mother care for him, I realized how much I had to offer, even with all of my limits.

David: I used to watch people shun you, and felt angry. Now I look inward and ask, "How am I still afraid of Daniel?" You're a challenge and an asset for me. I love you dearly, but I'm only just beginning to learn how.

Bruce: I'm a relative newcomer to Magic. I never knew you as a walking, biking person. I find your symptoms and diagnosis vague and difficult to understand. I have some appreciation for all you've done in the past to make Magic, but I know that only secondhand. You were on medical leave for most of the year before I came and you've been searching for ways to serve without worsening your condition since then. So I have a pretty skewed picture. I enjoy our time together, and I'm looking forward to knowing you better. But I confess, I hesitate to make a long-term commitment to you.

Ellen Steiner

Living with nature measures the quality of our own lives and our contributions to humankind.

Daniel: Have I been difficult for you in any ways?

Bruce: As house manager, I sometimes wonder how hard to push on you to live up to the standards everyone else maintains. I think about what David was saying earlier about "style."

Daniel: I'm learning to live differently from the way I did in the past. I want to be able to do more than I'm doing now. Sometimes I'll hurry and cut corners. I guess it's a way of asking for help without saying anything, leaving loose ends for others to handle. I can do a bit more. Learning to value being as I am, rather than striving to be as I used to be or think I should be, is pretty tough.

Bruce: I'm sometimes a corner-cutter, too. I keep hearing these "faster! Faster!" voices in my head. But somebody is left with my cut corners, and besides I think "slower, slower," may be a better life.

Daniel: You face a different set of choices.

Bruce: Maybe, but at root we both need to figure out how to be satisfied, and either of us can choose to listen to "faster, faster" to the point where we feel we're not enough.

Robin: I often wonder what you actually can do, Daniel. Sometimes I feel that you're just stuck in your own way, and it has nothing to do with your feet. Then I think about how I might feel in your position, and wonder what right I have to second-guess you. What can I really know about how you feel, anyway?

David: That's a tough part for me, too. I want to trust you to know what you can and cannot do. Then I think, "Are you just pandering, David? Are you actually getting in the way of his successful adaptation?" We're such a small community that getting perspective is difficult.

Daniel: Having a recognized health condition with a name, I'm less likely to be accused of malingering. Marfan's is a strange complex of symptoms, and my case is more than just Marfan's. Fortunately at Magic we live closely. As I evidence integrity, you and others come to trust me.

Joan: You manage to do a fair amount here. You just need to be accommodated. I appreciate how much of the kitchen duty you take, and I think you're almost a therapist to a lot of visitors, and even to the rest of us Magicians.

Daniel: I'm glad that people here can do the things I can't, and that I'm able to contribute as I do. Usually I'm really glad to be here with all of you.

I feel I benefit so much. For example, going out is next to impossible for me much of the time. The classes and workshops at Magic bring the world to my door. Last year we served more than a thousand guest dinners. More than a hundred people from a dozen different countries came to visit. All of us together generate this scene. Any individual would have a hard time doing it alone.

Bruce: You asked me about ways you've been challenging for me. I feel you present me with some tough choices. I have an opportunity to tutor at Stanford next quarter. But you've asked for some help with your writing. My parents, grandparents, and friends will understand and approve tutoring at Stanford. I'd feel more "on track" with my peers in graduate programs and conventional jobs. As I listen to others' voices in my head, I make their questions my own. Explaining what you and I do would be difficult.

David: That's the heart of the matter for me. The "Daniel payout" is in becoming more loving. The other payouts are in terms of wealth, power, and status, which most of us Magicians have been encouraged and carefully prepared to seek since early childhood. What do we value? Really? To what extent do we show it with our lives?

David: People who think about becoming part of Magic sometimes ask me about your contribution. I explain that you qualify for a pension and health benefits as a result of your prior work experience. They worry about your being a financial burden, even though you've been a net financial contributor to the community every year since you've been here.

Jeffrey: Even if you weren't, I want to feel that we can take care of some people here. About half of us in this country are too young, or too old, or too something to care for ourselves. I want Magic to carry its fair share, and I much prefer the idea of directly caring for people in the community to paying someone else to take care of people we don't know.

Daniel: People who feel burdened by me almost always feel burdened by the rest of you. I often feel a little sad for those who have so much, yet seem so needy. I like the way we're able to flush out feelings of dissatisfaction, resentment, blame, just in the course of living and working together.

Robin: Sometimes when I'm in over my head with my own responsibilities, I'll feel put upon by a request from you. You live so much of your life in

> ...every person arrives here with some mix of ability and disability, and that mix is constantly changing.

your own particular ways. I have difficulty bridging from my way to yours.

Daniel: I avoid asking for unnecessary help. I think that showing self-reliance is a way for me to build your confidence in me. I just built a six- by two-foot planter box and hoisted it into place outside my window, and surprised even myself! But hardly a day goes by when the rest of you don't offer me assistance; and most of the time, you respond pretty cheerfully to my requests. I appreciate that a lot!

David: Thanks in large part to you, I'm coming to understand that every person arrives here with some mix of ability and disability, and that mix is constantly changing. If we think that each day, each hour, with each person, must be tit for tat, we'll live in perpetual fear that we'll fail to uphold our side of the bargain and be shunted aside. This is the consciousness of the commercial exchange economy. I live in community to shed it.

Daniel: A serious disability may require more resources than something more benign. I want to think that I will be able to choose a path supportive of the community, if I become a drain. People often discourage me from even talking about this, but I'd rather live less long—with the knowledge that I contributed to the success of a community that gave generously to the world—than suck the community dry for a few extra years of my own.

Jeffrey: I returned to Magic after a five-year hiatus. You were no obstacle to me, Daniel. I think you've been great. You've always done whatever you were able. I remember back in the early days when we needed to raise some cash fast to pay off a loan on our house. You went straight out and got a job the next day. I'm grateful that you put up with the rest of us.

Bruce: I agree. Every day I think about how people in my circumstances step on people in your position. From you I'm learning that a big part of what makes disability so frightening is the treatment it elicits from others. And I realize that this is true at all levels of society. The subgenius feels inferior to—and dominated by—the genius. The All-American takes a back seat to the Olympian. What do we gain by all this competitive feeling? I want to live differently.

Daniel: I meditate on being calm with those who are afraid around me. I think that they are reminded of their own vulnerability, that they are confused and uneasy about withdrawing from me. Everybody wants to imagine that they'll still be loved, even after losing their power. But too often we build relationships to share power. If one of us can't deliver, "poof" goes the relationship.

Hilary: Daniel, you inspire me. You're so good about looking for ways to grow, doing your best, and coping with the result. You seem really adept at being as you are at any moment, and accepting it. Sure you have your moods; but overall, you seem really good at making the best of your circumstances. Seeing you continue to adapt to your changing condition is a powerful lesson.

Joan: Sometimes everybody else here is so engaged in operating the household and the Magic programs. But not you, Daniel. I've watched you introduce visitors and new arrivals to Magic. You seem almost infinitely patient. Like any good teacher, you have a knack for seeing the steps to understanding, and laying them out so a person can take them one at a time.

Daniel: Some of these new people come initially for a specific project or program. I usually wait for them to indicate a broader interest in Magic before I engage them. A surprising number want to console me. Once they understand that I can enjoy my days, many are quick to offer help or engage me in other ways. Over time, I get a sense of who wants to share what with me.

Robin: You're so positive, Daniel. That's one of your biggest gifts to me. I've been spoiled...ready to be grumpy at the slightest provocation. Seeing you laughing with all your wires and equipment and your wheelchair, I often think, "If you can laugh, I can laugh."

Daniel: I can laugh, but sometimes I dread that my condition will worsen. How long will I be able to forestall further decline? How long and how well will I live? I don't know, but I like the feeling that I am part of a community that stands for what I care most about. I think of all the disabled people who struggle to live "independently" whether they are recognized as disabled or not, and I wish they were able to live more as I do.

So there you have a few slices of Magic. We're up against all the familiar stuff. We're learning that we're disabled mostly by ourselves, and mostly enabled by each other. We're actively seeking to expand our circle of collaborators. Write us. Call us. If we get on, we'll find a way to be face-to-face. 🐾

Padanaram Village School

by Steve Fuson, Padanaram Settlement, Williams, Indiana

At Padanaram Settlement's founding in 1966, the few children of school age attended public school in Shoals, a long bus ride from home—but an even longer distance philosophically and spiritually from the basic needs of the communal family. Then, six years later, a community homeschool was started. The settlement's founder, Daniel Wright, had held forth this goal from the beginning, and it became reality when Marjorie began meeting with five students in a small trailer. There was no pretense of formality in that one-room "schoolhouse." Resources were few. The simplicity and plain living of a logging and sawmill camp provided the backdrop for all educational activities. Donated books were shelved in a broken refrigerator and creek fish were raised in a bathtub. From the first, book learning and practical learning were joined together in our school.

The second year brought three teachers and 11 more students. The school met in a three-floor log cabin, which had previously served as a hay barn and hog pen. This cabin was the schoolhouse from 1973 until 1976. We fondly remember the experiences shared during those three years. The qualities of smallness, intimacy, and family allowed us freedom to explore, reach out, and try new ways. I recall the group relaxing with mid-morning snacks from the communal kitchen, some lounging about with a book or puzzle, some going across the road to sit on waiting ponies. Sometimes our pet deer, Bucky, might stop by for crackers.

Our present wood-frame schoolhouse was built in 1976 with a large addition in 1990. Padanaram's village school now has eight full-time teachers and averages 60 students a year. Padanaram Settlement funds all school expenses.

The Educational Program

Early elementary students, between five and eight years of age, are taught in small groups roughly based on age and reading level. These younger groups move from room to room, supervised by a teacher who teaches all subjects by day's end. Experiencing different rooms helps provide both variety and a stimulating challenge for teachers and students. In the mornings, early elementary students are usually involved with math, English, and language art subjects, while the afternoons are devoted to science and social studies.

The Learning Center is for students aged nine to 17 years. This group of about 30 students shares a large central space with several side rooms. Each student has their own personal study carrel. During the mornings, the children study the core curriculum—math, English, science, social studies, and spelling. Learning groups work independently with four teachers supervising. Students raise a small flag on the side of their carrel if help is needed.

This independent style of learning places much individual responsibility on each of the students.

For 21 years now it has been my joy to lead and teach in our village school. Living together as we do, I have been privileged to witness the fruits of my labor. Former students manage and work in our communal business, run the common kitchen, and teach in our schools. I am honored to stand arm-in-arm with these, my spiritual brothers and sisters.

My other major responsibility is management of our orchards and vineyards. We have over 500 fruit trees and over 400 grape vines. During the busy harvest and canning season, the school children provide much help.

I write poetry and songs. I've written two books—though they are not yet published. My carpentry skills have proven invaluable.

I hike for pleasure and health, and I am learning the value of meditation. Attendance of our weekly spiritual meetings keeps my life buoyant. My wife, Mary Jo, and my son, Samuel, are one with me in this walk.

*Research and discovery are
part of the school curriculum.*

Steve Fuson, Padanaram

Each must learn to follow directions, read for comprehension, answer questions in writing, and check the majority of their work at the Score Table—by themselves. The teachers are there to clarify instructions, untangle those who get bogged down, pronounce unfamiliar terms, check tests, encourage, admonish, and generally act as facilitator/coordinator of the morning curriculum.

Afternoon schedules in the Learning Center are very different from the mornings, offering a greater variety: Research and Discovery, Arts and Crafts, Spelling Alert, Quest, and Recreation. In Research and Discovery (R&D), students are divided into four small groups based loosely on reading skills, each group with a teacher. The R&D groups meet in the side rooms and other locations three afternoons a week, pursuing a subject chosen by the group. These interage, "family-like" student groups focus on note-taking, outlining, and writing reports and research papers.

For Arts and Crafts, students are divided into small groups meeting about three times a week. "A&C" groups delve into any number of hands-on activities—jewelry making, wood carving, sewing, cooking, painting, drawing, wood working, or leaf collecting. The R&D and A&C formats are limited only by the interests, know-how, and resources of the teachers and students. Of course, other members of the community contribute to these small group minicourses, too. Generally these courses last from three to five weeks; then the students are reorganized into new interest groups.

Together, the core curriculum, R&D, A&C, and other learning formats offer a balance of stability and flexibility that maintains student interest. Mornings provide the stable time frame for concentration upon core curriculum academics, while the afternoons offer flexible diversity in movement, interaction, and interests. The entire student body and teaching staff come together in general meetings to start each morning, and meet again directly after lunch. In these meetings we take care of attendance records, share general information, and discuss school-related issues.

Parent-teacher conferences are scheduled at least annually, and the school is open to parent visits at any time. There is also a public open house once a year.

At Padanaram School, math, English, and science challenge the minds of some very free-spirited children. Learning really happens without many of the bureaucratic encumbrances and alienation problems that often beset public schools. From earlier years until present day, our community school has emphasized reading, writing, and math as building blocks and learning tools. Informality and openness have been intermeshed with formal planning, scheduling, and a strong academic curriculum.

Long-Term Student-Teacher Friendships

The school enjoys an innate stability from the long-term relationships teachers and students build together over the years from kindergarten to high school. Time is on our side—what is missed one year can be dealt with the next.

The teachers share in the complete growth pattern and mental development of each child from five to 17 years of age. Often a "slow" student, who had teachers in the throes of frustration and dismay, can emerge later as a fine learner. Disinterest, apathy, lack of comprehension, immaturity—whatever the traits keeping a student from meeting the school agenda, each student eventually finds a way—in the time frame of their own growth and maturity.

Not all so-called "slow" students end up as great academics or outstanding book learners, but each learns according to their own potential, their own sense of need, their own motivation. In our communal school we are able to hold each child as unique and special, to cherish and protect the right of each one to grow up in self-confidence and acceptance.

School-Community Interdependence

Within the community environment of Padanaram, students know they have an accepted place and a personal identity. A vital job and a home-for-life await each student just outside the school doors. This communal reality provides each student with an inner confidence and sense of stability, enhancing the family quality of the school. Because each has a vested interest in the well-being of the other, and because teachers and students live the same communal lifestyle, we can all become friends for life.

Now a second generation of parents, many of them former Padanaram students, are sending their children to the school. Each skill developed or bit of knowledge acquired, each increase in student maturity, holds the promise of a stronger, more capable community member to share in the Padanaram Settlement of the future. ⚑

Informality and openness have been woven in with formal planning, scheduling, and the academic curriculum.

Steve Fuson, Padanaram

Movers of Mountains, Shapers of Worlds

by Kirsten Ellen Johnsen, Greenfield Ranch, Ukiah, California

I am now the age that many of them were when they began this place. Long ago, to a six-year-old child, they were giants...movers of mountains and shapers of worlds.

I'm not sure exactly when it was that I realized they were clumsy, not wise. There was a General Meeting that lingers in my memory; it was one of the first times that doubt and fear settled silently in a corner of my child's mind. I remember the sensation as I was kneeling down next to my mother who sat cross-legged on the lawn of the ranch house, perhaps to ask her a question as she shushed me. Suddenly there was shouting across the circle; someone was standing up and raging at other people in the meeting, as the old walnut tree towered over us all. Other voices rose and other bodies stood to yell over the heads of those seated, and I didn't wait to see what happened next. I ran, scared, to rejoin my friends playing in the dusty parking lot.

The next time I ran from a general meeting it was with some disgust and flippancy. As I grew older I began to assimilate the general attitude that the General Meetings of Greenfield Ranch Association were impossible. It was an attitude that circulated among the adults, filtering down to the kids around tables and fireplaces at home, and reinforced in our play together around the barn and parking lot and swimming hole.

School at the Ranch House

I think we felt we owned the place anyway, since we were at the ranch house every day for school, which was taught by a few dedicated parents. We knew all the hiding places in the barn, all the secret passageways and best routes for getaway from the enemy in boys-chase-the-girls. Long hours we played, or sat around on the porch listening to Zephyr read stories from *The Jungle Book* as we ate lunch.

School would often center around morning lessons, beginning as soon as the teacher and enough kids arrived from our respective hikes and horserides to the ranch house. In the wintertime we would huddle around the wood stove, drying out our rainboots and wet clothes. After lunch we'd often gather in the kitchen, sometimes working on art projects like sewing or batiking, or else English and math skills. It seems we were a pretty tough group for the teachers to control. As summertime approached, many school afternoons ended early with a successful mutiny. We would simply refuse to return to class. As a group we would take off down the road, around the bend, tumble down the steep path of the meadow and jump in the pond. There we would spend the rest of the day frolicking and swimming.

Zephyr would round us up every once in a while for a "nature walk," usually along the creek that

---

Kirsten Johnsen grew up in an alternative community in northern California during its hippie commune phase in the 1970s. After surviving the culture shock of public schools, she attended and, in 1992, graduated from The Evergreen State College in Olympia, Washington. She currently rents a small yurt on Greenfield Ranch, her home community, and works as assistant manager at the local hot springs resort. She recently finished guest editing *Communities* magazine on the subject of "Growing Up in Community" (Fall 1994). Her future aspirations include graduate study in cultural anthropology, travel, writing, and singing.

leads from the dam to the ranch house bridge. We played and discovered all kinds of plants, flowers, and creatures; pouring plaster of paris into the tracks of the wild things that came down to the creek; pressing new wildflowers into the pages of the school journal. I'm sure it was a joy as much to the adults watching us as it was to us.

There were many adults that passed through the Annie Greenfield School. Parents, other community members, and travelers passing byn taught both basic and special classes—woodworking, pottery, sewing, reading, math. I remember when Gwydion taught us about homemade water systems, a subject to which we could all relate as our parents struggled with their homesteads. And how mad Molly would get when we would deliberately make mistakes in grammar! There were singing lessons with Phyllis at the piano, poetry sessions with Sun Bear on the back porch, French taught in the barn by Silvianne.

Arrowheads and Acorn Meal

One memorable time a man passing through the community demonstrated to an eager crowd of us kids how to chip out arrowheads. It was a daily passion among us to dig through the rich black soil around the Commonland searching for artifacts from the distant past. The land that now houses the community center, ranch house, and barns was a Pomo Indian village site, so we could never absorb enough information about the people before us, who had lived here for hundreds of generations. We experimented with making acorn-meal mush, and learned about basket weaving from our field trips to the Willits Museum.

One of our first field trips was to a neighboring community to see an ancient rock with petroglyphs. We were eager to learn the mysteries of the land. We explored every corner of it, observing the mating rituals of the newts in the creeks, rummaging through the dumps of the 1860s cattle ranch that was the origin of our beloved but dilapidated barn, and playing in the ranch house around which everything in our world revolved.

So when the adults came to their once a month General Meetings on the lawn, we kids felt inherently superior to their long process of talking and squabbling and fighting. We knew the land from the ground up, the secrets of the past beneath the

100 Mile Lodge

The movement to create alternative lifestyles requires commitment from one generation to the next.

black dirt and in the maze of rotting stalls; we knew the joy of cool water to splash in as we hunted for baby salamanders in the creeks; we knew when to run away from the obnoxious shouting that erupted during the meetings—we knew how to play!

Communal Celebrations

Not that the adults didn't play as well. The whole community played. It seemed in those times that the annual Summer Solstice parties went on for several days. Everybody looked forward to the horse races and water ballets, the watermelon races and homemade ice cream. One year the Flying Karamazov Brothers entertained us, but all I

Doug Jones, Birdsfoot Farm

Enjoying the wealth of creative energy in an intentional community.

remember of that night was dancing in the dusty parking lot in an oversized old-fashioned man's suit, jealous of the twirling skirt that my friend Aileen was wearing. We had just performed a skit to "Up The Lazy River."

The next year someone lifted Aileen and me up to the back of a flatbed truck, where we pranced around in flapper suits and sang songs from the '20s. It seemed we were often entertaining each other in the community with plays, skits, and other events.

There were many, many outrageous parties: a pyramid-raising party at John's, when we rode up Stay High Drive on a hay wagon. My friend's dad got so high that night he stole Peggy's truck. I know, because my dad and I hitched a ride with him. We didn't realize something was amiss until the 55-gallon barrels of water—kept full for fire safety—started falling over on us. We got out as soon as we could and walked home!

The Halloween parties were always a scene, the ranch house packed with people in all sorts of costumes. We bobbed for apples and had haunted houses in the barn. Troll and Marylyn made a hit with the kids when they brought real caramel candied apples. We didn't care how our purist parents frowned—for once we got real candy!

Musicals and Nude Movie Makers

One of our first plays we kids put on with Marylyn's help...something about cats and raccoons fighting and somehow reuniting under an effigy of the historic "Annie Greenfield" which was lowered from the barn loft. We danced around her and sang "Them bones, them bones, them...dry bones." Another time I played Dorothy, with a group of neighbors dressed up as the Scarecrow, Tin Man, and Cowardly Lion. We danced into the ranch house and barn complex singing "Follow the Yellow Brick Road," which we had practiced for weeks.

I can't recall all the happenings, though long-time community members remember and retell the stories: nude weddings in the summer, Christmas caroling, the time when the movie makers from Belgium came and strolled around the pond naked behind their cameras, trying to fit in I suppose. There were work parties for the roads and for house-raisings, and a great many potlucks.

Culture Shock

Slowly but surely though, the pall of the impossible General Meetings spread over the spirit of community. People burned out and issues became too complex to smooth over with a potluck dinner and a joint passed around the circle. We kids grew up and turned our eyes outward to the larger world: the inevitability of Ukiah High School. Parents started driving us to school in town, and soon we were separated from each other in classes and grades. We lost contact.

It felt very strange to me that the mountains that were moved and the worlds that were shaped in the back to the land movement seemed to disappear so easily. The society that we had retreated from, that had been loudly denounced in the whirl of activism around Simple Living Workshops and United Stand court battles, was suddenly very threatening to me. I felt unprepared for it. I was not prepared for classes that graded me, for town kids that sneered at me unless I did my best to fit in. I had to hide the fact that I loved to run naked and free in the woods and meadows with my friends. I let no one know that I really wasn't grossed out by a compost privy. I brushed down my wild crazy hair into managed curls and slipped into the back of the classrooms, hoping not to be noticed.

Communal Values Shaken

Somehow as a young kid I had nurtured a feeling in the back of my mind that the world these giants had shaped for me to live and play in was the best world. Naturally I had overheard the conversations and arguments at meetings about the "right" way to live...and other "righteous" concerns. My friends and I played games that ridiculed city kids, and felt very proud of our freedom and wildness. Perhaps it

> **We knew the land from the ground up, the secrets of the past beneath the black dirt and in the maze of rotting stalls; we knew the joy of cool water to splash in as we hunted for baby salamanders in the creeks...we knew how to play!**

was also because I had been taught to watch out for the younger kids that I developed a tangible sense of responsibility to the community and that I knew I'd get in big trouble with everybody if I misbehaved.

Our version of "the way to live" was supposed to be the answer to the problems of larger society. Now this feeling of purpose and identity struggled to survive against the onslaught of the Reagan Youth, the New Republicans of the 1980s, and, worst of all, the internal cynicism of the Greenfield Ranch Association at its own perceived failure.

I realize now that they were never giants. They were kids, too, leaving the suburbs and cities in droves to escape the oppression and social unrest of the 1960s. The age range of these people with visions of a new alternative society was from 18 to 35, most of them in their twenties.

Adulthood Brings Perspective

I am 27 now, amazed to know how young the Ranch founders really were back then. The mistakes that they made were mistakes that every generation makes, so that the next may learn and go on with a better understanding—if anyone is paying attention. How could these predominantly white children of the affluent 1950s suburbs have any understanding

Children at The Farm School in rural Tennessee.

of community, or know how to recognize it, encourage it, preserve it, when it happened to them? Their parents' generation had already been largely cut off from their roots of extended family during the preceding historical waves of farm-to-city urbanization and social change.

It was a truly gallant gesture, the movement to create lifestyles based once again upon the values of the land and reliance upon one's neighbors. Did any of these child-giants grasp the enormity of their vision, or the amount of commitment through generations that it would require?

The Righteous Survive

The world they shaped and lived in was the foundation of my childhood. Confused as I was coming out of high school, I held on to the images of that world, that "once-upon-a-time" life. It hurt me to hear the cynicism and despair of my community members as they ridiculed their own efforts. I felt self-conscious and foolish that the community had meant so much to me.

Then I began to realize that it had been a different experience for them. I hadn't been involved in the long, arduous meetings, the struggles to build and maintain community. Nevertheless, I had learned something very valuable as I darted between the clamoring adults to snatch the best of the potlucks. I learned a sense of place, an identity among people, and a belonging that lasts beyond "success" or "failure."

A New Generation Hears the Call

The values that I learned in my community at Greenfield Ranch are very much a part of my adult life. I still feel a great sense of responsibility and belonging. Two years after finishing my college degree I moved back home to the Ranch. Someday when I have children, I know that they will have a lot of people around keeping an eye out for them, like cousins and uncles and aunts.

I continue to enjoy the stories told about the "old days." These tales give me a sense of place in history, because I know the intentional communities movement is vast, and that our local history as a community arises from a long tradition of folk struggle. Now I can understand my community in the context of this historical struggle. This awareness gives me patience and tolerance, which I need if I'm to accept the hard lessons that come with living together and putting up with all the crazies!

Bozos for Christmas

Alongside all the bozos, drunks, and psychopaths, is a feeling of family and belonging that I would not trade for anything. Last Christmas it delighted me that Fred carved the turkey, playing out the role of one of our benevolent patriarchs. He told jokes to the kids about absent community members, jokes that only we would have understood. We laughed about the old days while my mom rushed around looking for a knife sharpener. Finally, a neighbor produced one from his jacket pocket, whetted the carving blade, and we started the feast.

Later, we all crammed around the Christmas tree and gave out simple presents to each other. The traditional Christmas carols were banged out on the piano, the ever present "rumor mill" was grinding away, and once again the whole event had all the familiar trappings of our annual extended family gathering.

Meeting Blues Meet the Nineties

Over all the years, what of those mountains and worlds that were once so earnestly moved and shaped? Well, it's obvious that my community was not successful in creating a "New Society." The internalized "evils" of the Establishment came with these back-to-the-landers from the city and made an awful mess of our meetings, contributing to—maybe even creating—the frustration and disillusionment that our community experienced throughout the 1980s.

Still, through it all, we have maintained the ingenuity and perseverance to carry forward our dreams and our longings for a better life, inevitably overcoming the disillusionment. Community members started putting their energy back into the larger society, and incredible creative ventures sprang up on all sides. Food and business co-ops, alternative technology research and development, theater, music, political and social activism of all kinds, midwifery, ecological restorations, art, dancing, teaching, law, therapy, solar engineering, bizarro paganism, computer weirdness, you name it—the wealth of our creative energies poured into the surrounding community.

Along with this outpouring, our personal definitions of community expanded to encompass these new territories. And while the wind sometimes still blows a bitter whiff of a sense of community "failure" (or perhaps it is a sense of impossibility), I believe that underneath it all there is a knowing that we will come through for each other when and if we have to.

A Happy Future for Mountain Movers?

Now, after more than two decades together, the lessons of respect and patience in our meeting

> **I realize now that they were never giants. They were kids, too, leaving the suburbs and cities in droves to escape the oppression and social unrest of the 1960s.**

processes might be finally beginning to take hold. It is a difficult road, with many backward steps and disillusionments. Conflict resolution is a spicy stew, made of trial and error, perseverance, immense tolerance, and a great deal of humor. I believe that it is *humor*, the ability to laugh at ourselves, that brings us through the worst storms.

I don't believe that there is any goal to community living—there isn't a state of perfection or realized potential that we are striving to reach. Instead, our "goal" is the daily fabric of life and the relationships we weave together, out of long-time familiarity. It seems to me that the work of moving mountains and shaping worlds can only be realized on all the levels of relationship. It is a dynamic interplay between self, home, family, community, and society at large. 🐾

Raising and Educating Children in Community

by Diana Leafe Christian, Managing Editor of Communities *magazine, Ft. Collins, Colorado*

When you think of kids and intentional community, do you envision a flock of happy children frolicking in a meadow? Although this picture may be accurate in some ways, according to experienced community residents, it can be misleading and idealistic.

We've noticed three aspects of the children-in-community issue. First, one of the reasons people join or form communities (now, as well as in the '60s and '70s) is for a safe and wholesome environment for families and their children. Second, many say that unless a community provides good facilities for children, it won't attract as many new members. And third, perhaps no issue may be more personal, sensitive, or potentially explosive for community members than the issue of children and their place in the community.

Happy, Confident Children

In 1989–90 Daniel Greenberg surveyed 219 intentional communities and visited 25 communities around the United States for his doctoral dissertation in Child Psychology.[1] He found a number of striking differences in children's lives from their noncommunity counterparts. Most communities Daniel visited had an extended-family-like atmosphere, where people had ample opportunity to form close, nurturing relationships with members of all ages. He found community children had many more adult role models than simply their parents, relatives, and teachers, and tended to develop friendships with many nonrelated adults.

In addition, he found that the world of grownups was largely demystified for children because they had an excellent sense of what adults *do*. Daniel observed constant informal learning experiences—regarding, for example, leadership, negotiation, the use and abuse of power, conflict resolution, consensus building or voting, financial planning, budgeting, meditation, ceremonies and rituals, cooking, food storage, recycling, organic gardening, composting, building construction, solar energy devices, and auto repair! As a result of these friendships with adults and exposure to their daily tasks, community children are often more socially mature, confident, outgoing, competent, and verbal (and at far younger ages), than their noncommunity counterparts. It's not uncommon for a community visitor to be startled by the articulate welcome and precocious comments of a four or five year old.

Community children do not usually play just with kids their own age, unlike public schools where they are segregated into same-age groups, or regular neighborhoods where there is strong peer pressure not to associate with younger kids. Community children, by contrast, hang out with all the other kids, regardless of age differences. Jan Gudmand-Høyer, the architect who originated cohousing in Denmark, says kids of all ages in his

Diana Leafe Christian had a long history in alternative media before assuming editorship of *Communities* magazine. She was research editor for *The Earth Changes Report*; writer/editor for the Institute of Noetic Sciences; book review editor for *Yoga Journal* magazine, and Editor/publisher of *Growing Community* newsletter (now a part of *Communities* magazine). For four years she hosted and produced a radio interview show on community-related topics.

Diana helped organize two cooperative households in Honolulu in the 1970s and has a passion for communities, permaculture, CSA farms, and low-cost, nontoxic, "natural" home building. She currently lives in Ft. Collins, Colorado and hopes to someday live in a child-oriented agricultural community. This article is reprinted from *Growing Community* newsletter, number 5, January 1994.

Mary Ann Kenny, Glen Ivy

Community provides a kind of carefree safety with options and choices of where to play.

community play together and show love and respect for each other, including those as young as a year and a half—"Like one big family," he says. These multi-age friendships also seem to help make community children confident, outgoing, and socially comfortable.

In larger intentional communities, Daniel found that shared child care tended to free up parents for other activities, giving more adults more free time. But in small intentional communities, child care took up an inordinate amount of time relative to the number of adults available. He also found that children were generally physically safer in communities than if they lived elsewhere.

Lonely, Grieving, or Confused Children.

But Daniel also found disadvantages. For example, in small, rural communities there might be fewer children to play with than in a regular neighborhood, and those community children would be lonely. And if there is high turnover in a community, the children left behind can grieve for years over the loss of friends, who felt like brothers and sisters (and mothers and fathers). Grieving for lost friends was also mentioned by several members of the "Adult Children Raised in Community" panel at the August '93 Celebration of Community conference.[2] Other research has found that in communities where children didn't have strong bonds with

• •

One child from a rural Colorado community... raised a stir in his grade school for easily and confidently approaching his teachers and principal as peers. "Hi there, Ralph. How's it going?"

• •

one or more adults, a high member turnover rate seemed to cause the children to exhibit apathy or hostility. However, in communities in which children did have nurturing and secure attachments with a few adults, a high turnover seemed to affect children positively.

Sharing child care among community adults, either occasionally or consistently, can create, among the care-givers, expectations of sharing important decisions about the children's care and behavioral norms—tough for parents who are unwilling to give up sole authority over their kids. Also, any inconsistency among the adults about behavioral expectations and discipline for children can be confusing for them—and frustrating for the adults, too! Daniel points out that these issues are more likely to arise in the early stages of forming community, when child care may get less attention than shorter-term projects such as building houses and starting gardens.

Community Education: Opportunity, Expense

Daniel found that of the 170 communities he surveyed that had children, 46 percent had some sort of schooling, including elementary-grade classes or homeschooling, and 17 percent (in larger communities, usually with over 50 kids) actually had formal schools. Because of the costly resources needed—classroom space, trained teachers (and legal barriers in some states)—creating community schools can be very difficult, especially for small communities. The commitment to extensive child care and/or formal

schooling takes one or more adults away from the rest of the work force, and educational materials—from books to science kits to computers—can be prohibitively expensive!

However, there are many wonderful advantages to community schools. Children can be protected from undesirable aspects of mainstream culture, such as aggressive consumerism, media hype, or racial and cultural prejudice, as well as the social cliques, crowded classrooms, discipline problems, deadening pedagogy, or outright violence often present in public schools. Community schools can opt for creative curricula and innovative, experimental learning methods. The parents and the whole community are usually deeply involved in their school, and the children's relationships with their teachers are usually based on years of mutual understanding and friendship.

There are also advantages to homeschooling in a community setting. "We make our schooling very brief," a seven-year-old boy explains on the "Follow the Dirt Road" video.[3] He adds that lessons are no longer than two hours at most, but, "We figure I learn a lot just helping out with people. And people make a point of explaining everything I want to know, in detail. And it doesn't feel like schooling to me, but I am learning pretty much all I want to know."

"Strangers in a Strange Land"

However, sending intentional community kids to public schools can also be a problem. Community children may be considered odd, or even feared, especially after one of the occasional, well-publicized reports accusing a community of cultlike behavior. Or the children may face genuine cultural and value differences with their classmates, which can be emotionally painful. One community child was considered strange by her classmates because she wanted to hug everyone. Another was avoided because she recycled her lunchsack!

Of course the confidence and social skills of community children can be very positive in public schools—although sometimes disconcerting. One child from a rural Colorado community, whom we met as a young man, had raised a stir in his grade school for easily and confidently approaching his teachers and principal as peers. "Hi there, Ralph. How's it going?"

Questions Seekers Might Ask

Here are some of the issues community veterans suggest we ask about before joining or forming communities.

Are children welcome in the community? Are there safe places for them to play?

Jan Gudmand-Høyer from Denmark told the October '93 Rocky Mountain Cohousing Association conference that he originated cohousing primarily to create safe, friendly places for raising children. In Danish cities, most children have limited outdoor play areas and are forbidden to cross busy streets. But Jan and his friends wanted their children to grow up in the kind of carefree safety not usually possible in a city, with options and choices about where to play. So, beginning with the first cohousing community, Jan designed large kitchen windows facing out onto children's play areas so parents could easily keep an eye on their children. He and other parents calculated the farthest acceptable distance they wanted their toddlers to wander from their front doors, doubled that distance, and placed the front doors of each unit that distance apart. Thus in the cohousing communities, buildings were literally designed around the needs of parents and children.

Does the community have organized child care?

Many older intentional communities, from spiritual retreat centers to secular communes and cooperatives, also provide child care. The Danish cohousing communities have a children's room in the Common House, where teenagers and adults often take care of younger kids. At the Winslow cohousing community on Bainbridge Island, Washington, the first thing parents did was organize an after-school child care co-op in the children's room of the Common House. Each adult in the community (if possible) takes care of the kids one afternoon a month. Whenever parents can't get home from work on time they can call a neighbor or friend in the community to look after their children. That's one of the best things about living there, says cofounder Chris Hanson.

Neglected Children

Are children welcome in some or all community activities? Are community adults so busy with a service or activist agenda, spiritual practice, or survival-level

> ...the world of grown-ups was largely demystified for children because they had an excellent sense of what adults *do*.

issues, that the children are inadvertently neglected?

Several years ago two of our friends and their children joined a large, successful, spiritual community in California. The parents wanted to live and work in a setting that would encourage and enhance their spiritual practice through group meditations, frequent teachings, and the atmosphere of the group's common spiritual heritage. They found, however, that time for family life at home was not valued or scheduled into the tight work schedule, and children were rarely included in the community activities. Children were considered a logistical problem to be handled with child care, and were not really members of the community. Our friends left after a few years, not willing to choose between their spiritual lives and the well-being of their children. (The community has subsequently become more family friendly.)

At the Celebration of Community conference, Kat Kinkade, cofounder of Twin Oaks, described what she termed a big mistake in child rearing during their early days. Influenced by Behaviorist developmental theories, Twin Oaks members believed their children would be better off away from their parents; so they created a separate children's building and designated full-time child-care workers. But the turnover in members (and thus child-care workers) was high, the children didn't have consistent norms and role models, and the parents and children missed each other terribly.[4]

In the "Adult Children Raised in Community" panel at the Celebration, a young mother described her experience growing up in a Christian international service community. She described how she and the other children experienced emotional abuse because of the community's beliefs and rules. She said the parents forced the community's values on

Just because children are in community doesn't mean all their emotional and physical needs are taken care of.

fields and meadows. But they had also wished their own parents had taken more time to love and care for them *especially*.

A member of the audience related that, in her present-day community, the adults had also once believed that just by living in a community their kids were provided for. Although the kids related more to each other than to the parents, all seemed well for a time. Then a child-pack "began preying on the adults in various ways," she said. Each parent protected his or her children from blame and accused the other children. It took them literally years, she said, to realize that all the children were involved, and it wasn't a kids' problem, but a symptom of something fundamentally wrong in the community. The parents came to the painful realization that they had neglected their children. When they all started talking together in the healing process, the kids said they wanted karate lessons. Though initially appalled, "We're a nonviolent community," the adults finally agreed. With the opportunity to channel their energies into ritualized karate, the children were delighted.

Problem Children

Do the parents and/or all adults in the community agree on what are dangerous or undesirable behaviors for children on community premises? Do the parents and/or all adults supervise children at large in the community, or reprimand children when they get out of line? How do adults handle grievances with someone else's child? Do limits or restrictions vary by children's age groups, or by individual parents' norms? If the entire community agrees on certain rules, who determines and administers the consequences if children break the rules?

What if eight-year-old Sarah becomes hyperactive and destructive when she eats sugar, and her parents are oblivious to healthy diet or the effects of sugar on children? In fact, what if they try to placate her with ice cream and candy? What if Sarah, revved up by her latest biochemical stimulation, hurts another child? What if other parents demand that Sarah stop being given sugar? And her parents, outraged and hurt, tell their friends to mind their own business? This kind of conflict, and many others you can imagine, could create serious conflict, heartbreak, and division in a community.

their children. One white family sent their son to an inner-city school so he'd appreciate African Americans and get a multicultural education. Instead, he was beat up frequently, and felt abandoned and abused by the community norms, and especially by his parents.

Another woman, raised in a Quaker activist community, felt the adults were "so busy saving the world" that they hardly had any time for the kids. Each participant on the panel related that community parents generally seemed to think that just because their children were in community, their lives were fine and their emotional and physical needs were taken care of. Not true! While their parents were busy with activist work or building the houses and homesteading, the panelists said, they had often felt neglected. As children they did have many adult friends, and frolicked in happy flocks with friends of all ages—literally the golden days in

Geoph Kozeny, Community Catalyst Project

Children at Risk

What are the limits or restrictions for the adults in their behavior around children? What is considered appropriate or inappropriate, and who determines this?

A woman on the "Adult Children" panel said she felt alienated as a child by the denial and falseness she found growing up in her community. The community was proud that it was comprised of peace activists who all took care of each other. But the children knew some of their friends were regularly beaten severely by their (apparently) alcoholic parents. Their own parents knew of these beatings, but did nothing. "They didn't protect our friends," the woman said.

Another woman ventured that it *wasn't* physically safer for children in communities than on the outside, even if some research findings indicate otherwise. She said the same kinds of dysfunctional and dangerous behaviors parents abhor in the wider culture can go on inside intentional communities. She told, for example, of sexual suggestiveness by an adult when she and a friend reached puberty. "Be very careful who you let into your community. Check them out," the panelists advised us sternly, "and don't fall into denial!"

Children and Rites of Passage

Do the adults acknowledge and honor transitions the children go through, such as puberty, or graduations? Are teenagers allowed more freedom or given responsibility regarding community matters?

Jan Gudmand-Høyer said that, although a teen room was built in the Common House of the first Danish cohousing community 22 years ago, the teenagers who first moved in didn't know each other, couldn't agree on how to use the teen room, didn't use it, and were bored. Years later, when another group of children had grown up to become teenagers, they were all great friends and took over the teen room with relish. Now Jan advises community founders *to include their teenagers in the planning phase* of any new community.

A woman on the "Adult Children" panel said that at puberty she and the other children were separated from their parents and sent to live at a youth school operated by her international service community, with only seven adults to supervise 150 teenagers. The result was chaos. Once again the youngsters felt abandoned and angry, she said.

> ●
>
> ...the same kinds of dysfunctional and dangerous behaviors parents abhor in the wider culture can go on inside intentional communities.
>
> ● ● ● ● ● ● ● ● ● ● ● ● ● ● ● ● ● ●

Two women on the panel mentioned the sadness they felt when they reached puberty, and instead of being welcomed into maturity by the adults in their communities, the young people felt a subtle and sometimes overt discrimination, such as receiving snide remarks when they stopped swimming nude or began to wear makeup. "Oh, now you're a *teenager*, you'll start becoming obnoxious."

At the community where the formerly aggressive kids demanded karate lessons the adults belatedly realized they had to honor and acknowledge their children's passages. So they instituted rituals where women welcomed teenage girls to womanhood and the men welcomed teenaged boys to manhood. The teenagers loved it, and were radiant in their new status as young men and women.

Favorite Stories

Are there informal learning experiences for children? Homeschooling? Do the adults organize classes for children in various skills or subjects in which one or more adult has knowledge?

Ten-year-old Tokeen, of Mettanokit Community in New Hampshire, created a wonderful situation for himself when he entered the fifth grade. This confident and curious child, who had been homeschooled from an early age, wanted to try public school so he could meet other children his age, but wasn't sure he'd like it. After trying it out for a month, he found that he liked the teacher and other children; was disconcerted by the regimented subjects—math at ten o'clock, reading at eleven; was disappointed that most "learning" was really just reading comprehension and involved short-term memory, rather than the in-depth learning of math and science he got at home; was interested in continuing pottery making; and found the school's arbitrary rules amusing and ridiculous.

Tokeen concluded he was getting something from public school that he couldn't get in homeschooling, but there were things he didn't like about public school either. So this young boy designed his own ideal school-and-home education program. With the help of his parents and community friends, and the cooperation of the local school board, Tokeen negotiated for and got less homework; shorter school days and optional time off; continued homeschooling of math, science, and history; and access three hours a week, with supervision, to the high school's pottery studio. Best of all he made lots of new friends at school—the reason he started the project in the first place![5]

The Gift of Learning

In the 1970s, several parents started a small community in Ojai, California, solely for the purpose of creating a multiparent homeschooling environment for their children. According to one cofounder, besides learning the basics, the children were taught courses in whatever subject was the passion of various adult members. So in addition to reading, writing, math, science, and history, the children learned woodworking, gymnastics, yoga, massage, astronomy, astrology, marble sculpture, gourmet cooking, and how to run a small "restaurant" business. The community kitchen was in fact the focus of an ongoing learning seminar in this community, as the adults taught the kids to cook and serve elegant meals for the whole community, organize and run the kitchen, and master principles of inventory and volume buying. So the adults served the children as teachers and mentors, and the children in turn served the adults—literally, as the kitchen team.

The cofounder said all of the children have remained the closest of friends, and since they have grown up each one of them has sought her out to thank her, saying that their community education was one of the most meaningful and empowering experiences of their lives. (AA)

Endnotes

1. Greenberg, Daniel, "Children in Community," in *Directory of Intentional Communities* (Langley, WA: Fellowship for Intentional Community, 1990), 328 pp. (out of print). A more detailed overview of Daniel Greenberg's research. Greenberg, Daniel, "People Start as Children" in *One Earth: The Findhorn Foundation & Community Magazine* (Summer 1993). An overview of his dissertation research. Send $4.50 to: One Earth, Ltd., The Park, Findhorn, Forres IV36 0TZ, Scotland. (0309) 691641. Greenberg, Daniel, "Children in Community and Their Education," audiotaped lecture from Celebration of Community conference, August '93, 120 minutes. Send $9.50 to: FIC Tapes, Rt 1 Box 155-D, Rutledge, MO 63563, 816-883-5545.

2. "Adult Children Raised in Community," audiotape panel discussion from Celebration of Community conference, August '93, 120 minutes. Send $9.50 to: FIC Tapes, Rt 1 Box 155-D, Rutledge, MO 63563, 816-883-5545.

3. Gauthier, Monique, *Follow the Dirt Road: An Introduction to Intentional Community in the 1990's*, VHS videotape, 1992, 53 minutes. Send $28 to author at: FTDR, 207 Evergreen Court, Landenberg, PA 19350, 215-274-2402.

4. Kinkade, Kat, "Founders Panel: Large Rural Communities," in *Communities* 83 (Summer 1994), 62 pp. Send $4.00 to: Communities, Twin Oaks, Rt. 4, Box 169, Louisa, VA 23093, 540-894-5126.

5. Rainwalker, Emmy, "Tokeen's Story: Our Homeschooler Goes to School," *FEC Systems & Structures Guide*. Send $1 to: Community Bookshelf, East Wind Community, Tecumseh, MO 65760, 417-679-4682.

Social Action

Jonathan Roth of Twin Oaks

Fellowship in the Nineties: A Continental Network Open to All

Fellowship for Intentional Community board members explain the Fellowship's ambitious projects for helping people get accurate information about today's intentional communities, promoting contact between communities, and relating products of the movement to the wider culture.

Innisfree: Lifesharing with Adults with Mental Disabilities

Marianne Roberts describes how her community provides a unique home for people with mental disabilities. She examines both what this can mean for residents with disabilities, and for the members attracted to the community to engage in this work.

An Ecovillage Retrofit for Los Angeles: Healing an Inner-City Neighborhood

Lois Arkin offers a snapshot of the ecovillage movement, another example of a community-based initiative to develop working models of sustainability. Lois describes in depth the evolution of her ecovillage in downtown Los Angeles. It is one way community can happen—even where the social conditions may be challenging.

Bioregionalism and Community: A Call to Action

David Haenke explains that bioregionalism picks up where environmentalism leaves off, challenging everyone to emphasize sustainability and define community to include the nonhuman as well. The North American bioregional movement has held biennial meetings since 1984 and is steadily building awareness of the task ahead. In line with this, David makes the case for a necessary partnership between communitarians and bioregionalists.

Central Living in the Netherlands: The Influence of Architecture on Social Structure

Dorit Fromm looks at collaborative living in the Netherlands. Contemporaneous with cohousing developments in Denmark, the Dutch see this form of shared housing as an opportunity for wide-scale housing reform, and have secured government support for their initiatives. Unlike their Danish counterparts, the Dutch units have attracted more singles and renters. They are learning some interesting things about the dynamic relationship between building design and social structure.

Fellowship in the Nineties: A Continental Network Open to All

by the FIC Editorial Board

*F*ormed as a regional network in 1948, the Fellowship for Intentional Community (FIC) shifted to a continent-wide focus in 1986. We began holding semiannual board meetings the following year, and set about identifying the intentional community movement's needs and selecting projects to meet those needs. In a sense, this reaching out was a test to see if communities were ready to act in concert, working together to explore the diversity and promote the strengths of cooperative living. Now, several years into the experiment, we know with certainty that the sustaining interest and energy are there.

The Fellowship's work is based on four common values:
- cooperation,
- nonviolence,
- inclusivity, and
- unrestricted freedom to leave a group at any time.

To promote these values, the Fellowship has pursued four main goals:
- to act as a clearinghouse for up-to-date information about intentional communities, including referrals to match groups seeking new members with people in search of a group;
- to build trust among communities by encouraging communication, friendships, visits, and cooperative activities;
- to facilitate exchange of skills, technical information, and practical experience among communities—both those that are well established and those newly forming; and
- to broaden the wider culture's awareness of cooperative alternatives and the practical value of the structures and "tools" developed by intentional communities.

How Do We Accomplish These Goals?

Publications

The Fellowship's first major project was creating the 1990 *Directory of Intentional Communities*. This comprehensive sourcebook took more than two years to compile, and has become the standard reference about intentional community living today. The *Directory* has been highly successful—selling out three printings, over 18,000 copies in all.

Encouraged by the popularity of the *Directory*, the Fellowship decided to revive a companion publication, *Communities* magazine. Founded in 1973, the magazine had been declining since the mid '80s, and a substantial debt had accumulated. In 1992, the Fellowship completed negotiations to become the magazine publisher. We have now paid off the debt and assembled a dedicated staff that has expanded the scope, tightened up the editing, and returned *Communities* to the magazine racks on a quarterly basis.

The editorial board of the Fellowship for Intentional Community publicizes news of interest to communitarians and others engaged in cooperative lifestyles. The editorial board seeks to increase awareness of intentional communities and related projects through Fellowship publications: the *FIC Newsletter*, *Communities* magazine, *Communities Directory*, and various occasional mailings. Board members and intentional community members are listed in this article.

Fellowship Board Meetings

The Fellowship is administered by a board of directors, comprised of members who are highly active in the organization. The board gathers twice yearly for three-day meetings, hosted each time by a different community or support organization. In an attempt to make meetings accessible to participants from all corners of the continent, the location is rotated from region to region across North America.

Meeting agenda topics range from the nitty-gritty of project details, to the exploration of long-term visions; from detailed budget analysis, to the delicate feelings surrounding personal changes. Board meetings are open to all, and are operated by consensus in a way that encourages input from all participants. The meetings provide a great opportunity for newcomers to get involved in a variety of Fellowship activities.

Each gathering is a time to meet new people and renew established friendships—expanding the personal connections that are the ultimate wealth of our organization. Fellowship members receive copies of the quarterly *Newsletter*, and notice of all meetings. In addition, board meeting invitations are sent to everyone on our mailing list who lives within a day's drive of the meeting site.

1993 Celebration of Community

In pursuit of our goals, and to gauge the burgeoning energy in the communities movement, the Fellowship organized the Celebration of Community held in

1994 FIC Member Communities

Abode of the Message	Earth Family Farm	Miccosukee Land Co-op	Society of Family Solidarity
ACCESS	Earthaven	Midwest Community	Sonnenhof
Acorn	East Wind Community	Monan's Rill	Southside Park Cohousing
Adirondack Herbs	Edges	Mount Madonna Center	Spaulding Unit
Alcyone Light Centre	Elkhorn Ranch	New Family Experiment	Springtree Community
Alpha Farm	Farm, The	North Mountain Land Trust	Still Water Sabbatical
Atmasantulana Village	Farm Home Center	One World Family Commune	Sunnyside Farm
Bear Creek Farms	Futures, Inc.	Ozone House	Sunset House
Birdsfoot Farm	Gabriel Farm	Panterra	Sunship Community
Bright Morning Star	Gaia Permaculture	Peaceful Gardens Village	Talking Circle
Bryn Gweled Homesteads	Ganas	Philoxia	Tekiah
Camphill Soltane	Gesundheit! Institute	Phoenix Community	Teramanto
Camphill Village, Copake	Goodenough Community	Pilot Mtn. Eco Community	Toadhouse
Canadian Life Colleges	Green Pastures Estate	Ponderosa Village	Twin Oaks
Cantine's Island Cohousing	Griffin Gorge Commons	Port Centauri	Union Acres
Celo Community	Hale Byodo Corazon	Prag House/Evergreen Trust	Uppity Womyn & Friends
Center for Experim. Design	Harbin Hot Springs	Quaker House	Vale, The
Center for Harmonious Living	Hawk Circle Cooperative	Rainbow Hearth Sanctuary	Veiled Cliffs
Center for Sacred Sciences	Hearthaven	Rapha Community	Walker Creek Farm
Cerro Gordo Community	Heartwood Institute	REF	We'Moon Healing Ground
Chester Creek House	Hei Wa House	Rejenneration House	Wellspring
ChristiansbrunnBrotherhood	ICA—Phoenix	Renaissance Community	Wellspring House
Chrysallis Farm	IDA	River City Housing Collective	Wild Earth
Common Place Land Co-op	Jubilee House Community	River Farm	Windward Foundation
Common Unity	Kidstown	Rowe Camp & Conf. Center	Winslow Cohousing Group
Communities Connexion	Lamborn Valley Community	Sandhill Farm	Wiscoy Valley Land Co-op
Cooper Street Household	Lichen Co-op	Seeds of Peace	World Academy of Keristan Educ.
Desiderata	Light Morning	Shannon Farm	Yoga Society of Rochester
Du-má	Magic Tortoise Foundation	Short Mountain Sanctuary	Zendik Farm
Dunmire Hollow	Magic, Inc.	Sky Woods Cosynegal	Zion's Order

For information about becoming a supporting member of the FIC, see page 438.

August 1993. Over 800 people from 15 different countries came together at The Evergreen State College in Olympia, Washington. We listened to a variety of inspiring speakers, participated in workshops, connected in small groups, learned to juggle, networked for future projects, sang, laughed, and hugged. While no dates have been set for the next event of this type, the Fellowship expects to build on this success by hosting future gatherings.

Regional Gatherings

The Fellowship helps publicize regional gatherings hosted by local communities and support organizations. These regional events are excellent opportunities for face-to-face contact with seekers from the area and with members of nearby communities. Regular regional gatherings are currently hosted in Virginia by Twin Oaks, in Indiana by Padanaram, and in the Seattle area by the Northwest Intentional Communities Association.

Academic Conferences

The Fellowship cosponsors the annual conferences of the Communal Studies Association (CSA) and the triennial conferences of the International Communal Studies Association (ICSA). These meetings bring together a diverse mix of people, including scholars, curators of historic communal sites, and members and former members of contemporary communities. Presentations range from academic papers on historic communities, to discussions of contemporary community relations with the wider society.

Canbridge

Consensus And Network Building for Resolving Impasses and Developing Group Effectiveness—CANBRIDGE is a process collective, organized on the premise that community experience offers unique insights into group dynamics. This offshoot of the Fellowship provides assistance to established and forming communities in skill areas such as group process, conflict resolution, consensus building, organizational development, decision making, and meeting design. Communities, cooperatives, businesses, and other groups may contact the Fellowship for referrals to experienced communitarians willing to offer consultations, facilitate challenging meetings, and conduct training.

FIC Board of Directors, April 1996

Betty Didcoct
Director of Outreach &
Program Development

Caroline Estes
Alpha Farm

Dan Questenberry
Shannon Farm/Deer Rock

Ella Peregrine
(Alpha Farm, 1994)

Elph Morgan
Hei Wa House

Geoph Kozeny
c/o Sandhill Farm

Harvey Baker
Dunmire Hollow

Ira Wallace
Twin Oaks/Acorn

Laird Schaub
Sandhill Farm

Lois Arkin
CRSP/L.A. Eco-Village

Associates

Ben Lipman
Solstice Foundation

Chad Fuller
(Sirius, 1992–93)

Diana Christian
Communities Magazine

Earl Loftfield
Sirius Community

Jillian Downey
Miep House

Loren Schein
(Ganas, 1993)

Paul DeLapa
(Esalen Inst., 1989–93)

Valerie Oaks
Twin Oaks

Velma Kahn
Abundant Dawn

Zev Paiss
Nyland Cohousing

Board members serve staggered three-year terms in a volunteer capacity. Those who might be interested in serving are encouraged to attend board meetings and become involved in committee work. The FIC board may be reached by email at fic@ic.org.

Revolving Loan Fund

The Fellowship assumed management of a long-established Community Loan Fund when the Community Educational Services Council (CESCI) dissolved in the summer of 1994. Since 1952 this fund has loaned out over $200,000—in amounts up to $5,000—to help intentional community businesses with start-ups or expansions. The Fellowship is attracting additional assets, and plans to expand community business-loan activities across the continent. Looking ahead, this loan fund could provide a base in the future for launching a community credit union or bank that could finance larger ventures.

Speakers Bureau

The Speakers Bureau can provide experienced presenters on intentional community topics for college classes, civic groups, churches, and other organizations. A list describing the areas of each speaker's expertise is available from the Fellowship office. Topics of general interest include the following: overview of the communities movement, workplace cooperation, sustainable living, Christian communities, cooperative parenting, land trusts, barter systems, communal education, Eastern religious communities, intentional community history, and archeology.

Future Projects

The Fellowship is considering several other initiatives—projects awaiting the time, energy, or dollars to move ahead. These include

- pamphlets on cooperative living—such as how to start a community, legal options for incorporating, or choosing an appropriate decision-making process;
- curricula for undergraduate and graduate programs in the study of historic and contemporary communities;
- mutual savings funds for major medical expenses such as that operated by the Federation of Egalitarian Communities;
- outreach programs to mainstream businesses—offering to share our considerable experience in cooperation, group process, and alternative ways of managing human resources; and
- support materials for communities struggling

• •

Each gathering is a time to meet new people and renew established friendships—expanding the personal connections that are the ultimate wealth of our organization.

• • • • • • • • • • • • • • • • • • • •

with local government over such issues as zoning, building codes, health department regulations, and tax status.

How Do We Work Together?

Consensus is the decision-making process used at Fellowship board meetings, although members come from living groups using many different styles of governance—only some of which include a form of consensus. Without judging how other groups make decisions, the Fellowship has chosen consensus for our work because of its potential for inclusivity and bridging different perspectives. Consensus supports the full expression of divergent views, encourages the input of all participants, and creates openings for a wide range of communitarians to get involved in communities movement work.

The Fellowship has a pattern of assessing where there's a need, then jumping into the work whether or not we possess the required skills. This has resulted in a lot of on-the-job training—over the last decade Fellowship members have become publishers, editors, accountants, distribution and marketing experts, computer wizards, bulk-mail coordinators, consensus trainers, conference planners, database managers, public speakers, writers, and diplomats.

As we work together, mutual understanding deepens, trust builds, and Fellowship meetings and projects become rich sharing experiences—much more than just occasions for doing business. As a decentralized organization, different tasks are managed

The closing ceremony at the August 1993 Celebration of Community organized by the FIC.

Leslie Goldman, Enchanted Gardener

from different sites around the country, and it's not uncommon for a project team to be scattered across the continent. In this electronic age, location is not the limiting factor it once was, as a quick review of Fellowship work assignments illustrates.

The *Directory* is managed in Missouri while articles are edited in Virginia—with substantial help from folks as widespread as California, Oregon, Texas, and Tennessee. The *Directory* Listings are updated by a networker who travels around the country continuously while coordinating with the database manager who resides in Virginia. For *Communities* magazine, the managing editor lives in Colorado, the Reach editor lives in Massachusetts, and the guest editor may live anywhere. The membership *Newsletter* is edited in Virginia, layed out in California, printed in Illinois, and mailed out of Missouri (the current home of the Fellowship office), and the organization is incorporated in Indiana.

Who Joins the Fellowship?

In a word—anyone. That is, anyone interested in supporting the intentional communities movement and the vision of the Fellowship. A member community may be an ecovillage, a cohousing group, a residential cooperative, a hippie farm, or a monastery. Individual members may live in a cooperative situation, or may be completely unaffiliated. Alternative businesses and networking organizations can join as nonresidential affiliates (see membership card on the last page for details).

Send your written inquiries to the Fellowship Office, Route 1 Box 155-CD, Rutledge, MO 63563, or call us at 816-883-5545. If you call long distance and reach our answering machine, your call will be returned "collect"—unless you leave your mailing address.

A Dream Come True

For many of us, the Fellowship is the realization of a long-sought vision: a continental association dedicated to the nurturing and promotion of intentional community living, and to helping people find the right home in community for themselves and their families. This dream can grow only as fast as more people feel the call to share their energy with other communitarians; if you're inspired to participate in the flowering of the intentional communities movement, please get in touch. We'd love to hear from you.

Innisfree: Lifesharing with Adults with Mental Disabilities

by Marianne Roberts of Innisfree Village, Crozet, Virginia

*I*magine a place where there is no discrimination and where everyone is treated with respect and has an opportunity to contribute. Innisfree is trying to create this kind of place in a village next to the Blue Ridge Mountains.

We are a community with adults with mental retardation and mental illness. Formed in 1971 by families who were concerned about the lack of quality care for their loved ones with disabilities, Innisfree offers a productive, progressive alternative to institutional or home-bound care for our coworkers (residents with disabilities). We are a secular community and welcome all people, regardless of race, ethnic origin, religion, sex, or age.

About 60 people—37 coworkers and 25 volunteer staff members—live here in our village on 550 acres of farmland next to the mountains of Shenandoah National Park. Our village consists of 11 residential houses, a large com-

A road sign at Innisfree Village.

munity center, a weavery/woodshop/bakery complex, a greenhouse, an office, a retreat cabin, outdoor recreational facilities, several farm buildings, and breathtaking scenery. We also maintain two group homes in the nearby town of Charlottesville.

Weekdays are spent in our houses and work stations. Four days a week, we work together in the woodshop, weavery, bakery, and garden. One day a week, we clean our houses and run errands.

Marianne Roberts first came to Innisfree Village in 1986 as a full-time volunteer house parent. Her move to Innisfree was intended to be a hiatus for her investment banking career on Wall Street, but eight years later she still prefers the simple life. Marianne uses her banking experience and MBA training from Harvard in overseeing Innisfree fundraising efforts. As a vegan and animal rights activist, she supports a reverence-for-all-life philosophy that encompasses all the earth's creatures.

Innisfree, Inc.

Volunteers at Innisfree give of themselves to advance society and extend dignity and respect to all people.

have come from more than 30 states to live and work in this village nestled against the mountains. Others have come from all over the world. At last count, Innisfree volunteers had come from 21 other countries.

We come to Innisfree as volunteers to take time out to assess career goals or life direction, or because of the appeal of living in an intentional community in a beautiful rural setting, or to experience the satisfaction of helping people with disabilities. You see, just as Innisfree is an alternative for our coworkers, it is an alternative for the volunteers, too, allowing us to integrate the values of our personal lives with the ideals of our working lives.

Some volunteers have no experience working with people having disabilities. Others are mental health professionals looking to broaden their experience. We have teachers, ministers, lawyers, MBAs, doctors-in-training, and nurses, and some volunteers straight out of college. Some have majored in English, religion, business administration, sociology, art, psychology, or horticulture, and some have simply majored in life. Some are in their early twenties, and some are in their mid-sixties. Some stay for a short time, and some stay for years. Many bring special interests, talents, or hobbies to add to the mosaic of community life, enriching all our lives. We've had jewelry and paper makers, musicians, and people who work for social change.

What do we take with us when we leave? Precious memories—of hugs, smiles, tears, even of tantrums. And we remember having penetrated beyond the labels of disabilities to the unique personhood of the coworkers we come to know and cherish.

We also remember the experience of living in a community—the endless meetings, the demands on our time, the fact that everything we do and everywhere we go becomes common knowledge. Of course, the flip side is knowing what interdependence means; experiencing the synergy of individuals working together; and finding support when all the chips are down.

We ask at least a one-year commitment from volunteers. Beyond that, our primary requirements are that volunteers (1) work patiently and nonjudgmentally with people who experience life in different ways than the norm, (2) have stamina to live in an extended family "fishbowl," and (3) have energy and a sense of humor.

Evenings we spend in our houses or in our community center, socializing and relaxing. Two days each week, we take off.

Innisfree has been on the cutting edge of care for people with disabilities since it was founded; the village has become a model for similar communities around the country and abroad.

Volunteer Staff

Except for a few core positions, our staff are technically all volunteer, receiving a small monthly stipend plus room, board, medical coverage, vacation pay, and a parting allowance.

We attract dedicated, hardworking idealists who believe strongly in voluntarism, in giving of themselves for the advancement of society, and in extending dignity and respect to all people. Volunteers

Homelike Atmosphere

Innisfree has a "life-sharing" environment rather than the traditional shift system that creates a distance between staff and clients. We live in small homes like families because we want to foster a sense of community and stability. We spend our days working alongside each other at home—where we cook, clean, and socialize—or at work—where we produce goods for ourselves and for the greater Charlottesville, Virginia, community.

In this close-knit environment where both the caring and the conflicts are magnified, we share the responsibilities, frustration, and joys of everyday living. And we try to learn and grow with each other, knowing that the inclusivity and diversity we encourage give us and our community strength and depth. By spending frugally and engaging volunteer staff, we operate at considerably less than the cost of state institutional care and have never needed government funding. Our costs are met entirely through private sources. In fact, we pride ourselves on using creative, nongovernment solutions to operate our community, and we strive to be a model for public institutions through prudent use of these private resources. A noted commentator in *The Washington Post* observed, "Government money can purchase professional competence, and can increase society's supply of such competence. But the mysterious dedication that makes Innisfree a community is, like all love, mysterious."

Two-to-One Ratio

A two-to-one ratio of coworkers to volunteers is maintained, which melds well with our philosophy of community and family. Small-group interaction and individualized relationships foster learning and growth for both coworkers and volunteers. Personalized attention helps us to continually be aware of the unfolding needs of coworkers, who, in a sense, become guides and show what the village focus should be. Our close relationships help us maintain a sense of community with coworkers, not for them. This is important to us because we do not come to Innisfree to *care for* persons with disabilities; rather we join a community that *includes* people with disabilities.

> **In this close-knit environment where both the caring and the conflicts are magnified, we share the responsibilities, frustration, and joys of everyday living.**

Stories of Community Life

People at Innisfree enjoy sharing stories about favorite community experiences. Stories about the sweat and toil of haying during the summer are especially plentiful; something very special happens when the sound of the baler echoes in our hollow. The whole experience of community living seems to crystallize out there in the hay fields.

When farm manager Joe Coleman starts up the baler, work station and house schedules are rearranged, clothes are changed, and people gather at the barn to jump on the hay wagon and take to the fields. Almost everyone helps; even people with allergies or bad backs can help by bringing water to the thirsty crew or driving the tractor. Gloves are a necessity as, solo and in pairs, we hoist the hay bales onto the wagon. It's hot, sticky, manual labor, and the teamwork grows as muscles begin to tire. The hay is carefully stacked on the wagon, yet even the best packing job can topple in the rutted fields or when climbing onto the roadway. Back at the barn, each wagon full is unloaded onto a conveyor and stacked in the hayloft for the winter season ahead.

Why do we recall haying with such fondness? Maybe because most of us are new to farm life. Maybe because the typical routine is broken, and we can sweat and laugh in the fields. Maybe because of the conversation that follows exhaustion. And just maybe it's the true equalizer...a time when all from Innisfree can join together and concretely see the

The Lake Isle of Innisfree

I will arise and go now,
and go to Innisfree,
And a small cabin build there,
of clay and wattles made:
Nine bean-rows will I have there,
a hive for the honey bee,
And live alone in the bee-loud glade.

And I shall have some peace there,
for peace comes dropping slow,
Dropping from the veils of the
morning to where the cricket sings;
There midnight's all a glimmer,
and noon a purple glow,
And evening full of the linnet's wings.

I will arise and go now, for always
night and day
I hear lake water lapping with low
sounds by the shore;
While I stand on the roadway,
or on the pavements gray,
I hear it in the deep heart's core.

—William Butler Yeats

work of community. It's when we learn again that together we can make it!

The Innisfree Drama Group

The Wizard of Oz was the last play produced by the Innisfree drama group. The group also performed the love story *Miss Lonely Hearts* on Valentine's Day, and the comedy *Off Guard* on April Fool's Day.

"Judith" starred as Dorothy in *Oz*. When asked about acting, Judith said, "I love it. I like rehearsals. They're not hard for me." Acting in the play even inspired her to visit Dorothy's homeland of Kansas.

The volunteer who founded the group brought drama to Innisfree for therapeutic reasons. "It's one of the things that gets people together to learn as a group," he said. "Whether it's drama or anything else, with people working in a group, they fall out with each other, and make up. It's about learning and growing. And it's fun." It's also hard work. Most of the plays take about a month's preparation.

"Louise" played Glinda, the Good Witch of the North. "I really enjoyed being in *The Wizard of Oz*," she said. "Nobody recognized me with my makeup on."

"Jane," the Wicked Witch of the West, echoed Louise's sentiments. "I enjoyed it very much," she said. "Everyone really pitched in, and we all did a good job...."

Remembering a Good Friend

One perfect day, we planted 12 trees around our community center. The holes had been dug earlier in preparation for the planting; on the appointed day, the sun was shining on the garden crew as the soil was prepared for the trees. Everyone worked together to move mounds of soil and mix it with compost. By lunchtime, a lot of sweat was flowing.

After lunch, everyone joined to move the trees to their planting positions. What a great feeling it was to create a sanctuary for the trees as well as a memorial to our friend "Susie," a coworker who died in 1987. What community spirit we felt as the sugar maples and the willow oaks went into the ground. And what a symbol of the ebb and flow of life at Innisfree.

As coworkers and volunteers we try to make this corner of the world a more gentle place. With advance notice, we welcome and enjoy visitors. Come and experience for yourself what life is like here at Innisfree Village.

An Ecovillage Retrofit for Los Angeles: Healing an Inner-City Neighborhood

by Lois Arkin of L.A. Eco-Village, Los Angeles, California

Sowing Seeds for L.A. Eco-Village

On Christmas Eve, I was on my nightly schmoozing walk around the block. My neighbor Jem was standing outside leaning over his old Cadillac having a smoke. I paused to chat. Then a car sped by, to my expletive.

"You know, yesterday," Jem offered, "183 cars went by in an hour, and about 75 percent of them were doing over 40!"

"How do you know that?" I queried, astonished.

"I stood here and counted them, "Jem replied, going on to describe the traffic patterns throughout our central-city neighborhood. I was delighted—we have to begin collecting traffic statistics to prepare for major changes on the two streets that comprise our neighborhood.

"What we really need help with is getting some of those speed bumps in here," he concluded, asking if I knew the people in local government who could help us do that.

I was elated at discovering this interest of Jem's. In urban neighborhoods techniques for traffic calming—slowing down auto traffic—are a major component of urban ecovillage and eco-city development. Jem's interest in this issue meant that others will get involved. He manages the 40-unit apartment building across the street from the four-plex where CRSP and the Eco-Village Center are headquartered, and he's a major energy on the block. Jem knows just about everyone and has a great sense of fair play.

Definition of an Ecovillage

Robert Gilman, of the Context Institute and *In Context* magazine, Bainbridge Island, Washington, defines an ecovillage as,

"...a human-scale, full-featured settlement in which human activities are harmlessly integrated into the natural world in a way that is supportive of healthy human development and can be successfully continued into the indefinite future."

That's a chunk to repeat for your friends when they ask, "What is an eco-village, anyway?" So we've learned to tell a little story that doesn't sound much different from how folks might describe living in any healthy small town or intentional community:

"In an ecovillage, or sustainable neighborhood, people can be close to where much of their food is grown and their livelihoods. The physical and economic environment is arranged so that quality time with family, friends, and community is possible. Leisure, recreational, and civic activities, too, along with work and family life are within walking or short nonpolluting commute distance."

Lois Arkin is the founder and Executive Director of CRSP, Cooperative Resources and Services Project, a 14-year-old non-profit organization committed to small cooperative ecological communities. CRSP is the coordinating organization for L.A. Eco-Village. She was coeditor of *Sustainable Cities: Concepts and Strategies for Eco-City Development* (Eco-Home Media, 1992) and *Cooperative Housing Compendium: Resources for Collaborative Living* (U.C. Davis, Center for Cooperatives, 1993) (both available from CRSP). Lois serves as a board member with the Fellowship for Intentional Community. She can be reached at 3551 White House Place, Los Angeles, CA 90004, 213-738-1254.

For ongoing news of the ecovillage movement, see the regular "Ecovillage" column in *Communities Journal of Cooperative Living*.

School children at the Primary Center next to the L.A. Eco-Village display the worm composting box they painted together.

Eco-Village Staff, L.A. Eco-Village

We're lucky. We can feel confident about the traffic-calming projects with people like Jem involved. He'll talk with most everyone on the block and help people get to public hearings when needed.

Earlier in the day, I was talking with Esfandiar, the garden coordinator for our block, about recycling the four-foot stack of cardboard from the boxes of produce clippings for our compost pile. He told me the city had started picking up cardboard for recycling—but we had to bind it up first.

I've been collecting twine for years, convinced that some day there would be a use for it. This was it! Out came my box of one- to two-foot strips of nylon twine. Soon, Ming Gook and Dai Han, Johnny and James were gathered around Esfandiar and me, curi-ous and wanting to help. These neighbor children, aged four to 12, made a game of tying the strings together. Esfandiar talked with the children about gardening, composting, art, sports, Christmas, his native Iran, and listened to their thoughts and concerns as we tied. In an hour, the string was stretched around poles across the street, down the block, maybe 1,500 feet of it. Four-year-old James insisted on rolling it all up on a stick when we were through, and a fine job he did of it, too.

After the job was done, they all went out on the street to play touch football, except for ten-year-old Johnny who practiced tennis on the sidewalk with me. Then Mary, one of our organic gardeners, came by to share a box of her wonderful ginger cookies with us.

We are finding more and more occasions for such spontaneous gatherings here in our neighborhood. The night before Christmas Eve, 1992, several members of our Eco-Village Working Group joined together for Christmas carolling. I'd lived on the block for 12 years. Never before had there been any carolling. As the five of us carolled down the street, we met many new folks in our two-block neighborhood and gathered information on their skills for the local barter system we're helping to organize.

Some Basic Ingredients for Inner-City Retrofits

These seemingly unrelated events are typical of the seeds needed to grow a sustainable neighborhood or ecovillage. Spontaneous encounters and working together build trust and a sense of community. In fact, we are a neighborhood in the process of becoming an intentional community by virtue of our prior residential choices.

Being on the streets helps reclaim them as important community space, apart from automobiles and crime. When neighbors see people of good will having fun on the streets, they are more likely to join in, expanding a healthy sense of play and neighborliness.

People who are multiskilled and public spirited can create a healthy neighborhood presence which, in turn, can motivate other residents to recapture hope and move into cycles of empowerment. This is whole-systems or cyclic thinking, recognizing that everything is related to everything else—spotting the unrelatedness or holes in our community systems, and closing the loops.

There can be many reasons for taking a walk. For example, I wait for Dianne so we can walk down the block together. We can chat with each other, get our exercise, share the synergy of our joyous togetherness with anyone we meet during our walk, look for recyclable "trash" for the garden and other projects, and more easily include neighbors in spontaneous conversations that one of us alone might be somewhat shy about.

A whole-systems approach to sustainable neighborhood planning and development is interactive and collaborative. A systems approach to planning works at transferring information to people living and working in the neighborhood. This kind of planning recognizes the value of spontaneity and

> ...we are a neighborhood in the process of becoming an intentional community by virtue of our prior residential choices.

chaos as essential to innovation and creativity. Whole-systems thinking promotes sensitivity and respect for the pace at which people can learn, plan, own, and incorporate changes.

An urban neighborhood on the path to sustainability is not isolationist within the city! Nor will it be when it has achieved significant self-reliance. The Eco-Village processes set a tone for participation. We engage adjacent neighborhoods and the city at large in our processes or share resources as appropriate.

For example, the Los Angeles Eco-Village Working Group concentrates on our two-block area for organizing the local barter system (local-exchange trading system or LETS). But we enthusiastically include others nearby who hear about the Eco-Village and want to be included. We participate in tree-planting projects in adjacent neighborhoods. We provide technical assistance to any neighborhood that seeks it. We invite others who live outside our neighborhood to participate in our working groups and neighborhood gatherings.

A neighborhood is sustainable when its economic, social, and physical systems are sustainable. The emphasis is always on the people and how they can take care of themselves and their environment in healthy ways—ways that do not jeopardize the ability of future generations to do the same.

Among those who are planning and advocating for sustainable neighborhoods, there is an emphasis on cooperative relationships, cyclic thinking, and quality of life. In addition to our basic need for a decent standard of living—that is, material sustenance and comforts, "quality of life" recognizes people's basic need for good relationships with other people and the environment—the place, the

111

community around them, and especially life-support systems of air, water, and soil.

At first, sustainable thinking has to be consciously practiced. For example, going shopping becomes a challenge, since one is constantly questioning how a product is made, transported, marketed, where packaging goes when we're through with it, what the nature of its by-products are, and what happens to all of it! Retraining ourselves to think this way—in cycles rather than in linear isolation—automatically cuts down on nonessential purchases. Much of the time previously spent on shopping, and driving to shop, is available for community activities such as gardening, composting, dialogue, community-based learning conversations, renovations, eco-businesses, and mutual aid. This is how ecovillages are created—by gathering a critical mass of people who regularly think and act in a whole-systems context. Interactions based on good will and a sense of mutual aid build trust and attract action-oriented energy. Opportunities for building healthy relationships and trust should receive priority—the more trust there is, the less bureaucracy will be necessary,

leaving more time and energy for community development and socializing.

Automobiles and Whole-Systems Thinking: An Exercise

As in nature, everything is constantly changing in an ecovillage. Being designed for sustainability, the social, physical, and economic systems of an ecovillage are all under constant readjustment—because they are understood to be interactive. For example, if we are in inner-city Los Angeles, and we want to breathe cleaner air (inner-city children here have the lowest lung capacity in the nation), we have to rethink our relationship to our private automobiles. When we do that as a community, there will be a number of options and actions emerging, all with social and economic impacts.

Some car owners will give up their autos altogether. This will save, on average, $5,000 to $8,000 per year for other uses, or simply provide freedom from having to earn so much. Lives will change substantially as work and social activities become more neighborhood based. In turn, the neighborhood economy will be strengthened. Other car owners will organize vehicle cooperatives, reducing the overall number of autos, pooling their auto-related expenses. Still others will simply reduce miles driven by rearranging their lives a little. Some will trade their fossil-fueled autos for electrics or other less polluting vehicles, and some will switch to bicycles and local mass transit options. All of these choices have positive social and economic effects.

As community members learn more and more about the car's role in the degradation of life in our city, some will become activists in organizations such as the Alliance for a Paving Moritorium and the Eco-Cities Council. They will help others to understand why changes are necessary and how to make changes in ways that enhance the quality of life for all species living in and around this and other cities.

When neighborhood people begin to think through, plan, and act in other areas of their lives, more and more of them will learn how to be involved in rebuilding our community. Child care, for example, is primarily a social system, but with obvious relations to the economic and physical systems of a neighborhood.

Public Interest Purposes of Ecovillages

- To demonstrate low-impact, high-quality lifestyles;
- to reduce the burden of government by increasing neighborhood self-reliance;
- to reverse the negative environmental, social, and economic impacts of current growth and development practices;
- to model sustainable patterns of development in the industrialized world, especially the United States, to encourage developing communities to bypass our unsustainable patterns; and
- to showcase the talents and skills of those working toward a sustainable future.

Learning to think and act in whole systems is fun. It's like a puzzle, challenging and full of surprises. Once there is a common vision, commitment, and action among even a small group of three or four people, then the pieces always start to fall into place. There's a certain magic to it. For instance, the Eco-Village wanted to acquire a building to establish a process for nonprofit community ownership. Just at that time, one of the four-plexes on our street came onto the market at an affordable price.

Then we made a longer-term decision to explore restoring the Bimini Baths, the hot mineral springs 2,000 feet below the surface of our neighborhood. We assumed it would take five to ten years to acquire the industrial building we had targeted for restoration as a bath house. Now the building is likely to become available this year! As our community awareness emerges, more opportunities for community building will appear—as if by magic!

Techniques for Developing Eco-Village Systems

We have experimented with a variety of techniques for planning and developing Eco-Village systems. For example, at one point we began holding monthly community gatherings. Project descriptions and sign-up sheets were brought to each meeting. We took these lists with us on daily strolls down the street to encourage more folks to get into a project group. We held group meetings in highly visible places like the sidewalk at the intersection of our two blocks, or in one of the building lobbies, or on the front lawn of an apartment building. At each meeting, we had a big sign that indicated what group was at work. This established an expanding presence for change in the neighborhood, and kept our processes open and accessible to all.

People are becoming friendlier on our two blocks as more and more of us actually get to know one another and share a friendly spirit with others on the block who haven't yet begun to participate. Current work groups are based on personal interests and consensus. The groups change regularly depending on the energy of neighbors and volunteers. At least one Working Group member familiar with Eco-Village systems participates with neighbors and other volunteers on each project group. This way Eco-Village culture can expand among residents more consistently.

> Once there is a common vision, commitment, and action among even a small group of three or four people, then the pieces always start to fall into place.

A sampling of project groups during the first year of the L.A. Eco-Village included earthquake preparedness, children and youth activities, composting and organic vegetable gardening, fruit-tree planting and stewardship, local exchange trading system (LETS—a local currency), traffic calming, neighborhood eco-business development, and monthly potluck gatherings and dialogue groups.

Students from a local church-based urban planning school worked with us on various surveys. Graduate students in urban planning, ecosystem design, and architecture from several local universities have developed Eco-Village plans for their academic projects. We have also been working closely with the White House Place Primary Center, a public school (K-2) located next to our CRSP/Eco-Village Center. Here youngsters in the Eco-Village and adjacent neighborhoods are learning whole-systems thinking in a community context with two of our city's prominent mentor-teachers. There is beginning to be real continuity between school and neighborhood.

We have facilitated workshops and brought resource people into the neighborhood on a variety of issues, including earthquake preparedness, traffic calming, water flow forms, eco-cities, composting, organic fruit trees and gardening, organic pest control, intentional communities, limited-equity co-op housing, and conflict resolution.

Many fruit trees have been planted and are being stewarded by youngsters who, in turn, engage other children to work with them for ongoing care of the trees. As these other children become ready to steward

• • • • • • • • • • • • • • • • • • •

...the social, physical, and economic systems of an ecovillage are all under constant readjustment—because they are understood to be interactive.

• • • • • • • • • • • • • • • • • •

a tree of their own, they select the type of tree, locate a site, plant it, and name it. The trees then become part of the children's "circle of friends." Involvement of young inner-city children with fruit-tree care and nurturing is the vision of one of our earliest project team members, Maria Davalos. It is so heartening to see her vision become real.

Factoring in Physical Size, Population, and Other Basics

In our two-block area, there are four apartment buildings with 184 households, seven four-plexes, two single-family dwellings, and a drug and alcohol recovery home—about 500 people all together. We have spoken with others in the city striving to create more livable neighborhoods. Some have sought to include much larger geographical areas. Los Angeles, even our inner city, often sprawls way beyond practical considerations. We encourage neighborhood development groups to narrow it down, starting with a set geographical boundary of one to three blocks and a population of no more than 500.

Our population is ethnically diverse and stable in its proportions of Asians, African Americans, Latinos, and whites. We are multigenerational with a wide spread of incomes from very low to moderate, although proportionately residents are primarily at the lower income levels. Our land uses are already substantially mixed with four strip malls within one block of the community, other commercial and industrial areas within a few more blocks.

We are one block away from the best mass transit in Los Angeles, and will be within walking distance of two stops for the new underground subway—scheduled to open in 1996.

The hot mineral springs beneath our neighborhood were the base for an international resort here until the early '50s. We plan to participate in the restoration of these hot springs to public use. Bimini Baths, as they were known, attracted people from all over the world. Bimini means "sacred site of healing," a perfect match for the Eco-Village vision.

Anthropological studies indicate that 500 is about the limit for an ecovillage-type community. It is about the maximum size group for those involved to be able to know and be known to one another, by name and face, and still give individuals the feeling that they can have some influence in the community's direction. Five hundred people in agreement on common issues and concentrated in a single geographic location can also be a powerful economic and political force.

The Eco-Village Planning and Advisory Group

There are about 25 members of the L.A. Eco-Village Planning and Advisory Group, and another 100 or so that have participated in some way during the past several years. After the April 1992 Los Angeles riots, the Planning Group decided to select the inner-city neighborhood around the CRSP center as the L.A. Eco-Village site.

A few members of the core group live in the Eco-Village neighborhood; some are considering moving in; others simply want to be part of the process of helping to make it happen. Some in the group who already live close by have committed to a regular presence in the neighborhood. They may eventually begin similar activities in their own and other neighborhoods—this is a learning laboratory for them. The Planning and Advisory Group meets in a variety of ways. There are biweekly dinner and dialogue gatherings, sometimes with special speakers. We have an electronic bulletin board in which we share information and dialogue, seek advice, and build community. For additional information sharing and community building, some of us participate in wider telecommunications networks—like those operated by the Institute for Global Communications, the Fellowship for Intentional Community, and other

Eco-Villagers reading the Neighborhood News.

Eco-Village Staff, L.A. Eco-Village

groups. We have Saturday morning potluck brunches, Friday night front-porch hang-outs with neighbors, and unstructured Monday night gatherings. A seven-member core group is in almost daily contact with each other.

The Planning and Advisory Group includes community organizers, professionals, graduate and undergraduate students in a variety of disciplines: ecosystem designers, architects, planners, environmentalists, educators, social change activists, waste management specialists, artists, writers, and others with a variety of eclectic interests.

A Brief History of L.A. Eco-Village

Prior to December 1992, the energy of Eco-Village was focused on a vacant 11-acre landfill site owned by the city, and on the surrounding neighborhoods in northeast Los Angeles. That site is about seven miles away from the current location. The vacant

landfill has a rural feel to it, though it is only about five miles from downtown. The volunteer Planning and Advisory Group used the landfill site to focus its energies for over five years. There have been four exploratory design studies and some significant public-policy work, including the establishment of eco-village concepts in the City of Los Angeles Housing Policies.

The Eco-Village Planning Group learned a lot about landfills; but when it came right down to it, no one in the group felt right about moving there. The Group had tried, over the years, to establish a presence in the neighborhoods surrounding the landfill. Although many of the existing neighbors expressed an interest, none assumed an active involvement, and some actively opposed our proposals.

After the violent uprisings of April 1992, many of us began to seriously reevaluate our priorities for inner-city Los Angeles. How could we help heal our city? How could we most effectively introduce whole

115

• • • • • • • • • • • • • • • • • • • •

The skills and knowledge are present within to heal ourselves, our neighborhoods, our cities, our planet—and we have the public responsibility to *do it*.

• • • • • • • • • • • • • • • • • • • •

systems planning into "rebuilding" neighborhoods? At the same time, how could we rethink our positions concerning urban development and open space issues? How could we protect, restore, and preserve our remaining open space? After much thought, those of us in the Planning Group realized that our hearts were no longer into the idea of creating yet another new development. The landfill should remain as open space.

It all added up! In mid-December 1992, 25 of us came together and enthusiastically consensed on changing the focus from the landfill site to this neighborhood. At that time, we had a 12-year presence here, and there were four major fires within two blocks of our community during the riots. We realized that the Eco-Village could have greatest impact where it was needed most—in our own built-out neighborhood.

An ecovillage is not a standard concept that can be designed and plunked down anywhere. Whether new development or retrofit of an existing neighborhood (urban, suburban, or rural), an ecovillage is a complex set of interactive processes. These processes are inextricably linked to a core group of people working to integrate the public interest with their individual needs, desires, resources, and networks.

Nothing has been lost in refocusing L.A. Eco-Village energy to the new site. In fact, progress is accelerating now because of the learning curve established in the process of working with the old site.

Eureka: Eco-Village Is a State of Mind! Share It!

Now others are moving here because energy is starting to concentrate on our Eco-Village retrofit. Those who begin similar processes in other neighborhoods will begin to share transformative energy here as well. There are so many people with large reserves of knowledge and skills, people isolated in their efforts to create change, and frustrated at not having an appropriate place or community in which their talents and energies can be utilized and validated. Hopefully, this is the decade in which more and more of us will find one another and create the synergies for accelerating planetary transformation.

New alignments are taking place for many of us as we realize our transformations must begin where we are. The skills and knowledge are present within to heal ourselves, our neighborhoods, our cities, our planet—and we have the public responsibility to *do it*. There is no more time for waiting and searching for "the place where I can live happily ever after."

Ecovillage is the form of community we have chosen to transform or retrofit our neighborhood. Recently, Dianne Herring, an L.A. Eco-Village core group member and ecosystem designer, enthusiastically commented to one of our dialogue groups,

"Eco-Village is a state of mind. You think; you play around; you talk about and work on all these interactive systems; then other people join with you. And soon, it just jumps out at you—you start thinking in Eco-Village systems about everything."

We believe our city, our bioregion, and the world at large desperately need inner-city models of sustainable neighborhoods. Those of us in the Planning Group have a longing for community and meaningful work in response to the pain of our city, and the pain that Los Angeles has brought to the planet through its giant media machine. We are elated to be doing something about it. ⚭

Bioregionalism and Community: A Call to Action

by David Haenke, Newburg, Missouri

*B*ioregion. A life region. A geographical area whose boundaries are roughly determined by nature rather than human beings. One bioregion is distinguished from another by characteristics of flora, fauna, water, climate, rocks, soils, land forms, and the human settlements, cultures, and communities these characteristics have spawned.

"Local community is the basic unit of human habitation. It is at this level that we can reach our fullest potential and best effect social change. Local communities need to network to empower our bioregional communities.

Human communities are integral parts of the larger bioregional and planetary life communities. The empowerment of human communities is inseparable from the larger task of reinhabitation—learning to live sustainably and joyfully in place."
—First North American Bioregional Congress, 1984

Bioregionalism is a comprehensive "new" way of defining and understanding the place where we live, and living in that place sustainably and respectfully. What bioregionalism represents is new only for people who come out of the Western industrial-technological heritage. The essence of bioregionalism has been reality and common sense for native people living close to the land for thousands of years, and remains so for human beings today. At the same time, bioregional concepts are rigorously defensible in terms of science, technology, economics, politics, and other fields of "civilized" human endeavor.

While the bioregional movement is only 20 years old, the essence of bioregionalism is what we can best remember and piece together of the oldest earth traditions and wisdom, tracing back to the beginnings of humanity,...and before that into the root ecological principles of life itself. It is upon these essences and principles that bioregionalism is ultimately based.

Using ecology as the screen, bioregionalism takes the best and most presently relevant of the old, and synthesizes it with the most appropriate of the new. Bioregionalism is the most thoroughly ecological of twentieth-century movements, after those of native and indigenous peoples.

Beyond the ecology movement, bioregionalism is far more than "environmentalism" as it is generally known. Indeed, we would say that there is no such thing as "the environment." Webster's dictionary defines "environment" as "The surrounding conditions, influences, or forces which influence or modify"; or "The aggregate of all external conditions and influences affecting the life and development of an organism."

Bioregionalists know that each of us is a living ecosystem that is completely immersed in, a part of, and utterly dependent upon the larger fabric of life on Earth. The "environment" is not "out there." It is in us, and we are in it.

In 1971 David Haenke moved from Ann Arbor, Michigan to an Ozarks farmstead with family and friends on a quest for an earth-honoring way of life and work. Immersed in whole-systems applied ecology ever since, David cofounded the Ozark Area Community Congress (OACC)—the first bioregional congress—(1977), conceptualized and organized the North American Bioregional Congress (1984), was one of the five original conveners of the U.S. Greens-Green Party (1984), and founded the North American Conference on Christianity and Ecology (1984). He currently directs the Ecological Society Project of The Tides Foundation, and is the Coordinator of the Bioregional Project of the Ozarks Resource Center. His current focus is the integration of Bioregionalism and ecological economics in the context of "total ecology." "Total ecology" covers all dimensions of interaction between the earth and the human species, including 35 ecological movements and disciplines.

Innisfree, Inc.

"The environment is not 'out there.' It is in us, and we are in it."

In contrast, the environmental movement today is primarily concerned with "saving what's left" of "out there," usually through legal adjustments to business as usual. Yet, despite all the Earth Days and political actions, ecological damage is accelerating. While environmentalism does much good work in consciousness raising, it is only a part of what must be done. Eco-awareness fails to propose comprehensive and systemic change at all levels—based on ecology. Bioregionalism does, reaching for something far deeper and more holistic that must be manifested.

Bioregionalism: An All-Inclusive Way of Life

Bioregionalism is an all-inclusive way of life, embracing the whole range of human thought and endeavor. It advocates a full restructuring of systems within a given bioregion, orienting toward regeneration and sustainability of the whole life community. This inclusion of the nonhuman in the definition of community is vital. Indeed, one of the basic tenets of bioregionalism is the notion of "bio-centrism," or "eco-centrism," where reality is viewed from a life-centered or ecologically centered perspective, rather than from a human-centered focus (anthropocentrism).

Bioregionalism speaks to the heart of community. If we are to continue to live on Earth, the definition of community has to include all the living things in our ecosystem. Without the flowers, mammals, insects, trees, birds, grasses, and the living soil and waters in community with each other, we would not be here at all. Humans need other life forms in order to survive. Without a respectful, cooperative relationship with others, we are both physically and spiritually impoverished. Without their ecological teachings we are ignorant and cannot know how to live. One oak tree can teach us more about sustainable economics than all the economists of the world put together. Altogether, nature has volumes to teach us about how to create sustainable community life.

The ecosystem, the watershed, the bioregion: these are the context, the boundary, the basic foundations of community. Lest our communities be parasitic and unsustainable, rights equal to our own human rights must be secured for all the living things of the ecosystem community in which our human communities are embedded. There is nothing new about any of this—except in the sense that contemporary society has forgotten what indigenous peoples around the earth have always remembered. It is for us to remember, to relearn, and to put into practice.

In order to be sustainable, our ways of making a living must be ecological. Ecological economics means bioregional self-reliance, deriving as much as possible of our livelihood from within, and close to, our community, only moving farther afield when we must. To be sustainable, we must better see our reliance on and interdependence with the nonhuman members of our community. We must rely on each other for health, sustenance, and wisdom.

Bioregional Gatherings

The periodic bioregional gatherings are presently evolving a theory of integrated systems: ecologically based economics, agriculture, forestry, technology, law, governance, politics, education, health care, energy, and everything necessary for the human dimension of a given bioregion to function sustainably. The Bioregional Gatherings are working out the

Daniel Greenberg

If we are to continue to live on Earth, the definition of community has to include all the living things in our ecosystem.

principles of ecological decentralism. If humanity is to survive, our systems of production and distribution of vital physical goods must be decentralized. The bioregion is the natural context for the practice of ecological economics and sustainable communities.

Starting with the Ozark Area Community Congress in 1980, there have been dozens of these congresses in bioregions around North America. Beginning in 1984, the North American Bioregional Congress has met every two years. Now called the Turtle Island Bioregional Gathering (from an indigenous term for the continent), this meeting serves as the continental and international gathering of the bioregional movement.

All five continental Gatherings have offered some focus on small communities and intentional communities. The Gatherings themselves have been examples of a vibrant community—albeit only for a week—where the group as a whole takes care of food preparation, child care, education, celebration, recycling, cleanup, shelter building, creating a newsletter, cultural presentations, and many more of the functions of a community. Altogether, Bioregional Gatherings have always concerned themselves with advancing the ideas of ecologically responsible communities.

Come Home to Earth

The bioregional movement offers hope for saving the human species and bringing "thrival" (not just survival) and sanity back into the human family, while preserving the integrity of the rest of life on Earth.

What bioregionalism is uncovering and remembering is a way for everyone, of any culture or background, to come home to Earth. We can draw upon the deep and perennial sources of knowledge to create a sustainable life in the present, no matter where we live, even in the largest cities.

Bioregionalism shows us that these sources of knowledge have no cultural or political copyright. They are available to us wherever there is a tree or a few square feet of uncontrolled life zone. There are points of contact and cooperation for all people who immerse themselves in the loving, honoring, and healing of the earth. We must heed our instinctive understanding of the ancient, current, and future ecological principles of the earth and the processes of life.

Bioregionalism is the making of active alliance with the earth in virtually every dimension of our individual and collective existence. Such an alliance is a basis for creating sustainable communities, and why bioregionalism and the communities movement are inextricably linked.

For more information about Bioregionalism, contact the following.

(1) Planet Drum Foundation, Box 31251, San Francisco, CA 94131, 415-285-6556.

(2) The Turtle Island Office, c/o Learning Alliance, 494 Broadway, New York, NY 10012, 212-226-7171. (Contact for Turtle Island Bioregional Gathering schedules.)

(3) The Bioregional Project, c/o David Haenke, Rt. 1, Box 20, Newburg, MO 65550, 314-762-3423.

Central Living in the Netherlands: The Influence of Architecture on Social Structure

by Dorit Fromm, Berkeley, California, reprinted from Collaborative Communities

Dutch "centraal wonen" (central living) began in 1969 when Lies van Dooremaal, a mother overwhelmed by the combination of professional work, housekeeping, and child care, published a plea in the local newspaper. She called for housing with common amenities to break the cycle of parental isolation and overwork. She reasoned that other parents shared her problems, and that they could help each other instead of living in isolation.

A few years earlier similar articles in Denmark had sparked enthusiasm for the cohousing movement. The newspaper advertisement in the Netherlands also met with positive responses, but there was a distinct difference between the groups that formed. While Danish cohousing attracted predominately married couples, the Dutch groups grew to include more singles, single parents, and elderly people—almost half are

single and a third are single parents. Yet in both countries the motivations were similar concerning design of communities for more social contact, including shared amenities and management.

The National Association of Centraal Wonen (LVCW) was created in 1971 as an umbrella organization for the new collective housing movement. LVCW proclaims that central living is "for the emancipation of man, woman and child" (Ren Krabbe). The Dutch view collaborative housing as a

Robby Ekara, National Association of Central Living, Netherlands

The National Association of Central Living was created as an umbrella organization for the new collective housing movement in Holland.

Dorit Fromm is a partner in the design firm of Riggs and Fromm in Berkeley. She is researching cohousing for seniors aged 55 and older, and has had many articles about housing published in *Progressive Architecture, Architectural Review*, and other professional publications. Dorit was awarded a grant from the National Endowment for the Arts to research new forms of housing with

shared services. The result of that earlier research was *Collaborative Communities*, which is now a standard English reference on cohousing in Holland according to the Landelijke Vereniging Centraal Wonen—the Dutch National Association of Central Living. *Collaborative Communities* is published by Van Nostrand Reinhold, New York, 1991, $45.95, 800-842-3636.

Cooking and eating together is one of the fundamental ways that groups create a sense of community.

tool for reforming society—not only relieving the isolation of the one-family home, but also that of the nuclear family structure itself.

In 1970, a group of 25 households organized to build collaborative housing in Hilversum, a small city not far from Amsterdam. The group wanted to make housing affordable to all levels of society. Although the group had concepts similar to cohousing, Dutch political structures produced a different outcome in the Netherlands.

In Holland, social (subsidized) housing has traditionally been built by local nonprofit housing associations with government funding. Since the beginning of this century, such nonprofit sponsors have been the channel for government subsidies to build rental housing. In 1992, there were 63 "centraal wonen" developments with some 2,000 dwellings, typically concentrated in large, urban buildings. At that time, an additional 15 to 20 more communities were being developed. About half of the Dutch developments have over 40 households, with the architecture physically dividing the households into clusters.

Dutch housing co-ops are designed to create levels of socializing between the private dwelling and the collaborating community by designing smaller common areas for the exclusive use of specific clusters of households. For instance, Hilversumse Meent contains a private level for each dwelling, shared semiprivate backyards, a semicommon space in the cluster kitchen-dining room, the common workshops and pub, and the public pedestrian paths in front of the homes.

Dividing the larger community into smaller groups fosters a greater sense of intimacy, allowing decisions about organization to be tailored more closely to specific clusters. Yet, because of their intimacy, groups of 12 households or fewer have more small-scale social problems than larger groups. Also, there may be confusion between the jurisdiction of the cluster and that of the community as a whole. For example, should the cluster or the whole community select new members?

The architecture at Hilversum reinforces small social groupings by connecting each housing unit to a specific cluster kitchen, providing few opportunities to mix or eat with the larger community. However, new central living communities are more flexible, supplementing the closed clusters with other clusters designed for more openness to wider social groupings.

Newer Dutch central living projects have a wide range of housing types and common kitchen arrangements. At least two different types of clusters are now planned into the larger projects. The traditional closed cluster, as at Hilversumse Meent, provides common rooms that are physically connected only to the dwellings in that cluster. Alternatively, open clusters rely on common rooms that are not connected to any one particular cluster of dwellings.

When the kitchen-dining areas are not centralized, but scattered among the clusters, the sense of community is altered substantially. Cooking and eating together is one of the fundamental ways that groups create a sense of community. In fact, a strong social grouping can become similar to a family or clan, and the size and strength of these clusters of households influences the strength of the community. Thus, architectural design can be viewed as a basic factor in the community experience.

Taking Care of Business

Jonathan Roth of Twin Oaks

The Tyranny of Structurelessness

by Joreen

*A*bsence of structure in many intentional communities is a natural reaction against the overstructured society in which most of us found ourselves, and against the inevitable control this gave others over our lives. The idea of structurelessness, however, has moved from a healthy counter to those tendencies to becoming a goddess in its own right.

Contrary to what we would like to believe, there is no such thing as a structureless group. Any group of people that comes together for any length of time for any purpose will inevitably structure itself in some fashion. The structure may be flexible; it may vary over time; it may evenly or unevenly distribute tasks, power, and resources among the members of the group. But a structure will be formed regardless of the abilities, personalities, or intentions of the people involved. The very fact that we are individuals, with different talents, predispositions, and backgrounds makes this inevitable. Only if we refused to relate or interact on any basis whatsoever could we approximate structurelessness; but that is not the nature of human groups.

The idea of structurelessness does not prevent the formation of informal structures, only formal ones. A "laissez faire" ideal for group structure becomes a smoke screen for the strong or the lucky to establish unquestioned hegemony over others. Thus, structurelessness becomes a way of masking power. As long as the structure of the group is informal, the rules of how decisions are made are known only to a few, and awareness of power is limited to those who know the rules.

For everyone to have the opportunity to be involved in a group and to participate in its activities, the structure must be explicit, not implicit. Decision making must be open and available to everyone, and this can happen only if it is formalized.

This is not to say that formal structure in a group will destroy the informal structure. But it does hinder the informal structure from having predominant control and makes available some means of formal negotiation if the informal leaders are not at least responsive to the needs of the group at large.

Once a group has given up clinging to the ideology of structurelessness, it is free to develop those forms of organization best suited to its healthy functioning. This does not mean blindly imitating traditional forms of organization or blindly rejecting them either. Some traditions will prove useful, and some will give us insights into what we should and should not do to meet the objectives of the members. But mostly we will have to experiment with different kinds of structures, both traditional and contemporary.

While engaging in this evolutionary process, there are some principles we can keep in mind that are essential to effective democratic structuring.

(1) Delegation of specific authority to specific individuals for specific tasks by democratic procedures. If people are selected to do a task after expressing an

Joreen, Jo Freeman, wrote this article while studying political science at the University of Chicago. She completed her Ph.D. in 1973, incorporating the ideas of this article into her dissertation, entitled *The Politics of Women's Liberation*, and has since earned a law degree as well. Jo is Editor of *Women: A Feminist Perspective* (five editions) and *Social Movements of the Sixties and Seventies*, 1983 (out of print since 1987). This article was also published in *Second Wave*, 2(1)—a women's periodical in the '70s, and reprinted soon after by KNOW, Inc., Pittsburgh, a feminist publishing group active in the '80s.

interest or willingness, they have made a commitment that cannot easily be ignored.

(2) Responsiveness of those to whom authority has been delegated to those who delegated it. Individuals may exercise power, but it is the group that has ultimate say over how the power is exercised. This is how the group exercises control over people in positions of authority.

(3) Distribution of authority among as many people as is reasonably possible. This prevents monopoly of power and requires those in positions of authority to consult with many others in the process of exercising their authority. Such decentralization also gives many people the opportunity to have responsibility for specific tasks and thereby to learn different skills.

(4) Rotation of tasks among individuals. Responsibilities that are held too long by one person, formally or informally, come to be seen as that person's property, and are not easily relinquished or controlled by the group. Conversely, if tasks are rotated too frequently the individual does not have time to learn the job and acquire satisfaction from doing it well.

(5) Allocation of tasks along rational criteria such as ability, interest, and responsibility.

(6) Diffusion of information to everyone as frequently as possible. Information is power. Access to information enhances one's power.

(7) Access to needed resources. Skills and information are resources as much as physical equipment, space, or dollars. Skills can be made available equitably only when members are willing to teach what they know to others.

Organization structures developed according to these principles can be controlled by the community as a whole. These principles encourage flexibility, openness, and modest terms of office for those in positions of authority. Since ultimate decisions will be made by all group members, those individual members with positions of authority will not be able to institutionalize their power easily. As communities go through various stages of development and positions of authority are rotated among different members, the group will gain experience in determining which of their members can provide the effective leadership needed to meet different challenges and opportunities. Over time, as more and more group members gain experience in positions of authority, the organization can realize increasing

Decentralization gives people the opportunity to learn different skills.

effectiveness and creativity in group endeavors—joining personal growth and community growth to a common end! 🜔

Intentional Communities as Laboratories for Learning about Direct Democracy

by Mildred Gordon of Ganas, Staten Island, New York

Thomas Jefferson said,

"I know of no safe depository of the ultimate power of the society but the people themselves, and if we think them not enlightened enough to exercise their control with a wholesome discretion, the remedy is not to take it from them, but to inform their discretion."

Almost everyone agrees with Mr. Jefferson. Attempts at effective, universal participation in direct democracy date back to early Athens at least, and possibly to the first time Homo sapiens stood upright. In the intervening years, countless groups, large and small, have had a go at it, but nobody has yet succeeded in making direct democracy work consistently, effectively, economically, humanistically, and/or replicably. Few empower themselves to create cooperative worlds the way they want them. This seems so even when the world in question is as small as one couple, a few children, and several friends and associates. Failure to self-empower seems as widespread personally as it is politically, precisely because people everywhere tend not to be (in Mr. Jefferson's words) "enlightened enough." The mandate therefore is to "inform their (our) discretion." The catch is that Mr. Jefferson didn't say how to do it. I think it might be the responsibility of intentional communities to try to figure it out.

Ganas, a New York City intentional community of about 80 people, of which I am one of six founding members, considers itself an experimental laboratory established primarily for this purpose. We spend a lot of time at Ganas learning how to exchange information effectively enough and truthfully enough to govern cooperatively and well. In the process, we have found it necessary to take a hard look at the problems involved, and what needs to be done about them.

Requirements for Cooperative Self-Governing (Participatory Democracy)

(1) Direct participation in cooperative self-government needs everybody to stay involved most of the time at all levels of planning, problem solving, and decision making. This seems necessary in spite of the inevitable frustrations and failures, because even a small number of negative, disruptive, or even just uninvolved individuals can do quite a lot of damage to the well-being and work of a cooperative group. It has been truly noted that if you are not part of the solution, you are inevitably part of the problem (sooner or later).

Good participation requires constant and active interest in issues, even from people not directly involved or those who have no jurisdiction in the matters at hand. There is a common idea among people in cooperatives and participatory democracies that nobody is going to be interested in most issues except owners, those directly affected, and the people who normally bulldoze their way through

---

Mildred Gordon was one of the cofounders of the Feedback Learning Institute in 1978. Her community interests include Feedback Learning and communications skill development, negotiation and conflict resolution, group facilitation, systems, product design and display, food purchasing, and gardening.

group process. But issues need to be considered important just because they matter to others in the group or to the group as a whole. Everyone who has ever done this kind of work knows that, unfortunately, such interest rarely happens.

(2) To work well, direct democracy needs all participants to inform themselves as fully as possible about each situation. This applies not only to the objective matter under discussion, but also to the feelings of all those concerned. Suppose the group is discussing the remodeling of their kitchen and has not reached agreement about what kind of fixtures to use for the new sink. Everyone in the group needs to know what fixtures are available at what price, and what the higher priced ones offer that the cheap ones don't. In addition, however, they need to know that one person fervently believes it always pays to buy the highest quality plumbing, another has a lifetime habit of buying things cheap and has almost made a life's philosophy out of it, two people are having a jealous conflict over a rival, and somebody else compulsively disagrees with everybody.

In addition, the information needs to be up to date. Maybe the jealous couple worked out their problem yesterday, or maybe there is a new fixture on the market that solves everybody's problem. Everybody who is in on the decision needs all this information. In its absence, not only the faucet decision, but the whole community could be the worse for it.

We also need to understand the information in context. How important is the sink fixture choice to the entire kitchen remodel, and how important is the remodel in the whole scheme of the group's overall goals and purposes? How much time can be given to this discussion, and what is the worst that can happen if the fixture decision turns out to be wrong? Is this the best time and place to deal with some of the emotional issues that surfaced, or should they be tabled for another time?

Clearly, not only does all this information have to be available to everyone involved, but everyone has to want to receive it—and this is not always the case. Not even usually. Often not even partially!

(3) Competitive feelings among the members of the group are a major barrier to good information exchange. Often we don't understand these competitive feelings (our own or each other's) or even acknowledge them. That doesn't make them go away, but drives them beneath the surface where

> **Many communities have evolved complex rule structures that tend to become as irrationally rigid as the outmoded social norms they are trying to replace.**

they continue to interfere with clear thinking and communication. What results are power plays rather than cooperative thinking. Conflicted thoughts and feelings remain unresolved. Good ideas, as well as good problem solving, get lost in the process. In fact, most of us spend most of our time dealing with the endless and fruitless competitions that plague our interactions.

New ideas leading to new decisions require undefensive, interactive group discussion. This can't happen when pet notions, values, and habituated thoughts get contradicted and people choose to feel bad or angry about the implied criticism. Unfortunately, defensive reactions are most likely precisely when new critical input and good interactions are most needed.

Uninformed, misinformed, or defensive participation in group process can be worse than no participation at all. There are those who refuse to listen with interest to opposing views. Some will listen but absolutely won't change their minds, no matter what. We've heard the familiar statement, "Don't confuse me with the facts; my mind is made up." Active participation of this kind can be a demoralizing time waster and a liability for the group.

(4) To understand fully what is going on, we have an even more difficult task to undertake. Interactive group process in a participatory democracy won't work well unless each participant is committed to learning how to present thoughts and feelings clearly and to respond to what other people present, both verbally and non-verbally. If we are not prepared to expose feelings or to be exposed to them,

> The trust that is
> needed is trust in our
> own ability to handle
> the consequences of
> an interaction, even if
> it goes badly.

we are in danger of losing touch with our direct experience of our own thought and emotion, as well as those of others (as in the faucet example). It is important that we continue to hold to this commitment, even when others make it difficult to do.

Whatever we say, no matter how we say it, there is a good chance our input will be received inappropriately. It may be unwelcome (though true) or welcome (though untrue.) Worse, nobody is immune to expressing occasional absurdities that might be ridiculed. We have all experienced feeling contradicted before being understood or having a well-meant comment met with indifference, hostility, or outright aggression. Politeness, masking of negative feeling, comments withheld or feelings submerged to avoid offending—all these contribute to still more misunderstanding. It is hard to keep on trying in the face of all this. The ability to persevere depends on learning to cope with frustrations, mistakes, criticism, feelings of humiliation—even occasional rages.

Attempts to establish trust in order to feel safe enough to open up haven't always done too well, either. When people are open, they sometimes can't be trusted to be nice. Conversely, if people can be trusted not to be hurtful, they are probably also not very open. They're just trying to follow the group's norms, often at considerable cost of awareness, spontaneity, and honesty, not to mention thoughtful intelligence.

The trust that is needed is trust in our own ability to handle the consequences of an interaction, even if it goes badly. If we need to be sure that nothing uncomfortable will come of it, we probably won't engage, or at least not very truthfully.

(5) The most difficult requirement of all is maintaining a strong positive motivation to participate. This dream is hard to attain, and even harder to maintain, given the predictable presence of a few "participants" who take their energy largely from power battles. Occasionally we even have to contend with the senseless raging fights that can bring everybody down, because it is hard to resist the strong desire to counterattack.

It is important to remember that negatively motivated people won't get more cooperative when they are judged and punished. They need understanding and help. The trouble is that rivalrous people usually don't want any help, however well intentioned. They are likely to view benevolent intervention as more competitive than helpful. Worse, most of us who have tried to maintain positive motivation have had frequent occasion to doubt our own purity of purpose.

Given all the above, it is not surprising that direct democracy and cooperation don't tend to work very well, either in or out of community. In fact, it is surprising that effective cooperative effort ever happens at all, but it does.

Learning how to do these things better than we do or have done is clearly necessary, but certainly not easy. Intentional community has good reason to be motivated to try to develop the learning methods and opportunities that could make it possible.

Intentional Communities Have Good Reason to Learn How To Do the Job of Building Better Worlds.

(1) Political Motivation: None of the governmental approaches used by today's communities is really fully satisfactory. Each offers some benefits, and each has its problems.

Strong Central Leaders. There are many good reasons for a community to avoid the kind of government in which a single person holds all of the authority and makes all the decisions. These days community people are generally in agreement that this kind of decision making is undesirable and probably dangerous, so there is no reason to preach to the converted by drawing out the arguments here.

Moral Law. Relying on agreed-upon religious or moral principles has only limited value. True, it provides some stability and can occasionally still the anxieties that we all struggle with. But it cannot itself

A display room at the second-hand furniture store operated by Ganas members.

Geoph Kozeny, Community Catalyst Project

as irrationally rigid as the outmoded social norms they are trying to replace. We have all seen legislation proliferate into restrictive tangles of contradictory concepts. New rules can be more tyrannical than either controlling morals or strong leaders. What makes them dangerous is that so many people take comfort from their promise to prevent problems. In reality, rules rarely prevent trouble. They are more likely to interfere with attempts to find good solutions. Laws that were meant to guide current thought too often eliminate it.

effectively relate to the problems that need answers every day. Somebody has to interpret, and in the interpretation the group faces the same problems as groups without a guiding vision. Generally speaking, inherited or even group-evolved fixed morality lacks the flexibility demanded by day-to-day issues.

Philosophic or Political Dogma. Many groups that consider themselves far beyond the strictures of religion or traditional morality still use some of the same assumptions and techniques called by more modern names. Particularly noticeable are the dogmas of the political left or the various faces of environmentalism. Neither of these movements stands still long enough for any systematic approach to become popular, and in the meantime, it is up to leaders to interpret what any particular community does with them. In one place, recycling is everything; in another, getting off the grid is the overall goal. Some groups are principally concerned with diet, others with occult powers. People are attracted for a variety of reasons to all of such groups, and their conflicting views present each community with decision-making problems that often are beyond the ability of their presumably shared belief systems to manage.

Rules and Agreements. Many communities have evolved complex rule structures that tend to become

Furthermore, just as with rule by charismatic leaders, enforcement of rules, law, norms, or moral codes requires some kind of punishment as a backup when people defy them, as somebody inevitably will. The usual leverage applied in community is peer pressure (in the form of personal rejection or expulsion of noisy nonconformers). Such measures tend to either get compliance without agreement, or they fail to deter or control at all. In any event, they rarely change anyone's mind about anything. Too much peer pressure can result in both conformity and rebellion alternately—or, in very dysfunctional people, simultaneously.

Mostly, trying to enforce rules just gets rid of difficult (and often good) people. When unquestioning compliance does happen, it is often at too great a cost to creative communication, and therefore effective participation itself becomes unaffordable.

Moral codes, norms, policy guidelines—even the written law itself—are weak substitutes for good group process. Any of them may work for a while, but when they fail, dangerous chaos, bad management, poverty, and ultimate failure to survive as a group are likely results.

A view of the common backyard that connects the five group houses at Ganas.

Geoph Kozeny, Community Catalyst Project

In order to avoid the emergence of strong leaders (or the disasters that can happen without them), and because good group process is so hard to come by, most communities ultimately do rely heavily on rule systems. But the rules are never wiser than the people who create them. They are not necessarily responsive to here and now reality, and for the most part they don't work very well. When leaders do appear, they mostly stay behind the scenes. Some combination of open and hidden leadership, some political policy arrived at by vote or by consensus, a proliferation of rules or agreements—these are the clumsy but commonly accepted compromises.

When such settlements are arrived at, the need for widespread effective participation in economic and political management may not come up for consideration again for years. For a while, people think they've solved the problems. Everyone tends to get more content and to bother less about the issues,

because things seem to be working well enough—as long as nobody looks too closely.

Maintaining the status quo in this way is often possible long after real trouble has set in, but before the consequences of that trouble are visible. In business, sales may be down, costs up, and productivity a disaster. In fact, the undertaking may already have failed. But maybe not all the bills have come in yet, and cash flow may still be good enough for the people involved to be unaware that their venture is already bankrupt. The same process can happen in relationships, families, or society at large. It happens frequently in community.

(2) Economic Motivation. Communities are composed of people who got together to satisfy their personal and collective lifestyle desires. They need to maintain economic stability, secure a moderate standard of living, and enjoy a range of occupational choices. It is important to have the opportunity to develop skills, employ talents, and allow for preferences.

Poor management often gets in the way. People frequently take positions they are not qualified for and may not even like, but hang onto because of the authority or status involved. Fearing to be found out, they avoid exposure or feedback and do an even poorer job. Eventually someone objects, dialog turns to arguments, and arguments to fights. People blame each other for work problems instead of getting together to solve them. Power struggles proliferate, everyone gets discouraged, and productivity sinks. Resources are wasted, and economic deterioration may follow. If strong, wise leaders don't take over, there is a pretty good chance that poverty and/or bankruptcy will.

Communities aware of such threats ought to be motivated to keep the direction of their economic lives where it belongs, in the hands of "the people themselves."

(3) Loving relationships that are secure, happy, and mutually supportive are a major value in communities. We can all agree on that, but how to get them is not well understood. What is needed are truthful exchanges, freedom from moral absolutes, a rejection-free social environment, and a flexibility sufficient to allow individuals to be different from but supportive of each other.

Economic, political, or personal interactions all call for relationships that are strong enough to handle open exchanges of feelings and perceptions. They all rely on truth. If we choose to lie to each other by omission (to prevent hurt feelings or to avoid trouble of whatever kind), other, more explicit lies tend to proliferate in the cover-up.

The kind of complex behavioral learning that a community needs in order to make participatory democracy work is a high-risk undertaking calling for a truly secure social base. Creating such a base requires us to keep up the positive motivation for the task of learning to think together creatively.

(4) Intentional communities can create the kind of environment needed, because we have control of many of the social reinforcers that facilitate or prevent change. Since we are literally in charge of creating our worlds as we want them to be, possibly we can learn how to reshape the forces that shaped us in the first place.

Most of that shaping was done in the past by usually random approval and disapproval. Essentially, we tend to repeat what felt good and avoid anything that threatens disapproval. We need to realize that we ourselves created the rush of pleasure we associate with approval, and our fears of the consequences of disapproval are almost never realistic.

In the big world, "winning" is rewarded with approval, material goods, or even security in relationships. Competitive "wins" may be applauded even when the action involved is clearly socially destructive. Emotional expression is almost universally discouraged. Learning from mistakes is often viewed as weakness. The outcome of telling the truth can be ostracism. Intelligent input to economic management can get you fired. Meaningful participation in politics is at least disheartening and generally just not an option.

In community, because we are empowered to decide almost everything together, we can hope to change these things. It is possible for us to allow and reward individual self-empowerment. We can celebrate occurrences of whatever behaviors we choose. We can support honesty and understanding in dialogue. We can open up to performance feedback and learn how to feel good about it, because we want to. We can learn to listen as actively as we speak, as eager to hear and understand as we are to speak and be understood. Maybe we can even learn to welcome new ideas.

• • • • • • • • • • • • • • • • • •

We can learn to listen as actively as we speak, as eager to hear and understand as we are to speak and be understood.

• • • • • • • • • • • • • • • • • •

We need to learn to allow others their responses of approval and disapproval of our behaviors, be glad to have their input, and give them a full hearing. We need to weigh it all out and then chart our own course, accepting that everyone else will also do whatever they decide, and that each of us has the responsibility to learn to accept and adjust to whatever comes of it. When these things are possible, we can finally hope to make open dialog a reality instead of just an exciting dream.

(5) Experimentation with alternative lifestyles is the stated purpose of many nonreligious communities. Historically, small communities have regarded themselves primarily as path blazers and social innovators. Because so many intentional communities hold these dreams in common, they are the logical choice of places in which to build our laboratories for learning the art of loving, cooperative autonomy, and creative self governing. ⚉

Consensus Ingredients

by Caroline Estes of Alpha Farm, Deadwood, Oregon

During the past few decades, while we have been searching for new ways of doing things in order to be inclusive, the decision-making process known as consensus has begun to be used increasingly and in many different situations. Government is using it to try to find ways that do not involve court cases on controversial laws, such as in the Forest Service. Hewlett-Packard uses it in its factories; and many social services are beginning to use it in their work.

In simple terms, consensus refers to agreement on some decision by all members of a group, rather than a majority or a select group of representatives. The consensus process is what the group goes through to reach this agreement. The assumptions, methods, and results are different from Robert's Rules of Order or traditional parliamentary procedure.

Over the past nearly 40 years, since I was first introduced to the use of consensus in Quaker business meetings, I have been in widely different situations in which it has been used, and I have been teaching it for the past 15 years. The Greens Party of North America used it in the beginning of its organization, and the bioregional movement of North America uses it exclusively in its biennial meetings. Many intentional communities use the process, as well as the board of the Fellowship for Intentional Community (FIC). Departments within government and universities, school faculties, and administrations are beginning to find it useful and efficient.

The Basis

Consensus is based on the belief that each person has some part of the truth and no one has all of it (no matter how much we like to believe that we ourselves know it all). It is also based on a respect for all persons involved in the decision being considered.

In our present society the governing idea is that we can trust no one, and therefore we must protect ourselves if we are to have any security in our decisions. The most we will be willing to do is compromise, and this leads to a very interesting way of viewing the outcome of working together. It means we are willing to settle for less than the very best— and that we will often have a sense of dissatisfaction with our decisions unless we can somehow outmaneuver others involved in the process. This leads to a skewing of honesty and forthrightness in our relationships.

In the consensus process, we start from a different basis. The assumption is that we are all trustworthy (or at least can become so). The process allows each person complete power over the group. For example, the central idea for the Quakers is the complete elimination of majorities and minorities. If there are any differences of view at a Quaker meeting, as there are likely to be in such a body, the consideration of the question at issue proceeds with long periods of solemn hush and meditation, until slowly the lines of thought draw together toward a point of

Caroline Estes is a founding member of Alpha Farm and a board member of the Fellowship for Intentional Community. She is a facilitator of mass meetings, including Turtle Island Bioregional Gatherings and meetings of the FIC. Caroline is a Quaker with long experience as a trainer in consensus decision making and is

writing a book on the subject. This article is adapted from a piece published in the Fall 1983 issue of *In Context: A Quarterly of Humane Sustainable Culture*, Bainbridge Island, Washington (reprinted by permission).

unity. Then the clerk frames a minute of conclusion, expressing the "sense of the meeting."

Built into the consensual process is the belief that all persons have some part of the truth in them, or what in spiritual terms might be called "some part of God." We will reach a better decision by putting all of the pieces of the truth together before proceeding. There are indeed times when it appears that two pieces of the truth are in contradiction with each other, but with clear thinking and attention, the whole may be perceived including both pieces, or many pieces. The traditional either/or type of argument does not advance this process. Instead, the consensus process is a search for the very best solution—whatever the problem. That does not mean that there is never room for error—but on the whole, in my experience, it is rare.

The consensus process makes direct application of the idea that all persons are equal—an idea that we are not entirely comfortable with, since it seems on the surface that some people are "more equal than others." But if we do indeed trust one another and do believe that we all have parts of the truth, then we can remember that one person may know more of the truth at one time, while another person may know more at another time. Even when we have all the facts before us, it may be the spirit that is lacking; and this may come forth from yet another who sees the whole better than anyone else. Everybody's contributions are important.

Decisions which all have helped shape, and with which all can feel united, make the necessary action go forward with more efficiency, power and smoothness. This applies to persons, communities and nations. Given the enormous issues and problems before us, we need to make decisions in ways that will best enable us to move forward together. When people join their energy streams, miracles can happen.

The Process

How does the consensus process actually work? It can be a powerful tool, yet like any tool, this process needs to be used rightly. To make the most of its possibilities we need to understand the parts and the process.

Consensus needs four ingredients—a group of people willing to work together, a problem or issue that requires a decision by the group, trust that there is a solution, and perseverance to find the truth.

● ● ● ● ● ● ● ● ● ● ● ● ● ● ● ● ● ● ●

Built into the consensual process is the belief that all persons have some part of the truth in them...

● ● ● ● ● ● ● ● ● ● ● ● ● ● ● ● ● ● ●

It is important to come to the meetings with a clear and unmade-up mind. This is not to say that prior thinking should not have been done, but simply that the thinking must remain open throughout the discussion—or else there is no way to reach the full truth. Ideas and solutions must be listened to with respect and trust, and must be sought from all assembled. This means everyone, not just some of the group. Consensus is the practice of oneness for those who are committed to that idea, or it is the search for the best possible solution for those who are more logic-based.

The problems to be considered come in all sizes, from "who does the dishes" to "how to reach accord on limiting the arms race." The consensus process begins with a statement of the problem—as clearly as possible, in language as simple as possible. It is important that the problem not be stated in such a way that an answer is built in, but that there be an openness to looking at all sides of the issue—whatever it may be. It is also necessary to state the problem in the positive: "We will wash the dishes with detergent and hot water," not "We will not wash the dishes in cold water." Or "We need to wash the dishes so they are clean and sanitary," not "The dishes are very dirty, and we are not washing them correctly." Stating the issues in the positive begins the process of looking for positive solutions and not a general discussion of everything that is undesirable or awful.

The meeting needs a facilitator/clerk/convener, a role whose importance cannot be too strongly emphasized. It is this person whose responsibility it is to see that all are heard, that all ideas are incorporated if they seem to be part of the truth, and that the final decision is agreed upon by all assembled.

Traits that help the facilitator are patience, intuition, articulateness, ability to think on one's feet,

Communities Directory

> The facilitator needs to be able to keep the discussion from being dominated by a few and to encourage those who have not spoken to share their thoughts.

and a sense of humor. It is important that the facilitator never show signs of impatience. The facilitator is the servant of the group, not its leader. As long as the group needs the clerk, he/she should be there. It is also important for a facilitator to look within to see if there is something that is missing—a person who is wanting to speak but has been too shy, an idea that was badly articulated but has the possibility of helping build the solution, anything that seems of importance on the nonverbal level. This essence of intuition can often be of great service to the group by releasing some active but unseen deterrent to the continued development of a solution.

The facilitator must be able to constantly state and restate the position of the meeting and at the same time know that progress is being made. This helps the group to move ahead with some dispatch.

And last but by no means least—a sense of humor. There is nothing like a small turn of a phrase at a tense moment to lighten up the discussion and allow a little relaxation. Once you have found a good clerk or facilitator, support that person and encourage them to develop their skills as much as possible. Often there are participants who want to talk more than necessary and others who don't speak enough. The facilitator needs to be able to keep the discussion from being dominated by a few and to encourage those who have not spoken to share their thoughts. There are a number of techniques for achieving this. One method is to suggest that no one speak more than once, until everyone has spoken; another is for men and women to speak alternately if those of one gender seem to be dominating the discussion.

However, it is not good to use any arbitrary technique for too long. These methods can bring balance into the group, but artificial guidelines should be abandoned as soon as possible. For instance, the technique of alternating men and women speakers might be used in only one session. My experience is that a single two- or three-hour session using such techniques will establish a new pattern, and there will be little need for guidelines to be continued any longer.

No matter how well the discussion is carried forward, how good the facilitator, and how much integrity there is in the group, there sometimes comes a point when all are in agreement but one or two. At that point there are three courses open. One is to see whether the individuals are willing to "step aside." This means that they do not agree with the decision but do not feel that it is wrong. They are willing to have the decision go forward, but do not want to take part in carrying it out.

If more than two or three persons start to step aside from a decision, then the facilitator should question whether the best decision has been reached yet. This would depend on the size of the group, naturally. At Alpha it is OK for one person to step aside, but as soon as others step aside also, the facilitator begins to watch and to reexamine the decision. At such a time the facilitator might ask for a few minutes of silence to see if there was another decision or an amendment that should have been considered but had been overlooked, something that would ease the situation.

Another possibility is to lay aside the issue for another time. Although this alternative always seems to raise serious questions, we need to have some perspective on what we are doing. It is likely that the world will continue to revolve around the sun for another day, week, or year, whether we come to a decision at this moment or at another. The need to make a decision promptly is often not as important as the need to ultimately come to unity around a decision that has been well seasoned.

Personal experience has shown me that even the most crucial decisions, seemingly time-bound, can be laid aside for a while—and that the time, whether a few hours or days, is wisely allowed if a later meeting can create a better decision than was possible in the first attempt.

The third possibility is that one or two people may stop the group or meeting from moving forward. At that time there are several key considerations. Most important, the group should see those who are with-

134

FIC board meeting,
November 1994.

Michael McIntyre

son concerning alignment of basic values and goals.

Consensus is a very conservative process—once a decision has been made, another consensus is required to change it. So each decision must be well seasoned and generally be relied on for some time. While decisions should not be made in haste, they can be tried on a temporary basis by including expiration dates. At Alpha Farm we have made temporary decisions on a number of occasions, usually trying the decision for a year and then either making a final decision or dropping it entirely. This necessitates keeping minutes, which is another aspect of consensus that needs consistent attention.

holding consensus as doing so out of their highest understanding and beliefs. Next, the individual(s) who are holding the group from making a decision should also examine themselves closely to assure that they are not withholding consensus out of self-interest, bias, vengeance, or any other such feeling. A refusal to consense should be based on a very strong belief that the decision is wrong—and that the dissenter(s) would be doing the group a great disservice by allowing the decision to go forward.

This is always one of those times when feelings can run high, and it is important for the group not to use pressure on those who differ. It is hard enough to feel that you are stopping the group from going forward, without having additional pressure exerted to go against your examined reasons and deeply felt understandings.

In my personal experience of living with the consensus process full-time for 23 years, I have seen meetings held from going forward on only a handful of occasions, and usually the dissenter(s) was justified—the group would have made a mistake by moving forward.

Sometimes, though rarely, one person is consistently at odds with everyone else in the group. Depending on the type of group and its membership, it would be well to see if this person is in the right organization or group. If there is a consistent difference, the person cannot feel comfortable continuing, so the group needs to meet and work with that per-

Minutes on each decision should be stated by the clerk, facilitator, or minute-taker at the time of the decision, so that all present know they have agreed to the same thing. It is not sufficient for minutes to be taken and then read at the next meeting, unless there is to be another meeting very soon. Copies of the minutes should be distributed promptly, because those who make the decisions are also the ones to carry them out. If the minutes are not distributed until the next meeting, some of the original decision makers may not be present. The minutes may or may not be correct, but the time for correction is past. This is a particularly important but little respected part of the process.

Several years ago, I was privileged to facilitate the first North American Bioregional Congress, held in Missouri. Over 200 persons arrived from all over the continent, and some from abroad. We worked together for five days, making all decisions by consensus. Some of those present had used the process before or were currently using it in the groups they worked with at home, but many had not used it. There was a high degree of skepticism when we began as to whether such a widely diverse group of

> **The need to make a decision promptly is often not as important as the need to ultimately come to unity around a decision that has been well seasoned.**

people could work in the degree of harmony and unity that consensus demands. On the final day of the Congress, there were very many resolutions, position papers, and policies put forward from committees that had been working all week long. All decisions made that day were made by consensus—and the level of love and trust among the participants was tangible. Much to the surprise of nearly everyone, we came away with a sense of unity and forward motion that was near miraculous.

A Second Point of View
by Ianto Evans

Thirteen years of experience at Aprovecho Institute have taught us some valuable lessons about consensus and our practice of consensus-minus-one.

Initially, coming from conservative backgrounds and fearing an inability to achieve unanimous agreement, we decided to ratify decisions if all but one person agreed. We saw this as a way to get business done without some obdurate individual holding up the whole show. Our bylaws say something like "with one member dissenting." What it means is if two people oppose something, they can block it, but an individual can't.

In fact, we seldom get a dissenter, but we're protected against unaccountable insanity or temporary bouts of grumpiness. Neither has ever been an issue, but we've found that if one person strongly opposes something, we usually try to discuss it to a point where they at least feel OK about the group going ahead. Then the dissenter can say, "Well, I still dissent but I don't feel unsupported in my views."

Effectively, this gives everyone a vote, as of course they have with total consensus, but there's a difference. In total consensus, one individual can gradually take control of an organization by cumulatively swaying what doesn't get done in a direction s/he wants to see it go. By refusing to agree to black, the group is left only with white to dark grey. Later the options can be narrowed further by refusing to support darker shades of grey. Over a period, and sometimes going unnoticed, a single subversive can push the whole group to accepting only white.

Reflections on Consensus-Minus-One
by Caroline Estes

At one level, the differences between these two approaches are slight—in practice probably hardly noticeable. Yet there is a difference in spirit that harks back to the difference between unitary and adversary democracy. Total consensus assumes and requires a high level of trust and maturity. If these qualities can be developed in the group, then using total consensus is well rewarded by a bonding that goes deeper than the reserve implied in consensus-minus-one. But even with the most unpromising groups a good facilitator can do wonders.

On the other hand, there are many groups—especially with loosely defined memberships—where it would be naive to assume that every member will act in "unitary good faith," especially since our society trains us to act as adversaries. Consensus-minus-one can permit these groups to gain many of the benefits of consensus and avoid risking the subversion that Ianto fears. The lesson, it seems to me, is to have lots of tools in your toolbox, and use each where it fits. ⚙

Bibliography

Auvine, Brian et al., *A Handbook for Consensus Decision Making: Building United Judgement*, 1981, Center for Conflict Resolution, 731 State St., Madison, WI 53703, 608-255-0479.

Auvine, Brian et al., *A Manual for Group Facilitators*, 1978, Center for Conflict Resolution.

(*In Context: A Quarterly of Humane Sustainable Cultures*, is available for $18 per year, $25 surface or $36 air mail outside the United States, from Context Institute, Box 11470, Bainbridge Island, WA 98110.)

The Rhythms of Home: Perspectives on a Communal Lifestyle

by Tom Starrs of Green Pastures Estate, Epping, New Hampshire

*E*very day Jack from Maine feeds and grooms the draft horses, Bob from Tennessee tackles a long list of odd jobs to keep our buildings in good repair, Alice from Massachusetts works at the reception desk in the front office, Glenn from Ohio arranges details for an upcoming retreat over the telephone, Diana from England does a little vacuuming, Tamara from Minnesota changes her daughter's diaper, Gale from California plans menus and works in the kitchen, Pat from Rhode Island goes off to massage school, and Helen from New Hampshire balances the petty cash before making a trip to the bank. What is so special about these individuals performing daily tasks? They all live together with about three dozen others in a 30-year-old spiritual community in Epping, New Hampshire called Green Pastures Estate. What sets them apart from those who

see the repetitive activity of daily chores as a boring rut, is that each of these folks has his/her own vision about the value of their presence in doing the job at hand. Each brings a particular sense of personal purpose, warmth, and movement into the daily routine, lifting the activity above the level of mechanical chores, into something that exudes a sense of meaningfulness, of going someplace, of having rhythm. And where there is rhythm, there is life.

Green Pastures Estate

"Residents and guests examine...being awake and alive in the world as it is."

Tom Starrs is the Program Director at Green Pastures where he has lived since 1980. He is a former board member of the Fellowship for Intentional Community, and was the Editor of the *FIC Newsletter*. In addition to being on the board of trustees for The Emissaries in New England, he is on the board of directors for the Northeast Organic Farming Association in New Hampshire.

. . . .

It's a rare human grouping, beyond the nuclear family, that has more than a superficial level of relatedness among its members...

. . . .

A Deeper Sense of Attunement

The rhythm of life at Green Pastures seems remarkable since community experience is so seldom found in society at large. Who knows the reality of a genuinely intimate community? Who has first-hand knowledge of living consistently over years in a creative, interdependent setting with neighbors beyond one's kin? Who has a personal understanding of being at peace individually and with others? It's a rare human grouping, beyond the nuclear family, that has more than a superficial level of relatedness among its members, let alone a deeper sense of attunement with the larger whole. This is what is being developed at Green Pastures: friendship, ease in living, and a sense of spiritual communion within, with life, with all the forms of life.

The hallmark of life at Green Pastures is change. What is done today may need to be approached differently tomorrow. Sometimes, describing the practices and policies of our community is a bit like trying to nail Jell-O to the wall. There are no hard and fast rules to govern people's behavior; people are responsible for what they do within the community.

Whenever my own perception of this collective dynamic gets set, inevitably people and circumstances come along with new factors to figure into the equation, requiring me to shift my understanding of what is. If I take an inflexible stance and refuse to acknowledge or receive the elements right in front of me, I very quickly find I'm having a hell of a time managing the details of the situation. And this is the heart of the matter, with implications far beyond examining a communal lifestyle: what is the state of *my* heart? That is my supreme responsibility regardless of external circumstance. When my mind and heart are clear, then I can deal practically with the situation at hand.

Emissaries of Divine Light

These are some basic principles for The Emissaries, a spiritually based association begun in the early 1930s. The Emissaries invite people to experience the fullness of their own potential as mature men and women by "letting their light so shine" in every endeavor, by revealing their own integrity in all areas of living.

There are 12 primary Emissary communities around the world—eight in North America, two in Europe, one in South Africa, and one in Australia. The New Hampshire community is a regional center for Emissaries of Divine Light, and the oldest currently active "commune" in New England. Actually, we don't use the word commune to describe ourselves since that word has lots of connotations. Instead, we use the word "unit," which has useful associations with the basic ideas of unified agreement and moving together as a whole community.

Green Pastures Estate was first formed in 1963 by six adults and five children in two homes on an old estate. Today there are approximately 40 people in ten residences on 160 acres, facilities for hosting 75 overnight guests for seminars and conferences, a chapel seating over 200, and a cemetery. Green Pastures is a working farm as well as a center for classes, workshops, and seminars of many sorts.

Draft horses are used in the certified organic garden and for gathering firewood. There are over 100 organic fruit and nut trees, and a small dairy and beef herd. We raise 200 turkeys a year, and keep a few pigs to handle dining room excesses. We are very much into recycling and composting. Farming and gardening operations provide for about two-thirds of our community food needs. Generally meals are eaten communally in the central dining room, although some unit members opt to eat in their homes. While not all meals are vegetarian, an alternative is provided whenever meat is served.

Financial Self-Sufficiency

Residents of Green Pastures keep track of their own finances and are responsible for their own belongings. Income is derived from retreats and workshops.

"Farming and gardening operations provide for about two-thirds of Green Pasture's food needs."

Green Pastures Estate

draft horses work, or to experience community living, or because they saw a news article or TV report about Green Pastures, or because the community somehow got listed in *Arthur Frommer's Guidebook to Utopian Vacations* or another directory—such as this one!

Visitors come to our intentional community in southeastern New Hampshire just about every day of the year. Generally, they receive a walking tour of Green Pastures' grounds, which includes a brief overview of our communal operations as well as a thumbnail sketch of the "personal responsibility" philosophy that is foundation to the Emissary program. Those on tour see the buildings are clean and well painted inside and out, the lawns are groomed regularly and there is virtually no litter anywhere to be seen. The garden is relatively weed free, the barnyard is in good order, and community members are fairly well dressed and in good spirits.

A few residents have jobs off the property. All residents have an ever-changing variety of roles and responsibilities within the community. And with each area of responsibility comes a large part of community life: *meetings!* Almost everyone is in some committee or team that meets regularly: office, kitchen, barnyard, garden, homekeeping, food production, attunement, housing, travel, and service. In addition, there are men's and women's meetings once a week, and no-agenda "family meetings" once a month for everyone. Plus, any number of special interest groups that gather to do their thing: choir, instrumental music, movement and dance, chant, seniors, teens, children, watercolor artists, and writers. There is no shortage of meetings at Green Pastures.

Exploring Existential Questions

The home atmosphere in this community provides an intimate, safe setting for personal growth and spiritual education, for exploring basic existential questions like Who am I? Where did I come from? Why am I here? Residents and guests examine the implications of being awake and alive in the world as it is. People considering these basic questions come from all over the planet to conferences, lectures, and seminars at Green Pastures.

In addition to visitors coming for our public events, others come out of curiosity, or to see the

Exploring Financial Questions

Initial visual impressions often are favorable; newcomers describe what they see with words such as "This is sorta like a spiritual country club." Inevitably they get around to asking specific, money-related questions like "What does it cost to run this place? How do you finance your lifestyle? How do you pay your full-time community members? What do they get paid?" As a once-in-a-while tour guide for hundreds of visitors to Green Pastures over the last 14 years, I don't think I have ever answered such questions in quite the same way twice.

Let me say that I get a little edgy—or perhaps I should say "protective"—when someone I've just met asks me within half an hour of being introduced

• • • • • • • • • • • • • • • • • •

Finances, business, money—these are not dirty words; indeed they open large doors of connection...

• • • • • • • • • • • • • • • • •

what my annual salary is, or makes an inquiry about the bottom line of our balance sheet. Perhaps this is one of my own cultural taboos, but there are times when I feel it is perfectly appropriate to say (as politely as possible), "It's none of your business." Then there are also times when it seems perfectly clear to state baldly and openly, "I make $250 a month" or "This is a $400,000-per-year operation."

Quite frankly, it all depends on my own quite subjective perceptions: What feels safe in the moment? And what is the invisible, energetic quality of "the flow?" Is this a two-way street of giving and receiving, or is the questioner just seeking to *get* answers out of me? Are we in a mutually vulnerable space right now? Such cautious thinking may seem a bit evasive to a hard-liner, or more related to spiritual dynamics than it is to simple facts. But to me, being aware of the flow with an individual in conversation indeed does relate to one's attitude and ability to handle the flow of money.

Monitoring "The Flow"

In this community, we keep a tight watch on income and expenses via regular meetings of Budget and Finance Committees, which work together to plan for the needs of each upcoming year. They make reasonable income and expense projections. If there is a shortfall, we operate like any other family might: we cut expenses somewhere or we sell assets or we seek alternate sources of income. If nothing works, some of us take outside jobs. What is different from a nuclear family is that our extended family has many more people with more experiences, creating a more complex and dynamic interplay.

Another element that affects this interplay is the nature of the players. Because we are a spiritually

based community and one needs a healthy right brain to be spiritually active, there are proportionately fewer in our midst with a strong left-brain capacity, which is essential to function responsibly with finances. So we must be sensitive; the accurate stewardship of money and the ability to let it flow properly cannot be left to a simple acquiescence to a few spiritual principles, or to a blind trust that "it will all work out (somehow)."

Sensitivity and wisdom are both required in the right handling of money. If an attitude of generosity is behind both spending and earning, it is true that one can come to know and experience a seemingly magical sense of providence, of life providing for emergencies, and even having enough at times to assist a worthy cause beyond our borders. On the other hand, frugality also has its rewards. Following the principle, "Do not spend what you do not have" (which makes "deficit spending" an oxymoron), means never having to worry about an insurmountable debt load. Indeed, we own over 90 percent of our assets.

So, how do we finance our lifestyle? It depends. It depends on a patient weighing of perceptible factors. It depends on balancing the value of incoming "needs" and a clear-eyed seeing of what is on hand to spend. It depends on our collective vision and our unified support for that vision. It depends on the balance of logic and intuition and how we choose to translate that into action. It depends on our ability to see the small as well as the large picture. Finances, business, money—these are not dirty words; indeed they open large doors of connection and, just incidentally, provide the means for our continuing operation and ability to live together.

Note: For a schedule of our seminars, conferences, and other events, write or call Green Pastures Estate. Visitors are encouraged to call ahead, particularly if attending a meal. Donations for meals are appropriate. Overnight accommodations are not guaranteed (or free) and must be reserved, preferably at least 48 hours in advance. ⚭

Legal Options for Intentional Communities

by Allen Butcher, Albert Bates, and Diana Leafe Christian

*I*ntentional communities generally arise from a specific idea or philosophy. Community members may be seeking an egalitarian, cooperative lifestyle; a self-reliant, back-to-the-land lifestyle; or a contemplative or spiritual lifestyle. They may want to educate or serve others, provide a nice place for a group of friends to live, or advance a combination of these goals. In any case, once an intentional community arises, attention begins to focus upon what kind of formal, legal organization best suits the group.

Why Should an Intentional Community Be Concerned with Legalities?

If it does not have a legal structure, problems can arise with regard to property rights for new members, compensation for departing members, personal liability, holding title to property and assets, or community agreements. Legal structures provide, if not a solution, at least a means to resolve problems fairly and equitably.

However, in the United States, the main imperative for organizing formally is taxes—a community must comply with the requirements of the federal Internal Revenue Service and state tax laws.

Since there are no legal forms created specifically for intentional communities—except perhaps 501(d) nonprofits, created for the Shakers and groups like them—communities often borrow from the various legal structures used in business organizations. Even though community members may not see their community as a "business operation," forming a legal entity derived from the business world offers distinct advantages to an emerging community. First, any agreements the group makes as part of its legal structure, such as partnership agreements or corporate bylaws, will be compatible with state law and legally enforceable. Second, using a legal structure such as a partnership or corporation to form an intentional community offers advantages when buying land together. And third, the IRS and state tax officials will tax a community according to the legal form it has taken.

Community Ownership and Legal Structures

The distinction between intentional communities and other forms of social organization is difficult to define from an inclusive legal perspective. It's like trying to define a religion in the legal sense—it can't

Allen Butcher first got involved with tax law in the early '80s as a board member of the New Destiny Food Cooperative Federation and New Life Farm. He was a board member of the Fellowship for Intentional Community during the period of expansion from regional to continental organizing. He served as Treasurer of the School of Living Community Land Trust. Allen lived at East Wind and Twin Oaks communities for 13 years, becoming a student of comparative economic systems in intentional communities. He has written a series of resource booklets for understanding and developing intentional community. While he was at Twin Oaks, Allen conceived the forerunner of this article for the last *Directory*. He now lives in Denver.

Albert Bates joined The Farm in Tennessee in 1972 after graduating from law school. He is a member of the Bar in Tennessee; General Counsel to Plenty-USA—The Farm's international relief and development organization; Director of Plenty's Natural Rights Center—a public interest law project; Editor/publisher of *Natural Rights* newsletter; and a former board member of the Communal Studies Association. As project manager of The Farm's Ecovillage Training Center, Albert travels to Russia, where he works with an emerging ecovillage near St. Petersburg. Albert collaborated with Allen on the incorporation article in the last *Directory*.

Diana Leafe Christian, who lives in Ft. Collins, Colorado, is Managing Editor of *Communities* magazine and former Editor/publisher of *Growing Community* newsletter (now a part of *Communities* magazine). She has extensive professional experience in editing and other news media work. Diana wrote a five-part series in *Growing Community* about legal options for intentional communities, some of which was adapted for this article.

• • • • • • • • • • • • • • • • • • • •

...it may seem impossible to come up with a definition of what your community is or is not. But if you don't do it, then the IRS will.

• • • • • • • • • • • • • • • • • • • •

be done in a truly descriptive way. Still, unless you understand the different legal forms of organization, it may seem impossible to come up with a definition of what your community is or is not. But if you don't do it, then the IRS will.

It is the kind of *ownership* a community has, as well as how its money is channeled, which will generally determine what kind of legal structure, or combination of structures, it should have. For example, in some intentional communities, each member-household owns its own lot, house, vehicles, tools, and equipment—little or nothing is owned in common. In other communities, the land, buildings, and all private property are owned in common, and shared.

In *communal communities*, not only does the community own property in common, but the members also have a common treasury—they contribute all or a portion of their income to the community, and the community in turn takes care of all or most of their needs. In still other communities, the members hold all land, buildings, and other assets in common, through a corporation, with individual members owning individual shares of these joint assets.

Many communities operate using several legal entities in an interactive fashion. In many "economically diverse" communities, the land and some buildings and equipment are held in common, while houses, cars, and bank accounts are held privately. The legal structure(s) that best satisfy the needs of one of these communities may be all wrong for another.

As far as possible, the object of choosing a legal structure is not to shape the community to fit the law, but to fashion legal forms that fit the community. Still, we have to admit, sometimes it's easier just to shape the community.

Legal Options for Communities

Theoretically, any form of intentional community may be organized under any of the types of organized legal structures normally recognized by state governments. These include simple partnerships, Subchapter S corporations, Limited Liability Companies (recognized in some states), limited partnerships, cooperative corporations, and nonprofit corporations. The latter include nonprofits for charitable, religious, or educational purposes; title-holding nonprofits, religious "common treasury" nonprofits, community land trusts, condominium associations and other homeowners associations, and housing co-ops. Economically diverse communities often use more than one of these legal structures in an interactive fashion.

Simple Partnerships

In this elementary form of legal association, two or more individual proprietors operate a common business. Each partner takes a share of the profits and pays the taxes on that amount, whether it is actually distributed or retained by the business.

The biggest advantage of the partnership form is its simplicity. In most states, the partners aren't required to file any papers with the state; in fact, they can set up their partnership with just an oral agreement or a handshake. (If a community is formed without any formal legal structures, the IRS and the courts would usually consider the community to be a partnership.)

A second advantage is that while the individual partners' incomes are taxed, the partnership is not itself taxed, unlike corporations, which are subject to "double taxation."

The biggest disadvantage of a partnership can occur if something in the community changes. This is because property rights and compensation of the partners are established by the original Partnership Agreement. If the Agreement is vague or does not anticipate every potential contingency, misunderstandings, disagreement, or other problems can arise if a partner or partners leave, new ones enter, or the Agreement dissolves.

A second problem with partnerships is that each partner is personally liable for the partnership's debts. For this reason, the business entrepreneurs of the nineteenth century created the corporation.

For-Profit Corporations

A corporation is an "artificial person," set up to be a legal entity apart from its owners. Corporations are created by registering, and filing "articles of incorporation," with officials of the state in which the business or intentional community is located. A community corporation can make contracts, accumulate assets, do business, sue, and be sued in its own name. The owners, or shareholders, decide on the management of the corporation but are not liable for the debts or lawsuits of the corporation. This feature of *"limited liability" is the principal advantage of creating a corporation.*

The principal disadvantage is double taxation. Corporations are normally taxed on any profits before the profits are distributed to the shareholders as dividends. Then the shareholders may have to pay taxes a second time when they report their dividends as income.

Subchapter S Corporations

This kind of corporation was created to help small businesses. The Subchapter S enables a small business (or community) to escape unfair situations, such as double taxation, while still obtaining the benefits of limited liability. To qualify for Subchapter S, a corporation must have no more than 35 shareholders, none of whom is another corporation or trust (married couples are treated as one shareholder). *A Subchapter S must operate a business that does not receive more than 20 percent of its income from passive sources such as rents and investments,* and must obtain the consent of its shareholders to apply for the classification. Subchapter S corporations pass any profits through to their shareholders, who must report that income, whether distributed or not, on their tax forms. The corporation itself, like a partnership, is tax exempt.

Limited Liability Companies

This legal structure, which is *not* a corporation, is recognized in some states but not others. Like a Subchapter S corporation, an LLC offers the advantages of a corporation's limited liability. Similarly, it provides a way to tie decision-making rights directly to financial contribution—one "share," one vote. An LLC has a partnership's taxation status in that

> A corporation is an "artificial person," set up to be a legal entity apart from its owners.

the LLC's profits aren't taxed directly; all profits and losses are passed through to the owners who pay income tax on their individual tax returns.

An LLC has advantages over an S corporation, including more flexible tax rules; more than 35 shareholders (called "members") can participate; trusts, estates, corporations, partnerships, and non-American individuals and businesses can be members of the LLC; there are no restrictions on income sources; and it can have greater planning flexibility in reimbursing any founding members who leave.

LLCs have recently become more popular following a 1988 IRS ruling that an LLC in Wyoming would be taxed as a partnership, thereby allowing any profit and loss to be passed through to the members for their individual tax returns. Viewed conservatively, however, we won't know how LLCs will be taxed in other states until courts in each state that now recognize the LLC decide whether it's a partnership or corporation.

The main disadvantage of an LLC is that, theoretically, *LLC members could be personally liable for damages or debts incurred while conducting business in a state that didn't recognize this business structure.* States recognizing LLCs include Arizona, Colorado, Florida, Georgia, Idaho, Illinois, Iowa, Kansas, Louisiana, Maryland, Michigan, Minnesota, Montana, Nevada, New Mexico, North Dakota, Oklahoma, South Dakota, Texas, Utah, Virginia, West Virginia, and Wyoming. States now considering LLCs include Hawaii, Indiana, Missouri, Nebraska, Pennsylvania, Rhode Island, South Carolina, and Tennessee.

Limited Partnerships

This legal structure, which is also *not* a corporation, allows a business or intentional community to raise money, especially in times when loans are tight or interest rates high.

A limited partnership has "general partners" and "limited partners." The general partners found the organization, assume all the responsibilities and take all the risks. They are personally liable for any lawsuits or debts incurred against the limited partnership. A general partner can be a person, a partnership, or a corporation. There can be one or more general partners.

The limited partners are investors who contribute money (or land or other assets) and take the entrepreneurial risks. They have no say in the day-to-day management of the organization and are protected from liability for the partnership or community's debts. If the organization fails, the most the limited partners could lose would be their original investment.

Limited partnerships come under state and federal securities regulations, and each state has different requirements to establish limited partnerships. They are usually more complex and costly to set up than other legal structures.

Nonprofit Corporations

Unlike all legal options mentioned so far, which are expected to make money, nonprofits are primarily organized to serve some public benefit, and are not expected to make money. Hence, a nonprofit may obtain IRS and state approval for special tax exemption.

Most intentional communities have elected to organize as nonprofit corporations and to apply for tax-exempt status.

As with for-profit corporations, a nonprofit corporation is created by registering with the state—filing a list of corporate officers and articles of incorporation. After receiving state approval, the organization may apply for a federal tax exemption with the IRS.

Of course, some nonprofit intentional community corporations will not seek federal tax exemption because members view their communities as basic political units, to be operated separately from their spiritual or religious practice. On the other hand, there are communities with several corporations, some of which might be tax exempt while others are for profit, or nonprofit without tax exemption.

Community land trust...ensures the original purpose for the land continues unchanged....

100 Mile Lodge

For those seeking to form tax-exempt corporations, there are several IRS tax exemptions to choose from. It is best to decide which category of tax exemption you are seeking before filing articles of incorporation, because the articles may have to conform to certain language that the IRS expects before it will grant a particular exemption.

Cooperative or Mutual Benefit Corporations

"Co-ops" are often used by consumer cooperatives (such as food-buying co-ops or credit unions), worker cooperatives, or producer cooperatives and are another legal option for communities with good state laws governing cooperative corporations. Co-ops are usually organized as nonprofit corporations; however, some states offer a special "cooperative corporation" category that is neither nonprofit or for profit.

In either case, to qualify as a co-op, the articles of incorporation must usually provide for open membership, democratic control (one member, one vote), no political campaigning or endorsing, and no profit motive—that is, a limited return on any invested capital. A co-op also provides limited liability to its members. In some states, members get nontransferable membership shares (instead of shares of stock) with an exemption from federal and state securities regulations. Any members who also serve as employees get tax-deductible fringe benefits.

501(c)(7)—"Social and Recreation Clubs"

Nonprofit mutual benefit corporations can use the IRS tax exemption 501(c)(7), which was created for private recreational or other nonprofitable organizations, where none of the net earnings goes to any member. This exemption can be used by a community with land which cannot legally be subdivided, yet whose members are required to put money into the community in order to live there, *and* who wish to recoup their equity if they leave. Members of a community organized this way "buy" a membership in the mutual benefit corporation. They can later sell their membership (at a profit if they wish) to an incoming member.

The advantages are that, *if organized properly*, the community would not be subject to state and local subdivision requirements—because members

> It is best to decide which category of tax exemption you are seeking before filing articles of incorporation...

wouldn't own specific plots of land or specific houses. Rather, in a strictly legal sense, they would simply have *use rights* to any plots or dwellings (although the members' internal arrangements could specify which plots or dwellings each would have preferred rights to use). In addition, members could pay for their membership with a down payment and installments rather than in one lump sum. They would be afforded some liability for the actions of the mutual benefit corporation. They would also have the right to choose who joined the community, which could be an advantage over other land-owning legal entities such as P.U.D.s or other subdivisions, wherein the landowners would be subject to federal antidiscrimination regulations if they attempted to choose who bought into their community.

The disadvantages are that 501(c)(7) nonprofits can be quite complicated to set up and may require a securities lawyer, as they are regulated by the Securities and Exchange Commission. As such, a 501(c)(7) *cannot advertise publicly* for new members, who are legally "investors." Rather, existing members or staff may only approach people they know personally to join them. A 501(c)(7) may have no more than 35 investor/members. No donations to such a community are tax deductible.

There are no dividends or depreciation tax write-offs; members are taxed on any profit if and when they sell.

501(c)(3)—Educational, Charitable, or Religious Corporations

Nonprofit 501(c)(3) corporations must provide educational services to the public, offer charitable services

• • • • • • • • • • • • • • • • • • • •

...the IRS interprets "religious" and "apostolic" very liberally; this can include self-described spiritual beliefs or practices, or secular beliefs that are strongly, "religiously" held.

• • • • • • • • • • • • • • • • • • • •

to an indefinite class of people (rather than to specific individuals), combat negative social conditions, or provide a religious service to its members and/or the public. (The IRS interprets "religious" very liberally; this can include self-described spiritual beliefs or practices.) 501(c)(3) nonprofits may receive tax-deductible donations from corporations or individuals, and grants from government agencies or private foundations. They are eligible for lower bulk mailing rates, some government loans and benefits, and exemption from most forms of property tax. Religious orders that qualify under 501(c)(3) may also be exempt from Social Security, unemployment, and withholding taxes in some cases.

In order to qualify for recognition as a 501(c)(3), an intentional community must meet two IRS tests. It must be *organized*, as well as *operated*, exclusively for one or more of the above tax-exempt purposes. To determine the organizational test, the IRS reviews the nonprofit's articles of incorporation and bylaws. To determine its operational test, the IRS conducts an audit of the nonprofit's activities in its first years of operation.

Many communities have difficulty passing the operational test because of the requirement that no part of the net earnings may benefit any individual (except as compensation for labor or as a *bona fide* beneficiary of the charitable purpose). If the primary activity of the organization is to operate businesses for the mutual benefit of the members, it fails this operational test.

Even if the community passes the operational test by virtue of other, more charitable, public benefits—running an educational center, providing an ambulance service, or making toys for handicapped children, for instance—it can still be taxed on the profits it makes apart from its strictly charitable activities.

This catch, called *unrelated business taxable income, has been a source of disaster and dissolution for some nonprofits* because of the associated back taxes and penalties, which can assume massive proportions in just a few years of unreported earnings. Unrelated business taxes prevent tax-exempt nonprofits from unfairly competing with taxable entities, such as for-profit corporations. The IRS determines a nonprofit's unrelated business trade income in two ways: the destination of the income and the source. If a community uses profits from bake sales to build a community fire station (presumably a one-time project related to the community's purpose), the IRS may consider that income "related" and not tax it. If, however, the bake sales expand the general operations of the community, or pay the electric bill, the IRS may consider that "unrelated" income, and tax it.

A Section 501(c)(3) nonprofit may not receive more than 20 percent of the corporate income from passive sources, such as rents or investments. If they are educational in purpose, they may not discriminate on the basis of race and must state that in their organizing documents. 501(c)(3) are not allowed to participate in politics—they can't back a political campaign, attempt to influence legislation (other than on issues related to the 501(c)(3) category), or publish political "propaganda." If they disband, they may not distribute any residual assets to their members; after payment of debts, all remaining assets must pass intact to a tax-exempt beneficiary—such as another 501(c)(3).

501(c)(2)—Title-Holding Corporations

This legal structure is a useful option for owning, controlling, and managing a nonprofit group's property. The 501(c)(2) is designed to collect income from property—whether it is a land trust, a retail business, or a passive investment such as space rental. All income is turned over to a nonprofit tax-exempt parent corporation, which is usually a 501(c)(3). The tax-exempt parent must exercise some control over the 501(c)(2) holding company, such as owning a majority of its voting stock or appointing its directors. The two corporations file a consolidated tax return. Unlike a 501(c)(3), a 501(c)(2) may not actively engage in "doing business," except for certain excluded categories such as renting real estate or negotiating investments...and *a 501(c)(2) can receive more than 20 percent of the corporate income from rentals or investments.*

Many nonprofit communities, especially community land trusts (see below) find that having both 501(c)(3)s and 501(c)(2)s provides a needed forum to both run businesses and manage land and housing. The 501(c)(2) limits the community's exposure to conflicts with the IRS over questions of income and possible personal "inurement," or illegal benefits.

501(d)—Religious and Apostolic Associations

If a nonprofit community has a spiritual focus and a common treasury, it may apply for this tax-exempt status. (Again, the IRS interprets "religious" and "apostolic" very liberally; this can include self-described spiritual beliefs or practices, or secular beliefs that are strongly, "religiously" held.)

In any case, the 501(d) is like a partnership or Subchapter S corporation, in that any net profits after expenses are divided among all members pro rata, to be reported on the member's individual tax forms. Unlike the 501(c)(3), the 501(d) corporation cannot confer tax deductions for donations.

501(d) nonprofits make no distinction between related and unrelated income. All income from any source is related. However, if a substantial percentage of community income is in wages or salaries from "outside" work, the 501(d) classification may be denied. A 501(d) can engage in any kind of businesses it chooses, passive or active, religious or secular. The profits are taxed like those of a partnership or S corporation. But a 501(d) doesn't have the restrictions of a partnership (it doesn't have to reform itself with each change of members), and it isn't limited to 35 shareholders like the Subchapter S.

501(d) corporations have no restrictions on their political activity—they can lobby, support candidates, and publish political "propaganda." They may or may not elect to have a formal vow of poverty. Upon dissolution, the assets of the 501(d) nonprofit may be divided among the members as

> **A land trust can be set up by an intentional community that has a specific purpose for the land, or simply to preserve it for future generations.**

far as federal law is concerned. However, state law generally requires that any assets remaining after payment of liabilities should be given to another nonprofit corporation.

The substantial advantages of the 501(d) may be outweighed in communities that would prefer to hold property privately. If the common ground between members is just that—the common ground—one of two other types of exemption may be more suitable.

Private Land Trusts

A private land trust is a legal mechanism to protect a piece of land from various kinds of undesirable future uses, like being sold for speculative gain; or to preserve land for various specific purposes—public use as a wilderness area, as rural farmland, or for low-cost housing. A land trust can be set up by an intentional community that has a specific purpose for the land, or simply to preserve it for future generations.

There are three parties to a land trust: the donor(s), who gives the land to the trust for a specific purpose or mission; the board of trustees, who administer the land and protect its mission; and the beneficiaries, who use or otherwise benefit from the land. People or institutions on the board of trustees are selected for their alignment with the goals and mission of the trust and their pledge of support. The trustees represent three separate interest groups: the beneficiaries, people in the wider community, and the land itself. The beneficiaries can be people who visit a wilderness preserve or park, the farmers who

• • • • • • • • • • • • • • • • • • • •

**The original owners of
the land and assets
cannot get their money
out of a community land
trust once they have
made the donation.**

• • • • • • • • • • • • • • • •

farm the land, the owners or residents in low-cost housing on the property, or the members of an intentional community who live and work on the land. The donor, trustees, and beneficiaries can be the same people in a private land trust.

Community Land Trusts

A CLT is designed to establish a stronger and broader board of trustees than a private land trust. This is accomplished by creating a board with a majority of trustees that are not land users. Usually only one-third of the trustees can live on the land or benefit directly from it, while two-thirds must live elsewhere and receive no direct benefit from the land. This ensures that any donors or land-resident beneficiaries who are also trustees cannot change their minds about the purpose or mission of the trust, use the land for some other purpose, or sell it. The two-thirds of the board of trustees from the wider community serve to guarantee the mission of the trust since they are theoretically more objective, and will not be tempted by personal monetary gain.

Private land trusts can be revocable by the original donors; community land trusts are usually not revocable.

Private land trusts and community land trusts are set up as nonprofit corporations, sometimes with a 501(c)(3) tax-exempt status. The trust holds actual title to the land, and grants the land residents long-term, renewable leases at reasonable fees.

The original owners of the land and assets cannot get their money out of a community land trust once they have made the donation. A CLT is an option for those who wish to ensure that the original

purpose for their land and activities continues unchanged into future generations, and is not altered by subsequent requirements for quick cash, loss of commitment, or personality conflicts among the land residents.

Homeowners Associations, Condominium Associations

Some communities may choose to organize as a "Planned Community"—a real estate term, in which members individually own their own plots of ground and dwellings, and are each members of a nonprofit corporation—a "Homeowners Association." The association, rather than the individual members, owns any community buildings and all the common areas, including land other than the individual plots.

Or a community may organize as a "Condominium," where the members each individually own the air space within their dwellings, and—as members of a nonprofit corporation, or "Condominium Association"—they own an undivided interest in the common elements of the property. The common property includes the structural components of the individual dwellings (roof, walls, floors, foundation), as well as the common areas and community buildings.

Planned communities and condominiums aren't legal structures; they are simply methods of purchasing land. In a planned community, the homeowners association owns everything but the individual units, and they must manage and maintain everything. In a condominium, the condominium association owns nothing, but must manage and maintain everything. Both kinds of associations are often organized as nonprofits, under the Internal Revenue Code, Section 528.

Under Section 528, such an association is exempt from taxation in acquiring, constructing, managing, and maintaining any property used for mutual benefit. Such tax-exempt "association property" may even include property owned privately by members, such as a greenhouse, meeting house, or retreat. But to qualify, the private property must affect the overall appearance of the community, the owner must agree to maintain it to community standards, there must be an annual pro rata assessment of all members to maintain it, and it must be used only by association members and not rented out.

The Association must also receive at least 60 percent of its gross income from membership dues, fees, or assessments. Also, at least 90 percent of its expenses must be for construction, management, maintenance, and care of association property.

Homeowners or condominium associations that want to use the 528 tax-exempt status don't apply for this exemption; they simply incorporate under I.R.C. Section 528 and file an 1120-H tax return each year.

Housing Cooperatives

This is a very specific kind of cooperative corporation, also called a mutual benefit corporation. Housing cooperative nonprofits vary slightly from state to state. In general, however, members own shares in the housing cooperative, which gives them the right to live in a particular dwelling. Although nonprofits don't usually allow shares of stock or stockholders, a housing cooperative does. The number of shares the members buy are based on the current market value of the dwelling in which they intend to live.

The members don't own their individual houses or apartments; the housing cooperative does. The members have simply bought the shares, which gives them the right to occupy the dwelling of their choice. They pay a monthly fee—a prorated share of the housing cooperative's mortgage payment and property taxes, combined with general maintenance costs and repairs. The monthly fee is based on the number of shares each of the members holds, which is equivalent to the dollar value assigned to their individual dwellings.

Intentionality

In designing a new community, or transforming an existing one, it is imperative that mutually respectful relationships evolve among the participants. Often the process of choosing the legal organization is the first opportunity a community has to develop a convivial style of interpersonal relationships. Community members should be aware that creating formal bylaws and gaining corporate recognition is of a lower level of importance than *the group's actual process of self-definition—that is the crux of the intentionality in intentional community.* While debate

• • • • • • • • • • • • • • • • • • • •

While debate over structure is occasionally the last act of a group, it is often the debate that is most fondly remembered in the years and generations to come.

• • • • • • • • • • • • • • • • • • • •

over structure is occasionally the last act of a group, it is often the debate that is most fondly remembered in the years and generations to come. ⓦ

Bibliography

Butcher, Allen, *Community, Inc.*, P.O. Box 1666, Denver, CO 80201.

Christian, Diana, "Legal Options for Communities, A Five-Part Series," *Growing Community* newsletter, 2–6, $5 ea. P.O. Box 169, Masonville, CO 80541.

Alternatives Center, *Co-op Housing*, 1740 Walnut Street, Berkeley, CA 94709, 510-540-5387.

Cohen, Lottie, and Lois Arkin, *The Cooperative Housing Compendium* (Davis, CA: Center for Cooperatives, University of California).

Federation of Egalitarian Communities, *Systems and Structures Packet*, Federation Desk, Box CD-5, Tecumseh, MO 65760.

Institute for Community Economics, *The Community Land Trust Legal Manual*, 57 School Street, Springfield, MA 01105.

For consultation and workshops on nonprofit tax exemption 501(c)(7)s and other financial/legal/real estate issues for forming new communities and retreat centers: Stephan Brown, 303 Hardister, Colverdale, CA 95425, 707-894-9466.

Buying Your Community Property

by Frances Forster and Byron Sandford of Quakerland, Austin, Texas

*B*uying your community property will be a lot like buying a home. If you've ever done that you know it can be a roller coaster ride, but eventually it does end! The process itself will provide many good opportunities to practice your group decision-making procedures, and test your abilities to trust that your decision to pursue this venture is right.

So where do you start? By answering three simple questions:

(1) Where do you want to be (geographically)?
(2) What do you need?
(3) How much can you afford?

After you've addressed these questions, the next steps are a little more mechanical—after all, there are only so many ways of identifying property and paying for it. Just trust that your decision makers will stay focused on the big picture and not get distracted by the zillion and one (sometimes insignificant) details.

Where Do You Want to Be?

Consider what your members are going to be doing for work and recreation. What are your needs for land, water, transportation, proximity to towns? What are your needs for an audience or market, for schools and continuing education? What about climate, rainfall, or soil types?

Make your lists and consult some maps. Chambers of commerce, local governments, newspapers, and libraries can be good sources of information about places you're considering.

What Do You Need?

A number of things need to fit together, or be developed hand in hand, so you need to have a rough idea of the number and types of people, animals, buildings, cars, and land uses that are going to be a part of the planned picture. For example, your county health department may require a certain type or size of septic system based on the number of people, and the septic fields need to be a certain distance from wells, waterways, and swimming areas.

Operations that require special permits, like the use of chemicals or machinery, merit special consideration, as do services or activities that will bring traffic or require animal management. Check out local ordinances or restrictions related to such special issues now, before you start the property search.

Sketch out a couple of rough site plans showing the desired relationships between buildings or functions. Having these will help in the site-selection process.

How Much Can You Afford?

Unless someone is giving you all the funds (or the land) with no strings attached, you will most likely need a loan from a mortgage company, bank, savings and loan, the actual seller, or other lender. This

Frances Forster and Byron Sandford are part of a new community, Quakerland, west of San Marcos, Texas, to be based on land currently used as a retreat by Quaker meetings in the area. They have traveled to Friends' Meetings throughout the region, building consensus for intentional community use of the retreat land, and recruiting folks to join the Quakerland community. Frances is a licensed real estate broker and Byron, a former mortgage banker, renovates dwellings and apartment buildings for rent or resale.

will apply whether you need funds for land alone, improvements (buildings), or both.

The lender will assess your borrowing power based on the collective income, assets, and debts of the persons who will be responsible for the note. These persons will sign the mortgage and deed documents for your community, based on whatever internal agreement you have. It may be to your advantage to have as many people as possible for cosigners, because it will boost your assets—the lender will like having lots of responsible parties.

To determine where you are financially, gather all your financial records and add up four sets of figures: (1) gross monthly incomes, interest, dividends, child support received, and other predictable income; (2) bank accounts, IRAs, trusts, whole life values, stocks, bonds, and other assets; (3) total of all debts (credit cards, loans, child support owed, etc.), and (4) the monthly obligation for these debts.

Once you have your totals, a lender can give you an estimate of how much you can borrow. While the figures will vary from lender to lender, you can get a ballpark estimate of what the lenders are thinking by doubling your cosigners' total annual gross income—this approximates the loan amount; one percent of that amount is your monthly payment. For another approximation, if your cosigners already have a debt load, multiply your cosigners' total monthly gross income by 29 percent—this is your maximum monthly payment (PITI: principal, interest, taxes, and insurance); unless your group already owes monthly debts of more than ten percent of the total monthly income. If your debts are higher, the amount available for the monthly land payments is reduced proportionately. If you put these calculations on paper you'll see how easy they are to figure.

Points of caution about your cosigners: (1) get credit reports for each cosigner early on and take a good hard look at them—you don't want surprises later; and (2) if cosigners are self-employed, make sure the lender considers their income eligible; if you do include future business income in your financial picture, be sure to provide profit and loss statements reflecting past experience.

Visit with Lenders

At this point you have a fairly good idea of where you want to be, what you need, and how much

> **After visiting with a few real estate brokers, you'll have to decide whether your group has the time, experience, and contacts to manage the land purchase without professional assistance.**

money you have to work with. Now it's time to make introductory visits to senior officers of some lenders in your area. Ask for information on rates, loan alternatives, what other things you need to look at, and if they would consider loaning money to your group (not all lenders make all types of loans). Provide possible lenders with an overview sheet. Remember, you're just gathering information, not making a formal loan application.

Visit with Appraisers and Real Estate Brokers

Make brief visits with some appraisers and brokers who specialize in farm and ranch properties, or commercial or multi-family properties if your community will be in an urban location. Again, your goal is to gather information about the vicinity, the market, the possibilities. You should be able to learn about good areas to consider, what the average cost per acre or per square foot is in those areas, and which factors are most significant in determining price in your vicinity. Significant factors include size, location, view, water, type of soil, trees, and proximity to major roads.

Broker Commissions, Inspections, and Appraisals

You may not be responsible for the broker commission—in some places it is customary for the seller to pay the commission to the listing broker, who shares it with the buyer's broker. So payment may not be an issue. Yet, many folks will consider trying to save money by avoiding the use of brokers, or even

"So where do we start?"

inspectors and appraisers. On the other hand, professionals can save you money, and a lot of time and energy. Their experience and specialized training can help you to avoid making mistakes. Only if you feel you have enough expertise and time should you shepherd a real estate transaction by yourselves.

Innisfree, Inc.

Another word about brokers. There is some debate in the realty world at this time about whether the buyer's broker will actually represent the buyer or the seller. There's no need to get caught up in that concern if you are honest, fair, shop in the price range you can afford, and don't play games. Then, you'll do fine.

Inspections are usually performed soon after you enter into a contract. The private inspection is a very thorough inspection of structures and systems (electrical, plumbing, heating, and air conditioning, etc.). The inspector is hired and paid by the buyer, and costs in the vicinity of $200. The purpose of the inspection is to acquaint the buyer with the workings of the property and the condition of the dwelling systems.

Appraisals are also sometimes called inspections, but their role is different. Appraisers provide an independent estimate of the dollar value of a property for the lender, usually, or the buyer or seller. The general rule for pricing a property is to learn what comparable properties (comps) have sold for in the last six months. If the market is rapidly changing, and there are enough comps, the time limit may be shortened to three months, or appropriate adjustments can be factored in for market price changes.

Finding Your Property

After visiting with a few real estate brokers, you'll have to decide whether your group has the time, experience, and contacts to manage the land pur-

chase without professional assistance. If you decide to contract with a broker instead, select one that understands your needs, has appropriate expertise, and is willing to put in the time that you'll need, because you'll need plenty of time. Everything about an intentional community buying property is unusual, so you'll need a strong, creative advocate who can help with the other professionals who are part of the purchase process.

The obvious places to look for properties are the local newspapers and free real estate brochures. Another way of locating property, especially in the country, is to drive around the area you're considering. There may be properties for sale by owners, or listed by licensed agents who are not members of the local board. A broker will also have other resources, which will vary in format from place to place, but will include new listings and properties that are for sale but may not have signs.

For-sale-by-owner is simply that—the owners themselves are handling the sale without the involvement of a listing agent. Sometimes owners have enough expertise to do the job right, sometimes not; they may not realize what is involved other than saving the cost of a commission. Be sure to find out what the picture really is. And if you decide to pursue a transaction with no agents involved, for sure get an appraisal, survey, inspection, and especially title insurance, even if you must pay for it yourself. (Please note: For-sale-by-owner is different from owner financing, which is discussed later.)

Properties on the market should have an owner's disclosure statement, or a list showing any problems with appliances and systems, structural items, environmental factors, and any legal issues that may affect the property. These statements are now required in some states for the protection of both the sellers and the buyers. If the property you want doesn't have a disclosure statement, insist on one!

Also check on deed restrictions and zoning regulations for your selected property to make sure you can operate the kind of business you want, or build the kind of buildings you need. Review your rough sketches and needs lists—don't overlook something important!

You've Found the Property, Now What?

Submit an offer. If you've done your homework you know everything you need to know to make a realistic offer. Your offer, generally on standard contract forms, will propose your sales price, method of financing, closing date, and other details. Keep it as simple as possible, and don't ask for insignificant concessions. It's OK to make your price a little below where you want to end up, but you don't want to make it so low you insult the seller. You may be buying a family home, not just some corporate tax shelter. The seller may sign (accept) your offer or make a counter, in which case the house is still on the market. Hopefully you will come to terms quickly and move into the closing period—the evaluation period between contract signing and the closing, or actual property title transfer.

You've Signed, So You're Ready to Move In? Whoa!

Give yourself enough time in the closing period to work up a good case of the jitters—if not this whole process is no fun! Actually, from this point a lot depends on the property and the financing method.

In a nutshell, during the next two weeks you'll do the inspection (if there are any structures), the appraisal, and start the loan process, if you haven't already. The loan is usually the part that takes time—anywhere between two weeks and two

> ...check on deed restrictions and zoning regulations...to make sure you can operate the kind of business you want, or build the kind of buildings you need. Review your rough sketches and needs lists—don't overlook something important!

months, depending on how much information on how many people the lender wants. After the loan is approved, the boundary survey is ordered and any other contingencies are resolved—which can take a while, too. Then you can close, and that just takes an hour or so. Then you can move.

While the lender is doing its thing, the title company is researching the property records to make sure, for one thing, that the person selling the property has the right to do so, and that the title will be clear when it is transferred to you. That means that no back taxes, liens, judgments, or other claims will be transferred to you, and that any easements, encroachments, rights of way, mineral rights, or anything else that will affect your usage and enjoyment of the property will be made known to you prior to closing. Your insurance on the title is forever, so they like to be sure about these things!

The title insurance is usually paid by the seller, with a second document going to the lender. The cost to the seller is usually around one percent of the sales price, and to the lender about $200. A copy to the buyer costs a little less. A copy for yourselves would be a good idea—and if you order it up front the cost is a lot less than if you do it later.

Let's Talk Attorneys

Attorneys have a place in the transaction if you want them, and they can be invisible if you prefer.

● ●

...you may be tempted to forego the appraisal, boundaries survey, title search, and title insurance to save money. Think again....Honest mistakes are made every day, and your community's future is at stake.

● ●

They can prepare and review contracts prior to submittal, during negotiations, and after; they can prepare loan and deed documents; they can order title work from a title company; and attorneys can be helpful at closings. If you and the seller prefer to close with the title company, the title company and the lender will simply have their usual attorneys draw up the papers and send them to the title company for closing. Also, in some states, attorneys can still act as brokers. A broker can tell you about local regulations.

Let's Talk Owner Financing

In owner financing, the owner is willing to forego receiving his full equity all at once, and instead will earn interest on his equity from you. Normally the seller will want 25 to 30 percent down payment, and monthly payments at or above market rates, although he may be flexible on this point. It is very common for rural properties to be financed this way.

Sometimes the owner agrees to carry the note for only a few years until it's a good time (for you or him) to refinance, or sell the note. Don't let the idea that your note might be sold scare you—the note is a commodity, like stocks, that can be bought and sold, but your terms remain the same.

In setting up this note, the seller most likely will want to see your financial documents just as a banker would. The difference is that a private seller may be a little more flexible than regular lenders, which are highly regulated and in most cases must meet required guidelines.

By the same token, you should also ask to see the seller's documents to ascertain either that the note has been paid off, or that the seller has the right to sell the property without paying the note off. If the note has a "due on sale" clause, then the owner cannot sell the property this way, at least not without written authorization from the lender. And that should be reviewed by an attorney.

Also, with owner financing you need to be clear, in your documentation, about who will be responsible for paying the taxes and insurance, and when the title will transfer. Even if you don't use a lawyer or a broker, you should still close with a title company to make sure everything is done correctly and recorded with the county clerk. A flawed title can be a long-term cause for insecurity and legal expenses, dragging on for years to a very uncertain outcome.

With owner financing you may be tempted to forego the appraisal, boundaries survey, title search, and title insurance to save money. Think again. And if you decide you can do without one of them, think yet again! Honest mistakes are made every day, and your community's future is at stake.

Aren't you chomping at the bit to get started on this community adventure? Just think of all the things you'll learn, and think of all the opportunities you'll have to practice your group-decision-making skills! It will all be worth it in the end. And you'll know it! ⚲

Tips on Financing Realty

by Robert H. Watzke, Milwaukee, Wisconsin

*I*f you are in the market for real estate, come to know all you can about property for sale in your area of interest. That means one or more of your group is going to have to invest time in searching and researching. Cruise the area where you want to live, looking for "For Sale" signs. Contact real estate brokers to learn what they have available. Go to the County Registrar of Deeds and review recent sale prices.

Comparable Sales Data before Appraisal for Loan

Once you find a desirable property, you need comparable sales to evaluate the proposed purchase prices. While a comparable sales study may cost as much as or more than an appraisal of a specific property, "comparables" provide the necessary insight into your local real estate market.

Bankers today work almost exclusively with their own approved appraisers. Go to the bank(s) that you think you'll be using, and ask which appraisers they might recommend to appraise the type of property you are purchasing.

Later, a bank-financed appraisal will be required, but it is important for you to build your own market awareness—separate from the bank's. The cost of comparables is modest compared to what you save when you're well informed and can negotiate from a position of knowledge.

You can gain maximum effectiveness from specific appraisals by knowing market values, getting your appraisals ahead of time, and paying the appraisers yourself. Review the appraisal to make sure the work is documented and includes the comparables that your research indicates are representative and supportive of what you are seeking to accomplish. If the work is not satisfactory, you may request the appraiser to redo the work or you may seek another appraiser.

When applying for a bank loan, it will be to your advantage if the bank sees the appraisal supporting your loan request and recognizes the signature at the bottom as that of one of their appraisers. Then the bank simply sends the appraisal out for updating or "recertification" by the appraiser. You will have to pay for the recertification, but the cost should be nominal. By the way, the bank will give you a copy of the updated appraisal if you ask for it.

Financial Strategy

Always protect your asset base. Provide a contingency fund for emergencies or unexpected opportunities. Estimate how much you will need; establish a purchase plan and a budget that provide enough money to both buy *and* operate—plus a contingency reserve for both the short term (1–5 years) and long term (6–25 years). The long term should be no less than the amortization period of your indebtedness on the property.

Robert H. Watzke has been self-employed since 1958 in the real estate, insurance, and securities industry as an appraiser, broker, and dealer/developer/investor. He has been licensed in Wisconsin. He has served as an officer in professional associations and worked as a real estate consultant and fee appraiser for attorneys, lenders, and government agencies. Bob is a former board member of the Fellowship for Intentional Community and the FIC's Community Business Loan Fund.

Banking Relationships

Before you meet with the banker, review the bank's Profit and Loss Statement for last year and this year to date. Examine size and assets, learn who the operating officers are, and the directors. Ask one of the front office loan managers by phone whether the bank is making loans on the general type of realty you're interested in buying. Ask their loan rates, and what their lending practices are. Then you will know in advance about the bank's terms, policies, and procedures. When you visit the banker, dress the way he or she dresses even if you have to go out and buy, rent, or borrow the "costume."

Your goal is to make a reasonable loan request and get a loan commitment on the least expensive terms available from the competing banks in the area. You may need to negotiate simultaneously with more than one potential lender.

Supporting Documents for Your Loan Requests

First, secure an appraisal for the property which is at least equal to— preferably greater than—your purchase price. The ratio of your loan request to appraisal value should be better than what the bank normally allows, adding to their margin of safety. This margin could make a substantial difference with the Board or Loan Committee that gives final approval to your request.

A copy of your net worth statement should also be included, and those of other cosigners and the community corporation. Get net worth statement forms from the various lenders in your area to see what they're using. The forms are short and simple for individuals, more lengthy and complex for corporations. Keep your responses simple. Remember that whatever you tell your lender will be "public knowledge." The bank may give your credit reports to credit agencies for confirmation, and your reports may be passed around among various agencies.

Find out which credit agency the bank or the lenders in the area generally use. Purchase a copy of your credit records from each one of those credit agencies *before* making any loan applications. Be aware that each time a credit agency provides someone with a report on you, that inquiry is listed in your credit file. In that way, they all know from whom you have been seeking credit.

Provide the lender with credit reports on all cosigners and the community corporation, even though the lenders have to procure these reports on their own. That way, you know what credit information agencies are saying about you before your prospective lender knows. Credit agencies often dredge up incorrect data; so advance review of your credit report enables you to correct any discrepancies or outdated records before the credit report goes to your lender(s).

Real Estate Agents

Unless you have entered into a "Broker With Commission/Buyer Contract" with a real estate agent, remember that agents are paid by the sellers. The Broker/Buyer Contract specifies your payment of the agent for help in finding and purchasing realty. Without such a contract, an agent has an obligation to act in the seller's best interests—which do not necessarily parallel your interests as a buyer.

Attorneys

Do you need one? Yup!

Get one who specializes in real estate. Ask your attorney to review everything you're supposed to sign, *before* you sign it. Your attorney can do little for you once you've signed.

If you feel that you must enter into a contract before the attorney has seen it, then insert this clause: "This contract is subject to our attorney's review and written approval within forty-eight (48) hours after acceptance or this contract shall become null and void, at the buyers option."

These are some of the lessons I've learned from over 35 years of buying, selling, and financing realty for myself. Use this information to help your community secure the home you envision. ⚘

Communal History

Jane Evershed

For the Next Seven Generations: Indigenous Americans and Communalism

Native American Glenn Morris provides an historic overview of political organization and community life among native peoples before Europeans arrived in North America. While the social structures are varied, it's instructive that communal, nonhierarchic forms were common. With the rising interest in resource-conscious living, it is important to recapture accurately the wheels of sustainability that have already been invented.

Dreams and Other Products of Nineteenth-Century Communities

History Professor Lyman Tower Sargent debunks the myth that historic communities withdrew from the societies in which they lived. Then, as now, communities contributed culturally in a wide variety of ways, both philosophically and materially—from the abolitionists of Hopedale to the public schooling of New Harmony, from the quality manufactured goods of Amana to the austere lines of Shaker furniture. Last century's communities tended to be hierarchically run, yet economically democratic; they were philosophically liberal and accorded labor more dignity than the society at large.

A Look at Student Housing Cooperatives

Deborah Altus traces the roots of student co-ops back to the early part of this century, and reports that social activism tends to attract co-opers as much as inexpensive housing. For many, student housing is their first taste of group living. Increasing contacts between student residential cooperatives and other intentional communities can provide students opportunities to extend their cooperative experiences into lifetime careers.

For the Next Seven Generations: Indigenous Americans and Communalism

by Glenn T. Morris of the University of Colorado, Denver

*I*n 1492, over 600 distinct indigenous nations existed in what is known today as the United States. With all of the colonization, destruction, and forced assimilation that has transpired since then, over 500 nations survive, representing 2,000,000 indigenous Americans, with 200 native villages in Alaska alone. A common misconception about these indigenous peoples is that they were homogeneous. Although some common characteristics can be found, indigenous peoples in the Americas were, and remain, as distinct from each other as Swedes are from Basques are from Armenians.[1]

This diversity spanned over 300 languages and dialects, distinct spiritual traditions and practices, and differing social organizations. But there are some common threads through the indigenous world that are helpful in discussing communalism—especially as it may be useful in constructing sustainable, egalitarian social models for the future.

Communalism for indigenous peoples is not an aberrant social practice; it is, instead, the social norm. This is quite distinct from the infrequent examples of communalism in Western societies. Notions of land held in common, consensus decision making, and respect for the environment, though considered deviant within Western culture, are neither new nor controversial in traditional indigenous societies.

Haudenosaunee Confederation, 400 Years of Multinational Government

Before 1600, five indigenous nations—the Cayuga, Mohawk, Oneida, Onondaga, and Seneca—formed the Haudenosaunee Confederation, or League of the Iroquois, with homelands then covering what is now upper New York State. (Since then, the Tuscarora and remnants of other indigenous nations have joined.) The Haudenosaunee system is consensual in design and operation. The Onondaga are the fire keepers, acting as executives and mediators. They also guard the wampum belts, which are read and serve as the Iroquois constitution. The other nations of the Confederation serve in either upper or lower houses of the Iroquois legislature.

In the Haudenosaunee system, there has never been a concept of a dictatorial leader, let alone a male one. The Haudenosaunee were, and continue to be, matrilineal. When a man and woman marry, the man moves to the woman's family, and newborn children enter the clan of their mother. The clan mothers select the political leadership of the nations, and possess the authority to remove leaders from office for malfeasance. In addition to leadership selection and removal, the clan mothers also serve as the judiciary.

Haudenosaunee Political Organization Inspires U.S. Constitution

Benjamin Franklin, Thomas Jefferson, James Madison, and most probably other members of the U.S. Continental Congress, had extensive contact with indigenous culture, and borrowed major portions from the Haudenosaunee system for use in the U.S.

Glenn Morris is an Associate Professor of Political Science at the University of Colorado at Denver and he directs the Fourth World Center for the Study of Indigenous Law and Politics. He also serves on the Leadership Council of the American Indian Movement of Colorado, and he has participated in the delibera-tions of the United Nations Working Group on Indigenous Peoples and the U.N. Commission on Human Rights. Glenn is of Shawnee Heritage. Some portions of this article were presented to the 1990 Communal Studies Association Conference at Hancock Shaker Village, Pittsfield, Massachusetts.

The ethic of respect for the earth and for future generations is foremost for many indigenous Americans.

100 Mile Lodge

when a major issue could not be settled to everyone's satisfaction. If a member or several members of a talwa [Muscogee town] continued to disagree with the majority on a policy, they were free to move and establish their own community, with the support—not the enmity—of those whose talwa they were leaving. When a dissident group established a new town—and also when a neighboring tribe joined the Muscogee Confederacy, an ember from one of the mother talwas was used to start the fire of the new settlement as a symbol of continuity and unity.[4]

Constitution.[2] The political philosophies and institutions of the indigenous American peoples, from the Haudenosaunee to the Delaware to the Cheyennes, are reflected in the development of every major Western political philosophy in the past 300 years. From Rousseau to Thomas Paine, from John Locke to Proudhon and Kropotkin, their theories of natural rights and egalitarianism, and their belief in individual liberty, are all found in indigenous societies. In reality, indigenous societies played a vital role in the evolution of modern political thought.[3]

Communal Harmony among the Muscogee

A second example of advanced indigenous social organization is the Muscogee (Creek) Nation. Originally located in Alabama and Georgia, the Muscogee have the oldest political institutions in North America, with a continuing, recorded history going back beyond 400 years. The decentralized, matriarchal, communal nature of the Muscogee permeates every aspect of life, from familial relationships to the administration of criminal justice. Muscogee society provides balance and harmony, while fostering a large degree of personal autonomy and freedom.

As Sharon O'Brien describes,

Harmony was so highly valued among the Muscogees that a special system was devised to maintain it even

The Muscogee exhibit some essential characteristics of the communalism found in many indigenous societies:

- the importance of spirituality and respect for all life;
- the absence of hierarchical, coercive authority with the goal of consensus in decision making;
- the liberty of the individual coupled with the individual's consciousness of responsibility to the whole;
- the importance of extended family with concomitant respect for both the children and the elders; and
- the operation of systems of justice that focus on the healing of society and the restoration of balance, rather than retribution or vengeance.

It has been rare to find an indigenous society run by a dictator, an oligarchy, or even by majority rule—since majority rule creates an out group, the minority. Political authority truly emanates from the consent of the entire nation when consensus decision making is used. In 1727, New York Lieutenant Governor Cadwallader Colden observed that

"The authority of these (indigenous) rulers is gained by and consists wholly in the opinion that the rest of the Nation's (members) have of their wisdom and integrity. They never execute their resolutions by force upon any of their people."[5]

Similarly, Georgia governor, James Oglethorpe, in describing the Muscogee political system in 1764, stated,

"There is no coercive...power....(Their leaders) can do no more than persuade....They reason together with great temper and modesty till they have brought each other into some unanimous resolution."[6]

These examples of advanced indigenous society are a far cry from the mainstream portrayals of Indians as primitives ruled by brute force through the principles of social Darwinism. Instead, indigenous social systems are characterized by humanity and foresight, as expressed in the centuries-old

U.S. Indian Policy: Extermination and Assimilation

A destructive foreign ethic was introduced into the Americas from Europe in 1492, an ethic that places a premium on competition, private property, and subordination of the environment to human desires. As the United States expanded and invaded more indigenous regions, this European ethic shaped U.S. policy toward Indian peoples. U.S. Indian policy views indigenous Americans, their territorial claims, and their cultural and social practices as impediments to the spread of "true" civilization. While government policy has vacillated between extermination and assimilation, one end has been evident throughout—indigenous practices of communalism, shared land tenure, extended families, and grassroots consensus have been replaced, forcibly if necessary, by Western models of social organization and behavior.[1]

At various times, policies of extermination and assimilation have been embodied in legislation and regulations to force the removal of indigenous peoples, outlaw traditional spiritual practices, prohibit the speaking of traditional languages, sanction wholesale kidnapping and indoctrination of indigenous children in missionary or government boarding schools hundreds of miles from their communities, destroy indigenous legal and political systems, and undermine the moral and social authority of indigenous societies.

United States colonial policy has had a dramatically negative impact on the consciousness of indigenous peoples in the Americas.[2] Many traditional values have been supplanted by techno-industrial beliefs; many indigenous children identify more closely with dominant-culture media personalities than with the messages and heroes of their own indigenous nations.[3] The continuing erosion of traditional indigenous values and principles convinced many parents that traditional, indigenous wisdom was anachronistic—of no value in a complex, computer-driven society; so parents often consciously decided not to pass down much of the knowledge of past generations.[4] Of course, the indigenous renaissance has done much to influence these negative attitudes, but there is still a long way to go.

As the noted Lakota and American Indian Movement leader Russell Means once observed,

European faith—including the new faith in science—equals a belief that man is God....American Indians know this to be totally absurd....American Indians have been trying to explain this to Europeans for centuries, but...Europeans have proven themselves unable to hear....It is the role of American Indian peoples, the role of all natural beings, to survive. A part of our survival is to resist.

(Continued on next page)

Haudenosaunee philosophy that all major decisions of a nation must be based on how those decisions will affect at least the next seven generations.[7]

The ethic of respect for the earth and for future generations is translated into social practice in every activity, from child rearing to crop planting to decisions on where to establish new communities. This socialization process results from centuries, if not millennia, of wisdom about the earth, about the fruits of the earth, and about human settlement over time in any particular part of the earth.

Indigenous American Renaissance

Despite centuries of erosion by extermination and assimilation, traditional indigenous culture began a comeback in the seventies that continues today. After experiencing technological society run amok,

---

(Continued from previous page: U.S. Indian Policy: Extermination and Assimilation)

We resist not to overthrow a government or to take political power, but because it is natural to resist extermination, to survive. We don't want power over white institutions, we want those institutions to disappear. That's revolution....I trust the community and the culturally based vision of all the races that naturally resist industrialization and human extinction.[5]

Endnotes

1. Churchill, Ward, and Jim Vander Wall, *Agents of Repression: The FBI's Secret Wars Against the Black Panther Party and the American Indian Movement* (Boston: South End Press, 1988). Debo, Angie, *And Still the Waters Run: The Betrayal of the Five Civilized Tribes* (Norman: University of Oklahoma Press, 1940, 1989). Eckert, Allan W., *A Sorrow in Our Heart: The Life of Tecumseh* (New York: Bantam, 1992). Harding, Sidney L., *Crow Dog's Case: American Indian Sovereignty, Tribal Law, and United States Law in the Nineteenth Century* (New York: Cambridge University Press, 1994). Hoxie, Frederick, *A Final Promise: The Campaign to Assimilate the Indians 1880–1920* (Cambridge: Cambridge University Press, 1989). Jaimes, Annette, *The State of Native America: Genocide, Colonization and Resistance* (Boston: South End Press, 1992). Matthiessen, Peter, *In the Spirit of Crazy Horse* (New York: Viking Press, 1983, 1992).

2. *Denver Post*, August 16, 1992, 15A, cites 1990 Census data: American Indians continue to have the lowest family income, the highest unemployment, a poverty rate of 23.7 percent compared to 10.3 percent nationally, and the highest incidence of teenage suicide in the United States.

3. Mander, Jerry, *In the Absence of the Sacred: The Failure of Technology and the Survival of the Indian Nations* (San Francisco: Sierra Club Books, 1991), examines the connection between the spread of the techno-industrial world view and the destruction of indigenous peoples. Churchill, Ward, "Another Dry White Season," *Bloomsbury Review* (April/May 1992), critiques Mander from an indigenous viewpoint. Adams, Michael, *Machines as the Measure of Men: Science, Technology and Ideologies of Western Dominance* (Ithaca, NY: Cornell University Press, 1989).

4. Prucha, Francis Paul, editor, *Americanizing the American Indian: Writings by 'Friends of the Indians,' 1865–1900* (Cambridge, MA: Harvard University Press, 1973). Weyler, Rex, *Blood of the Land: The Government and Corporate War Against the American Indian Movement* (New York: Everest House, 1984).

5. Means, Russell, "Fighting Words on the Future of the Earth," *Mother Jones* (December, 1980), 22, reprinted as "The Same Old Song," in Ward Churchill's *Marxism and Native Americans* (Boston: South End Press, 1983).

Debunking Myths for Species Survival

For many people socialized in the United States, the only exposure to indigenous political leaders is an image of a "Big Chief" on the cover of their grade school writing tablet.[1] This image, coupled with Hollywood distortions of indigenous peoples and societies, has convinced nonindigenous Western society that sociopolitical structure among American Indians was male/warrior dominated, barbaric, and autocratic, without room for individual liberty or dissent. However, these traditional Western descriptions of indigenous society could not be farther from reality.[2]

Prejudiced myths about indigenous peoples were developed early and planted deep in Western historical writings. By the nineteenth century, such notable authors as Lewis Henry Morgan, John Locke, and Frederich Engels were describing indigenous social organization in terms ranging from the backhanded "primitive communism" to the pejorative "barbaric." They anticipated the day when indigenous peoples would evolve into an industrial, presumably "civilized," form of capitalism or communism.[3]

Now, ironically, indigenous peoples watch the system based on Engels' version of advanced communism disintegrate, and watch the Lockean capitalist system move ever closer to the environmental precipice. Meanwhile, the "primitive" political systems of the Haudenosaunee (Six Nations Iroquois) and other indigenous nations continue to function effectively after at least four centuries despite continuous oppression from "civilized" society.[4] The idea that indigenous communalism is an archaic relic of the past, holding no lessons or usefulness in the late twentieth century, reflects an ignorance about the nature of indigenous North American social organization. Sadly, this ignorance and lack of respect prevent consideration, or even awareness, of fundamental solutions to some of the most pressing problems of our time.

At the 1992 U.N. Conference on Environment and Development in Rio de Janeiro, called the Earth Summit, the organizers from the industrial nations offered few serious proposals for reversing the negative effects of Western development vision. Indigenous peoples from around the world felt compelled to offer their own vision of how to retrieve the species from the brink of destruction. Known as the *Kari-Oca Declaration*,[5] after the community in which it was decided, this statement proposes to move the planet toward a saner environmental vision and demands justice for the world's indigenous peoples—the most immediate victims of technological expansion. In the indigenous people's viewpoint, the dominant paradigm cannot shift if Western governments fail to recognize the similarities between their historic policies of extermination and their contemporary attitudes and actions.

Endnotes

1. Bataille, Gretchen, and Charles L.P. Silet, editors, *The Pretend Indians: Images of Native Americans in the Movies* (Ames, IA: Iowa State University Press, 1980), discusses the shaping of the collective consciousness of the United States regarding indigenous peoples, as do the following titles. Berkhoffer, Robert F., *The White Man's Indian: Images of the American Indian from Columbus to the Present* (New York: Vintage Books, 1978). Deloria, Vine, *God Is Red* (New York: Dell, 1973), reissued by Fulcrum, 1993. Drinnon, Richard, *Facing West: The Metaphysics of Indian Hating and Empire*

(Continued on next page)

many indigenous young people made conscious decisions to remember the indigenous truths that have evolved over millennia in the Americas. Through this renaissance, indigenous people began communicating with the traditional elders of their nations to learn their languages, their ceremonies, and their native histories. Consequently, there has been an enormous rebirth of indigenous spirituality, a resurgence of indigenous political and social sovereignty, and a willingness to express an indigenous alternative to the ecological, social, and political crises of the late twentieth century.[8]

Indigenous Communalism: Cultural Threat or Path to the Future?

Indigenous communalism presents the same ecological challenge to the Western world view today that it did in 1492—providing sustainable alternatives to environmental destruction, to the inequality created by capitalist competition, and to the continuing fragmentation of human beings in an expanding industrial milieu.

The future of transformational thought, be it communitarian, utopian, green, or otherwise, can only be enhanced and strengthened by the respectful inclusion of indigenous views. This inclusion must not be an afterthought, or a patronizing attempt to appear multicultural;[9] it must be a serious evaluation of indigenous perspectives. Such an inclusion could lead to a new, sustainable society that will promote cooperation, equality, and deep ecological principles, while simultaneously celebrating diversity, individual liberty, and dissent on a postindustrial planet. ⦿

Endnotes

1. Debo, Angie, *A History of Indians of the United States* (Norman: University of Oklahoma, 1979, 1989), describes the diversity of indigenous peoples and their experiences with invader or settler states, as do the following titles. Jaimes, Annette, *The State of Native America: Genocide, Colonization and Resistance* (Boston: South End Press, 1992). Prucha, Francis Paul, *Documents of United States Indian Policy* (Lincoln: University of Nebraska Press, 1975). Williams, Robert A., Jr., *The American Indian in Western Legal Thought: The Discourses of Conquest* (Oxford: Oxford University Press, 1990).

(Continued from previous page: Debunking Myths for Species Survival)

Building (New York: Shocken Books, 1990), 2nd edition. Horsman, Reginald, *Race and Manifest Destiny: The Origin of American Racial Anglo-Saxonism* (Cambridge, MA: Harvard University Press, 1981) (especially Chapter 10). Stedman, William Raymond, *Shadows of the Indian: Stereotypes in American Culture* (Norman: University of Oklahoma Press, 1982).

2. Schusky, Ernest, editor, *Political Organization of Native North Americans* (Washington: University Press of America, 1970). Vogel, Virgil, *This Country Was Ours: A Documentary History of the American Indian* (New York: Harper and Row, 1972).

3. Engels, Frederich, *The Origin of the Family, Private Property and the State* (New York: International Publishers, 1942, 1975). Locke, John, *The Second Treatise of Government* (New York: Liberal Arts Press, 1952). Morgan, Lewis Henry, *Ancient Society, or Researches in the Lines of Human Progress from Savagery through Barbarism to Civilization*, 1877. League of the Ho-De-No-Sau-Nee, Iroquois, 1851.

4. Colden, Cadwallader, *The History of the Five Indian Nations* (Ithaca, NY: Cornell University Press, 1958) (originally published in 1727). "A Basic Call to Consciousness," *Akwesasne Notes*, 1978, Mohawk Nation, Rooseveltown, NY 13683.

5. The *Kari-Oca Declaration* is available from the author at the Fourth World Center for the Study of Indigenous Law and Politics, Department of Political Science, University of Colorado at Denver, Campus Box 190, P.O. Box 173364, Denver, CO 80217.

2. Barriero, Jose, "Indian Roots of American Democracy," *Northeast Indian Quarterly* (Ithaca, NY: Cornell University). Grinde, Donald A., Jr., *The Iroquois and the Founding of the American Nation* (San Francisco: Indian Historian Press, 1977). Johansen, Bruce, *Forgotten Founders: Benjamin Franklin, the Iroquois and the Rationale for the American Revolution* (Boston: Harvard Common Press, 1982). Johansen, Bruce, and Donald A. Grinde, *Exemplar of Liberty* (Los Angeles: UCLA, American Indian Studies Program, 1991). Unfortunately, the framers of the United States Constitution were not ready to integrate some of the more liberating elements of the Iroquois system, such as suffrage and political power for women, abolition of slavery, and periodic redistribution of societal wealth.

3. Ibid. Brandon, William, *New Worlds for Old: Reports from the New World and Their Effect on the Development of Social Thought in Europe, 1500–1800* (Athens, OH: Ohio University Press, 1986). Commager, Henry Steele, *The Empire of Reason: How Europe Imagined and America Realized the Enlightenment* (Garden City, NY: Doubleday, 1978).

4. O'Brien, Sharon, *American Indian Tribal Governments* (Norman: University of Oklahoma Press, 1989), 23. Debo, Angie, *The Road to Disappearance: A History of the Creek Indians* (Norman: University of Oklahoma Press, 1941), describes Muscogee (Creek) sociopolitical systems and United States subversion, as do the following titles. Green, Donald E., *The Politics of Indian Removal: Creek Government and Society in Crisis* (Lincoln: University of Nebraska Press, 1977). Moore, John H. "The Muskoke National Question in Oklahoma," *Science and Society* 52(2) (1988): 163.

5. O'Brien, Sharon, *American Indian Tribal Governments* (Norman: University of Oklahoma Press, 1989), 16.

6. Ibid., 22.

7. "A Basic Call to Consciousness," *Akwesasne Notes*, 1978, Mohawk Nation, Rooseveltown, NY 13683. Jaimes, Annette M. with Theresa Halsey, "American Indian Women: At the Center of Indigenous Resistance in Contemporary North America," and accompanying notes in *The State of Native America: Genocide, Colonization and Resistance* (Boston: South End Press, 1992), describe the roles of women in indigenous societies. Llewellyn, Karl and E. Adamson Hoebel, *The Cheyenne Way* (Norman: University of Oklahoma Press, 1941), describes traditional indigenous systems of justice. Noon, J., *Law and Government of the Grand River Iroquois* (New York: The Viking Fund, 1949). Strickland, Rennard, *Fire and the Spirits: Cherokee Law from Clan to Court* (Norman: University of Oklahoma Press, 1975), 10, describes a Cherokee perception of law that was at odds with the encroaching European view: "To the Cherokees, law was the earthly representation of a divine spirit order. They did not think of law as a set of civil or secular rules limiting or requiring actions on their part. Public consensus and harmony, rather than confrontation and dispute, as essential elements of the Cherokee world view, were reflected in ancient concepts of law."

8. Steiner, Stan, *The New Indians* (New York: Harper and Row, 1968), documents the genesis of the transformational indigenous renaissance. Gedicks, Al, *The New Resource Wars: Native and Environmental Struggles Against Multinational Corporations* (Boston: South End Press, 1993). Waley, Rick and Walter Bresette, *Walleye Warriors: An Effective Alliance Against Racism and for the Earth* (Philadelphia: New Society Publishers, 1994). Rose, Wendy, "The Great Pretenders: Further Reflections on Whiteshamanism," in *The State of Native America: Genocide, Colonization and Resistance* (Boston: South End Press, 1992), distinguishes the indigenous renaissance from the emergence of the nonindigenous new age movement, which often seeks to appropriate indigenous knowledge for its own purposes.

9. Churchill, Ward, "Another Dry White Season," *Bloomsbury Review* (April/May 1992). Notable indigenous spokespersons are providing valuable contributions to transformational politics. But only a few are recognized, such as Lakota leader Russell Means, Anishinabe activist Winona LaDuke, Seneca historian and SUNY Buffalo professor John Mohawk, and Wisconsin Greens leader Walt Bressette. Most "Green" publications don't cite indigenous sources, and fail to give credit to indigenous philosophy and practice as the foundation for much of the green agenda.

Dreams and Other Products of Nineteenth-Century Communities

by Lyman Tower Sargent, University of Missouri–St. Louis

*E*xcept for the Shaker influence on design, the use of the ever popular Shaker song "Simple Gifts" by Aaron Copland, and a fascination with the sexual relations at Oneida, early American intentional communities tend to be treated as if they had withdrawn from all contact with the wider culture. This was emphatically not the case.

While communities did withdraw to practice their chosen lives, they were always in touch with the wider culture, both drawing from it and contributing to it. Even the most isolated communities—foreign-born religious groups with limited English language skills—interacted with their neighbors through trade and sharing ways of dealing with the unfamiliar environment. Of course these interactions had definite limits. Many communitarians, then as now, had decided that the wider culture was deeply flawed, corrupt, even evil. Hence, while the impulse for withdrawal was real, it was never complete.

The origins of cultural influences are notoriously difficult to demonstrate, and the great majority of nineteenth-century intentional communities remain largely unstudied. Even so, much is known about the practical influence some of these groups had on American culture. These practical aspects that we actually know about are the first focus of this survey, followed by a consideration of communitarian social and political ideas—where the most important influences are found.

Early Religious Communities Enriched American Culture

Nineteenth-century religious communities made important contributions to American material culture. The Shakers, Oneida, Amana, and other groups mass-produced industrial and agricultural products and fine handcrafts. In upper New York State, Oneida made silk, canned fruit, and manufactured animal traps for the fur trade. After decades of successful operation, communal businesses were converted to a stock corporation in 1881 with community members, mostly native New Englanders, becoming stockholding employees. Today, Oneida Ltd. continues as a thriving corporation producing stainless steel and silver tableware.

The Amana villages near the Iowa River produced high-quality woolen goods and print cloth for wholesale distribution nationally. Lumber, produce, honey, meat, flour, and many other products were retailed locally. To this day, Amana is still well known for high-quality foods (fruit and hams), electric appliances, generous wages, and scrupulous business ethics.

The Inspirationists of Amana are Pietist dissenters from the Lutheran Church—refusing to take oaths of allegiance or give military service—and were inspired by divine revelation to migrate from their individual homes in Germany. The Inspirationists moved to New York State in 1842 and formed a communal economy, moving again in 1855 to Iowa.

Lyman Tower Sargent is a Professor and Chair of the Political Science Department, University of Missouri–St. Louis. He is Editor of *Utopian Studies: Journal of the Society for Utopian Studies*, and a past board member with the Communal Studies Association. Lyman has abridged this essay from a much longer article, "The Social and Political Ideas of the American Communitarians: A Comparison of Religious and Secular Communes Before 1850," in Michael S. Cummings and Nicholas D. Smith, editors, *Utopian Studies III* (Lanham, MD: University Press of America, 1991), 37–58. Lyman is also the author of *British and American Utopian Literature, 1516–1985: An Annotated Chronological Bibliography* (New York: Garland, 1988).

While retaining the Amana Church and common spiritual beliefs, the communal businesses were changed to a stock corporation in 1932. Today the Amana Society has a stable population of 1,400 people.

Shaker Influences Stand Out

The Shakers had the widest impact in many areas of American culture, most clearly in architecture, furniture, decorative arts, and music. The Shakers became communal in 1787, and grew to include several thousand members living in 19 communities across the northeast by the mid-1800s. However, their vows of celibacy made the Shakers completely dependent on new-member recruitment to sustain their communities. After 1830, Shaker membership declined slowly for the next hundred years—to less than 100 by 1940 and only a handful now.

Simplicity was central to Shaker life. While the tune for "Simple Gifts" may be the best-known Shaker music, the words symbolize the Shaker quest for purity and unity.

Simple Gifts
'Tis the gift to be simple, 'tis the gift to be free,
'Tis the gift to be simple, come down where we ought to be,

And when we find ourselves in the place just right,
'Twill be in the valley of love and delight.

When true simplicity is gain'd,
To bow and to bend we shan't be asham'd,
To turn, turn will be our delight
'Till by turning, turning we come round right....

Simplicity Leads to Full, Rich Life

The most famous expression of simplicity was Shaker furniture, which came to exemplify all of Shaker life. Their furniture was very simple; straight lines were preferred, with no decorative flourishes. The result was an austere beauty that has attracted much attention in recent years. All Shaker artifacts were designed to fit a lifestyle that, while emphasizing the role of work as worship, stressed an economy of motion and effort that led to the development of many labor-saving devices. For example, most

Shaker chairs were designed to be hung from pegs on the wall to ease floor cleaning.

The Shakers were particularly adept at designing ways of easing housework; they spent much time and effort on improving washing machines and developing various devices to make ironing easier. Ease of work was always one of the goals, but that aim was first and foremost a way of removing impediments to work as worship. Exhaustion makes it much less likely that one will see work as a way of getting closer to God. Therefore, the Shakers aimed at simplicity— simplicity in work, simplicity in design, simplicity in life. Simplicity, they believed, led to a full, rich life.

Social and Political Ideas of Early American Religious Communities

The greatest contributions made by early American intentional communities were the principles on which they based their lives. Often founded on idiosyncratic interpretations of the Bible, these nineteenth-century communes look back to a long tradition of Christian communitarianism, radicalism, and heresy, and are sometimes linked to the developing tradition of socialism. The Shakers and the members of Oneida and Hopedale were explicitly socialists, and many socialist theoreticians— including Friedrich Engels—looked to these religious American communities as exemplars of the possibilities of socialism.

To a great extent, the early American religious communities were authoritarian, patriarchal, and hierarchical. Political power derived from religious charisma and authority and religious leaders who delegated authority as they chose. Even where democratic forms existed, as at Oneida and Hopedale, the personalities of the religious leaders gave them considerable power, whatever legal forms existed. Adin Ballou and Hopedale came closest to overcoming this problem.

Economically, all these communities practiced some form of common ownership. A few practiced communal ownership only for prudential reasons; some for political reasons; but most were following a biblical injunction to do so. On the whole, communities were successful economically and provided a comfortable life for their members. Normally community members worked hard, but they lived at least as well as—in many cases better than—they would have in the wider culture. When communities dissolved, generally their members were left reasonably well off.

But esoteric theology, not material well-being, was the focus of communal life. For instance, the most fundamental theological propositions of the Shakers were concerned with the dual nature of God. This duality pervaded Shaker life from governance to architecture. All Shaker buildings were constructed to reflect this duality. Each of the buildings had at least two entrances and two staircases, often directly next to each other, so that men and women would never meet in a doorway or on the stairs. This extreme separation of the sexes was a combined result of theological dualism and the rejection of physical sexual relations taught by Mother Ann Lee.

The Practical Christians of Hopedale

Hopedale (1841–1856), near Milford in eastern Massachusetts, was an egalitarian commune of up to 235 people. Founder Adin Ballou tried to make the teachings of Christianity real through the lives of the members. He sought, as the title of one of his periodicals has it, to develop Practical Christians. One aspect of this process was the vision of a community withdrawn from the evils of the world, where it would be possible to live a better life.

Hopedale served as a center for various reform movements. The community was an important center of abolitionist and temperance activities, as was Oneida to a lesser extent. Hopedale and Oneida were both active in the women's rights and labor movements. But it was Oneida, based near Lake Oneida in upper New York State, that was the most infamous group in the history of the communitarian movement.

Oneida: Christian Perfectionists Establish Successful Complex Marriage

The Oneida Community of Christian Perfectionists was founded in Putney, Vermont, by John Humphrey Noyes in 1840. A communal economy was established in 1844, and three years later the main community site was moved to former Oneida Indian Reservation lands (purchased by the community from New York State). Oneida grew to include well

"Normally community members worked hard, but lived at least as well as—in many cases better than—they would have in the wider (nineteenth century) culture."

Institute for Social Ecology

over 200 people with branch communes in Wallingford, Connecticut, and, for a time, at four other sites. The fact that Oneida was one of the most successful American communities economically and socially gets lost in the popular concern over their communal sexual relations.

The practice of what Oneidans called "complex marriage" has fascinated the popular press for over a century. Bible Communism and complex marriage meant nonpossessiveness and sexual fidelity within the group, and was based on descriptions of heaven found in the biblical Gospels of Matthew and John. At Oneida, complex marriage required considerable discipline of community members. Every woman was free to refuse or accept any, or every, man's attention; but "special love" (sexual exclusivity) or jealousy for single individuals had to be given up. Oneida women and men shared the

167

• •

The fact that Oneida was one of the most successful American communities economically and socially gets lost in the popular concern over their communal sexual relations.

• • • • • • • • • • • • • • • • • • • •

freedom to love other Oneida men and women—but only if there was a mutual attraction confirmed by the community, and only if the community agreed the pair were a proper match, most especially regarding experience in male continence. The people of Oneida were quite disciplined in their practice of male continence (coitus interruptus), which was vital to avoiding unplanned pregnancy.

The community could not afford many children in the early years, and the equality-minded Oneida women did not want to stay pregnant most of the time. While the wider society operated without any effective awareness of family planning and contraception, the Oneida system worked very well: In the two decades between 1848 and 1869 only 35 children were born to a community of some 40 sexually active couples and many singles (beginning at puberty). During the following decade of planned—but still limited—pregnancies, 58 children were born.

Mutual Criticism and Stirpiculture: Paths toward Perfection

Another basic Oneida institution was mutual criticism. This system of pointing out the personal strengths and weaknesses of community members has been used by Mao's China and some contemporary communities, although it is doubtful whether Oneida was the inspiration for these modern practices. In Oneida, mutual criticism was a formal process in which each member was criticized and given the chance to correct faults. Most members, consciously striving for perfection, welcomed it. Mutual criticism was designed to help each member maintain a clear view of their social, familial, and economic responsibilities to other individual members and the community as a whole.

In 1869, after 20 years of male continence, the community was secure enough to afford more children. Oneida undertook a eugenic experiment they had envisioned for years, which they called "stirpiculture." The community had long since decided it made the most sense if they were to have children, to have the best children possible. A board of community members decided who should have children. The experiment was successful on almost any measure including the physical and intellectual quality of the Oneida children.

Of course, the quality of the children was due as much to child-rearing practices as to breeding practices. Children were raised communally. They went into community nurseries at an early age, where they were looked after as much as possible by women other than their mothers to avoid "special love" and exclusive attachments. Children were given some productive work at a fairly early age, but they also enjoyed a great deal of freedom.

The community consciously saw itself in the forefront of the women's rights movement, providing women the chance to experiment with various changes in dress and style. But, of course, the dramatic changes in sexual behavior, child rearing, and variety of work opportunities were of primary significance in women's daily lives.

Most religious communitarians believed that their experiments would be short-lived because the Second Coming was near—they were preparing themselves for the heavenly life soon to come. But the Oneida Perfectionists were notably different. The Perfectionists thought that the Second Coming had already occurred, and that they were creating the perfect life that God intended for all of His children.

Oneida and the other intentional groups are appropriately labeled experimental communities, or communal experiments. Members were willing—even eager—to experiment with their own lives in their search for a better society. These were all remarkable communities of people willing to move from belief to practice, willing to change their lives dramatically to fit a vision of a better life.

New Harmony: A First Attempt at Cooperative Community

New Harmony, a residential cooperative from 1825 to 1827, is located in southern Indiana near Evansville. This cooperative was the most influential secular community of the era, even though it was a disastrous experiment as an intentional community. Robert Owen, the founder, was involved with the emerging cooperative movement at his textile mills in Scotland when he purchased the town of New Harmony from the Harmony Society.

A German Pietist commune (1805–1916) that founded the settlement in 1814, the 800 Harmonists had established a regional trading center with 180 buildings—dwellings, factories, mills, stores, school, library, church—and public gardens surrounded by 2,000 acres of improved fields and pastures and almost 18,000 acres of woodlands. The Harmonists sold it all to Robert Owen for $125,000 and moved back to Pennsylvania where they had already built one town and proceeded to build another one.

Owen sought to introduce the new cooperative concepts to North American society through New Harmony—20 years before a group of English weavers developed the Rochdale Principles for effective co-op management. In converting New Harmony from a religious commune to a secular cooperative, every mistake that could be made was made. Cooperative organizing wasn't started until months after the town was purchased and many of the residents already established, along with a variety of personal and ideological conflicts. There was never any agreement on basic community rules and regulations; candidates for membership were not screened. Owen spent most of his time traveling to promote the community, or living in and managing his model company town in Scotland (which included the largest cotton-spinning mills in Great Britain). There was never any cohesive leadership at New Harmony, and there were constant disputes.

Even so, in its brief existence as a cooperative, New Harmony was a focal point for major reform activities. Neither the American labor movement nor the women's movement would have developed in quite the way they did without the people and ideas from New Harmony. The community attracted a number of outstanding European scientists, architects, and educators who had a tremendous impact

> In converting New Harmony...to a secular cooperative, every mistake that could be made was made.

on the development of these professions in the United States, especially education.

Frontier Leadership and Education Radiate from New Harmony

For good or ill, the state capitals of a number of midwestern states were designed by a man from New Harmony; an important early geologist of the midwest was headquartered at New Harmony; and Owen's children stayed in the United States and became active in various reform movements. One, Robert Dale Owen, was involved in the statehood of Indiana, was an early member of Congress from Indiana, wrote the legislation establishing the Smithsonian Institution, and chaired the committee that set up the Freedman's Bureau to actively protect the rights of former slaves after the Civil War.

Robert Owen believed in mass education, and the United States is one of the few countries where the idea has ever been taken seriously. New Harmony, then on the frontier at the Wabash River, had the first educational system in the United States to provide public schooling from childhood through adult education. To this day, adult education in the town of New Harmony is enhanced by the imposing Workingmen's Institute, the first of 160 libraries funded by William Maclure.

An educator who came to New Harmony with Owen, William Maclure had a vision of higher education as we know it today in the great universities. For Maclure, higher education had to include research and publication together with teaching. He wanted New Harmony to be the first true university in the United States.

Regarding university education, Maclure's vision exceeded that of Owen, but both men found a

• •

At the base of these communitarian ideals was...the belief that people would choose to change— to improve—themselves, their children, and their environment.

• •

common cause in vocational education. Maclure believed that from their earliest years students should be taught agricultural and industrial occupations as well as intellectual ones. Further, he believed that the best way to do this was through experience. Students should work and learn skills while also getting a formal education. Maclure argued that students should be in income-producing jobs to help defray the expenses of their education; he aimed at making all schools self-supporting through cooperative work-study programs.

This last point was part and parcel of the cooperative approach that communities like New Harmony were preaching. Cooperative work, it was believed, would be more productive and provide a better life than individual, competitive jobs.

Nashoba and Brook Farm

Although New Harmony excluded "persons of color" from cooperative membership, one of those who spent time there, Frances Wright—a famous lecturer and women's rights advocate—tried intentional community as a means of helping slaves to buy their freedom. Deep in the slave-holding south, on the Wolf River outside Memphis, Tennessee, Wright founded Nashoba (1825–1835). This community was home to several white abolitionists and 30 slaves working to educate themselves for freedom, while buying their way out of bondage.

The members of Brook Farm, near Boston, Massachusetts, undertook a major experiment in social reform by establishing a community that

sought to abolish the status differences between mental and physical labor. Nathaniel Hawthorne, faced with a pile of manure to be moved and his first set of blisters, scathingly satirized the experiment. Brook Farm was both an unusual and important intentional community. Preschool or day-care education was specifically designed with two purposes: to provide early educational experiences for the children, and to free their parents for other productive labor. Founded in 1841, Brook Farm grew to over 70 members before it was destroyed by fire in 1846.

Many Secular Communities Emphasized Education and Equal Rights

The history of American education would have been much different without New Harmony and other secular communities that emphasized education. Many of the people who joined these communities wanted to better educate themselves and their children, and they wanted to educate the outside world by their example.

At the base of these communitarian ideals was a form of environmental determinism combined with the belief that people would choose to change—to improve—themselves, their children, and their environment. Members believed that intentional communities could provide a better life than could be achieved through private ownership and competition. Even with the high failure rate and the personal struggles involved, many communitarians continued to believe in cooperative lifestyles.

Most of the early secular communities were democratic although not consensual; they aimed at equality and generally practiced it. Economically, most groups were communal, holding all property in common and distributing goods on the basis of need.

Conclusion: Dreams Can Come True, for a Short Time or for Lifetimes

In reviewing more than a century of dreams involving several thousand people, a number of interesting conclusions emerge. First, nineteenth-century communities were generally successful economically— compared to their other plans, community economic goals were relatively simple to define. Second, the members of many communities bickered and fought continually. Third, and probably connected to the second point, leadership was erratic. This was true partly by choice; some communities did not want leadership—they wanted to control their own lives individually. Sadly, some of the secular communities did not last long enough for the ties of friendship and communal feeling to overcome disagreements about implementation of group ideals.

Both authoritarian and democratic processes can produce viable intentional communities. Authoritarianism seems to be most successful with a religious sanction. Democracy requires hard work and all involved must be willing to participate in lots of meetings. Just as in the wider culture, achieving group goals can be hindered by the egos of group members, and by open or poorly defined membership policies. The most important conclusion is that social equality within an intentional community is damned hard, but can be achieved given sufficient determination. Some nineteenth-century intentional communities realized gender, racial, ethnic, or religious equality, and/or accepted both mental and physical labor as of equal worth. Outside of community, realization of such egalitarian dreams is hard to achieve, and virtually impossible to maintain.

I don't believe that any dream can ever truly fail. And even though most of these aren't my dreams, I find it hard to call them nightmares; none of these communal societies ever developed the nightmarish idea of imposing their vision on outsiders. We know now, to our cost, that dreams can become nightmares. Hence, we must approach dreams—perhaps our own most of all—with both respect and caution.

The dreams of communitarians from the last century gradually changed—from the Shakers' millennial waiting for the end of history, to the secular and religious activism of New Harmony, Oneida, and Hopedale. In their waiting, preparing themselves for their future heavenly abode, the Shakers accomplished a great deal—changing their own lives and the way the rest of us perceive the objects around us.

Oneida, Hopedale, and the secular communitarians developed a democratic egalitarianism that had been presaged in the nondemocratic millennial communes. The Shakers' separation of the sexes was later followed by more political empowerment of women in communities like Oneida, Nashoba, and Hopedale. Racial equality was the norm at Hopedale, the mission of Nashoba, and a practice of

> The Shakers' separation of the sexes was later followed by more political empowerment of women in communities like Oneida, Nashoba, and Hopedale.

most other religious and secular communities—or at least one of their dreams.

Thus, while the religious communities were generally patriarchal, hierarchical, and authoritarian, they were also generally economic egalitarians and provided a rich intellectual, religious, and cultural life for all members. While Brook Farm and New Harmony specifically addressed the problem of balancing mental and physical labor, all the communities gave greater dignity to labor than was available in the wider society.

Even though many women remained tied to traditional occupations, communes like Oneida, the Shakers, Hopedale, New Harmony, and Brook Farm tried to equalize the reward system, and encourage more active political participation. The secular groups took particular care to empower elements of their communities that were disenfranchised in the world around them. Formal participation was extended beyond the white, male, property-owning class to include women, blacks, and poor people. Variations of New England town-meeting democracy were developed in nineteenth-century intentional communities just as this form of community empowerment was beginning to disappear elsewhere.

Intentional communities of the last century had dreams of creating better lifestyles for their members. On the whole, they succeeded in realizing their dreams—some for only a short time, others for generation after generation after generation. This rich American heritage will provide inspiration for many future generations of communitarians as the quest for perfection continues. ⚙

A Look at Student Housing Cooperatives

by Deborah Altus, University of Kansas, Lawrence, Kansas

Student housing cooperatives provide an ideal opportunity for members to learn skills for intentional community living. In a student housing cooperative, members share living quarters that they themselves manage. Resident self-management provides co-op members with a degree of autonomy often coveted by their dormitory-residing counterparts. But with autonomy comes the responsibility of managing a household in which members play the dual roles of tenant and landlord. While this level of responsibility may be unwelcome to some, many student co-op members enjoy the opportunity to learn skills ranging from baking bread and repairing faucets to overseeing financial records and running group meetings.

Student housing cooperatives offer the immediate tangible benefit of cutting living costs. But, in the long run, the less tangible benefits received from group living and member management probably outweigh any direct financial savings. Co-op members live in a situation that requires them to share resources, set and work toward goals, make decisions, reach compromises, and learn how to get along with each other. The active, daily practice of cooperation that goes on in student housing co-ops prepares members for a life beyond the ivory tower that can be both individually rewarding and helpful to the broader community.

The Six Cooperative Principles

The roots of student housing cooperatives can be traced back to a group of weavers in mid-nineteenth-century England, the Rochdale Society of Equitable Pioneers. They formed a cooperative business to escape from the horrendous conditions in the factories where they worked and also to gain greater control over their lives. They established a set of principles, six of which are practiced today by cooperatives around the world: open membership; one member, one vote; limited return on share capital; not-for-profit operation; continuous education, and cooperation among cooperatives.[1] Although student housing cooperatives vary widely in their practices, most follow these six principles.

Rochdale-model cooperative housing in the United States dates back to the late 1800s to several apartment associations that operated cooperatively in New York City.[2] Students first became involved in the cooperative movement around the same period, as shown by the founding of the Harvard Cooperative Society in 1882. A few student housing cooperatives opened their doors around the turn of the century, with Northwestern University opening what may have been the first student housing co-op in 1886.[3] The first wave of student housing co-ops typically served self-supporting women students for whom economical housing was essential to remaining in school.

Deborah Altus is a cooperative movement historian. She is an active board member with the Communal Studies Association, a former Fellowship for Intentional Community alternate board member, and she served as the guest editor of the spring 1994 issue of Communities magazine on the theme of "Women in Community: Yesterday and Today." A former member of several housing cooperatives, Deborah remains active in her local food co-op. She works as a researcher at the KU Gerontology Center where she studies shared housing arrangements for older people. Deborah gratefully acknowledges Commonwealth Terrace Co-op, Falcon Heights, Minnesota, for their financial support of her research.

Student Housing Co-ops for Women

The Universities of Wisconsin, Michigan, and Kansas all offered cooperative housing for self-supporting women students during the teens and 1920s. Although financial concerns were an important deciding factor for women to join these co-ops, the residents clearly reaped additional benefits. Helen Hanely, a student housing co-op member in 1920, described the benefits as she saw them: "A cooperative house...is an advantage to a Freshman girl because she has the opportunity to become readily acquainted with a large group of girls. Besides lessening expense, the girls produce a home atmosphere which to me means a great deal....Each girl in the house must give and take as circumstances dictate, and in this way, she learns the spirit of cooperation."[4]

Indeed, membership in Helen's co-op, the Wita Wentin House, was so meaningful to members that a group of the women kept up a round-robin letter for 60 years following their residence at the co-op.

The number of student housing cooperatives grew rapidly during the 1930s, but, despite conventional wisdom, the depression was not the sole motivating factor for starting new co-ops. The students who began the co-ops were concerned not only with the economics of cooperation but with pressing social issues ranging from peace to racism. Some were inspired by the teachings of Toyohiko Kagawa, a Japanese clergyman who preached that cooperatives were the foundation for world peace.[5] In the 1940s, racially integrated student housing co-ops began to appear on college campuses across the nation and were dubbed "a triumph over racial superstition and prejudice."[6] In many cases, these co-ops offered the first racially integrated housing on campus.

Jayhawk Co-op members at the University of Kansas pose for their graduation picture in the 1940s.

Luther Buchele

173

Sunflower House members today.

Today's Campus Co-ops

Student housing cooperatives remain active on college campuses across North America, and, in some places, are expanding. At the University of California, Berkeley, 1,220 students live in cooperative houses, and at the University of Minnesota, 500 students are housed in cooperative apartments. The Inter-Cooperative Council at the University of Michigan houses 560 students in co-ops, while 811 students live cooperatively at the University of Texas. In Waterloo, Ontario, 984 students at the University of Waterloo live in cooperatives, and co-ops house over 1,200 students in Toronto, Ontario.[7]

Student housing cooperatives differ widely from place to place. Some co-ops are small, homey groups, housing only a dozen or so students. Others are enormous high-rises, serving hundreds of members. Some co-ops have a long history of leftist political involvement, dating back to 1930s socialist activities. Others, like some of the farm-affiliated co-op houses in the Midwest, are more conservative.

North American Students of Cooperation

The organization of student housing cooperatives goes beyond the local level. Students have formed a binational cooperative organization, the North American Students of Cooperation, or NASCO, which provides education, development, and support services for student cooperatives around the United States and Canada. NASCO's precursor, NASCL (the North American Student Cooperative League) started during the co-op boom in the 1940s. The energy of NASCL members compensated for slim budgets (NASCL operated for a time out of a broom closet in a co-op house at the University of Kansas), and the league played an active role in organizing cooperatives throughout North America in the 1940s and 50s.[8] After remaining dormant for about a decade, NASCL was rejuvenated in 1968 in the form of NASCO—an organization that has been energetically promoting student cooperatives for over 25 years.

NASCO offers many important services to its member co-ops.[9] It began the Campus Cooperative Development Corporation, which has helped to establish co-ops at a number of different universities over the past decade. NASCO offers a yearly institute, where co-opers from across North America come to learn about the principles and practices of consumer cooperation, to share ideas, to enjoy each other's company, and to renew their commitment to a cooperative society.

NASCO Networks with Other Types of Intentional Communities

NASCO also offers a summer internship program that places student co-op members in short-term jobs in the cooperative sector, including other intentional communities. These internships not only further the intern's cooperative education, but they provide the hosts with enthusiastic workers who are eager to promote the cooperative movement. NASCO summer interns helped to organize the Celebration of Community conference in 1993, and a former NASCO member serves on the board of the Fellowship for Intentional Community (FIC). Members of both organizations have attended each other's meetings to establish wider networks.

The recent cooperation between NASCO and the FIC is exciting. In the past, the intentional communities and cooperative movements—despite their similarities—have often followed separate paths. In fact, the cooperative movement has sometimes deliberately dissociated itself from communitarian activity—a practice dating back to James Peter Warbasse, the first president of the Cooperative League of the United States of America. Warbasse wanted the cooperative movement to be free from the negative public opinion sometimes accompanying communal activities.[10]

For nearly a century, student housing cooperatives have been a presence on college campuses. They have survived tumultuous events in our society—several wars, the Depression, student uprisings—to represent one of the more durable forms of student housing. Amid the enormous problems facing society today, the student cooperative movement serves as an important reminder of the benefits of pooling resources, energy, and talent for the common good.

Endnotes

1. Sekerak, E., and A. Danforth, *Consumer Cooperation: The Heritage and the Dream* (Santa Clara, CA: Consumers Cooperative Publishing, 1980). Provides a good overview of consumer cooperation.

2. Siegler, R., and H.J. Levy, "Brief History of Cooperative Housing," *Cooperative Housing Journal* (1986), 12–19.

3. Stiebeling, H., *Survey of Student Housing Cooperatives* (Emporia, KS: Kansas State Normal School, 1921).

4. Hanely, H.A., "How 3,400 K.U. Students Are Living: As the Students Tell It," *The University of Kansas Newsletter*, 20(4) (1920), 1.

5. Schildgen, R., *Toyohiko Kagawa: Apostle of Love and Social Justice* (Berkeley, CA: Centenary Books, 1988). Describes the work of Kagawa in detail.

6. *Central League of Campus Co-ops* (Kansas City, MO: Consumers Cooperative Association, September 1, 1947). I am grateful to Jim Jones, Executive Director of the Inter-Cooperative Council at the University of Michigan, for providing me with a copy of this pamphlet.

7. *1991–1992 Guide to Campus Co-ops*, (Ann Arbor, MI: NASCO).

8. Buchele, Luther, former executive secretary of NASCL and former general manager of the Inter-Cooperative Council, University of Michigan, in personal conversations about NASCL and early student housing cooperatives.

9. North American Students of Cooperation, Box 7715, University of Michigan, Ann Arbor, MI 48107, 313-663-0889. The NASCO main office is in the University of Michigan Student Union.

10. Spann, E. K. *Brotherly Tomorrows: Movements for a Cooperative Society in America, 1820–1920* (New York: Columbia University, 1989), 268–269.

(ADVERTISEMENT)

About the Maps

*T*o our delight, we have so many communities to list that we need nine pages to show the ones in North America. The gray boxes overlaying the U.S. map below will give you an idea of the area covered by each of the following eight pages. The maps of Canadian and Mexican communities are on page 186.

Because we have much fewer off-continent listings, we are not supplying maps for communities abroad. However, we do provide lists of all communities in this book sorted geographically. The North American Community List begins on page 187, and is sorted first by country, then alphabetically by state or province. The International Communities List is found on page 344, and is sorted alphabetically by country.

For ease of identification, we have placed community names directly on the maps. For economy of space, we have shortened community names to twelve characters or less and included this abbreviation in the Charts, along with the community's full name, for reference.

While we have done all we reasonably can to insure accuracy in locating communities, the scale of these maps is large and positions are approximate. For your convenience, we have indicated with light gray lines the locations of interstate highways. While these maps may be reliably used to rough out a travel plan, we strongly encourage you to get full directions from each community you intend to visit and not rely solely on these maps to get you to anyone's front door.

The map below gives a graphic depiction of how communities in this directory are distributed in the U.S. It is tempting to interpret this as representative of the strength of interest in alternative living, yet we caution you against drawing conclusions too quickly.

On the one hand, the maps show concentrations of community activity in several regions—up and down the whole West Coast; throughout New England and upstate New York; around the Blue Ridge Mountains of Virginia and Smoky Mountains of North Carolina; along the Front Range in Colorado. We believe this to be an accurate indication of what's happening in those areas.

On the other hand, there are no communities shown in the Northern Plains states, and this masks the existence of hundreds of long-standing Hutterite communities, which are covered in this directory under a group listing in the Resource section but not listed individually (a rough distribution of the 392 North American Hutterite communities is indicated on the map below and the Canadian map on page 186). Further, we are aware of several existing or forming groups in the Utah, Idaho, Montana, Wyoming region which prefer to keep a low profile and hence are not listed. The maps would suggest there is not much community activity in that area, yet we believe it to be otherwise.

So please be careful which thousand words you extract from the picture below.

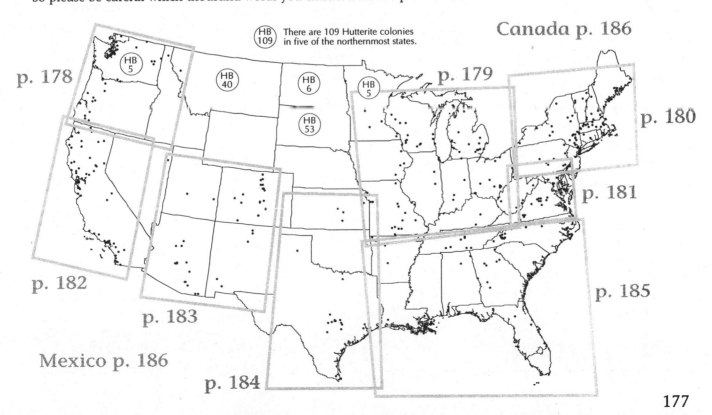

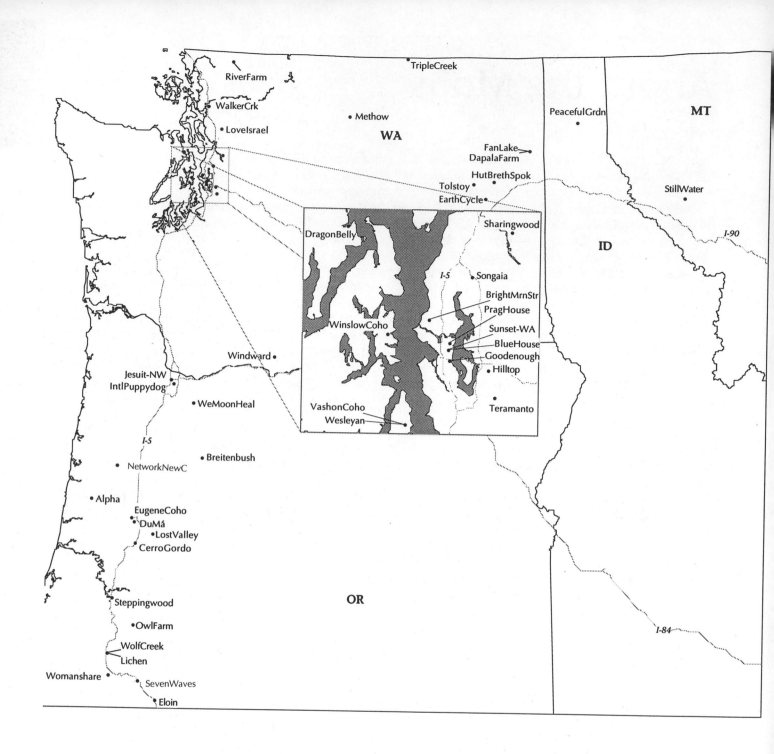

RiverFarm

WalkerCrk

LoveIsrael

TripleCreek

Methow

WA

FanLake
DapalaFarm

HutBrethSpok

PeacefulGrdn

MT

StillWater

I-90

ID

Tolstoy
EarthCycle

Sharingwood

DragonBelly

Songaia

I-5

BrightMrnStr
PragHouse

Sunset-WA
BlueHouse
Goodenough

Hilltop

WinslowCoho

Windward

Jesuit-NW
IntlPuppydog

WeMoonHeal

VashonCoho
Wesleyan

Teramanto

I-5

Breitenbush

NetworkNewC

Alpha

EugeneCoho
DuMá
LostValley
CerroGordo

OR

I-84

Steppingwood

OwlFarm

WolfCreek
Lichen

Womanshare
SevenWaves
Eloin

Northwest

← EFE

MN

• ChesterCrk

• NorWoodVegan

• Camphill-MN

MI

• Dorea

WI

• SongOfMorng

TwinCitCoho •

• Riverside-WI

• PrairieRidge

• Starland

• ChristineCn

• MikecoRehtl

DOE-Farm

• Dreamtime

• NewJahRuslm

WiscoyVall

ZephyrVall

• DanceWatter

HighWind

LandStewCen

YaharaLindn

Wellsprg-WI

MI

• BalancdLife

IonExchange

MarthasCoop

• MadisonCoop

FarmHome

SkyWoods

Jesuit-Midw

CircleSanct

WomensCoop

Sichlassen

Rivendell

FriendsLake

InterntlCoop

CasaMaria

HouseLavendn

Vivekan-MI

Osterweil

InterCoop-MI

• Communia

ICA-Chicago

RebaPlace

LakeVillage

Elderwood

WhiteHouse

• HawkCircle

JesusPeopUSA

Maxworks

Heartlight

HeiWaHouse

IA

Vivekan-IL

Remar

• RiverCity

Qumbya

CathWork-OH

CoventCmty

QuakerHouse

OberlinStuCo

• Maharishi

IL

• Stelle

IN

OH

• Sandhill

• CenPeaceLif

Greenhous-OH

Edges

NewVrndaban

CmtyInStJo

CasaGrande

Currents

Sunflower-OH

YellowHouse

ValeThe

SusBAnthony

FarValley

KS

Hearthaven

DeepWoods

Glendower

EsseneSkoola

NewJerusalm

EdenSanct

NewCovent

HarvestHills

StudtCoopOrg

CarpentrVil

Sunflower-KS

Sheprdsfld

• Lothlor-IN

RainbHouse

Sunnyside

SistrDivProv

• Padanaram

VeiledCliff

WV

OneThouSmPhm

Meramac

• Zirkle

MO

Goodwater

HighHorizons

Sassafras

ShiningWater

KY

ZionsOrder

SevenSprgs

• FolkCorps

Sweetwater

• Greenwood

AnandaMrga

CranberryCrk

• Shiloh

• EastWind

• SpiralWimm

Midwest

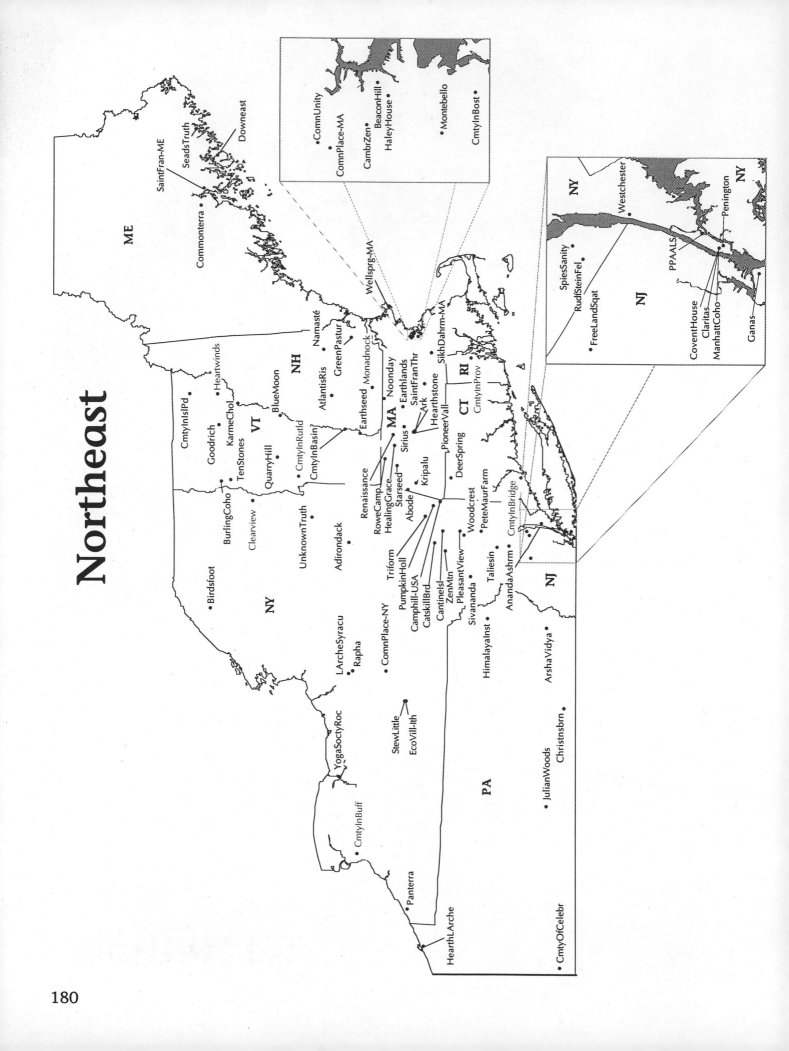

Northeast

ME

SeadsTruth
SaintFran-ME
Downeast
Commonterra

Inset (upper, Boston area):
CommUnity
CommPlace-MA
CambrZen
BeaconHill
HaleyHouse
Montebello
CmtyInBost
Wellsprg-MA

Inset (right, NY/NJ area):
NY
Westchester
Penington
NY
SpiesSanity
RudfSteinFel
PPAALS
FreeLandSqat
NJ
CoventHouse
Claritas
ManhattCoho
Ganas

VT / NH / MA area:
Heartwinds
CmtyInIslPd
Goodrich
KarmeChol
TenStones
QuarryHill
BlueMoon
CmtyInRutld
CmtyInBasin
Namasté
GreenPastur
AtlantisRis
Earthseed
Monadnock
Noonday
Earthlands
SaintFranThr
Ark
Hearthstone
SikhDahrm-MA
Sirius
PioneerVall
CmtyInProv
RI
CT
DeerSpring
PeteMaurFarm
CmtyInBridge
Renaissance
RoweCamp
HealingGrace
Starseed
Abode
Kripalu
Woodcrest
AnandaAshrm

NY area:
Birdsfoot
BurlingCoho
Clearview
UnknownTruth
Adirondack
LArcheSyracu
Rapha
CommPlace-NY
Triform
PumpkinHoll
Camphill-USA
CatskillBrd
CantineIsl
ZenMtn
PleasantView
Sivananda
Taliesin
HimalayaInst
YogaSoctyRoc
StewLittle
EcoVill-Ith

PA area:
CmtyInBuff
Panterra
HearthLArche
YogaSoctyRoc
JulianWoods
Christnsbrn
CmtyOfCelebr

NJ:
ArshaVidya

180

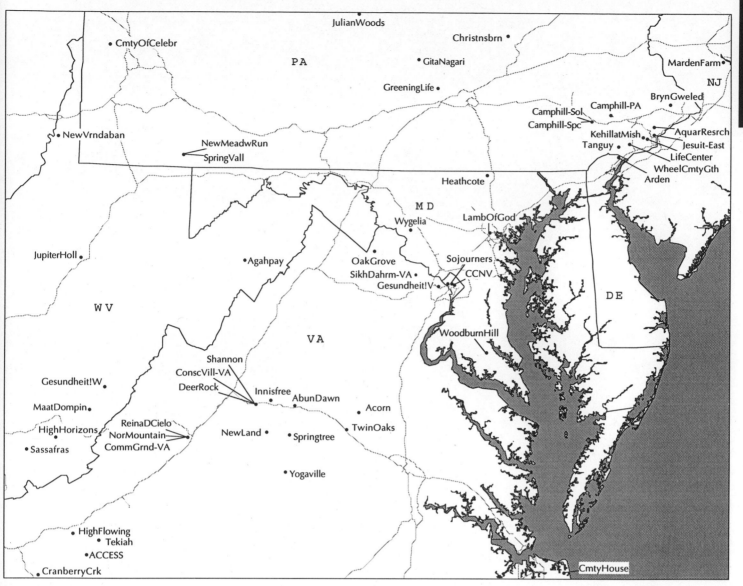

JulianWoods

Christnsbrn •

CmtyOfCelebr

PA

MardenFarm •

• GitaNagari

NJ

GreeningLife •

BrynGweled •

Camphill-Sol

Camphill-PA

NewVrndaban

Camphill-Spc

KehillatMish

AquarResrch

NewMeadwRun

Tanguy

Jesuit-East

SpringVall

LifeCenter

WheelCmtyGth

Heathcote •

Arden

MD

LambOfGod

Wygelia •

JupiterHoll •

• Agahpay

OakGrove

Sojourners

SikhDahrm-VA •

CCNV

Gesundheit!V •

WV

DE

VA

WoodburnHill

Shannon

ConscVill-VA

DeerRock

Innisfree •

Gesundheit!W •

AbunDawn

• Acorn

MaatDompin •

HighHorizons •

ReinaDCielo

TwinOaks •

NorMountain

NewLand •

• Springtree

• Sassafras

CommGrnd-VA

• Yogaville

HighFlowing

• Tekiah

•ACCESS

• CranberryCrk

CmtyHouse

Mid-Atlantic

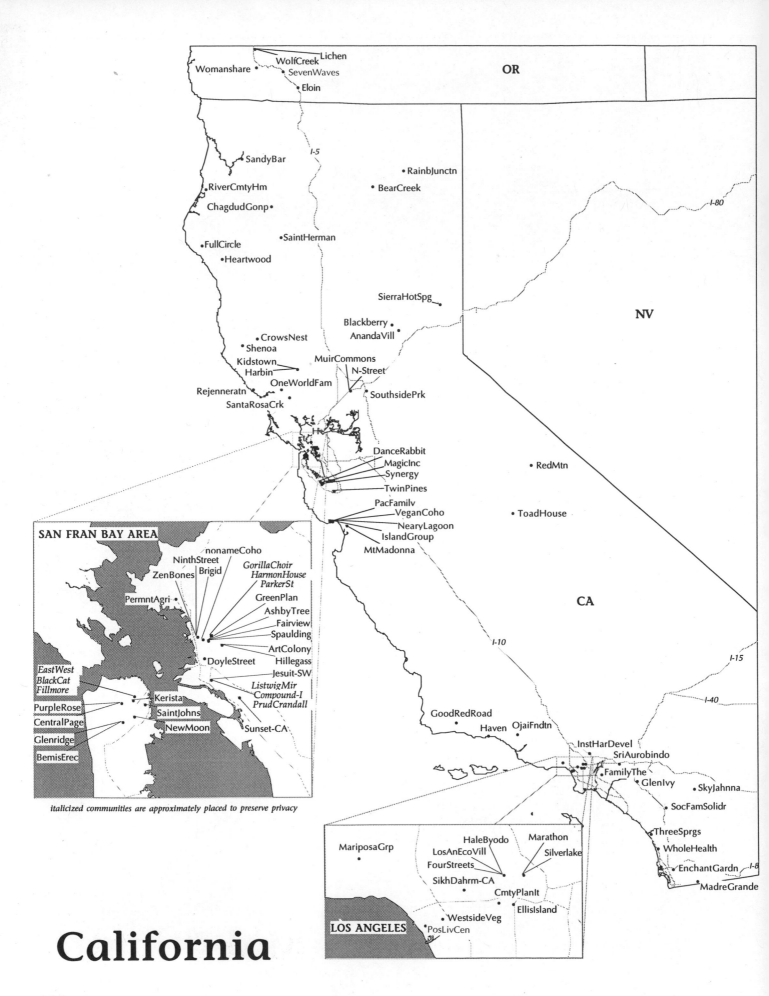

OR

NV

CA

Lichen
WolfCreek
Womanshare
SevenWaves
Eloin

SandyBar

RiverCmtyHm
ChagdudGonp•

•SaintHerman

RainbJunctn
BearCreek

FullCircle
Heartwood

SierraHotSpg

I-5

I-80

CrowsNest
Shenoa
Kidstown
Harbin
OneWorldFam
Rejenneratn
SantaRosaCrk

Blackberry
AnandaVill

MuirCommons
N-Street
SouthsidePrk

DanceRabbit
MagicInc
Synergy
TwinPines
PacFamily
VeganCoho
NearyLagoon
IslandGroup
MtMadonna

RedMtn

ToadHouse

I-10

I-15

I-40

GoodRedRoad
Haven OjaiFndtn

InstHarDevel
SriAurobindo
FamilyThe
GlenIvy   SkyJahnna

SocFamSolidr

ThreeSprgs
WholeHealth
EnchantGardn   I-8
MadreGrande

SAN FRAN BAY AREA

nonameCoho
NinthStreet
ZenBones Brigid
GorillaChoir
HarmonHouse
ParkerSt
GreenPlan
PermntAgri•
AshbyTree
Fairview
Spaulding
ArtColony
DoyleStreet Hillegass
Jesuit-SW
ListwigMir
Compound-I
PrudCrandall
EastWest
BlackCat
Fillmore
Kerista
PurpleRose
SaintJohns
CentralPage
NewMoon
Glenridge
Sunset-CA
BemisErec

italicized communities are approximately placed to preserve privacy

LOS ANGELES

MariposaGrp

HaleByodo
LosAnEcoVill   Marathon
FourStreets   Silverlake
SikhDahrm-CA
CmtyPlanIt
EllisIsland
WestsideVeg
PosLivCen

California

182

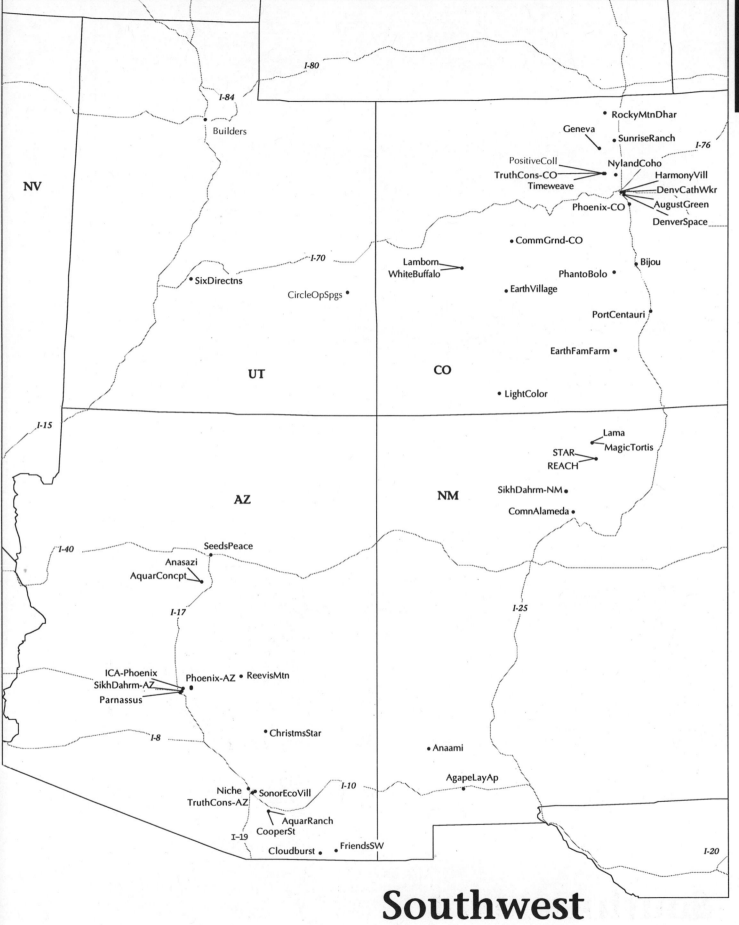

NV

UT

CO

AZ

NM

Builders

I-80

I-84

I-76

RockyMtnDhar

Geneva

SunriseRanch

PositiveColl

NylandCoho

TruthCons-CO

HarmonyVill

Timeweave

DenvCathWkr

Phoenix-CO

AugustGreen

DenverSpace

CommGrnd-CO

I-70

Bijou

SixDirectns

Lamborn

WhiteBuffalo

PhantoBolo

CircleOpSpgs

EarthVillage

PortCentauri

EarthFamFarm

LightColor

Lama

MagicTortis

STAR

REACH

SikhDahrm-NM

ComnAlameda

I-40

SeedsPeace

Anasazi

AquarConcpt

I-17

I-25

ICA-Phoenix

Phoenix-AZ

ReevisMtn

SikhDahrm-AZ

Parnassus

ChristmsStar

I-8

Anaami

AgapeLayAp

Niche

SonorEcoVill

I-10

TruthCons-AZ

AquarRanch

CooperSt

I–19

Cloudburst

FriendsSW

I-20

I-15

Southwest

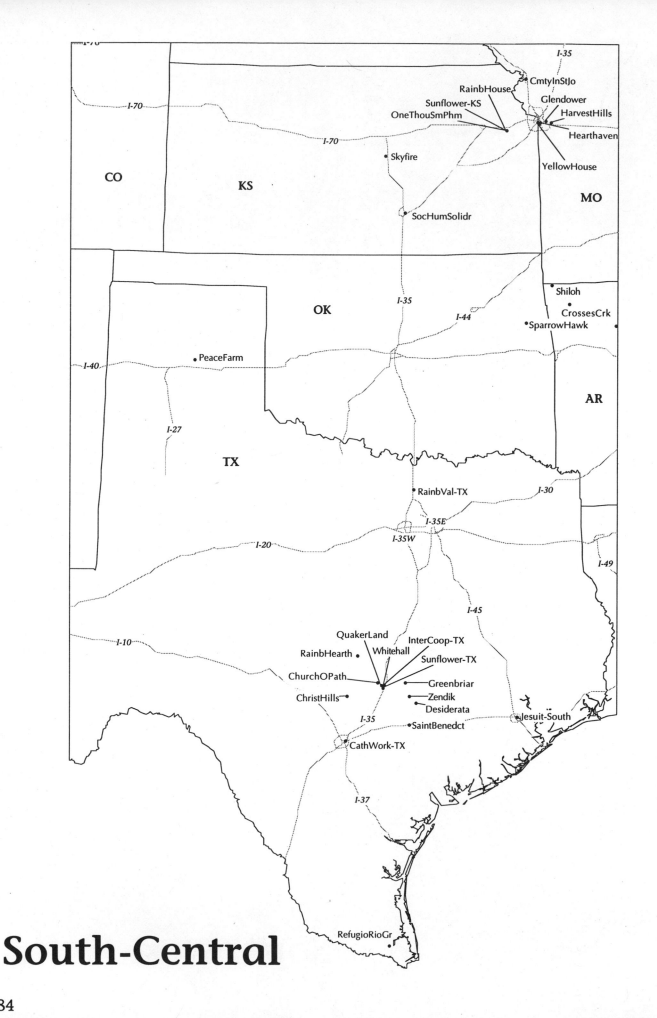

CO

KS

MO

I-70

I-70

I-70

CmtyInStJo

RainbHouse

Glendower

Sunflower-KS

HarvestHills

OneThouSmPhm

Hearthaven

Skyfire

YellowHouse

SocHumSolidr

I-35

OK

Shiloh

I-44

CrossesCrk

SparrowHawk

AR

PeaceFarm

I-40

I-27

TX

RainbVal-TX

I-30

I-35E

I-20

I-35W

I-49

I-45

I-10

QuakerLand

InterCoop-TX

RainbHearth

Whitehall

Sunflower-TX

ChurchOPath

Greenbriar

ChristHills

Zendik

Desiderata

Jesuit-South

I-35

SaintBenedct

CathWork-TX

I-37

RefugioRioGr

South-Central

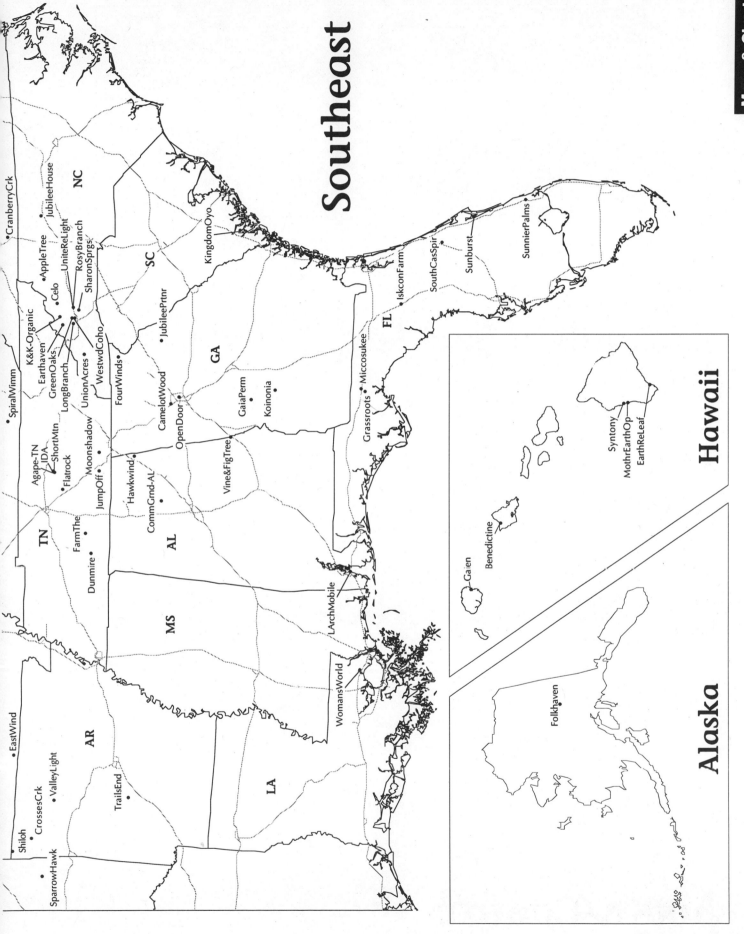

Southeast

Hawaii

Alaska

NC
SC
GA
FL
TN
AL
MS
AR
LA

CranberryCrk
JubileeHouse
AppleTree
UniteReLight
RosyBranch
SharonSprgs
Celo
SpiralWimm
K&K-Organic
Earthaven
GreenOaks
LongBranch
UnionAcres
WestwdCoho
FourWinds
KingdomOyo
JubileePrtnr
CamelotWood
OpenDoor
GaiaPerm
Koinonia
Vine&FigTree
Grassroots
Miccosukee
IskconFarm
SouthCasSpir
Sunburst
SunnierPalms
Agape-TN
IDA
ShortMtn
Flatrock
Moonshadow
JumpOff
Hawkwind
CommGrnd-AL
FarmThe
Dunmire
LArchMobile
WomansWorld
EastWind
CrossesCrk
ValleyLight
TrailsEnd
Shiloh
SparrowHawk

Gaien
Benedictine
Syntony
MothrEarthOp
EarthReLeaf

Folkhaven

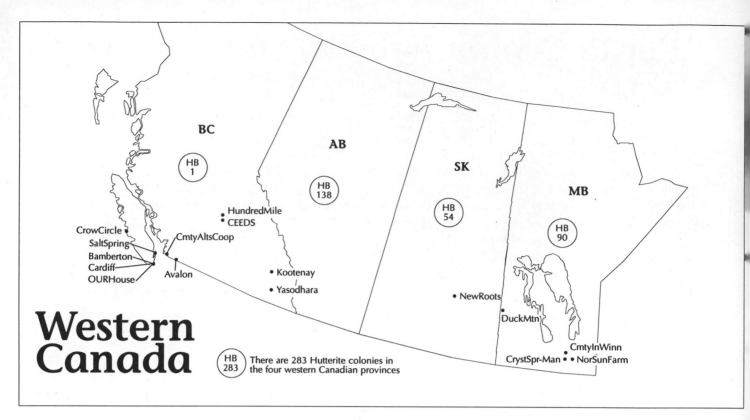

Western Canada

BC

HB 1

AB

HB 138

SK

HB 54

MB

HB 90

HundredMile
CEEDS

CrowCircle
SaltSpring
Bamberton
Cardiff
OURHouse

CmtyAltsCoop

Avalon

Kootenay

Yasodhara

NewRoots

DuckMtn

CmtyInWinn
CrystSpr-Man • • NorSunFarm

HB 283   There are 283 Hutterite colonies in the four western Canadian provinces

Eastern Canada

ON

PQ

LArchHomefi

NS

Morninglory

Dragonfly • • Lothlor

Stonehedge

Philoxia • • Headlands

Rowanwood
KingView
TorontoTORI

LArchDaybrk
Spiricoasis
BuddhistSoc

Mexico

Krutsio

LosHorcones

Arcoiris

Huehuecoyotl

Key to Communities by State/Province

WHAT FOLLOWS is a list of North American communities alphabetized by state or province within each country. If you are interested in looking for communities within a state, begin your search here and then look up the information in the cross-reference Charts (a highlighter is handy for this) or in the Listings.

The abbreviated community names are used in the Maps (p. 178), in the Index (p. 418), and are also used on right-hand pages in the cross-reference Charts (p. 190) where the left-hand page contaits the full names.

For each entry in this list, the abbreviated community name is followed by a comma, and then the town associated with the community's mailing address.

UNITED STATES

AK–Alaska
Folkhaven, Wasilla

AL–Alabama
CommGrnd-AL, Blountsville
Hawkwind, Valley Head
LArchMobile, Mobile
Vine&FigTree, Lanett

AR–Arkansas
CrossesCrk, Springdale
Shiloh, Sulphur Springs
TrailsEnd, Hot Springs
ValleyLight, Deer

AZ–Arizona
Anasazi, Snowflake
AquarConcpt, W Sedona
AquarRanch, Vail
ChristmsStar, Winkleman
Cloudburst, Bisbee
CooperSt, Vail
FriendsSW, McNeal
ICA-Phoenix, Phoenix
Niche, Tucson
Parnassus, Phoenix
Phoenix-AZ, Phoenix
ReevisMtn, Roosevelt
SeedsPeace, Flagstaff
SikhDahrm-AZ, Phoenix
SonorEcoVill, Tuscon
TruthCons-AZ, Tucson

CA–California
AnandaVill, Nevada City
ArtColony, Berkeley
AshbyTree, Berkeley
BearCreek, Fall River Mills
BemisErec, San Francisco
BlackCat, San Francisco
Blackberry, North San Juan
BlackOak, (N California)
Brigid, Berkeley
CentralPage, San Francisco
ChagdudGonp, Junction City
CmtyPlanIt, Los Angeles
Compound-I, Oakland
CrowsNest, Ukiah
DanceRabbit, Menlo Park
DoyleStreet, Emeryville
EastWest, San Francisco
EllisIsland, Los Angeles
EnchantGardn, San Diego
Fairview, Berkeley
FamilyThe, Whittier

Fillmore, San Francisco
FourStreets, Los Angeles
FullCircle, Honeydew
GlenIvy, Corona
Glenridge, San Francisco
GoodRedRoad, Solvang
GorillaChoir, Berkeley
GreenPlan, Berkeley
HaleByodo, Los Angeles
Harbin, Middletown
HarmonHouse, Berkeley
Haven, Santa Barbara
Heartwood, Garberville
Hillegass, Berkeley
InstHarDevel, Flintridge
IslandGroup, Santa Cruz
Jesuit-SW, Oakland
Kerista, San Francisco
Kidstown, Middletown
ListwigMir, Oakland
LosAnEcoVill, Los Angeles
MadreGrande, Dulzura
MagicInc, Stanford
Marathon, Los Angeles
MariposaGrp, Topanga
MonansRill, (N California)
MtMadonna, Watsonville
MuirCommons, Davis
N-Street, Davis
NearyLagoon, Santa Cruz
NewMoon, San Francisco
NinthStreet, Berkeley
nonameCoho, Berkeley
OjaiFndtn, Ojai
OneWorldFam, Santa Rosa
PacFamily, Santa Cruz
ParkerSt, Berkeley
PermntAgri, Richmond
PosLivCen, Venice
PrudCrandall, Oakland
PurpleRose, San Francisco
RainbJunctn, Adin
RedMtn, Crowley Lake
Rejenneratn, Jenner
RiverCmtyHm, Arcata
SaintHerman, Platina
SaintJohns, San Francisco
SandyBar, Orleans
SantaRosaCrk, Santa Rosa
Shenoa, Philo
SierraHotSpg, Sierraville
SikhDahrm-CA, Los Angeles
Silverlake, Los Angeles

SkyJahnna, Idyllwild
SocFamSolidr, Temecula
SouthsidePrk, Sacramento
Spaulding, Berkeley
SriAurobindo, Lodi
Sunset-CA, Oakland
Synergy, Stanford
ThreeSprgs, Oceanside
ToadHouse, San Francisco
TwinPines, Santa Clara
VeganCoho, San Francisco
WestsideVeg, Los Angeles
WholeHealth, Cardiff
ZenBones, Berkeley

CO–Colorado
AugustGreen, Denver
Bijou, Colorado Springs
CommGrnd-CO, Aspen
DenvCathWkr, Denver
DenverSpace, Denver
EarthFamFarm, Gardner
EarthVillage, Gunnison
Geneva, Boulder
HarmonyVill, Golden
Lamborn, Paonia
LightColor, Pagosa Springs
NylandCoho, Lafayette
PhantoBolo, Cripple Creek
Phoenix-CO, Englewood
PortCentauri, Pueblo
PositiveColl, Boulder
RockyMtnDhar, Red Feather Lk
SunriseRanch, Loveland
Timeweave, Boulder
TruthCons-CO, Boulder
WhiteBuffalo, Paonia

CT–Connecticut
DeerSpring, Norfolk

DC–District of Columbia
CCNV, Washington
Finders, Washington
Sojourners, Washington

DE–Delaware
Arden, Arden

FL–Florida
Grassroots, Tallahassee
IskconFarm, Alachua
Miccosukee, Tallahassee
SouthCasSpir, Cassadaga
Sunburst, Cocoa
SunnierPalms, Ft Pierce

GA–Georgia
CamelotWood, Marietta
FourWinds, Tiger
GaiaPerm, Mauk
JubileePrtnr, Comer
Koinonia, Americus
OpenDoor, Atlanta

HI–Hawaii
Benedictine, Waialua
EarthReLeaf, Naalehu
Gaien, Kapaa
MothrEarthOp, Honaunau
Syntony, Captain Cook

IA–Iowa
Communia, Iowa City
HawkCircle, Tipton
IonExchange, Harpers Ferry
Maharishi, Fairfield
RiverCity, Iowa City

ID–Idaho
PeacefulGrdn, Sandpoint

IL–Illinois
CasaGrande, Urbana
CoventCmty, Chicago
EsseneSkoola, Golden Eagle
ICA-Chicago, Chicago
JesusPeopUSA, Chicago
Maxworks, Chicago
QuakerHouse, Chicago
Qumbya, Chicago
RebaPlace, Evanston
Remar, Chicago
Stelle, Stelle
Vivekan-IL, Chicago

IN–Indiana
CenPeaceLif, Muncie
Lothlor-IN, Bloomington
Padanaram, Williams

KS–Kansas
OneThouSmPhm,
RainbHouse, Lawrence
Skyfire, Lindsborg
SocHumSolidr, Wichita
Sunflower-KS, Lawrence
YellowHouse, Kansas City

KY–Kentucky
Folkcorps, Berea
SpiralWimm, Monticello

LA–Louisiana
WomansWorld, Madisonville

MA–Massachusetts
Ark, Amherst
BeaconHill, Boston
CambrZen, Cambridge
ComnPlace-MA, Cambridge
ComnUnity, Somerville
CmtyInBost, Dorchester Center
CmtyinHyan, Hyannis
Earthlands, Petersham
HaleyHouse, Boston
HealingGrace, Shelburne Falls
Hearthstone, Shutesbury
Kripalu, Lenox
Montebello, Jamaica Plain
Noonday, Winchendon Springs
PioneerVall, Amherst
Renaissance, Gill
RoweCamp, Rowe
SaintFranThr, Worcester
SikhDahrm-MA, Millis
Sirius, Shutesbury
Starseed, Savoy
Wellsprg-MA, Gloucester

MD–Maryland
Heathcote, Freeland
LambOfGod, Baltimore
WoodburnHill, Mechanicsville
Wygelia, Adamstown

ME–Maine
Commonterra, Monroe
Downeast, Bar Harbor
SaintFran-ME, Orland
SeadsTruth, Harrington

MI–Michigan
BalancdLife, Davisburg
Elderwood, Manchester
FriendsLake, Chelsea
Heartlight, Sturgis
HeiWaHouse, Ann Arbor
InterCoop-MI, Ann Arbor
Jesuit-Midw, Detroit
LakeVillage, Kalamazoo
LandStewCen, Columbiaville
MikecoRehtl, Big Rapids
Osterweil, Ann Arbor
Rivendell, Lansing
SkyWoods, Muskegon Heights
SongOfMorng, Vanderbilt
TorontoTORI, Ann Arbor
Vivekan-MI, Fennville
WhiteHouse, Ann Arbor

187

Communities Directory

MN–Minnesota
Camphill-MN, Sauk Centre
ChesterCrk, Duluth
Starland, Gibbon
TwinCitCoho, Minneapolis
WiscoyVall, Winona
ZephyrVall, Rushford

MO–Missouri
AnandaMrga, Willow Springs
CmtyInStJo, St Joseph
EastWind, Tecumseh
Glendower, Independence
Goodwater, Bourbon
Greenwood, Mountain View
HarvestHills, Independence
Hearthaven, Kansas City
Meramac, Bourbon
Sandhill, Rutledge
SevenSprgs, Mountain Grove
Sheprdsfld, Fulton
ShiningWater, Fredericktown
SistrDivProv, St. Louis
Sunnyside, Mokane
Sweetwater, Mansfield
ZionsOrder, Mansfield

MT–Montana
StillWater, Plains

NC–North Carolina
AppleTree, Blowing Rock
Celo, Burnsville
Earthaven, Marshall
GreenOaks, Asheville
JubileeHouse, Winston-Salem
K&K-Organic, Marshall
LongBranch, Leicester
RosyBranch, Black Mountain
SharonSprgs, Fairview
UnionAcres, Whittier
UniteReLight, Black Mountain
WestwdCoho, Asheville

ND–North Dakota
EFE, Grand Forks

NH–New Hampshire
AtlantisRis, Bradford
CmtyInLancas, Lancaster
GreenPastur, Epping
Monadnock, Temple
Namasté, Barnstead

NJ–New Jersey
FreeLandSqat, West Milford
MardenFarm, Somerset

NM–New Mexico
AgapeLayAp, Deming
Anaami, Silver City
ComnAlameda, Santa Fe
Lama, San Cristobal
MagicTortis, San Cristobal
REACH, Taos
SikhDahrm-NM, Espanola
STAR, Taos

NV–Nevada
Builders, Wells

NY–New York
Abode, New Lebanon
Adirondack, Broadalbin
AnandaAshrm, Monroe
Birdsfoot, Canton
Camphill-USA, Copake
Cantinelsl, Saugerties
CatskillBrd, Elka Park
Claritas, New York
Clearview, Moriah
ComnPlace-NY, Truxton
CoventHouse, New York
EcoVill-Ith, Ithaca
Ganas, Staten Island
LArcheSyracu, Syracuse
ManhattCoho, New York
Panterra, Westfield
Penington, New York
PeteMaurFarm, Marlboro
PleasantView, Ulster Park
PPAALS, New York
PumpkinHoll, Craryville
Rapha, Syracuse
RudfSteinFel, Spring Valley
Sivananda, Woodbourne
SpiesSanity, New City
StewLittle, Ithaca
Taliesin, Maybrook
Triform, Hudson
UnknownTruth, Warrensburg
Westchester, Hastings
Woodcrest, Rifton
YogaSoctyRoc, Rochester
ZenMtn, Mt. Tremper

OH–Ohio
CarpentrVil, Athens
CathWork-OH, Cleveland
Currents, Glouster
DeepWoods, S. Bloomingville
EdenSanct, Athens
Edges, Glouster
FarValley, Amesville
Greenhous-OH, Columbus
NewCovent, Athens
NewJerusalm, Cincinnati
OberlinStuCo, Oberlin
RavenRocks, (SE Ohio)
StudtCoopOrg, Athens
Sunflower-OH, Amesville
SusBAnthony, Millfield
ValeThe, Yellow Springs
VeiledCliff, Scottown

OK–Oklahoma
SparrowHawk, Tahlequah

OR–Oregon
Alpha, Deadwood
Breitenbush, Detroit
CerroGordo, Cottage Grove
DuMá, Eugene
Eloin, Ashland
EugeneCoho, Eugene
IntlPuppydog, Portland
Jesuit-NW, Portland
Lichen, Wolf Creek
LostValley, Dexter
NetworkNewC, Philomath
OwlFarm, Days Creek
SevenWaves, Central Point
Steppingwood, Roseburg
WeMoonHeal, Estacada
WolfCreek, Wolf Creek
Womanshare, Grants Pass

PA–Pennsylvania
AquarResrch, Philadelphia
ArshaVidya, Saylorsburg
BrynGweled, Southampton
Camphill-Sol, Glenmoore
Camphill-Spc, Glenmore
Camphill-PA, Kimberton
Christnsbrn, Pitman
CmtyOfCelebr, Aliquippa
GitaNagari, Port Royal
GreeningLife, Shermans Dale
HearthLArche, Erie
Himalayalnst, Honesdale
Jesuit-East, Philadephia
JulianWoods, Julian
KehillatMish, Upper Darby
LifeCenter, Philadelphia
NewMeadwRun, Farmington
SpringVall, Farmington
Tanguy, Glen Mills
WheelCmtyGth, Rose Valley

SC–South Carolina
KingdomOyo, Sheldon

TN–Tennessee
Agape-TN, Liberty
Dunmire, Waynesboro
FarmThe, Summertown
Flatrock, Murfreesboro
IDA, Dowelltown
JumpOff, Sewanee
Moonshadow, Whitwell
ShortMtn, Liberty

TX–Texas
CathWork-TX, San Antonio
ChristHills, Blanco
ChurchOPath, Austin
Desiderata, Smithville
Greenbriar, Elgin
InterCoop-TX, Austin
Jesuit-South, Houston
PeaceFarm, Panhandle
QuakerLand, Ingram
RainbHearth, Burnet
RainbVal-TX, Sanger
RefugioRioGr, Harlingen
SaintBenedct, Waelder
Sunflower-TX, Austin
Whitehall, Austin
Zendik, Bastrop

UT–Utah
SixDirectns, Monroe
CircleOpSpgs, Moab

VA–Virginia
AbunDawn, Check
ACCESS, Floyd
Acorn, Mineral
CommGrnd-VA, Lexington
CmtyHouse, Virginia Beach
ConscVill-VA, Staunton
CranberryCrk, Hillsville
DeerRock, Afton
Gesundheit!V, Arlington
HighFlowing, Riner
Innisfree, Crozet
LightMorn, (Central Virginia)
NewLand, Faber
NorMountain, Lexington
OakGrove, Round Hill
ReinaDCielo, Lexington
Shannon, Afton
SikhDahrm-VA, Herndon
Springtree, Scottsville
Tekiah, Check
TwinOaks, Louisa
Yogaville, Buckingham

VT–Vermont
BlueMoon, South Strafford
BurlingCoho, Burlington
CmtyinBasin, Bellow Falls
CmtyInBello, Bellow Falls
CmtyInBurl, Burlington
CmtyInIslPd, Island Pond
Earthseed, Saxtons River
Goodrich, Hardwick
Heartwinds, Lyndon Center
KarmeChol, Barnet
QuarryHill, Rochester
TenStones, Charlotte

WA–Washington
BlueHouse, Seattle
BrightMrnStr, Seattle
DapalaFarm, Elk
DragonBelly, Pt Ludlow
EarthCycle, Waukon
FanLake, Elk
Goodenough, Seattle
Hilltop, Bellevue
HutBrethSpok, Reardon
LoveIsrael, Arlington
Methow, Twisp
PragHouse, Seattle
RiverFarm, Deming
Sharingwood, Snohomish
Songaia, Bothell
Sunset-WA, Seattle
Teramanto, Renton
Tolstoy, Davenport
TripleCreek, Oroville
VashonCoho, Vashon
WalkerCrk, Mt Vernon
Wesleyan, Vashon Island
Windward, Klickitat
WinslowCoho, Bainbridge Isld

WI–Wisconsin
CasaMaria, Milwaukee
ChristineCn, Willard
CircleSanct, Mt Horeb
DanceWatter, Gays Mills
DOE-Farm, Norwalk
Dorea, Turtle Lake
Dreamtime, Viola
FarmHome, Milwaukee
HighWind, Plymouth
HouseLavendr, Milwaukee
InterntlCoop, Madison
MadisonCoop, Madison
MarthasCoop, Madison
NewJahRuslm, Soldiers Grove
NorWoodVegan, Ashland
PrairieRidge, Fall Creek
Riverside-WI, Colfax
Sichlassen, Milwaukee
Wellsprg-WI, Newburg
WomensCoop, Madison
YaharaLindn, Madison

WV–West Virginia
Agahpay, Moorefield
Gesundheit!W, Hillsboro
HighHorizons, Alderson
JupiterHoll, Weston
MaatDompin, Auto
NewVrndaban, Moundsville
Sassafras, Hinton
Zirkle, West Hamlin

CANADA

BC–British Columbia
Avalon, Clearbrook
Bamberton, Victoria
Cardiff, Victoria
CEEDS, Lone Butte
CmtyAltsCoop, Vancouver
CrowCircle, Tofino
HundredMile, 100 Mile House
Kootenay, Argenta
OURHouse, Victoria
SaltSpring, Salt Spring Island
Yasodhara, Kootnay Bay

MB–Manitoba
CmtyInWinn, Winnipeg
CrystSpr-Man, Ste. Agathe
DuckMtn, Boggy Creek
NorSunFarm, Steinbach

NS–Nova Scotia
LArchHomefi, Wolfville

ONT–Ontario
BuddhistSoc, Toronto
Dragonfly, Lake Saint Peter
Headlands, Stella
KingView, Aurora
LArchDaybrk, Richmond Hin
Lothlor-ONT, Perth
Morninglory, Killaloe
Philoxia, Marlbank
Rowanwood, Oro Station
Spiricoasis, Toronto
Stonehedge, Enterprise

SK–Saskatchawan
NewRoots, Wynyard

MEXICO

Baja Calif. Sur
Krutsio, Guerrero Negro

D.F.
Arcoiris, Cuauhtemoc

Morelos
Huehuecoyotl, Tepoztlan

Sonora
LosHorcones, Hermosillo

Explanation of the Charts

IT ALL BEGAN with a question…or actually, eight pages of questions, distributed to every community we knew. We created and started mailing out questionnaires in 1992 and continued through the beginning of 1995, tinkering all the time with what we asked, and cajoling groups to respond. Our hope was to completely refresh the data published in the previous *Directory*. For the most part we succeeded.

Caveats and Keys

Some information (such as total population) may be outdated quickly, while other figures (such as year founded) will never change. For your convenience, we have indicated the date of the questionnaire responses, as we have done for the Listings (beginning on page 212). We have printed here each community's responses to a set of uniform questions, and are not in a position to verify the accuracy of what a community says about itself. We suggest using the data as a guide to each group's situation as of the date listed.

Empty space indicates that we have no information from the community in that category. Some communities did not send in a questionnaire and thus have blanks in every column. We nonetheless included them here because there is information about them in the Listings section and we didn't want you to inadvertantly miss them, or think that we had information we forgot to include. A grayed-out community name indicates that the community was pulled since the first printing. See the listing for details.

The Dietary section of our questionnaire is an area where we asked more detailed questions at first and later simplified. In view of this, we offer the following amplication of Chart terms: *Community does not allow this in members' diets* became "none." *Not provided/used by community but ok to buy on own or use when away* became "OK." *Eaten/used occasionally* became "some." *Eaten or used daily/often* became "often." *Emphasized by the community* became "yes!"

A Brief History of the Charts

Back when we created the first edition of this directory, we developed a questionnaire asking groups to supply objective answers to what we believed were the most commonly asked initial questions about communities. We had seen attempts at this in prior directories and thought it a good way for people to quickly screen the hundreds of listings for the ones most in alignment with their interests and values.

After receiving the initial responses to our first version of the questionnaire, we developed a profound respect for the profession of surveying; it was hard to craft the questions to get clear and informative answers. Many questions had to be thrown out because groups sensed there was a "correct" answer and they didn't want to be portrayed as "incorrect" (everyone, for example, characterized themselves as supporting a value of voluntary simplicity—no matter how many cars they owned or individual houses they built).

So…we tinkered with the questions and winnowed the answers down to those most usable. Then we faced the challenge of formatting all this painstakingly collected and collated data. The eight pages of dense-packed Chart we ultimately published in the last *Directory* were the most labor-intensive section in the book.

Reader response to the charts was illuminating. For some, it was a gold mine; it was just what they wanted, and they couldn't stop poring over the columns and comparing the figures. For others, it all looked impressive, but they tended to get a headache staring at the numbers and hurried over to the paragraph descriptions.

In short, we got another chance to learn what we already knew: people absorb information in different ways, and charts and symbols are not an easy language for many to converse in.

For this edition, we overhauled the questionnaire right at the start, and enlisted our academic friends with survey experience to better word the questions. Despite this, we *still* had some questions that didn't produce workable answers. We were probably too ambitious in what we wanted to accomplish, and the length of the questionnaire (eight pages!) discouraged careful responses (who has the time?).

What we're saying is that the Charts are a work in progress. We think we've made significant improvements from last time—the layout is less crowded and the data is displayed using abbreviations that seldom need translation—yet we know we're still a ways off from Chart perfection.

Being in the information business, the Fellowship is committed to discovering what is happening in intentional communities today, keeping current on new developments (no easy task!), and figuring out the best ways to offer all this to a hungry public. Keeping in mind the wide variety in preferred information cuisines (quizines?), you might say that what follows is our "a la Chart" menu. *Bon apetit!*

Community	Forming/Reforming Non-Residential	State/Prov. or Country	Year Established	Rural, Urban or Both	Open to More Adults?	Open to More Children?	Total Population	# Adults	# Children (<19yrs)	Percentage Women	Identified Leader	Leadership Core Group	How are Major Decisions Made?	Join Fee	Income	Who Owns Land	Acres of Land	Survey Date
Abode of the Message		NY	75	R	Y	y	57	41	16	54%	N		O	Y		cmty		12/94
Abundant Dawn	F	VA	94	R	Y	y	11	9	2	70%			C	N	mixed	cmty		12/94
ACCESS	F	VA		R	Y	y	2	2	0	50%	N	N	C		shared			10/93
Acorn		VA	93	R	Y	y	21	20	1	50%	N	N	C	N	shared	cmty	72	4/95
Adirondack Herbs	RF	NY	82	R	Y	y	8	8	0	25%	Y	Y	C L G	N		mix	120	10/92
Agahpay Fellowship	RF	WV																10/92
Agape Cmty	F	TN	72	R	Y	y	6	2	4				C M	N	shared		300	PrevDir
Agape Lay Apostolate Cmty		NM	83	R	Y	y	20	8	12	57%	Y	Y	G	N	indep	cmty	10	11/93
Alcyone Light Centre																		
Alpha Farm		OR	72	R	Y	y	19	14	5	57%	N	N	C		shared	cmty	280	4/92
Anaami	F	NM	92	R	Y	y	4	4	0	25%	N	N	C	N	indep			1/93
Ananda Ashram		NY	64		N	n	20											3/94
Ananda Marga		MO	85	B	Y	y	120	120	0	38%	Y	Y	C G	N		mix	140	12/92
Ananda Village		CA	69	R	Y	y	356	253	103	53%	Y	Y	C M L G	Y	indep	cmty	750	9/92
Anasazi Ranch	F	AZ	94	R	Y	y	6	2	4				C	Y	shared	clt	40	7/94
Apple Tree Acres		NC	76	R	Y	y	12	10	2	50%	N	N	C O	N	indep	indiv	25	9/93
Aquarian Concepts	F	AZ	89	B	Y	y	100	76	24	54%	Y	Y	L G O	N	indep	mix		6/94
Aquarian Research Foundation	RF	PA	69		Y	y	5	3	2				C	N				PrevDir
Aquarius Ranch	RF	AZ	85	R	Y	y	5	5	0	20%	N	N	C	N	indep	mix	30	9/92
Arcoiris	RF	Mex.	84	U	Y	y	7	5	2	40%	Y	Y	C M	N	indep	indiv		7/92
Arden Village		DE	1900	B	Y	y	550	410	140	50%	Y	Y	M	N	indep	mix	162	11/93
Ark, The		MA	84	R	Y	y	12	5	7	60%	N	N	M	N	indep	indiv	1.5	7/94
Arsha Vidya Gurukulam		PA	86	R	Y	y	23	20	3	50%	Y	Y	L	N		n profit	14	11/92
Art Colony at Eden Falls	F	CA	93	R	Y	y	6	4	2	50%		Y	C	N	indep	other	35	2/93
Ashby Treehome		CA																12/94
Atlantis Rising		NH	76	R	N	n	12	6	6	50%	N	N	C M	Y	indep	n profit	128	8/93
August Green Cohousing	F	CO	soon	U	Y	y	16	8	8	70%	Y	Y	C	N				1/95
Avalon	F	BC	86	B	Y	y	4	2	2	50%	Y	Y	G	N				11/93
BabaDas																		
Balanced Life Center	RF	MI	70	B			3	3	0	67%			L		shared			7/93
Bamberton	F	BC	90	U	Y	y	?			50%	N	Y		N	indep		2100	12/94
Beacon Hill Friends House		MA	58	U	Y	n	16	16	0	56%	N	Y	C	N	indep	clt		6/94
Bear Creek Farms	F	CA	88	R	Y	y	6	4	2	50%	N	N	C	N	indep	other	26.3	4/92
Bemis Erectus		CA	89	U	Y		6	6	0	0%	N		C	N	indep	ldlord		9/94
Benedictine Monastery of Hawaii		HI	84	R			6			17%	Y		L G		shared	n profit		7/94
Bijou Cmty		CO																11/93
Birdsfoot Farm		NY	72	R	Y	y	7	7	0	43%	N	N	C	N		cmty	73	12/92
Black Cat House		CA	86	U	N	n	8	7	1	71%	N	Y	C	N	indep	subgrp		7/94
Black Oak Ranch			65	R	M	m	28	26	2	50%	N	Y	C	N	indep	cmty	440	PrevDir
Blackberry	RF	CA	83	R	Y	y	3	2	1	50%	N	Y	C	N	shared	indiv	50	6/92
Blue House, The		WA	82	U			5			0%	N		C	N	indep			7/94
Blue Moon Cooperative		VT	86	R	N	n	18	10	8	60%	N	N	C	Y	indep	cmty	165	8/94
Breitenbush		OR	77	R	Y	y	47	39	8	41%	Y	Y	O	Y	indep	other	86	4/92
Bright Morning Star	RF	WA	79	U	N	n	6	4	2	50%	N	N	C	N	indep	indiv		9/93
Brigid House		CA	85	U	N	n	7	6	1	57%	N	N	C		indep	indiv		6/92
Bryn Gweled Homesteads		PA	40	B	Y	y	199	149	50	54%	N	N	C M	Y	indep	cmty	240	5/92
Buddhist Society of Comp. Wisdom	RF	ONT	79	U	Y	?	4	4	0		Y	Y		N	shared	cmty		4/92
Builders, The		NV	69	B	Y	y	25			50%	Y	Y	G	N	indep	cmty		5/92
Burlington Cohousing Group	F	VT	89	U	Y	y	33	23	10	57%	N	N	C	Y	indep			7/94
Caerduir																		
Cambridge Zen Center		MA		U	Y	y	135				Y	Y	C L G	Y	indep	clt		5/93
Camelot-of-the-Wood		GA																NQ
Camphill Soltane		PA	88	R	Y	y	44	42	2	50%	Y	Y	C L	N	shared	cmty	50	10/93
Camphill Special Schools		PA																NQ
Camphill Village		PA	72	R	Y	y	125	108	17	51%	N	Y	C O	N	both	cmty	430	12/92

KEY *Provinces:* BC = British Columbia, MB = Manitoba, NS = Nova Scotia, ON = Ontario, SK = Saskatchewan. *Decisions:* C = Consensus, M = Majority, L = Leader, G = Group of leaders or elders, O = Other. *Who Owns Land:* CLT = Community Land Trust, Cmty = Community, Indiv = Individual, Ldlord = Landlord, Subgrp = Subgroup of members. *Income:* Shared = Members Share Income, Indep = Handle Own Finances. *Survey Date:* PrevDir = Previous Directory, NQ = No Questionnaire, Date is when survey questionnaire was completed or last updated by community.

North American Cross-Reference Chart

Map / Index Name	Eat Together How Frequently?	What % of Own Food Is Grown?	Organic Food in Diet	Diet	Caffeine in Diet	Alcohol in Diet	Tobacco in Diet	# Children (<19yrs)	% Home Schooled	% Cmty Schooled	% Private Schooled	% Public Schooled	Spiritual Path	Primary Purpose and/or Focus
Abode	nearly all meals	>50%						16	50	50	0	0	Sufi	spiritual freedom to fulfull ideals in life
AbunDawn	nearly all lunches	>50%	yes!					2						joy, activism, healing, green
ACCESS	nearly all meals	1–5%		veg	ok	often	ok	0						implement sustainable systems
Acorn	nearly all dinners	6–20%		omni	ok	ok	ok	1	0	0	0	100		equality, ecology, liberation
Adirondack	rarely	6–20%		omni	often	some	often	0						herbs, conservation, technology
Agahpay														coop, common purse
Agape-TN								4	100	0	0	0	Christian	shared spiritual life
AgapeLayAp	1 time/wk	1–5%						12	0	10	0	90		prayer service family
Alcyone														
Alpha	nearly all dinners	21–50%		omni	often	some	ok	5	0	0	0	100		extended family, group process
Anaami	nearly all dinners	>50%		vgn	ok	ok	ok	0						spiritual, self-sufficiency
AnandaAshrm														spiritual, educational center
AnandaMrga	1–3 times/mo	1–5%	often	veg	ok	none	none	0	0	0	50	50	Eastern	self-realization and social service
AnandaVill	rarely	1–5%	often	veg	some	none	none	103	2	78	0	20	Eastern	spiritual community
Anasazi								4	50	50	0	0	NAm,E,Ecl	no alcohol or drugs
AppleTree	rarely	1–5%	often	omni	often	some	often	2	0	0	0	100	Other	health of earth and occupants
AquarConcpt	1 time/wk	6–20%	often	veg	ok	ok	ok	24	100	0	0	0	Other	cont. fifth epochal revelation
AquarResrch								2					Chr,O	concern about world situation
AquarRanch	1 time/wk	1–5%		omni	often	often	ok	0						100% personal fulfillment
Arcoiris	2–5 times/wk	None		omni	often	some	some	2	0	0	0	100		egalitarian, spiritual, political
Arden	1 time/wk	1–5%						140	0	0	15	85		community, single tax, arts
Ark	nearly all dinners	1–5%		veg				7	0	0	0	100		living together peacefully (& efficiently)
ArshaVidya	nearly all meals	None		veg	often	none	ok	3	0	0	0	100	Eastern	ashram for study of vendanta
ArtColony	1–3 times/mo	>50%		omni	some	some	ok	2	0	0	0	100		realization of full potential
AshbyTree														see GreenPLAN
AtlantisRis	rarely	6–20%						6	0	0	0	100		ecological agriculture solar
AugustGreen	1–3 times/mo	None						8	0	0	0	100		cohousing community
Avalon				omni	often	some	ok	2	0	0	0	100	Pagan	pagan education
BabaDas														
BalancdLife	nearly all meals	21–50%						0					Other	balancing mental, physical, spiritual
Bamberton		1–5%												sustainable new town community
BeaconHill	nearly all dinners	None	some	omni	often	ok	ok	0					Quaker	quaker residential community
BearCreek	2–5 times/wk	6–20%			ok	ok	none	2	100	0	0	0	Other	holistic, artistic, extended family
BemisErec	1–3 times/mo	None						0					Pagan	gay/bi, spirituality, healing, arts
Benedictine	2–5 times/wk	6–20%											RomanCath	ministering, retreat center
Bijou														simple living, peace & justice
Birdsfoot	nearly all dinners	21–50%		veg	ok	ok	ok	0						farm friends simple mobius
BlackCat		1–5%						1	0	0	0	100	Pagan	maagic; direct action politics
BlackOak	nearly all dinners	21–50%	yes!					2						humor, friendship, extended family
Blackberry	nearly all dinners	1–5%		no red	some	some	none	1	100	0	0	0		intimacy, ecology, homeschooling
BlueHouse	rarely													easy livin', good people
BlueMoon	1–3 times/mo	1–5%		omni	often	often		8	0	0	25	75		cooperative musical neighborly
Breitenbush	1 time/wk	None		veg	ok	ok	ok	8	50	0	0	50		business as spiritual practice
BrightMrnStr	2–5 times/wk	1–5%		omni	often	ok	none	2	0	0	0	100		musical loving close family
Brigid	1 time/wk	1–5%		no red	some	some	none	1	0	0	0	100		collective co-ownership
BrynGweled	1–3 times/mo	6–20%		omni	often	often	often	50	10	0	30	60		cherish diversity & autonomy
BuddhistSoc	nearly all meals	None	often	veg	some	none	none	0	0	0	0	100	Buddhist	urban zen buddhist community
Builders	rarely	1–5%							0	0	0	100	Ecu,Ecl	self or god realization
BurlingCoho	rarely	None						10	50	0	25	25		cohousing
Caerduir														
CambrZen	nearly all meals	1–5%	often	veg	ok	ok	ok		0	0	0	100	Buddhist	zen practice
CamelotWood														egalitarian new age earth religion
Camphill-Sol	nearly all meals	6–20%	yes!	omni	often	none		2	0	0	100	0	Humanist	lifesharing with mentally handicapped youth
Camphill-Spc														anthroposophy
Camphill-PA	rarely	>50%	yes!	omni	some	some	some	17	0	0	100	0	Other	community with disabled adults

KEY *Food codes:* omni = includes red meat, no red = no red meat—includes fish or poultry and dairy, veg = vegetarian—no meat—includes dairy, vgn = vegan—no meat or dairy. *Spiritual path:* B = Buddhist, Chr = Christian, E = Eastern, Ecl = Eclectic, Ecu = Ecumenical, EDL = Emissaries of Divine Light, HB = Hutterian Brethren, NAm = N.American Indian, NSOM = New Social Order in Messiah, O = Other, P = Pagan, Prot = Protestant, Qk = Quaker, RC = Roman Catholic, UU = Unitarian Universalist.

Communities Directory

Community	Forming/Reforming/Non-Residential	State/Prov. or Country	Year Established	Rural, Urban or Both	Open to More Adults?	Open to More Children?	Total Population	# Adults	# Children (<19yrs)	Percentage Women	Identified Leader	Leadership Core Group	How are Major Decisions Made?	Join Fee	Income	Who Owns Land	Acres of Land	Survey Date
Camphill Village Minnesota		MN	80	R	Y	y	41	30	11	41%	N	Y	C	N	shared	n profit	~400	5/92
Camphill Village USA		NY	61	R	Y	y	220			50%	N	N	C	N		cmty	700	5/92
Cantine's Island	F	NY	92	R	Y	y	22	16	6	53%	N	N	C	Y	indep	subgrp	8	5/93
Cardiff Place	F	BC	94	U	Y	y	22	16	6	81%	N	N	C	Y	indep	other		10/94
Carpenter Village	F	OH																12/92
Casa Grande Colectiva		IL	70	U	N	n	7	7	0	57%	N	N	C	N	indep	ldlord		7/94
Casa Maria		WI	66	U	Y	y	24	21	3	60%	N	N	C	N	indep	mix		4/92
Catholic Worker Cmty, Cleveland		OH	86	U	Y		20				N	Y	C	N		mix		5/92
Catholic Worker House	RF	TX	85	U	Y	y	26	14	12	38%	N	Y	C	N	shared	other		7/93
Catskill Bruderhof		NY	90	R	M	m									shared	cmty		PrevDir
CCNV: Cmty for Creative Non-Violence		DC	77	U	Y		50									other		6/94
CEEDS		BC	74	R	Y	m	15	15	0	40%			C	N	shared	other	640	12/92
Celo Cmty		NC	37	R	N	n	72	52	20	50%	N	N	C M	Y	indep	clt	1200	8/94
Center for Peace & Life Studies	RF	IN	76	R	Y	y	9			50%	N	Y	C	N	indep	n profit	60	6/94
Center for the Examined Life																		
Central-Page Limited Equity Co-op		CA	83	U			14	13	1	46%	N	N	C	Y	indep	co-op		9/94
Cerro Gordo Cmty		OR	78	R	Y	y	30	22	8	50%	Y	Y	C M O	Y	indep	mix	1164	12/92
Chagdud Goupa Foundation		CA	79	R			30			40%	Y		L			n profit	260	7/94
Changing Water Ministries																		
Chester Creek House		MN	81	U	Y		6	6	0	100%	N	N	C	N	indep	cmty		1/94
Christ of the Hills Monastery	RF	TX	72	R	Y		18	15	3	09%			C L		shared	n profit		6/94
Christiansbrunn Brotherhood	RF	PA	88	R	Y	n	3	3	0	0%	N	N	C	N		cmty	63	6/92
Christine Center	F	WI	81	R	Y	y	18	14	4	64%		Y	C	N	indep	clt	251	11/93
Christmas Star		AZ	80	R	Y	y	28	19	9	53%	N	Y	C	N	indep	mix	41	10/93
Chrysallis Farm																		
Church of the Path	F	TX	93	B	Y	y	16	13	3	54%	Y	Y	O	N	indep	cmty	4	4/94
Circle Op Springs	F	UT	93	R	Y	y	6	6	0	17%	N		C	Y	indep	cmty	124	2/94
Circle Sanctuary	NR	WI	74	B	Y	y	200	160	40	50%	Y	Y	O	N	indep	n profit	200	12/94
Claritas	F	NY	soon		Y	y	1	1	0				O					1/95
Clearview	F	NY	94	R	Y	y	10	8	2		N	N	C O	Y	indep	n profit	575	4/96
Cloudburst Community	F	AZ	94	R	Y	y	2	2	0	0%	N	N	C	Y	both	n profit	36	1/95
Common Ground (VA)		VA	80	R	Y	y	18	12	6	58%	N	N	C	Y	indep	other	80	12/92
Common Ground Cmty		AL	87	R	N	n	13	10	3	60%	N	N	C O	N	indep	clt	80	9/92
Common Ground Housing Assoc.		CO	94	U	S	s	41	30	11	57%	N	Y	M	N	indep	other	2	10/94
Common Place		MA	73	U	N	n	33	25	8	55%	Y	Y	C	N	indep	cmty		9/93
Common Place Land Co-op		NY	76	R	Y	y	24	15	9	50%	N	N	C	N	indep	clt	432	4/92
Common Unity		MA	91	U	Y	y	15	13	2	46%	N	N	C	N	indep	mix		11/93
Commons on the Alameda		NM	92	U	Y	y	43	32	11	56%	N	Y	C	Y	indep	cmty	5	10/94
Commonterra		ME	77	R	Y	y	16	9	7	56%	N		C	Y	indep	clt	150	6/94
Communia	NR	IA	75	B	Y	y	20			50%	N	Y	C	N	indep	indiv	300	5/93
Community Alternatives		BC	77	B	Y		43	32	11	65%	N	N	C	Y	indep	cmty		1/95
Community House		VA	89	U	Y	s	7	7	0	71%	Y		C L	N	indep	indiv		12/94
Community in Basin Farm		VT	89	R	Y	y	50				Y	Y	C L G O	N	shared	other		12/95
Community in Boston		MA	81	U	Y	y	120				Y	Y	C L G O	N	shared	other		12/95
Community in Bridgeport		CT	93	U	Y	y	40				Y	Y	C L G O	N	shared	other		12/95
Community in Buffalo		NY	93	U	Y	y	60				Y	Y	C L G O	N	shared	other		12/95
Community in Island Pond		VT	78	R	Y	y	1125	625	500		Y	Y	C L G O	N	shared	other		12/95
Community in Providence		RI	92	U	Y	y	75				Y	Y	C L G O	N	shared	other		12/95
Community in Rutland		VT	92	U	Y	y	80				Y	Y	C L G O	N	shared	other		12/95
Community in St. Joseph		MO	89	U	Y	y	60				Y	Y	C L G O	N	shared	other		12/95
Community in Winnipeg		MB	93	U	Y	y	10	10		48%	Y	Y	C L G O	N	shared	other		12/95
Community of Celebration		PA	73	U	Y	y	20	16	4	58%	Y	Y	O	N	both	n profit		6/94
Community Plan-It	F	CA									Y	Y	C	Y	indep	cmty		8/92
Compound "i"		CA	93	U	N	n	7	7	0	29%	N	Y	C M			ldlord		9/94
Consciousness Village (CA)																		

KEY *Provinces:* BC = British Columbia, MB = Manitoba, NS = Nova Scotia, ON = Ontario, SK = Saskatchewan. *Decisions:* C = Consensus, M = Majority, L = Leader, G = Group of leaders or elders, O = Other. *Who Owns Land:* CLT = Community Land Trust, Cmty = Community, Indiv = Individual, Ldlord = Landlord, Subgrp = Subgroup of members. *Income:* Shared = Members Share Income, Indep = Handle Own Finances. *Survey Date:* PrevDir = Previous Directory, NQ = No Questionnaire, Date is when survey questionnaire was completed or last updated by community.

Map / Index Name	Eat Together How Frequently?	What % of Own Food Is Grown?	Organic Food in Diet	Diet	Caffeine in Diet	Alcohol in Diet	Tobacco in Diet	# Children (<19yrs)	% Home Schooled	% Cmty Schooled	% Private Schooled	% Public Schooled	Spiritual Path	Primary Purpose and/or Focus
Camphill-MN	rarely	>50%		omni	often	some	some	11	50	0	0	50		anthroposophy
Camphill-USA	rarely	21–50%												anthroposophical community
Cantinelsl	2–5 times/wk	1–5%						6						small-scale cohousing
Cardiff	2–5 times/wk	1–5%						6	0	0	0	100		caring & sharing cohousing
CarpentrVil														simple living, independence, cooperation
CasaGrande	2–5 times/wk	1–5%						0						co-op living; support of Community
CasaMaria	rarely	6–20%						3	0	0	0	100		nonviolence lifestyle
Cathwork-OH	nearly all dinners	6–20%	some	omni	often	ok	ok		0	0	0	100	RomanCath	radical christianity
Cathwork-TX	nearly all dinners	1–5%	often	omni	often	none	ok	12	0	0	0	100	Ecu	house of hospitality
CatskillBrd									0	100	0	0	HB	hutterian brethren
CCNV	nearly all dinners	1–5%												resist injustice; homelessness
CEEDS	nearly all meals	>50%		omni	often	often	some	0						organic food movement
Celo	rarely	6–20%						20						neighborliness and social concern
CenPeaceLif		1–5%											Christian	justice, faith
CenExamLife														
CentralPage	rarely	None						1						limited equity housing co-op
CerroGordo	rarely	6–20%						8	0	0	0	100		prototype symbiotic community
ChagdudGoup	nearly all meals								0	0	0	100	Buddhist	dharma
ChangingWtr														
ChesterCrk	2–5 times/wk	None		veg	some	ok	ok	0						lesbian feminist
ChristHills	nearly all meals	21–50%						3	100	0	0	0		seek mystical union w/ god
Christnsbrn	nearly all meals	6–20%	yes!	omni	often	ok	ok	0					Other	gay men's religious community
ChristineCn	nearly all meals	1–5%	yes!	no red	some	ok	ok	4	50	0	0	50	Ecu,Ecl	foster spiritual realization
ChristmsStar	2–5 times/wk	21–50%	yes!	veg	some	ok	ok	9	100	0	0	0	Ecl,O	esoteric path of evolving knowledge
Chrysallis														
ChurchOPath	2–5 times/wk	None	often	omni	often	some	ok	3	0	0	0	100	Other	self-actualization, service
CircleOpSpgs								0						sustainable systems
CircleSanct	1–3 times/mo	6–20%						40	10	0	10	80	Pagan	pagan community / wiccan church
Claritas								0						individual recognition/growth
Clearview	2–5 times/wk	21–50%						3	100	0	0	0	NewAge	education / demo ecovillage
Cloudburst	nearly all meals	21–50%		veg				0	100	0	0	0		sharing loving land-based community
CommGrnd-VA	1–3 times/mo	>50%		veg	often			6	100	0	0	0		personal/community empowering
CommGrnd-AL	1 time/wk	6–20%						3	0	0	100	0		community, ecology and humor
CommGrnd-CO	2–5 times/wk	None						11	0	0	25	75		affordable employee community
ComnPlace-MA	1–3 times/mo	None	often	omni	often	often	ok	8	0	0	0	100	Prot	community, intentionality
ComnPlace-NY	1 time/wk	6–20%		omni	some	some		9	57	0	29	14		cooperative ecological community
ComnUnity	1–3 times/mo	1–5%		veg	some	some	ok	2	100	0	0	0		spirituality/social change
ComnAlameda	2–5 times/wk	1–5%						11	15	0	15	70		convivial neighborhood
Commonterra	rarely	6–20%						7	33	33	0	33		housing
Communia	2–5 times/wk	>50%							0	0	0	100		creation of spiritual retreat center
CmtyAltsCoop	1 time/wk	6–20%						11	0	0	0	100		intentional community
CmtyHouse	nearly all meals	1–5%						0					Other	deep healing work
CmtyinBasin	nearly all meals	21–50%	yes!	omni	some	none	none		100	0	0	0	NSOM	new social order in messiah
CmtyinBost	nearly all meals	21–50%	yes!	omni	some	none	none		100	0	0	0	NSOM	new social order in messiah
CmtyinBridge	nearly all meals	21–50%	yes!	omni	some	none	none		100	0	0	0	NSOM	new social order in messiah
CmtyinBuff	nearly all meals	21–50%	yes!	omni	some	none	none		100	0	0	0	NSOM	new social order in messiah
CmtyinIslPd	nearly all meals	21–50%	yes!	omni	some	none	none	500	100	0	0	0	NSOM	new social order in messiah
CmtyinProv	nearly all meals	21–50%	yes!	omni	some	none	none		100	0	0	0	NSOM	new social order in messiah
CmtyinRutld	nearly all meals	21–50%	yes!	omni	some	none	none		100	0	0	0	NSOM	new social order in messiah
CmtyinStJo	nearly all meals	21–50%	yes!	omni	some	none	none		100	0	0	0	NSOM	new social order in messiah
CmtyinWinn	nearly all meals	21–50%	yes!	omni	some	none	none		100	0	0	0	NSOM	new social order in messiah
CmtyOfCelebr	1 time/wk							4	0	0	0	100	Prot	live among oppressed; hospitality
CmtyPlanIt														a model to change the world
Compound-I	nearly all dinners	1–5%		vgn				0						vegan collective performance
ConscVill-CA														see Consciousness Village/Rebirth Int'l

KEY *Food codes:* omni = includes red meat, no red = no red meat—includes fish or poultry and dairy, veg = vegetarian—no meat—includes dairy, vgn = vegan—no meat or dairy. *Spiritual path:* B = Buddhist, Chr = Christian, E = Eastern, Ecl = Eclectic, Ecu = Ecumenical, EDL = Emissaries of Divine Light, HB = Hutterian Brethren, NAm = N.American Indian, NSOM = New Social Order in Messiah, O = Other, P = Pagan, Prot = Protestant, Qk = Quaker, RC = Roman Catholic, UU = Unitarian Universalist.

Name	F/RF/NR	State/Prov. or Country	Year Established	Rural, Urban or Both	Open to More Adults?	Open to More Children?	Total Population	# Adults	# Children (<19yrs)	Percentage Women	Identified Leader	Leadership Core Group	How are Major Decisions Made?	Join Fee	Income	Who Owns Land	Acres of Land	Survey Date
Consciousness Village (VA)																		
Consciousness Village/Rebirth Int'l		VA	76	R	Y	y	100	83	17	57%	Y		C	Y		mix		9/94
Cooper Street Household		AZ	70	B	Y	y	7	6	1	50%	N	N	C M O	N	indep	subgrp	22	6/92
Covenant House Faith Cmty		NY	76	U									M		indep	ldlord		6/94
Covenental Cmty		IL	79	U	Y	y	47	33	14	67%	N	Y	M	N	indep	cmty		6/93
Cranberry Creek Cmty		VA	90	R	Y		7	7	0	33%	N	N	C	N	shared	cmty	55	7/93
Crosses Creek Youth Ranch		AR	70's	R	Y	n	9			63%	Y	Y	C L	N		indiv	10	5/92
Crow Circle Collective	RF	BC	89	B	Y	y	23	19	4	29%	Y	Y	M L	N	indep	indiv	20	5/93
Crow's Nest	NR	CA	77	R	Y	y	63	53	10	53%	N	Y	C	N	indep	n profit	55	9/94
Crystal Spring		MB		R	M	m								N	shared	cmty		PrevDir
Currents		OH	80	R	Y	y	21	12	9	42%	N	N	C O	Y	indep	cmty	163	2/93
Dance Hawaii!																		
Dancing Rabbit Project	F	CA	93	R	Y	y					N	N	C	Y	indep			9/95
Dancing Waters		WI	83	R	M	m	13	11	2	55%	N	N	C	N	indep	cmty	130	6/92
Dapala Farm	F	WA	90	R	Y	y	4	4	0	50%	N	N	C O	N	indep	cmty	16	4/94
Deep Woods Farm		OH	82	R	Y	y	5	5	0	40%	N	Y	C		indep	clt	282	9/93
Deer Rock		VA	92	R	Y	y	17	12	5	57%	N	Y	C	Y	indep	cmty	330	1/96
Deer Spring Bruderhof		CT		R	M	m								N	shared	cmty		PrevDir
Denver Catholic Worker		CO	78	U	Y	y	14						C		shared	ldlord		6/94
Denver Space Center		CO	79	U			6	6	0	33%				N		indiv		11/92
Desiderata		TX	75	R	Y	y				47%	Y	Y	M	N	indep	indiv		9/94
DOE Farm		WI	77	R	Y		35	35	0	100%	N	Y	C	Y	indep	co-op	80	9/94
Dorea Peace Cmty		WI	80	R	N	n	13	6	7	50%	N	N	C	N	indep	mix	87	6/92
Downeast Friends Cmty	RF	ME	78	U	Y	y	9	9	0	33%	N	Y	C	N		subgrp		3/94
Doyle Street Cohousing		CA																1/94
Dragon Belly Farm	F	WA	89	R	Y	y	5	4	1	75%	N	Y	C	Y	indep	indiv	26	11/92
Dragonfly Farm		ONT	77	R	N	n	7	7	0	29%	N	N	C		indep	cmty	250	11/93
Dreamtime Village	F	WI	85	R	Y	y	7	6	1	17%	N	Y	G	N		mix	85	8/92
Du-má		OR	90	U	Y	y	7	7	0	57%	N	N	C	Y	indep	cmty		10/93
Duck Mountain Circle	F	MB	88	R	Y	y	6	2	4	50%	N	N	C	N	indep	indiv	160	4/92
Dunmire Hollow		TN	73	R	Y	y	15	10	5	50%	N	N	C	Y	indep	cmty	160	4/92
Earth Cycle Farm	RF	WA	75	R	Y	y	6	3	3	33%	N	N	C	N	shared	cmty	80	12/92
Earth Family Farm	RF	CO	88	R	Y	y	13	11	2	38%	N	Y	G	N			50	1/93
Earth Re-leaf	RF	HI	89	B	Y	y	3	3	0	0%	N	N	C	N	indep	indiv	1	11/92
Earth Village Institute	F	CO	92	R	Y	y	7	5	2	50%		Y	C L	N	indep	indiv	146	6/92
Earthaven	F	NC	92	R	Y	y	22			43%	N		O		indep	n profit	368	10/94
Earthlands	RF	MA	92	R	Y		15	15	0	50%	N	Y	C	Y	indep	indiv	300+	9/94
Earthseed	F	VT		R	Y	y	3	3	0			N	C	N				6/94
East Wind		MO	73	R	Y	y	60	55	5	36%	N	N	C M	N	shared	cmty	428+	9/95
East/West House		CA	57	U	M		13	12	1	54%	N	N	C			n profit		9/94
Ecovillage at Ithaca	F	NY	92	B	Y	y	45	29	16	64%	N	Y	C	Y	indep	other	176	7/93
Eden Sanctuary	F	OH		R	Y	y					N	Y	C	N				2/93
Edges	F	OH	92	R	Y	y	19	15	4	50%	N	N	C	N	indep			1/92
EFE	F	ND	91	B	Y	y	2	2	0	100%			C	N	shared	other	<1	7/92
Elderwood Farm	F	MI	92	R	Y	y	4	2	2	50%	Y	Y	C	Y	shared	indiv	35	1/95
Ellis Island		CA	69	U	M	m	11	11	0				C	N		cmty		PrevDir
Eloin Cmty		OR	90	R	Y	n	21	12	9	67%	Y	Y	G	N	shared	cmty	80	12/92
Enchanted Garden	RF	CA	76	U	Y		8	8	0	50%	Y	Y	M L	N	indep	ldlord		6/94
Essene Skoola Phish (E.S.P.)	F	IL	soon	R	Y	y						N	L	N	indep	mix		6/92
Eugene Cohousing	F	OR	90	U	Y	y					N	Y	C					1/93
Fairview House		CA	92	U	M	m	13	10	3	50%	N	N	C	Y	indep	indiv		9/94
Family, The		CA	89	B	Y	y	31	10	21	60%	Y	Y	M	N	shared	ldlord		8/94
Fan Lake Brethren		WA	90	R	Y	y	7	6	1	50%	Y	Y	M	N	shared	cmty	122	7/94
Far Valley Farm		OH	80	R	N	n	17	10	7	40%	N	N	C	Y	indep	n profit	234	12/94
Farm Home Center	F	WI	87	U	Y	y	3	3	0	33%	Y	Y	C	Y	indep			5/93

KEY *Provinces:* BC = British Columbia, MB = Manitoba, NS = Nova Scotia, ON = Ontario, SK = Saskatchewan. *Decisions:* C = Consensus, M = Majority, L = Leader, G = Group of leaders or elders, O = Other. *Who Owns Land:* CLT = Community Land Trust, Cmty = Community, Indiv = Individual, Ldlord = Landlord, Subgrp = Subgroup of members. *Income:* Shared = Members Share Income, Indep = Handle Own Finances. *Survey Date:* PrevDir = Previous Directory, NQ = No Questionnaire, Date is when survey questionnaire was completed or last updated by community.

Map / Index Name	Eat Together How Frequently?	What % of Own Food Is Grown?	Organic Food in Diet	Diet	Caffeine in Diet	Alcohol in Diet	Tobacco in Diet	# Children (<19yrs)	% Home Schooled	% Cmty Schooled	% Private Schooled	% Public Schooled	Spiritual Path	Primary Purpose and/or Focus
ConscVill-VA														see Consciousness Village/Rebirth Int'l
ConscVillReb	nearly all meals	6–20%		veg				17	10	0	10	80	Other	total mastery of mind & body
CooperSt	1 time/wk	1–5%						1	0	0	0	100		improved life for all
CoventHouse	2–5 times/wk													service and spirituality
CoventCmty	1 time/wk	6–20%	often	omni	often	ok	ok	14	0	0	0	100	Prot	christian urban extended family
CranberryCrk	2–5 times/wk	21–50%		veg	often	some	ok	0						living deliberately/consciously
CrossesCrk	nearly all meals	21–50%		omni	often	none	ok		0	100	0	0		to be a family
CrowCircle	1 time/wk	1–5%		omni	some	often	some	4						clean sustainable culture
CrowsNest	1–3 times/mo	21–50%						10	25	0	25	50	Pagan	save planet, establish community
CrystSpr-Man									0	100	0	0	HB	hutterian brethren
Currents	1–3 times/mo	1–5%		omni	some	some		9	0	0	12	88		co-op homestead w/ social change
DanceHawaii														
DanceRabbit	1–3 times/mo	1–5%	yes!											environmentally sustainable town
DanceWatter	1–3 times/mo	21–50%		omni	some	some		2						cooperative rural community
DapalaFarm	nearly all dinners	>50%		no red	ok	ok	some none	0						homesteading educational center
DeepWoods	1 time/wk	6–20%		omni	some	none	none	0						rural land trust consensus
DeerRock	1–3 times/mo			omni	some	some	some	5	40	0	60	0	Ecu,Ecl,P	new mountain settlement
DeerSpring									0	100	0	0	HB	hutterian brethren
DenvCathWkr	nearly all meals	6–20%											Other	hospitality, voluntary poverty, personalism
DenverSpace	1–3 times/mo	1–5%						0						stimulating friends convenient
Desiderata	1–3 times/mo	1–5%							0	0	0	100		love the land & livin country
DOE-Farm	2–5 times/wk	6–20%						0					Pagan	recreation & education for womyn
Dorea	2–5 times/wk	1–5%		omni	often	some	ok	7	0	0	0	100		peace and justice
Downeast	2–5 times/wk	21–50%	often	no red	often	ok	ok	0					Quaker	ecology art
DoyleStreet														cohousing
DragonBelly	2–5 times/wk	6–20%		no red	ok	ok	none	1	0	0	0	100		personal & planetary transformation
Dragonfly	1–3 times/mo	21–50%		omni	yes!		often	0						enjoy life
Dreamtime	nearly all meals	21–50%		omni	often	often	ok	1	100	0	0	0		permaculture hypermedia village
DuMá	nearly all dinners	6–20%		veg	ok	ok	ok	0						ecology, personal growth, egalitarian
DuckMtn	nearly all meals	21–50%		omni	ok	ok	ok	4	100	0	0	0		gently living on the earth
Dunmire	1 time/wk							5	40	0	0	60		small rural community
EarthCycle	nearly all dinners	>50%	yes!	omni	ok	some	ok	3	100	0	0	0	Other	harmony, ecology, earth-honoring
EarthFamFarm	1–3 times/mo	1–5%		veg	ok	ok	ok	2	0	0	0	100		living sacred loving being
EarthReLeaf	rarely	21–50%		vgn	ok	ok	ok	0						consensus land trust & family
EarthVillage	2–5 times/wk	1–5%		omni	often			2	0	0	100	0		energy-efficient cohousing
Earthaven	1 time/wk	6–20%	ok	omni	ok	ok	none						Ecu,Ecl	spiritual ecology
Earthlands	nearly all dinners	6–20%		vgn				0						environmental activism
Earthseed								0					Pagan	deep ecology, creativity, diversity
EastWind	nearly all meals	6–20%		omni	ok	ok	ok	5	33	0	0	66		economic, social equality
EastWest	nearly all dinners	None						1						low-cost communal living
EcoVill-Ith		6–20%		veg				16	0	0	28	72		ecological cohousing village
EdenSanct													Other	based on vow of non-violence
Edges				veg	ok	ok	ok	4	25	0	25	50		respect and sustainability
EFE	nearly all meals	1–5%		omni	often	some	ok	0						low-income co-op retrofits
Elderwood	nearly all dinners	>50%		veg				2	100	0	0	0	Pagan	organic food production
EllisIsland								0						no dogmas
Eloin	nearly all meals	21–50%		vgn	none	none	none	9	100	0	0	0		physical and spiritual evolution
EnchantGardn	1–3 times/mo	1–5%		veg		some	ok	0						grow together
EsseneSkoola	nearly all dinners			veg		none	none						Other	heaven on earth
EugeneCoho	nearly all dinners													cohousing
Fairview	nearly all dinners	1–5%						3	0	0	50	50		affordable progressive community
FamilyThe	nearly all meals	None	some	omni	some	some	none	21	100	0	0	0	Christian	share love of jesus w/others
FanLake	nearly all meals	21–50%	some	omni	some	some	none	1	0	0	0	100	HB	reliance on god through jesus
FarValley	1 time/wk	21–50%						7	15	0	0	85		diversity, cooperation, stewardship
FarmHome	rarely	None			ok	ok	ok	0						agriculture, health

KEY *Food codes:* omni = includes red meat, no red = no red meat—includes fish or poultry and dairy, veg = vegetarian—no meat—includes dairy, vgn = vegan—no meat or dairy. *Spiritual path:* B = Buddhist, Chr = Christian, E = Eastern, Ecl = Eclectic, Ecu = Ecumenical, EDL = Emissaries of Divine Light, HB = Hutterian Brethren, NAm = N.American Indian, NSOM = New Social Order in Messiah, O = Other, P = Pagan, Prot = Protestant, Qk = Quaker, RC = Roman Catholic, UU = Unitarian Universalist.

	F/R/NR	State/Prov. or Country	Year Established	Rural, Urban or Both	Open to More Adults?	Open to More Children?	Total Population	# Adults	# Children (<19yrs)	Percentage Women	Identified Leader	Leadership Core Group	How are Major Decisions Made?	Join Fee	Income	Who Owns Land	Acres of Land	Survey Date
Farm, The	RF	TN	70	R			320						M	Y		clt	1750	1/93
Fillmore House		CA	81	U	N	n	7	7	0	43%	N	N	C O	N	indep	indiv		8/94
Finders, The		DC	71	B	Y	y	14	14	0	36%		Y	M O	N	both	mix	600	7/94
Flatrock Cmty	RF	TN	79	R	Y	y	12	8	4	63%	N	N	C	N		clt	27	6/92
Folkcorps	F	KY	92	R	Y	y	1	1	0	0%	Y	Y	C	N		cmty	48	4/92
Folkhaven	F	AK	94	R	Y	y	3	3	0	0%	Y	Y	C L G	N		cmty	1	11/93
Four Streets Co-op		CA	84		Y	y	400	200	200		N	Y	M	Y	indep	co-op		9/94
Four Winds Village	F	GA	71	R	Y	y	10	10	0	60%	Y		C G	N	indep	cmty	80	12/92
Free-the-Land NYC Squatters' Cmty		NJ																NQ
Friends Lake Cmty		MI	61	U	Y	y	20					Y	C	Y	indep	cmty	90	9/94
Friends Southwest Center		AZ	73	R	Y	y	11	11	0	64%	N	Y	C	N	indep	clt	68	12/92
Full Circle Natural Farm	F	CA	93	R	Y	y	3	2	1	50%	N	N	C	N	indep	cmty	20	9/93
Gaia Permaculture	F	GA	89	R	Y		8	6	2	50%		Y	C	N	indep	other	15	12/92
Gaien	F	HI	92	R	Y	y	6	5	1	50%	N	Y	C	N	shared	indiv	2.5	12/92
Ganas		NY	80	U	Y	y	57	55	2	40%		Y	C O	N		subgrp		10/92
Geneva Cmty	F	CO	soon	R	Y	y	22	16	6	50%		Y	C	Y			176	8/94
Gesundheit! Institute (VA)		VA																NQ
Gesundheit! Institute (WV)		WV																NQ
Gita Nagari Village	RF	PA	75	R	Y	y	47	29	18	46%	Y	Y	G	N	indep	mix	300	5/92
Glen Ivy		CA	77	R	Y	y	83	70	13	56%	Y	Y	C L G	N	indep	cmty	75	5/92
Glendower	F	MO	94	U	Y	s	3	3	0	50%	N	N	C	N	indep	indiv	.5	4/96
Glenridge Co-op		CA	74	U	Y	y	275 fu				N	Y	M	Y	indep	co-op		9/94
Good Red Road, The	F	CA	92	R	Y	y	2	2	0	50%	N	Y	C O					2/94
Goodenough Cmty	NR	WA	81	U	Y	y				67%	Y	Y	C G	N	indep			1/93
Goodrich Farm Cooperative	F	VT	92	R	Y	y	6	4	2	0%	Y	Y	C	N		clt	54	2/93
Goodwater Cmty	F	MO	88	R	Y	y	3	1	2	0%	Y	Y	C O	N		mix	5	1/93
Gorilla Choir House		CA	86	U	S	s	4	4	0	50%	Y		C O	N	indep	indiv		8/94
Grassroots Cmty		FL	81	R	M	m	86	45	41	50%	N	Y	C M	N	indep	indiv	45	7/94
Green Oaks Cmty	F	NC	92	R	M	m	7	7	0	43%	N		O			n profit	6	10/94
Green Pastures Estate		NH	25	R	Y	y	25	23	2	58%	N	Y	C G		indep	cmty	150	4/96
Greenbriar Cmty		TX	69	R	N	n	55	33	23		N	N	C			other	171	8/93
Greenhouse Cooperative		OH	92	U	Y	y	15	8	7	43%	N	N	C	Y	indep	indiv		11/92
Greening Life Cmty		PA	74	R	Y	y	12	10	2	50%	N	Y	C	Y	indep	cmty	135	6/92
GreenPLAN	F	CA	94	U	Y	y	8	8	0	63%	N	Y		N	indep	indiv		5/94
Greenwood Forest Association	RF	MO	80	R	Y	y	145				N	Y	M	N	indep	mix	1000	10/92
Griffin Gorge Commons																		
Hale Byodo Corazon	F	CA	86	U	Y		7	7	0	14%	N	N	C	N	indep	indiv		1/93
Haley House Catholic Worker		MA	66	B			7			0%			C		indep		11	7/94
Harbin Hot Springs		CA		R	Y	y	146	133	13		Y	Y	C M L G	Y		n profit	1160	12/92
Harmon House		CA	74	U			6			50%	N		C					6/94
Harmony Village	F	CO																NQ
Harvest Hills Association	RF	MO	72	R	Y	y	150	100	50	55%	N	N	M	Y	indep	mix	45	1/95
Haven	F	CA	94	U	Y	y	5	4	1	50%	N	Y	C	N		ldlord		8/94
Hawk Circle		IA		R	Y	y	6	4	2	25%	N	N	C	N		other	5.5	2/93
Hawkwind Earth Renewal	F	AL	88	R	Y	y	6	5	1	33%	Y	Y	G	Y	indep	mix	77	8/92
Headlands	RF	ONT	72	R	N		9	5	4	40%	N	N	C	N	indep	subgrp	2	4/92
Healing Grace Sanctuary	F	MA	79	R	Y	y	2	1	1	100%	N		C			indiv	85	1/93
Hearth (L'Arche)		PA	72	U			52			69%	Y	N	M L	N	indep	n profit		6/94
Hearthaven		MO	87	U	Y		5	5	0	60%	N	N	C	N		cmty		12/92
Hearthstone Village	NR	MA	84	R	Y	y	90				N	N	O	N				7/94
Heartlight Center		MI	87				16	15	1									7/92
Heartwinds	F	CA	93	R	N	n	10	5	5	60%	N	N	C	N	indep	mix	50	12/95
Heartwood Institute		CA	78	R	Y	m	100	95	5	60%	N	Y	C O G	N	indep	indiv	240	12/95
Heathcote Center	RF	MD	92	R	Y	y	14	7	7	71%	N	Y	C M	Y	indep	clt	37	6/94
Hei Wa House		MI	85	U	Y	dk	8	8	0	75%	N	N	C	Y	indep	ldlord		2/95

KEY *Provinces:* BC = British Columbia, MB = Manitoba, NS = Nova Scotia, ON = Ontario, SK = Saskatchewan. *Decisions:* C = Consensus, M = Majority, L = Leader, G = Group of leaders or elders, O = Other. *Who Owns Land:* CLT = Community Land Trust, Cmty = Community, Indiv = Individual, Ldlord = Landlord, Subgrp = Subgroup of members. *Income:* Shared = Members Share Income, Indep = Handle Own Finances. *Survey Date:* PrevDir = Previous Directory, NQ = No Questionnaire, Date is when survey questionnaire was completed or last updated by community.

North American Cross-Reference Chart

Map / Index Name	Eat Together How Frequently?	What % of Own Food Is Grown?	Organic Food in Diet	Diet	Caffeine in Diet	Alcohol in Diet	Tobacco in Diet	# Children (<19yrs)	% Home Schooled	% Cmty Schooled	% Private Schooled	% Public Schooled	Spiritual Path	Primary Purpose and/or Focus
FarmThe	rarely	6–20%	yes!	veg	some	ok	ok		10	30	5	55	Ecl	open-ended experiment
Fillmore	nearly all dinners	None		vgn				0						political artistic lifestyle
Finders	nearly all meals	None						0						all the world's a stage
Flatrock	2–5 times/wk	1–5%		veg	often	ok	ok	4	0	0	0	100		personal growth, equality, growth
Folkcorps	nearly all dinners	>50%						0	50	0	0	50		self-help, work crews, replicate
Folkhaven	nearly all meals	21–50%	yes!	omni	often	some	ok	0					Pagan	family tribe and folk
FourStreets	rarely	None						200	0	0	10	90		limited equity housing co-op
FourWinds	1 time/wk	1–5%		veg				0	100	0	0	0		service to others practicing light!
FreeLandSqat														urban homesteading, activism
FriendsLake	2–5 times/wk	None							50	0	0	50	Quaker	quaker
FriendsSW	rarely	1–5%						0						peace and human rights
FullCircle	2–5 times/wk	>50%	yes!	no red	ok	ok	ok	1					Ecu	artlife
GaiaPerm	1–3 times/mo	6–20%		no red	some	some	ok	2						permaculture sustainable design
Gaien	nearly all dinners	>50%		veg	often	some	none	1	100	0	0	0		eclectic egalitarians, conscious evolution
Ganas	nearly all dinners	1–5%		omni	often	ok	ok	2	0	0	100	0		feedback learning
Geneva	nearly all dinners			veg				6	0	0	90	0		cohousing model
Gesundheit!V														model health care community
Gesundheit!W														model health care community
GitaNagari	1 time/wk	6–20%	often	veg	none	none	none	18	10	70	0	20	HK	pure devotional service
GlenIvy	nearly all meals	6–20%	often	omni	some	ok	ok	13	0	0	0	100	EDL	living together creatively
Glendower	nearly all meals	1–5%	some	omni	some	some	none	0					Ecu,P	polifedility and pagans
Glenridge	rarely	None							0	0	10	90		limited equity housing co-op
GoodRedRoad	2–5 times/wk	21–50%						0						growth, family, sharing, security
Goodenough		None							0	0	50	50		relationship skills, covenant community
Goodrich	nearly all meals	>50%		omni	yes!	often	often	2	0	0	0	100		collective living in formative stage
Goodwater	nearly all meals	6–20%	yes!	omni	some	ok	ok	2	100	0	0	0	Other	healing waters and healing people
GorillaChoir	nearly all meals	1–5%		veg				0						heart songs
Grassroots	1–3 times/mo	6–20%						41	0	27	18	55		high quality neighborly living
GreenOaks	1 time/wk	6–20%	often	no red	some	some	some	0					Ecl	spiritual ecology
GreenPastur	nearly all dinners	>50%	often	omni	ok	ok	ok	2	100	0	0	0	EDL	attunement with life
Greenbriar	1 time/wk	6–20%						23	100	0	0	0		non-coercive education; kids
Greenhous-OH	1 time/wk	1–5%		veg	often	some	some	7						cooperation awareness ecology
GreeningLife	1 time/wk	21–50%		omni	often	often	some	2	0	0	100	0		growth in spirit; balance
GreenPlan	nearly all dinners	1–5%		veg	often	some	none	0						ending greed and waste
Greenwood	rarely	6–20%		omni	some	some	some		50	0	0	50		land stewardship
GriffinGorge														
HaleByodo	2–5 times/wk	1–5%		omni	often	often	ok	0						shared housing, musical
HaleyHouse	2–5 times/wk	1–5%											Other	service for self and others
Harbin	rarely	1–5%		no red	some	some	some	13	25	0	0	75		heart consciousness
HarmonHouse	1 time/wk			veg										ecological, family, stability, friendly, food
HarmonyVill														cohousing
HarvestHills	1–3 times/mo	1–5%						50	5	0	0	95	Chr,Ecl	general christian environment
Haven	2–5 times/wk	None		veg	ok	ok	none	1	0	0	0	100		cooperative sharing/counseling
HawkCircle	nearly all dinners	1–5%		omni	often	some	ok	2	0	0	0	100		consensus, sharing, diversity
Hawkwind	2–5 times/wk	6–20%	yes!	omni	some	none	often	1	50	0	0	50	NAm	harmonius earth-healing for all
Headlands	1–3 times/mo	>50%		omni	often	ok	ok	4	0	0	0	100		inexpensive rural co-op living
HealingGrace	nearly all dinners	>50%	yes!	omni	none	none	none	1	100	0	0	0	Ecl,O	unravel roots of social ills
HearthLArche													RomanCath	mutual relationships with people with disabilities
Hearthaven	1 time/wk	1–5%	ok	omni	ok	ok	none	0					Ecu,Ecl	living from the heart
Hearthstone	2–5 times/wk	6–20%												sharing/supportive neighborhood
Heartlight								1						seek first the kingdom of god
Heartwinds	1–3 times/mo	6–20%		omni	some	some		5	0	100	0	0		good neighbors, friends, family
Heartwood	nearly all meals	6–20%	yes!	ok	none	ok		5					Ecu	heal planet via personal transformation
Heathcote	2–5 times/wk	1–5%		no red	often	some	ok	7	100	0	0	0		equality, sustainability, joy
HeiWaHouse	2–5 times/wk	1–5%		veg	often	ok	ok	0						cooperative urban household

KEY *Food codes:* omni = includes red meat, no red = no red meat—includes fish or poultry and dairy, veg = vegetarian—no meat—includes dairy, vgn = vegan—no meat or dairy. *Spiritual path:* B = Buddhist, Chr = Christian, E = Eastern, Ecl = Eclectic, Ecu = Ecumenical, EDL = Emissaries of Divine Light, HB = Hutterian Brethren, NAm = N.American Indian, NSOM = New Social Order in Messiah, O = Other, P = Pagan, Prot = Protestant, Qk = Quaker, RC = Roman Catholic, UU = Unitarian Universalist.

Community	Forming, Reforming, Non-Residential	State/Prov. or Country	Year Established	Rural, Urban or Both	Open to More Adults?	Open to More Children?	Total Population	# Adults	# Children (<19yrs)	Percentage Women	Identified Leader	Leadership Core Group	How are Major Decisions Made?	Join Fee	Income	Who Owns Land	Acres of Land	Survey Date
High Flowing Cmty		VA	89	R	Y	y	9			43%	Y		G		indep	ldlord	100	7/94
High Horizons	F	WV	94	R	Y	y	1	1	0	100%			O	N	indep	indiv	260	12/94
High Wind Association		WI	81	R	N	n	17	14	3	50%	N	Y	C	N	indep	mix	128	11/92
Hillegass House		CA	76	U	Y	y	8	8	0	63%	N	N	C	N	indep	subgrp		9/94
Hilltop Cmty		WA	51	R	Y	y	70			58%	Y	Y	M	N	indep	mix	63	3/94
Himalayan Institute		PA	71				105											6/94
Holy City Cmty																		
HOME																		
Homestead Cmty																		
Horcones Two																		
House of Lavendar		WI	74	U	Y	y	4	4	0	25%	N	N	C M	N	indep	cmty		6/92
Huehuecoyotl		Mex.	71	R	N	n	36	22	14	50%	N	N	C	Y		cmty	5	6/92
Hundred Mile Lodge	RF	BC	48	B			51	44	7	66%	N	Y	C	N	indep	cmty		1/95
Hutterian Brethren of Spokane		WA	60	B	M	m	45	45	0						shared	cmty		PrevDir
ICA/Chicago		IL																NQ
ICA/Phoenix	RF	AZ	88	U	Y	y	20	14	6	64%	N	N	C	N	indep	n profit		6/92
IDA	F	TN	93	R	N	n	8	8	0	0%	N	N	C	N		other	243	1/94
Innisfree Village		VA	71	B	Y	y	50	50	0	52%	Y	Y	C	Y		cmty	600	5/92
Institute for Harmonious Dev	F	CA	92	B	Y	n	5	5	0	40%	Y	N	C L	N	indep	indiv		4/94
Inter-Cooperative Council (MI)		MI	37	U	Y	n	600	600	0		Y	Y	C M	Y	indep	co-op		6/93
Inter-Cooperative Council (TX)		MI	37	U	Y	n	162	162	0		Y	Y	M	Y	indep	co-op		1/95
International Co-op House		WI	64	U	N		30	30	0	50%	N	Y	C	Y	indep	cmty		6/94
International Puppydogs	F	OR	92	U	Y	n	5	5	0		N	N	C					12/94
Ion Exchange Village	F	IA	84															10/92
Iskcon Farm		FL	65	R	Y	y	30			50%	Y	Y	G	N		cmty	127	6/94
Island Group, The	F	CA		R	Y	y	300			33%	Y	Y	C					7/94
Jesuit Vol Corps East		PA		B	Y	n					Y	Y	C G	N		n profit		12/94
Jesuit Vol Corps Midwest		MI		B	Y	n					Y	Y	C G	N		n profit		12/94
Jesuit Vol Corps NW		OR	57	B	Y	n	181			64%	Y	Y	C G	N		n profit		12/94
Jesuit Vol Corps South		TX		B	Y	n					Y	Y	C G	N		n profit		12/94
Jesuit Vol Corps SW		CA		B	Y	n					Y	Y	C G	N		n profit		12/94
Jesus People USA		IL	72	U	Y	y	500	350	150	50%	N	Y	G		shared	cmty		1/95
Jubilee House Cmty		NC	79	U	Y	y	9	5	4	80%	N	N	C	N	shared	other		12/92
Jubilee Partners		GA	79	R	Y	n	17	9	8	56%	N	N	C L	N	shared	cmty	258	4/92
Julian Woods Cmty	RF	PA	70	R	Y	y	24	17	7	41%	N	N	C	Y	indep	cmty	140	2/93
Jump Off CLT	F	TN	92	R	Y		11	10	1	44%	N	N	C	Y	indep	cmty	1200	5/92
Jupiter Hollow		WV	76	R	Y	y	12	7	5	43%	N	N	M	Y	indep	cmty	178	1/93
K&K Organic Health Farm	F	NC		R	Y		12	12	0	42%	Y		O	N	shared	clt	300+	6/94
Kailash Kunj																		
Karmê-Chöling		VT	71	R	Y	y	53	46	7	50%	Y	Y	C L G	N	indep	other	540	5/93
Kehillat - Mishpakhot	NR	PA	82	U	Y	y	40					Y	O	Y	indep			12/92
Kerista Global Village	RF	CA	56	U	Y	y				50%	N	Y	C M	N	indep			3/93
Kidstown	RF	CA	90	R	Y	y					N	N	C M G	N	indep	indiv		7/92
King View Farm	RF	ONT	72	R	S	s	33	30	3	52%	Y	Y	C G	N	indep	n profit	86	4/92
Kingdom of Oyotunji		SC	70	R	Y	y	57			56%			G		indep	n profit	10	6/94
Koinonia Partners		GA	42	R	Y	y	27	15	12	53%	Y	Y	C	N	shared	other	1500	1/93
Kootenay Cooperative		BC	69	R			34	24	10	45%	N	N	C	Y	indep	cmty	200	4/92
Kripalu Center for Yoga & Health	RF	MA	72	R	Y	y	300+				N	Y	G			n profit	428	1/95
Krutsio		Mex.	76	R	Y	y	6	4	2	50%	Y	Y	C M	N	shared	clt	7000	6/92
L'Arche Daybreak		ONT	69	B	Y	y	117	101	16	50%	Y	Y	C L G	N	indep	cmty	20	6/92
L'Arche Homefires	F	NS	79		Y	y	46	35	11	57%	Y	Y	C	N	shared	cmty		7/93
L'Arche Mobile		AL	74	U	Y		44	41	3	43%	Y	Y	C G			cmty		11/93
L'Arche Syracuse		NY	74	U	Y		30				Y	Y	C G		indep			6/94
Lake Village		MI	67	B	Y	y	40	29	11	58%	Y	Y	G	N	indep	cmty	115	12/92
Lama Foundation		NM	68	R	Y	y	9	8	1	50%	Y	Y	O	N	indep	cmty	107	5/92

KEY *Provinces:* BC = British Columbia, MB = Manitoba, NS = Nova Scotia, ON = Ontario, SK = Saskatchewan. *Decisions:* C = Consensus, M = Majority, L = Leader, G = Group of leaders or elders, O = Other. *Who Owns Land:* CLT = Community Land Trust, Cmty = Community, Indiv = Individual, Ldlord = Landlord, Subgrp = Subgroup of members. *Income:* Shared = Members Share Income, Indep = Handle Own Finances. *Survey Date:* PrevDir = Previous Directory, NQ = No Questionnaire, Date is when survey questionnaire was completed or last updated by community.

Map / Index Name	Eat Together How Frequently?	What % of Own Food Is Grown?	Organic Food in Diet	Diet	Caffeine in Diet	Alcohol in Diet	Tobacco in Diet	# Children (<19yrs)	% Home Schooled	% Cmty Schooled	% Private Schooled	% Public Schooled	Spiritual Path	Primary Purpose and/or Focus
HighFlowing	rarely	6–20%												galactic synchronization
HighHorizons		21–50%						0					Other	teach environmental living
HighWind	rarely	>50%		veg	some	some	some	3	0	0	50	50		ecology, whole-systems learning
Hillegass	nearly all meals	1–5%						0						communal family-like living
Hilltop	rarely	1–5%							0	0	10	90		self-governed residential park
HimalayaInst.				veg										holistic, health, yoga, meditation
HolyCity														
HOME														
Homestead														
HorconesTwo														
HouseLavendr	2–5 times/wk	1–5%		omni	ok	ok	none	0						urban housing co-op
Huehuecoyotl	1–3 times/mo	1–5%		omni	often	some	some	14	0	50	50	0		developing ecotopian village
HundredMile		21–50%						7					EDL	integrating influence to human affairs
HutBrethSpok								0	0	100	0	0	HB	hutterian brethren
ICA-Chicago														global network, human development
ICA-Phoenix	nearly all dinners	1–5%		omni	some	ok		6	0	0	0	100		cooperative simple lifestyle
IDA	nearly all meals	21–50%	yes!	veg	ok	ok	ok	0					Pagan	queer spiritual faerie art
Innisfree	2–5 times/wk	1–5%		omni	often	ok	ok	0						adults with mental disabilities
InstHarDevel	nearly all meals	None	often	veg	none	none	none	0					Ecu,O	fourth way living food
InterCoop-MI	nearly all dinners	None		omni	often	often		0						affordable student cooperative housing
InterCoop-TX	nearly all dinners	None						0						affordable student cooperative housing
InterntlCoop	nearly all dinners	1–5%		omni	some	ok	ok	0						cooperative living education
IntlPuppydog	2–5 times/wk	6–20%						0						extended intimate family
IonExchange														parenting by "good life" principles
IskconFarm	nearly all meals	21–50%		veg					0	100	0	0	HK	simple living, high thinking
IslandGroup									100	0	0	0		create a psychedelic community
Jesuit-East	nearly all dinners	6–20%											Chr,RC	service and education
Jesuit-Midw	nearly all dinners	6–20%											Chr,RC	service and education
Jesuit-NW	nearly all dinners	6–20%											Chr,RC	service and education
Jesuit-South	nearly all dinners	6–20%											Chr,RC	service and education
Jesuit-SW	nearly all dinners	6–20%											Chr,RC	service and education
JesusPeopUSA	nearly all meals	None						150	0	100	0	0	Christian	evangelical christian ministry
JubileeHouse	nearly all dinners	None	often	omni	some	some	ok	4	0	0	0	100	Prot	god's call: peace/justice; play
JubileePrtnr	nearly all dinners	6–20%	often	no red	often	ok	ok	8	0	0	0	100	Other	refugee resettlement
JulianWoods	rarely	21–50%		no red	often	some	ok	7	0	0	25	75		land stewardship gentle living
JumpOff	1–3 times/mo	1–5%		veg	some	some	ok	1	0	0	0	100		eco-village land trust
JupiterHoll	rarely	6–20%		omni	often	some	ok	5	0	0	0	100		home with friends and nature
K&K-Organic	2–5 times/wk	>50%		no red	ok	ok	ok	0						organic self supporting community
Kailash														
KarmeChol	nearly all meals	6–20%		omni	often	ok	ok	7	0	0	0	100		meditation practice and study
KehillatMish	1–3 times/mo	None							25	0	0	75	Jewish	sustainability experimental
Kerista	2–5 times/wk	None		omni	often	some	often							neotribal paranational design
Kidstown	2–5 times/wk	6–20%		vgn	ok	none	none							sharing, cooperating, having fun
KingView	nearly all meals	21–50%	yes!	omni	some	ok	ok	3					EDL	spiritual regeneration
KingdomOyo	rarely	None							0	100	0	0	Other	west african culture and traditions
Koinonia	nearly all dinners	>50%		omni	often	some	ok	12	0	0	0	100		living witness to gods kingdom
Kootenay								10						we inhabit the land
Kripalu	nearly all meals	None		veg					100	0	0	0	Eastern	spirit and personal growth
Krutsio	nearly all meals	21–50%	often	omni	ok	none	none	2	100	0	0	0	Ecu	unit of ascending integration
LArchDaybrk	rarely	None						16	0	0	0	100	RC,Prot	creating homes for persons with disabilities
LArchHomefi	1–3 times/mo	1–5%						11	0	0	0	100	Quaker	solidarity/friendship/valuing
LArchMobile	1–3 times/mo	1–5%						3						permanent family-like home
LArcheSyracu	nearly all dinners												Christian	helps developmentally disabled
LakeVillage	rarely	>50%						11	11	0	24	85		live well with less
Lama	nearly all meals	1–5%	often	veg	some	none		1	0	0	0	100	Ecu,Ecl	awakening of consciousness

KEY *Food codes:* omni = includes red meat, no red = no red meat—includes fish or poultry and dairy, veg = vegetarian—no meat—includes dairy, vgn = vegan—no meat or dairy. *Spiritual path:* B = Buddhist, Chr = Christian, E = Eastern, Ecl = Eclectic, Ecu = Ecumenical, EDL = Emissaries of Divine Light, HB = Hutterian Brethren, NAm = N.American Indian, NSOM = New Social Order in Messiah, O = Other, P = Pagan, Prot = Protestant, Qk = Quaker, RC = Roman Catholic, UU = Unitarian Universalist.

Community	Forming, Reforming, Non-Residential	State/Prov. or Country	Year Established	Rural, Urban or Both	Open to More Adults? / Open to More Children?	Total Population	# Adults	# Children (<19yrs)	Percentage Women	Identified Leader / Leadership Core Group	How are Major Decisions Made?	Join Fee	Income	Who Owns Land	Acres of Land	Survey Date
Lamb of God Communities	NR	MD	71	U	Y y	200			50%	N Y	C G	N	indep			6/94
Lamborn Valley Cmty		CO	87	R	Y y	21	11	10	50%	N Y	C	Y		mix	120	12/92
Land Stewardship Center	F	MI		R	Y n										150	4/92
Laurel Hill Plantation																
Lichen Co-op		OR	71	R	Y y	5	5	0	60%	N N	C	Y		cmty	140	6/92
Life Center Association		PA	71	U	M m	37	36	1	53%	N Y	C	N		n profit		12/94
Light and Color Foundation	F	CO	93	B	Y y	16	16	0	50%	N Y	C	N	indep			1/94
Light Morning			73	R	Y y	6	5	1	40%	N Y	C	N	indep	indiv	150	7/93
Listwig Mir		CA	83	U	N n	8	6	2	50%	N N	C	N		subgrp		8/94
Long Branch		NC	74	R		9	6	3			C			clt	126	PrevDir
Los Angeles Eco-Village	F	CA	92	U	Y y	100	60	40	50%	Y Y	C O	N	indep			12/94
Los Horcones		Mex.	73	R	Y y	32	21	11	29%	N N	O	Y	shared	cmty		1/95
Lost Valley Educ Center		OR	89	R	Y y	15	10	5	40%	N Y	C G O	N	indep	indiv	90	5/92
Lothlorien (Elf Lore Family)		IN														NQ
Lothlorien Farm		ONT	72	R		15	13	2	46%	N	C	Y	indep	cmty	700	8/92
Love Israel Family		WA	68	R	Y y	81	33	48		Y Y	C L G	Y	shared	other	300	1/93
Maat Dompin Project	F	WV	soon	R	Y y	5	5	0	100%	Y Y	G		indep	n profit		12/94
Madison Cmty Cooperatives		WI	70	U	Y y	179				Y	C	Y		co-op		9/93
Madre Grande Monastery		CA	75	R	Y y	20	20	0	50%	N Y	G	N	both	n profit	264	5/92
Magic, Inc.		CA	76	U	Y y	8	8	0	25%	Y Y	C O	N	both	other		4/92
Magic Tortoise Foundation	RF	NM	73	R		6	5	1	40%	N Y	C			cmty	46	1/93
Maharishi International University		IA	73	B		7600	5700	1900	50%	Y Y	G O		indep	n profit	260	1/95
Manhattan Cohousing	F	NY	90	U	Y y					N Y	C	Y	indep			5/93
Marathon Co-op		CA	85	U	Y y	170	120	50		N Y	C M	Y		co-op		9/94
Marden Farm, The	F	NJ	85	R	Y y	3	3	0	67%	N	C		both	indiv	123	7/94
Mariposa Group, The		CA	84	B	Y y	4	3	1					Y		cmty		PrevDir
Martha's Housing Cooperative		WI	70s	U	Y y	30	30	0					Y		cmty		PrevDir
Maxworks Cooperative		IL	84	U	Y y	12	12	0	25%	N Y	C		indep	mix		7/94
Meramec Valley CLT	RF	MO	88	R	Y y	1 FU				Y	C O	N	indep	mix	213	1/93
Methow Center of Enlightenment		WA	90	R	Y y	5000				Y	M				88	6/94
Miccosukee Land Co-op		FL	73	R	Y y	216	142	74	54%	Y Y	M	N	indep	mix	319	8/94
Mikeco Rehtle	F	MI	89	R	Y y	5	4	1	75%	Y Y	C	N				6/92
Molly Hare Cooperative																
Monadnock Geocommons Village	F	NH	89	R	Y y	5	5	0	40%	Y Y	C O	Y	indep	indiv	75	8/93
Monan's Rill			74	B	Y y	32	23	9	62%	N	C O	Y	indep	cmty	440	10/92
Montebello Cmty		MA	82	U		7	7	0	43%		C	N	indep	indiv		1/93
Moonshadow	F	TN	65	R	N n	10	9	1	40%	N N	C	N	indep	indiv	200	3/93
Morninglory		ONT	69	R	N n	16	6	10	67%	N N	O	N	indep	clt	100	12/92
Mother Earth Church of Opihihale	RF	HI	79	R	Y y	7	4	3	25%	N Y	C	N	indep	mix	11	5/92
Mount Madonna Center		CA	78	R	Y y	107	84	23	54%	N Y	G	N	indep	cmty	355	9/92
Muir Commons		CA	91	U	Y y	65	37	28	57%	N N	C	N	indep	mix	3	1/95
Multiple Chemical Sensitivity Park																
N Street Cohousing		CA	86	U	Y y	52	36	16	53%	N Y	C	N	indep	mix		10/93
Namasté Greens	F	NH	73	R	Y y	7	5	2	40%	N Y	C	N	shared	indiv	49	12/92
Neary Lagoon Co-op		CA	92	U	Y	144	86	58		N Y	M	Y	indep	co-op		9/94
Network for a New Culture	F	OR	94													3/94
New Covenant Fellowship	RF	OH	72	R	Y y	16	8	8	57%	N N	C	N	shared	cmty	120	6/92
New Jah-rulsalem	RF	WI	71	R	Y y	26	8	18	50%	N N	C O	N	indep	clt	5	1/93
New Jerusalem Cmty	NR	OH	71	U	Y y	250	155	95	50%	N Y	C G	N	indep	other		5/92
New Land		VA	79	R	Y y	54	44	10	66%	N N	M	N	indep	indiv	200+	12/94
New Leaf																
New Meadow Run Bruderhof		PA	57	R	M m	150						N	shared	cmty		PrevDir
New Moon		CA	83	U	P m	13	13	0	~50%	N N	C	N	indep	indiv		5/94
New Roots CLT	RF	SK	78	R	Y y	20					C	N	indep	clt		7/94
New Vrndaban		WV	68	R	Y y	227	148	79	51%	Y Y	C L G	N	both	mix	4000	12/92

KEY *Provinces:* BC = British Columbia, MB = Manitoba, NS = Nova Scotia, ON = Ontario, SK = Saskatchewan. *Decisions:* C = Consensus, M = Majority, L = Leader, G = Group of leaders or elders, O = Other. *Who Owns Land:* CLT = Community Land Trust, Cmty = Community, Indiv = Individual, Ldlord = Landlord, Subgrp = Subgroup of members. *Income:* Shared = Members Share Income, Indep = Handle Own Finances. *Survey Date:* PrevDir = Previous Directory, NQ = No Questionnaire, Date is when survey questionnaire was completed or last updated by community.

Map / Index Name	Eat Together How Frequently?	What % of Own Food Is Grown?	Organic Food in Diet	Diet	Caffeine in Diet	Alcohol in Diet	Tobacco in Diet	# Children (<19yrs)	% Home Schooled	% Cmty Schooled	% Private Schooled	% Public Schooled	Spiritual Path	Primary Purpose and/or Focus
LambOfGod													Ecu	ecumenical community
Lamborn	2–5 times/wk	>50%	yes!	omni	ok	ok	ok	10	45	45	0	10	Prot	living our spiritual beliefs
LandStewCen				vgn			none							sustainable land stewardship
LaurelHill														
Lichen	1–3 times/mo	1–5%		no red	ok	ok	ok	0						environmental co-operative
LifeCenter	2–5 times/wk	1–5%						1						cooperative ownership of housing
LightColor	rarely	None		no red	ok	ok	ok	0						nature, cultural arts, holism
LightMorn	nearly all meals	>50%	yes!	veg	ok	some	ok	1	100	0	0	0	Ecl	simplicity and abundance
ListwigMir	nearly all dinners	1–5%						2	0	0	0	100		neo-social culinarism
LongBranch								3						environmental education
LosAnEcoVill	1 time/wk	1–5%		veg	some	ok	ok	40	0	0	2	98		healing urban neighborhoods
LosHorcones	nearly all meals	>50%						11	0	100	0	0		behaviorism equality sharing ecology pacifism
LostValley	nearly all dinners	6–20%		veg	ok	ok	ok	5	100	0	0	0		sustainable models & education
Lothlor-IN														nature sanctuary & education center
Lothlor-ONT	rarely	1–5%						2	0	0	0	100		land stewardship
LoveIsrael	rarely	6–20%	often	omni	ok	ok	ok	48	0	70	0	30	Other	living as one, in love
MaatDompin								0					Ecu,O	womyn of color empowerment
MadisonCoop		1–5%		veg										affordable housing
MadreGrande	nearly all dinners	6–20%		veg	often	some	some	0						positive spiritual path
MagicInc	nearly all meals	1–5%		omni	ok	ok	ok	0						ecological approach to value
MagicTortis	1–3 times/mo	6–20%						1	0	0	100	0		human development workshops
Maharishi	rarely	6–20%						1900	35	0	50	15	Other	community focused on consciousness
ManhattCoho		None												urban cohousing in new york city
Marathon	rarely	None						50	0	0	20	80		limited equity housing co-op
MardenFarm	2–5 times/wk	6–20%						0					Other	living in harmony with nature
MariposaGrp								1	0	0	0	100		honesty
MarthasCoop								0						cooperation, consensus
Maxworks	2–5 times/wk	1–5%						0						reutilize urban wastes, espec. wood
Meramac	1–3 times/mo	1–5%												ecological land stewardship
Methow	21–50%												Other	provide community for all
Miccusukee	rarely	1–5%		omni	often	some	some	74	2	0	15	83		rural cooperative community
MikecoRehtl	2–5 times/wk	None	yes!	vgn	ok	ok	none	1	100	100	0	0	Ecu,Ecl	appropriate, self-sufficient, sustainable
MollyHare														
Monadnock	1–3 times/mo	6–20%	often	veg	ok	ok	ok	0	0	0	50	50	Other	sustainable & mindful living
MonansRill	1–3 times/mo	6–20%	often	omni	some	some	some	9	0	0	0	100	Quaker	consensus/greens/gardening/fun
Montebello	2–5 times/wk	None		omni	often	ok	none	0					Other	urban evangelical christian
Moonshadow	nearly all dinners	>50%		no red	often	often	some	1						learn/teach sustainable living
Morninglory	1–3 times/mo	21–50%	often	omni	often	some	often	10	0	80	0	20	P,Ecl	respect for earth and each other
MothrEarthOp	1–3 times/mo	6–20%		omni	some	some	?	3	0	0	0	100		cooperation and self improvement
MtMadonna	nearly all meals	6–20%	yes!	veg	often	ok	none	23	0	100	0	0	Eastern	spiritual & personal enlightenment
MuirCommons	2–5 times/wk	6–20%						28	0	0	20	80		to be a good neighbor
MultChemSens														
N-Street	2–5 times/wk	1–5%		omni	often	often	ok	16	0	0	12	88		cohousing community
Namasté	nearly all dinners	6–20%	yes!	omni	ok	ok	ok	2	0	0	0	100	UU,P,Ecu	to enhance/sustain all of life
NearyLagoon	rarely	None						58	0	0	0	100		limited equity co-op
NetworkNewC														living without fear or violence
NewCovent	nearly all meals	>50%	yes!	omni	ok	none	ok	8	0	100	0	0	HB	christian social action
NewJahRuslm	2–5 times/wk	21–50%		omni	some	none	ok	18	0	66	0	33		god in man, and man in god
NewJerusalm	rarely	1–5%	some	omni	often	often	some	95	2	0	10	88	RomanCath	a lay, catholic, eucharistic community
NewLand	rarely	1–5%						10	0	0	20	80		develop our spiritual paths
NewLeaf														
NewMeadwRun									0	100	0	0	HB	hutterian brethren
NewMoon	nearly all dinners	1–5%		veg	yes!	often	often	0	0	0	0	100		crazy world—just duck
NewRoots	rarely													land trust, prairie ecology
NewVrndaban	2–5 times/wk	21–50%	often	veg	none	none	none	79	0	70	0	30	HK	wholistic god-conscious living

KEY *Food codes:* omni = includes red meat, no red = no red meat—includes fish or poultry and dairy, veg = vegetarian—no meat—includes dairy, vgn = vegan—no meat or dairy. *Spiritual path:* B = Buddhist, Chr = Christian, E = Eastern, Ecl = Eclectic, Ecu = Ecumenical, EDL = Emissaries of Divine Light, HB = Hutterian Brethren, NAm = N.American Indian, NSOM = New Social Order in Messiah, O = Other, P = Pagan, Prot = Protestant, Qk = Quaker, RC = Roman Catholic, UU = Unitarian Universalist.

Communities Directory

Name	Forming/Reforming	Non-Residential	State/Prov. or Country	Year Established	Rural, Urban, or Both	Open to More Adults?	Open to More Children?	Total Population	# Adults	# Children (<19yrs)	Percentage Women	Identified Leader	Leadership Core Group	How are Major Decisions Made?	Join Fee	Income	Who Owns Land	Acres of Land	Survey Date
Niche	F		AZ	92	U	N	y	5	4	1	50%	N		C	N	indep	clt	2.2	12/92
Ninth Street Co-op			CA	86	U			7	6	1	67%	Y		C	Y	indep	co-op		9/94
no name yet Cohousing	F		CA	94	U	Y	y	18	13	5	77%	N Y		C	Y	indep	cmty		10/94
Noonday Farm			MA	84	U	N	n	7	5	2	43%	N			N	indep	cmty	18	5/93
North Cottonwood Ecovillage																			
North Mountain CLT			VA	72	R	Y	y	5	3	2	67%	N N		C		indep	clt	127	5/92
North Woods Vegan Cmty	F		WI	94	R	Y	y	5	5	0	40%	N N		C		indep	ldlord	2	10/94
Northern Sun Farm Co-op			MB	82	R	N		20	11	9	55%	N N		C		indep	cmty	160	7/92
Nyland Cohousing			CO	93	U	N	n	122	84	38	53%	Y		C	Y	indep	cmty	42	10/94
Oak Grove	F		VA		R	Y	y	1	1	0	100%	N N		C	N	indep	indiv	80	4/93
Oberlin Student Co-op Assoc	·		OH	50	U	Y	n	600+	600	0		Y		C M	Y	indep	co-op		9/94
Ojai Foundation			CA	79	R	Y	y	8	8	0	50%	Y		C O	N	indep	other	40	9/92
1000 Small Pharmabusters			KS	88	U			6	4	2	60%	N N		C	N	indep	subgrp		7/94
One World Family Commune			CA	67	B	Y	y	15	13	2	100%	Y N		C	N	shared	ldlord		6/94
Open Door Cmty			GA	81	U	Y	y	30			27%	N Y		G	N	shared	mix		
ORCOM (Orgone Committee)																			
Osterweil House			MI	47	U	N	n	13	11	2	54%	Y Y		C M		indep	cmty		10/93
O.U.R House			BC																NQ
Owl Farm			OR	76	R	Y	y	6	5	1	100%	N N		C	N	indep	clt	147	9/92
Pacific Family Co-op			CA	91	B	Y	y	113	98	15		Y		M	Y		co-op	10	9/94
Padanaram Settlement			IN	66	R	Y	m	160	90	70	44%	Y Y		G	N	shared	clt	2000	6/92
Pansy Farm																			
Panterra	F		NY	92	R			2	2	0				C					6/94
Parker Street Co-op			CA	88	U	Y	y	26	24	2	50%	N Y			Y		cmty		8/94
Parnassus Rising	F		AZ	90	B	Y	y	2	2	0	50%	Y Y		M	N		cmty	100+	5/93
Peace Farm			TX	86	R	Y	y	8	6	2	43%	Y Y		C	N	indep	mix	20	5/92
Peaceful Gardens Village	F		ID	90	R	Y	y	6	3	3	50%	N Y		C	Y	indep	indiv	44	4/93
Penington Friends House			NY	1897	U	Y	y	29	23	6	47%	Y N		C	N	indep	other		7/92
Permanent Agriculture Land Trust	F		CA	93	B	Y	y	7	5	2	20%	N Y		C O	N		clt		4/93
Peter Maurin Farm			NY	93	R	Y	y	15	13	2	20%	N N		O		indep	other	50	6/94
Phanto Bolo	F		CO	93	R	Y	y	9	8	1	44%	N Y		C	N	indep	indiv	43	1/93
Philoxia			ONT	74	R	Y	y	12	10	2	40%	Y Y		M G	N	both	indiv	400	6/92
Phoenix Cmty			CA	83	U	Y	n	3	3	0	67%	N			N		subgrp		4/92
Phoenix Cmty Forming	F		AZ	93	U	Y	y	7	5	2	40%	N Y		M	N	indep			12/93
Piceon Farms																			
Pilot Mtn EcoCommunity																			
Pioneer Valley Cohousing	F		MA	94	R			77	57	20	55%	N N		C	N	indep	cmty	25	1/94
Pleasant View			NY		R	M	m								N	shared	cmty		PrevDir
Ponderosa Village																			
Port Centauri	F		CO	90	R	Y	y	8	8	0	50%	N Y			N	indep	subgrp	3000+	12/92
Positive College	F		CO	94	R	Y	y					Y N		C M L G O	N				4/94
Postive Living Ctr & Cmty	F		CA	91	U	Y	n	40	40	0	38%	Y Y		L	N	indep	ldlord		1/95
PPAALS	F		NY	94	U	Y	n	5	5	0	60%	Y N		C L	N	indep	indiv		3/94
Prag House			WA	71	U	N	n	16	11	5	55%	N N		C	N		clt		8/92
Prairie Ridge Cmty	F		WI	90	R	Y	y	8	6	2	40%	N N			Y	indep		200	11/92
Prudence Crandall House	RF		CA	72	U	N	n	6	4	2	75%	N Y		C	N	indep	indiv		12/92
Pumpkin Hollow Farm			NY	37	R	Y									N		cmty	130	10/93
Purple Rose			CA	78	U	N	n	10	10	0	40%	N N		C	N		subgrp		12/92
Quaker House	RF		IL	90	U	Y	y	9	8	1	63%	Y Y		C	N	indep	n profit		10/93
Quakerland	F		TX	81	R	Y	y	11	11	0	58%	N Y		C			cmty		5/94
Quarry Hill			VT	46	R	M	m	90	65	25	54%	N Y		G	N	indep	other	200+	1/95
Qumbya Co-op			IL	88	U	Y	n	34	29	5	50%	N Y		M	Y	indep	other		7/92
Rainbow Hearth Sanctuary	RF		TX	81	R	Y	y	18	12	6	57%	N Y		O	N	indep	mix	20	10/93
Rainbow House			KS	79	U	Y		10	10	0	40%	N N		C	N	indep	indiv		1/93
Rainbow Junction	F		CA	92	R	Y	y	5	3	2	33%	N N		O	N	indep	indiv	40	4/92

KEY: *Provinces:* BC = British Columbia, MB = Manitoba, NS = Nova Scotia, ON = Ontario, SK = Saskatchewan. *Decisions:* C = Consensus, M = Majority, L = Leader, G = Group of leaders or elders, O = Other. *Who Owns Land:* CLT = Community Land Trust, Cmty = Community, Indiv = Individual, Ldlord = Landlord, Subgrp = Subgroup of members. *Income:* Shared = Members Share Income, Indep = Handle Own Finances. *Survey Date:* PrevDir = Previous Directory, NQ = No Questionnaire, Date is when survey questionnaire was completed or last updated by community.

Maps & Charts

Map / Index Name	Eat Together How Frequently?	What % of Own Food Is Grown?	Organic Food in Diet	Diet	Caffeine in Diet	Alcohol in Diet	Tobacco in Diet	# Children (<19yrs)	% Home Schooled	% Cmty Schooled	% Private Schooled	% Public Schooled	Spiritual Path	Primary Purpose and/or Focus
Niche	2–5 times/wk	1–5%		veg	ok	ok	ok	1	0	0	0	100		affordable urban housing, permaculture
NinthStreet	rarely	21–50%						1	0	0	0	100		limited equity housing co-op
NoNameCoho	2–5 times/wk	1–5%						5	0	0	100	0		living in community
Noonday	nearly all dinners	6–20%		veg				2	0	0	100	0		food for the poor
NorCottonwd														
NorMountain	1 time/wk	21–50%		veg	some	some	ok	2	0	0	0	100		the dance of community living
NorWoodVegan	nearly all meals	6–20%		vgn	some	ok	ok	0						rural vegan sustainable living
NorSunFarm	rarely	6–20%		omni	often	some		9	75	0	0	25		living lightly on the land
NylandCoho	2–5 times/wk	1–5%						38	0	0	15	85		to live more simply with others
OakGrove	2–5 times/wk	6–20%						0					Qk,NAm,E	alternative living spiritual center
OberlinStuCo	nearly all meals	None		veg				0						student owned co-op
OjaiFndtn		1–5%		no red				0	0	0	100	0		educational retreat vision
OneThouSmPhm	nearly all dinners	6–20%						2						create sustainable way of life
OneWorldFam	nearly all dinners	1–5%	often	vgn	ok	ok	ok	2	50	0	0	50	Other	world transformation - utopia
OpenDoor	nearly all meals	None							0	0	0	100	Christian	serving the poor
ORCOM														
Osterweil	2–5 times/wk	None		omni	often	ok	ok	2						we bake our own fresh bread!
OURHouse														community-based youth program
OwlFarm	rarely		yes!	veg	ok	ok	ok	1	100	0	0	0	Pagan	land accessibility to wimmin
PacFamily	rarely	None						15	2	0	0	13		co-op mobile home park
Padanaram	nearly all meals	21–50%		omni	often			70	0	99	0	1		international communal utopia
PansyFarm														
Panterra		None		veg				0					Other	universal oneness of consciousness
ParkerSt	rarely	1–5%						2	0	0	0	100		resident owned, affordable
Parnassus	1–3 times/mo	None		omni	often	ok	none	0						the brave new world vision
PeaceFarm	1–3 times/mo	1–5%		veg	some	some	ok	2						peace and social justice
PeacefulGrdn	nearly all dinners	>50%		no red	ok	ok	ok	3	50	0	0	50		spirituality, cooperation, love
Penington	nearly all dinners	None		omni	often	none	none	6						quaker sponsored living community
PermntAgri	1–3 times/mo	6–20%		omni	some	some	ok	2	100	0	0	0		permaculture land trust
PeteMaurFarm	2–5 times/wk	21–50%						2	0	0	0	100	RomanCath	the liturgy and the land
PhantoBolo	1 time/wk	None	often	omni	often	ok	ok	1					P,NAm	growing together on earth
Philoxia	nearly all meals	21–50%		veg		ok		2	100	0	0	0		to exemplorate wholeness and truth
Phoenix-CO	2–5 times/wk	None						0					E,B	juicy growthful group marriage
Phoenix-AZ	rarely	None		omni	often	some	ok	2	100	0	0	0		cooperation and human growth
PiceonFarm														
PilotMtn														
PioneerVall	2–5 times/wk			omni	often	some	none	20	10	0	0	90		blend of privacy and community
PleasantView									0	100	0	0	HB	hutterian brethren
Ponderosa														
PortCentauri	1 time/wk	6–20%		omni	ok	ok	none	0						self sufficient new civilization
PositiveColl														truth–trust–love–friendship–happiness–freedom
PosLivCen	1–3 times/mo	None		veg	some	ok	ok	0						positive, conscious, healthy
PPAALS	2–5 times/wk	None				ok	ok	0						sponsor child/mental aid tv thon
PragHouse	1–3 times/mo	None						5	0	0	50	50		secular humanist political
PrairieRidge	nearly all dinners	>50%		omni	some	some	ok	2	0	0	0	100		family, ecology, wholeness
PrudCrandall	2–5 times/wk	6–20%						2						4 generations, feminist, stable
PumpkinHoll	nearly all meals	21–50%		veg									Other	theosophy: study, service, meditation
PurpleRose	nearly all dinners	1–5%		veg	ok	ok	ok	0						collective affordable living
QuakerHouse	nearly all dinners	1–5%	often	veg	some	ok	ok	1					Ecu	quaker-based eco/peace emphasis
QuakerLand								0					Quaker	community through consensus
QuarryHill	rarely	1–5%						25	0	100	0	0		creative expression + nonviolent parenting
Qumbya	nearly all dinners	1–5%		omni	often	some	ok	5						student-owned cooperative housing
RainbHearth	rarely	6–20%	often	omni	ok	none	none	6					Other	semi-intentional neighborhood community
RainbHouse	1 time/wk	1–5%		omni	some	some	some	0						peace-seeking economical living
RainbJunctn	1 time/wk	21–50%		omni	often	none	ok	2						spiritual simplicity peace

KEY *Food codes:* omni = includes red meat, no red = no red meat—includes fish or poultry and dairy, veg = vegetarian—no meat—includes dairy, vgn = vegan—no meat or dairy. *Spiritual path:* B = Buddhist, Chr = Christian, E = Eastern, Ecl = Eclectic, Ecu = Ecumenical, EDL = Emissaries of Divine Light, HB = Hutterian Brethren, NAm = N.American Indian, NSOM = New Social Order in Messiah, O = Other, P = Pagan, Prot = Protestant, Qk = Quaker, RC = Roman Catholic, UU = Unitarian Universalist.

Community	Forming, Reforming, Non-Residential	State/Prov. or Country	Year Established	Rural, Urban or Both	Open to More Adults? / Open to More Children?	Total Population	# Adults	# Children (<19yrs)	Percentage Women	Identified Leader / Leadership Core Group	How are Major Decisions Made?	Join Fee	Income	Who Owns Land	Acres of Land	Survey Date
Rainbow Valley	RF	TX	81	R	Y	6	2	4	47%	N Y	C M	Y	indep	cmty	220	5/92
Raj-Yoga Math and Retreat																
Rapha Cmty	NR	NY	71		Y y	42	31	11	61%	N N	C	N	indep			10/93
Raven Rocks			70	R	Y y	11	11	0			C	N		cmty	1047	PrevDir
R.E.A.C.H.	F	NM	90	R	Y y	40	39	1	30%	Y Y	L G	Y	indep	cmty	55	11/93
Reba Place Fellowship		IL	57	U	Y y	95				Y	C	N	shared	cmty		10/92
ReCreation Center																
Red Mountain	F	CA	94	R	Y y	1	1	0	0%	Y N	O		indep	indiv	1	3/94
Reevis Mountain		AZ	80	R	Y n	15	13	2	33%	Y Y		Y	indep	mix	13	6/92
Refugio Del Rio Grande		TX	85	R	Y y	6	6	0	33%	Y	C	N	both	n profit	4	1/95
Reina del Cielo		VA	72	R	Y y	25	15	10		N Y	C	N	indep	other	50	7/94
ReJenneration House	F	CA	89	R	Y m	5	5	0	40%	Y Y	C	N	indep	indiv	5	5/92
Remar		IL	92	B	Y y	50			12%	Y Y	G	N	shared	ldlord		1/95
Renaissance Cmty	RF	MA	68	R	N n	38	20	18	60%	N Y	C	N		mix	88	4/96
Rivendell Cooperative		MI	73	U	Y y	6	6	0	50%	N N	C	Y	indep	cmty		5/92
River City Housing Collective		IA	77	U	Y y	40	29	11	50%	Y Y	O	Y	indep	mix		1/93
River Cmty Homes		CA	84	R		88	48	40	73%	Y	C M		indep	co-op	30	9/94
River Farm		WA	?	R	M m	11	8	3	56%	N N	C	N	indep	clt	80	6/92
Riverside Cmty	F	WI	93	R	Y y	8	6	2	50%	N N	C	Y	indep	cmty	133	7/93
Rocky Mountain Dharma Center		CO	71	R	Y n	39	38	1	41%	Y Y	G	N	indep	n profit	500	3/93
Rosy Branch Farm		NC	87	R	N n	24	11	13	55%	N N	C	Y	indep	mix	50	7/93
Rowanwood Conservers Society		ONT	85	R		28	15	13	53%	N N	C	Y	indep	cmty	92	9/92
Rowe Camp & Conference Center		MA	73	R	Y y	9	9	0	78%	Y	L O	N	indep	other		4/93
Rudolf Steiner Fellowship		NY	66	R	Y y	124	100	24	59%	N Y	G	N	indep	cmty	25	5/92
Saint Benedict's Farm		TX	56	R	Y n	5	5	0	40%	Y N	C L	N		indiv	105	8/93
Saint Francis Cmty		ME	76	R	Y y	20	13	7	58%	Y Y	C	N		cmty	180	6/93
Saint Francis & Therese		MA	32	U	Y	7	4	3		N N	C	N	shared	clt		6/94
Saint Herman of Alaska Monastery	F	CA	70	R	Y n	13	13	0	0%	Y Y	L G	N		indiv	100+	7/92
Saint John's Order	RF	CA	69	U	Y y	5	5	0	40%	Y	G	N	shared	ldlord		9/94
Salt Spring Centre		BC	81	R	Y	11	7	4	43%	Y Y	M	Y		n profit		4/92
Sandhill Farm		MO	74	R	M n	10	7	3	43%	N N	C	N	shared	cmty	135	8/92
Sandy Bar Ranch	F	CA	92	R	N y	6	6	0	50%	N N	C	N	shared	indiv	42	1/93
Santa Rosa Creek Commons		CA	79	U	Y y	44	34	10	57%	N Y	C	Y	indep	co-op		8/94
Sassafras Ridge Farm		WV	72	R	N n	18	9	9	60%	N N	C	N	indep	mix	240	4/92
SEADS of Truth, Inc.	F	ME	80	R	Y y	8	6	2	50%	N Y	C L O	Y		subgrp	60	8/92
Seeds of Peace		AZ				5	4	1								NQ
Seven Springs Farm		MO	72	R	N n	14	13	1	43%	N N	C	N		mix	120	4/92
Seven Waves	F	OR	88	R	Y y	6	6	0	50%	Y Y	G	Y		other	130	1/93
Shannon Farm		VA	74	R	Y y	90	63	27	49%	N N	C	N	indep	cmty	520	1/96
Sharingwood		WA	84	R	Y y	35	25	10	44%	N Y	C	Y	indep	mix	38	10/93
Sharon Spring Cohousing	F	NC	92	R	Y y	16	7	9	29%	N Y	C	N		mix	29	8/93
Shenoa		CA	90	R						Y Y	C	N		n profit	160	1/94
Shepherdsfield		MO	79	R	Y y	29	29	0	62%	Y Y	C G	N	shared	cmty	95.5	7/92
Shibboleth, The																
Shiloh Cmty		AR	42	B	Y y	31	25	6					N		cmty		PrevDir
Shining Waters Retreat	RF	MO	83	U	Y	49	33	16	60%	Y Y	C G	N	indep	other	55	8/93
Short Mountain Sanctuary		TN	73	R	Y m	11	11	0	0%	N N	C	N	indep	clt	200	5/92
Sichlassenfallen		WI	65	U	N n	7	7	0	57%	N N	C M	N	indep	co-op		8/92
Sierra Hot Springs		CA	89	R	Y y	16	14	2	50%	Y Y	G	Y	indep	other	700	2/93
Sikh Dharma (AZ)		AZ	69		Y y					Y Y	O	N	indep	n profit		1/95
Sikh Dharma (CA)		CA	69		Y y	900 fu				Y Y	O	N	indep	n profit		1/95
Sikh Dharma (MA)		MA	69		Y y					Y Y	O	N	indep	n profit		1/95
Sikh Dharma (NM)		NM	69		Y y					Y Y	O	N	indep	n profit		1/95
Sikh Dharma (VA)		VA	69		Y y					Y Y	O	N	indep	n profit		1/95
Silverlake Co-op		CA	84	U		100				Y	M	Y	indep	co-op		9/94

KEY *Provinces:* BC = British Columbia, MB = Manitoba, NS = Nova Scotia, ON = Ontario, SK = Saskatchewan. *Decisions:* C = Consensus, M = Majority, L = Leader, G = Group of leaders or elders, O = Other. *Who Owns Land:* CLT = Community Land Trust, Cmty = Community, Indiv = Individual, Ldlord = Landlord, Subgrp = Subgroup of members. *Income:* Shared = Members Share Income, Indep = Handle Own Finances. *Survey Date:* PrevDir = Previous Directory, NQ = No Questionnaire, Date is when survey questionnaire was completed or last updated by community.

Map / Index Name	Eat Together How Frequently?	What % of Own Food Is Grown?	Organic Food in Diet	Diet	Caffeine in Diet	Alcohol in Diet	Tobacco in Diet	# Children (<19yrs)	% Home Schooled	% Cmty Schooled	% Private Schooled	% Public Schooled	Spiritual Path	Primary Purpose and/or Focus
RainbVal-TX	rarely	1–5%		omni	some	some	some	4	20	0	0	60		sustainable living
RajYogaMath														
Rapha	1–3 times/mo	None						11	0	0	0	100	Prot,Ecu,Ecl	commitment to spiritual growth
RavenRocks								0						education, ecology, sharing
REACH	rarely	6–20%						1						eco-sound-self-sufficient
RebaPlace	1 time/wk	1–5%		omni	some	some	none		15	0	0	85		radical christian community
ReCreation														
RedMtn	1 time/wk	1–5%		no red	ok	ok	ok	0						spiritual and personal growth
ReevisMtn	nearly all meals	>50%		no red	none	none	none	2						self reliance w/spiritual orientation
RefugioRioGr	nearly all meals	21–50%						0						refugee camp support community
ReinaDCielo	1–3 times/mo	1–5%						10					Other	spiritual
Rejenneratn	2–5 times/wk	21–50%	yes!	veg	some	some	ok	0					Ecl	diversity stewardship health
Remar	nearly all meals	None											Christian	christian attention to needy people
Renaissance	1–3 times/mo	21–50%	yes!	omni	often	ok	ok	18	0	0	10	90	Ecu,Ecl	individual freedom resposibility
Rivendell	1–3 times/mo	1–5%		no red	ok	ok	ok	0						cooperative housing
RiverCity	nearly all dinners	1–5%		omni	ok	ok	ok	11						cooperative affordable housing
RiverCmtyHm	rarely	None						40	0	0	5	95		limited equity housing co-op
RiverFarm	1–3 times/mo	6–20%		omni	often	some	often	3	0	0	0	100		land stewardship and education
Riverside-WI	1–3 times/mo	1–5%		veg	some	some	ok	2	0	0	50	50		rural cohousing healthy living
RockyMtnDhar	nearly all meals	None	often	omni	often	some	some	1					Buddhist	contemplative practice
RosyBranch	1–3 times/mo	1–5%		omni	some	some	some	13	10	0	10	80		modeling cooperative options
Rowanwood	1–3 times/mo	6–20%		omni	often	some	ok	13	0	0	0	100		extended family, caring, stewardship
RoweCamp	2–5 times/wk	None		no red	often	some	ok	0						personal & spiritual growth
RudfSteinFel	nearly all meals	>50%		omni	often	none	ok	24	0	10	90	0		spiritual growth through service
SaintBenedct	nearly all meals	None	often	omni	often	some	none	0					RomanCath	to seek god completely
SaintFran-ME	2–5 times/wk	21–50%		no red	often	often		7	0	0	0	100		community of dispossessed
SaintFranThr	nearly all dinners	1–5%		veg				3	0	0	0	100	RC,O	peace & justice cmty
SaintHerman	nearly all meals	6–20%	often	no red	often	some	none	0					Eastern	"Give ye them to eat" (Mt. 14:16)
SaintJohns	nearly all dinners	None						0					B,Chr	to practice the dharma
SaltSpring	nearly all dinners	6–20%	often	veg	some	none	none	4	0	33	33	33	E,Ecl	positive thought & action
Sandhill	nearly all dinners	>50%	yes!	omni	often	often		3	100	0	0	0	Pagan	sustainable ecology & equality
SandyBar	2–5 times/wk	21–50%		omni	some	some	some	0						sustainable living and education
SantaRosaCrk	1 time/wk	1–5%						10	0	0	10	90		cooperation; ecological living
Sassafras	rarely	21–50%	often	omni	often	often	ok	9	43	0	14	43	P,Ecl	decentralized cooperation
SeadsTruth	2–5 times/wk	6–20%		no red	often	ok	ok	2						do yourself solar organizing
SeedsPeace								1						political action support collective
SevenSprgs	1–3 times/mo	1–5%						1	0	0	0	100		rural living/cooperation
SevenWaves	2–5 times/wk	>50%	often	omni	ok	none	none	0					Other	actively benefit poverty poor!
Shannon	1–3 times/mo	6–20%	some	omni	some	some	some	25	12	0	16	72		cooperative rural lifestyles
Sharingwood	2–5 times/wk	1–5%		omni	some	ok	ok	10	50	0	0	50		rural co-housing large greeenbelt
SharonSprgs	rarely	1–5%		veg				9	50	0	0	50		support friendship sound living
Shenoa	nearly all meals	1–5%		no red	often	some	some		0	0	0	100		retreat & learning center
Sheprdsfld	nearly all meals	1–5%	often	omni	ok	ok	none	0	0	100	0	0	Prot	to follow the way of jesus christ
Shibboleth														
Shiloh								6					Christian	spirituality, bakery
ShiningWater	2–5 times/wk	None		veg	ok	ok	ok	16	0	0	0	100		cultural educational health yoga
ShortMtn	nearly all dinners	21–50%		no red	some	ok	ok	0						queer safe space
Sichlassen	1–3 times/mo	1–5%		omni	often	some	some	0						common life style
SierraHotSpq	1 time/wk	None	some	veg	often	none	some	2	50	0	0	50	mix	spiritual lifestyle, holistic health
SikhDahrm-AZ		None		veg									sikh/yogic	see Sikh Dharma - CA
SikhDahrm-CA		None		veg					0	33	33	33	sikh/yogic	sikh, yoga
SikhDahrm-MA		None		veg									sikh/yogic	see Sikh Dharma - CA
SikhDahrm-NM		None		veg									sikh/yogic	see Sikh Dharma - CA
SikhDahrm-VA		None		veg									sikh/yogic	see Sikh Dharma - CA
Silverlake	rarely	None												limited equity housing co-op

KEY *Food codes:* omni = includes red meat, no red = no red meat—includes fish or poultry and dairy, veg = vegetarian—no meat—includes dairy, vgn = vegan—no meat or dairy. *Spiritual path:* B = Buddhist, Chr = Christian, E = Eastern, Ecl = Eclectic, Ecu = Ecumenical, EDL = Emissaries of Divine Light, HB = Hutterian Brethren, NAm = N.American Indian, NSOM = New Social Order in Messiah, O = Other, P = Pagan, Prot = Protestant, Qk = Quaker, RC = Roman Catholic, UU = Unitarian Universalist.

Community	Forming, Reforming, Non-Residential	State/Prov. or Country	Year Established	Rural, Urban or Both	Open to More Adults?	Open to More Children?	Total Population	# Adults	# Children (<19yrs)	Percentage Women	Identified Leader	Leadership Core Group	How are Major Decisions Made?	Join Fee	Income	Who Owns Land	Acres of Land	Survey Date
Sirius Cmty		MA	78	B	Y	y	33	20	13	53%	N	Y	C G	N	indep	cmty	86	5/92
Sisters of Divine Providence	F	MO	32	U	Y	n	66	66	0	100%	Y	Y	C M	N	shared	cmty		8/93
Sivananda Ashram Yoga Ranch Colony		NY	75	R	Y	y	18	18	0	50%	Y	Y	C L G	N	indep	other	77	12/92
Six Directions	F	UT	89	R	Y	y	42	23	19		N	Y	C M L G O	N	indep	mix	170	12/93
Sky Woods Cosynegal		MI	73	B	Y	y	6	6	0	33%	N	N	C M	N	shared	cmty	20	8/92
Sky-Jahnna, The	F	CA	80	B	Y	y	6	2	4	83%	N	Y	C G	N	shared	other		7/93
Skyfire	F	KS	94	R	Y		2	2	0	0%	N		C		indep			12/94
Society for Human Solidarity	F	KS	83	U	Y	n	2	2	0	50%	N	N	C	N	shared	other		11/93
Society of Family Solidarity	F	CA	93	B	Y	y	9				Y	Y	M	Y	indep			9/94
Sojourners Cmty	RF	DC	71	U	Y	y	13	10	3	50%	N	Y	C G	N		cmty		7/93
Song of the Morning	F	MI	70	R	Y		12	12	0			Y	C M	Y	indep	n profit	800	9/94
Songaia Cmty		WA	87	R	Y	y	16	11	5	31%	N		C	N	indep	mix	11	7/92
Sonoran Eco-village	F	AZ	91	B	Y	y	6			50%	N	Y	C					4/93
Southern Cassadaga Spiritualist Camp		FL	94	B	Y	n	280	280	0	50%	N	Y	G	Y	indep	other	55	7/93
Southside Park Cohousing		CA	93	U	Y	y	38	24	14	69%	N	Y	C M	Y	indep	indiv	1.4	12/92
Sparrow Hawk Village		OK	81	R	Y	y	90	76	14	74%	N	N	C	N	indep	mix	432	9/94
Spaulding Unit		CA	78	U	N	n	10	10	0	50%	N	Y	C	N	indep	subgrp		12/92
Spies for Sanity	F	NY		B	Y	y	4	4	0	50%	N	N	C	N				9/94
Spiral Wimmin's Cmty		KY	87	R	Y	y	7	7	0	100%	N	N	C	N	indep	clt	250	4/92
Spiricoasis	F	ONT	91	R	Y	y	6					Y	G	Y	indep	cmty		12/93
Spring Valley Bruderhof		PA	90	R	Y	y	170	80	90	59%			C	N	shared	cmty	150	6/92
Springtree Cmty		VA	71	R	Y	m	5	4	1	50%	N	N	C M	N	shared	cmty	120	4/92
Sri Aurobindo Sadhana Peetham	RF	CA	72	B	Y	n	6	5	1	17%	N	Y	O		both	other	3.5	7/94
S.T.A.R.	F	NM	92	R	Y	y	61	53	9	47%	Y	Y	L G	N	indep	cmty	640	11/93
Starland Hutterian Brethren		MN		R	M	m								N	shared	cmty		PrevDir
Starseed Cmty	F	MA	87	R	Y	y	6			71%		Y	C	N	indep	indiv	130	7/94
Stelle Cmty		IL	73	R	Y	y	93	72	21	44%	N	N	M	N	indep	mix	240	1/93
Steppingwoods	F	OR	75	R	Y		1	1	0	100%	N		C	N	indep	indiv	120	5/92
Stewart Little Co-op		NY	72	U	Y		16	16	0	50%	N	N	C	N	indep			6/94
Still Water Sabbatical	F	MT	91	R	Y	y	13	13	0	54%	N	Y	C M G O	N	indep	cmty	.25	4/93
Stonehedge Farm	RF	ONT	75	R	Y	y	13	6	7	50%	N	N	C	N		cmty	50	4/93
Student Cooperative Organization Inc		OH	92	U	N	n	10	10	0	50%	N	N	C M	Y	indep	n profit		3/94
Sunburst	F	FL	92	U	Y	y	4	4	0	25%	Y	Y	C	N		clt		2/93
Sunflower Co-op		TX	80	U	N	n	8	8	0	50%	N	N	C	N	indep	cmty		8/93
Sunflower Farm		OH	74	R	N	n	17	15	2	47%	N	N	C	N	indep	mix	100	7/94
Sunflower House		KS	69	U	Y	n	30	25	5	33%	N	Y	M	Y	indep	cmty		4/92
Sunnier Palms	F	PA	92	R	Y	y	17	14	3	47%	N	N	M O	Y	indep	cmty	23	6/92
Sunnyside Farm	F	MO	93	R	Y	y	8	2	6	50%	Y		L	Y	shared	indiv		11/93
Sunrise Ranch	RF	CO	46	R	Y		140	130	10		Y	Y	C	N	indep	clt	360	1/93
Sunset House (CA)	RF	CA	77	U	Y	y	7			43%	N	N	C	N	indep	cmty		12/92
Sunset House (WA)		WA	74	U			6			67%			C	N		clt		6/94
Susan B Anthony Mem. Unrest Home		OH	79	R	Y	n	4	4	0	100%	N	N	C	N	indep	clt	152	5/92
Sweetwater CLT		MO	89	R	Y	y	14	9	5	67%	N	N	C	N	indep	clt	480	4/92
Synergy		CA	72	U	Y		35	30	5	49%	N	Y	C	N	indep	other		6/93
Syntony	F	HI	81	R	Y	y	3	3	0	33%	N	N	C	N	shared	indiv	1	5/92
Taliesin Cmty	F	NY	93		Y	y							C O		indep	clt		1/94
Tanguy Homesteads		PA	45	U	Y	y	100	70	30	50%	N	Y	C	Y	indep	co-op	100	1/95
Tekiah	RF	VA	91	R	Y	y	5	4	1	66%	N	N	C	N	shared	cmty	5	9/92
Ten Stones	F	VT	93	R	Y	y	23	14	9	50%	N	Y	C	Y	indep	cmty	88	5/93
Teramanto		WA	75	B	Y	y	9	8	1	33%	Y	Y	C	Y	indep	mix	1.5	7/92
Three Springs	F	CA	92	R	Y	y	9	9	0	44%	N	Y	C	Y	indep	clt	160	1/93
Timeweave																		
Toad House	NR	CA	75	R	Y						N	N	C M O	Y	indep	other		7/92
Tolstoy Farm		WA	63	R	M	m	35	26	9	35%	N	N	C	N	indep	n profit	240	10/93
Toronto TORI Cmty	NR	MI	~68	B	Y	y	200	48	18		N	N	C	N	indep			8/94

KEY *Provinces:* BC = British Columbia, MB = Manitoba, NS = Nova Scotia, ON = Ontario, SK = Saskatchewan. *Decisions:* C = Consensus, M = Majority, L = Leader, G = Group of leaders or elders, O = Other. *Who Owns Land:* CLT = Community Land Trust, Cmty = Community, Indiv = Individual, Ldlord = Landlord, Subgrp = Subgroup of members. *Income:* Shared = Members Share Income, Indep = Handle Own Finances. *Survey Date:* PrevDir = Previous Directory, NQ = No Questionnaire, Date is when survey questionnaire was completed or last updated by community.

Map / Index Name	Eat Together How Frequently?	What % of Own Food Is Grown?	Organic Food in Diet	Diet	Caffeine in Diet	Alcohol in Diet	Tobacco in Diet	# Children (<19yrs)	% Home Schooled	% Cmty Schooled	% Private Schooled	% Public Schooled	Spiritual Path	Primary Purpose and/or Focus
Sirius	2–5 times/wk	6–20%	yes!	veg	ok	ok	ok	13	0	0	36	54	Ecu,Ecl	planetary transformation
SistrDivProv	nearly all dinners	None						0					RomanCath	hope, love for creation, justice
Sivananda	nearly all meals	21–50%	yes!	veg	ok	none	none	0					Eastern	yoga and vedanta
SixDirectns	1–3 times/mo	1–5%	often	veg	ok	ok	ok	19	50	0	0	50	P,NAm,O	optimal family health (eclectic)
SkyWoods	nearly all meals	1–5%		omni	some	some	ok	0						wholism synergy equality
SkyJahnna	2–5 times/wk	None	often	omni	some	none	some	4	100	0	0	0	Eastern	meditation/children/new-tribe
Skyfire	nearly all dinners	6–20%	yes!	omni	some	ok	none	0					Quaker	think and do tank
SocHumSolidr	nearly all meals	None	some	veg	some	some	none	0					Other	promoting "creative interchange"
SocFamSolidr	rarely					some	none		33	33	33	0		enhancement of fratnl families
Sojourners	1–3 times/mo	None						3	0	0	50	50	Other	living our faith, social injustice
SongOfMorng	nearly all meals	1–5%		veg				0	20	0	80	0	yoga	yoga
Songaia	2–5 times/wk	21–50%		no red	often	ok	ok	5	0	0	50	50		earth centered extended family
SonorEcoVill														healing sustainability fun
SouthCasSpir	rarely	None		omni	often	some	some	0					Other	spiritual enlightenment
SouthsidePrk	2–5 times/wk	None		omni	some	ok	ok	14	0	0	0	100		shared community living
SparrowHawk	1 time/wk	1–5%						14	0	0	0	100	Ecl,O	spiritual growth, serve humanity
Spaulding	2–5 times/wk	1–5%		no red	ok	ok	ok	0						diversity, integrity, growth
SpiesSanity	2–5 times/wk							0						human good-will power
SpiralWimm	2–5 times/wk	6–20%	often	omni	some	none	none	0					Pagan	ecofeminism
Spiricoasis	2–5 times/wk	6–20%		veg		none	none							personal & planetary brilliance
SpringVall	nearly all meals	1–5%		omni	often	some	none	90	0	85	0	15	HB	practical christian living
Springtree	nearly all meals	>50%		omni	often	often	ok	1	0	0	100	0		living lightly; cooperation
SriAurobindo	2–5 times/wk	1–5%						1	0	100	0	0	Eastern	practice of sri aurobindo's yogo
STAR	rarely	6–20%						9						eco-sound-self-sufficient
Starland									0	100	0	0	HB	hutterian brethren
Starseed	nearly all meals	21–50%		veg									Other	safe, loving environment for healing
Stelle	rarely	1–5%	often	omni	often	some	ok	21	33	28	0	38	Other	personal growth/ balanced living
Steppingwood		6–20%		no red	some	none	none	0						lesbian feminist personal recovery
StewLittle	nearly all dinners			veg				0						community living and consensus
StillWater	rarely	6–20%	yes!	omni	often	ok	ok	0					Ecl	nonagressive bible living/educ
Stonehedge	1–3 times/mo	>50%		omni	often	some	often	7	0	0	0	100		rural co-op; housing; co-ops
StudtCoopOrg	1–3 times/mo	1–5%		veg	some	ok	ok	0						student cooperative housing
Sunburst	2–5 times/wk	6–20%		omni	often	some	ok	0						alt. technology education, holistic living
Sunflower-TX	2–5 times/wk	1–5%		veg	often	none	none	0						personal growth open communication
Sunflower-OH	1–3 times/mo	1–5%						2	0	0	0	100		independence and cooperation
Sunflower-KS	nearly all dinners	None		omni	ok	ok	ok	5						student housing cooperative
SunnierPalms	2–5 times/wk	6–20%		omni	often	some	some	3						body acceptance
Sunnyside	nearly all meals	21–50%	often	veg	none	none	none	6	0	100	0	0	Other	christian bible church
SunriseRanch	nearly all meals	>50%	yes!	omni	some	ok	ok	10	0	0	0	100	EDL	practical spirituality
Sunset-CA	1 time/wk	1–5%		veg	ok	ok	none							cooperative urban home; diversity
Sunset-WA		1–5%												collective group house
SusBAnthony	1 time/wk	21–50%		omni	some	some	often	0						feminist activism
Sweetwater	1–3 times/mo	6–20%		omni	some	some		5	100	0	0	0		rural community land trust
Synergy	nearly all dinners	1–5%		veg	often	some	ok	5						student alternative living
Syntony	nearly all dinners	6–20%	yes!	no red	ok	some	none	0					Ecl	family clusters, networking, polyfidelity
Taliesin													Pagan	stewardship self-sufficiency growth
Tanguy	1 time/wk	1–5%						30	5	0	20	75		friendly neighborhood co-op values
Tekiah	nearly all lunches	21–50%		no red	some	some	ok	1						sustainable living
TenStones	1 time/wk	21–50%		omni	often	some	none	9	15	0	25	60		cohousing community
Teramanto	1 time/wk	6–20%		omni		ok	ok	1						responsible free creating
ThreeSprgs				no red	ok	ok	ok	0						caring for person and planet
Timeweave														
ToadHouse	rarely	None												recreation housing co-op
Tolstoy	1 time/wk			omni	some	some	some	9	0	0	10	90		decentralized rural living
TorontoTORI	nearly all meals							18						learn how to build community

KEY *Food codes:* omni = includes red meat, no red = no red meat—includes fish or poultry and dairy, veg = vegetarian—no meat—includes dairy, vgn = vegan—no meat or dairy. *Spiritual path:* B = Buddhist, Chr = Christian, E = Eastern, Ecl = Eclectic, Ecu = Ecumenical, EDL = Emissaries of Divine Light, HB = Hutterian Brethren, NAm = N.American Indian, NSOM = New Social Order in Messiah, O = Other, P = Pagan, Prot = Protestant, Qk = Quaker, RC = Roman Catholic, UU = Unitarian Universalist.

Name	Forming Reforming Non-Residential	State/Prov. or Country	Year Established	Rural, Urban or Both	Open to More Adults?	Open to More Children?	Total Population	# Adults	# Children (<19yrs)	Percentage Women	Identified Leader	Leadership Core Group	How are Major Decisions Made?	Join Fee	Income	Who Owns Land	Acres of Land	Survey Date
Trails End Ranch		AR	83	R	Y		9	9	0	33%	Y	Y	C	N	indep	indiv		12/92
Triform Camphill Cmty		NY	79	R	Y	y	38	29	9	52%	N	Y	C	N	shared	cmty	81	10/93
Triple Creek		WA	80	R	Y	y	22	13	9	46%	N	N	C M	Y	indep	cmty	530	12/92
Truth Consciousness (AZ)		AZ	74	R	Y		24			54%	Y		O	N	both	n profit		6/94
Truth Consciousness (CO)		CO	74	R	Y		24			54%	Y		O	N	both	n profit		6/94
Twin Cities Cohousing Network	F	MN																NQ
Twin Oaks		VA	67	R	Y	m	99	85	14	55%	N	N	O	N	shared	cmty	460	2/95
Twin Pines Co-op		CA	69	U			156	106	50			Y	M	Y	indep	co-op		9/94
Union Acres		NC	89	R	Y	y	53	37	16	51%	N	N	C	Y		mix	126	5/92
United Research Light Center		NC	70	R									O			n profit	200	6/94
Unknown Truth Fellowship Workers	F	NY	43	R	Y	y					Y	Y	O	N	shared	indiv		2/94
Vale, The		OH	61	R	Y	y	32	19	13	53%	N	Y	C	Y	indep	other	40	4/92
Valley of Light	RF	AR	79	B	Y	y	5	5	0	20%	Y	Y	C M	Y		indiv	55	5/92
Vashon Cohousing Group		WA	93	R	Y	y	14	7	7	57%	N	N	C M	Y	indep	cmty		11/93
Vegan Cohousing Working Group	F	CA	97	U	Y	y	25 fu							Y	indep	cmty		9/94
Veiled Cliffs Cmty	F	OH	90	R	Y	m	4	4	0	25%	N	N	C O	N	shared	indiv	145	6/94
Victor Trading Co-op																		
Vine & Fig Tree		AL	86	R	Y	y	6	6	0	50%	N	N	C O	N		other	240	11/92
Vision Foundation																		
Vivekananda Monastery		MI	68	R	Y	n	12	12	0						shared	cmty	108	PrevDir
Vivekananda Vedanta Society		IL	65	B	Y	n	15	14	1	20%	Y	Y	L G	N		cmty	120	4/92
Walker Creek Farm		WA	84	R	N	y	15	8	7	63%	N	N	C	N	indep	clt	20	4/92
We'Moon Healing Ground	RF	OR	91	R	M	m	4	4	0	100%							52	12/92
Wellspring	F	WI	88	R	Y	n	4	4	0	75%	Y		C L O	N	indep	other	31.5	11/92
Wellspring House	RF	MA	81	U	Y	y					N	Y	C	N		other	10	6/92
Wesleyan Christian Cmty		WA	77	R	Y	n	48	28	19	52%	Y	Y	C	N	indep	clt	68	4/92
Westchester Cohousing	F	NY	91		Y	y	34	23	11	63%	N	N	C	Y	indep			1/95
Westside Vegetarian Cmty	RF	CA		U	Y	n	8	8	0	50%	N		C M	Y	indep	subgrp		6/93
Westwood Cohousing	F	NC	soon	U	Y	y					Y		C M	N	indep	mix		6/94
Wheel Cmty Gathering	F	PA	90	B	Y	y	55	40	15	50%	N	Y	C	N		other		11/92
White Buffalo Farm		CO	75	R		n	10	10	0	50%			C		shared	cmty		6/94
White House		MI	79	U	Y	m	6	6	0	50%	N	N	C	N	indep	other		2/95
Whitehall Co-op		TX	49	U	S		13	13	0				C	Y		cmty		PrevDir
Whole Health Foundation		CA	73	U	Y	m	10	10	0	50%	Y	Y	C L	N	indep	indiv	.2	3/93
Windward Foundation		WA	80	R	Y	y	20	19	1	53%	Y	Y	C	N	indep	cmty	80	7/92
Winslow Cohousing Group		WA	92	B	Y	y	80	51	29	51%	N	Y	C	Y	indep	cmty	5	8/92
Wiscoy Valley		MN	75	R	N	n	32	24	8	46%	N	N	C	Y	indep	cmty	356	6/94
Wolf Creek Sanctuary		OR	86	R	Y	y	4	4	0	0%	N	N	C	N	indep	other	80	11/93
Woman's World	F	LA	92	R	Y	m	6	6	0	100%	Y	Y	L	Y	indep	indiv	100	6/92
Womanshare		OR	74	R	M		4	4	0	100%	N	N	C	N	indep	subgrp	23	11/93
Women's Co-op		WI	91	U	Y	n	8	8	0	100%	N	N	C	N	indep	co-op	.25	12/94
Woodburn Hill Farm		MD	75	R	Y	y	38	35	3	49%	N	Y	C	N	indep	cmty	128	5/92
Woodcrest Bruderhof		NY	54	R	M	m	300							N	shared	cmty	100	PrevDir
Wygelia	F	MD	87	R	Y	y	3	3	0								65	9/94
Yahara Linden Co-op		WI	74	U	N	n	7	6	1	50%	N	N	C	N	indep	clt		7/94
Yasodhara Ashram		BC		R	Y		15	15	0	67%	Y	Y	O	Y	shared	cmty	140	11/93
Yellow House, The		KS	80	U	Y	m	4	4	0	50%	N	Y	C	N	indep	indiv		7/94
Yoga Society of Rochester		NY	72	U	Y	n	10	7	3	43%	N	N	C	Y	indep	cmty		6/94
Yogaville - Satchidananda Ashram		VA	67	R	Y		200			55%	Y	Y	G	Y		cmty	1000	10/92
Zen Bones Intentional Spirit	F	CA	93	U	Y	m	6	5	1	60%	N	N	C L	N	indep	indiv		12/93
Zen Mountain Monastery		NY	80		Y		25	25	0	~50%	Y	Y	G		indep	n profit	230	6/94
Zendik Farm		TX	69	R	Y	y	45	30	15	44%		Y	C	Y	shared	indiv	300	5/92
Zephyr Valley Cmty Coop	F	MN	95	R	Y	y	7	6	1	50%	N	N	C	Y	indep	cmty	550	6/94
Zion's Order		MO	51	R	Y	y	32	15	17	60%	Y	Y	G	N	shared	cmty	1175	1/93
Zirkle's Branch	RF	WV	91	R	Y	y	1	1	0	0%			C		indep	indiv	70	6/92

KEY *Provinces:* BC = British Columbia, MB = Manitoba, NS = Nova Scotia, ON = Ontario, SK = Saskatchewan. *Decisions:* C = Consensus, M = Majority, L = Leader, G = Group of leaders or elders, O = Other. *Who Owns Land:* CLT = Community Land Trust, Cmty = Community, Indiv = Individual, Ldlord = Landlord, Subgrp = Subgroup of members. *Income:* Shared = Members Share Income, Indep = Handle Own Finances. *Survey Date:* PrevDir = Previous Directory, NQ = No Questionnaire, Date is when survey questionnaire was completed or last updated by community.

Map / Index Name	Eat Together How Frequently?	What % of Own Food Is Grown?	Organic Food in Diet	Diet	Caffeine in Diet	Alcohol in Diet	Tobacco in Diet	# Children (<19yrs)	% Home Schooled	% Cmty Schooled	% Private Schooled	% Public Schooled	Spiritual Path	Primary Purpose and/or Focus
TrailsEnd	nearly all meals	6–20%		omni	often	some	none	0						wellbeing, equality, self-sufficiency
Triform	rarely	21–50%		omni	often	ok	ok	9	0	100	0	0		social therapy
TripleCreek	rarely	21–50%		omni	some	some	some	9	0	0	0	100		collective land stewardship
TruthCons-AZ	nearly all dinners	6–20%		veg									Other	spiritual awakening
TruthCons-CO	nearly all dinners	6–20%		veg									Other	spiritual awakening
TwinCitCoho														cohousing network
TwinOaks	nearly all meals	21–50%	often	omni	some	some	some	14	25	0	50	25		equality, ecology, nonviolence
TwinPines	rarely	None						50	0	0	5	95		limited equity housing co-op
UnionAcres	2–5 times/wk	6–20%	yes!	veg	ok	ok	ok	16	80	0	20	0	Ecl	earth stewardship co-creation
UniteReLight	1 time/wk	1–5%												heal the earth, thus the individual
UnknownTruth		None		vgn	none	none	none							believe now and seek unknown true religion
ValeThe	rarely	6–20%		omni	some	ok		13	0	0	50	50		family and envrionment oriented
ValleyLight	nearly all meals	>50%						0	100	0	0	0		self-awareness sustainability
VashonCoho	1–3 times/mo	None						7	75	0	0	25		cohousing
VeganCoho	2–5 times/wk			vgn										vegan-friendly cohousing
VeiledCliff	nearly all dinners	6–20%	often	omni	some	some	ok	0					Other	self growth and oneness
VictorTradCo														
Vine&FigTree	nearly all dinners			omni	often	often	ok	0						where all live in peace & unafraid
VisionFdtn														
Vivekan-MI								0					Eastern	work, acceptance; see Vivekan-IL
Vivekan-IL	nearly all dinners	6–20%		veg	often	none	ok	1	0	0	0	100		to realize god
WalkerCrk	rarely	6–20%		omni	often	some	none	7	10	0	0	90		protect & develop our land sustainably
WeMoonHeal	1 time/wk	21–50%	often	omni	some			0					Other	womyn, earth, process
Wellsprg-WI	nearly all meals	>50%	often	veg				0					Ecu,Ecl,O	harmony with self, others, earth
Wellsprg-MA	nearly all meals	6–20%	often	omni	often	some	ok						Other	hospitality education housing
Wesleyan	2–5 times/wk	6–20%	often	omni	ok	some	none	19	0	0	65	35	Prot	loving, caring, supportive, helpful
Westchester								11	0	0	20	80		community lifestyle
WestsideVeg	1–3 times/mo	1–5%		veg	some	some	none	0						vegetarian and personal growth
WestwdCoho	2–5 times/wk													privacy and community both
WheelCmtyGth	1–3 times/mo	21–50%	yes!	vgn	ok	ok	ok	15	100	0	0	0	Ecu,Ecl	sharing & support of community life
WhiteBuffalo		21–50%						0	0	100	0	0		participation in realization of the divine
WhiteHouse	nearly all dinners	1–5%		veg	ok	ok	none	0						affordable cooperative housing
Whitehall								0						support, family bonding
WholeHealth	1–3 times/mo	>50%		vgn	ok	ok	none	0						holistic group vegetarian home
Windward	nearly all dinners	>50%		veg				1	100	0	0	100		sustainable, holistic living
WinslowCoho	2–5 times/wk	None		omni	some	some	some	29	0	0	10	90		community / privacy in balance
WiscoyVall	1–3 times/mo	21–50%						8	0	0	0	100		sustainable (agri) culture
WolfCreek	nearly all dinners	6–20%	often	veg	often	some	often	0					Other	gay men's spirituality
WomansWorld	rarely	1–5%						0						private rural lesbian world
Womanshare	nearly all dinners	21–50%		no red	ok	ok	none	0						lesbian collective shared work
WomensCoop	2–5 times/wk	1–5%		veg				0						women's cooperative
WoodburnHill	rarely	21–50%						3	66	0	0	33		spritual re-creation space
Woodcrest									0	100	0	0	HB	hutterian brethren
Wygelia	nearly all meals	6–20%						0	0	0	0	100		respect self and others
YaharaLindn	1–3 times/mo							1	0	0	0	100		learn to live with other folks
Yasodhara	nearly all meals	6–20%						0						spiritual cmty, yoga & retreat center
YellowHouse	1 time/wk	1–5%						0						urban neighborhood development
YogaSoctyRoc	nearly all dinners	1–5%	often	veg	ok	ok	ok	3					Eastern	yoga, personal transformation
Yogaville	nearly all meals	6–20%	often	veg	none	none	none		0	100	0	0	Ecu,Ecl	all faiths, world peace, integral yoga
ZenBones	rarely	None		omni	some	ok	ok	1						clean & sober self-sufficient
ZenMtn	nearly all meals	1–5%						0					Buddhist	enlightenment
Zendik	nearly all meals	>50%		omni	none	none	none	15	100	0	0	0		practice and teach ecolibrium
ZephyrVall		21–50%		omni	often	often	ok	1						rural land co-op
ZionsOrder	nearly all meals	1–5%		omni	some	none	none	17	33	0	0	67		apostles times living
Zirkle	nearly all dinners	21–50%		omni	often	ok	often	0						commitment to the earth

KEY *Food codes:* omni = includes red meat, no red = no red meat—includes fish or poultry and dairy, veg = vegetarian—no meat—includes dairy, vgn = vegan—no meat or dairy. *Spiritual path:* B = Buddhist, Chr = Christian, E = Eastern, Ecl = Eclectic, Ecu = Ecumenical, EDL = Emissaries of Divine Light, HB = Hutterian Brethren, NAm = N.American Indian, NSOM = New Social Order in Messiah, O = Other, P = Pagan, Prot = Protestant, Qk = Quaker, RC = Roman Catholic, UU = Unitarian Universalist.

The Federation of Egalitarian Communities

More than sixteen years ago, five North American communities founded the Federation of Egalitarian Communities (FEC) because they shared a dream of cooperation. Since then, the Federation has been evolving and maturing, realizing the original dream and fostering new ones. Today, the member communities are East Wind, Sandhill, Tekiah, and Twin Oaks, with six groups affiliated as Communities-in-dialog—Acorn, Blackberry, Ganas, Krutsio, Northwoods, and Veiled Cliffs. Altogether, over 200 people are living in these ten communities.

To Be A Federation Member, A Community Must:

1) hold its land, labor and other resources in common;
2) assume responsibility for the needs of its members;
3) practice non-violence;
4) use a form of decision-making in which members have an equal opportunity to participate, through either consensus, direct vote, or right of appeal or overrule;
5) work to establish equality of all people and not permit discrimination on the basis of race, class, creed, ethnic origin, age, sex, or sexual orientation;
6) act to conserve natural resources for present and future generations while striving to continually improve ecological awareness and practice;
7) create processes for group communication and participation, and provide an environment which supports people's development.

WHAT DOES IT MEAN TO BE A FEDERATION COMMUNITY?

In addition to aligning with our seven basic principles, member communities create operating funds for the Federation by taxing themselves $200 per year plus 1% of net revenues. We create a labor pool by committing 10 hours annually for each working member, plus the time it takes for delegates to attend the twice yearly assemblies. In exchange for these resources, the member communities receive many benefits, including:

RECRUITMENT—Each year, the FEC places over $1000 worth of ads in alternative periodicals. In response to the hundreds of responses we receive, we send out a brochure which describes each member community in detail. So whenever an inquiry comes in to one community, information about all ten goes out. In addition, we have a slide show and other materials for use in lectures and presentations.

SECURITY FUND—In 1986 the FEC began collecting funds from member communities to create a joint security fund for protection against the economic burden of large medical bills. We manage this fund ourselves, so the money remains ours to use for short-term cash needs and other desirable investments, until major medical expenses arise. If necessary, a community can withdraw from the program at any time and get 90% of its investment back.

EXPERIENCE—Our communities have a varied and extensive wealth of knowledge about community living. We can help new (and not-so-new) communities with the challenge of creating appropriate structures, offering models that have worked (and advice about what hasn't worked) on nearly every aspect of community living.

INTERCOMMUNITY CONTACT—Federation activities provide opportunities for contact with like-minded folk, interrupting the feelings of cultural isolation that some communities experience, while reinforcing our choices not to swim in the mainstream. Delegates from member communities get together twice a year to discuss FEC programs and issues. These assemblies are open to all and represent a major forum for the exchange of news and views.

LABOR EXCHANGE—Members of one community often lend a hand at another community. This can really help when there's a big project to be done, and really helps to build a sense of the Federation as an extended family.

TRAVEL EXPENSES—The FEC pays the cost of delegate travel to assemblies, sets aside money to help make labor exchange between member communities possible, and subsidizes participation in outside events of interest to our members.

CAN THE FEDERATION HELP YOU?

The Federation seeks contact with like-valued communities interested in exploring membership or other forms of regular exchange. For information about any aspect of Federation affairs, write or call: *Don Rust,* Federation Secretary, Rt. 3 Box 6B-D, Tecumseh, MO 65760, (417) 679-4682 ❖

Are you forming a community? Or struggling with an existing one? Maybe the Federation can lend a hand.

Our ten member communities have accumulated over 100 years of experience at figuring out how to make community work. Along the way, we've learned a lot about the kinds of systems and structures that match our values of cooperation and equality.

We have gathered many of the written documents from our affiliated communities into a collection—the **Systems & Structures packet**. It includes everything from bylaws to property codes, from behavior norms to labor and government systems, from visitor policies to ideas about what to do when you have too many dogs.

This collection of materials runs to hundreds of pages and is available for about the cost of copying and postage. For a free catalog describing each document and how to order, write: Federation Desk, Box 6B-D, Tecumseh, MO 65760.

About the North American Listings

Archives: Hundred Mile Lodge

*T*his section contains descriptions of well over 500 intentional communities, including addresses and phone numbers (except where groups requested that some or all contact information remain unpublished). You may choose to browse them randomly, or devour them systematically—your intuition and a glance at page 5 ("How to Use This Directory") will determine which approach might best meet your personal needs and interests.

The Listings are arranged alphabetically for easy overall access—a person whose interests are geographically specific should probably start with the Maps (page 177) and the list of communities sorted by state/province (page 186). Acronyms have been considered as one word even though they might normally be spelled with periods between the letters. Numerals have been treated as if they were spelled out (e.g., 1st Street House would be sorted as if spelled "First Street").

A community's listing is where you're most likely to get a sense of how the group sees itself—that's where each group was given room to tell its own story...to share its vision, its history, its daily life. Hopefully these descriptions will give you a feeling for the community, beyond the facts and figures. However, there's a lot of information in the Chart (see key on page 188) that doesn't appear in the Listings, so use both for the best overview of each community.

Some frequently used abbreviations:

SASE – Self-addressed stamped envelope; groups that emphasized this in their listing are unlikely to respond if you don't. enclose one.

[cc] – The group cannot commit to responding promptly to letters.

2/1/95 – The date (at the end of a listing) that the entry was submitted, or that the group last confirmed the accuracy of the information.

[2, 9] – Numbers in brackets at the end of some listings refer to back issues of *Communities* magazine that feature information on that group. An index of back issues begins on page 434.

A few general disclaimers: First, we can't guarantee that the information in the Charts and Listings is accurate—each community decided what to say about itself. We edited only for length and clarity (if a community's listing exceeds 36 lines, they paid us to print those extra lines). We caution each reader to verify all information before deciding to get involved with any of the groups listed. This is why we decided to include *Communities* back-issue references with the listings; though most of the information is favorable, some is critical.

Second, these listings are useful primarily as a "snapshot" of how each community saw itself at some point in the recent past. You may see things in the picture differently from how the community sees them. Also, communities change. Information that was accurate when submitted may now be outdated (hence, our decision to date the entries). The community may be open to change—even desirous of change. Some groups wrote explicitly about their plans for the future; for others you'll need to "read between the lines."

Third, community descriptions, and even Chart "facts," may vary depending on which person filled out the forms. An individual committed to a particular value may find (or help create) a climate supportive of that value—yet they may also write a listing that describes their personal vision rather than the community's.

Fourth, it's hard to predict what factors will be most important to an individual who is searching for satisfaction in community, especially for a person new to the idea. To choose or exclude communities on the basis of a single factor—diet, for example—may be to exclude a very real possibility for growth, change, new understanding, and happiness. (Are you absolutely sure you can't live with meat-eaters...or vegetarians?)

We encourage you to explore community with an open mind, an open heart, and a willingness to grow and experience—rather than with rigid ideas about your personal Utopia. (◭)

ABODE OF THE MESSAGE

Route 1, Box 1030-D
Shaker Rd.
New Lebanon, NY 12125
(518)794-8090/794-8060 Fax

A thriving spiritual community of 41 adults and 16 children living on 430 acres in the Berkshire Mountains. It was founded in 1975 by Pir Vilayat Khan, head of the Sufi Order in the West. The Abode has many purposes. It is an expression of spiritual freedom in which people of diverse interests are striving to fulfill their spiritual ideals in everyday life. It is an esoteric school for the Sufi Order in the West, and a spiritual center for the message of the unity of all religions and all people. It is a retreat center for those who seek the opportunity to withdraw from the world for a period so they may commune with their innermost being.

The Abode was started to provide an environment conducive to the fulfillment of human potentialities, and a supportive and creative framework within which self-discovery would be fostered. It was formed as an experiment, with the hope that individuals of varying beliefs, interests, and desires could live together harmoniously and successfully, learning how to share cooperatively the bounty which life offers. This vision, this ideal, is the Abode's continuing purpose and goal.

Most members earn a living in the surrounding community or are self-employed. Each is responsible for his or her financial contribution to the community, paying a fixed monthly fee for housing and food. Community members share kitchen and cleaning responsibilities (each contributing 3–4 hrs/wk). One half day each month is set aside as "community workday," sharing chores such as gardening, wood gathering, cleaning of common areas, etc. Common meals are served three times daily, and all community members have private rooms or houses on community property.

Decision making is democratic, with community members participating in policy formation through committees that make recommendations to an appointed executive committee. A sincere effort is made to consider the wishes and interests of all community members when making decisions. Write or call for further information. 12/16/94 [29, 53]

ABUNDANT DAWN

(Forming)
Rt 1, Box 35
Check, VA 24072
(540)651-3412
1014 Grove Street
Charlottesville, VA 22903-3404
(804)977-1872

We are a group of experienced communitarians (most of us have lived at Twin Oaks, Sandhill, and/or East Wind) creating a small village of cooperative and communal households and clusters. Each subgroup makes its own economic and membership decisions, within general guidelines of the Community.

Our core values are commitment to clear communication and self-awareness, Earth stewardship, and self-realization through service. Consensus is used for community-wide decisions.

We recently merged with Tekiah Community (see listing). Tekiah is the first income-sharing subgroup of Abundant Dawn. We have another group (as yet unnamed) which is not income-sharing.

We are currently developing income generating businesses (portable sawmill, farmer's market, etc) on the land. We have dreams of a healing center someday.

We support the passions of our members, including artisanry and music, feminism and environmental activism, healing and spiritual work, ecologically sound construction and energy conservation, and sustainable agriculture. Gay positive. Write or call with specific questions. SASE requested. 10/24/95

ACCESS

(Forming)
Route 1, Box 576-H
Floyd, VA 24091
(540)745-3452

ACCESS (A Center for the Creation of Environmentally Sustainable Systems) is currently located on 67 acres of wooded land in southwestern Virginia. We are working to create a rural community based on principles of egalitarianism, shared income and work, consensus decision making, truly sustainable living systems, and the development and practice of sustainable interpersonal systems—all with a healthy balance of fun and humor. We believe it is vitally important to question, research, develop, and implement environmentally sustainable systems for "energy" production, dwellings, food production and preservation, etc. We are committed to finding new ways for people to live together with respect for our natural environment and each other. We support alternative relationships, including non-traditional sexual partnering and bonding, extended families, and shared responsibility for children. We are open to many possibilities and are interested in other individuals or groups who share these goals and beliefs.

We plan to offer how-to and resource information on each of the projects we pursue, as well as workshops and apprenticeship programs. We welcome inquiries and we will be happy to discuss any of these issues with you. Please get in touch with us before planning a visit. 10/3/94

ACORN

1259-D6 Indian Creek Rd
Mineral, VA 23117
(540)894-0595
AcornFarm@aol.com
http://www.ic.org/acorn/

Acorn is a thriving new community (started in April 1993) seeking ways of living that are cooperative, caring, and ecologically sustainable. We are building a diverse egalitarian society that embraces feminism, multiculturalism, diverse sexual and gender orientations, and personal spiritual growth. We value energy spent on improving interpersonal communication and exploring nontraditional relationships. Acorn is committed to keeping our policies flexible in order to meet the varied needs of each individual. Our decisions are made by consensus. We enjoy a close relationship with Twin Oaks Community, seven miles down the road.

As of this writing, 20 members live here, and we would like to grow quickly to 30–60 members. Our ages range from 1 to 68 years. We delight in the company of our toddler, and hope to have more children living here soon.

Our beautiful 72 acres border on the South Anna River and include an oak woodlot, 25 acres of prime farmland, and 20 acres of rich bottom lands. Our renovated white clapboard farmhouse is surrounded by mature oaks and flowering shrubs, with a pond nearby for cooling off. Our large multipurpose residence and community center, Heartwood, was designed and built almost entirely by community members.

Acorn's money and resources are held in common. Earning income from the established Twin Oaks industries of hammocks and tofu, we have also been developing our own businesses, mainly crafts so far. We plan to develop facilities for hosting workshops and conferences on permaculture and a variety of progressive topics. Individually and in teams, members take responsibility for work areas such as building, organic gardening, auto maintenance, cooking, accounting, and forestry. Some members have chosen to maintain careers working outside the community. We also welcome ideas for new home-based businesses.

We take great pleasure living together on the land; work and play are often closely intertwined. Gathering to swim in the river, sing folk songs, or soaking outdoors in our wood-fired hot tub are just a few of the things we do to relax and enjoy ourselves. Many parties, celebrations, and rituals occur spontaneously; others are planned for seasonal holidays. Many members also take advantage of social and cultural opportunities at nearby Twin Oaks, Charlottesville, Richmond, and Washington D.C. We are actively seeking new members; please write or call for more information. 11/4/94

ADIRONDACK HERBS

(Re-Forming)
Fish House Road
Galway, NY 12074
(518)883-4196/883-3453

Two farms, 30 miles apart, in the Adirondack foothills—50 acres near Sacandaga Lake, and 70 acres further west. We grow medicinal herbs, produce tea bags, sell to health food stores, build wood-fired water heaters. We expect to open a health food store and a shop repairing/selling used electronics and light machinery.

Seventeen hours of work/week keep us on bare subsistence level; any additional work counts toward land/profit shares. You can start your own business here, or join a cooperative business here. We have a good library, piano, sailboats, windsurfer, ought to get hang glider, ultralight. We are very interested in bees, flywheels, alternative energy vehicles, small air-

ships, steel fiber reinforced ferrocement, aquaculture, and winter ice refrigeration.

We prefer using dumped or surplus materiel, such as paper, envelopes, lumber, steel, bananas with brown spots. We'd rather pick firewood at the town dump than cut down trees. We respect all religions/spiritual paths, propose herbal medicine as an adjutant rather than an alternative to regular medicine. We take very seriously environmental degradation, the destruction of indigenous peoples, cruelty against humans and animals, television, waste, war, peace, and science. We take a bit less seriously astrologers, therapists, political correctness, the New Age, disco, and the New World Order. For more info, please send a long SASE. 10/19/94

AGAHPAY FELLOWSHIP

(Re-Forming)
HC70, Box 111
Moorefield, WV 26836

Want to be first-century-type Christian community with rural location/lifestyle, conserving the planet's resources. Wanted: people to join us to re-establish/re-form said community. Suggestions: eating low on the world's food scale. Having area/neighborhood contacts including witness to beliefs and outreach to needy people. Wanted: members of all ages. Families with children welcome. Suggested eventual goals: having our own school system because of dissatisfaction with public school system; having our own business(es) to assure members' employment. Proposal: we make decisions by consensus. Opportunity: charter membership with chance to help form basic policies/rules instead of waiting years for necessary seniority—thus better chance to follow one's interests or felt callings. Opportunity: help with newly affiliated local Habitat for Humanity to provide decent housing for low income people. Very important: no unexpected visits; correspond first. [cc] 10/10/92

AGAPE COMMUNITY

(Forming)
118 Orthodox Way
Liberty, TN 37095

Agape Community is a residential settlement of the Russian Orthodox Church Outside of Russia. It is located in a remote rural area of mountain hollows some 60 miles SE of Nashville. Permanent residence is open to those who share fully

with the Community in the Faith, either as landholders purchasing neighboring property, or as leaseholders on community-owned property (presently one family and visitors). Temporary residence on community property is possible for those who seriously seek instruction in the Faith. Visitors who seek information concerning the Orthodox Christian Faith and an experience of a life centered therein are welcome for short periods of time by prior arrangement...but should be prepared for primitive living conditions and a diet and daily life conditioned by the discipline of the Church.

The community operates a small religious press and publishes a bimonthly magazine, *Living Orthodoxy*, at $8/year (USA). For further written information and recent newsletter, send $5 to cover the cost of response...our resources are severely limited (SASE appreciated too). [cc] 10/30/93 [13]

AGAPE LAY APOSTOLATE COMMUNITY

c/o 1401 W. Birch
Deming, NM 88030
(505)546-4940/546-8281

The Agape Lay Apostolate Community is a Catholic nonprofit organization dedica-ted to a life of prayer, service to others, and a strong family-oriented lifestyle. There are presently two married couples with children, one celibate woman, and the man and wife who founded the community living on the same property in single family dwellings. The buildings on the property are owned collectively. All families are responsible for their own bills.

The community meets once a week for a meal together and adult evening discussions. Saturday nights are reserved for a home church "Agape" liturgy of the word celebration. Everyone ten years and older is invited to attend.

The mission outreach of the community is the St. Vincent de Paul Thrift Store that makes money to shelter and feed the homeless and transient population who pass through the town. Members donate time to work at the store and take care of needy people and families. Wives are homemakers and the men have jobs in town. The children are schooled publicly except for religious education which is home-schooled. Children are encouraged to go on mission in their teenage years. SASE requested. 11/10/93

ALCYONE LIGHT CENTRE

(Forming)
Hornbrook, CA 96044

(COMMUNITY LISTING REMOVED)

Lost their land July '95 (foreclosed). Former members remain interested in teaching other communiites about sustainable architecture, especially straw bale construction. 9/26/95

ALPHA FARM

Deadwood, OR 97430

(541)964-5102 Farm
(541)268-4311 Alpha-Bit

Alpha Farm is a close-knit extended-family style community on 280 acres in the Coast Range of Oregon. Consensus, our decision-making process, is also a metaphor for the ideal world we seek to create here—and so help create in the larger world. We seek to honor and respect the spirit in all people and in nature; to nurture harmony within ourselves, among people, and with the Earth; and to integrate all of life into a balanced whole. We value service and work as love made visible. Group process is a strong point; we meet regularly for business and sharing.

Founded in 1972, we average 15–20 adults, and now have four children. New people spend a year as residents (trial members) before admission to membership. Members and residents work on the farm, in community-owned businesses (a café-bookstore, contract mail delivery, and construction), and in freelance professional work. We also offer workshops on consensus and facilitation several times a year. All income and resources are held in common. Individuals have private rooms; other living space is common, and evening meals are communal.

We are open to new residents; visitors are welcome for a three-day initial visit. Please call or write well ahead. 4/5/93 [Cmtas1, 34, 82, 83]

ANAAMI

(Forming)
P.O. Box 1726
Silver City, NM 88062

(505)388-5162/535-2452

We are a small group of diverse individuals whom the Spirit has brought together to begin a community in the mountains of southern NM, near the beautiful Gila Wilderness. We share a commitment to sustainable organic farming and conscious stewardship of the Earth. We are trying to buy part of a cattle ranch and turn it over to permaculture—healing the damaged land and providing healthy food for ourselves. We are hoping that enough resources will come together so that we don't have to be paying off the land, and can focus on our spiritual growth and service to others and move toward a trade-barter type economy. We are spiritually oriented, and share a respect for all spiritual paths. We hope to dance, play, eat, meditate, work, and farm the land together. We hope that Quaker Meeting, Sufi Dancing, sweat lodges, group meditation, free-style dancing, and working with kids will be an integral (though not compulsory) part of our lives together. We are open to others who feel called to seek a lifestyle based on togetherness, self-sufficiency, and love and respect for all God(dess)'s creation. If you would like more information on the current status of our group, please contact us by mail. We wish you peace, love, and good fortune! SASE required. 1/15/93

ANANDA ASHRAM

Sapphire Road
Route 3, Box 141
Monroe, NY 10950

(914)782-5575 9am–7pm

A spiritual community (est. '64) that also serves as an educational center. Current population is at full capacity (20 members). One would need to visit for a long time before being considered for membership. [cc] 6/20/94

ANANDA MARGA

Route 2, Box 45
Willow Springs, MO 65793

(417)469-4713 MO Center
(718)898-1603 NY Office

Ananda Marga is a global socio-spiritual movement which teaches that it is the duty of every individual to use all of his or her potential for the all-around advancement of one's self and the society as a whole. Ananda Marga provides free instruction in meditation and yoga practices. Its social service projects have included disaster relief; community development; nutrition, health, and medical programs; group homes for young people and ex-offenders; schools and education programs from kindergarten to college level; volunteerism; and ecology awareness.

Ananda Marga's women's welfare department is women-managed and seeks to elevate the dignity of women through political, economic, and social equality. It provides seminars on spirituality, self development, and leadership.

"The Renaissance Movement aims for an enlightenment and a resuscitation of subtler and higher thinking in human beings. It wants that every person should be guaranteed the minimum physical requirements of life, and every person should get scope for the full exploitation of psychic potentiality. Every person should get equal opportunity to attain absolute truth and is endowed with all the glories and achievements of the world. Every person should march toward the absolute. In and through this movement human beings should be made conscious of the purpose and meaning of life." 12/19/92

ANANDA VILLAGE

14618 Tyler Foote Road
Nevada City, CA 95959

(916)292-4100/292-9009 Fax
(800)545-4569 Toll-Free

Ananda World Brotherhood Village is a spiritual community based on the communitarian principles taught by Paramahansa Yogananda. Founded in 1968 by the master's disciple, Kriyananda (J. Donald Walters), Ananda now has several branch communities, including one in Europe, and numbers some 500 members.

Dedicated to a life of high ideals and simple living, members of Ananda share their teachings and way of life through The Expanding Light Retreat, through tours and pilgrimages, and through urban teaching centers and meditation groups. Summer work exchange is also available. Ananda embraces 750 acres of woods and meadows in the Sierra Nevada foothills, in Northern California. Members support themselves through a variety of community and private businesses. The Ananda "how to live" school is open to children from both within and without the community.

Voluntary cooperation is the norm in community activities. We seek a mood of friendship and harmony, together with a cheerful spirit of service to God; respect for individuals and their privacy; and freedom to learn and grow at one's own pace. A balance is sought between spiritual guidance and self-motivation. Ananda is not affiliated with Self-Realization Fellowship. 9/18/92 [3, 9, 16, 21, 53]

ANASAZI RANCH

(Forming)
P.O. Box 2066
Snowflake, AZ 85937
(520)536-3445

Anasazi is a cross-cultural, inter-tribal, inter-racial community of families with children and those who align themselves in a commitment to the community as a whole. We are a family of 2 adults and 4 children, seeking others and searching for land or ranch with potential for a spiritual, self-sustaining community. The love of God (our true self) in its myriad forms is our central focus—by working together, supporting each other, and serving others (future plans include a working ranch for troubled youth).

We honor the saints of all religions with the balance of East and West. Our personal growth is deeply rooted in the Native American way of life. Daily meditation is a primary practice, and the purification ceremony is an intrinsic part of our personal/collective growth process to maintain individual balance and collective harmony. All are facilitated by a traditional Native American in a manner acceptable to traditional elders. We home-school and home-birth.

Our goals include utilizing the best of alternative energy, organic gardening, greenhouse, community kitchen/dining, cohousing...all ingredients incorporated in a working ranch/farm, growing ultimately toward self-sufficiency. Our decision-making process is by consensus, the ancient custom of traditional native peoples. Members and visitors abstain from alcohol and drugs. Due to space limitations, we are unable to accommodate visitors; however, camping is available in the national forest/wilderness nearby. Write with SASE, or send $18 (includes P&H) for a comprehensive prospectus. 7/15/94

APPLE TREE ACRES

P.O. Box 887
Blowing Rock, NC 28605
(704)295-7390/295-3013

Apple Tree Acres, formerly Harmony Mountain Acres (est. 1976), is a small mountain community in the Pisgah National Forest. Located five miles from Blowing Rock, a beautiful no-crime, no-pollution, low-traffic (except during tourist season) village with excellent school, shopping, parks, and lakes. We value nature; clean air, water, and soil; the wildlife; the

scenery; and our solitude. Our common bond is *consciousness* of our oneness with all life. Our common purpose is to improve the health of Earth and its occupants. We are devoted to healing by the will of the God who lives within all parts of life. We believe that all pain, poverty, and disease are caused by a belief in separation from the one reality/God, and have been strongly influenced by the Course in Miracles. We work in our chosen careers; own our own land, and share work on roads and other agreed upon projects; buy food, etc. cooperatively through a member-owned natural food store. Open to forming community-owned business. Diverse skills in home design and construction; plumbing; electrical; solar power; spring-fed water systems; organic gardening; herbal medicine, etc. Seek like-minded neighbors to buy adjoining land. One house and several 10-acre tracts available at $2,000 to $3,000 per acre. SASE requested. 1/3/94

AQUARIAN CONCEPTS

(Forming)
P.O. Box 3946
West Sedona, AZ 86340
(520)204-1206/204-1252 Fax
http://www.sedona.net/sd/
aquarian/

Aquarian Concepts Community is a God-centered community located in Sedona, AZ. The guidelines for the community and its members are based on the teachings found in the Fifth Epochal Revelation as set forth in *The Urantia Book* and *The Cosmic Family Volumes*, with an emphasis on the life of Jesus of Nazareth, known as Christ Michael, the Sovereign Creator Son of Nebadon.

Members come from all parts of the world, with a majority having moved here from within the United States. Founded in 1986 by Gabriel of Sedona and his wife Niann (who co-shares with Gabriel the mandate of the Bright and Morning Star of Salvington), the community has about 100 full-time members. New members align monthly, and hundreds of others worldwide are connected by affiliation. The Extension Schools of Melchizedek, located at the community center, are for starseed children, teenagers, and adults —and are unique on this planet. This sacred school is not only for mindal development and book learning, it is very much a school for soul growth.

The community is organizing and developing extensive organic farms and

gardens; additional land is being purchased and set aside for long-range plans. The community has a music ministry, operates a publishing company, and supervises a cottage industry. We have a medical clinic and a healing center. The Aquarian Concepts Community Healing Team incorporates both spiritual and scientific techniques such as psycho-spiritual counseling, personal transmissions, light body visualization, and Tron therapy.

Weekend seminars on Continuing Fifth Epochal Revelation are held at the end of every second month. Classes for community members are held four nights a week, and visitors are invited to a weekly social gathering and/or tour of the community by appointment. SASE requested. 6/10/94 [80/81]

AQUARIAN RESEARCH FOUNDATION

(Re-Forming)
5620 Morton Street
Philadelphia, PA 19144-1330
(800)641-6545 Community Info
(215)849-1259/849-3237
(Call to send Fax.)
arosenblum@mcimail.com

Tax exempt since 1970, Aquarian works on a positive future for the planet. World problems and opportunities are now too great for present staff, so we seek gifted people, including computer networkers, to work full time communally for a world based on love. We share what we have, but permit no drugs or tobacco. We're mostly vegetarian and use natural healing. We've worked at videos on communal living (*Where's Utopia?*), new systems of organic agriculture that might even regrow rainforests, and getting CNN to do films on a positive future showing everyone how good the Earth could be. We publish a positive future novel-on-disk which you may add to and distribute. Currently we're living in a poor part of the city, with room for only an intimate community sharing four bedrooms, an office, and a printing shop with our family of four (Joel 10, April 15, Judy, and Art). We accept responsible non-monogamy and seek a larger, ZEGG-inspired community with room for an airstrip for our 4-place Cessna. Serious co-workers are welcome. We suggest sending $5 for newsletters and other information before planning an extended visit. Single newsletters are sent free with your 55¢ SASE. We have a free computer BBS for newsletter readers, and help folks get amazing rates on phone service—sometimes totally free long distance for a month. We use our four-place Cessna to fly people on visits we can arrange to communal groups. Aquarian seeks to build a worldwide movement toward community and all kinds of lifestyles that could lead to a positive future for our planet. For phone rate details, see Resources listing. 1/10/95

AQUARIUS RANCH

(Re-Forming)
P.O. Box 69
Vail, AZ 85641-0069

(520)449-3588/323-6351 Fax

Reach full potential and 100% fulfillment at Aquarius. We try to live by consensus, not adding more rules to our already over-regulated lives. Our ranch is 100% solar energy sufficient and due to its success, we have developed a solar-based cottage industry as well as doing the service to DC power (batteries and components) for phone and utilities. Other plans include raising exotics (parrots, monitors, or ostriches).

Our textile-free ranch is available for camping to registered guests as a safe base camp for mountain exploration. We feel that we have the best of all worlds, a million miles from civilization, yet only an hour's drive to metropolis and jobs. We have pollution-free air and water, a terrific mountain view, and great weather—warm winter, cool summer—at 4000' elevation.

Come for a visit. If we find that we like each other, a mutually beneficial set of

agreements will surely be found. You may find very rewarding support in industrial sales (commission basis), and someone between jobs and broke may accept an inside "mother" position in exchange for room and board. An inactive person may appreciate free RV space in exchange for adding a human voice to an answering machine. We try to live in harmony with each other and pure, unpolluted nature. Your textile-free visit may grab you for a lifetime. SASE required. 3/29/94

ARCOIRIS (COMUNIDAD)

(Re-Forming)
Apartado Postal 24-514
06700, Cuauhtémoc
Mexico DF, MEXICO

25-549-2234/207-2306

Comunidad Arcoiris (est. 1984) is an egalitarian, intentional, urban, spiritual group. Committed to alternative lifestyles, economic cooperation, spiritual development and conscience, extended family childcare, open sexual preferences and relationships, moderate consumption, appropriate technology, ecological and libertarian awareness, political activism. We try to have equal relation among members, with consensus decisions in a non-sexist, -ageist, -racist context. Our interests are intellectual, spiritual, emotional companionship, encouragement, and providing a financially secure base.

We have mostly separate incomes, rooms, possessions. We share some income-producing activities and have formally

registered 3 cooperatives and 4 business corporations, some of which are operating, and some of which are latent. We intend to increase their significance and income. Some members practice and teach Kundalini, tantra yoga, metaphysics, shamanism. Some do writing, editing, publishing. Others are consultants in process, environmental engineering, political science, future studies. We are all highly educated, but have made only vague advances in spiritual, moral growth. Population has ranged from 6 to 15 part- or full-time associates. We need, seek more highly motivated, knowledgeable members. SASE preferred if in Mexico, $1 if outside Mexico. 7/16/92

ARDEN VILLAGE

The Highway
Wilmington, DE 19810

(302)475-3912

Arden is an intentional community founded in 1900 by social reformers Frank Stephens, sculptor, and Will Price, architect, to create a society based on Henry George's single tax economics and William Morris' arts and crafts philosophy. Their ideas and land use plan live on in the 162-acre community, open to people of all beliefs, creeds, and cultures.

Arden was incorporated in 1967 and has 550 residents currently. All residential land is held in a trust. Leaseholders pay one property tax (land rent determined by elected assessors) and own their homes. The town meeting government is a model

of direct democracy. Forty-five percent of the land is in greens, roads, pedestrian paths, two large forests. Arts and crafts activities flourish here with over 40 professional artists currently living and working in the village. Arden is located 7 miles north of Wilmington, DE, near an exit on I-95. Write for more information; SASE appreciated. 11/15/93 [85]

ARK, THE

**91 Baker Road
Amherst, MA 01002-9602
(413)259-1701**

The Ark is in the early stages of creating extended family together. We are located in a friendly, cooperative neighborhood called Hearthstone Village (pop. 80+), and are also part of a larger friendship network. The house is 7500 sq. ft. of mostly finished, flexible spaces—designed to support needs for both community and personal sanctuary. We are looking for a family and children-loving folk who: •connect energetically with us, •are interested in exploring long-term community, •want to be learning relationship skills in the context of living together, •enjoy creating gatherings and events, and •are interested in exploring co-ownership.

The "village" is in the Pioneer Valley of western Massachusetts, where major cultural, political, artistic, and alternative events abound. We aspire to a state of dynamic stability in which we may expect miracles in our daily life while also knowing that our lives and our lifestyles are an integral part of the manifestation of miracles on a planetary scale. Please write (SASE)—share your vision of living together, and we'll send more information about us. 7/27/94

ARSHA VIDYA GURUKULAM

**P.O. Box 1059
Saylorsburg, PA 18353
(717)992-2339**

Arsha Vidya is a traditional ashram in the Pocono Mountains of Pennsylvania founded by Swami Dayananda Saraswati in 1986. The ashram is a place of contemplation and traditional study of the scriptures of Vedanta and the Sanskrit language. Meditation and yoga are also practiced as aids to gaining spiritual insight. Swami Dayananda, a traditional teacher from India, is the spiritual director and main teacher. He stresses the need for true spiritual knowledge as the means for self-realization.

Presently, 23 people reside at the ashram. Some are staff members, others are students. All residents work together to support the daily operations. Students generally participate in a work-study program instead of paying for room and board.

Throughout the year, a variety of residential spiritual retreats are offered for those who are unable to reside at the ashram year-round. In keeping with the gurukula tradition of India, no tuition is charged for any of its programs. The ashram is supported primarily by generous donors and volunteer labor. Anyone interested in the spiritual teachings of Vedanta is invited to visit the ashram and participate in its programs. 11/30/92

ART COLONY AT EDEN FALLS

**(Forming)
P.O. Box 5426
Berkeley, CA 94705
(510)943-3291**

New Age community of friendship and love looking for co-creators in harmony with the forces of nature to help us evolve and enlarge. Join us if you understand that a possible way to happiness is to accept that we have an intellectual, emotional, spiritual, and physical self—and that growth in each of these areas allows the infinite variety of our own potential to emerge. Through growth we become our own sun with our own light of revelation. Join us on 35 ruggedly beautiful wooded acres with creek and major waterfalls 150 miles northwest of San Francisco.

The community is a loosely knit association of artists, retirees, and nature lovers of all ages, races, and religions. We come together because of our desire to live in a beautiful and healthy environment, in company with other loving and caring people with whom we can share work, dreams, healthy food, ideas, business ventures, leisure, and self-realization.

The gardens, pond, and hiking trails will be developed by community effort and used by all of us. Those of us coming together because of our commitment to painting, sculpture, music, pottery, writing, and photography will build a large communal studio. Some of us own a home. Others rent or lease from neighbors.

Everyone needs to be financially responsible for themselves. At the same time, community members will assist each other with

information and opportunities to the extent possible. Lucia and I are supplementing our income from art by building doors as works of art. We also design and build houses. Some of you may join together to develop vineyards, organic truck farms, mail order nursery, or health care facilities.

There are presently two new homes available for rent. One has four bedrooms at $900 a month. The other has two bedrooms at $700 a month. A small cottage is available for $350 a month. The two bedroom we just moved out of is available at $400 a month. The mobile home is $200 per month. We know of other adjacent properties for sale, rent, or lease.

If you wish to conduct your business to recognize the interconnectedness of people and go beyond your own self definition in ways that nurture, encourage, and support life—join us. Join us if you can understand that conclusions are not something to feud with a neighbor over. Conclusions depend on interchangeable premises which vary with our own needs, the society we live in, and our own emotional, intellectual, and spiritual development. SASE requested. 8/9/94

ASHBY TREEHOME

**1639 Prince Street
Berkeley, CA 94703
(510)849-9673
greenplan@igc.apc.org**

Ashby Treehome is a multi-house community for communitarians who haven't found their ideal permanent home yet. Contact with other urban and rural communities is a priority, and we have openings when members move on to other communities and also when we expand. We are associated with the GreenPLAN community [see separate listing].

Our values and lifestyle are liberal, discouraging competition and favoring individuality, better communication, conservation, and respect for others. We share organic vegetarian food in a poison- and addiction-free home. We favor bicycles and mass transit, and wish to share cars to further reduce auto dependence. Reducing private property is important, so we budget for expansion and also support other nonprofit enterprises. 12/2/94

Drop in on our Web site...

http://www.ic.org/

ATLANTIS RISING, INC.

P.O. Box 85
Bradford, NH 03221
(603)938-2723

We are a rural community that started in 1975. There are presently 3 member families, one on the land, the others in the Boston area. The 128-acre parcel is mainly wooded and abuts a 1585-acre state forest. One homestead is being constructed presently; it's a passive solar conservation house. Owner-built post-and-beam solar electric saltbox design. There are curly horses and a small organic orchard. Visions include more biodynamic agriculture and permaculture, bioregional networking, and biodiversity preservation. We may take on new member(s). SASE requested, and please include phone number with inquiries. [cc] 9/4/93

AUGUST GREEN COHOUSING

(Forming)
P.O. Box 1666
Denver, CO 80201-1666
(303)355-4501/377-5160

August Green was founded in the summer of 1994 by a small group of single parents, most of whom were living in transitional housing. By autumn a number of other people joined the group, which is now comprised of many different family structures and income levels.

Although a few members of our group are interested in suburban or even rural cohousing communities, most of the sites we are investigating are urban. One important aspect of our vision of urban community is the intention to develop neighborhood outreach programs wherever our community locates. For this reason, and because many of our members are low- or moderate-income, we expect to work closely with government and nonprofit agencies to identify a site and secure funding for our community.

We welcome the involvement of anyone interested in supporting or joining our project. Please call or write. 1/5/94

AVALON

(Forming)
P.O. Box 2205
Clearbrook, BC V2T-3X8
CANADA

Avalon is a community-in-formation based on neo-Pagan Witchcraft. We intend to be a teaching community which will offer year-long intensive residency training to Priest-hood in Witchcraft. This will involve the skills of gardening, wildcrafting, hunting, and herbalism. The central people in Avalon presently are in their 30s, with children. Our hope is to gather together a dozen people and relocate to the interior mountains of British Columbia before the turn of the century. We will be open to women and men, all sexual preferences and ages, with a particular interest in parents and children. The community will not be vegetarian, and the land is unlikely to be owned in common. SASE requested. 11/3/93

BABADAS

(Re-Forming)
Athens, GA 30603

(COMMUNITY LISTING REMOVED)

Letters returned "No Forwarding Address." Phone has been disconnected and there's no new listing with directory assistance. 3/1/96

BALANCED LIFE CENTER

(Re-Forming)
P.O. Box 0173
Davisburg, MI 48350-0173
(313)634-4571

A small community (est. '70) focused on universal spirituality and seeking to balance the mental, physical, and spiritual. Presently three members (two women and one man) who share all income and nearly all meals (vegetarian). Please include SASE. [cc] 6/20/94

BAMBERTON

(Forming)
749 Yates Street
Victoria, BC V8W-1L6
CANADA
(604)389-1888

Bamberton is a proposed new town for 12,000 people that is to be built over 20 years on the site of an old industrial works, 20 miles north of Victoria, British Columbia, Canada. The community is being designed around the principles of commu-

nity wholeness, ecological sustainability, and a positive vision of the future. The design incorporates pedestrian mobility, traditional village neighborhoods, ecological protection, sustainable transportation systems, energy efficiency, etc. The town will have a complete fiber-optic network, and a multilayered economy designed for the 21st century—emphasizing building, eco-tourism, the arts, environmental technologies, home-based business, and telecommuting. The community's development is being funded by four Canadian labor union pension funds.

The project is currently undergoing a series of government studies, prior to approval. A group of future residents has formed the Bamberton Community Alliance, a nonprofit society which brings people together for social events, keeps them in touch with developments, and enables them to participate in the community's development. Government approval process is expected to extend into 1997, with resident move-in to follow that. Please include SASE with inquiries. 12/26/94 [80/81]

BEACON HILL FRIENDS HOUSE

6 Chestnut Street
Boston, MA 02108
(617)227-9118

Beacon Hill Friends House is a Quaker-run residential community and a center for Quaker outreach and programming, located in a large old house in central Boston. Our residents include students and working people who live here because they want to be in community, are interested in Quakerism, or are interested in peace and social justice. Residents share responsibility for cleaning the house, serving dinners, and welcoming our many guests. We work to build community with shared chores, regular retreats, and family-style dinners. At a biweekly business meeting held in the manner of Friends, residents plan events and set policy concerning personal conduct. A committee of current and former residents reviews applications to live in the house and tries to select residents from diverse religious and ethnic backgrounds, with a variety of interests and concerns to bring to the group. Residents may live here for up to two years. Major policy decisions are made by our Board of Managers, made up of Quakers from around New England, with resident representatives. Day-to-day operations, including shopping, cooking dinner, overseeing maintenance, and paying bills, are handled by staff. 6/25/94

BEAR CREEK FARMS

(Forming)
39701 Deaf Mule Trail
Fall River Mills, CA 96028

(916)336-5509

Escape from the maddening crowds. Evolve beyond the "lone homesteader." Focus your income production into three intensively exciting work days a week. If your mode is organic food growing, homeopathic remedies, and a long-range view to a land trust for future generations...we may have the ideal sanctuary without a need to devolve into a socialist "free-for-all" commune. Our neighbor has

the only other accessible private land in this million-acre timber preserve (no clear cutting) with four individual parcels for sale with duck/fish ponds. We have a partially completed huge community structure, hook-ups for two motor homes (off the power grid), a three-bedroom house on a half acre (in town), with large single apartments and commercial buildings suited to: bakery/grocery outlet; hardware/tool rentals; art gallery/print shop; a healing center; or private school facilities. We seek those who also hunger to be among sober, communicative, intellectual, artistically creative, honest folks striving for a "realistic divorce" from the uncivilized social order. This mountain apple orchard (ca. 1856) is 16 miles from county airport, PGA golf, full emergency hospital, and 350 miles from any nuclear power plants. Our theme is to be a small health-oriented extended family of monogamous couples with their individualities intact—no guru, group religion, or charity scams. Let us know SASE how your participation will improve Bear Creek Farms. 12/6/94

BEMIS ERECTUS (FINOCCHIO)

36 Bemis
San Francisco, CA 94131-3020

(415)334-6550 Gay/587-5939 Bi
(415)861-0371 Fax
fcook@igc.apc.org

We are a "family of choice" sharing values of open communication and cooperation among intimate equals (revisioning our male role training). We support each other in a diversity of health- and spirit-conscious, sex/love/intimacy-affirming lifestyles. Our spiritual sources are eclectic, including Native American, Buddhist, Quaker, Catholic, Wiccan, Taoist, and Liberation-Celebration-Methodist influences. Some of our members are "comfortably" coexisting with HIV. We have two teams which compete to provide delicious, low-fat (mostly vegetarian) gourmet dinners on alternate Thursday evenings. We tend to have either a "Heart Share" before dinner or a "go-around check-in" at dinner. We have both a consensus decision-making process and a house manager to handle administrative details.

We host numerous community events which put our values into practice (see Resource listing for Community Center for Gay/ Bi Spirituality, Healing, and the Arts) including: Gay Spirit Drumming & Healing Circles, Men Meeting Men Parties and Workshops, Dreambody Cinema Project, Geomancy, Citizen Empowerment, Peer Counseling classes, and Neighborhood Safety meetings. We also support Hospitality Exchange and other "visitor/host exchange programs." We keep a waiting list of people who want to join our family. Sublets are also available on occasion since most of us love to travel.

We rent a 4-story house that was originally a home for wayward boys; now it houses a fraternity of delightfully queer men. Several of us are practicing artists; the walls, halls, and stairs serve as a gallery to show off the gorgeous, sensual work of our members and friends. We're into networking and schmoozing, moon howling, and giant jigsaw puzzles on the coffee table. Let us hear from you. 1/2/95

BENEDICTINE MONASTERY OF HAWAII

P.O. Box 490
Waialua, HI 96791
(808)637-7887

Established in 1984, we are a charismatic Benedictine Catholic community of one woman and five men. Our primary focus is prayer and work, including ministering and running a retreat center. Members share all things in common, take a vow of poverty, practice celibacy, and fast on Wednesdays and Fridays. For the next few years, due to space restrictions we aren't able to accept new members. 7/15/94

BIJOU COMMUNITY

411 West Bijou
Colorado Springs, CO 80905
(719)635-5078

We are a loose affiliation of people, an ecumenical group that practices simple living and works for peace and justice. Our residences are held in a land trust, housing 3 adults and 2 children. We have a Hospitality House for people in need, and a soup kitchen that serves 350 people a day. There are 10 to 15 others active in our extended network. Our work is supported through donations. 11/3/93

BIRDSFOOT FARM

CR25, Box 138
Canton, NY 13617
(315)386-4852

We are a 20-year-old agricultural community in a very rural area near the Adirondack Mountains. We grow most of our food and sell vegetables, herbs, fruits, and crafts for part of our income. We average 8-11 adult members; our population swells each growing season as we host several apprentices who come to learn about farming, community life, and other skills. Several members have part-time jobs off the farm.

Our 73-acre farm has fertile loam,

woods, a stream, two barns, and five houses. The land and buildings are owned by the community. The vegetable business is a separate partnership. We envision a cautious expansion in membership, including kids. New members have a year trial period. We each pay monthly "rent" for living expenses, purchase equity in the property, and buy our food together.

We are concerned with problems of sexism, racism, violence, and environmental destruction. We care a lot about each other, and find time for many kinds of sharing—such as communal meals, group work, rituals, parties, etc. Each person follows his/her own path. Some of us are exploring and borrowing from many spiritual traditions. We create our own rituals. If you would like more information about our community or our apprenticeship program, please feel free to send a note about yourself and a SASE. 1/11/95

BLACK CAT HOUSE
San Francisco, CA

Black Cat Collective is a housing collective with two bases of unity—Feminist Witchcraft (or compatible spiritual focus: we have an engaged Buddhist, etc.) and Direct Action Politics. We have a large house owned by several of the members, located in the Mission district of San Francisco. We were formed as a group of friends who decided to live together; some of the friends have since moved on, and we have some new members—friends from the larger community who have subsequently joined us.

We are seven adults and a 12-year-old, and we enjoy a lot of good team spirit. All major decisions are by consensus. We eat together regularly, though when our schedules get full the cooking schedule gets sparse. We garden and have a rock & roll band. 7/28/94

BLACK OAK RANCH
Northern California

We are an extended family, not a collective or commune. We have many family units and individuals within the Hog Farm. Twenty-six Hog Farmers are partners in our rural land, others are not. Not all of our land partners live on our property. Those of us living together on our land cook together for the most part. We have individual sleep spaces.

Some of us are hippies, some of us are

yuppies, some defy description. We are farmers, doctors, storekeepers, artists, clowns, musicians, nurses, carpenters, chefs, etc. We have children of all ages, and some of our friends also spend time living with us.

We have built a beautiful camping facility on our land which we rent to our own performing arts and circus camp—Wavy Gravy's Camp Winnarainbow for kids and adults. We are also open to renting to other groups. 11/10/94

BLACKBERRY

(Re-Forming)
P.O. Box 208
North San Juan, CA 95960
(916)288-3600

Blackberry (formerly Community Evolving) is a close-knit intentional family committed to living, working, learning, and growing together in the Sierra foothills north of Nevada City, California. We place much value on raising our children and ourselves in a nonviolent, healthy emotional and physical environment.

We are an income-sharing group, working to perfect our egalitarian, collective economics. The adults gather regularly for business and emotion-sharing meetings, and for family meetings where children participate fully. All our decisions are made by consensus.

In our daily lives we like to experiment with various forms and rituals gleaned from many sources. We share an Earth-based spirituality, celebrating the seasons together.

The main focus of our community is responsible stewardship of the Earth, starting with this 50 acres of mixed conifer and hardwood forest. We are looking to create an environmental learning center here, to help people appreciate the integrity of the forest ecosystem.

We need initiators for this project: people with design experience in educational curriculum, architecture, organic agriculture, permaculture, forest management, and nonprofit corporations. We also need people with skills in building, teaching, gardening, and bookkeeping. We see the community being active in local and global issues of health, peace, and the environment. Underlying all this is the desire to be deeply involved in each others' lives, to be sources of inspiration and learning for each other, and to grow older and wiser together. 5/5/94

BLUE HOUSE, THE

318 – 17th Avenue
Seattle, WA 98122
(206)329-1804

A cooperative household established in '83, the Blue House has a history of being for easy-living good people. Current membership is nine men; house decisions are by consensus. We have a nice garden. SASE required with inquiries. [cc] 7/15/94

BLUE MOON COOPERATIVE

HCR 65, Box 54
South Strafford, VT 05070

This cooperative neighborhood on a gorgeous old farmstead in central Vermont was established by a group of friends who met in the early 1980s while working together in regional anti-nuclear, feminist, and disarmament coalitions. Initially we gathered as an informal study group to learn about land trusts and collective living. We spoke with people who had lived in communes and collectives and began to explore alternative legal and financial structures with a lawyer who specializes in cooperatives and worker-owned businesses. Our goal was simplicity, not to underestimate the importance of fairness and flexibility. Fortunately, it meanwhile took us more than two years to find land that we could afford, by which time we had a strong basis of understanding among our members (during those two years we met together at least monthly, and sometimes semimonthly), as well as a solid set of bylaws. Being a cooperative instead of a land trust has been important to all of us; also important has been the fact that we live "off the grid"—our homes are powered by solar photoelectricity. Our present shared

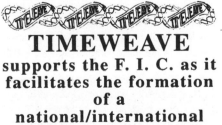

TIMEWEAVE

supports the F. I. C. as it facilitates the formation of a national/international network of communities. (Our listing is in the N. American section.)

projects include maple sugaring, woodland stewardship, and building a community swimming pond. We're a musical, good-humored group, very tuned in to our kids. SASE requested. [cc] 8/21/94

BREITENBUSH HOT SPRINGS RETREAT & CONFERENCE CENTER

P.O. Box 578
Detroit, OR 97342
(503)854-3320
http://www.wvi.com/
~hotspring/community/

We are an intentional community and worker-owned cooperative which operates Breitenbush Hot Springs Retreat and Conference Center, located 60 miles east of Salem, Oregon on the west slope of the Cascade Mountains. Currently our community ranges from 45 to 70 including adults and children. We honor all spiritual traditions and are intentionally creating an energy self-reliant model for ourselves and the world. We are involved in raising public consciousness about ecology issues, and are deeply involved in trying to save the remaining temperate rain forest of our area. We strive to serve the highest social good, and to achieve our own highest individual good.

Breitenbush Hot Springs is a rustic hot springs resort that was built in the late 1920s and early 30s. The resort went through many changes until 1977 when we purchased the idle and deteriorating property and spent several years restoring the old resort and getting it ready to host guests again. In 1985 the community purchased the land from the founding member and in 1989 formed the worker-owned cooperative. The members of the worker-owner cooperative participate in a profit/loss sharing program, make most of the major decisions about community and business affairs, and elect our board of directors. To be a worker-owner, a community member must be employed for one year, be a community member and employee in good standing, and pay a membership share of $500. Currently over thirty of our community members are worker-owners. Maintaining the retreat and conference center provides the livelihood for those of us who live here.

The community lives across the river from the retreat and conference center in a village-like setting. We have regular community sharings and three times a year we close our guest facilities for a four day community renewal where we join together for sharing, fun, and community processing.

As each year passes more and more people come to Breitenbush. A whole book could be written about all our adventures, explorations, and lessons learned in this grand experiment over the years. We live a rich, full life here. We have an abundance of diverse people, new ideas, healing practices, friendships, challenges, Spirit, and nature. SASE requested. 9/8/95

BRIGHT MORNING STAR

(Re-Forming)
302 NW 81st Street
Seattle, WA 98117
(206)782-9305

Bright Morning Star is a very musical and literate 6-person household in north Seattle. We are, among other things, opera singers, Quakers, advocates for the Fellowship of Reconciliation, folk singers, Aikido enthusiasts, sci-fi buffs, recyclers, a librarian, a counselor, and a Unitarian. We range in age from 13 to 43 and are 50-50 male/female. We share food, meals, and chores, and we meet weekly to check in and to address any budding issues. We make decisions by consensus. Due to an allergic member, many of our meals are dairy/wheat free. We have work days to honor the continued well-being of our home and fun times during celebrations and everyday events. Occasionally one of us spontaneously breaks into song.

We began in Philadelphia in 1979 via the Movement for a New Society as two couples (gay and straight) combining incomes and co-parenting 3 children. In 1985 we moved to Seattle and eventually jointly bought a large, airy house. After 8 years of continuity, recently 1 adult and 1 child departed and we welcomed a community-minded woman. We are committed to creating a pleasant, cooperative, and nurturing environment for personal growth and social activism. Invited guests are welcome. SASE required. 9/28/93

BRIGID HOUSE

2012 Tenth Street
Berkeley, CA 94710

Brigid is a collectively owned home in Berkeley, begun in 1985. We are looking for new members who want to explore the possibility of eventually becoming co-

owners. Currently there are two owners in their forties, the 14-year-old son of one of the owners, and four renters whose ages range from 23 to 37.

We are a combination of the following: activists, pagans, artists, doctoral student in social welfare, interning psychotherapist, job developer for adults with developmental disabilities, bodyworkers, hikers, cartoonist....

Our house (originally a duplex) has separate bedrooms, an assortment of common space, and a large yard with garden and hot tub. The house is our home—it is not an investment.

Our agreements include a weekly dinner/ meeting, sharing mostly organic food, regular upkeep and renovation of our home, and most important, clear communication and consensus process. We value diversity. Because of environmental sensitivities, we discourage smoking, fragrances, and most pets. We also discourage drug or alcohol abuse. We value our friends and family outside the house, our work and leisure. We strive to give each other space to grow, some continuity, and our listening side. SASE requested, and please be patient for our reply. Please write or call before visiting with your "bio." [cc] 4/2/94

BRYN GWELED HOMESTEADS

1150 Woods Road
Southhampton, PA 18966
(215)357-3977
http://ourworld.compuserve
.com/homepages/edkramer/
bryngwel.htm

Bryn Gweled Homesteads seeks to be a friendly neighborhood cherishing family autonomy and extreme diversity of culture, wealth, religion, politics, lifestyles, etc. Persons join by purchasing a home, such as from the estate of a deceased member, and signing a lease from BGH for a 2-acre lot. Only approved applicants can negotiate for a house. Applicants visit all 75 families. If an applicant gets at least 80% positive vote in secret written ballot, then they acquire approved applicant status. Each member owns a non-interest bearing debenture representing capital investment in land, roads, community center, swimming pool, etc. which is bought by the next owner of a house. Homes sell at prices typical for the area. Located one mile north of the northernmost tip of Philadelphia. BGH had many

alumni at its 50th anniversary in 1990. SASE requested. [cc] 4/29/94

BUDDHIST SOCIETY OF COMPASSIONATE WISDOM

(Re-Forming)
86 Vaughn Road
Toronto, Ontario M6C-2M1
CANADA
(416)658-0137

1214 Packard Road
Ann Arbor, MI 48104
(313)761-6520

(Formerly Zen Lotus Society.) We are a spiritual community focused on Zen training and manual work—under the guidance of Zen Master Samu Sunim of the Korean Chogye Order. We live a communal lifestyle based on the monastic model as it is adapting itself to North America. Some members hold jobs, others work within the temple(s) on projects including the publication of *Spring Wind—Buddhist Cultural Forum*, our international quarterly journal. We have an affiliate community in Michigan.

Our training is open to men, women, and couples (families, under special circumstances) and can lead to religious ordination (monk or nun) or lay orientation (Dharma teacher) for qualified individuals. Short visits can be arranged. A three-month trial residence period and a sincere mind for Zen training are prerequisites for full-time community membership. Inquiries welcome. SASE requested. 4/27/92

BUILDERS, THE

P.O. Box 2278
Salt Lake City, UT 84110

The Builders, founded in 1969 by Norman Paulsen, direct disciple of Paramahansa Yogananda, offers instruction in the Sun Technique of Meditation. A lifestyle incorporating Twelve Virtues and Eight Paths of right action assists us in accessing the higher brain and the cosmic sense of illumination. Individual commitment to, and relationship with Mother/ Father/Creator, "I am that I am" is vital. We also value our association with like-minded souls.

We are self-motivated, self-responsible individuals. There is no formal membership or membership committee. Builders reside in four western states, where Builder-owned businesses exist and Builder-owned property and/or housing is maintained.

Current businesses include: natural food stores & cafes, demolition & excavation, motel, gas station, mobile home park, apartment complex, and sailing ship restoration. We have 20 years experience in community living. We notice society's evolution toward cooperative community and responsible world citizenry. We invite hard-working sincere seekers of Truth to explore the possibility of working with us. Visitors by appointment only; please include SASE. 8/8/94

BURLINGTON COHOUSING GROUP

(Forming)
67 Penn Street
Burlington, VT 05401
(802)658-4857

Cohousing group with 4 households now, planning to grow to 12 households (20–40 members). The legal structure of the community is a cooperative, and the group makes its decisions by consensus. Deposit required ranges from $5,000–$10,000; and a typical unit costs $80,000–$100,000. Please include SASE with inquiries. [cc] 7/14/94

CAERDUIR

Kansas City, MO 64111
(COMMUNITY LISTING REMOVED)

Letters returned "Moved. Left No Address." 11/26/95

CAMBRIDGE ZEN CENTER

199 Auburn Street
Cambridge, MA 02139
(617)576-3229

The heart of the Kwan Um Zien School, founded by Zen master Seung Sahn, is the consistent daily practice which goes on in its Zen centers and affiliated groups. Practicing and working together, we discover what it means to be human. As we learn to let go of our illusions of separation, we are able to live our lives more openly with increasing clarity and compassion. The Cambridge Zen Center offers a daily schedule of bowing, sitting, and chanting, as well as monthly retreats and biweekly interviews with a master Dharma teacher. Our public talks every Thursday evening are free and open to the community, as is daily practice. 5/17/93

CAMELOT-OF-THE-WOOD

P.O. Box 674884
Marietta, GA 30067
(770)423-9585

Camelot-of-the-Wood is an egalitarian New Age and Earth Religion community which promotes the vision of the Earth Mother and Sky Father as a balanced duality. Camelot is an auxiliary of "The Church of Y Tylwyth Teg," an old religion for a new age. Camelot was founded by Rhuddlwn Gawr, an elder of the church

N. American
b c

who was initiated into the ancient religion in Wales in 1966. Camelot promotes a relinking of humanity with itself and nature. Camelot is a spiritual community which also includes a school of holistic healing. We are involved with environmental issues including alternative energy sources, organic agriculture, recycling, and resource conservation. Camelot has a manager/planner form of government using a democratic process of election and appointment of managers and planners. We try to keep the formation of committees to a minimum, relying instead on the capabilities of our facilitators. We have weekly and monthly membership meetings to air differences. SASE requested. 7/23/92

CAMPHILL SOLTANE

Nantmeal Road
RD1, Box 300-A
Glenmoore, PA 19343
(610)469-0933/469-1054
(610)469-0933 Fax

Camphill Soltane is a lifesharing intentional community based on Anthroposophy as developed by the Austrian educator Rudolf Steiner. Soltane is part of the worldwide Camphill movement with 85 locations in 18 countries. Our work is with mentally retarded young adults, on 50 acres in a beautiful part of Pennsylvania, one hour northwest of Philadelphia. We have biodynamic orchards and gardens, weaving and pottery studios, baking, painting, singing, drama, and many arts and crafts which we employ in building community together with handicapped people. Ours is a spiritual and service community with a reverence for life, for cooperation, and for celebration.

We have approximately 45 people living and working together, including children. A Waldorf School is located nearby, as are other communities with which we are closely associated. We welcome visitors, and have many. We usually request that people seeking long-term involvement make a one-year commitment to get to know us, our "students," and the many details, involvements, and activities of our life. Many people come from different countries, bringing a unique and lively atmosphere to Soltane. Altogether, this is a high-energy, full, and busy life...especially the very rewarding but demanding work with our handicapped companions. Give us a call,

write, or (best) visit! SASE requested. 5/10/94

CAMPHILL SPECIAL SCHOOLS

Beaver Run
Route 1, Box 240
Glenmoore, PA 19343
(610)469-9236

Camphill Special Schools, Inc., is a community of 60 adults and their children who live with, work with, and educate a population of about 60 children in need of special soul care. These are children with varying degrees of mental retardation or other handicaps.

The school offers a three-year seminar in Curative Education for those who come to live with and learn to educate the special child. The foundation of the work and education is based on Anthroposophy—a holistic approach to life developed by Rudolf Steiner, an Austrian philosopher, educator, and artist. Camphill is an international movement, with more than 70 centers throughout the world.

Life is intense and demanding here, but very enriching. Please call for further information. 7/13/94

CAMPHILL VILLAGE MINNESOTA, INC.

Route 3, Box 249
Sauk Centre, MN 56378
(612)732-6365

Camphill Minnesota is one of 70 Camphill communities around the world. 41 of us—children, adults, and adults with mental handicaps—live in extended families in seven houses on two adjoining farms totaling 300 acres (plus 200 rented).

We live together for a variety of reasons which all come together in the quest to bring the needs of the land, people, and animals into harmony with the needs of the Spirit. All of our work is based on Anthroposophy (literally, "the wisdom of man") which came about through Rudolf Steiner (1861–1925), an Austrian-born philosopher, artist, and scientist.

We farm and garden biodynamically—an approach that combines organics, the rhythms of the planets, and other factors. Through a creative approach which uses art to introduce subjects to the children, the goal of our home school is to bring the child's thinking, feelings, and will into harmony. In all that is done (including

our houses, weavery, woodshop, and bakery) the dignity of humanity is enkindled collectively and individually. We are open to new members as space is available. Please inquire by letter or phone. 5/6/92

CAMPHILL VILLAGE (PA)

Kimberton Hills, Inc.
P.O. Box 155
Kimberton, PA 19442
(610)935-0300

Camphill Village of Kimberton Hills is one of seven North American communities in the Camphill movement—each one unique, yet all with similar purposes. We seek to create a renewed village life, and to establish social forms of human interdependence between disabled and non-disabled people. Our approach is a nondenominational Christian way of life based on the inspirations of Rudolf Steiner's Anthroposophy, which allows each person to evolve to their potential as a respected individual.

Started in 1972, our 430-acre biodynamic farm is run by a community of 125 members, including some with mental disabilities. Scattered around the farm are fifteen houses which shelter "extended families" who work the farm, gardens, orchard, bakery, cheese house, and sell surpluses in the small coffee shop and farm store. We have a strong cultural life which involves many visitors and neighbors. Visitors are welcome to share in the life and work here—for shorter or longer periods as space permits. We also have a small apprentice program in biodynamic agriculture which brings 4–6 students per year for "on the job training." All visits are by appointment only —and letters are preferred to phone calls [SASE appreciated]. 5/9/94 [1, 76]

CAMPHILL VILLAGE U.S.A.

Camphill Road
Copake, NY 12516
(518)329-7924

Camphill Village USA, Inc., is an international community of some two hundred people, half of whom are mentally disabled adults. Situated on six hundred acres of wooded hills and farmland, the village includes farm buildings, workshops, a community center, a gift shop, a co-op store and 17 family-size houses shared by 6 to 8 mentally disabled adults and 2 to 4 co-workers and their children. Part of the wider Camphill Movement based on the innovative therapeutic work of Karl Koenig, MD, the village life includes farming, work, worship, and cultural activities. Co-workers live in Camphill Village as full-time volunteers, receiving no salary but working in answer to the needs of others while, in return, their own needs are provided for. Through this viable alternative to the wage system, it becomes possible to develop a sense of mutual responsibility and brotherhood.

Skills: Our only requirement is a dedication to maintain active interest, care, and concern for one's fellow man. Camphill Village offers a three-year training in Social Therapy. Contact: Julia Rasch, Associate Director, at (518) 329-4851. 8/21/92

CANTINE'S ISLAND

(Forming)
39 E Bridge St
Saugerties NY 12477
(914)247-0397

Cantine's Island is a small cohousing community forming on 8 waterfront acres in the Hudson Valley. We cherish both community and privacy, and will structure our homes, common house, landscape, and bylaws to maximize both. Our legal structure is based on a homeowners association, though not all households need to hold mortgages. Our decision-making structure is consensus-based. Our homes will be modular, designed using principles expressed in Christopher Alexander's Pattern Language. As of summer 1993 we are still looking for more households to join us. Please include SASE with inquiries. [cc] 5/19/93

CARDIFF PLACE

(Forming)
Victoria CoHousing
Development Society
1246 Fairfield Road
Victoria, BC V8V-3B5
CANADA
(604)480-5152/920-9984

On August 29, 1994, Cardiff Place became Canada's first completed cohousing community. It was intentionally designed by its future residents to combine the privacy of fully self-contained units with extensive common facilities to foster social interaction. We wanted a place where we know our neighbors, where it is safe to raise our kids, and where there are people of diverse ages and occupations.

We chose this site for many reasons: we're a comfortable walk from downtown, the ocean, and Beacon Hill Park; we're close to amenities such as schools, shopping, medical and recreational facilities, and a bus stop; and we live in an established older neighborhood with tree-lined streets and lots of green space. We have two buildings on a half-acre lot: one is a completely renovated manor with 6 units, and the other a new building with 11 units. Each building has 4 floors with the private units on the top three, and common facilities on the ground floor.

The heart of Cardiff Place is its common facilities. These include an indoor and outdoor play area for children, a lounge area with a fireplace, a workshop, a guest bedroom, a laundry, a storeroom, a pantry, and a kitchen/dining area. Our tradition is that residents have the option of eating together 2–5 times per week. Outdoor facilities include a vegetable garden, a patio, and a landscaped garden with a walkway. The group has business meetings every week where all decisions are made by consensus. 10/15/94

CARPENTER VILLAGE

(Forming)
P.O. Box 5802
Athens, OH 45701
(614)593-6562

[Formerly Paideia.] Carpenter Village is a new small forming community in a scenic area of S.E. Ohio, near Ohio University, which is congenial to alternative communities. Carpenter Village has been founded by people with considerable experience in helping establish such communities, house design and building, and the social services. Private 3+ acre tracts will be available for people from many different fields who want to work at home. 15 commonly owned acres will be for community use and cooperative activities including joint income-producing efforts. Along with simpler living, independence, and cooperation, we value ecological sensitivity, compassion, communication, participatory democracy, community-based economics, and personal/spiritual growth. To increase collaborative possibilities, our process to get acquainted will include a pre-community skills matching followed by weekend exploratory meetings. Interested people can write for more information and questionnaires. When clusters of shared skills/interests have been identified, the

weekends will be arranged. We would also like to encourage inquiries from existing worker-owned businesses which want to relocate. 7/24/94

CASA GRANDE COLECTIVA

Urbana, IL
(217)344-0300
glindber@uiuc.edu

La Casa Grande Colectiva, a 23-year-old housing cooperative, is situated on 2.5 acres of land in Urbana, Illinois. The town just grew up around this secluded little haven of an old farmstead, and our landlord is now trying to develop the property. In response, we're trying to organize a realistic plan for purchasing the land, a parcel at a time, and placing it in a land trust.

We provide low-cost, not-for-profit cooperative housing that is operated and governed in a participatory and democratic manner. The main thing that brings us together is a commitment to cooperative living, and an interest in maintaining a loose-knit, supportive, extended family environment. We also strive to be ecologically sound and egalitarian. 2/5/89

CASA MARIA

Catholic Worker Community
1131 North 21st, Box 05206
Milwaukee, WI 53205
(414)344-5745

The Casa Maria Catholic Worker House has been fundamental in housing and feeding the homeless for 50 years. It is based on the philosophy of nonviolence, voluntary poverty, and helping those in need. The community is large enough to house 4 families and 3 single women until they find another place to live. The community also gives out food, clothes, and used furniture to those in need. There are about 25 people who work at the house now. No one is paid because it is done in the Christian conviction that we should take care of our sisters and brothers in need without seeking any reward for this. We are interested in rooting out the violence in our society and the causes of hunger and homelessness. As a result, we do not cooperate with the governments of this society and its system. We receive no funding from the Church, government, or large corporations, nor do we accept tax exemptions.

We are always looking for new members—since the more people we have, the more we can do to care for the needy, to work to nonviolently destroy the causes of poverty, and to build a new society of generosity and caring. 4/28/92

CATHOLIC WORKER COMMUNITY OF CLEVELAND

3601 Whitman Ave
Cleveland, OH 44113
(216)631-3059

Deeply convinced of the radical truth of the Gospel, we strive to follow a Catholic Worker philosophy. We emphasize the corporal works of mercy—identifying with and ministering to the homeless, poor, sick, imprisoned—and radical action against the causes of poverty and oppression. We seek to be nonviolent and opposed to all war, and to answer Jesus' call to be peacemakers. We recognize the continual need to clarify our thought through prayer, reflection, dialogue, and action.

We are forming a loving and caring resistance community with a strong spiritual base which will enable us to share our lives with those who are broken—not just for their sake but ours as well, knowing that we are all sisters and brothers.

Come to Cleveland! We need new community members to live in our intentional community and to help in our work with the homeless on Cleveland's west side. Our ministry includes a cooperative community, a drop-in center, several small houses of hospitality, a newspaper, and efforts in resistance to violence and militarism. We invite those interested in this possibility to write us, or call (216)631-3059 and ask for Joe. 5/7/92

CATHOLIC WORKER HOUSE / SAN ANTONIO

(Re-Forming)
622 E. Nolan Street
San Antonio, TX 78202
(210)224-2932/271-3630

We at San Antonio Catholic Worker House open our home to families who need temporary housing, and provide a free soup lunch four times a week to the public. We are committed to consensus decision making, spiritual pluralism, green revolution (organic gardening, recycling, and ecological living), discovering and teaching the simple life, communal living, economic justice, cheap ice cream, and

the revolution that starts with the self. Each community member is responsible for helping with the day-to-day running of the house, including cooking, household maintenance, counseling, helping with the newsletter, and childcare. Each member has the potential for individually initiated projects, learning Spanish, political involvement, and tutoring. SASE requested. 8/2/93

CATSKILL BRUDERHOF

Hutterian Brethren
Elka Park, NY 12427
(518)589-5103
http://www.bruderhof.org/

Begun in 1990. [See main listing for "Hutterian Brethren" in the Resources section.] 6/1/92

CCNV: COMMUNITY FOR CREATIVE NON-VIOLENCE

425 Mitsnyder Place NW
Washington, DC 20001
(202)393-1909

The Community for Creative Non-Violence is a 22-year-old community of resistance and service that is rooted in spirituality. We attempt to share our lives and our resources with the poor whom we encounter daily through our soup kitchen, shelter, and drop-in centers. At the same time we seek to educate, confront, and change those institutions and structures that make each of us a victim.

We see community as a means of living which is healthy, and one which frees us up to do our work. Our resident staff, ages 18–90, includes 15 women and 35 men. Open to new members; volunteers must serve for six months before they have the option of becoming a voting member. We provide beds and dinners for 175 women and 1100 males.

Brochures will be sent upon request. Visitors with a serious interest in sharing our life must contact us in advance so that housing can be arranged. 6/22/94

CEEDS

C-184, Horse Lake Site
RR#1, Lone Butte
100 Mile House, BC V0K-1X0
CANADA
(604)395-4225/296-3216

Members of the Community Enhancement & Economic Development Society (CEEDS) look upon ourselves as the seeds

of a movement to change the disastrous present-day methods of agriculture. The majority of our members are in their early thirties, and have spent their entire adult lives working toward that aim. During our early years we squatted on a natural meadow, and were known as hippies. We are still part of the hippie back-to-the-land movement. We are ecologists deeply concerned with and actively working in the defense of Mother Nature.

CEEDS rents and operates four small farms in the South Cariboo. We raise and breed cattle, pigs, workhorses, sheep, goats, a variety of poultry, and honey bees. Surplus organic meat and vegetables are sold at farmers' markets and at the farm gates. Special activities include our sheep project (which proves that sheep are a viable alternative to herbicide spraying for weed control), horse logging, preservation of rare breeds of plants and animals, providing a home and meaningful lifestyle for street people, apprentice training for our labor-intensive organic farming methods, and working for and bartering with neighbors and friends.

We have fifteen full-time members, both Indian and White, who live on and manage our farms. There is no private property. There are also Indian street people who live and work with us, fluctuating between town and the farms. We have twenty-five sustaining members who have supported us financially and are entitled to first call on organic produce. Our long-term goal is to establish more CEEDS farms throughout the province. Our deeds do match our words. Brochure available. 12/1/92

CELO COMMUNITY

1901 Hannah Branch Road
Burnsville, NC 28714

Celo Community, founded in 1937, is located in the mountains of western North Carolina. It comprises 1100 acres occupied by 34 households living separately and making their livings independently. Members purchase "holdings"— a form of land trust. Before building on a holding members must get community approval of their plans. They can't mortgage a holding at a bank, but can borrow against it from the community.

A minimum 6-month trial membership is required before becoming a member, and there is a very long waiting list. However, numerous neighbors take part in Celo Community activities, thus enjoying most of the advantages of membership.

Ernest Morgan is community secretary, and visitors are welcome to camp in a pleasant spot near his house, with access to washroom, electricity, and phone. Alternately, rooms are available at the Celo Inn: (704)675-5132. A complete set of community documents is $6 post-paid. 8/29/94 [77(D)]

CENTER FOR EXPERIMENTAL CULTURAL DESIGN

[renamed Network for a New Culture.]

CENTER FOR PEACE & LIFE STUDIES

(Re-Forming)
P.O. Box 1238
Muncie, IN 47309
(317)396-3508

CPLS is really a community within a community. The families that live on the grounds form the nucleus of a larger Christian community which meets regularly to promote peace and foster our own spiritual growth. In the summer the CPLS offers family campers recreational and community-building experiences. Six cabins and a dining hall are available from spring through late summer. A chapel/meeting hall and a winterized cabin are available year-round for group gatherings.

Community members are dedicated to building a peaceful world, to living simply, and to sharing resources with those in need. We welcome inquiries about participating in family camp, using facilities for a group sharing, or joining the residential core group. Please include a SASE with inquiries. [cc] 6/24/94

CENTER FOR THE EXAMINED LIFE

San Diego, CA

(COMMUNITY LISTING REMOVED)

Disbanded in '93 after core group members left to pursue other interests. 10/22/95

CENTRAL-PAGE LIMITED EQUITY CO-OP

200-B Central Avenue
San Francisco, CA 94117
(415)431-5610

A turn-of-the-century Victorian house on a quiet street in the center of "The Haight"—an ultra urban, diverse neighborhood. The co-op, formed in '82, is housed in a building containing 8 apartments (renovated by the owners) with no yard and no common areas except storage and laundry.

All owner residents make decisions as the Board of Directors, and all serve on one of two committees: maintenance or management. The work of the co-op is done in these committees with occasional hired skilled labor. The owner residents did all the work in remodeling the kitchens in 1993. The co-op will probably need a new roof in 1995, and we'll be looking for a co-op roofing company. Please include SASE with inquiries. 9/12/94

CERRO GORDO COMMUNITY

Dorena Lake, Box 569
Cottage Grove, OR   97424
(541)942-7720
http://www.efn.org/
~andrewm/Cerro_Gordo/
Cerro_Gordo.html

Our goal is a symbiosis of village, farm, and forest for up to 2500 people on 1200 acres—a whole valley on the north shore of Dorena Lake, near Eugene, Oregon. Homes, businesses, and community facilities are being clustered in and near a pedestrian solar village, preserving over 1000 acres of forest and meadow.

We're planning a self-supporting settlement, with organic agriculture and a variety of small businesses on site: Our first manufacturing business sells Equinox bicycle trailers nationally; our Forestry Cooperative preserves a diverse forest ecosystem while perpetually producing enough lumber for 25 homes a year; and we're planning a lakeview lodge for visiting members and workshops on sustainable community development worldwide.

While homes and businesses are privately owned, all residents will be members of the Community Cooperative, which owns open space and utilities, and facilitates democratic self-government. We're seeking to create a life-enhancing community which reintegrates the human community and our inner selves with the larger community of the biosphere. The community building process emphasizes participation in a diverse yet mutually

supportive community. We invite you to join our extended community of residents, future residents, and supporters who are working together to create Cerro Gordo. Send for the introductory package, which includes plans and progress, membership information, and a visitor's guide (available for $5). 12/14/92 [16, 32, 71/72, 74, 80/81]

CHAGDUD GONPA FOUNDATION

P.O. Box 279
20 Red Hill Road
Junction City, CA 96048
(916)623-2714

A community of 30 adults based on Vajrayna (Tibetan) Buddhism as taught by Chagdud Tulku Rinpoche, a Tibetan llama who came here 15 years ago. All activity is to follow the Dharma. Shared income, separate housing, all meals eaten together (no special diet). We are open to visitors. 7/7/94

CHANGING WATER MINISTRIES

(Forming)
24 Mellon Street
Newport News, VA 23606
(804)930-3806

Changing Water Ministries (CWM) is an intentional community in the forming stages, dedicated to mastery of self through spiritual study. By mastering the self, we can experience true joy. We have studied the teachings of many masters and schools of thought to develop our own system that produces measurable results. We intend to continue our explorations until we discover most of the secrets of the universe.

Our banner paraphrases Plato: there are no bad people in the world, only dummies. We believe that all problems and personality quirks have their source in specific spiritual barriers. We have developed a method for removing these barriers, called LASER (Learning About Soul Experiences via Regressions) that allows us to tap the knowledge that each of us holds within ourselves. Our community is based on the consistent application of this method from each of us to the others.

We in the community have seen that the reason for our existence as humans is to master relationships and experience true joy. By continually interacting with one another we create the opportunity to attain that mastery. As Gurdjieff said, the best method for mastering one's life is to expose oneself to the unpleasant manifestations of others.

Our training is rigorous and certainly not for everyone. As the saying goes, "many are called and few choose to answer." We have answered the call and dedicated ourselves to it. Are you looking for such a commitment? SASE required. 8/11/92

CHESTER CREEK HOUSE

1306 E. 2nd Street
Duluth, MN 55805

(218)728-5468

Founded as a community in 1971, Chester Creek House became a community of lesbian women in 1981. We currently have 6 members and are seeking new members; at this time we are populated by adults only. We are primarily a vegetarian, non-smoking, chem-free household living in a three-story Victorian home in the city of Duluth (pop. 90,000). We make decisions by consensus. Though it is not a prerequisite for joining, women living in the household tend to be active in social justice movements (anti-nuclear, peace, sanctuary) and the women's community (battered women's shelter, rape crisis hotlines, domestic violence, women's studies, women's action group). The house is a gathering place for community events and parties, and provides shelter to women in transition. The house is owned by the household, and each member has her own room. Chores are rotated monthly, and every member contributes a fixed amount to the upkeep of the house and to food. House members cook and eat together 2–3 times weekly, and hold weekly house meetings. We welcome visitors who

are community-minded. Please write for more information. SASE required. 1/25/94

CHRIST OF THE HILLS MONASTERY

(Re-Forming)
P.O. Box 1049
Blanco, TX 78606

(210)833-5363

A spiritual community (est. '72) based on Russian Orthodox principles. Current population is 19 adults and 3 teens; we're open to visitors and more adult members. Members are celibate, share all income and nearly all meals. Our primary purpose is to seek a mystical union with God. [cc] 6/20/94

CHRISTIANSBRUNN BROTHERHOOD

NEW NAME:

MAHANTONGO SPIRIT GARDEN

(Re-Forming)
Route 1, Box 149
Pitman, PA 17964

Mahantongo Spirit Garden is a non-Christian hermitage and retreat center for gay men. Located on 63 acres in the mountains of central Pennsylvania, the Garden provides a safe place removed from the world, where gay men can explore their own spirituality freed from dogma and conventional beliefs. The Garden is a self-sustaining farming community that emphasizes crafts and a life without electricity, phones, or running water. Short-term visits are encouraged and workshopsare offered in traditional

building skills, baking, and a variety of crafts. Write Johannes Zinzendorf for information. 4/18/96

CHRISTINE CENTER FOR UNITIVE PLANETARY SPIRITUALITY

(Forming)
W 8291 Mann Road
Willard, WI 54493

(715)267-7507

The Christine Center for Unitive Planetary Spirituality is an inclusive, intentional, transpersonal, spiritual community embracing an eclectic practice and supporting a new mythology for the emerging global culture. This practice, called Unitive Planetary Spirituality, is the embodiment and recognition of mystical unitive spirituality in individual and community life.

The primary purpose of the Christine Center is to foster individual, community, and global spiritual development. The community of both resident and non-resident members is dedicated to spiritual realization and to assisting others in their spiritual process by giving retreats, seminars, and spiritual guidance. Our 251-acre farm consists of a house where meals are served, a barn transformed into a library and meditation hall, a silo chapel, 18 hermitages, a sauna, and hot tub. The tranquil forest setting includes an organic vegetable garden, an orchard, a pond, and nature trails abundant with wildlife to nurture the re-creation of body, mind, and spirit. Work/study programs also available. Call or write for a brochure. 3/17/94

CHRISTMAS STAR

**2444 Dripping Springs Road
Winkleman, AZ 85292**

The road which unites all levels of perception is the esoteric pathway of evolving knowledge. The higher one's level of attainment, the greater the benefits one derives. These benefits serve the real work of evolution which is not based upon the individual but upon our physical environment. We are fools to pollute it. In this landscape exists a world/media-linked society in which the tests of multiple points of view, of trivial temptation, of corruption and sellout "prove" the self-perceived value of one's identity. This is truly a test of revelation where clarity of vision is required to raise one's degree of metaphysical comprehension. Spiritual growth requires commitment to a process and constant attention. The spiritual journey will inexorably lead to the creation of centers of exchange wherein competition and war will be replaced with cooperation and intimate communications. Unless such a place is made, the growth of Spirit cannot take place. The vision of Christmas Star seeks to be such a place—at which art, music, planting, building, and dancing become the crops in a field of ultimate reality tended by people who don't abandon the process of sifting the useful from the useless (weeds) at the first sign of conflict. We have everything we need, not by ourselves but together with grace, over time. Write (SASE) or call anytime, and bring your best self.
10/3/93

CHRYSALLIS FARM

Montague, CA 96064
(COMMUNITY LISTING REMOVED)

Has sold its land and the members are joining another community. 3/23/96

CHURCH OF THE PATH

(Forming)
**207 S. Commons Ford Road
Austin, TX 78733**

(512)263-9435

Self-responsibility and the application of the law of cause and effect are the fundamental bases of our teachings. Thoughts and feelings are actions; we are responsible for them as well as our actions. Therefore, loving and caring for one another involves revealing to each other and purifying our thoughts, our

feelings, and our actions. We practice this in our training activities, thus helping each other find the only true and lasting happiness, the one found through honesty and integrity. Anyone interested in our lifestyle is invited to give it a try. Inquirers should clearly and honestly identify themselves. 4/5/94

CIRCLE OP SPRINGS

(Forming)
**P.O. Box 1171
Moab, UT 84532**

(801)259-5610
**http://rene.ma.utexas.edu/
~kwalker/op/op.html**

[Previously listed as Sky Ranch.] Our forming community is on 124 acres, 30 minutes south of Moab, with a perennial creek and springs adjacent to public lands. The land is characterized by pinion forest, canyons with cottonwoods, agricultural fields, wildlife, and quiet. The property is owned by a company whose shareholders are the community members. Individual shareholders have half-acre lots on which they may build a home. Although land outside the homelots is available for agriculture, business, and other individual and community structures and projects, the group as a whole approves site selection and sets guidelines to maintain quality of life for everyone.

Our vision of community includes developing sustainable lifestyles in terms of food and energy production, resource use, and architecture; decision making by consensus; a mix of private and community control of land; a balance between group and private life; and deepening our ties with the world of wild things. In the process of developing our relationships with each other, we share a commitment

to honest communication and awareness of discrimination based on sex, sexual orientation, race, and other diversities. We value growth, change, and fun. The community is seeking new members and welcomes inquiries. SASE requested with inquiries. 2/26/94

CIRCLE SANCTUARY COMMUNITY

(Non-Residential)
**P.O. Box 219
Mt. Horeb, WI 53572**

(608)924-2216/924-5961 Fax

The Circle Sanctuary Community is a Pagan spiritual community of women, men, and children associated with Circle Sanctuary (also known as Circle), a legally recognized Wiccan church and international Pagan resource center (see resource listing for "Circle Network"). Circle Sanctuary is based on a 200-acre sacred nature preserve about 30 miles west of Madison, Wisconsin. At Circle Sanctuary Nature Preserve, community members share rituals, ideas, support, and celebration with each other at seasonal festivals and other events throughout the year. Some community members have homes near Sanctuary land. Most members live in Wisconsin and neighboring states, but others are from more distant places. Within the community we have a Volunteers Circle which meets monthly to help with various aspects of Circle's work, including networking correspondence, other office work, festival preparation, publications, facilities upkeep, gardening, research, and nature preservation projects. Visits to Circle Sanc-tuary land must be arranged in advance with staff, and timed to coincide with community gatherings. The community's newsletter, *Sanctuary Circles*, is published eight times yearly and includes news of members as well as details about festivals and other events.
12/15/94

CLARITAS

(Forming)
**c/o Vern Squires
225 W. 23rd Street
New York, NY 10011**

xverns@cairn.org

Seeking to attract truly individual-minded persons who can contribute financially and/or with skills and occupations to the creation of an individual-oriented, self-reliant community. Location search now under way in the NY-NJ-PA areas. We want simplicity of life, but emphasize clarity of individual purpose and priorities (which we assist the individual in finding) in the belief that simplicity follows clarity, just as form follows function. Our ends-directed systems approach is for structure, definitely not stricture. Not intended for lip-service-jargon types, the overly collectivist-minded, or chronic sentimentalists. All others please apply. Singles, couples, children, all age ranges welcome. 1/27/95

CLEARVIEW

Center for the Celebration of Life

P.O. Box 335
Moriah, NY 12960

[Previously listed as Alegres.] Spiritually, ecologically focused community, 8 adults, 2 children on 575 acres in Adirondack Mountains on Lake Champlain. Currently we all live in a beautiful 7,000 sq. ft. hilltop lodge with extraordinary mountain views, barns, lake front cabin, beach, 100' waterfall, 80 acres fields, southfacing house sites for planned off-grid, clustered eco-village for 60 people. Economic sustainability and employment a reality now with established recycled rope business. Conference/retreat center, natural forestry/wood products business, permaculture/cash crop agriculture, alternative school, etc., underway. Modified consensus, co-creation with nature and spiritual realm; fun, play and recreation, balance of freedom and cooperative creating.

Community Values: We create our reality and manifest our dreams by how we think, feel and flow energy. Choose positive focus, abundance, well-being, and connection to godforce as a natural state of existence. Looking for like-minded, emotionally mature, and financially secure pioneers ready to live their dreams. $10,000 land share, sweat equity possible. Internships and visitors programs. Arrange in advance. Vision statement package $3. 4/20/96

CLOUDBURST COMMUNITY

(Forming)
P.O. Box 373
Bisbee, AZ 85603

The Cloudburst Community is an intentional community being formed at 6500' above Bisbee, Arizona, near the Mexican border. We envision a community of sharing individuals with a goal toward

sustainable nature-centered living. On 36 acres of hillside in the Mule Mountains, we are building our vision. Imagine gardens, brilliant mud huts, straw bale houses, buildings that blend with the curvature of the Earth, and architecture that is a reflection of the soul. Our current vision is to have individual living spaces, each individual building their own dwelling with help from other people in the community.

Cloudburst is a place to create home, to grow trust, cultivate friendship, and encourage passionate living. We would like to start with a small group of five to ten people. We are open minded and do not permit discrimination on the basis of race, class, creed, ethnic origination, age, sex, or sexual orientation. We value honesty and a willingness to share in all aspects of community life. We have community workdays and make decisions in a weekly meeting. We share meals, sweats, gardens, and each other's pain and joy. We also have a faded blue '47 International truck used as a conduit for spiritual matters of the universe and the mundane passing of human affairs. And, oh yes! A sense of humor is crucial! 1/29/95

COMMON GROUND

Route 3, Box 231
Lexington, VA 24450
(540)463-9451 / 463-9422

Our small intentional cooperative community holds a perpetual lease on 80 acres of land owned by the School of Living—a regional community land trust. Our members hold lifetime subleases, and own the improvements. We wish to live in harmony with nature, to maintain a conscious balance between the personal and social needs of people, and to educate and empower ourselves and others by using the techniques of nonviolent conflict resolution.

Members follow their own spiritual leadings. Most prefer a vegetarian diet. Our children (ages 5–15) are homeschooled by choice, and meet with other home-schooled children three times a week in our Learning Center.

We have monthly business meetings which use consensus decision making; meetings are open. Managers are selected to coordinate and supervise community work; it is common to have Work Days where the whole community turns out to work in the community garden, on building the shop shed, etc.

Each household has two-plus acres to

develop privately. Over half of our acreage is being developed cooperatively by the community. A yearly budget is adopted, and each household is assessed a monthly rental fee to cover expenses. We have two carpenters, a car mechanic, a home-maker, a lawyer, an entrepreneur, a teacher, an audio-video specialist, and three retired persons. Several times a month we party, and in summer swim in our pond. Visitors are welcome upon pre-arrangement; tenting and camping space is available. SASE requested. 12/28/92

COMMON GROUND COMMUNITY

442 Red Maple Road
Blountsville, AL 35031
(205)429-3088 / 429-3090

We are 10 like-spirited adults and 3 children. Our purpose includes harmony with our environment, nurturance, celebration of spiritual diversity, and social change. The community leases 80 acres of farmland from Gaia Land Trust, created in 1980, and members sublease holdings. The Trust's purpose is to own and preserve land and improvements, promote community, honor ecosystems, and prevent abuse of resources. The community pays monthly rent to the Trust. Community members pay dues and rent equally, and in-kind service is an option. Each member is economically independent. The Trust pays taxes, fire protection, maintenance, etc. With no community members, the land would devolve to a party committed to preservation.

We gather monthly for a day of work, play, and business (using modified consensus). Working through difficult decisions and writing our Guidelines have developed deep trust and extended family. In ten years as a community, only one full member has left. We dream of all being on the land full-time, and half of us are now. We live in owner-built structures heated with wood and solar, passively cooled. Power varies from solar to conventional to mixed, but conservation is key in all. We enjoy visitors, but our membership is closed. Visitors must write in advance and enclose a SASE. 9/20/92

Community Referrals: Networking People Places & Projects for Intentional Community

Roommate, Household & Community Referrals

Kathey Sutter (503) 235-9098
P.O. Box 3804, Portland OR 97208
bv407@freenet.carleton.ca

COMMON GROUND HOUSING ASSOCIATION

701 Independence Place
Aspen, CO 81611
(970)925-1961

A public "Employee Housing" project, built on county-owned land, developed as affordable housing based on the cohousing model. Because Aspen is a resort area, all adjacent land has been bought up, and people living/working here can't afford their housing. Therefore the city/county tries to develop affordable housing for construction workers, architects, secretaries, loan officers, elderly, graphic artists—spanning from semi-skilled to professional.

Members found out about this project through newspaper ads. A group formed, then got involved in the design process. The entire project was put together on a speculative basis, including all professional services, and then the county came through with the funding. We now have 100% occupancy and a waiting list. Members will be required to work a certain number of hours per month (4–6?, yet to be determined) or pay $10/hr. 10/15/94

COMMON PLACE

141 Oxford Street
Cambridge, MA 02140
(617)864-8947

Common Place is an intentional, cooperative community in Cambridge, Massachusetts. We came together as a group of members of a social justice-oriented church community. We hoped for a more shared life and a chance to live a more responsible urban life. Our first meetings were in 1972, and we bought land and moved into our building in 1973. Of the eight families who now live at Common Place, six are from the original group, and a seventh has been here 18 years. We are celebrating our 20th anniversary this year with great joy and gratitude.

We have been deeply committed to each other, being present in both hard times and moments of great joy. Many rituals have grown over time—an annual progressive dinner of gala proportions at Christmas time, retreats twice a year, graduation and birthday parties, monthly meetings, regular potlucks, etc. The 21 children who have been born and nurtured here are some of our greatest joys. We have also tried to be more efficient in our use of the world's natural resources

and to be responsible citizens of our neighborhood, city, state, nation, and world. Members of Common Place are activists on issues happening at all of those levels. Finally we are conscious of our need to continue to seek spiritual grounding for our lives. [cc] 9/20/93

COMMON PLACE LAND COOPERATIVE

4211 Route 13
Truxton, NY 13158
(607)842-6849 / 842-6858

CPLC is a rural cooperative land trust located in the rolling hills of central New York State. We are 14 adults and 8 children, and are actively seeking new members. We expect to evolve into a small-scale community of 35–40 households, aiming at greater food and energy self-sufficiency. We have six owner-built solar homes on the land, and the farmhouse serves as rental space for prospectives or home builders.

Over ten years we have come to agreement on 11 core ideals which define and guide our community, including land stewardship and trust, consensus decision making, voluntary simplicity, welcoming diversity, and community participation. Interests include organic gardening, ecological land use planning, solar and wind power, political activism, home birth, natural continuum parenting, home-schooling, puppet theater, and worker-owned businesses.

We invite participation at a variety of levels, from weekend camping at $2 per night, to meeting attendance, to work parties. We hold two festivals on the land each year—the late June Strawberry Festival, and the August Summer Gathering—a fun way to meet the larger Common Place community. Initial contact in writing is strongly encouraged (SASE requested). 4/26/92

COMMON UNITY

P.O. Box 441713
Somerville, MA 02144-0014

A community of people who support each other in personal growth, work for progressive social change, and celebrate and learn from our spiritual diversity. We have a few group households and a network of folks who come to events and help us plan our future. We are looking for people interested in building long-term community. We are currently urban-based, but may have a more rural component in the future. SASE requested. 5/4/94

COMMONS ON THE ALAMEDA

2300 W. Alameda
Santa Fe, NM 87501
(505)471-9176

A nontraditional cohousing community of 28 households in a traditional adobe-style compound with courtyards ("placitas"), a central plaza, and office/studio spaces situated on 5 acres in a low-density area of Santa Fe. What makes us nontraditional is that our core group included a full complement of professionals—we used no outside professionals whatsoever (including engineering, architectural, legal, and financial). A subgroup did the site plan and defined the placitas; individual families developed their own units; and each placita was developed by the households that surround it. We tried to "mainstream" the project in a way that made it seem accessible as a "possibility" to the general population. Two more sites are available; condominium-style ownership. Average cost: $40,000 plus house construction at $70–$100 sq. ft.; financing available.

N. American

c

We share 2 meals per week in the common house (more once we're full and the kitchen systems are debugged). Members each cook and clean up 1 meal/month. Members are also required to put in 4 hours/month of community work (though in fact there are a lot of us who put in substantially more than that). We have two community meetings per month, and group decisions are by consensus—with a lot of the work delegated to committees; those willing to do the work end up with a lot of authority. 10/15/94

COMMONTERRA

Route 1, Box 3000
Monroe, ME 04951

(207)525-7740

Commonterra (est. '77) is five households, total population 9 adults and 7 children, living on 150 acres held in common through a community land trust. Open to new members who must go through a one-year provisional process. Individual families own their own houses, and are responsible for their own finances and domestic arrangements; community decisions are by consensus. [cc] 6/20/94

COMMUNIA: DEEP MOUNTAIN RETREAT CENTER

(Non-Residential)
P.O. Box 1188
Iowa City, IA 52240

(319)245-1006/338-2826

Communia is a lay contemplative non-sectarian community devoted to the practice of offering, and to a spiritual life of work, prayer, and service. It is open to all spiritual traditions, and is focused on the nurture of spiritual growth, practice, and discovery.

Deep Mountain Retreat Center, on 278 acres of hilly farm and bottom land in the Turkey River Valley, in the "Driftless area" of northeast Iowa, is the central expression of the community and provides a silence and solitude which nurture the inward journey toward peace. Except for the staff, Deep Mountain Retreat Center is now non-residential—though we also provide for extended residence through our Associate Program. Service to others continues to be the primary expression of the community. We offer Deep Mountain as a year-round spiritual retreat and practice facility for individuals, couples, families, and groups that come

for silence and meditation, reflection, recreation, rest, restoration, renewal, and rediscovery of spirit. It is both a healing environment and, through organized workshops and retreats, a spiritual educational opportunity. Communia's agenda is an open-ended one which transforms with the participation of those who help in creating a place for exploring inner peace. Please include SASE with inquiries. 5/16/93

COMMUNITY ALTERNATIVES CO-OP

1937 West 2nd Avenue
Vancouver, BC V6J-1J2
CANADA

(604)733-3744 Fax

We are 43 members (ages 0–66) living in a cooperative community located in the city of Vancouver. We are interested in and working on/toward alternate family groupings, community-scale economics, meaningful employment, appropriate technology, consensus decision making, and collective social action. Projects initiated by some of our members include a cooperative restaurant, a gourmet garnish and salad company, a retail/wholesale muffin business which trains mentally disabled young people and adults, and another communal housing cooperative in our neighborhood (which shares a similar vision of community). We are part of the Community Alternatives Society which has 10 nonresident members, and which also owns a 10-acre organic farm one hour from town. Prospective visitors should please write first (and please include a SASE). [cc] 1/26/95

COMMUNITY HOUSE

1308 Graham Road
Virginia Beach, VA 23454

(804)481-7948

Community House, VA Beach, is one home of a living and working community of the New Family. The New Family is an association of individuals whose primary interest is to help overcome the multitude of segregational aspects within humanity on all levels of life. We offer circumstances, assistance, and guidance to develop your senses for your innate qualities, talents, and potential for healing and creative action; our attention and efforts to assist you in focusing on the spiritual relationship between all things and all beings (heal relationship conflicts); support for

your courage, willingness, ability, and effort to face the truth of your inner "unholy" conditions that are in the way but are there for a reason (they need to be recognized, understood, and healed—Community in worship and application). Visitors or long-term "students" of life are welcome upon written expression of intent. For more information, please write with SASE or call. 12/16/94

COMMUNITY IN BASIN FARM

New Social Order in Messiah
P.O. Box 108
Bellows Falls, VT 05104

(802)463-1342

The Basin Farm Community began in 1989 as an organic vegetable farm. Our vision here is to feed the organic food grown here to all our people in all the Association's communities in New England. Getting back to the land these days sounds good as long as everyone's self-interest is the same. But when birds of many different feathers try to have a life together with a higher motivation than self-interest, it inevitably fails. This self-interest that has caused many communities since the '60s to come apart at the seams is the same self-interest that is destroying the present social order. At the Basin Farm we are very sympathetic toward all those who have been hurt in community, and that's why we want you to know about us. [See network listing for the "Community In" Association in the Resources section.] 12/26/95

COMMUNITY IN BOSTON

New Social Order in Messiah
92 Melville Avenue
Dorchester, MA 02124

(617)265-6265

The Community in Boston began in 1981. We do odd jobs and operate the Common Ground Cafe and Common Sense Store which sells our products made in cottage industries throughout New England. We also make clothes and children's furniture as cottage industries. People of different nationality, gender, temperament, background, education, status, and race are living together here in a unity which is rooted and grounded in the forgiveness we have received. We are under authority in this new social order. There is a government in this community and each of the other Association communities that brings stability, order, and care to our lives. The New Testament is our Constitution, and the Sermon on the Mount is our Bill of Rights. This life is visible because it actually empowers us to love each other without any denominational differences, without any dissension, without even differences of opinion. Yahshua's word is teaching us what true empowerment really is. [See Resource listing for the "Community In" Association.] 12/26/95

COMMUNITY IN BRIDGEPORT

New Social Order in Messiah
2403 North Avenue
Bridgeport, CT 06604

(203)367-2866

The Community in Bridgeport, located about an hour from New York City, began in the summer of 1993. We are about 40 people here, and we are working toward the opening of a first quality used clothing store. We are eager to share our hospitality with anyone passing our way. We extend our warmest welcome to come and visit our community, for a day, or to stay. [For additional information see the network listing for the "Community In" Association located in the Resources section.] 12/26/95

COMMUNITY IN BUFFALO

New Social Order in Messiah
2051 North Creek Road
Lakeview, NY 14085

(716)627-2098/649-4967

The Community in Buffalo began in 1993 when a handful of people from western New York wanted to go back there and start a community. Now we have grown in numbers to about 60, which includes many children of all ages. We build and remodel homes and small businesses. In June of '95 we opened our Common Sense Store where we sell handcrafted futons, furniture, soaps, candles, leather, and ironworks—all created in sister communities. If you are seriously tired of "community" being a disappointing or hurtful experience, if you are ready for a radical new life, a covenant of love with others, come and visit. If you still believe that love is the answer, come and live with us for a while and see for yourself. [See network listing for the "Community In" Association in the Resources section.] 12/26/95

COMMUNITY IN ISLAND POND

New Social Order in Messiah
P.O. Box 443
Island Pond, VT 05846

(802)723-9708

The Community in Island Pond began in 1978 when the communities in Tennessee began to move up to Vermont at the request of a few Vermont families. The community grew to about 350 people by the mid–eighties living in 14 community houses. Since the beginning, Island Pond has been the center of cottage industry, printing, and the development of curriculum for our children. In 1992, we started sending out many families to start new communities all over New England. As a result, the Island Pond Community is down to one household housing about 30 people. The sole cottage industry is Simon Tanner, a retail store selling and repairing shoes. Since our beginning in Tennessee in 1972 we have not tried to reform something old but rather to restore what was begun but soon lost by the early church in the first century—communities of believers who surrendered all to live together in faith. We invite you to come and join in this emerging new social order. [See network listing for the "Community In" Association in the Resources section.] 12/26/95

COMMUNITY IN PROVIDENCE

New Social Order in Messiah
167 Cole Avenue
Providence, RI 02906

(401)861-5691

The Community in Providence began in 1992. There are about 75 men, women, and children living in two large households. We make all natural futon mattresses and sell them along with other items made in the cottage industries of our sister communities. We also operate a print shop where we publish community Freepapers. We want this life we have found in our Master, Yahshua. to go out to the entire earth. We especially appreciate the freedoms we have here to express our beliefs and to demonstrate our life due to the influence of Roger Williams, founder of Rhode Island. [See network listing for the "Community In" Association in the Resources section.] 12/26/95

COMMUNITY IN RUTLAND

New Social Order in Messiah
115 Lincoln Avenue
Rutland, VT 05701

(802)747-7217/773-0582

The Community in Rutland began in 1992 when we moved the Common Sense Soap factory here from Island Pond. There are about 80 people here living in two households. We work in the soap shop daily and sell our products to retail stores all over the U.S. as well as to individuals through mail order. We extend to you our warmest welcome to come and visit us or

any of our communities listed in this Directory. In a world of confusion and mistrust, you may have many questions and doubts about us, our lifestyle, and our beliefs. We welcome you to come and visit and see for yourself if our life is true. (John 7:17). [See network listing for the "Community In" Association in the Resources section.] 12/26/95

COMMUNITY IN ST. JOSEPH

New Social Order in Messiah
1923 Clay Street
St. Joseph, MO 64501
(816)232-0095

The Community in St. Joseph began in 1989 when we became aware that St. Joseph was in the center of the "heartland." We are about 60 people who want to see a solution to loneliness demonstrated here in the center of the U.S. The only solution that will work is to believe in Yahshua, obey His word, and follow Him into the new social order that He is building according to His instruction. This is only possible where God's love dwells, in His holy habitation. Here, He makes a home for the lonely, bringing them into families (Psalms 68:5,6). Now there is a home for the homeless and hope for the hopeless. We offer a place to belong, a place where the commands of Messiah can be lived out. And this is His commandment, that we love one another in the same way that He loves us (John 13:34,35), and that we be one as He and his Father are one (John 17:22,23). [See network listing.] 6/15/93

COMMUNITY IN WINNIPEG

New Social Order in Messiah
484 Wardlaw Avenue
Winnipeg, MB R3L-0K3
CANADA
(204)475-3362/284-4445

The Community in Winnipeg, which began in 1993 as 120 of us moved here from Nova Scotia, operates the Common Ground cafe in Osborne Village and takes an active part in the many folk festivals hosted in Winnipeg each year. We are not Christians or Jews or any other religion, but a preserved seed, a new sprout that has sprung up from the dusty parched land. We are a tender little shoot, like a new branch snipped from a tree that was cut down and planted again in good soil to begin anew (Ezekiel 17:22); like a stone

cut out of a perverse mountain to become something totally new and fresh (Daniel 2:34,35); like a new wineskin especially fashioned to contain the new wine (Luke 5:38). [See network listing for the "Community In" Association in the Resources section.] 12/26/95

COMMUNITY IN WOODSTOCK

New Social Order in Messiah
P.O. Box 628
Woodstock, NY 12498
(914) 679-5915

The Community in Woodstock began in 1995 with a vision of opening a music conservatory in this culturally rich New York town known for decades as ". . . the colony of the arts". Our desire is to demonstrate a life of music, celebration, and festivals in a town once teeming with the hope of the "Woodstock Nation". People from every nation will respond to this demonstration and join in so that this present social order can finally come to an end. [See network listing for the "Community In" Association in the Resources section.] 12/26/95

COMMUNITY OF CELEBRATION

P.O. Box 309
Aliquippa, PA 15001
(412)375-1510

An Episcopal community (est. '73) with 20 lay people and ordained clergy living in an oppressed, poor, urban area. Our shared purpose is to live our baptismal vows among the poor and the oppressed; to pray and work for renewal and reconciliation in the church and in the world; to offer hospitality, retreats, and conferences (at home and away) on various topics including worship, leadership, Christian education, liturgical renewal, and prayer. We share daily morning and evening prayer. SASE required. 6/21/94

COMMUNITY PLAN-IT

(Forming)
3500 W. Adams Boulevard
Los Angeles, CA 90018
(213)735-4344

It is important to be clear that we are in a planning process but do not yet have the community. We believe that the way we live together and relate together in community is the basic building block that is

needed to change the world; Community Plan-It has as its goal the transformation of the planet.

We are designing a planned cooperative community that enables us to live in greater harmony with ourselves, each other, and our environment. In this community it is necessary that our lifestyle not only be abundant and successful, but also nurturing and fun. In creating such a model, others will be able to see how we can all cooperate and enjoy a higher standard of living. We envision that the replications of our community and similar models around the world will eventually have a transforming effect on the environment, world peace, and the prosperity of all humankind—as we finally learn the benefit of choosing to live for the highest good of all life.

Currently we are in the process of locating land in California, gathering resources, and securing funding on the scale needed to build the initial community of up to 500 people. Our vision has been articulated in a 45-page document which is available for $3. 8/5/92

COMPOUND "I"

Oakland, CA

Compound "i" is a vegan collective living in a warehouse space in an urban industrial area in Oakland. We share most dinners, and enjoy the convenience of having a basketball court (which doubles as a performance space) in our living/dining room. Most of us are artists in one way or another, and we frequently host performances organized to benefit various progressive causes. We share cooking and chores as equally as possible, and make most major decisions by consensus. 9/18/94

CONSCIOUSNESS VILLAGE / REBIRTH INTERNATIONAL

P.O. Box 1026
Staunton, VA 24402
(540)885-0551

Consciousness Village/Rebirth International is an international rebirthing center for the purpose of spiritual purification using earth, air, fire, and water. Our founder is Leonard Orr, the originator of the rebirthing movement. We have a weekly training session which includes three seminars, three rebirths, and one day of fasting and fire purification. We also have special guests come from outside once a month to give trainings and seminars, usually on weekends. It takes six weeks to become a permanent resident, including three weeks of training and three weeks of working guest status. Most members are between the ages of twenty and forty, and are into high levels of spiritual purification. We are open to more people who share these interests and would like to join our community. For information about training and/or membership, please write or call. The Chico center is the community's main office. 9/8/94

COOPER ST. HOUSEHOLD / TRIANGLE F RANCH COOPERATIVE

P.O. Box 238
Vail, AZ 85641

Cooper Street Household is a cooperative intentional household living in a suburban home in Tucson and on a 22-acre primitive "ranch" in an isolated foothills canyon. These two settings permit flexibility in responding to differing needs for togetherness.

We are six adults living within an organizational structure which is loose. There are few rules, but tolerance for the lifestyles of others is expected. Consensus is used for major decisions such as the acceptance of a new family member.

We feel that we can lead a better life together, living in community, than separately. Despite the diversity of our occupations and cultural backgrounds, we have a common value system related to right treatment of ourselves, right treatment of others, and right treatment of the environment. Visitors

are welcome, but should be prepared to camp if facilities are crowded. [cc] 6/12/92

COVENANT HOUSE FAITH COMMUNITY

346 W. 17th Street
New York, NY 10011-5002
(212)727-4971

Covenant House serves homeless and runaway youth in six different locations: Anchorage, Los Angeles, Houston, New Orleans, Fort Lauderdale, Toronto, and New York. At each site we have a shelter and a separate community house.

Community members serve for 13 months and receive room, board, stipend, and health insurance. Prayer life supports community life; all forms of Christianity are welcome, and we practice simple living. A staff recruits and coordinates the volunteers for their year of service and community life. Interested people can call or write for brochure or application. 5/18/92

COVENENTAL COMMUNITY OF UNIVERSITY CHURCH

P.O. Box 377530
Chicago, IL 60637
(312)493-9225 eves

In late '77, through the sponsorship of a local Christian church active in issues of social justice, a group began to form to explore becoming an urban Christian community. Although people came and left, by '79 a core of people had committed themselves, and housing that group became a focus. We purchased and occupied in July '79 a property in an adjoining deteriorated neighborhood. The

building was in bad shape and consumed much time and energy for ten years until we declared it rehabilitated.

Our goals are to be an extended family of choice (multi-racial, -cultural, -generational) and to exhibit shared Christian values in our behavior among ourselves and with others. We manage the property as a co-op and share in the work. People continue to join, and others have left. Two leavings have been difficult, but all others remain in relationship despite the distance. We currently have 33 adults and 14 children.

We struggle with issues of racism and classism in the group and in the neighborhood. We do not share income but try to be sensitive about the differences in our resources. We annually re–covenant and review how well we are individually and collectively acting out the covenant. Our building is a typical city courtyard complex with 21 units of various sizes. Not all can or want to live in this building (we might get another) so there are both old and new members living nearby. In the basement we created common space where we meet for all purposes. We commit to being together once a week where we follow a loose liturgy of prayer, eating, singing, sharing joys and concerns, and some serious discussion. SASE requested. [cc] 6/4/93

CRANBERRY CREEK

Route 3, Box 531
Dugspur
Hillsville, VA 24343
(540)728-7568

Cranberry Creek Community was founded to provide a setting within which mem-

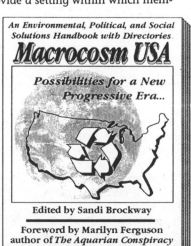

bers can live in a way that respects and nurtures all life, to live in greater balance, with greater simplicity.

The members of Cranberry Creek Community are committed to living interdependently, to healing and maintaining the land, and to dedicating themselves and others in the stewardship of creation. The many ways we work to attain our goal of education for others include providing a model of a working community, extending hospitality to others, publishing the "Simple Living Newsletter," and offering retreats and workshops.

Since our lives are intimately connected to the human family and to the Earth, we live simply to increase our awareness that the way we live can contribute to the health of the human family and the Earth. Cranberry Creek Community recognizes the importance of the individual and therefore respects and supports the rights of each member to privacy and personal growth/development. 7/12/93

CROSSES CREEK YOUTH RANCH & CHRISTIAN COMMUNITY

1021 Ritter Street
Springdale, AR 72764-2329

(501)643-2338

Crosses Creek is a small community established to give spiritual healing to youth and adults, where individuals and families are living on the premises and working together. We are located on a river in the midst of the scenic Ozarks.

We maintain a number of cottage industries, both to provide income for the community, and valuable work experience for our youth. We desire new members with skills in building, maintenance, housekeeping, kitchen service, education, sewing, crafts, and greenhouse work. Must be willing to work. All members share income. SASE requested. 5/1/92

CROW CIRCLE COLLECTIVE

(Re-Forming)
Box 372
Tofino, BC V0R-2Z0
CANADA

(604)725-2112/725-3102

We live in Clayoquot Sound at the edge of the last large temperate rainforest. One million people visit Tofino yearly to feel the beauty of nature. CCC is open to 30 campers, especially those interested in sustainable culture, and we have 8 homesites available by joint ownership. We are 4 years young, open to teachers: more family members willing to enjoy household-level solar, wind, and composting power.

One project is to reach out through the Green network to buy and co-steward private land endangered by clearcut logging, and have base camps there to go deeper into the wilderness experience, gently. We also monitor what our governments will not protect: a trust company is being formed through Turtle Island Earth Stewards (see TIES listing in Resources section).

A progress report and information are available with SASE of 2 dollars to CCC. Land trust shares are 10 Canadian dollars each to TIES. The shares give the bearers the option to visit wilderness, trek, climb trees and mountains. We surf the clean edge and fly driftwood with class into the sweetest shelters. The sauna cabin soothes after a 4–6 hour hike...spark up and sweat down, then open the door, dry the cabin, and move in for the night. Leave the woodshed full, as found, like stepping stones across Vancouver Island. All is well, M. Poole. 5/28/93

CROW'S NEST

(Non-Residential)
P.O. Box 1542
Ukiah, CA 95482

(707)485-0481

Crow's Nest is a small, non-residential, Neo-Pagan/ecological community of folks living near Annwfn, our sacred land [55 wooded acres in Northern California owned by the Church of All Worlds—see Resource entry] where we hold many of our seasonal rites, festivals, handfastings, work parties, workshops, retreats, and meetings. We treat this land as sacred and see ourselves as stewards, not owners. When Annwfn has resident caretakers, they are usually members of the Crow's Nest.

Our nest, one of many in the CAW network, has two levels of focus: 1) the philosophical/educational level, which includes our work with magic and special projects; and 2) the community level, which provides support and nurturing, extended family, and a context for personal growth. Our nest has meetings once a week to do circles, encounter groups, and lectures (other nests meet more or less often, varying with the interests and enthusiasm of their membership). The *Green Egg* magazine, published by CAW, gives a good general overview of the network of nests, our common values, and our collective endeavors. If you have a purpose for visiting our sanctuary at Annwfn, please write for our Visitors' Policy. 9/21/94

CRYSTAL SPRING

Hutterian Brethren
St. Agathe, Manitoba
R0G-1Y0 CANADA

(204)433-7634

[See main listing for "Hutterian Brethren" in the Resources section.] 6/1/92

CURRENTS

13177 Concord Church Road
Glouster, OH 45732

(614)448-4141/448-2504
(614)448-3400/448-4801

Currents Community formed in the late '70s as an outgrowth of our regional food co-op network. We became a legal entity in 1981 and bought a 163-acre farm, home to the 10 members, 2 residents exploring membership, and 9 children. Located in the Appalachian hills of southeast Ohio, we are 15 miles from the university town of Athens, a very supportive macro-community environment. We are attempting to create a replicable model of joint land ownership and stewardship based on cooperative principles and requiring only modest capital investment.

One common bond is a commitment to nonviolent social change activism. This same orientation is expressed within the community as a commitment to open communication and to the nurture and empowerment of each member to become a full and equal participant.

Home-based economic enterprises and development of sustainable land use practices are in their beginning stages. We are currently building new housing and expect to have room for a few new residents in the near future. SASE requested. 2/21/93

DANCE HAWAII!

(Re-Forming)
Hilo, HI

(COMMUNITY LISTING REMOVED)

Folded up shop after 20 years of trying. Couldn't find the right folks to make it work. 1/7/96

DANCING RABBIT PROJECT

(Forming)
P.O. Box 414
Palo Alto, CA 94302

(415)325-3562
sirna@xenon.stanford.edu
http://www.1reality.org/
dancing-rabbit/DR.html

The Dancing Rabbit Project is a group of individuals who desire true environmental sustainability. Rather than the "quick fixes" or band-aid efforts of the mainstream, we are interested in long-term societal and technological changes that will ensure the integrity of the ecosphere, and the well-being of humans, far into the future.

We believe that it is impossible to live sustainably while enmeshed in the consumer culture, but humanly difficult to live independently in isolation. Therefore, we envision a locally self-reliant town committed to radical environmental sustainability—a place where one can get one's livelihood and happiness without causing environmental degradation. We intend to build such a town.

Fully realized, Dancing Rabbit will be a small town with about 1000 residents. We will be housed in a variety of living arrangements, eat a variety of foods, and work on varied projects. It will be a society flexible enough to include egalitarian communities, cohousing, individual households, and hermits. But while we may have different approaches to some issues, the common desire for environmental sustainability will underlie all key decisions at Dancing Rabbit.

Although Dancing Rabbit will strive for self-sufficiency and economic independence, we will not be sequestered from mainstream America. Rather, outreach and education are integral to our goals. We will vigorously promote ourselves as a

viable example of sustainable living and spread our ideas and discoveries through visitor programs, academic and other publications, speaking engagements, and the like.

Currently, Dancing Rabbit has some members living cooperatively in Berkeley, CA as a stepping stone to forming our eventual rural community. There, we have meetings with the larger membership of DR to discuss our progress and work together towards our goals. At this point, we make decisions by consensus.

We also have an extensive e-mail discussion list and publish a newsletter. If you are interested in being a part of Dancing Rabbit please write, call, or email us to get more information, find out when our next meeting is, or arrange a visit. We are especially looking for preexisting groups interested in pooling resources with us and/or forming a community within the town of Dancing Rabbit. We hope to be moved to a rural site somewhere in the US by spring of 1997. 9/25/95

DANCING WATERS

Route 2, Box 69
Gays Mills, WI 54631
(608)872-2333/872-2498

DW Co-op is on a 130-acre farm among beautiful hills and hollows of Southwestern Wisconsin. We are 11 adults and 2 children who own land and buildings in common. We gather twice monthly for potluck and meetings. Decisions are made by consensus. Housing is clustered, so we bump into each other as we go about our daily lives—sharing food, work, song, and spirit on a less structured basis. Though rural, most of us make our incomes off-farm. We have large common gardens, hay fields, orchards, and extensive woods. We are open to more homesteading, (non-pet) small animal raising, and cottage industry.

We are surrounded by an extensive alternative community including food co-op/cultural exchange, Waldorf school, and organic marketing pool. The wider community helps us create a home that is more than a refuge from the mainstream. Occupations and interests include music making; writing; computer work/play; Green and Central American politics; orcharding; carpentry; weaving; counseling; meditation; yoga; natural foods; alternative energy; volleyball; smithing; health care; wine making; teaching; Native,

Buddhist, and other spiritualities; and trying to figure out what Permaculture means to our land, buildings, and relationships. Visitors required to make advance arrangements. SASE please. 8/14/92

DAPALA FARM

(Forming)
c/o Daniel & Patti Christman
E. 15014 Laurel Road
Elk, WA 99009
(509)292-0423

We're Dapala Farm, a sustainable technologies educational center. Our community has developed to teach self-sufficiency skills and lifestyle, with working examples in the following: organic gardening, greenhouse gardening, composting/soil building, raised beds, drip irrigation, vegetarian cookery, food preservation, root cellaring, low-cost energy efficient housing, alternative energy, gravity-fed water systems, wood heating, homestead organizing strategies, barter, community/ extended family, and live-in apprenticeships. We've followed the examples of Helen and Scott Nearing in our wish to inspire others to develop practical lifestyle alternatives. We'd like to reach those who wish to learn, and those called to teach. We'd like to keep our community small (under 12 people) on our small acreage (16 acres). We've two bedrooms in our home, dormitory space in an underground building, a 20' tipi, and space for campers. Vegetarian meals are coordinated as a communal affair. We'll be doing cottage industries such as organic produce to local markets, co-ops, and restaurants; prepackaged dried meals; community supported agriculture; and homestead arts/crafts. Write or call. Be well and happy. SASE requested. 4/26/94

DEEP WOODS FARM, INC.

24851 State Route 56
S. Bloomingville, OH 43152
(614)332-6602

282 acres, 1 hour SE of Columbus OH in Hocking Hills region, with 5 buildings, 3 large waterfalls, cliffs, caves, and abundant wildlife. *Goals:* land preserved as community for 10 households, people, caring, simple, self-reliant, all ages. Enhancement of environment, charitable works, congenial interaction with nearby community and other intentional communities. Members from diverse generations, ethnic backgrounds, cultures, education, philosophies, religions. No tobacco, no illegal drugs or mood altering substances. *Membership process:* information exchange and visits precede mutual decision for year-long trial residency followed by mutual decision for household membership and lease of up to 2.5 acres for homesite. SASE requested. 9/18/93

DEER ROCK

Route 1, Box 381
Faber, VA 22938
(804)263-6970
(804)263-6997/6512
http://www.ic.org/deerrock/

Deer Rock (formerly Monacan Ridge) is a community created by a group of veteran communitarians and enthusiastic new members—a seasoned team which combines experiences from many places: intentional communities including Twin Oaks, Ananda Village, North Mountain, East Wind, Shannon Farm, Ganas, Claymont (Gurdjieff), kibbutzim and moshavim, as well as mediation centers, the Peace Corps, Quaker meetings, and worker-owned companies.

Based on our ideals and experiences, we have consensed on a thoughtful Membership Agreement which commits us to cooperation, justice and sustainable living, nonviolence, and peaceful conflict resolution. Our bylaws are based on consensus with back-up provisions for a 70% vote (no voting so far). Dues are 7% of after tax income for land residents; minimum dues are $60 per month ($400 maximum) plus eight hours of labor. Off-land member dues are at half rate. Nonresident supporters enjoy limited community benefits for $10 per month.

The land is held in common, leased to School of Living, and leased back under a Community Land Trust lease. Deer Rock members will hold long-term dwelling leases ($3,000 fee with installment options) and own the lease equity in homes we build, or leases we purchase from other members. Housing options will include homesteads and cohousing in addition to clustered family homes. We are renovating a large apple packing house into our community meeting hall, common kitchen and conference center dormitory. Farm animals and pets are welcome if treated kindly. We envision a multifaceted life in tune with Nature—a life of love, work, play, free inquiry and expression, art, music, and diverse spiritual practices. We expect to grow to approximately twenty households, including some group housing.

Deer Rock strives for a wholehearted, sane, balanced, community of friends, a place where we practice common sense and fairness and avoid rigid doctrine and authoritarianism. We intend to nurture multiple generations and cultural backgrounds while exercising vigilance against oppressions such as sexism, racism, ageism, and homophobia.

In September 1994 we purchased Deerrock Orchard, a 330-acre mountain valley with three houses and 16,000 sq. ft. of industrial space, perennial streams, a pond, 80 acres of old orchard, and two farm tractors. A forest which has not been harvested in twenty-two years covers 220 acres of high ridges enclosing the property. We enjoy a moderate climate year-round with a 7–8 month growing season, dependable rainfall, and winters providing 8–12 inches of snow.

Two on-land businesses provide immediate income opportunities: weaving hammocks for Twin Oaks, harvesting organic apples, and selling cider. There is plenty of room to set up more hammock looms on the second floor of the packing shed. The other business, Deerrock Apple Cider harvests our organic Golden/Red Delicious, Jonathan, Winesap and York apples, contracts for off-land cider pressing, and wholesales to local food stores and communities. Most members commute to jobs in Charlottesville, home of the University of Virginia, which is thirty minutes away through the Blue Ridge foothills.

We work on our decision-making process using C.T. Butler's book *Formal Consensus* as a common reference source, and seek to improve our personal relationships using conflict resolution techniques. Deer Rock members get plenty of group decision-making practice on project teams and committee meetings as well as the monthly meetings. Site planning for Nelson County Planning Commission approval, and coordination of dwelling construction are major projects. In 1995 we joined the School of Living, a mid-Atlantic Community Land Trust that finances and coordinates the development of Deer Rock and four other communities in MD, PA, and VA.

Deer Rock now includes over 12 adult members, 5 children, and about 10 supporters. With a target membership of 75 adults, we are actively seeking more new members and supporters. If you want more than an introductory letter, please send $5 for an information package including bylaws and Membership Agreement.

We appreciate your interest in Deer Rock and the intentional communities movement, and wish you well in your search for a home in intentional community. 1/14/96 [85]

DEER SPRING BRUDERHOF

Hutterian Brethren
207 West Side Road
Norfolk, CT 06058

(860)542-5545
http://www.bruderhof.org/

[See main listing for "Hutterian Brethren" in the Resources section.] 11/1/93

DENVER CATHOLIC WORKER

2420 Welton Street
Denver, CO 80205

(303)296-6390

We are a faith community committed to voluntary simplicity and hospitality. Our core group is currently three members, and we live with temporary guests (numbering an average of 12) who join us based on their financial and housing needs. Food and household goods are received through donations and some neighbors join our hospitality efforts. We welcome new members who are serious about living a lifestyle committed to service. If so, please write about arranging a trial visit. Please include a SASE with inquiries. [cc] 6/30/94

DENVER SPACE CENTER

Northeast Denver, CO
(303)296-8061

We are an urban cooperative household established in 1979—more intentional

than a boarding house, less intense than a commune; more civilized than a fraternity, less crowded than a dormitory. We have relatively few rules, though relatively much experience in this lifestyle. We share the rent, the common spaces, the housework, a piano, a big yard with gardens, and make decisions by consensus when possible. We encourage friendships, good company, interesting conversations, aesthetic ruminations, and connections to a developing circle of friends. We have a non-biological resemblance that eludes prosaic description. [cc] 11/24/92

DESIDERATA

Route 1, Box 69
Smithville, TX 78957-9703

(512)360-5046

We are a group of 10 families who each own 2 acres and jointly own 101 acres. We have come together because we love living in the country and we love living close to the land—the Earth. We are not bound by any particular race, creed, religion, or politic. We are bound by our love of the land and our desire to take care of it and enjoy it. The land provides us with a home; a community of like-minded people; solitude and companionship; food if we plant or gather it; water for the drinking; woods for the hiking; a pool, a creek, and a river to cool off in; more than 50 varieties of wildflowers to enjoy, the smell of the wild, the out of doors. SASE requested. [cc] 9/27/94

DOE FARM

Wisconsin Womyn's Land Co-op
Route 2, Box 150
Norwalk, WI 54648

(608)269-5301

D.O.E. (Daughters of the Earth) Farm is a beautiful 80-acre farm/campground/home located in west central Wisconsin. The land was acquired in '77 by the Wisconsin Womyn's Land Co-op, our organizational structure. Two presently live at the farm full time, though our organization is strong and spread out over the entire Midwest. Membership in WWLC is required of all womyn who use the land, and is based on a sliding scale of $3 per $1000 of net annual income, adjustable for womyn with special circumstances.

Our founding vision includes self-sufficiency, an environment conducive to personal and collective growth, a non-

hierarchical political and social structure with consensus among members (WWLC decisions are made at monthly open business meetings), being open to visits from nonresident womyn, organic gardening (but NOT large-scale farming), and an atmosphere of learning and skill sharing. All womyn living on the land needn't necessarily live together, but must meet a minimum energy exchange with regard to the land, maintenance, and other womyn in the living collective.

Our structure gives power to members who take responsibility, who commit themselves to do the work. Directions have changed; policies have come and gone; some policies have been kept for a very long time. More members and any womyn willing to contribute money, time, labor are especially welcome in order to preserve this open womyn's sanctuary. Womyn wishing more information should write, and please enclose SASE (two stamps). 9/8/94

DOREA PEACE COMMUNITY

1645 – 60th Street CTHD
Turtle Lake, WI 54889

We are a community of married couples who own their own homes, and each family supports itself. We work in the surrounding towns and participate in the life of the larger community. We have 89 acres of which 78 acres are held as a nature reserve, 7 acres are held in common, and four 1-acre homesites are owned by individual families. Our children attend Amery public school. We gather 4 times a week to share meals together and hold regular community meetings. Besides common meals, we do equipment sharing, have a common garden site and orchard, justice fund, etc. 6/3/92

DOWNEAST FRIENDS COMMUNITY

(Re-Forming)
122 Cottage Street
Bar Harbor, ME 04609

(207)288-3855 (msg.)

"We envision a community that nurtures the individuality of each member. We envision a community that practices a way of living that is sustainable for generations to come, a way of living that defines by practice and direction the meaning of human ecology. We envision a community that strives to work out our personal difficulties between members through its own ingenuity."

Established in 1978 as a collective working to create a whole grain bakery, it has evolved into a group of artists and human ecologists. Located in town, we have been a source of housing and support for College of the Atlantic people for 15 years. Some of our members are actively involved in protecting the environment of Maine through grassroots and legislative involvement.

In practice, we are economically independent with an individual contribution toward upkeep and taxes of the building, phone, electric, and recycled paper products. Physically, our community consists of one large commercial building, one large organic garden, and one large shed. We have a complete woodworking shop, and dream of a pottery studio. SASE requested. 5/13/94

DOYLE STREET COHOUSING

5514 Doyle Street
Emeryville, CA 94608-2502

(510)601-7781/655-7399

We are a small urban cohousing community. Our building has twelve condominium units and a common area (kitchen, dining, sitting, workshop, laundry, playroom, storage, and hot tub) newly built largely within the walls of an existing industrial building. Eleven units are owner-occupied. We are twenty adults, ages 18 to 66, and four children, ages 1–13. We started living here in the spring of 1992 after more than two years' work by a core group of 5 households. We meet monthly to discuss community issues, plan work sharing and expenditures, make policy, and do planning. We share up to four common dinners every week. 4/22/94

DRAGON BELLY FARM

(Forming)
3882 Larson Lake Road
Port Ludlow, WA 98365

(360)732-4855
http://www.cohousing.org/
specific/dragonbelly

Developing community a ferry ride and 30 miles from Seattle, near Port Townsend (previously listed as Tamlin Hollows). We have forests, meadows, wetlands, creeks, ponds, lots of spring and well water, and soil that needs work—glacial moraine and peat that has never been previously farmed. We're planting an organic orchard, herb and vegetable gardens; chickens seem to be a good combination with the orchard. We also have ducks, goats, and an assortment of other creatures (founders don't eat animals). Small-scale aquaculture may be viable. We are planning a retreat center and/or alternative B&B, and are open to other cottage industries. Local jobs are limited.

We think there is room for about five houses and some smaller cabins, yurts, tipis. Building houses would necessitate co-ownership, but we are also open to some renters. We are looking for other responsible, holistically growth-oriented, communicating, natural food eating, non-smoking, nature lovers who can share our dreams. We are particularly looking for an organic gardener, preferably with biodynamic knowledge. We are spiritually eclectic and committed to personal and planetary transformation. SASE required. 11/30/92

DRAGONFLY FARM

Mink Lake Road
Lake Saint Peter
Ontario K0L-2K0 CANADA
(613)338-2709/338-3316

Situated just east of Algonquin Park amid the rolling, pre-Cambrian hills of the Canadian Shield is Dragonfly Farm. Our small collection of people persist on 250 acres of trees, marginal agricultural land, in a rather severe climate. Our seasonal businesses include a commercial greenhouse offering a plurality of flowers, and organic vegetable and herb starts; a mobile sawmill which custom cuts local people's logs; and a wreathing co-op. There are also a horse, cow, chickens, cats and dogs. Our gardens provide us joy and bounty.

Presently we are not seeking new permanent members. We welcome visitors, especially those from foreign lands who wish to experience rural Canada and need a place to stay. Accommodations are primitive. We heat with wood, have electricity, and use an outhouse since there is no indoor running water. In the summer months camping is available (on the back 40). During winter we can always find a way to squeeze people into our homes. Donations of monies from visitors go toward taxes etc. A few hours of assisting in farm activities are welcomed.

Here at Dragonfly the "politics of anarchy" rule within a sense of "communal individualism." Communication is preferred before arrival. [cc] 3/18/94

DREAMTIME VILLAGE

(Forming)
Route 2, Box 242-W
Viola, WI 54664
(608)528-4619 (Office)
(608)625-2217 (School)

Dreamtime evolves from the meeting of hypermedia and permaculture. Hypermedia is the entire range of tools for information exchange and resources for creative production; permaculture refers to sustainable use of land and resources. Emphasis will be made at Dreamtime on hybrid, experimental, educational, and networking activities which promote the creation and sustenance of alternative culture and organized using the model of a loose-knit microvillage with individual autonomy but still sharing collective responsibility for the buildings and land.

Dreamtime properties include the old West Lima School which is two-story brick with an attached gymnasium and quonset hut on 3 acres. This site is slowly being converted into an educational center complete with woodshop, music studio, pottery studio, performance and gallery space, library, perennial sculpture garden, orchards, and more. Other properties total 70 acres of undeveloped woods, field, and wetland. Titles will eventually be held by Driftless Bioregional Land Conservancy.

Interested visitors are welcome. Overnight visitors are charged $5 a day, plus they are expected to contribute an hour or two of labor. Please call or write in advance, or send $3 for a copy of our newsletter. 11/20/92

DUCK MOUNTAIN CIRCLE

(Forming)
Box 41
Boggy Creek
Manitoba R0L-0G0
CANADA
(204)937-3238

Duck Mountain Circle is a developing intentional community located in the hills of western Manitoba. Our goal will be to create a "people garden" where life will co-evolve and flourish indefinitely into the future, and will provide individual residents with the opportunity to be directly responsible for meeting their needs in a gentle way.

We now offer apprenticeship programs on various aspects of "gentle living on the Earth." These are custom designed for each individual participant and include such areas as organic beekeeping, alternative energy generation, no-intervention childbirth, organic gardening, nature study, natural foods cooking, wild foods foraging, homeschooling, etc. We also provide retreats for individuals and small groups.

We are based on 160 acres which is designated as an "ecological significant area" by the World Wildlife Fund, The Nature Conservancy, and the government of Manitoba.

We are actively encouraging individuals and families to become involved to help actualize the development of Duck Mountain Circle. We are also open to visitors who would like to experience a unique part of Canada. Please write or phone for more information. 4/11/92

DU-MÁ

2244 Alder Street
Eugene, OR 97405
(541)343-5023

We are a stable urban community formed in 1988 based on five values—ecological responsibility, diversity, personal growth, egalitarianism, and community. Ecological responsibility includes growing vegetables, recycling, and buying used products. We embrace diversity by respecting differences and seeking members from different backgrounds. We pursue personal growth through various methods including co-counseling, music, art, and astrology. We strive for equality by using consensus and educating ourselves about internalized sexism. And to foster community we set time aside for activities such as singing and retreats.

Visitors often remark that we are neat, well-organized, and accountable

to our values. We eat vegetarian meals together, nurture relationships, and share the joys and responsibilities of owning a home large enough for nine members. We share expenses but not our incomes.

We seek new members who are compatible with us, have energy to contribute, are financially stable, and who are looking for an established community to grow with. We are not a quick housing fix. Our membership process helps us determine who will thrive and be happy here. 11/5/93

DUNMIRE HOLLOW

Route 3, Box 449
Waynesboro, TN 38485

(615)722-9201
(615)722-3078
(615)722-5096

Dunmire Hollow (est. '73) is a community of about a dozen people sharing their lives and 160 acres in a magic hollow in Tennessee. We have fields, orchards, gardens, woods, springs, creeks, a community center, woodshop, sauna, countywide food co-op, etc. Each family is economically independent; we make our livings in a variety of ways: construction, auto repair, teaching, woodworking, sewing, nursing, doctoring, truck driving, small engines sales and repair, crafts, and from providing for ourselves more directly through domestic economy and barter.

We are happy to communicate with people who are interested in rural community living. We enjoy visitors; please write for more information or to arrange a visit (include a SASE). 4/5/93 [83, 85]

EARTH CYCLE FARM

(Re-Forming)
Route 1, Box 9-C
Waukon, WA 99008

(509)236-2265

In 1975 Earth Cycle Farm's 80 acres were placed in a land trust for community members to develop and demonstrate diverse sustainable agriculture practices, including organic farming, cover cropping, permaculture, and reforestation. Residents work toward a self-sufficient lifestyle that provides a majority of food, shelter, and energy for simple living. Alternative technologies include windmills, solar electricity, draft animal power, and use of indigenous building materials. The possibilities are great for fruit and vegetable marketing, handicrafts, and other cottage industries.

This farm is an educational center for sustainable living, where people come to get hands-on experience with food production, appropriate technologies, and group processes. Teaching children these skills, and a basic respect for their environment, is a primary focus. College interns and apprentices will also play an important role.

We welcome people with an interest and desire in living in harmony with the land, cooperating with one another, and working for the future of community. Some of our ongoing projects include: food drying and canning, draft horse/oxen training, forestry management, and design and construction of housing and alternative energy systems. There are plenty of other areas and opportunities, depending on personal interest and inspiration. We invite visitors and trial residents to share this beautiful space. Please write or call to let us know your hopes and plans. SASE requested. 6/9/94

EARTH FAMILY FARM & ECOVILLAGE

(Re-Forming)
93 County Road 550
Gardner, CO 81040

(719)746-2332

Beautiful clouds above—vision of change. Sacred mountains below—standing in eternity. This is southern Colorado, home for Earth Family Farm. We are open to all who contribute to the Medicine Lodge by living a simple lifestyle in touch with spirit and nature, truly suckling from the Breasts of Mother Earth. We value sharing and encouraging each other's paths and gifts, with current focus on wild crafting, holistic healing and growth, eco-activism, and providing a base-camp for visitors doing mountain retreats. Massage, herb teas and baths, celebratory music/dance, medicine wheel, and pyramid meditations are current creative connections. Experience stillness while working with the land.

As a welcome home center we invite people who are: 1) committed to alternative lifestyles, 2) positively motivated, 3) deconditioned from the need for structures of status and "overlords," 4) actively seeking the best in others and quick to forgive mistakes. Creation of more eco-friendly shelters and vehicles, greenhouses, solar hot water, wind machines, gardens and trees, ongoing inner growth, gentleness, and love are our goals. Join the Council Table; lend a hand to create villages of intelligent labor, community service, and ecological soundness for a happier and peaceful world. Call us if interested in primitive vacationing. SASE requested. 12/6/94

EARTH RE-LEAF

(Re-Forming)
Box 599
Naalehu, HI 96772

(808)929-8003

Earth Re-Leaf, a co-op farm network-play organization, has as its goal furthering the availability of small decentralized homestead-type land situations to low-income people. This provides opportunities for the people to grow food and build shelter. We also offer holistic educational services and tools to purify the people and the land. A newsletter and other literature are published periodically in furtherance of these goals. We provide interested groups and supportive friends with information and research data that discourage dependency on government welfare programs and encourage self-sufficiency. We also promote international homesteading and tree planting as a major peace campaign and solution to world problems.

We are looking for small core groups of friends to pursue these goals using a simple consensus council based on the following agreements: 1) short silent period before speaking, 2) equal uninterrupted 3-minute speaking rotations, 3) division into groups of 12 or fewer speakers, 4) decisions by unanimous agreement. Using this council format we will also be exploring evolving relationship and sexuality concepts along with cooperative child care, adding agreements to this base as we grow. We now have one small piece of land with food and shelter available, and are looking into expanding to additional land as soon as a stable core group with serious intent has formed. 12/1/92

EARTH VILLAGE INSTITUTE

(Forming)
P.O. Box 23
Gunnison, CO 81230

(303)642-0020

Planning an ecological energy-efficient cohousing community 17 miles south of Gunnison on 120 acres at 9500 ft. elevation. Site has springs and lakes, and is bordered on two sides by national forest. The 3-1/2 story Common House/multi-household dwelling is almost completed. Plans include energy self-sufficiency, community businesses, in-house financing, land development, and building construction. 8/29/94

EARTHAVEN

(Forming)
P.O. Box 1107
Black Mountain, NC 28711

(704)683-1992

Earthaven is an evolving village community on 340 forested acres in the Blue Ridge mountains of Western NC. We are a living/learning community dedicated to an ever-deepening understanding of ourselves and our universe through real-life spirituality, neo-tribal culture, sustainable health/healing arts, consensus process, Earth-friendly building, permaculture, and Earth care. Looking for families, couples, and singles with vision, pioneering spirit, and skills to co-create ecospiritual culture now! 99-year leases, memberships, and internships available. SASE for workshop schedule; $15 for info and 6-mo newsletter subscription. 4/17/96

EARTHLANDS

(Re-Forming)
39 Glasheen Road
Petersham, MA 01366-9715

(508)724-3428/724-3530 Fax

Earthlands is a community-based organization in rural New England, where experiential learning and personal empowerment are the basis for living and learning in harmony with the Earth and all its creatures. We serve as a multi-purpose Center for Sustainable Living, with activist trainings, Earth-oriented programs, and personal and group retreats. Lasting community health and societal change depend on the empowered individual. To promote dynamic interrelationship, Earthlands endeavors to support and encourage individuals striving to live lightly, creatively, and lovingly; to develop the community as a model center for experiential learning and sustainable living; and to conduct educational and activist outreach at all levels, from local to international. Ongoing openings for resident community members and program center staff and interns. Please include SASE with inquiries. 9/9/94

EARTHSEED

(Forming)
PO Box 647
Saxtons River VT 05154

brobin@igc.apc.org
http://piney.wpine.com/earthseed/

We are in the process of co-envisioning and co-creating a community, sharing our experience with our neighbors and the world. We intend to be living simply and sustainably; radiating love and healing to the human family on Earth; releasing our patterns of oppression; listening to and honoring our whole selves, each other, the land, and its beings and spirit; speaking truth; reclaiming our power from within; feeling and expressing all feelings; co-creating sustainable culture; celebrating diversity; practicing Earth-centered spirituality; nurturing each individual's unique creative expressions; clear personal responsibility around all issues.

Key elements of our vision are Circles, Natural Cycles, Celebration, Consensus process. We are in the process of developing inclusive love (including self), self-responsibility, experience of communal living, communication and listening skills, group process skills, honesty, flexibility, financial responsibility, vision, and commitment to personal growth and social change.

Between us we will also need to have or acquire practical skills, including permaculture design, construction, organic gardening, legal, accounting, administration, waste/wastewater treatment, appropriate and solar technology, healing, crafts, program development, marketing, electronic communications, writing, and fundraising. We intend to co-own land with hills, mature forest, wildlife, water, a communal building, gardens, and personal dwellings. 6/10/94

EAST WIND COMMUNITY

Box CD-96
Tecumseh, MO 65760

(417)679-4682/679-4684 Fax
cath@eastwind.org
http://www.well.com/user/eastwind/

East Wind, established in 1973, is a community which is owned and operated by its members. All income and expenses are shared in common. We are located on 160 acres, lease 190, own an additional 268, and are in the process of purchasing an adjoining 427 acres of land in the beautiful Ozark mountains of southern Missouri.

Our community is supported entirely by the income which we derive from our successful Nut Butter and craft businesses (Twin Oaks Hammocks and Utopian Sandals). We maintain an organic garden, cows for dairy and beef, pigs, sheep and chickens for domestic use. Each member works an average of 40 hours per week in return for food, clothing, health care, and other needs and amenities.

East Wind is an active member of the Federation of Egalitarian Communities, a network of groups devoted to building communities rooted in the values of equality, cooperation, and nonviolence. Our decision making is primarily democratic, and we try to distribute authority and responsibility among our members.

Our population tends to fluctuate between 50 to 70 members. We want to grow in a sustainable manner and welcome visitors. Write or call (please *don't* drop in) for more information or to arrange a visit. 10/26/93 [10, 13, 18, 32, 41, 52, 73, 84, 85]

EAST-WEST HOUSE

San Francisco, CA

(415)346-2990

We at East-West House live in a large four-story, thirteen-bedroom Victorian house which is located in the North of Panhandle district of San Francisco. The name "East-West House" came from the original founders of the collective, who were studying Buddhism. Begun in 1957, the group rented at various locations before buying the current house in 1972. In 1990 the house, badly in need of repair, was sold to a nonprofit dedicated to providing low-income housing—with the condition that the house would be able to maintain its collective structure. Innovative Housing, the nonprofit that now owns the house [see Resource listing], was able to obtain state and city funding for the renovations, which were completed in 1992.

We have no stated theme or ideology other than a desire to live collectively. We have monthly meetings, share cooking and chores, buy bulk foods and supplies, recycle, and try our best to live harmoniously with our housemates. 9/24/94

ECOVILLAGE AT ITHACA

(Forming)
CRESP, Anabel Taylor Hall
Cornell University
Ithaca, NY 14853

(607)255-8276
http://www.cfe.cornell.edu/ ecovillage/

Located in the beautiful rolling hills of New York's Finger Lakes Region, EcoVillage at Ithaca is actively seeking new resident members. Our goal is to build a replicable model of a cooperative, environmentally sensitive community clustered in six neighborhoods of 25–30 attached houses each. The design provides for a pedestrian village surrounded by expansive gardens, orchards, woods, wetlands, ponds, and sustainable agricultural areas. Our plan incorporates energy-efficient, healthy housing with passive solar design features. Planning is underway for a biological waste treatment system that will also supplement village energy needs.

EcoVillage has purchased 176 acres of land located 1-1/2 miles from downtown Ithaca, and 3-1/2 miles from Cornell University and Ithaca College, with access to local services. Using the Cohousing model pioneered in Denmark, twenty households have been meeting for a year to plan the first neighborhood. Each neighborhood will feature cooperative dining in a common house which may include a day care facility, recreation area, workshop, guest quarters, and laundry room. The first resident group plans to move in here in 1995.

As a living laboratory and teaching center, EcoVillage will showcase systems that can be replicated nationally and internationally. We hope that you will join us. SASE requested. 7/27/93

EDEN SANCTUARY

(Forming)
c/o Wilson
3920 East 17th
Eugene, OR 97403

Inspired by the Community of the Ark in France, we wish to create a community in the U.S. similarly based on a vow of nonviolence. While open to all spiritual paths, our common denominator is a deep commitment to nonviolence and reverence for all life. We relate to the Biblical term "Babylon" as a way of describing a society that is existing in a state of alienation from God/our Higher Self and which perpetuates itself through a set of institutions based on violence and greed. Though we applaud the communities movement, we question whether its goals can truly be achieved unless we are willing to more completely sever ourselves from the ways of Babylon.

We affirm the demonstrated power of a vow of nonviolence and non-cooperation, taken in solidarity with others, to provide strength in resisting reassimilation. We seek nonviolent alternatives in economics, government, energy, diet, and interpersonal relationships. We affirm the Gandhian concept of "bread labor" and affirm the use of simple hand tools in achieving our independence. We are also creating a support network for those interested in taking the vow but not in being part of an actual physical community [see Resource listing for One By One]. Send SASE for more detailed information. 6/28/94

EDGES

(Forming)
Route 3, Box 452
Glouster, OH 45732

(614)448-2403

Edges (formerly the Athens Land Co-op) is a community growing from the need for ecologically sound processes for our essential systems. Our vision is to create a healthy, happy, sustainable way of life, both for ourselves and as a model for others. We are committed to exploring personal growth through healing ourselves and our relationships with each other and with the land. We meet regularly, and have recently acquired land.

Our goals include: 1) land stewardship using permaculture principles, 2) living in harmony, utilizing clear communication, responsibility for ourselves, and mediation when conflict arises, 3) interaction with the larger world community by offering examples of alternative systems through an Education and Resource Center, 4) encourage personal autonomy within a cooperative framework. We plan for 20–30 adult members, believe in strength through diversity, and in ending all forms of oppression.

Members work together on projects, and form groups to run businesses by choice. Housing is generally autonomous, though some may opt for group households. Maintenance is accomplished by a monthly labor/dollar assessment. Land and co-op are owned by the co-op/trust. Our vision of cooperation includes making decisions based on what will work best for each and the group as a whole. We use consensus for major decisions and, rather than emphasizing rules, we prefer living by principles, guidelines, and consciousness. SASE requested. 6/14/94

EFE / ENVIRONMENT-FRIENDLY ENTERPRISES

(Forming)
1120 University Avenue
Grand Forks, ND 58203-3654

Our vision: Co-op housing/social support/

livelihood; formal contracts; consensus and individual autonomy; and win-win, nonmanipulative interactions. We want to restore/retrofit old homes into rent-to-own co-ops for low-income housing/home ownership, and to develop a cooperative livelihood, especially involving green enterprises (nontoxics, alternative energy and appropriate technology, ecotourism, horticulture, etc.). We also want to make available rooms or apartments for displaced youth and others, including social support.

Our daily life: We live in a Victorian duplex with a rental unit in an older section of a small university city (a service center in a state dependent on agriculture, federal lands/installations, and tourism). We are presently one full-time resident, a self/community-employed adult responsible for property management and garden; and one part-time adult, a school employee with classroom responsibilities and school activities, who resides elsewhere during school year. "Pets" in residence, too.

New members wanted ("disabilities" as welcome as "normalcies"). We also desire networking, possible affiliations with nearby and regional co-op groups. Will consider relocation; prefer North Woods/North Plains/Rockies regions. SASE required. 1/11/95

ELDERWOOD FARM

(Forming)
15210 Schleweis Road
Manchester, MI 48158
jeff@trillium.soe.umich.edu

ElderWood Farm is located in southeastern Michigan, just southwest of Manchester. The goal of ElderWood is a commitment to provide high-quality organic produce, to create a healthy, respectful environment for children, and to strive toward self-sustainability. With this as its foundation, ElderWood looks forward to meeting like-minded individuals.

ElderWood Farm was established in 1993 and is in the process of developing its soil fertility on a modest-sized garden space. The farm is 35 acres, including 10 acres of woods. Garlic and potatoes will be the first crops to be marketed in the fall of 1996. Farming will increase as our population increases, and we have just begun to actively announce our existence. It is hoped that people become attracted to the surprisingly mild climate here in Michigan, and choose to come for a visit. 1/17/95

ELLIS ISLAND

1204 W. 27th Street
Los Angeles, CA 90007-2330
(213)748-7546

"Hang loose but don't fall apart." We are fond of certain slogans, including "Keep it clean, pay the rent, contribute...." Founded in 1969, we were a somewhat classic hippie commune. Over the years there have been plenty of changes, the house always reflecting its current membership. We're now more eclectic, maybe even with a touch of bourgeoisie in a member or two.

We are currently remodeling our 11-bedroom house, with some house members being hired by the group. Four members are the legal owners, but function as stewards rather than as landlords. It's definitely a mid-city urban environment. We're mostly anarchistic and nonhierarchical. We have no particular dogmas or religious focus, although we lean to the left politically and are generally anti-war. Several members have a background in Transactional Analysis; although it's not "practiced" here per se, it does provide a basis for "straight talk." Among our members there is also an incredible diversity of attitudes and interests—including some into cooperatives, creative arts, and/or loud music (Rock & Roll).

We are not soliciting new members— they come regularly through our network of friends and acquaintances (we have at least a 6-month waiting list for new residents). Prospective visitors need to make arrangements in advance, and should direct inquiries to Rush Riddle. 11/17/93

ELOIN COMMUNITY

P.O. Box 446
Ashland, OR 97520

We live in the wilderness of southern Oregon, embracing a simple life and learning to harmonize with nature and each other. We are a spiritual community, nondenominational, honoring the divine in all life. We draw wisdom from the Essene teachings of Professor Szekeley and other universal learnings. We do extensive organic gardens, build our own dwellings, and work toward turning our 80 acres into a botanical park. We are off the grid— with passive and active solar, hydroelectric, and wood systems. We are vegetarian, and no alcohol or drugs are allowed. We honor ourselves as a temple of God. We are seeking new members who are inter-

ested in our way of life, who are light-hearted, and who have skills in being a gardener, carpenter, or teacher for our homeschool. Written inquiries with photo are requested before visiting. SASE is requested. 1/27/95

ENCHANTED GARDEN

(Re-Forming)
6008 Arosa Street
San Diego, CA 92115
(619)582-9669

Eight of us live together on a 1/3-acre parcel surrounded by canyons in the state college area of San Diego. The land exists as an oasis of green with many aromatic herbs and simple foods growing. The work that has gone into preserving this natural environment for more than 14 years is an inspiration to many. The land is rich in nature spirits and life energies drawn here through many hands working together. We have an in-house library with books on gardening and natural healing.

The property is in private ownership, and is a house offering rental to those in the local community who would like to live as "extended family" and join together in house meetings and shared house duties. We live by basic agreements to keep the house orderly and maintain the property. Through local ads, we attract individuals with a "community" bent who bring new energies to the house. Rentals occur from time to time, and one space is available for work trade. Individuals who would like to live in this special environment and contribute to the intentional living focus are encouraged to call.

Our goals for the next few years are to increase food production and the fertility of the soil, and create more and more extended community around gardening together and shared rituals. The intent of the house is to demonstrate how much beauty anyone can create in their own backyard, even in an urban area, and to exemplify an alternative way of living together. 5/5/94

ESSENE SKOOLA PHISH (ESP)

(Forming)
Route 1, Box 169
Golden Eagle, IL 62036

Let's go fission! 12-Step people, Veg's, Eco-folks, Rainbows, Utopia builders— Welcome! Campin-parkin-garden space, bath etc. available 30 mi. W. of Alton, in Calhoun County. We ain't organized yet. Hills, bike trails, wildlife refuge, river nearby. OAHSPE said (c. 1881) that 'man is subject to unseen influences that cause nations to rise and fall in cycles; that it's not enuf for the prophet to accuse ignorance and war for the fall of civilizations, but that the unseen cause of causes must be found so that 'man in the future may "overcome these epidemic seasons of cycles." OAHSPE predicted that governments based on force (police/military) would soon fall into chaos and be replaced by spiritual communities (with consensus rule and without leaders) which would raise orphans (from the chaos) to be a new race on the Earth. Essene Skoola Phish seeks to be a learning ground for such communities and prophets, where all are students and teachers in the school of life. Besides nature, our textbooks include *OAHSPE Books of Prophecy, Ben, Judgment, Inspiration, Shalam, Discipline*; *Essene Gospel of Peace-1*; *Co-Dependence* (Schaef); *AA 12 Steps*; *Group Relationships Anonymous*; *Guidebook for Intentional Communities* (Morgan); *Universe of Motion*; and *The Great Reckoning* (Davidson). OAHSPE samples 5 pgs: $1+stamp. 6/22/92

EUGENE COHOUSING

(Forming)
711 West 11th
Eugene, OR 97402
(541)343-5739/484-2597

Eugene Cohousing is a group of 16-plus families forming to create a neighborhood within the Eugene city limits. We hope to build energy-efficient homes and a community garden. SASE requested with inquiries. 5/10/93

FAIRVIEW FOLKS

1801 Fairview
Berkeley, CA 94703
(510)658-3899

We are a 10-person organically evolving multigenerational household made up of educationists, spiritual aspirants, activists, musicians, and artists. We range in age from 3 to 50, and our three children bring much joy to our lives. Since our house is only two years old, we are still in the process of organizing ourselves. We cook dinners (vegetarian) five days a week, meet weekly, and are intently fixing up our house (we have purchased the two houses). We have a beautiful flower garden, a small vegetable garden, a dog, and several cats.

Though we don't believe in a specific dogma or religion, we are all progressively minded and share an interest in political, social, and spiritual matters. We are generally committed to making our house an affordable, pleasant place to live. Implicitly, there is a commitment to open, loving communication with each other. We also strive to be emotionally responsible and work out interpersonal issues as they arise. We are involved in our neighborhood, specifically in trying to get everyone in the area together to make our neck of South Berkeley a better place. Mail and phone inquiries only, and please include SASE. 9/24/94

FAMILY, THE

14118 Whittier Blvd #116
Whittier CA 90605
(800)4-A-FAMILY
(310)690-4930

The Family is a controversial Christian movement whose full-time members live in independent communities. We trace our origins back to '68 in Huntington Beach, CA, when our founder, Father David, began a ministry to the counter-culture youth of the '60s. Over the years The Family has grown and changed, but our basic goals remain the same: to help others find meaning in their lives through Jesus, and to give our children a good Christian upbringing. We believe in the Bible as the Divinely inspired Word of God, and that eternal Salvation is God's free gift to anyone who sincerely acknowledges his/her need for a Savior and asks for Christ's forgiveness.

About 3000 adults and 6000 children live communally as full-time volunteer missionaries in approximately 250 communities in 50 countries. Our members are required to uphold a code of conduct and maintain high physical standards. Nicotine, drugs, and excessive use of alcohol are forbidden. We hold Christ's law of love to be the supreme tenet upon which all conduct should be based; all acts motivated by unselfish love for others are acceptable to God. We believe that loving heterosexual relations between consenting adults, regardless of their marital status, is not a sin in the eyes of God, provided it hurts no one. 8/10/94

FAN LAKE BRETHREN

2762 Allen Road West
Elk, WA 99009
(509)292-0502

We follow the teachings and traditions of the Hutterian Brethren Church. We share all things in common, as the early Christians did, and commit our lives to God through Jesus, by the power of the Holy Spirit. We do our best to love God and to love one another, to reject the world and all its lusts. Jesus is the head of our church, and we hear his voice with the help of his Holy Spirit. [See main listing for "Hutterian Brethren" in the Resources section.] 7/20/94

FAR VALLEY FARM

12788 New England Road
Amesville, OH 45711
(614)448-4894

We are 10 adults and 7 children living in sub-Appalachia on 234 acres of open and wooded land in S.E. Ohio (near Athens, the home of Ohio University). We incorporated with the state of Ohio in 1980, and eventually renamed ourself "Far Valley Farm."

We are multi-skilled, and are moving toward a goal of relative self-sufficiency. We regard ourselves as stewards of this land, sharing sort of an overall respect for life and the life force which includes self-respect, growth, and love. We have grown fairly organically, are pretty tolerant, and tend to be honest and up-front with each other. We are presently full, and are not accepting new membership applications at this time. Please, written inquiries only (SASE appreciated). 12/20/94

FARM, THE

(Re-Forming)
34, The Farm
Summertown, TN 38483
(615)964-3574
http://www.thefarm.org/

The Farm is a cooperative community of families and friends living on 1750 acres in southern middle Tennessee. We started the Farm in 1971 with the hope of establishing a strongly cohesive, outwardly directed community—a base from which we could, by action and example, have a positive effect on the world as a whole. The Farm is a community where ideals can find expression in daily life, and it has pioneered in the fields of midwifery, soy technology, Third World relief, solar energy, and cooperative living.

The Farm School is a unique alternative education center, and since 1984 has been a member of the National Coalition of Alternative Community Schools. The Farm is still home to the Midwife School, and babies are delivered regularly. Although PLENTY's business offices have been moved to California, Trade Wind continues to market Guatemalan goods; the Natural Rights Center continues its groundbreaking work in environmental law; and Kids to the Country maintains a nature enrichment program for urban children.

Approximately 33 residents and about 40 businesses (including the Soy Dairy, Solar Electronics, the Book Publishing Co., and the Dye Works) contribute funds to maintain the community. Please write or call (SASE requested). [cc] 1/9/93 [4, 13, 14, 53, 65, 76, 77(D), 82, 83, 84]

FARM HOME CENTER

(Forming)
P.O. Box 1208
Milwaukee, WI 53201-1208
(414)463-8321

The Farm Home Center is a shareholder-owned company whose primary purpose is to establish a sustainable agricultural center—one which demonstrates natural (organic and/or biodynamic) methods of gardening and small-scale farming on an individual, family, and commercial basis. The basic philosophy of the FHC is that its shareholders and associate members are stewards of the soil, responsible for our own bodies, and that the health and well-being of the ecosystem and of themselves are of utmost importance.

The FHC will develop a Residential Home and Retreat Center for its participants who will establish gardens and farm animals—enabling FHC to become self-sufficient and self-sustaining. The FHC's vision incorporates social and environmental values which promote the development and management of the "Farm" as a living ecosystem. Future plans include the development of a Study and Conference Center which is nonsectarian

(open to all races, religions, and beliefs), and focused on alternative agriculture, holistic healing, and preventative health care. 5/2/93

FILLMORE HOUSE
San Francisco, CA

We're an ever-evolving community of politically and artistically active people attempting to live a caring lifestyle in an often uncaring world. It doesn't always work out smoothly, but we try. We make decisions by consensus, and our basic communication form is notes taped to door handles, on the refrigerator, on the piano, even on the ceiling. These are sometimes ignored, but usually listened to in some way or another. We usually fill house openings with friends and acquaintances.

The house's focus has shifted over time from artists to musicians to jugglers, and around again. Members are active in various collective endeavors around town such as Bound Together Books, Inner Sunset Community Foods, 848 Community Art Space, Wise Fool Puppet Intervention, and the Desert Site Works Project. Our varied schedules permit us to spend time with each other in many different formats and time frames (i.e., midnight rituals, early morning breakfasts, weekday beach parties, or just hanging out in the evening around a box of cookies).

Our historic house, built in 1894, will some day have a historical marker saying that this is where the world-famous song "I left my Heart in San Francisco" was written. We're surviving in the city, and you can too. 8/5/94

FINDERS, THE
Washington, DC

The Finders have been around for 23 years, living and working in a rather spontaneous non-organization. The group, now 14 adults, has no official name ("Finders" is the label most often used by outsiders to describe their community).

Their overall approach to life is to make it into a "Game"—a challenging and educational process where the rules change from week to week, day to day, sometimes even by the hour. Members often "volunteer" to each other, informally rotating leadership roles depending on the project at hand, the experience of the people involved, and the prevailing

mood of the moment. The head game caller is usually Marion Pettie, the originator of the adventure.

Their cooperative lifestyle is efficient, and a fertile arena for personal growth. They own an apartment complex; a huge warehouse (now a library, resource center, gathering space, and crash pad); a 600-acre farm four hours from town; and a movie theater. They often share communal meals, pool most resources, and operate several consulting and research businesses—for business organizations, computer users, and people in need of virtually any type of information. They thrive on challenges to their creativity.

The Finders welcome visitors who share their zest for learning and adventure. They'd enjoy hearing from you—if you're friendly, open minded, and resourceful enough to find them.... 7/25/94

FLATROCK COMMUNITY

(Re-Forming)
2720 Hutchinson Road
Murfreesboro, TN 37130
(615)895-2841

Flatrock Community is 8 adults and 4 children working to develop creative responses to competitive economics, sexism, racism, wasteful resource use, disintegration of supportive community, and other problems facing our society. The 13-year-old community owns 27 acres, predominantly cedar glade, three miles from a city of 50,000 with a medium-sized university and 32 miles from Nashville.

Current interests include organic gardening, personal growth, development of group living and communication skills, appropriate technologies, cottage industries, and further education for women is encouraged and supported. We are much interested in diversity of membership: diversity of age, culture/ethnicity, background. We live in simple houses and share a community house. Although separate finances are maintained, our monthly community dues are used to purchase tools and make improvements and repairs. We make group decisions through consensus. We welcome new members and visitors. Prior arrangements required. Please include SASE with correspondence. 6/19/92

 Exploring the Web?
http://www.ic.org/

FOLKCORPS

(Forming)
111 Bobolink
Berea, KY 40403
(606)986-8000

[Formerly: Future, Inc.]
Ready to start gardens and houses when we have: 1) eight dedicated workers, male and female, one skilled farmer (grow veggies, fruit, nuts, fish, herbs, plus reforestation); one skilled nurse (live in, health from womb to tomb); five skilled builders (community hall for big meals, gatherings, office, laundry, shop, clinic, library, plus small efficiency homes); one skilled business person (run the office and be guardian for those who can't cope).
2) Eight dedicated retired persons, a core group of comrades, a soul fraternity, with functions: pool 0% loans for capital, no-interest and no rent, refunded when next occupant moves in; help each other with custodial care, "cans help can'ts," pool experience for whole enterprise; work when and if they choose.

DESCRIPTION: 50 good acres for up to 200 residents; mountain location; access to good highway; spring or site for surface water lake. SET UP: 4 crews: Food, Health, Homes, Business; self-propelled but report weekly to total group. Consensus by total group. Daily Noon Gathering for unity, meal, fun, worship, business (crew reports). A major business gathering monthly (terminate war, AIDS, slums, homelessness). COSTS: Less than 1/2 of conventional. Self-help and non-sales eliminate money lender, landlord, huckster, and bureaucrat. Self-sustenance is "all for each and each for all." MISSION: This communal magnet will pull volunteers, they learn on Folkcorp's crews, then replicate. Groups network in fellowship, business, super government—new humanity. Get out of capitalist harness, into communal harness. Send SASE. 2/12/94

FOLKHAVEN

(Forming)
P.O. Box 878791
Wasilla, AK 99687
(907)376-9677

Folkhaven is an experiment based on common sense, history, and science. Our concept: start with what we know of instinctive human nature and build a just and fulfilling society around those human traits and needs. The extended family and tribal structure of pre-agricultural man provides our social model. We believe any attempt by ivory tower ideologues to force instinctive human behavior into unnatural social molds can only result in tragedy. Twenty-three extinct civilizations and today's social chaos bear witness.

We endorse and practice stewardship, permaculture, ecoregionalism, alternative energy, natural spirituality, and a holistic approach to life. These values notwithstanding, we take a realistic world view and believe in using science and technology to empower and enrich our lives.

Folkhaven is currently forming. Land has been acquired, facilities constructed, and an orchard and garden established. Today we seek vigorous intelligent folk to join us in shaping a better life for ourselves and our children. Ultimately, we seek to create a workable social model to replace our disintegrating society. 11/21/93

FOUR STREETS CO-OP

641 N. New Hampshire
Los Angeles, CA 90004
(213)913-0439

Four Streets is a scattered-site limited equity housing co-op made up of single family homes, duplexes, fourplexes, and apartments located on four streets—hence the name. The four streets are on an abandoned freeway corridor adjacent to Highway 101 in L.A. The neighborhood has a mix of business and residential property near L.A. City College.

The co-op is governed by a board that is elected by the membership. The board meets weekly on Tuesday evenings in open meetings. There are also three committees that meet weekly: Building & Grounds, Membership, and Finance. The committees report to the board every other week. The annual meeting is attended by 60% of the members. We sponsor a Christmas party and many planned children's activities throughout the year. Ethnically, Four Streets is 80% Latino from many countries, and 20% that is a mix of Asian, Black, and Anglo. Correspondence in Spanish is preferred; SASE appreciated. 9/9/94

FOUR WINDS VILLAGE GREAT SPIRIT RETREAT

(Forming)
Route 1, Box 2120
Tiger, GA 30576

(706)782-6939

At Four Winds Village Great Spirit Retreat, the call is now going out for open-minded people on the spiritual path to the All One Father, Creator of all life. We look to join with others of like mind to come learn, worship, and build together a community of people practicing love, peace, and service to others—providing the children with good role models for guidance and living the simple rural life, and helping them develop their own talents at their own private school. Our primary focus is for the children.

We are students of the book *OAHSPE*—revelations of earth, sky, and spirit for the new age of spiritual wisdom—and living it in community. Angel Guidance given through John Newbrough in 1882 is now a worldwide Faithists brotherhood which is little known. The Angel Intelligence calls us the Lighthouse of Enlightenment.

We publish books, and Four Winds News operates an Indian museum gift shop and a bed and breakfast. We have a community center, chapel, mobile homes, administration building, and campground on 80 acres in northeast Georgia mountains. Visitors welcome; write for more info (sample literature $2). Economic disasters and worldwide Earth changes are upon us, but they're bringing good and positive change for the better for those inspired to be pioneers in small cooperative groups worshiping the Great Spirit. 12/4/92

FREE-THE-LAND N.Y.C. SQUATTERS' COMMUNITY

c/o 46 Lindy's Drive
West Milford, NJ 07480

We are located in Manhattan's Lower East Side, near Tompkins Square Park, with 400 homesteaders living in 22 separate apartment houses. Each house has its own autonomy, most have workdays once a week, house meetings, and some have communal meals. We organize concerts, speakouts, demonstrations, and potlucks. Projects: theater/coffeehouse, future childcare center. We are currently in ambiguous legal status as many of the houses were originally abandoned by the city. We are a diverse group dedicated to free green spaces, community self-reliance, anarchistic decision making, anti-racism, and having fun. The best way to get involved is to come to Tompkins Square Park, find us, see the squats, and see if space is available. Mail inquiries can't set up visits, but if you are into working you can assist with workdays, and maybe a house member will take you as their guest. Families with children need to contact the individual squat. You're kinda on your own, but a SASE will answer your questions or correspondence. 4/15/93

FRIENDS LAKE COMMUNITY

1000 Long Lake Road
Chelsea, MI 48188

(313)475-7976

In 1961 a group of Quaker families formed a cooperative community which emphasizes simplicity, ecology, and caring. We are a complex organization, open to persons of every faith and color, with diverse backgrounds and many overlapping areas of interest—our common ground is living with Quaker ideas as our guiding values. All community decisions are made using consensus.

Our 90 acres now has six families living or building on the land, with room for six more. We also enjoy an extended community of 150–200 members who use the land for retreat and recreation, and participate in meetings and celebrations. All members are expected to contribute three hours of labor per year, and are invited to participate in our work parties, educational programs, and monthly community/Board meetings (followed by potlucks or evening campfires and singing).

Sustaining members may acquire lifetime leases on cabin sites and home sites. All members have access to the many community facilities—the beaches, the boats, the lake and woods, the community buildings, and the campgrounds. We have also established a wildlife sanctuary, and a subgroup is developing a conference facility for activities consistent with our principles. Our Michigan Friends Center, capable of handling retreats of up to 40 people, will be available for rent by early 1995. Please include SASE with inquiries. 9/12/94

FRIENDS SOUTHWEST CENTER

Route 1, Box 170
McNeal, AZ 85617

(520)642-3547

Friends Southwest Center is a small land trust in the high desert, with independent living and commitment to Quaker principles of truth, nonviolence, and simple living. We have excellent water, clean air, year-round cool nights—and this is possibly the most economical place to live in the United States. The corporation is not-for-profit, and is solvent. Few jobs are available. Our land is in the Gadsden Purchase, twenty miles from the Mexican border, and we shop in Mexico once a week. A sojourning period is required for your protection and ours. Hook-ups are available. Write (send SASE) or call for more information. 1/1/93

FULL CIRCLE NATURAL FARM

(Forming)
P.O. Box 126
Honeydew, CA 95545

We see the world transforming. The age of empire is giving way to a new age—a return to harmony, health, and wholeness. Our work is to become a seed group for this transformative vision.

We are currently one young couple with a baby boy living on twenty beautiful acres in the coastal Mattole River valley in northern California: forests, meadows, springs, fir, madrone, oak, deer, bear, owls, the sacred mountains, mother ocean. We are creating an organic, natural farm with complete self-sufficiency from "the grid"—with the empire as our goal. We live a simple life without electricity or running water. We seek to return art to life and life to art. The shelters we build, the clothing we make, the food we grow and cook; we dance and paint, make music, play, and work. We seek to return a shattered way of life to a whole way of art life. We would like to meet others who share this transforma-

Drop in on the FIC...

http://www.ic.org/

tive vision and who would like to join us in forming a community of peace, freedom, and love. 10/7/93

FUTURES, INC

[Renamed Folkcorps]

GAIA PERMACULTURE COMMUNITY

(Forming)
Route 1, Box 74-A
Mauk, GA 31058

(912)649-7700

Gaia Community began in 1989 on its beautiful secluded 15 acres in west central Georgia. We are an interracial group, currently five members, and many on the edges. We are sustainable oriented, instituting and practicing permaculture for Dear Life. We teach and share PC (Permaculture) practices with others in all its reality; limited resources, big dollars and all. A down-to-earth group of individuals of all persuasions, but with a central ethic of caring for the Earth, caring for Earth's people, and using excess resources toward these aims.

There are many projects planned for Gaia as we are into aquaculture, organics, animal husbandry, appropriate "low" tech and other sustainable related areas. We welcome others with like kind and sharing ways. There are sweat equity opportunities for those who may wish to

stay among our wilds and wake to the morning alarm clock of wild turkeys and the splendor of our climate and back sandy roads. There is also the beauty of work here with us and a discipline to face some adversities, continuing toward a sustainable future.

These are Gaia's building days and we welcome other inputs—so come and visit, our Rasta vibration and reggae music will welcome you! We are seeking too a carpenter female/male and animal husbandry person. Peace. SASE requested. 12/3/92

GAIEN

(Forming)
6335 Waipouli Road
Kapaa, HI 96746

Aloha! Gaien has formed. Gaien is a combination of Gaia and heaven—heaven on Earth. We are a community of authentic eclectic egalitarian vegetarian awakening decentralized cooperative peaceful simple harmonious dedicated joyful obsequious observant sharing enthusiastic beautiful probiotic ecologically and environmentally sensitive human beings, most of the time.

We are committed to conscious evolution. Our basic living philosophy is to be as present as possible in the moment while helping ourselves and the Earth regain wholeness. Our planet-side focus, at this time, is sustainable agricultural research. We operate Organic Kauai Produce, which provides ourselves and others with high quality vegetables, fruits, and herbs. This focus also includes research on low-impact cottage industries using locally produced and/or grown materials.

Our dream focus is to co-create a sustainable eco-village in a paradisical environment. We invite and welcome those who feel aligned with our vision to correspond. Support and contribution on any level will be joyfully received. Mahalo! SASE required. 12/29/92

GANAS

135 Corson Avenue
Staten Island, NY 10301

(718)720-5378/981-7365
http://village.ios.com/~wonder

At Ganas, about 75 people of all ages, many nationalities, races, religions, educational and political backgrounds, and every imaginable personality live together in surprising harmony. Perhaps we get along so well because of our commitment to diversity and open dialog. Work issues as

well as personal or interpersonal conflicts are identified and confronted before they can escalate into serious problems.

People at Ganas value personal privacy, awareness of each other, respect for individual preferences and differences, economic success, high living standards, and having a good time.

The community was founded in 1980 by the Foundation for Feedback Learning, a NYC non-religious, educational group, committed to learning to freely exchange feelings, ideas, and personal perceptions. We think of ourselves as a laboratory for learning how to learn these things—and we know we have a long way to go.

Ganas is populated by several relatively separate, but complementary, groups. The Core Group serves as the Board of Directors. It consists of 9 people who share all their resources and do whatever needs to be done.

An extended core group of 20–25 people do not share all their resources. They engage in discussion of Ganas issues, and in the community's activities and businesses as they choose. These two groups make most of Ganas' decisions, either by consensus or with authority delegated by the core group. Most of them work in the community, and are highly motivated to do the daily job of helping to create a great place to live. Both groups are very stable and have developed a lot of loving closeness over the years.

Another approximately 25 people live in the Ganas housing, and work or study in the city. They generally enjoy the community, but are not much involved with its goals or activities. Most of them make good relationships and tend to feel that they benefit a lot from the experience. Like everyone at Ganas, they are invited but not required to join whatever is going on. In fact, most of the extended core group is present for most events, and this group rarely is. Newcomers and visitors are welcome to join in wherever they like.

Ganas is located on Staten Island, in a mixed, lower middle class neighborhood, about a half hour ferry ride from Manhattan.

Five of the community's seven large, Victorian-like houses are connected by picturesque walkways. Because of the many trees (some fruit-bearing), berry bushes, flower and vegetable gardens, porches and pretty spots for hanging out, the place has a surprisingly rural feeling. Private and public spaces are comfortable, attractive, and well maintained.

We share excellent facilities for work, study, and play. Food is plentiful, pretty good, and varied enough to satisfy most people, including some vegetarians. People can eat in a common dining room or prepare meals for themselves in one of three stocked, equipped kitchens.

Our three retail stores are located a few blocks from the residences. They restore, repackage and recycle furniture, clothing, household goods, books, records, artwork, and crafts. We also sell new discount fabrics, toys, jewelry, cards, and a few imports. Work choices include housekeeping, construction, and maintaining our buildings and vehicles. We have plans to produce simple clothing, toys, and furniture; to wholesale some items; and we seek people who want to do these things. We're also open to supporting other business ventures proposed by members if they meet Ganas' criteria for profitability and social value.

If you want to visit, just call or write. You'll be welcome to come to dinner at no cost, or to stay for a few days at $15 a day. Visitors staying longer pay their expenses at the rate of $100–140 a week. If that's not affordable, we'll try to arrange a work exchange. If we decide to try living together, you can work in the city and pay $400–550 a month. If you prefer, depending on our needs and your skills, perhaps we can arrange for you to work with us for your expenses. For more information, see our four-page ad on pages 336-339. 9/7/94 [77(D), 80/81, 82]

GENEVA COMMUNITY

(Forming)
Site: Near Lyons, CO
Contact: P.O. Box 4488
Boulder, CO 80306

(303)443-6868

Geneva Community will serve as a model and long-term experiment. Ancient philosophies of living harmoniously with nature will combine with leading-edge technologies aimed at living lightly upon the land.

The physical design will consist of clustered homes of young and old, singles, couples, and families. A community center will incorporate a large dining area for dinners (each home will have its own small kitchen), recreation areas, meeting room, children's play rooms, studios, shop space, and guest quarters. Shared facilities enable each household to require less square footage.

The community will be designed and sited so that the existing vegetation and wildlife will be minimally disrupted. A large portion of the land will remain untouched. Permaculture techniques will be utilized for improving and reclaiming the ecological balance.

Geneva Community will be a place where we all know and care about one another, where we help one another accomplish our goals, and where we all take responsibility for raising our little ones and caring for our elders. Here is a home where we can combine our resources and wisdom to live together and grow in harmony. Please include a SASE with inquiries. 8/29/94

GESUNDHEIT! INSTITUTE

Volunteers to help build:

- **Kathy or Cheryl**
  HC64, Box 167
  Hillsboro, WV 24946
  (304) 653-4338

Tax-deductible donations
or to join the mailing list:

- **Patch Adams, MD**
  6877 Washington Boulevard
  Arlington, VA 22205
  (703)525-8169
  (703)532-6132 Fax
  achoo@well.com
  http://www.well.com/
  user/achoo/

Gesundheit! Institute is primarily a volunteer work camp building a holistically oriented model health care community. Our ultimate goal is the construction of a 40-bed, free, community-based hospital on 310 acres of land in rural West Virginia. Our dream is to create a truly ecumenical healing center with everything from Western allopaths to spiritual healers, treating all types of illness. Humor, clowning, art, nature, love, and friendship are important ingredients in our work.

We have already built a 4000 sq. ft. workshop and have plans completed for the residence hall, which will begin construction as soon as funds are available. A comprehensive land plan has been drawn up to develop our property in an ecological manner.

In West Virginia, 5 resident adults staff the volunteer program and maintain the property. Volunteers are being sought to help with the project, though at this time we are not seeking more long-term members. The "spirit of community" itself is used as a medicine. Help build a dream with a group of enthusiastic do-gooders! Call or write to arrange a 1–2 week visit! 6/25/94 [64]

GITA NAGARI VILLAGE ISKCON FARM

(Re-Forming)
Route 1, Box 839
Port Royal, PA 17082

(717)527-4101

"Plain Living and High Thinking" is the motto of Gita Nagari, the Hare Krishna movement's 600-acre farm community in central Pennsylvania's Juniata Valley. Begun in 1975 by the movement's founder, Srila Prabhupada, the community raises crops, protects cows, works oxen, schools children, publishes a farm journal, and lives life in the loving spirit of Lord Krishna's *Bhagavad-Gita*, Gandhi's favorite book of truth. Krishna's devotees love to share, and Gita Nagari has a lot to offer: farm-fresh vegetarian foods, spiritual ecology, bhakti-yoga culture, and deep friendship on the path to self-realization. Weary of the modern wasteland? Visit Gita Nagari and drink deep at the reservoir of pleasure—Krishna consciousness. For more information write to ISKCON Farm. 5/9/92

GLEN IVY

25000 Glen Ivy Road
Corona, CA 91719

(714)277-8701/277-8700 Fax

Glen Ivy (est. 1977) is the community name of the southwest regional center for the Emissaries [see main listing in the Resources section] located in the Santa Ana mountains east of Los Angeles. Approximately 85 people of all ages make Glen Ivy their home. Communal living is not an end in itself for us, but is a means to create a still, unified environment that encourages a greater experience of one's true identity. New members are not drawn from the general public; over the year we are host to hundreds of visitors from around the world who come for art of living classes or simply to share with us as they familiarize themselves with the spirit of the Emissaries.

The permanent residents have taken on the task of bringing this expansive spirit into practice in all of our everyday duties

We have intentional community on the Web.

http://www.ic.org/

and relationships. Our current operations include childcare; housekeeping; cooking shared meals for the entire community; tending our expanding gardens and orchards; design, construction, and maintenance of our physical plant; and gatherings for the shared radiation of the One Spirit. We invite visitors interested in the Emissaries to come on Sundays and share in our morning radiation service from 10:45 on. [See main listing for the Emissaries network in the Resources section.] [cc] 11/10/92

GLENDOWER

P.O. Box 520291
Independence, MO 64052
(816)252-6023

Currently a core group of 3 adults, formed in the summer of 1994 to encourage maximum ecological savings through sharing of resources, and to support each other emotionally and socially as much as possible. We recently bought a "common" property and have started sharing some living costs cooperatively. We are open to new members and especially hope to find those who are non-smokers, drug-free, and who want "open relationships" rather than monogamy. All races, singles, couples, pagans, freethinkers, atheists, and ecumenically oriented people are welcome. Glendower is Celtic for "Valley of Water." SASE required. 12/8/94

GLENRIDGE CO-OP

137 Addison Street
San Francisco, CA 94131
(415)587-5815

Glenridge Co-op is a combination of townhouses and 2-story apartments spread over seven city blocks of hills and valleys in San Francisco. GARCI, our 20-year-old resident council, in 1991 began a process to convert our structure to a resident-owned limited equity housing co-op, with HUD backing the loan. The conversion to "Glenridge Co-op" began in the winter of 1994. Of the 275 family units, many will become owners, and some will remain as tenants. The complex is ethnically and economically diverse. SASE requested. [cc] 9/9/94

GOOD RED ROAD, THE

(Forming)
P.O. Box 9008, Dept. 174
Solvang, CA 93464

After visiting and living in community, we are ready to bring together the best of what we experienced. We believe community should expand one's opportunities, and in no way limit personal choice or freedom. Commitment and dedication to the overall well-being of the group are important while retaining personal autonomy.

We visualize an extended family of 6 to 12 adults, plus children, in a rural setting (hopefully in the Ozarks) sharing meals, chores, long-term goals, and ideals. Family members will share in the ownership of the land, the establishment and operation of cottage industries, and all decision making. The financial base should be broad enough to allow varied interests and degrees of participation.

We wish to be in a health conscious environment where the use of alcohol and tobacco is minimal, and we take responsibility for stewardship of Mother Earth. We would like an eclectic, inclusive spiritual focus, open to a variety of love styles: gay, straight, bisexual, monogamous or not. The important aspects are open, honest communication, shared decision making, future security, personal growth, mental stimulation, and enjoyment.

We would like to hear from people who are interested in joining or anyone who has ideas or finances to contribute. We will respond. 3/2/94

GOODENOUGH COMMUNITY

(Non-Residential)
2007 – 33rd Avenue South
Seattle, WA 98144

(206)323-4653/322-3279 Fax

Through roots that go back over 25 years to prior communities, the Goodenough Community (the American Association for the Furtherance of Community, a nonprofit educational corporation) was founded in 1981.

We are an organized response to our members' need to participate in a social process that builds character, strengthens will, and teaches relational skills. We are multi-residential, using our relationships and our organizing systems to help us create a place for transformation, a place where we share responsibility for the relational environment in which to accomplish personal and social change. Our community provides culture, safety, order, and prioritization as expressed in our mission and covenant:

"The Goodenough Community is a learning community created and offered by an intentional covenental core of members. We create a culture that enables human growth. Through our relationships we develop and heal ourselves and each other, allowing spirit to emerge, thus freeing our creativity and vitality to serve the good of all.

"Since, by entering into this covenant we create and sustain our community, we agree to be accountable to each other for upholding it. As part of the Goodenough Community, I commit:
• To become the best version of myself;
• To make and keep agreements with great care;
• To be constant through conflict;

• To give myself fully to the process of transformation through the expression of love;
• To trust the good intentions of each of us;
• To relate with respect and acceptance;
• To enter fully into life's experiences;
• To awaken to my awareness of my unique role in the Universe;
• To acknowledge the inner- and inter-connectedness of all creation;
• So be it!"

We continue to gather our learnings on personal transformation and community building, and have several consultation options available. Please contact us for more information. 3/15/94 [83]

GOODRICH FARM COOPERATIVE

(Forming)
RD 1, Box 934
Hardwick, VT 05843

(802)472-6352

Goodrich Farm Cooperative, a collective that is living in one large farmhouse on 54 acres, is in the process of forming a land trust and seeking members capable of paying off the FmHA mortgage. We are interested in organic farming, maple sugaring, and logging. Some of our responses to the questionnaire are sketchy, and will inevitably be defined and sharpened by the people who join, interacting with the few already living on the farm. Four more house sites are available. SASE requested. 2/19/93

GOODWATER COMMUNITY

(Forming)
Star Route, Box 104
Bourbon, MO 65441

(573)775-2329

We are a newly forming spiritual community within Meramec Valley Community Land Trust. We are dedicated to healing waters through social transformation. Goals include running a center for natural birth; marketing ecological water-use systems and servies; coordinating natural rights civil litigation; providing ecological recreational and educational opportunities; promoting cooperative organic use of agricultural resources; helping people find right livelihood; networking with individuals and groups with similar purposes; and providing whatever other services we can to help make a better world.

We want to coordinate a network of volunteers that will live and share with us

for a month at a time or work on a specific project periodically as needed. Some special skills needed are holistic healers and counselors, EMTs, midwives, teachers, homemakers, plumbers, builders, engineers, laborers, lawyers, and farmers. We will work with people seriously interested in living together in community to develop temporary housing and permanent homesteading arrangements. Visitors are welcome for 2 or 3 days. We are about 80 miles southwest of St. Louis near I-44. Call or write with SASE for details. 1/1/93

GORILLA CHOIR HOUSE

Berkeley, CA
(510)841-5367

The Gorilla Choir has been meeting every week for over eight years, raising spirits in the flatlands of Berkeley. Our aim is to heal ourselves, heal the planet, demonstrate the Glory of the Presence in All, and have a good time. Each week 10–40 people get together to sing songs from all of the world's spiritual traditions. Our material is all-inclusive, ranging from silly to sublime, and is never sung the same way twice. As we deepen our ability to hold, express, and empower the vision, we align ourselves with the Sacred Hoop of Life—just breathing, making sounds, and monkeying around.

Our small household exists to indulge the Gorilla Project—participants in the weekly sing came up with a down payment to purchase the house. Choir members are all generic world servers; choir membership is determined by participation, and embraces a diverse range of individual philosophies (we have political radicals and pacifists, rich and poor, gay and straight...you name it). Four choir members live here, living fairly independent lives while enjoying each others' company. 8/3/94

GRASSROOTS COMMUNITY

5075 Sweet Basil Lane
Tallahassee, FL 32311

Grassroots is a land co-op community of 45 adults and 41 children. There are several values essential to our group's purpose: support for the environment; peace and disarmament; hunger and habitat issues; and a focus on the quality of life. Individuals own their own parcels and their own homes; as a community we hold 4% of the land in common, and the community assesses itself for road repair, etc.

(Continued...)

We make all major decisions by consensus, but fall back on majority rule if consensus fails three times. Currently all 27 parcels of land are sold. We are full and have a waiting list; we're open to new members only if we find more land or if existing members leave. SASE requested with inquiries. [cc] 2/5/89

GREEN OAKS COMMUNITY

(Forming)
7-C Green Oaks Road
Asheville, NC 28804

We began as a few friends linked together by the planetary lightwork we were doing. Our mutual love and respect for each other gave birth to the vision of a spiritually based community where we could live and work together. We grounded the summer of 1992 at Green Oaks which is a small community of five homes and six acres.

The community was created on the premise that we are living through a very special transition time on the Earth, and that certain people have chosen to be here at this time to play a midwifery role in this process and to model a vision of the future. We feel that the principles of Love, Respect, Balance, Transformation, Personal Freedom, Creativity, Truth, and Integrity are the foundation for community life. We are not actively seeking "members" but are in an allowing space for spirit to direct us. SASE requested. 2/5/94

GREEN PASTURES ESTATE

38 Ladd's Lane
Epping, NH 03042

(603)679-8149/679-5138 FAX
http://codemeta.com/~bob/
gpasture.html

Green Pastures is the New England headquarters (since 1963) for the Emissaries, a worldwide association of wholesome men and women devoted to allowing full release of the natural qualities of life's spirit in practical, everyday living. We love revealing true being by truly being. Green Pastures supports itself through public/private conferencing and retreats.

Twenty-five men, women, and children ranging in age from ten to eighty-seven live here in a spirit of agreement. The 150-acre estate is comprised of woodland pasture fields, orchards, and a garden of several acres (worked with draft horses). Animal life abounds: dogs, cats, parrots

and cockatiels, goats, cows, pigs, and turkeys. Visitors are welcome anytime. Overnight guests should make arrangements prior to arrival. Accomodations are on a "suggested donation" basis. Green Pastures is located one-quarter mile east of the intersection of Routes 125 and 27 in Epping, NH, about an hour's drive north of Boston. [See main listing for the Emissaries network in the Resources section.] 2/26/94 [74]

GREENBRIAR COMMUNITY

P.O. Box 466
Elgin, TX 78621

Established in 1969, we are a loose-knit community of 25 adults and 25 children living on 170 acres near Austin, Texas. What really holds us together is our school, which is based on "non-coercive alternative education." Our houses are arranged in a village cluster to allow lots of open land, including a 45-acre wildlife corridor. The community has no specific religion, but every aspect seems to be represented within our membership. Similarly, our dietary preferences range from vegans to meat-eaters. We have limited facilities, so are not looking for more members and are not open to unannounced drop-in visitors. SASE requested. [cc] 8/4/93 [26]

GREENHOUSE COOPERATIVE

220 E. 14th Avenue
Columbus, OH 43201

The Greenhouse Cooperative exists as a forum for people, primarily students, to explore cooperative living. We are actively involved in local and statewide activism, with interests in environmental, sexual, racial, and political justice. 15 individuals live in one campus-area home, with options for single, double, or triple occupancy in rooms. Sharing labor and food helps keep costs down while teaching members the value of living together as peacefully as possible.

Cooperatively purchased organic food is prepared nightly, and members cook delicious vegetarian meals for one another. Weekly house meetings encourage members to engage in sharing, consensus decision making, and problem solving.

The Greenhouse asks all potential visitors to write before visiting, and encourages those interested to attend a weekly

meeting. No "drop-ins." SASE required with inquiries. 11/9/92

GREENING LIFE COMMUNITY

Route 1, Box 265
Shermans Dale, PA 17090

(717)545-4761/545-4363

Greening Life was established in 1972 on a 135-acre farm in south central Pennsylvania. We are a planned, intentional community. We built our own homes, roads, and water system. We follow organic farming practices on our 50 acres of tillable land and in our 2-acre garden which produces the majority of our vegetables. Our orchard is providing us with fruit.

The effort to create a balance of cooperative living, with time for individual and family, has been a rewarding struggle. Growth in spirit, both individual and community, is an important part of our life together. We respect all persons and value their opinions as a voice to help guide us. We are open to share our spirit and resources with other individuals and groups. 6/18/92

GREENPLAN

(Forming)
3090 King Street
Berkeley, CA 94703

(510)845-5416
greenplan@igc.apc.org

Green Progressive Living Action Network's ideal is reducing greed and waste by providing an alternative to privately owned housing and automobiles. Our homes offer comfortable shared housing for responsible and dynamic people who desire to live ecologically and sustainably. The economic benefits of sharing and conserving resources should be directed toward good causes and sheltered from slackers.

We oppose competition, exploitation, authoritarian oppression, and social limitations that discourage people from living to their potential. Personal freedom and responsibility, visualization, dynamic freedom, and open communication are all vital. Happiness and consideration for others are crucial. Top group priorities include maintaining an enjoyable living environment; conserving resources; fewer autos; and continuing expansion by acquiring more houses. Important personality characteristics for members include

awareness of one's effect on the world and others; being happy; doing one's best; and also personal advancement.

Renters are welcome, even short-term guests, as long as you are a positive influence and pull your own weight. So far we include students, teachers, professionals, musicians, entrepreneurs, anti-car activists, Tom Robbins fans, and others. Freeloaders and those with untreated addictions will not be tolerated; nor will competitive, self-centered, or anti-group behavior. We are expanding, so please join us if you wish to live pro-socially with other responsible people.

Initial locations are in Berkeley near mass transit. We plan to expand into more homes, remodeling and organizing them for comfortable sustainable living. We can use help with all aspects of this expansion. Positive folks of all ages are welcome to live, work, or visit. Please e-mail, write, or call for info! 11/15/94

GREENWOOD FOREST ASSOCIATION

(Re-Forming)
Star Route, Box 70-H
Mountain View, MO 65548

(417)934-2566

Greenwood Forest is a land trust of 1000 acres in southern Missouri, in the heart of the beautiful Ozarks bioregion. Our property borders on 55,000 protected acres of Ozark Scenic Riverways land, with the Jacks Fork river just down the hill. Greenwood was created 12 years ago in order to preserve the natural beauty of this exquisite place.

We have 45 privately owned 5- and 10-acre parcels, and 540 acres of commonly owned land. The common land acts as a buffer between parcels and holds the more pristine spots for all to enjoy. Members elect a board of directors, and decisions are made by majority rule. Each owner can build their own home on their parcel and hold full title. Homes and land use must comply with some restrictions designed to protect the environment.

Greenwood members are diverse in our backgrounds, belief systems, and personal lifestyles—though the major conviction which binds us together is stewardship of the land. We meet for potlucks, swimming, annual meetings, etc. Some members are interested in cooperative homeschooling.

We have a few 5-acre and 10-acre

parcels available for resale, and welcome inquiries. Please enclose a SASE with inquiries. 10/26/92

GRIFFIN GORGE COMMONS

Wells, NY

(COMMUNITY LISTING REMOVED)

Bad address: "Forwarding Order Expired." Their unlisted phone numbers have also been disconnected. 8/1/95

HALE BYODO CORAZON

(Forming)
202 S. Kingsley Drive
Los Angeles, CA 90004-4308

(213)738-6054

[Formerly: Beverly-Kingsley Community.] Shared housing in multicultural mid-Wilshire area of Los Angeles. Musically rich household with frequent recitals and rehearsals, after dinner music making with house members and friends of the house. Twice weekly family-style dinners of 12–16 participants, each of whom takes turns cooking and cleaning up. Guests and travelers welcome with advance notice. Rent of $550–650/mo. includes utilities and share of common supplies, own room but some shared baths. Strong sense of community, and most decisions are made by consensus. Large California craftsman house with large, sunny, and quiet rooms, comfortably decorated. Supportive personalities, good listeners, and conversationalists. Socially active and engaged. Residents generally between 30 and 50 years of age, male and female, gay and straight. SASE requested. 12/30/94

HALEY HOUSE CATHOLIC WORKER

23 Dartmouth Street
Boston, MA 02116

(617)262-2940/424-0622

Haley House has been in existence for over 29 years, and its members continue to provide services for themselves and for others. Membership is presently 7 men; many are formerly homeless people who are now in positions of authority. Meals are shared several times a week, and decisions are made by consensus.

Though there's a spiritual focus, life here is interreligious rather than "religious." Members manage their own finances, and share 25% of their earnings. [cc] 7/15/94

HARBIN HOT SPRINGS

**Heart Consciousness Church
P.O. Box 782
Middletown, CA 95461**

**(800)622-2477 (CA only)
(707)987-2477**

Harbin Hot Springs is a clothing-optional, 1100-acre New Age community/teaching center nestled in a quiet valley with clean air and pure spring water. We have been in existence since 1972, and have well over 100 adult members who operate, maintain, and improve a hot springs retreat and conference facility.

There are many challenging opportunities here for those skilled in construction, mechanics, carpentry, housekeeping, healing, administration, computing, etc. If you are interested in applying for residency, or wish to consider establishing a program of your own here, your inquiry is invited. Financial assistance for projects is sometimes available.

There are many important details concerning visiting, meals, workshops, pets, children, and residency that are not covered in this listing—so we recommend calling or writing (Attn: Community Relations) before visiting us. Please enclose $1 for postage.

How to get here: Take Highway 29 north from the Napa Valley to Middletown, turn left (west) at the Union 76 gas station; then right at the stop sign and continue four miles, keeping left at the fork in the road. Use of drugs or alcohol is not permitted. Open 24 hours a day, 365 days a year. 12/18/92

HARMON HOUSE

Berkeley, CA

A politically progressive household of professionals and students (est. '74) with a current population of three women and three men in their 20s and 30s. Consensus decisions, vegetarian meals shared once a week. Ecological, family, stable, friendly group. 6/25/94

HARMONY VILLAGE

**(Forming)
3825 Clay Street
Denver, CO 80211**

(303)477-1155

Harmony Village is a forming cohousing community in Golden, Colorado, a few miles west of Denver. We are purchasing 9.5 acres of land near downtown Golden, but with a somewhat rural feel. We plan to build something in the range of 30 home units (mostly attached), southwestern/adobe style, on a few acres of the property, and leave the rest as open space. We were hoping to close on our land in late 1994, and to start building as soon as possible thereafter. 7/27/94

HARVEST HILLS ASSOCIATION

**8 Oak Hill Cluster
Independence, MO 64057**

(816)229-2490

Harvest Hills is still a viable entity after 20 years of learning about what it means to live in community. There are now 60 families with all ages represented— including 22 people over sixty-five years of age, and 46 children under the age of sixteen. The community owns outright about 45 acres of semi-wooded land, as well as two condominium units, a community center, and a community swimming pool.

Early members were involved in the Reorganized Latter Day Saints church; it's still a major influence, but not a restriction. Our current membership is multi-racial, and there are at least a half dozen different religious denominations represented in the resident families.

Our original philosophy remains intact, and many of the original signers of our covenant are still living in the community. Basically, we envisioned a community with all homes located around a common green in which children could play in view of all of the residents; automobiles are not allowed in this area. The arrangement of the community has been especially good for mothers and the rearing of children. Homes are owned by the individuals, and we have acquired some adjacent land for additional buildings. Though we're now creating a waiting list for those wanting to join, the community welcomes anyone who would like to be part of an intentional community based on Christ's values. For more information

please write to the attention of: President, Harvest Hills. 1/22/95

HAVEN

**(Forming)
512 E. Arrellaga Street
Santa Barbara, CA 93103**

(805)966-7771/963-3337

Haven is a newly formed small intentional family/community in Santa Barbara. We use co-counseling as our major shared growth process, encouraging emotional healing from past distresses while fostering an atmosphere of openness, practicality, prosperity, inner and outer success, and fun in "present time." We include adults and children, hoping to become ever more multi-generational. One of us is heterosexual; others are bi. We have monogamists and polyamorous among us. We are primarily vegetarian. Some of us have yoga and ashram backgrounds. Among our members are a software engineer/entrepreneur, an artist/teacher/yogi, a sociologist/bodyworker, and a massage therapist/hypnotherapist. We are not actively looking for new members, as we're still getting to know one another, but we eventually would welcome people with financial skills, food growing talent, and, always, strong co-counselors. SASE requested. 12/25/94

HAWK CIRCLE COOPERATIVE

**890 Green Road
Tipton, IA 52772-9255**

**(319)886-3624
http://www.ic.org/hawkcircle/**

Our Cooperative (formerly the Third Place House Collective) is intended to be a safe place, both physically and emotionally. We have specific values and policies concerning a number of issues. Basic to these is a respect for diversity and a desire to achieve a balance between the needs of members, our community, and the environment.

Using a consensus decision-making process, we work to combine the best ideas available when making decisions and solving problems. We encourage each other, working to improve our abilities to live cooperatively through discussions, workshops, and day-to-day living.

Our recently acquired land, approximately 6 acres, is near Tipton, Iowa.

We have a large 5–6 bedroom house, combination garage/workshop, large two-story Quaker barn, a pig barn, 3 acres tillable, and many trees. The house has a very large attic which we are planning to renovate. We are also just beginning to plan the long-term use of our land. If you would like to know more about us, please write or call. 3/21/93

HAWKWIND EARTH RENEWAL COOPERATIVE

(Forming)
P.O. Box 11
Valley Head, AL 35989

(205)635-6304 eves best

Our 77-acre primitive retreat is nestled in the northern Alabama mountains, and is home to a developing healing arts center. We have/are creating co-ops for membership, organic gardening, livestock, food storage, seminars, arts and crafts—plus we have summer and winter campgrounds, a timesharing tipi, and a seminar center. We hold classes and public gatherings on a regular basis; facilities are available for private gatherings with 30 days advance reservation.

Our spiritual path is a combination of Native American and Earth traditions; we have many elders from many tribes. The community makes its decisions by majority rule, using a council process.

Our resident population varies with the seasons, ranging from 6–10 adults in the winter up to 15 in the summer, with 2–10 children. We have a support network of over 1000 members. Members barter programs are available for services or materials. Please include a SASE with inquiries. 8/1/92

HEADLANDS

(Re-Forming)
Route 1
Stella, Ontario K0H-2S0
CANADA

(613)389-3444

Headlands is a nonprofit consumer cooperative. We are presently 3 men, 2 women, and 4 children (8 to 10 years old). Members are involved in a commercial sheep farm (680 ewes) and other revenue activities. Our livestock and gardens provide most of our food.

We live on Amherst Island on Lake Ontario near Kingston, Ontario. Individually, we are active in the social and political life of the surrounding

390-person un-intentional community that Headlands is a part of. Collectively we publish a monthly newsletter, the *Amherst Island Beacon*, keeping our neighbors up to date with all the local news and views that are fit to print in this somewhat conservative rural area. Please include a SASE with any correspondence. 4/10/92

HEALING GRACE SANCTUARY

(Forming)
Creamery Ave CD-4
Shelburne Falls, MA 01370

(413)625-9386 9am–7pm

So far Healing Grace is...A PLACE: an 85-acre nature sanctuary and meditative retreat embraced in a magical river bend with an old house and barn; quiet; drug free; unplugged; voluntary simplicity; voluntary service.

A DREAM: we envision a small family-centered clan of Gentle Souls living together and keenly devoted to ultra-wholesome choices in all realms, patterned after natural systems...truly sustainable lifestyle; warm loving relationships; trusting spirit for guidance; savoring life and each other; all ages intermixed.

POTENTIAL: focalizers needed for permaculture garden, land, trails, structures, editing, homespun crafts and arts, vocations, rituals and celebrations, household tasks, group process, healing, reEvolutionary education, innovative community service, social transmutation....

We aim to look in the mirror often via an enthused, open forum (lacking in our society and even most communities and reform groups). Sharing needs, offerings, loyal dissent, bold dreams, change. Asking ourselves: Are we nurturing all facets of what it means to be human? What do we like, and why? Do *we* do that? What don't we like, and why? Do *we* do that? Who practices what we preach? Do we notice, welcome, and embrace them? Let's detox from divisive social conditioning, living into and popularizing alternatives to Western Civilization's forms of organization. Aiming to replace all monoculture, oppression, doubletalk with ultra humaneness, win-win, and "How can we do better still?"

Is this your heartsong? Please call or write (with SASE) telling what you might focalize, plus your phone number and best time to call. Hugs abounding, and Namasté. [cc]. 3/29/94

HEARTH, THE (L'ARCHE)

523 West 8th Street
Erie, PA 16502
(814)452-2065/455-5732

A Catholic community (est. '72) with about 50 members living in seven households. Members share most meals and handle their own finances. Special focus is creating mutual relationships with people with disabilities. Open to more adult members. [See other L'Arche network listings for more background.] [cc] 6/21/94

HEARTHAVEN

3728 Tracy
Kansas City, MO 64109
(816)531-8164/561-0531

We are an urban community of five members who seek to model a way of living from the heart which includes living responsibly, nonviolently, and ecologically. We put a high value on the practice of hospitality to all beings, and of living life out of love rather than fear. We are open to being joined by one or two individuals at a time who wish to live in and contribute to the healing ways of our household. We are also open to visitors depending on schedules and needs. 3/21/94

HEARTHSTONE VILLAGE

(Non-Residential)
91 Baker Road
Amherst, MA 01002-9602
(413)259-1701 M–F 9–5 EST

Hearthstone Village is a group of more than 90 people living mainly on and around Baker Road in Shutesbury, Massachusetts, who identify themselves as a community of friends. Though we are not a residential community, subgroups in the village are—our neighborhood includes both the Sirius Community and The Ark Community, plus the Trusteeship Institute, a neighborhood bulk store, and a number of cooperatives. We publish a village newspaper, hold village meetings four times a year, and celebrate many of the major holidays together. The phone listed above is usually answered weekdays 9–5; if you end up talking to our answering machine, we will return your call collect. Please include a SASE with correspondence. 7/27/94

HEARTLIGHT CENTER

67138 Shimmel Road
Sturgis, MI 49091

(616)651-2234

Heartlight Center is a Spiritual Light Center for Peace and Wholistic Education. Its total focus is upon knowing our connection with our Heavenly Father, and then manifesting His Will for us in service to the world. It is a place where people are truly striving to live the Kingdom of God here on Earth.

If you are interested in discovering more about who you are, your relationship with the Heavenly Father, and to understand this beautiful life He has given to one and all, then please write or call for more information. We will be happy to help you in any way we can. 7/6/92

HEARTWINDS

(Forming)
P.O. Box 315
Lyndon Center, VT 05850-0315

A rural, small, low-density community with adequate space for personal privacy, freedom, and philosophy. We have individual ownership of homes and attendant acreage, with communal property held in a membership land trust. All income and personal property remain with the individual. We share ideas, camaraderie, help, and support in an atmosphere of good neighbors/good friends/good family. Communal activities are voluntary; decisions are by consensus. We have no dogma or overriding membership philosophy, relying instead upon mutual consideration, good land trust guidelines, and common sense—diversity with unity. We are alternative thinking, open-minded,

and responsible parents, considerate human beings. We have children and retired in the group. We're nonsectarian, financially secure, respectful of rights and responsibilities. Possibilities here include sharing gardening, food production, workshop, tools, sauna, children's education, animal husbandry, and any ideas on business enterprises—or just a nice place to live! We're currently looking at land across the nation. Please include a SASE with inquiries. 3/4/94

HEARTWOOD INSTITUTE

220 Harmony Lane
Garberville, CA 95542

(707)923-5000 Office
(707)923-5012 Work Exchg.
(707)923-5010 Fax

We are a unique and healing community providing a supportive environment for vocational training and personal growth. We are a teaching community of dedicated individuals who care how men and women live in balance with Mother Earth, who care about the truth of our experience with one another.

Our mission is to provide resources for attaining physical, psychological, and spiritual well-being. We see ourselves as a catalyst for planetary healing through personal transformation. Vocational training in the Natural Healing Arts, workshops, and wellness retreats are our vehicle.

We share three vegetarian meals a day, and make special provisions for food allergies. The resident staff members get room and board and a stipend. Participants in the work exchange program pay a portion of their Workman's Compensation and get meals and classes; most work exchange participants camp on the land. Management department and committee decisions are by consensus or not, depending on the circumstances. Our land is 240 acres of mountains, meadows, and woods. The air is clean, the sky is big, the nights starlit. 12/1/95

HEATHCOTE CENTER

(Re-Forming)
21300 Heathcote Road
Freeland, MD 21053

(410)329-6877

Heathcote is located 30 miles north of Baltimore, MD, nestled in a narrow wooded valley on a 37-acre community land trust. It's been home to many people

over the last 28 years. Though the members have changed as people moved along their paths, the spirit of the place remains one of conscious living with the Earth. We have recently expanded from being women-only to being a mixed community welcoming men and children. We are a community of friends and family who choose to live cooperatively and consciously create a better way of life. Our commitment is to foster gender balance and a diversity of culture, spirituality, and thought. We desire to build a beautiful community in which to nurture the Earth, our children, and ourselves. Our shared philosophy is to maintain an interconnectedness to the larger society by giving back through education and community outreach.

Members currently live in a 150-year-old grain mill and several outbuildings. We plan to build alternative, energy-efficient group houses with individual and family units. We will also renovate the mill to create an active conference center and homeschool resource center. Our members' interests include organic gardening, ritual, meditation, co-counseling, personal healing, the Deaf community, political activism, and women's and men's groups—and we plan to host events on these topics. The women of the community have a strong commitment to creating safe womonspace. A lesbian group house is also planned. We welcome people of all ages, races, and sexual orientations. We'd like to hear from those who are interested in transforming society and creating a peaceful future with Earth. SASE appreciated when you write. [cc] 2/8/93

HEI WA HOUSE

1402 Hill Street
Ann Arbor, MI 48104

(313)665-6186
http://www.ic.org/heiwa/

Hei Wa house was started in 1985. We are a vegetarian, cooperative, non-smoking household, with a membership fluctuating between 8 and 12 people. We are a diverse group with a wide range of occupations and interests. We are working folks, artists, healers, and students. We pride ourselves on the diversity of our sexual orientations.

A countercultural and anti-establishment feeling pervades the house. Having no fixed ideology, many of us are influenced by anarchism, ecology, feminism, nonviolence, paganism, and socialism. Housemates have been involved in various political issues: gay rights, AIDS activism, hemp legalization, radical agriculture, urban issues, community organizing, wimyn's rights, environmental issues, and anti-militarism.

We try to live ecologically by recycling, composting, and eating simple food grown locally and organically. We get most of our produce from a local biody-namic community-supported farm, and also get food from our local co-ops. We occasionally garden or wildcraft plants in our yard.

Our decisions are made by consensus. If you wish to visit, you must contact us in advance. SASE requested. [cc] 2/14/95

HIGH FLOWING COMMUNITY

Route 1, Box 477
Riner, VA 24149

(540)763-2651

A community of 3 women, 4 men, and 2 children with a shared focus on the advanced application of art, music, and dance for something we call "Galactic Synchronization." We're members of the Planet Art Network (PAN) and do international networking of the Mayan Calendar in the form of the dreamspell. Open to visitors and more members. Send SASE and $5 for additional infor-mation. [cc] 7/12/94

HIGH HORIZONS

(Forming)
RR 2, Box 63-E
Alderson, WV 24910

(304)392-6222

I have 250 very primitive beautiful acres of mountainside, a stream originating on the land, and about 9 acres cleared. My aim is to get a small group of people together to work within the ecological system and live on less: self-sufficiency, permaculture, organic gardening, natural health; all of it. No addictions! Little junk food and no communicable diseases, sex problems, dishonesty, or "weirdos"—just sensible people working to get a toehold (and who may later opt to move on to their own homesteads). Retired person with "can-do" attitude and fix-it abilities would do just fine. Single parents should work out well, as would those with aller-gies or chemical sensitivity.

The project has been inspired by my spirit guides, and I am open to the ideas and needs of those who are drawn here.

Brainstorm sessions will determine rules, finances, and small businesses we might create; working/studying outside will be encouraged. Those who wish to visit for a look-see will be sent directions upon request, and I'm happy to answer any questions not covered here. Please include a SASE with inquiries. 12/14/94

HIGH WIND ASSOCIATION

W7136 County Road U
Plymouth, WI 53073

(414)528-8488 Information
(414)528-7212 Registrations

High Wind started in 1981 and existed for 11 years as an intentional community. In the spring of 1992 we decided to release this image, to decentralize even more than we had been doing for several years, and to call ourselves an "ecological vil-lage." As part of the restructuring and assessing our future direction, we're holding off for now on accepting new members unless they are hired as staff members of our Learning Center or are part of the newly forming research/design team next door (the Plymouth Institute) that will concentrate on demonstrations for sustainable living. [See High Wind entry in the Resources section.] SASE requested. 10/8/93 [67]

HILLEGASS HOUSE

3056 Hillegass Avenue
Berkeley, CA 94705

Hillegass House is an eleven member, 18-year-old collective in Berkeley. We began as a (mostly) single-parent house made up of six adults who wanted to share the burdens (and joys) of parenting. The age spread of the current member-ship runs from the early thirties through early sixties, with the median age being 40-plus. Our group is relatively stable, and two of our original members still live in the house.

We are an exceptionally diverse group in most regards (i.e., interests, spirituality, diet, sexuality, employment, etc.) and we think that's important. We blend together so well because we balance a strong commitment to group living and a real enjoyment of group dynamics on the one hand with a healthy respect for another's privacy because we realize having time to one's self is absolutely vital.

Other factors of our success? Well, it helps that we live in a lovely house that

can accommodate our number pretty gra-ciously. Even more significantly, dinners are shared and we all perform at least honorably in the kitchen (and we have several really outstanding cooks in the crowd). Written inquiries only, with SASE (we're sometimes slow in answering corre-spondence). [cc] 9/14/94

HILLTOP COMMUNITY

14806 SE 54th Street
Bellevue, WA 98006

This owner-developed residential park of 409 homes was conceived by architects and incorporated in 1948. Situated on a scenic ridge near Puget Sound, it covers 63 acres—40 in private homesites and 23 in parklands owned in common, and a county road. The community functions through a committee system to maintain its trails, swimming pool, tennis court, natural wetland, and well-water system. Its strong themes are neighborliness and the preservation of native vegetation. SASE requested. [cc] 3/4/94

HIMALAYAN INSTITUTE

RR 1, Box 400
Honesdale, PA 18431

(717)253-5551

A nonprofit organization devoted to teaching holistic health, yoga, and meditation as means to foster the per-sonal growth of the individual and the betterment of society. People of all ages, nationalities, faiths, and professions come to our seminars, classes, and work-shops—which range widely from such subjects as meditation, Hatha yoga, and health awareness to stress management and biofeedback. Unique to the structure of our programs is a continuing synthesis of ancient teachings and disciplines with Western scientific and experimental traditions. Our research systematically explores such fields as medicine and psychotherapy—as well as diet, nutrition, and exercise in relation to their mutual influence upon an individual's growth in health and maturity.

Our courses emphasize the total integration of body, mind, and spirit. The faculty and staff have expertise in various professional fields and are also involved in their own self-training so that they bring reflective experience to their classes. In its practical philosophy the Institute looks upon the realization of human potentials as a lifelong experience leading to increased health, creativity, and happiness. Please include SASE with inquiries. 6/21/94

HOLY CITY

(COMMUNITY LISTING REMOVED)

Asked to be removed.

HOME

Marinette, WI

(COMMUNITY LISTING REMOVED)

Lost contact. 11/25/95

HOMESTEAD COMMUNITY

Middletown, CT

(COMMUNITY LISTING REMOVED)

No longer a community. 3/21/96

HORCONES TWO

Tucson, AZ

(COMMUNITY LISTING REMOVED)

Address and phone not good. 12/16/95

HOUSE OF LAVENDAR

2455 W. Juneau Avenue
Milwaukee, WI 53233

(414)933-3033

A "Community House" near the center of downtown Milwaukee. 5–6 members with a variety of backgrounds and experiences, but sharing a commitment to good energy conservation practices, nutritious food, progressive social changes, and alternative developments in our city. Since '68 we have had 50 members— educators, counselors, artists, public health workers, students, community activists. A few former members still live in the neighborhood and continue to enrich our lives. [cc] 6/30/92 [85]

HTTP://WWW.IC.ORG/

FIC Web Weavers
Rt 1 Box 155-D6
Rutledge MO 63563

(816)883-5545
ficweb@ic.org
http://www.ic.org/

The Intentional Communities World Wide Web site is where you can find information on ecovillages, cohousing, residential land trusts, communes, student co-ops, urban housing cooperatives and other related projects and dreams....

If you have access to the Internet and to the Web please stop by and pay us a visit. Check with us for Web addresses for communities. Drop-ins welcome. 4/30/96

HUEHUECOYOTL

A. P. 111, Tepoztlán
Morelos, MEXICO

Huehuecoyotl is an alternative village in the mountains of Mexico, founded by a group of adults and their children— artists, ecologists, artisans, and educators from seven different nationalities. In 21 years of existence and 10 years on the land, the community has developed into an extended family; a New Age experimental center; a model of rural, simple community living; and an important site where different traditions, cultures, and visions blend harmoniously with each other.

Ideal communities exist only in the imagination of visionaries, but real communities are a long daily process of understanding, hard work, patience, and love. Our village reflects both the frustrations of not being able to materialize our ideals, and also achievements that are beyond description in terms of solidarity, cooperation, harmony in diversity, and an example of libertarian, ecotopian visions functioning since the early seventies. We are now facing a new cycle of our growth, which implies moving into a more balanced relationship with our environment, and with our collective cultural center which we expect to become an alternative educational center for new communities, for the arts, networking, and communications. We try to bring together the best of all worlds, and we live a fairly happy life. SASE requested. [cc] 6/21/92

HUNDRED MILE LODGE

(Re-Forming)
Box 9
100 Mile House, BC
V0K-2E0 CANADA

(604)395-4077/395-3804
(604)395-2143 Fax

We are a 47-year-old community which was originally established as a gathering together of people involved in a spiritual network called the Emissaries of Divine Light. After some 40 years of living together, economically supporting each other, eating together, looking after each other's children, gardening, milking cows...we have now seen the line between commune and community blur. We now find our- selves in a new place. We're older and wiser, fewer in numbers, and more interested in living in a community than living communally; cooperative community is the concept we are in the process of defining. Spiritually, the modes of the previous four decades are making a unique transmutation. This transformation could be roughly described as a change from collective worship and lifestyle to the sometimes arduous but compelling path of individuation and community.

For those who resonate with the art of rebuilding, who wish to pioneer further the ageless challenge of living in community, whose incomes are their own responsibility, and who love living on the edge of the Cariboo Wilderness...come and visit us! Please make prior arrangements by letter or fax. [See main Resource listing for the Emissaries network.] 1/26/95 [36]

HUTTERIAN BRETHREN

[See historic overview in the Resources section.]

Individual Hutterian Brethren communities listed in this Directory: Crystal Spring (Manitoba), Darvell (England), Deer Spring (CT), HB/Spokane (WA), Michaelshof (Germany), New Meadow Run (PA), Owa (Japan), Pleasant View (NY), Spring Valley (PA), Starland (MN), Woodcrest (NY). 6/1/92 [82, 84]

HUTTERIAN BRETHEREN OF SPOKANE

Route 1, Box 6-E
Reardon, WA 99029

(509)299-5400

The Hutterian Brethren Church, founded in 1528, now has 360 settlements or communes worldwide, with a combined population of 40,000 members. We are largely agrarian people, though in former times in Europe we were potters and ceramics artisans. We do mixed farming of various kinds, which keeps the young people busy. Kindergarten is for children aged 3–6; students attend public and some private school until grade 9, some through grade 12, and some even attend college. Sunday is our worship day, and includes Sunday school for unbaptized students. [See main listing for "Hutterian Brethren" in the Resources section.] 4/27/92

ICA / CHICAGO

Institute for
Cultural Affairs
Information Services
4750 N. Sheridan Road
Chicago, IL 60640

(312)769-6363

An international organization with community centers in 29 countries [see main network listing in the Resources section, and individual community listings for ICA/Phoenix and Songaia]. 7/29/94

ICA / PHOENIX

(Re-Forming)
Institute of Cultural Affairs
4220 N. 25th Street, #4
Phoenix, AZ 85016

(602)468-0605/955-4811

The ICA Residential Community in Phoenix is one of an international network of communities originally formed by staff members of the ICA, a nonprofit human development organization [see main Resource listing]. Its current membership of 14 adults and 6 children includes present and past staff members and volunteers. Group decisions are made by consensus, with power shared equally among the members. Families and single individuals are responsible for their own economic support, renting apartments from the ICA and paying their own utilities and a fixed amount for food corporately bought and prepared. There are 14 mostly 2-bedroom apartments in two one-story buildings, in addition to offices and a community room and kitchen. There are no required religious beliefs or practices. Membership is open to others sharing our values. SASE requested. 7/29/94 [85]

IDA

(Forming)
904 Vickers Hollow Road
Dowelltown, TN 37059

(615)597-4409

Our goal is to create community that allows people to enhance the art of living their lives. We offer queer safe space for all.

We govern ourselves non-hierarchically through consensus decision making with as much anarchy as suits us. We believe that through mutual support we can create fertile ground for personal and spiritual growth. By working as little as possible for money, we free ourselves from the toil and drudgery of jobs and are freed to do what we truly want—freed to do work that directly supports ourselves, in harmony with the planet that supports us all. Our financial focus will be in crafts and arts. Through faerie magick and pagan spirituality, we, as third gender, can heal ourselves and find important roles in helping heal others and our planet. We intend to share all this with others by hosting workshops, seminars, gatherings, and art festivals, encouraging queer artists and faeries to share their knowledge, wisdom, and other resources, as we share ours. Inquiries welcome; no new members at this time. 1/4/94

INNISFREE VILLAGE

Route 2, Box 506
Crozet, VA 22932

(804)823-5400
(804)823-5027 Fax

Innisfree Village was founded in 1971 as a creative alternative to institutional or homebound care for adults who are mentally handicapped. Innisfree is a service-oriented community located on a 550-acre farm about 20 miles from Charlottesville. In both the Village and the two in-town group homes, residents live and work in an interdependent environment and share a mutual respect.

The 20–25 volunteer staff make a minimum one year commitment, and though personal needs are met by the Village, the most substantial reward is the satisfaction of building community through daily effort. Longer commitments are encouraged. Although as many decisions as possible are made on a consensus basis, Innisfree is not an egalitarian community. Policies and decisions about daily matters are made during weekly meetings, preceded by a Steering Committee which sets the agenda. The Board of Directors, composed primarily of parents of the handicapped residents, deals with finances, building, admissions, and areas of overall welfare.

All members of Innisfree live together in family-style homes and work in the bakery, garden, office, weavery, or woodshop. For the volunteer, Innisfree provides the opportunity to both live in a community

and contribute to the lives of persons often excluded from alternative communities. While self-sufficiency is one of our dreams, most of our energy is directed to creating and supporting a lifestyle for persons with special needs.

We invite you to visit Innisfree, but please write or call well in advance. Overnight visits can be arranged. 1/27/94

INSTITUTE FOR HARMONIOUS DEVELOPMENT

(Forming)
3791 Hampstead Road
Flintridge, CA 91011

(818)952-4940

An esoteric Essene-type community practicing Fourth Way (Gurdjieff/Ouspensky) principles for deep personal transformation and living food diet for optimum health. Founded in January 1992 by a Fourth Way facilitator and advocate of the living food lifestyle. The community accepts and respects members of any religious, philosophical, or devotional background; Fourth Way practice enhances any form of higher work. There are group meditations but no prescribed form. Hatha Yoga and similar gentle movement exercises are included in the community schedule. Fourth Way students are provided with opportunities and assistance in working on themselves to transcend the ordinary life of unconscious mechanicality. A unique living food system has evolved which includes many gently warmed dishes along with living bread and desserts. The system effectively simulates a normal cooked food diet and provides an enjoyable, non-austere sense of fulfillment. The community sponsors a health recovery and weight loss program for the public using its living food system. Some community members act as staff for the public program. Interactions with other community members and with the public provide ample opportunity for self-observation and self-remembering. 4/4/94

INTER-COOPERATIVE COUNCIL (ICC)

Ann Arbor, MI
http://www.umich.edu/~umicc

A network of 19 cooperative houses in Ann Arbor. [See Resources listing.] 6/28/93

INTER-COOPERATIVE COUNCIL (ICC)

Austin, TX

A network of seven cooperative houses in Austin. [See Resources listing.] 12/14/92

INTERNATIONAL CO-OP

140 West Gilman
Madison, WI 53703
(608)255-0818

International Cooperative House is a democratically governed, multicultural, gay affirming, feminist, politically and socially diverse housing community of 30 adults. We own a 19th-century house built by the Vilas family. We are located in a historic neighborhood close to downtown Madison and the University of Wisconsin campus. Our goals are international understanding and cooperative living education. [One of 9 houses in the Madison Community Co-op—see network Resource listing.] 1/15/94

INTERNATIONAL PUPPYDOGS MOVEMENT

(Forming)
Portland, OR
(503)231-2512

Puppydogs are known for warmth, humanity, and profoundly social patterns of living. The name "International Puppydogs Movement" originated at The Puppydogs Club, a communal household where two of us lived years ago. The Puppydogs Club became well-known for the fact that its residents liked to lie (sometimes sleep) very close together, curled up like puppies in front of the fireplace. Over time, we began to call our basic family unit the "pile," and a unique philosophy developed.

At present we are a small number of gay and bisexual men, geographically dispersed throughout the states of Oregon and Washington, who plan to live together as an extended family and intentional community. We are people attempting to love each other—willingness to accept an atmosphere of heightened communication and intimacy is perhaps the most important qualification for joining us in this search. We are pragmatic and practical about the financial basis of the community. Deadlines have not been set for the purchase of land, etc., but we expect to be living together before the end of the millennium (approximately 5 years from the date this was written). 12/25/94

ION EXCHANGE VILLAGE

(Forming)
Route 1, Box 48-C
Harpers Ferry, IA 52146
(319)535-7231

We are in the formative stages of developing our community. Currently there are two of us, husband and wife. Our purpose is to provide a safe, secure environment in a natural setting whereby children can be raised with their curiosities in a beautiful rural setting. We envision a community composed of parents or would-be parents who are willing to adopt needy children. Parents who have their own biological children are also welcome. We would all be living in private homes and be committed to the rearing of children based on the following "Good Life Principles": 1) Emotional, physical, and mental security; 2) Gaining knowledge for self-enhancement, to do good things, and to create beauty; 3) Recognizing and enjoying beauty; 4) Being courageous; 5) Seeking a balance in life, assuring temperance; 6) Caring for self and others; 7) Loving and being loved; 8) Sharing; 9) Pleasure; 10) Fairness; 11) Trustworthiness; 12) Making sense of the day. The ultimate goal is to provide children with the necessary human values and meet their human needs so that they may grow up and contribute to society by making this a better world for themselves and others.

We are also committed to conserving natural resources and managing the prairie, woodland, wetlands, and river ecosystems which include plant and animal life. Nestled in a remote valley in NE Iowa, the scenic Yellow River flows through the heart of the land and empties into the Mississippi River 6 miles downstream. Prairie meadows, wooded slopes, rock bluffs, and river bottom make up the 166 acres. There is plenty of room for vegetable and herb gardens. The two of us earn our living by collecting native wildflower seed and marketing it by mail order. With the land there are many possibilities for those interested in creating cottage industries based on natural resources. SASE required. 10/18/92

ISKCON FARM

P.O. Box 819
Alachua, FL 32615
(904)462-2017

An alternative religious community (est. '77) affiliated with the International Society for Krishna Consciousness. We are dedicated to pursuing the goal of life: understanding the absolute truth, simple living, and high thinking. There are 8 men, 8 women, and a dozen kids living here in our rural center, and we educate our own children. Major decisions are made by our leaders, and members contribute 10% of their incomes to support the community. We are vegetarians, and share nearly all meals. [cc] 11/2/94

ISLAND GROUP, THE

(Forming)
1803 Mission Street #175
Santa Cruz, CA 95060
(408)427-1942

Inspired by Aldous Huxley's utopian novel, the vision is to create a psychedelic community. At present we organize national conferences, host salons (and plan to host them in other communities), publish a newsletter, and plan to form a community. Decisions are by consensus; members pay dues of $30/year. Please include a SASE with inquiries. [cc] 7/16/94

JESUIT VOLUNTEER CORPS

Northwest Center
P.O. Box 3928
Portland, OR 97208-3928
(503)335-8202

The purpose of the JVC is to promote justice and peace through direct service with the poor and through structural change. Volunteers commit themselves for one year at a time (August to August) to do full-time ministry; the International Program requires a 2-year commitment. We strive to build community by a simple lifestyle and mutual encouragement of service. Volunteers must be 21 or over, either male or female, without dependents. They receive room & board, health insurance, and a stipend. We're interdenominational, but strongly affiliated with the Catholic Church. Needed: flexibility; enthusiasm; sense of humor; and commitment to values of community, simple living, spirituality, and social justice. 1/6/95

Other JVC Regional centers:

- **JVC East:**
  18th & Thompson Streets
  Philadelphia, PA 19121
  (215)232-0300

- **JVC Midwest:**
  5671 W. Vernor
  Detroit, MI 48209-2157
  (313)841-4420

- **JVC South:**
  P.O. Box 3126
  Houston, TX 77253-3126
  (713)756-5095

- **JVC Southwest:**
  P.O. Box 23404
  Oakland, CA 94623-0404
  (510)653-8564

- **JV International:**
  P.O. Box 25478
  Washington, DC 20007
  (202)337-6143

JESUS PEOPLE U.S.A.

920 W. Wilson Avenue
Chicago, IL 60640

(312)561-2450/989-2076 Fax
eric@jpusa1.chi.il.us

Jesus People USA is a Christian church/community in Chicago. As a community we number about 500 people who live together at a single address in the Uptown district. We hold our goods and property in a common purse, according to the example given in the Book of Acts; community-owned businesses provide 90% of our income. By living communally we find we can more effectively serve God, minister to others, and strengthen ourselves than by living independently. We do not believe God desires everyone to live the same way we do.

As a church we evangelize, baptize, worship, marry, and bury. Our fellowship was founded as an independent ministry in 1972, settled in Chicago the following year, and in 1989 joined the Evangelical Covenant Church (a denomination related to the Evangelical Free Church). Worship services are held at a rented building five blocks from our home. Community members run a shelter for over 50 homeless women and children, and offer a hot meal to street people six days a week. We believe the Lord wants us to identify with and serve the poor in our neighborhood.

We also sponsor *Cornerstone* magazine,

Cornerstone Festival (a music event which attracts about 10,000 people each 4th of July weekend), and several bands: Rez (heavy metal), Cauzin' efekt (rap), The Crossing (Irish/Celtic folk), and Crashdog (punk rock). Visitors are welcome here, but please write or call beforehand. 1/3/95

JUBILEE HOUSE COMMUNITY

2425 Spicewood Drive
Winston-Salem, NC 27106-9768

The Jubilee House Community, established in 1979, is an intentional Christian Community with 9 members, ages 3 mo. to 44 yrs. Our ministries are governed by a Board of Directors and are supported through contributions and the JHC's craft cooperative. Community members work both in and outside the Community. JHC has moved to Central America for 5+ years, to coordinate an appropriate technologies/agriculture project. In response to invitations from Nicaragua and El Salvador, a site was chosen Spring 1993, and the Community moved there several months later. We continue to welcome visitors for short- or long-term participation in Community life, worship, work, and play. Our Community size has ranged from 5–23, and has included diverse faiths, cultures, and family groupings. Children and adults have equal voice in Community decisions made by consensus. Members of the Community live together, sharing their income and household duties. In addition to our focus on Central American solidarity, the JHC's history of shelter work has resulted in continuing to offer hospitality to the homeless and counseling for rape victims. We work for peace and justice in the midst of hopelessness, and we try to remember to celebrate and play. 12/31/92

JUBILEE PARTNERS

P.O. Box 68
Comer, GA 30629

(404)783-5131

Jubilee Partners is a Christian service community that was started in 1979 on 258 acres of land in north Georgia. The community is comprised of approximately 20 adults and 10 children. Around half of these folks are resident partners, and half are volunteers who stay for periods of 3–5 months. Jubilee's ministries include resettling refugees from various countries, raising money to assist amputees who are victims

of the war in Nicaragua, and ministering to the needs of some of the people on Death Row in Georgia. We are open to new members, though everyone interested in living here must come as a volunteer for the first year. 4/27/92 [65, 77(D)]

JULIAN WOODS COMMUNITY

(Re-Forming)
Route 1, Box 420-G
Julian, PA 16844

(814)355-5755/355-8026

Julian Woods Community is 140 acres of hillside and woodland in central Pennsylvania. A guiding principle here is land stewardship. We enjoy our diversity and the challenge to live cooperatively on shared land. We have teachers, engineers, woodspersons, craftspersons, one lonely mechanic, and many folks working directly on the land. We live in families or small family-like groups clustered within a short walk of each other.

Organic, biodynamic gardening, foraging, and herbal healing are practiced. Simplicity, sustainable living, and farming habits leading toward self-sufficiency are primary goals. With the aid of a grant from the state, we have constructed an evapo-transpiration greenhouse for our sewage treatment. The greenhouse provides 6000 sq. ft. of growing space.

Adjacent to JWC a subgroup formed a 180-acre community land trust with School of Living. One resident family works an organic CSA endeavor. We seek people with resources to help realize ecologically based ideals. Contact us if you want to participate with us in whatever work it takes to make our dreams and decisions reality. Please include a SASE with correspondence. [cc] 2/25/93

JUMP OFF LAND TRUST

(Forming)
c/o Sanford McGee
P.O. Box 3254
Sewanee, TN 37375

(615)598-0307/598-5942 (msg.)

Jump Off CLT (formerly EarthStar Institute; Ecanachaca Land Trust) is a community of individuals living in a committed relationship with 1200 acres of beautiful land, most of it undeveloped, on the Cumberland Plateau. Our first priority is to protect and nurture this land, which in turn feeds us and is our home. As a young community, many of us do not yet live on the land, and others are only now building our homes; for the future, we envision ten to fifteen homesites, gardens, an orchard, a community center (where spiritual and educational gatherings can take place), and space for studios and cottage industry.

Our members (currently 10 persons, aged 2 to 59) love to work, love to play, and are committed to honest group process and consensus decision making. Many of us practice a spirituality centered on loving the Earth and honoring the cycles of nature. We are seeking ways to simplify our lives as part of our commitment to the land; this includes a commitment to organic gardening methods, limited energy consumption, and principles of permaculture. Each household is expected to be financially self-supporting. Jump Off is a place where we dare to dream, and dare to work to make our dreams come true. We envision ourselves growing, and are open to meeting like-minded persons. SASE requested. 1/2/95

JUPITER HOLLOW

Route 1, Box 279
Weston, WV 26452

(304)269-4875/269-6374

We are a small community in rural West Virginia started in 1976 when a group of friends bought our 180-acre farm and moved into the large farmhouse together. We subsequently built five more houses, gained members (up to 20), lost members, and are now 7 adults and 5 full-time children including several original members.

We are a corporation which holds title to all land, houses, and improvements. Beyond this our lives are mostly structured around our family units. Incomes are derived from outside jobs such as social work and teaching, as well as home-based businesses such as camera repair, writing, and crafts. Membership and maintenance fees are used to finance community projects. We do not have a central spiritual or political focus. What has kept us together for 16 years is the desire to live among friendly, cooperative, and compatible folks who share an interest in maintaining the beauty of our land while being free to pursue our own lifestyles. We are actively looking for a few individuals or families to help further our community goals. 6/3/94

K&K ORGANIC HEALTH FARM

(Forming)
Route 3, Box K&K
Mars Hill, NC 28754

(704)689-4998/689-4999 Fax

30 miles north of Asheville, NC, nestled on 390 sheltered mountain acres, with fresh spring water, clean air, and virgin soil. Home of "The Healing Triad" project: 1) K&K Organic Health Farm with modern greenhouses and support community; 2) Developing intentional, self-sustaining communities; 3) Developing a holistic health/conference center. The farm grows organic, chemical-free vegetables for community use and for the market. Unique dome structures being built for workshops and gatherings. Emphasis on spiritual development, learning and practicing self-sufficiency, healing the Earth and ourselves, respecting Native traditions, etc. Like-minded people welcome. 6/13/94

KAILASH KUNJ

Olympia, WA

(COMMUNITY LISTING REMOVED)

Lost contact. 3/1/96

KARMÊ-CHÖLING

Buddhist Meditation Center
RR1, Box 3
Barnet, VT 05821

(802)633-2384/633-3012 Fax

Karmê-Chöling provides an environment for meditation and study of the Buddhist teachings. Through an integrated schedule of meditation, study, and work, one can apply the teachings to everyday life.

Karmê-Chöling was founded in 1970 by the Vidyadhara, the venerable Chogyam Trungpa Rinpoche, a Buddhist meditation master who was formerly the abbot of the Surmang monasteries in Tibet. Rinpoche's son, the Sawang Osel Rangdrol Mukpo, now leads Shambhala International and its affiliated centers, including Karmê-Chöling.

Our schedule includes 5–7 hours of meditation each day. There is also a midday work period. We offer a variety of

weekend programs taught by visiting teachers and staff. Call or write to receive our brochure. 6/22/93

KEHILLAT MISHPAKHOT

(Non-Residential)
525 Midvale Avenue
Upper Darby, PA 19082-3607

(215)352-2689

Established in 1982. About a half dozen families, adults, and children. The goal of Kehillat Mishpakhot, or "Community of Families," is to develop a life pattern which improves two aspects of modern American society: 1) Relations of people with each other (Community), and 2) Relations between humans and Planet Earth (Ecology).

Kehillat Mishpakhot exists in Upper Darby (Suburban Philadelphia); our philosophy is "build where you are." The religious component of this subculture is Jewish; basically rational but with a dedication to protect and perfect Planet Earth as "stewards of the Creator." Kehillat Mishpakhot is egalitarian and cooperative, but focused on life in (expanded) families.

Kehillat Mishpakhot is like a Havurah; we live in our own homes. We celebrate life-cycle events and holidays together. There is an affiliated preschool, which is being expanded into a "Family School." Kehillat Mishpakhot is also planning to grow an appropriate business for our members. Please write for information about our program and philosophy. Please include a SASE; no collect calls accepted. 12/30/92

KERISTA GLOBAL VILLAGE

(Re-Forming)
P.O. Box 410068
San Francisco, CA 94141-0068

(415)863-1909/255-7263 (msg.)

Keristans are all members of the Confederation of Utopian Idealists. The group's newsletter is called "Worker's Paradise." Members of the Kerista Tribe can have the option of dual identity; i.e., they can also belong to other communities or kibbutz-type habitats. Adult fun and games include the gestalt-o-drama process and the dramatology acting workshop, bundled with lots of tribal cultural activities, conversational salons, and peer self-help techniques. Self-esteem enhancement is theater.

The Keristan philosophy of cooperative living and co-housing has been evolving since 1956. It has gone through 12 major transformations. Now, in its 13th reincarnation, it emerges as a high-tech global village network. The core group has organized a nonprofit corporation called "World Academy of Keristan Education, Inc." (also known as WAKE, Inc.).

Members of the neotribal community see themselves as pathfinders and pioneers on the peer frontier. Shared values and optimistic utopian idealism are the main glue that holds the group together. They have a plan called "The Kerista Community Prosperity Plan" which is now in the research and prototype development stage of actualization. Free newsletters, tracts, and booklets are available on request. Correspondence and phone calls are invited. 3/20/93 [14, 36, 41, 64, 71/72, 77(D), 80/81]

KIDSTOWN

(Re-Forming)
Solutions for Today
P.O. Box 826
Middletown, CA 95461

(707)987-0669

Kidstown is presently "creating a future worth living, in a world without fear and without violence." It is modeled/modified on the "city centers" of the German ZEGG community experience. Local clubs of adults and children are being formed around the ideal quoted above, and hopefully through meetings, activities, growth exercises, and shared experiences many of us will form community groups or arrange to live communally with other club members.

In Middletown this experiment is extending itself through an innovative approach to the town's desire to build a youth activity building. We at Solutions For Today (SOFT, a nonprofit organization) are providing seed money for teens to learn commodities trading systems and techniques to earn money for themselves and to build the town's activities building—with the additional benefit of boosting their own self-esteem. There are many other benefits to be derived from this intergenerational social and service club.

If you would like working toward these values and ideals, or wish to start a city center or club in your area, please write (SASE requested). 7/1/94

KING VIEW FARM

(Re-Forming)
P.O. Box 217
Aurora, Ontario L4G-3H3
CANADA

(905)727-9171/727-1013
(905)727-7031 Fax

King View is an Emissary Community located on an 86-acre farm, forty minutes north of Toronto, Ontario. Established in 1972, our community of 33 is involved in a transition to a more collaborative style of living and self government. The Emissary mission of "assisting with the spiritual regeneration of the planet and its people" has been and continues to be at the heart of King View. Much space is also available to explore our personal passions and diverse needs. Some residents work at King View while others have jobs in the surrounding area. We have a unique retreat and conference business, hydroponic lettuce business, and our organic farm and garden. [See main Resource listing for the Emissaries network in the Resources section.] 12/14/94 [85]

KINGDOM OF OYOTUNJI

Royal Ministry of Tourism
P.O. Box 51
Sheldon, SC 29941

(803)846-8900/846-9939

A Yoruba African village 50 miles south of Charleston, SC, established in 1970, sometimes referred to as "the Vatican of Voudon." Resident membership includes 25 women, 20 men, and a half-dozen children. Major decisions are by King Oseijeman Adefunmi and a group of chiefs under him. Members handle their own finances, and pay dues or rent to the community. All children are schooled at the community, and the community has had disagreements with the state over the practice of ritual scarring. Guided tours $3.50, camping $3, guest house $10. Please include SASE with inquiries. 6/25/94

KOINONIA PARTNERS

Route 2
Americus, GA 31709

(912)924-0391

An intentional Christian community and service organization committed to compassionate living, racial reconciliation, nonviolence, and good ecology. We support

ourselves by farming, gardening, and a mail-order business selling peanut/pecan products and books and tapes by Clarence Jordan. Our ministries include a child development center, low-cost housing, prison work, community development, and hospitality. More than 20 employees work in many areas of Koinonia's life.

We have an active volunteer program. Six to ten volunteers come for 1–3 month sessions that include work, worship, group-building, studying Christian faith and life. Hundreds of visitors come each year, some for a few hours, others for a week or more. Groups come for work/study experiences. We welcome visitors, and ask that they contact us before arriving.

Koinonia was founded in 1942 by Clarence and Florence Jordan, and is supported through industry and donations. It has always been nondenominational, and was founded as a "demonstration plot for the Kingdom of God." The community has people of all ages, and community members practice economic sharing and shared decision making. Come and check us out! 1/5/93

KOOTENAY COOPERATIVE LAND SETTLEMENT SOCIETY

General Delivery
Argenta BC V0G-1B0
CANADA

(604)366-4370/366-4380

We are 22 adults and 9 young people living on 200 acres of mostly forested hillside at the north end of Kootenay Lake in southeastern British Columbia. Our community, established in 1969, is striving for a balance of ecology and human economy on our land and within our group. We have a system of 12 individual homesites surrounded by common lands. Our decisions are by consensus.

There are several things about us that are unique: 1) Most people consider Argenta itself to be an alternative community, so in many ways we have a larger community. 2) We really are on the edge of the wilderness; the Purcell Wilderness Conservancy is only a 2.5-hour hike away.

We appreciate visitors and letters, but prospective visitors must write in advance. We occasionally look for new members. 4/13/92

KRIPALU CENTER FOR YOGA & HEALTH

Box 793
Lenox, MA 01240

(413)448-3400 /448-3274 Fax

Kripalu Yoga Fellowship is a nonprofit volunteer organization dedicated to providing holistic health education, spiritual inspiration, and humanitarian service. Since 1972, KYF's programs have educated well over 100,000 people about the relevance and applicability of yoga for today. Our main center, nestled in the Berkshire Mountains of Western Massachusetts, is an oasis where you can rediscover the beauty of your own life, a unique environment to support your search for greater health and happiness—your potential for abundant energy, long-lasting contentment, and limitless ability to love. We offer year-round programs in yoga, self-discovery, health and well-being, spiritual attunement, and bodywork.

At the heart of the organization is a 25-year-old community where up to 300 people have lived and worked together in service. As of mid-1995, the community is currently in a major transition which, as always, brings uncertainty and opportunity. The community will continue to do yoga in its largest sense, as union and integration. 9/1/95 [12]

KRUTSIO

Apartado Postal 174
Guerrero Negro
Baja Calif. Sur, MEXICO

I am writing this on a hill, in my egg-shaped stone room. The SW window shows the immense ocean, today particularly blue and calm. Through the south window I can see the uninhabited desert mountains. All that is visible belongs to us—as we belong to it.

During our 16 years here we have grown some plants, but this land is not good for agriculture. Now we are starting a project of mariculture. In our balanced way of life we work hard and efficiently about 6 hours a day doing the practical, everyday matters. Besides that, we work hard in ourselves, as we share the concern for self-knowledge and development. The communal stone buildings can be seen through the SE window. Looking around, people find expressions of our frugal way of living and our attunement with nature everywhere. It is very quiet, though my son talks to me once in a while. As usual,

I reply in Esperanto. When he finishes his studies today we'll go swimming in the sea. We're egalitarians, and value the family as well as individuality and the tribe. Above, a skylight allows a piece of sky to come to me. We feel like a tree with deep roots in the ground, steadily growing toward the light. When one is in darkness, the light is uncomfortable. Who, right now, would enjoy heaven? We are narrowing the gap. SASE required (a U.S. airmail stamp is sufficient). [cc] 6/30/92 [73]

L'ARCHE DAYBREAK

11339 Yonge Street N
Richmond Hill
Ontario L4C-4X7
CANADA

L'Arche is an international family of communities for people with developmental disabilities and those who wish to share life with them. Today there are 100 L'Arche communities around the world, including 40 in Canada and the US. The charter which unites them all states: "We believe that each person whether handicapped or not, has a unique and mysterious value. The handicapped person is a complete human being and as such has the right to life, to care, to education, and to work. We also believe that a person who is wounded in his capacity for autonomy and in his mind is capable of great love which the Spirit of God can call forth, and we believe that God loves him in a special way because of his poverty."

Assistants and persons with a disability live in the same home, sharing the daily tasks of life: preparing meals, house chores, helping with personal hygiene if needed. Sharing life in this daily way invites the assistant to develop bonds of friendship and trust that are mutually growthful and life-giving. Assistants initially come to serve, and slowly they discover that they are receiving more than they are giving. 6/4/92

Communities magazine on the Web…

http://www.ic.org/fic/cmag/

L'ARCHE-HOMEFIRES

(Forming)
Box 1296, Wolfville
Nova Scotia B0P-1X0
CANADA

(902)542-3520/542-9771

L'Arche-Homefires is basically a Christian community which is formed with and around men and women who have an intellectual handicap (problems doing algebra). It is important to us, however, that nobody should feel excluded due to his or her religious beliefs, or lack of religious beliefs.

Homefires is part of a world-wide organization called L'Arche (French for "ark," as in the story of Noah's ark, signifying a place of refuge). L'Arche was started in 1964 by a Canadian, Jean Vanier, and there are now about 100 such communities all over the world. L'Arche is not just an attempt to provide homes for people, it is an attempt to live out the gospel and put forth an alternative lifestyle. We presently have four homes and a cottage industry producing dried fruit, candles, and crafts.

L'Arche-Homefires is a place of friendships. It's a two-way street where everyone gives and everyone gets back—often far more than is given. 7/10/93

L'ARCHE MOBILE

151 S. Ann Street
Mobile, AL 36604

(334)438-2094

L'Arche Mobile is Christian Community where people with a mental handicap live with non-handicapped. L'Arche Mobile is a member of the International Federation of L'Arche [see listing in Trosly, France]. Our focus is to provide a permanent family-like home for those who are in need, with an emphasis placed on relationships which bring stability.

L'Arche Mobile has four homes and a workday program, and is located in the downtown area of Mobile. Our community began in 1994 and consists of 19 people with a handicap, 14 house assistants, 4 work assistants, office assistants, and a local board of directors.

We try to create a home centered on trust and compassion as well as the daily living activities that we encounter. We try to live a simple life discovering our own gifts, listening to the needs of others, accepting our differences, and deepening our relationships. 5/28/93

L'ARCHE SYRACUSE

1701 Jane Street
Syracuse, NY 13206

(315)437-9337

A Christian community (est. '74) with 30 members, living in five households. Members share nearly all dinners, and handle their own finances. Special focus on helping the developmentally disabled. Open to more adult members. [See other L'Arche network listings for more background.] [cc] 6/22/94

LAKE VILLAGE

7943 South 25th Street
Kalamazoo, MI 49001

(616)327-0614/327-5713
(616)387-8134 Office at W.M.U.

Lake Village grew out of the nonprofit Behavior Development Research & Educational Cooperative founded in 1967. The program was initially concerned with early childhood development, and established the Learning Village preschool which continues to date teaching children in the city of Kalamazoo.

The Lake Village farm was begun in 1971, dedicated to exploring a more sustainable environmental ethic. This extended family commune occupies a mile and one-half of Long Lake's northeast shoreline on approximately 115 acres of forest, meadow, and wetlands located east of Portage, MI, in Pavilion Township.

Over the past 20 years there have been approximately 300 different people from all over the world who have participated in the Lake Village program. Today there are 40 members in all who are a part of this cooperative farm effort. Most members live on an additional 200 acres of land purchased privately, bordering the Lake Village premises. Some members live off the farm while working there during the day. Others live on the commune and hold jobs in the Greater Kalamazoo area as teachers, social workers, secretaries, waiters and waitresses, plumbers, roofers, counselors, and, of course, as students in the various area schools.

We consider ourselves a large extended family, and are very much a part of the greater Kalamazoo community which we hope is likewise dedicated to promoting an ecological, sustainable lifestyle—so that our children's children may enjoy the future blessings of a healthy Mother Earth. Welcome to our home and yours. 12/3/92

LAMA FOUNDATION

P.O. Box 240
San Cristobal, NM 87564

(505)586-1269 M–F 9–11am

Lama, founded in 1968, is an ecumenical spiritual community located at an elevation of 8600 feet in the wilderness of northern New Mexico. Lama's stated purpose is to serve as an instrument for the awakening and evolution of consciousness. An ever-evolving resident body lives at the foundation year-round and is dedicated to caretaking Lama and maintaining the spirit of community. Each summer people join our family to experience a lifestyle rich in spiritual practice, community, and service as we operate a retreat program offering a variety of workshops.

Those wishing to participate in the yearly cycle of Lama come initially as summer staff, then apply for residency at our fall consensus meeting. Residents make a yearly commitment to the running and upkeep of the foundation.

In addition to retreats and spiritual practice in community, Lama maintains two rustic, comfortable hermit huts that afford the opportunity to look inside one's self in a beautiful, isolated mountain setting. We also operate a cottage industry silk-screening prayer flags from many religious traditions. Lama is a place where many teachings are brought into daily life—the teachings of community, nature, devotion, meditation, and spirit are all honored and practiced together. 5/5/92 [53]

LAMB OF GOD COMMUNITIES

(Non-Residential)
306-J North Chapel Gate Lane
Baltimore, MD 21229

(410)646-3196

An ecumenical community with 200 members living in their own houses and coming together once a week. Leadership is through a core group; community decisions of varying nature are made either by consensus or by the community elders. Open to more members. Please include SASE with inquiries. [cc] 6/22/94

LAMBORN VALLEY COMMUNITY

1559 – 4110 Drive
Paonia, CO 81428

Lamborn Valley Community's main focus

is spiritual. We try to take time to listen to "the still small voice of God within" and act accordingly. Christ is our primary, but not only, teacher. A major part of community life is work and play with children; we want our children to grow up among and learn with us.

The community's resources include a 120-acre organic farm and orchard, 10 dwelling units, a community center, a river, and plenty of irrigation water. Work is scarce and wages are low in the small town of Paonia one mile away. We are looking for one or two permanent families who share our vision and are willing to work hard to attain it. Please include SASE with inquiries. 12/15/92

LAND STEWARDSHIP CENTER

(Forming)
4107 Columbiaville Road
Columbiaville, MI 48421

(810)793-2511

The Land Stewardship Center is a new, nonprofit organization formed to promote the rediscovery and practice of land stewardship values and skills. Its first activity, now under way, is the restoration of a nature sanctuary around a small lake in the midst of a 150-acre farm located in the Great Lakes Bioregion. The sanctuary will be buffered first by a paradise gardening/living zone—landscaped for beauty, solitude, and foraging—and secondly, by a natural farming zone, based on the principles of Masanobu Fukuoka's *One Straw Revolution*.

It is hoped that people who are dedicated to land stewardship and who volunteer to work on the Center's restoration projects will form an ongoing residential community to demonstrate how such land stewards can both sustain themselves and live in harmony with the rest of nature. There are a house and small cottage on the land to accommodate community members and apprentices. Please write for more information or to arrange a visit. SASE requested. 1/21/95

LAUREL HILL PLANTATION

Natchez, MS

(COMMUNITY LISTING REMOVED)

Community has folded. 10/1/95

LICHEN

**P.O. Box 25
Wolf Creek, OR 97497**

(541)866-2665 7–8am best

Lichen, established in '71 as a cooperative land conservancy/trust, is a community of organisms living and growing together for mutual benefit. Our facilities include a community building, four satellite retreats, a lab, shop, small solar greenhouse, and garden area. Most of our 140 acres are devoted to a wildlife refuge and environmental sanctuary and, as a result, we now prohibit domestic animals.

Newcomers might develop their own livelihoods along these lines: present members derive their income from contract services and/or individual home industries—including lab electromechanics (non-defense); field recording, editing, and producing cassette tapes of nature sounds (especially of birdsong); and craft activities.

Environmentalism is our nearest approach to a community spirituality, and our philosophy of personal growth is based on the individual's development within the community context—rather than having the community be a hodge-podge of individualized traits. We expect members to commit substantial time and energy to community projects and issues. Agreed-upon expenses for space, utilities, food, taxes, and capital are shared; remaining personal earnings are used at individual discretion. We like a varied diet, mostly vegetarian. We come together for some meals, work projects, and meetings. Childcare is by family/parent(s), but shared at times by others. Visitors are welcome with advance arrangements. For more information, please write—include significant information about yourself and enclose a SASE. A couple of dollars to help with other correspondence expenses would be appreciated. 11/9/93

LIFE CENTER ASSOCIATION

**4722 Baltimore Avenue
Philadelphia, PA 19143**

Originally formed as a support community for MNS (Movement for a New Society), the LCA is now a democratically structured organization created to develop and promote nonprofit cooperative ownership and management of property. The LCA owns and holds property in trust, keeping it affordable and well-maintained for the long-term use of individuals and groups.

Six of our seven West Philadelphia properties are leased to communal houses of six or seven people each. The seventh property has two apartments, as well as offices for three nonprofit community organizations. Each household chooses its own members and is fairly autonomous. Many members are involved in community and political activities. Openings occur sporadically. Please include SASE with inquiries. 12/29/94

LIGHT & COLOR FOUNDATION

**(Forming)
P.O. Box 2947
Pagosa Springs, CO 81147**

(970)264-6250

Spiritually conscious group forming to

begin community of neighbors in southern Colorado. In part a nonprofit visual arts educational center, modeled somewhat after Findhorn's U. of Light in Scotland. Pristine natural environment with gardens, meadows, and stream. Studios for multiple media. Private dwellings of owner's choice. Consensus decisions. Off the grid. Some domes. Forged from the purpose and quality of members' lives. Individual development supported; self-responsibility for livelihood, or work for visual arts center.

Organic process dictated by those who join the group. Nonviolent, non-religious, though spiritual. A place for creation and recreation. Pottery, weaving, dyeing, painting, sculpture, photography, glass studios for members and students, other studios as needed. General ambience of peace and upliftment, natural serenity, and quiet industry. A gentle, healthful setting which promotes radiant health.

A core group and council to decide path of growth workshop and seminar schedules. Plans for shop and/or mail-order catalog as outlet for our work. Indigenous buildings when possible. Non-artists also welcome. Hope to purchase land in the vicinity of Durango/Pagosa Springs in 1994. May maintain Santa Fe homes or shop for contact. Mature, responsible, positive folks interested in community and privacy both, most welcome. SASE requested. 6/20/94

LIGHT MORNING

Copper Hill, VA

Light Morning is a small community of diverse folks who share meals, work, and a common vision. Since our arrival here in 1974, we have been exploring the following possibilities—that good health and self-esteem deserve cultivation; that a simpler lifestyle will enable us to live closer to the Earth; that the Earth itself is a living creature; that we, as a species, are ripening into an awareness that we co-create our personal and world circumstances; that a new kind of family can greatly assist in this ripening; and finally, that our daily life is the proving ground for such hypotheses.

Our experiments along these lines have resulted in varying degrees of success. What we have to offer is our lifestyle, our experience, and our tentative conclusions— as well as a good collection of unresolved issues and questions. We highly value our continuing exchanges with visitors, friends, and neighbors, many of whom are exploring similar growing edges. 9/10/93

LISTWIG MIR

Oakland, CA
(510)547-8935

Listwig Mir (formerly The Revolutionary Tomato) is a lively 12-year-old inter-generational household of 6.5 adults and two kids committed to low-impact urban living. Communal living as an intentional family is our preferred lifestyle for health, happiness, and conservation. By living collectively we hope to achieve an economy (and an ecology) of scale.

We share housework, gardening, and shopping. We believe in good living through fine dining, chocolate, and high cholesterol. We strive to eat semi-vegetarian meals together, and to create a child-centered environment emphasizing support for both children and adults. Our household is organized through a combination of formal consensus-reaching and benevolent spontaneity.

In addition to our commitment to environmentalism, housemates' interests include peace and social justice, feminism, nonsectarian humanism, and (often unsuccessful) attempts at philosophical cuteness. Diversity of opinion regarding politics, metaphysics, ethics, and religion keeps us entertained. 9/11/94

LONG BRANCH

Environmental
Education Center
P.O. Box 369
Leicester, NC 28748-0369
(704)683-3662

We are a small group of people who are deeply concerned about the interwoven and accelerating problems of population growth, natural resource depletion, and environmental degradation. We are a community of individuals who have chosen to live cooperatively and steward this land...caring for it in a way that it will be healthy and beautiful for our children's children. We align ourselves with all the groups and centers across the country that are dedicated to helping heal the Earth. As our particular focus we have chosen to demonstrate specific, practical strategies by which individuals can simplify their lifestyles and become more self reliant—with organic gardening, ecological agriculture, solar energy, and appropriate technology.

Our land is an ecological sanctuary and land trust, and we have developed a small, hands-on environmental education center. We have staff, interns, and a volunteer program. We are open to the public every Saturday, and frequently offer weekend workshops on a variety of topics including organic gardening, greenhouse design, country crafts, natural cooking, composting toilet systems, natural history, massage, and nutrition. 7/16/94

LOS ANGELES
ECO-VILLAGE

(Forming)
c/o CRSP
3551 White House Place
Los Angeles, CA 90004

(213)738-1254
crsp@igc.apc.org
http://www.ic.org/
la-ecovill.html

This demonstration-in-progess is a two-block built-out mixed use neighborhood of approximately 500 persons near downtown L.A. The mostly low-income neighborhood is ethnically and generationally diverse and located adjacent to public transit. A core group of 6 to 10 persons who live in and near the neighborhood facilitate and coordinate a variety of activities designed to retrofit the neighborhood for long term sustainability in its physical, social, and economic systems. This whole-systems approach to the development of community is based on our sense of interconnectedness with one another and the land in the context of the problems we have in our bioregion and political jurisdictions. We take a systemic approach to local problems so that we may contribute to improving our eco-systems—working toward environmental, social, and economic health. Our purposes are to demonstrate high-quality/low impact lifestyles, reduce the burden of government, and reverse the negative environmental impacts resulting from a long history of unsustainable growth patterns. We also want to provide an example of a radically different way of being in Southern California which might help to inspire Third World communities everywhere to bypass the unsustainable growth and development patterns which most aspire to. Call for orientation and tour schedule. Non-paid internships, work and vacation visits may be arranged. Send $1 for current information package before further inquiries. [See article on page 109.] 3/15/94

LOS HORCONES

Apartado Postal #372
Hermosillo, Sonora
MEXICO 83000
(52)(62)147219

Los Horcones began in 1973 and is located on 250 acres in the State of Sonora, which borders Arizona. In 1995 we are starting a branch, Horcones Two, in the southwestern USA [see separate listing].

Our basic objectives are to design a society where people cooperate for a common good; have shared or communal property; and reinforce egalitarian, pro-ecological, and pacifist behaviors.

Los Horcones is an ecologically oriented community, and as self-sufficient as possible. We have abundant orchards, organic gardens, and farm animals. We have communal child rearing, and all who participate in the care and education of our children are trained to do so. We have our own school where students learn personal and social behaviors (self-knowledge, interpersonal skills, etc.) as well as academics.

We have an experimental approach to the design of the community, basing our practices (education, economy, family, government, etc.) on scientific research, not on the personal beliefs of some members or any particular individual.

We are deeply concerned with personal growth and interpersonal relationships, so a main focus of the community is human behavior. We are a Walden Two community in that we use principles derived from the experimental analysis of behavior in our daily life to learn communitarian behaviors. This does not mean that we follow the novel *Walden Two*, written by B. F. Skinner, but rather that we apply the science on which *Walden Two* was based.

Los Horcones is an income-sharing community. It provides all the goods and services needed by its members. We have communal buildings (dining room, laundry, recreational center, shops, etc.) and private bedrooms.

We organize our labor not only for efficiency, but also for satisfaction and creativity. Generally, we work 6 hours/ 4 days a week, and 4 hours/2 days a week. Woman and men have equal opportunities to choose jobs. Members choose their own work and make their own schedules. All members' work schedules include study or reading time. Instead of set vacations, members can take time for travel or study whenever they prefer.

We derive our income from selling natural food products (yogurt, granola, etc.), organizing summer camps, teaching children with special behavioral needs, and consulting work with cooperatives and other groups (schools, intentional communities, etc.). New ideas for income areas are welcome. We want a diverse community.

We value and encourage the participation of every member in decision making, and we call our organizational structure Personocracy. Attending weekly general meetings is part of our work schedule. Coordinators organize each community area (agriculture, food, childcare, education, finances, cleaning, etc.). Any member can be a coordinator of any area they are interested in. Coordinators do not have special privileges.

Los Horcones is open to new members, and also to people interested in research projects in agriculture, animal farming, ecology, or any area related to cooperative life. We invite you to visit us. Please write or call in advance. 1/25/95 [32]

LOST VALLEY EDUCATIONAL CENTER

81868 Lost Valley Lane
Dexter, OR 97431
(541)937-3351

We are a young and growing intentional community, situated on 90 beautiful acres in a valley outside of Eugene, Oregon. Our land is comprised of a meadow, a coniferous forest, a clearcut that we are replanting, and a stream. We have a large organic garden and greenhouse, and are becoming a demonstration site for sustainable agriculture, ecological living, and alternative technology.

Our mission is to create and foster mutually beneficial relationships between humans and all parts of the web of life on Earth. We believe that interdependent relationships provide a means of attaining personal well-being and contributing to the successful survival of our planet. We are living an ethic that demonstrates right livelihood and encourages others in their healing and growth.

We are creating an extended family—comprised of single individuals, couples, and families—which is learning to live cooperatively and lovingly. We are establishing a home where we can learn, work, and relax. Currently we are 11 adults and 6 children, and are seeking new members to implement our vision.

Our residents live in modest cabins, private rooms, a yurt, and single family apartments. We are in the process of completing a modified "cohousing" unit which will expand our residential options. All residents of LVEC pay for food and housing, and fulfill a work commitment to the community. Some earn stipends for their work with the conference center; some are creating cottage industries to generate personal income; others work in the Eugene area.

We operate Lost Valley Educational Center as a tax-exempt, nonprofit organization. We have lodging for 150 visitors, classroom spaces, dining facilities, and a professional kitchen. Meals are vegetarian, mostly organic. The groups we attract are dedicated to peace and justice, personal growth, or ecological restoration. We welcome a diversity of racial, cultural, and spiritual backgrounds. If you are interested in learning more about us, or visiting, please write (include a SASE). 11/4/94

LOTHLORIEN (ELF LORE FAMILY)

P.O. Box 1082
Bloomington, IN 47402-1082
(812)336-5334

Lothlorien "green havens for elfinfolk" is a nature sanctuary, survival education center, woodland meeting grounds—a unique experiment in fusing land stewardship with creative mythology. Membership is $10/year. Magical campground, nature shrines, ritual spaces, festivals, educational events. Eclectic approach: synergy, synchronicity, synthesis, networking, mutual aid and support, biodiversity, solar energy, new shelter, terraculture, biospherics, sustainable lifestyles,"living as modern elves." Send $3 for wild magick guidebook, merging at the core of ecology, nexus, earth vortex, planetary changes, intergalactic resonance, tribal music, dance, shamanism, healing, exploration, ceremony, trance work, theater, art, crafts, UFOs, geomancy, currents, elements, connections, practical alchemy, good vibrations, people, flora and fauna, visions of the future, children are the path, tap the inner child, plant seeds, rainbow warriors of the whole with strong focus on the green ray heart tree balance point! Intentional community, extended family, electric gypsy haven, rebirth of elfin awareness. Never forget: "Terraform the Earth first, then head for Mars"—evolutionary perspectives. 4/21/93

LOTHLORIEN FARM

P.O. Box 2022
Perth, Ontario K7H-3M9
CANADA

Lothlorien Farm is a loose-knit land-based community in the forested lake country of the Canadian Shield. Since 1972 we have collectively held 700 acres in the Ottawa Valley watershed. Although Lothlorien is not too far from more settled parts of Ontario, the country is wild and peaceful. There are gardens, chickens, individually owned houses and workshops, a small lake, a maple bush, and cross-country ski trails.

On the farm currently there are four independent households with 6 adults and 2 children; the 7 other members and their families live elsewhere. Membership is stable, and commitment strong; in the past ten years only one member has moved away and one has joined. Life here involves few communal activities or responsibilities, but members share a lot informally and are quite involved in the surrounding community. Group decisions are generally made by consensus. Members purchase equity shares in the land and are responsible for their own housing and income generation. Most resident members are self-employed, while two commute to part-time jobs.

There is a one-year pre-membership period. We are not actively recruiting new members, but we are interested in sharing our experience of community with other individuals or communities. [cc] 8/4/92

LOVE ISRAEL FAMILY

14724 – 184th NE
Arlington, WA 98223
(360)435-8577 / 435-3799 fax

"When the seers come together, then the watchers will see."

Now that we've seen that we are the Family of God, what are we going to make of our relationships?

Now that we've seen that we are eternal beings, what kind of a culture can we create that will last forever?

Now that we know that we are One Person, how do we fit together to fulfill our wholeness?

Now that we can agree that Love is the Answer, how can we translate that love into on-going daily life together, forgiving and remaining loyal to one another?

After 25 years, we continue to address these challenges together: learning, growing closer, overcoming our weaknesses, and carving out a new reality for ourselves and our children.

Inspired by the revelation of Jesus Christ, the Family began gathering around Love Israel in 1968. Currently 85 people are integrating their lives on a 300-acre ranch, 50 miles north of Seattle, Washington. SASE requested. 8/16/95 [85]

MAAT DOMPIM

(Forming)
Auto, WV 24917-9999
(540)992-0248 VoiceMail (VA#)

The spiritual, educational, and cultural aims of this 501(c)(3) organization are to create an accessible and ecologically thoughtful environment that will foster intercultural respect and communication, and will particularly empower women of color by providing access to information, training, and other tools and resources. We are creating a retreat center that will primarily (but not exclusively) cater to women. One of our programs—The Institute of Ancient African Herstory—encourages, facilitates, and supports women of color who are researching their own cultures. There will most likely be a small revolving staff plus interns, residents, etc., on the land. Many of our decisions (finances, schooling, diet, community meals, etc.) have yet to be determined, and incoming members will influence those choices. 12/16/94

MADISON COMMUNITY COOPERATIVES (MCC)

Madison, WI
http://www.stdorg.wisc.edu/ mcc/home.html

A network of nine cooperative houses in Madison [see Resources listing]. MCC houses with listings in this directory:
• International Co-op   9/29/93
• Martha's Housing Co-op
• Women's Co-op

MADRE GRANDE

Monastery of the Paracelsian Order

18372 Highway 94
Dulzura, CA 91917-1216
(619)468-3810

As a New Age monastery, we have monks who are men and women of any spiritual persuasion. We require only that members be on a positive path to spiritual perfection. Residents are guests, students, and members. The members are monks who make all decisions and set community goals. Retreat guests take limited part in community functions according to their skills and conditions of residence. Students are studying for friar status in the Paracelsian Order, or priest status in the Johannine Catholic Church and Temple of the Absolute Light (our parent corporation). Membership in the monastery is necessary for permanent residence, but retreats can be extended for several years.

Leadership in the monastery is by annual election among the monk community. Ability to work cooperatively on group goals is valued above all else. Special skills are needed—especially organic gardening, maintenance, office

work, word processing, and a willingness to do even the menial to get our goals manifested. Our monks are all highly skilled in their abilities. We publish our own journal, *The Philosopher's Stone*. Write or call for current issue, and/or to make reservations for a visit. 6/6/92

MAGIC, INC.

P.O. Box 5894
Stanford, CA 94309

(415)323-7333
http://www.impactol.org/ iol/magic/

We live together to learn and to teach how humans may more effectively care for ourselves, each other, and the environment. We practice being grateful for each day, and we aim to strike a balance between utilizing the diverse resources of our Stanford University/Silicon Valley surroundings and maintaining contemplative, modest lives. (Though our P.O. Box is in Stanford, our house is in Palo Alto.)

Our everyday activities include lifeplanning, journaling, and reflecting; gardening, cooking, and eating vegetarian; building, repairing, cleaning, and sharing housing; sewing, washing, and wearing simple, comfortable clothing; being respectfully and joyously sexual; drawing, writing, and conversing; playing musical instruments, singing, and dancing; bicycling, running, walking, swimming, and stretching. With others we operate a nonprofit, charitable corporation which promotes the common good by teaching (through demonstration projects, workshops, classes, consulting, and publishing) about personal awareness and health, cooperation and peacefulness, environmental protection and restoration, and using the methods and principles of the science of ecology

to shed light on the questions, "To what purposes shall we live? How may we further our purposes? On what bases do we decide these things?" We welcome inquiries. SASE required. 10/1/94

MAGIC TORTOISE FOUNDATION

(Re-Forming)
Box 111
San Cristobal, NM 87564
(505)586-1652/586-0197

We are a small intentional community located in the foothills of the Sangre de Christo mountains of northern New Mexico. The basic purpose of the community is to foster human development, both individual and social. The Magic Tortoise is pursuing a direction which will provide facilities for research and education in areas of the fine arts, crafts, the environment, agrarian concerns, bodywork, and various spiritual disciplines. Our immediate and emerging goal is to offer a series of workshops that are focused on our primary purposes. SASE required. 1/26/93

MAHARISHI INTERNATIONAL UNIVERSITY

N. Main Street, Route 1
Fairfield, IA 52556
(515)472-7000/472-6929 Fax

Maharishi International University is a fully accredited university with teachings through the PhD level in many fields, with a curriculum based on a one-week block system. About one-third of the population of our small town is affiliated with the University. All in all, we have 600 faculty and staff, 1200 students, plus 2000 others associated with the T.M.

(Transcendental Meditation) movement. Most members moving into the community buy their own homes, and meditate in our large group domes. Students live and eat on campus.

There are now over three million T.M. meditators worldwide, and one of our goals is to get 7000 meditators living in one place on each continent—to create a spiritual coherence which will provide the basis to help establish world peace. We are also building a spiritual capital in the North Carolina mountains for up to 4000 people.

Nearby we are building a totally integrated 5000-room complex on 1500 acres (houses, cabins, and dorms) made of environmentally friendly materials. The project will stimulate a retirement community.

Long-range plans include the development of an electric car system—tying in well with our general tendency to pursue high-tech, environmentally friendly businesses. A high proportion of our members are new-age entrepreneurs, thus the local economy is booming in contrast to the rest of surrounding region. 1/4/95

MANHATTAN COHOUSING

(Forming)
P.O. Box 1801
Old Chelsea Station
New York, NY 10011

(212)642-8406

We are a cohousing group in formation which is developing a community in New York City. We are searching for sites in areas that offer safe, quiet, low-scale neighborhoods; good schools; interesting street life; and closeness to public transportation. Each household will have a complete, private apartment plus shared common facilities (e.g., common kitchen for those who wish to share meals, playroom), supporting a balance between community and privacy. We plan to have between 15–20 households and move in by the end of 1996. We intend to cooperatively design, develop, own, and manage the housing; be environmentally conscious; reflect the human diversity of NYC; be sensitive to the surrounding neighborhoods; and have fun. We will build or renovate a building which has lots of light and an outdoor space (rooftop suitable for a garden, interior courtyard, backyard, etc.).

We are looking for folks who want to live in NYC; like the idea of cohousing; want to actively take a hand in building

their community; and, above all, are really committed to working out differences early and consciously. Give us a call. 2/4/95

MARATHON CO-OP

743 Tularosa Drive
Los Angeles, CA 90026

(213)666-3002

A scattered-site limited equity housing co-op, eleven blocks long and one block wide, formed in an abandoned freeway corridor. Ethnically and economically diverse units range from single family homes to fourplexes, from studios to five bedrooms. There are units that are Section Eight subsidized, and units that are not.

There is an annual meeting, attended by two-thirds of the members, where the Board of Directors and the officers are elected. Intermittent meetings are called when important issues arise. Committees are very active. The Board and committees meet monthly, with a third of the members attending Board meetings.

The ethnic makeup of Marathon is 2/3 Latino from many countries, and a 1/3 mix of Anglos, African Americans, and Asians. There are are least two large social events a year for the entire housing co-op: a summer picnic and a Christmas party, both well attended. Marathon is a sister co-op (by way of Route Two Community Housing Corp., the developer) with Alexandria Co-op, Four Streets, Dayton Heights, and Silver Lakes. Please include SASE with inquiries. 9/8/94

MARDEN FARM, THE

(Forming)
c/o Philip W. Marden
8 Old Lane, Highwood
Somerset, NJ 08873

(908)247-7594

We have 123 acres of steep and heavily wooded land with two ponds, a stream, and a mountaintop with a 40-mile view —only 1-1/2 hours from Manhattan. We envision converting our old 6-bedroom farmhouse into a holistic health center, and creating an ecovillage complete with livestock and an organic farm. We make decisions by consensus, and new members will help shape our plans for how labor, food, and finances are shared, how children are schooled, and whether housing takes the form of individual units, co-housing, or an old-style village. Our real goal is to start a new religion based on protecting the biosphere, where everything we do to provide

for our needs—from extraction through manufacture to distribution and recycling— is done in a way that enhances all of life. Write or call for more information. 7/24/94

MARIPOSA GROUP, THE

21450 Chagall Road
Topanga, CA 90290

(818)340-1146

The Mariposa Group, a Conscious Community: We are creating an environment which promotes more joyful and fulfilling conditions for work, play, and interpersonal relationships. Our emphasis is on fully using the interpersonal support, personal skills, education, financial resources, and group energy available to us in a community—such that each of us may achieve our fullest human potential and happiness. We are actively seeking new members who are willing to commit to making themselves, and this community, all that they can be. Send SASE for more information. 11/17/93

MARTHA'S HOUSING COOPERATIVE

225 E. Lakelawn Place
Madison, WI 53703

(608)256-8476

Martha's Housing Cooperative is one of 9 houses in the Madison Community Co-op [see Resource listing]. All decisions are made by consensus at the house level, and by majority rule at the board level. Our particular house is a diverse group of 30 workers and students who strive for a high degree of intimacy and involvement with each other.

We are committed to cooperation, consensus, feminism, anti-racism, peace, caring for the environment, and many other issues. Individuals have their own rooms, and share the rest of the house. We share a vegetarian meal every evening, and all interested folks are invited to share our food. We ask a one year commitment of all new members. Children are welcome. [cc] 9/29/93

MAXWORKS COOPERATIVE

716 West Maxwell Street
Chicago, IL 60607

Pro-environment workers' cooperative, based in downtown Chicago's historic public market district. We undertake to retrieve, stockpile, reprocess, and remarket those rejected resources which are found in the waste stream of Chicago's markets, industries, and neighborhoods. Maxworks recycles cardboard, paper, glass, metals, plastics; designs and manufactures new products where possible rather than scrap the materials; converts pre-used lumber into workbenches, shelving, lofts, ladders, recycling and compost bins, alternative energy structures, birdhouses, artparts, educative hardwood toys, building repair and restoration, landscaping, gardening, etc. Guests and members contribute $25/week Maxtax and 14 hours/week productivity time.

Currently involved in legal efforts to acquire title to the various properties; need co-editor for the mire of paperwork. Also wanted: volunteers to help with materials sorting, lumber de-nailing, carpentry projects; in exchange you can learn a wide array of urban recycling skills. 7/24/94

MERAMEC VALLEY COMMUNITY LAND TRUST

(Re-Forming)
Star Route, Box 104
Bourbon, MO 65441
(573)775-2329

We are a land trust which in June of '88 bought 213 acres along a crystal clear, canoeable tributary of the Meramec River in rural Missouri. We comprise 22 families and individuals who mostly live and work in St. Louis; thus far only one family lives on the land full-time. Families are financially independent and make their own decisions about vocations, housing, diet (though we tend toward health consciousness in general), schooling, etc. A few of us have immediate plans to establish homesteads. Many plan to use the land for recreation.

We are a diverse group with ecological interests as our common factor. We practice a blend of consensus and majority rule in our decision making. Membership is currently fully subscribed, though we do maintain a waiting list of interested individuals. We'd also like to network with others who might want to purchase adjacent land.

We hold approximately 50% of our total land for common use and management. The most noteworthy qualities of our community land trust are the harmonious interaction of persons from diverse lifestyles, and the pristine environment which includes springs, caves, bluffs, creeks, fields, and forests. Visitors are asked to make advance reservations.

SASE required with inquiries. [cc] 1/1/93

METHOW CENTER OF ENLIGHTENMENT

P.O. Box 976
Twisp, WA 98856
(509)997-3147

The Holy Wise Ones have designated Methow as a major spiritual center in development upon this planet. It is the responsibility of each spiritual group upstairs to position their ground ambassadors, aligning them with their spiritual center of choice. It is unfortunate that so few can actually align with these centers, and ironic that the future of mankind lies in back country rural areas where natural uncontaminated resources are plentiful. Our inter-dimensional celestial project in north central Washington is designed to be a major Communications Command Post, Cultural Development Learning and Healing Center for all who have access to it. Space people (U.F.O. intelligences) from all dimensions will come and go freely from this Celestial City location.

We are reaching out to gather as many as Divine Guidance and time allow (Earth and economic changes); our goal is 2000 settlers. At Methow there are no rules or regulations of any kind, since the whole valley is our spiritual center, including everybody in it. It is a clean, simple plan, approved by the Holy Wise Ones, and allows for every one to do their thing naturally, finding their way in their own time. [cc] 6/25/94

MICCOSUKEE LAND CO-OP

Tallahassee, FL

The Miccosukee Land Cooperative (MLC) is a community of 100 families and individuals who together own 279 acres situated nine miles east of Tallahassee. Co-op members privately own their own homesteads which range in size from one acre to several acres each. A total of 90 acres is preserved in its natural state as common land, owned collectively and enjoyed by the entire membership.

MLC members are drawn together by a common desire to live in a rural environment where the land is respected and interaction between neighbors is a sought-after experience. All activities (other than paying assessments for necessities such as taxes and insurance) are purely voluntary, allowing each person to choose the level of sharing and social-

izing s/he prefers. While we are a diverse group in age, occupation, and religious practice, many adults are in the prime years of their careers. Time to do all one would like is scarce. Despite this busy pace, we make time to celebrate the milestones of our lives and to support one another in times of sickness or tragedy. Many of us carry the vision of more time for shared meals and sitting on the porch shelling peas, gossiping, and singing. In the meantime we walk more separate paths, but always give thanks for our land and precious neighbors. 12/26/94 [42]

MIKECO REHTLE

(Forming)
1127 Fuller Avenue #9
Big Rapids, MI 49307-2151

Mikeco Rehtle is an expanded/extended family tribe based on spiritual, social, and psychological values. We will hold land in a community or stewardship land trust, and all other property and assets will be held communally. Each adult member (14 years old and up, depending upon the individual) is expected to work 5-1/2 hours a day, 6 days a week, 44 weeks a year—doing community-sustaining or income-producing labor—or pay an equivalent amount of money based on the current minimum wage.

Housing is assigned by community consensus, with options of family-style, dormitory-style, cohousing, and private rooms. Most units will have private bathroom and kitchen facilities; privacy is a high priority.

We envision our community as a living demonstration of appropriate, sustainable, natural being and doing—emphasizing clean air and water; healthy food, clothing, shelter, and energy—plus health care, economics, governance, politics, education, transportation, communications, architecture, construction technology, etc. Our economics will revolve around hosting conferences, hosteling, retreats, and workshops; writing, teaching, and speaking about our work; and establishing a foundation to offer grants and no-interest loans to assist folks in their conversion to appropriate, sustainable, community-based endeavors. We are also interested in soy food production as a primary aspect of our community income. Miso, tamari, tempeh, tofu, etc, is envisioned. We'd like to hear from folks with experience, interest, ideas, referals, resources, etc, in this area. Send SASE with questions, suggestions, etc. 11/22/93

MOLLY HARE COOPERATIVE

Durham, NC

(COMMUNITY LISTING REMOVED)

Community has folded. 2/1/95

MONADNOCK GEOCOMMONS VILLAGE

(Forming)
Derbyshire Farm
Temple, NH 03084

(603)654-6705
http://www.ic.org/geo/

Monadnock Geocommons Village is an educational ecovillage for residents working on Gaia Education Outreach Institute projects [see Resource listing]. In 1994 we are three staff members plus design team friends wishing to integrate jobs, family, farming, meditation arts, celebration, and learning in one sustaining place of community. Our site is a beautiful hill farm bordering 2000 acres of protected mountain wilderness. Present housing could serve 20 guests. We are exploring ways to raise funds and transfer farm ownership into an educational land trust. Our village design will include cohousing, Geocommons College, Monadnock Life Education Center, agriculture/permaculture, retreat camp, and green businesses. We welcome participants of diverse ages, skills, and backgrounds. This work requires strong commitment to education, community building, personal inquiry, sustainability, voluntary simplicity, and mindfulness. SASE requested. 11/26/94

MONAN'S RILL

Northern California

(707)538-7354

Monan's Rill, established in 1973, is an intentional community of 30 people ranging in age from infancy to the 70s. We live on 440 acres of beautiful wooded hills about one hour north of San Francisco. Our name comes from a small creek running through the property.

We are committed to helping each other and caring for the land. Some of us are Quakers, and our business meetings are conducted after the manner of Friends. Decisions are by consensus.

We are a general partnership, and no one holds individual title to houses or land. We share the responsibilities of our garden and orchard (certified organic), the roads, the water and septic systems. We are teachers, carpenters, nurses, and volunteers for nonprofits. As a group we have no creed, but we all share a concern about the present social and ecological crisis; we each reach out to do what we can. We do not claim to have a solution to the world's problems—or even our own. We believe we are taking steps in the right directions, and we know that good things are happening here. If you get an answering machine when calling, please leave your address. 5/18/94 [77(D)]

N. American m

MONTEBELLO COMMUNITY

74 Montebello Road
Jamaica Plain, MA 02130

An urban intentional Christian community, located in a less affluent, racially mixed Boston neighborhood. We encourage church involvement and living by scriptural values. We have in-house worship, and stress hospitality and building relationships. We tend to be a "community of individuals" as each one of us chooses their own church and social group; we try to have 2–4 meals together each week and have a weekly community meeting. 1/1/93

MOONSHADOW

(Forming)
Route 1, Box 304
Whitwell, TN 37397

(615)949-5922

Moonshadow is deeply integrated with the land, a forested Appalachian valley with caves, creeks, and bluffs. Our deliberate existence has a minimum impact on the forest ecosystem. We combine traditional knowledge with appropriate scientific methods to interact intelligently with nature. Our hand-crafted buildings are made of natural materials. Our energy is from the sun and the forest. Trees and shrubs are integrated with food crops and herbs for self-sufficiency. We experiment with native and exotic plants for nutrition and medicine. Artistic expression fulfills personal, functional, and political needs. As organizers in the environmental and social justice movements, we network with other groups and individuals.

We are striving to facilitate an evolutionary process which will radically change the system—the dominant paradigm—to ensure a sustainable future and equality for all life. We have created a solar-powered office space where MEDIA RIGHTS, an alternative nonprofit production company, is now based. Education is our major goal: to share our collectively gained wisdom through publications, video, radio, workshops, music, computer networking, and gatherings. We are in the process of obtaining nonprofit status (educational/ scientific) for our community, and are seeking outside sources of support. We hope that sharing our experience and vision will help people move more gently on the Earth. Ecology! 9/3/95

MORNINGLORY

RR4, Killaloe
Ontario K0J-2A0
CANADA

10 children and 7 adults live on the land now (6 of the kids are home birthed, a practice we highly value). An essential value of our group is respecting the Earth. As an intentional community we seek to preserve and foster a simple way of life, and to protect the land and the wildlife for the enjoyment of future generations. Morninglory's 100-year-old log farmhouse is now the home of a parent-operated ungraded alternative school of 15 children, aged 4 to 14.

Organic gardens and orchards. Only electricity that's homemade and off the grid; 6 phones. Seven private all-weather dwellings scattered on 100 stony, hilly, and wooded acres in the foothills overlooking the Bonnechere Valley and Algonquin Park. A beautiful location that is blessed with sufficient bugs in early summer and cold enough winters to keep the local population from getting crowded.

Maple syrup, swimming and skating pond, and great hills for sliding and skiing. We have lots of interaction with the high quality artistic community living nearby. We enjoy music and dance.

Anyone wanting to visit, please write ahead. Yes, we may wish new members. No, we're not quick correspondents—we're child oriented, and their needs and survival come first. Please include SASE with correspondence. [cc] 12/10/92

MOTHER EARTH CHURCH OF OPIHIHALE

(Re-Forming)
Box 172
Honaunau, HI 96726

(808)328-8202/326-5188

We are a cooperative community of 4 adults and 3 children living on 11 acres of rainforest on the Kona coast of the island of Hawaii. Rain, mosquitoes, few nearby beaches or jobs, 20 miles from town.

We're planting orchards, raising kids, earning a living in town to keep our bills paid and our projects going. Eventually, we may make the land available for workshops, trainings, and retreats to help pay expenses, but for now it all comes out of our pockets.

If you're honest, keep your word, and are willing to do your share; if you prefer living with people who resolve conflicts as they arise; if the idea of community service appeals to you—drop us a line.

Short-term internships are available in landscaping and gardening. Skills training in conflict resolution and communication available. Short-term visitor camping space and work trade arrangements available. Long-term partnership/membership available to the right person/family. 5/8/92

MOUNT MADONNA CENTER

445 Summit Road
Watsonville, CA 95076

(408)847-0406/847-2683 Fax

Mount Madonna Center is a 355-acre intentional community, retreat, and seminar facility in the mountains east of Santa Cruz. As a public nonprofit educational organization, the Center teaches adults in programs on personal growth, spiritual pathways, and alternative health sciences —plus has a fully accredited private school of over 100 children from preschool through high school, including boarding school facilities for both boys and girls. Groups of up to 300 can be accommodated with programs/retreats lasting for a weekend or longer.

The inner life of the Center is inspired by its spiritual leader, Baba Hari Dass. It is a home to people on a quest for spiritual and personal enlightenment. Although it is not mandatory, many residents follow daily meditation practice.

The Center's approximately 30 buildings were built through major contributions of time and money. Residences range from single family homes to single room cabins. Five campgrounds provide tent housing in mild weather. An organic garden provides vegetables for the Center's vegetarian diet and flowers to beautify the buildings.

Community staff members pay fees covering room and board based on their work commitment at the Center. These fees can be as low as zero for five days work. There are few paid positions at the Center, and these are mostly with the School.

The members of the Center are closely integrated with people who are not residents but who participate in Center activities. In addition, residents and non-residents both support a theater group, a choir, The Pacific Cultural Center, Gateways Book Store, and a children's orphanage in India.

The administration of the Center consists of a board of 10 directors, elected by the membership, a 7-person administration who are heads of main areas, and a middle management group who are in charge of other areas. SASE requested. 9/15/92 [76]

MUIR COMMONS

**2323 Muir Woods Place
Davis, CA 95616**

(916)758-5202 (msg.)

We are a cohousing community located on a 2.83-acre site within a subdivision of Davis, CA. As future residents, we designed our site to promote interaction between neighbors.

We are resident-managed and provide 90% of the energy required to run the place. We strive for community while balancing our individual needs for privacy. We have a "Video Tour" tape available for rent ($25 deposit required; we refund $16 when it's returned). Please include a SASE with any inquiry. [cc] 1/12/95

MULTIPLE CHEMICAL SENSITIVITY PARK

Dripping Springs, TX

(COMMUNITY LISTING REMOVED)

Community has folded. 12/17/95

N STREET COHOUSING

**708 "N" Street
Davis, CA 95616
http://www.cohousing.org/
specific/n_street/**

N Street Cohousing is a nurturing environment that offers a practical use of shared resources, cultivates personal relationships, and strives for diversity. While there is an individual level of responsibility to the community, the community acknowledges personal choices and needs. Please include a SASE with inquiries. [cc] 11/11/93

NAMASTÉ GREENS

**(Forming)
Route 2, Box 578
Center Barnstead, NH 03225**

(603)776-7776

Attempting to be a Green movement bio-circle by values. Focused on permaculture,

polyfidelity, integrity, service...working toward land trust, biodiversity, cohousing, local co-op, extended multi-mate families, commitment!!!

We seek maturity (of all ages), nature lovers, industrious, creative, peace loving partners to co-create a Permaculture Integrity Polyfidelity (P.I.P.) ecovillage. We have 49 acres, 5 housing units, a water test and purification and construction business. Our focus is enhancing life via sustainable lifestyle. Visitors by pre-arrangement; send SASE. 1/23/93

NEARY LAGOON CO-OP

**81 Chestnut Street
Santa Cruz, CA 95060**

(408)457-2424

Neary Lagoon was developed from the ground up by the Santa Cruz Community Housing organization. Neary is a limited equity housing co-op, and consists of two-story apartments, eight units per building, twelve buildings in all. Facilities include a community room, an office, and a maintenance shop. The community room hosts kids' activities, tutoring, Girl Scouts, birthday parties, and Salvation Army visits one day a week to offer assistance to families. There are numerous other member activities such as potlucks, Christmas, Halloween, and Easter events.

Members elect the Board of Directors at an annual meeting. Residents must be low income to qualify for membership. The ethnic mix is 85% Latino, primarily from Mexico and El Salvador, and 15% Anglo and African American. 9/9/94

NETWORK FOR A NEW CULTURE (NFNC)

**(Forming)
NFNC Information Center
P.O. Box 205
Philomath, OR 97370**

**(800)624-8445
nfnc@cvo.oneworld.com**

[Previously listed as Center For Experimental Cultural Design.] Network for a New Culture (NFNC), formerly Center for Experimental Cultural Design, is an association of several hundred people thoughout the U.S. inspired in part by the ideals and goals of the ZEGG community in Germany. NFNC sees community as a means to social change, and one of our goals is to establish communities which serve as models of healthy ways of relating to the Earth and to each other. To

put it simply, we see community as a means to producing a world without fear, violence, coercion, or sexual repression. We believe that there are several key components to realizing this vision: self-responsible individuals; mutual support; honesty and openness in interpersonal relationships; a realization that means determine ends; and a realization that the personal is political—that is, a commitment to personal growth and change.

At present, there are NFNC "city groups" in Arizona, Oregon, and Virginia; and there are plans for several small start-up communities. To facilitate the community-forming process, NFNC holds several conferences, workshops, and camps every year, and publishes two newsletters, "New Culture" (our quarterly journal) and "The NFNC Quickie" (our monthly update sheet). For a free copy of "New Culture," contact our information center. 4/9/96

NEW COVENANT FELLOWSHIP

**(Re-Forming)
13206 Dutch Creek Road
Athens, OH 45701**

(614)592-4605

We are seeking to live out the radical vision of Jesus, living together in love, sharing our lives, living an alternative lifestyle, and confronting violence and injustice in the world around us.

Our main income is from raising organic vegetables. We have been active in peace and social justice activities, the environmental movement, prisons, and serving the homeless. We seek to live simply, and identify with the poor. 11/2/92

NEW JAH-RULSALEM

**(Re-Forming)
Commonwealth Village
RR1, Box 1210
Soldiers Grove, WI 54655**

(608)734-3886 / 734-3513

Commonwealth Village of New JahRulsalem's basic philosophy: We are the ground floor of a revitalization of principles and morals first brought to the U.S. 20 years ago. These principles and traditions are based on the original "Christian" concept of God: God in man/ man in God. This fundamental concept requires us to look for the God (good) in every person. To live this concept with a whole heart is not only to know God, but to experience the very being of God. This is the foundation by which we seek to build the future. Love, truth, justice, and peace are the cornerstones of our being and our greatest gift to one another—and are therefore the only acceptable reality. Reasoning is a basic ritual in the community. By reasoning we learn and teach. By reasoning we open the heart and find causes for unity. We see that every living creature has been endowed with an inherent blessing. It is this blessing that each of us brings to share with one another.

Daily and future activities: school, organic gardening, woodworking, research, playing, praying, music, talking, alternative energy, aquaponics, eco-habitats, a caring non-predatory community designed by those that live it. A life of living, a way of life that requires a commitment to self-government. SASE requested. 1/30/93

NEW JERUSALEM COMMUNITY

(Non-Residential)
745 Derby Avenue
Cincinnati, OH 45232

(513)541-4748
(513)541-2377

New Jerusalem, established in 1971, is a lay Catholic community of 250 adults and children. We have chosen to center our lives together in an integrated, working-class neighborhood in Cincinnati. Each Sunday and Wednesday we gather for worship and discussion. During the rest of the week we seek to live out the gospel of Jesus as extended family to one another and to brothers and sisters down the street and around the globe.

Some of our current involvements include the care of Central American refugees, housing rehabilitation, and work to protect the environment. 10% of our annual income is given away to those in need and those working for change.

After our founding by a Franciscan priest, and his departure in 1985, we have struggled to give authority to one another, to re-choose the community for what it is, and to accept responsibility for our own lives. While maintaining a good relationship with the church and respecting the tradition, we are also listening to the Holy Spirit and honoring our own experience. Our life is rich, full, and challenging as we integrate our personal journeys, families, careers, and community. We are happy to welcome you and to serve you as God leads, trusting that God will continue to

bless us all with more abundant life together. 5/15/92

NEW LAND

Route 1, Box 175-P
Faber, VA 22938

The New Land is an intentional community of individual homesites in a beautiful rural setting, with mountain views, access roads, and a lake—on land shared with the Monroe Institute, a research and educational organization dedicated to the study and development of human consciousness through the use of audio-stimulated brain hemispheric synchronization and other scientific techniques. Residents and landholders who chose to join the New Land come mostly through experience with the Institute.

Homes are privately owned, and most members are self-employed (in a wide range of professional fields) or retired. The only common land is at the nearby Monroe Institute. Personal freedom and evolving consciousness are shared values. Occupations, types of homes, and land use are a matter of individual choice (i.e., gardens, greenhouses, horses, llamas, etc.). Members get together as desired to share in special projects, social affairs, and spiritual growth. Some homesites are available. SASE appreciated. 12/18/94 [77(D)]

NEW LEAF COMMUNITY

Cincinnati, OH
(COMMUNITY LISTING REMOVED)

Lost contact. 4/10/96

NEW MEADOW RUN BRUDERHOF

Hutterian Brethren
Farmington, PA 15437

(412)329-8573
http://www.bruderhof.org/

[See main listing for "Hutterian Brethren" in the Resources section.] 6/1/92

NEW MOON

1516 Guerrero
San Francisco, CA 94110

(415)826-5452

We are a house established in '83, living together without a formal structure or community goal. We are presently 13 young to middle-aged adults. We live in an old Victorian house with an extensive

garden, on a noisy city street, coming together for dinner occasionally. Music is a common interest in the house. All expenses and chores, including food, are shared. Individual rents range from $220 to $400 per month. We also have a travelers room available for $75 per week. 5/24/94

NEW ROOTS COMMUNITY LAND TRUST

(Re-Forming)
Box 909, Wynyard
Saskatchewan S0A-4T0
CANADA

(306)554-2985

We are a land trust formed in 1978. We organically farm rye, alfalfa, and hay. Currently a handful of families live here at various times of the year. Although a nonprofit organization, we use consensus to make decisions. We are eager to network with other prairie ecological groups and encourage visitors or prospective members (must write ahead). [cc] 7/7/94

NEW VRNDABAN

City of God
Route 1, Box 319
Moundsville, WV 26041

(304)843-1600

The City of God is a place to get serious about bringing God into your life in an atmosphere free from so many of the problems that plague our modern world. Pilgrims to the City of God find a place to live, work, worship, and grow surrounded by spiritual purity. We started out 25 years ago as a traditional Hare Krishna community. Now, while retaining the spiritual essence of Krishna Consciousness, we are eager to reach out and share with lovers of God from all traditions who have dedicated their lives to the development of faith. We are accepting applications from spiritual preceptors who would like to establish their own spiritual community within the City of God.

We have 5000 acres of beautiful, hilly land, so there's lots of room to grow and glory in God's natural gifts. The City of God is also a place for spiritual retreats, interfaith gatherings, self-sufficient living, and—don't forget—the mystical presence of Prabhupada's Palace, always reminding us of the powerful message of the spiritual master. We welcome people from other communities to write, visit, connect—we know we can benefit from your experiences, and we are grateful for the opportunity to share the great blessings that have been showered upon us. Love of God lives and thrives at the City of God. SASE requested. 12/6/92 [16]

NICHE: TUCSON COMMUNITY LAND TRUST

(Forming)
1050 S. Verdugo
Tucson, AZ 85745

(520)882-0985

We are an eclectic community dedicated to preserving urban land for affordable housing. Both resident and supporting members may use our newly acquired residence near downtown Tucson to promote the ideals of alternative education, appropriate technology, permaculture, etc. Our main requirement is that members be respectful and supportive of diversity. We particularly encourage members to step outside stereotyped gender roles (e.g., men in parenting, women in construction). Current projects include straw-bale construction, expansion of our board of directors, and the development of a homeschooling network. As we are in our fledgling state, expect big changes by the time you read this. Se habla Español. SASE requested. [cc] 12/16/92

NINTH STREET CO-OP

1708 – 9th Street
Berkeley, CA 94710

(510)524-7896

Ninth Street Co-op is a limited equity housing cooperative owned by its residents. The co-op consists of two duplexes and one cottage with a common area, fruit trees, and an organic garden in an urban neighborhood of working class,

ethnically diverse people. Members are low-to-moderate income. All resident members serve as members of the Board of Directors that meets monthly. Ninth Street Co-op is self-managed and has a vision of continuing and increasing affordable housing in the City of Berkeley. The group became a co-op in 1993. Please include SASE with inquiries. 9/10/94

NO NAME YET— COHOUSING

(Forming)
2220 Sacramento Street
Berkeley, CA 94702

(510)549-3749

...no name yet. We are a cohousing community enjoying living together as friends and neighbors while we plan the renovations and new construction which will make our community complete. Because we are acting as our own developer, we meet very often—once a week all together, plus one or two committee meetings per week. We eat together twice a week, with two cooks and three clean-up people. We cook for 20 at these meals, and have smaller, informal meals at other times.

We are currently 13 adults and 5 kids (ages 2 to 12) and look forward to more relaxed time with each other in a couple of years when we complete our development phase. We recycle, compost, and swap cars—trying to reduce our consumption levels to something reasonable. We have some solar lighting and look forward to more...and perhaps to a grey-water system. We are too busy to enjoy visitors often at this point, but look forward to being a more active part of the broader network in the future. Please include a SASE with inquiries. [cc] 1/12/95

NOONDAY FARM

P.O. Box 71
Windsor Road
Winchendon Springs,
MA 01477

(508)297-3226

Noonday Farm is a small spiritually based Catholic Worker community which grows food for homeless and elderly persons in Massachusetts, and provides hospitality. We have sister communities in Soweto and Nicaragua. We are also the base for the Noonday Singers. 5/8/93

NORTH COTTONWOOD ECOVILLAGE

Hillsboro, KS
(COMMUNITY LISTING REMOVED)
Lost contact. 12/16/95

NORTH MOUNTAIN COMMUNITY LAND TRUST

Route 2, Box 248-C
Lexington, VA 24450

(540)463-1760

North Mountain began in 1972 as a rural commune. We have a beautiful piece of land—127 acres, mostly hilly woods, about 10 of it tillable. We are located in a valley encircled by the ancient Allegheny Mountains. The commune continued with many comings and goings through the '70s and into the mid-'80s. As our members grew older and most began having families, the need for individual housing grew. In 1990 we changed our structure to that of a land trust.

The land is owned by the community, with members having lifetime leases to individual 2-acre plots; homes are owned by the individuals. There is a work commitment each month as well as a monetary one. We have meetings monthly, potlucks regularly, and labor exchanges amongst us. We now consist of 5 members—2 homes, 3 adults, 2 children, various dogs, cats, chickens, a barn, a shop, and a granary. We do some gardens together, others individually. We have hopes to grow in the future but no desire to grow too quickly or too large, remaining at 6 to 8 households at most. If interested, please write and schedule a visit. We want to ensure that you know us and we know you, and that we all know what's involved when we join together in the dance of community living.

Come dance with us at North Mountain Community. SASE requested. 5/12/92 [32]

NORTH WOODS VEGAN COMMUNITY

(Forming)
P.O. Box 953
Ashland, WI 54806

We are a fledgling community located in Northern Wisconsin near Lake Superior, surrounded by the Chequamegon National Forest. Safe and sane food, sharing in food preparation and in meals, consensus decision making, conflict resolution, organic gardening, medicinal herbs, playing, dancing, dreaming, simplifying, and an anti-consumer lifestyle leading into self-sufficiency are the intended focus. Members currently support themselves economically, but sharing is ever present. We are now acquiring funds to ransom a part of Mother Earth from slavery. We are looking for kindred souls (the Sesame Street Posse taught us to share). Guests welcome. Funky considerations never nil. All serious inquiries will be promptly answered. 10/21/94

NORTHERN SUN FARM CO-OP

P.O. Box 689, Steinbach
Manitoba R0A-2A0
CANADA

(204)434-6887 / 434-6143

Northern Sun Farm Co-op is a rural community with the land being cooperatively owned by all members. We have both resident and nonresident members. Our focus is on alternative energy, appropriate technology, simple lifestyles, and self-reliance. We live in family groups and we promote individual responsibility for life choices. Northern Sun Farm is always open to visitors. 1/20/93

NYLAND COHOUSING COMMUNITY

3525 Nyland Way
Lafayette, CO 80026

(303)499-8915

The Nyland CoHousing Community is one of the first completed CoHousing communities in the US. Nyland began as Colorado CoHousing in 1988 after a few friends got together to talk about the new book CoHousing by McCamant and Durrett. In May of '90 we optioned the land, in August '92 we began moving in,

and all residents were in by May of '93.

Our community of 122 people includes 87 adults, 6 teens, and 29 kids—with an assortment of visiting children and friends of the community. We own 42 acres of land, annexed by the town of Lafayette, in a rural area just outside the city of Boulder. There are 42 homes, a 6000 sq. ft. common house, an 860 sq. ft. shop building, and a 600 sq. ft. greenhouse. Houses are individually owned, and common properties are being held in unison through a homeowners association. All properties are maintained and managed by the residents of Nyland.

Our decision-making structure consists of committees and consensus. We meet two times a month in general gatherings, and smaller work groups handle the tasks of managing the land and community affairs. Daycare is provided during the day, and we generally have shared meals four nights a week in the common house. Tours of the community are available at 11:00AM the last Sunday of each month. 11/21/94

OAK GROVE

(Forming)
Route 1, Box 455
Round Hill, VA 22141

Oak Grove is an 18th century mountain farm/center—on the edge of the Blue Ridge Mountains, 60 miles from Washington, D.C. Located between an old Native American spring and ceremonial ground, the Appalachian Trail, and a 1200-acre nature preserve, the farm's 80 acres of exceptionally verdant land possess the magic and mystery of the Blue Ridge, the oldest mountains in the world. Mountain laurel, old stone walls, ancient trees, ley lines provide beauty and peaceful creativity.

Part of the community's emphasis is the development of a center for more simplified, alternative living—in harmony with nature—with a spiritual orientation. Small conferences and workshops, "Insight Meditation," solstice/equinox gatherings already take place here.

Prospective members with professional or strong experience in house building or

organic gardening or orcharding can be added to develop a community of six or eight households. Yurts and trailers, as at Findhorn, are possible housing.

At this very beginning stage, Oak Grove consists of one writer (a Quaker), a medium-sized passive solar house, several tipis, and visitors. Please include a SASE with inquiries, and include a description of yourself, goals, and experience with house building or organic agriculture! SASE required. [cc] 4/21/93

OBERLIN STUDENT CO-OPERATIVE ASSOCIATION

Wilder, Box 86
Oberlin, OH 44074

(216)775-8108
http://www.oberlin.edu/
inside/stuorgs/OSCA.html

A network of self-managed student co-op houses. [See main listing in the Resources section.] 9/13/94

OJAI FOUNDATION

9739 Ojai-Santa Paula Rd
Ojai, CA 93023

(805)646-8343

Located on a 40-acre ridge of semi-wilderness land in Ojai, California, the Ojai Foundation is an educational sanctuary for both youth and adults, a place of personal retreat, and a community devoted to sharing practices, personal stories, and visions of a more peaceful planet while living and working together close to the earth.

One of our primary focuses is on our New Visions of Education Program. The core of this program is a group process called "council" which involves speaking and listening "from the heart." Many schools in California and other parts of the country have been incorporating council in their curriculum. Classes from these schools in the greater L.A. area, both private and public, have the opportunity to come to the land and participate in individually designed retreat programs: 6th graders come for a two-day retreat to have the opportunity to appreciate the Earth in a healthy way, to work and create together; 7th graders to experience a three-day ropes course retreat; and 12th graders to do rites of passage and a sweat lodge in a five-day retreat. This program is expanding rapidly to include retreats for other grades as well. We also offer Teen Rites of Passage programs for 14–18 year olds which are not connected to any particular schools.

Our adult programs revolve around "Foundation Studies" which include training in the Council Process, Storytelling, Mindfulness in a variety of traditional and contemporary settings, Permaculture, and the study of Intimate Relationships. We offer programs for people interested in community building, education, business, and the arts. Wilderness Rites of Passage and adult private retreat opportunities for both individuals and/or groups are available.

The community itself is an essential part of this work: staff, guests, teachers, and students all create and explore how to learn and live together with care for self, each other, and the Earth. Our common practices include daily morning meditation, council, and service to the vision of making the Foundation a haven for the programs we offer. We have six residential core staff positions and offer work retreat to four individuals each month. Core staff positions usually arise from the pool of work retreatants. Please call or write for our brochure or more information. 7/10/94

1000 SMALL PHARMABLISTERS

P.O. Box 1313
Lawrence, KS 66044

Yes, we are 1000 Small Pharmablisters, also known as the Country Folks. Both of our names are recycled from found objects, as is much of the rest of our way of life. We are the grass growing through the pavement, literally and metaphorically. Lately we are 5 adults and 1 child, and usually the four-leggeds have us outnumbered. The things we do together include aspiring to raise smart, happy, and healthy children; growing organic herbs and vegetables; making art; cooking yummy vegan feasts; and almost completing the *New York Times* cross word puzzle. Future projects include moving to the country, opening a Last Supper museum, and fixing the roof. We generally like visitors, but please write first. 8/27/94

ONE WORLD FAMILY COMMUNE

• **535 Spencer Avenue**
  Santa Rosa, CA 95404
  (707)527-8380

• **502 N Sweetzer**
  Los Angleles CA 90048
  (213)655-3019

We began in 1967 in San Francisco where we ran our first natural food restaurant, The Here & Now. We recognize Allen

Michael to be the entity prophesied to come as "the comforter" in St. John 14:16 and 16:7-14. We have published 4 books of Allen Michael's channelings in the "Everlasting Gospel" series, produced hundreds of public-access video shows, and are now producing our own videos.

We are not a religion, but live according to our spiritual awareness and are chartered as the Universal Industrial Church of the New World Comforter. We go by the name, One World Family Commune. After having been spread out, we are now coming back together in Sonoma County (except two small groups), where we presently have one house in Windsor with six people, and one house in Santa Rosa with nine people. We look forward to having a large complex where we can have our many workshops for publishing, videos, music, art, woodshop, gardening, clothing, healing arts, and guest facilities. 6/6/94

OPEN DOOR COMMUNITY

910 Ponce de Leon Avenue NE
Atlanta, GA 30306-4212

(404)874-9652/876-6977

The Open Door Community is a residential Christian community which shares life with the homeless and hungry and those in prison, especially those under the sentence of death. We live together to enable our work for justice and righteousness rooted in the nonviolent love of the cross. We struggle to resist the idols of money, power, violence, sexism, racism, death, war, and the self. We share worship, work, parenting, visiting, playing, meals, friendship, and study.

Everyone participates in daily decisions; our leadership team (members with lifetime commitments) make financial and policy decisions. Our ministries include permanent housing for 30, breakfast and soup kitchens, showers and clothing, visitations and letter writing to prisoners, anti-death penalty advocacy, advocacy for the homeless, medical services, free eye exams, a "Hospitality" newsletter, daily worship, weekly Eucharist, and Bible study. Members are expected to NOT earn any income. Visitors are limited to a one-month stay. 6/25/94

Communities Directory on the Web…

http://www.ic.org/fic/cdir/

ORCOM / ORGONE COMMITTEE

Brooklyn, NY

(COMMUNITY LISTING REMOVED)

Bad address—lost contact. 4/16/96

OSHO CENTERS OF NORTH AMERICA

[See main network entry in the Resources section.]

http://www.osho.org/ commune/oci.htm

Osho was a spiritual master, also known as Bhagwan Shree Rajneesh, who passed away in 1990. The main ashram is in Poona, India [see International listings]. In the US there are about 50 centers, but none are nearly as large as the commune developed in Antelope, Oregon, which folded in 1985 after the U.S. Government forced Rajneesh to return to India. [See also the community listing for the Positive Living Center]. 10/22/93

OSTERWEIL HOUSE

338 E. Jefferson
Ann Arbor, MI 48104-2309

(313)996-5956

We are a student cooperative household of 13 folks in a homey three-story house with shared meals and a living space with no TV. Osterweil tends to be slightly apart from the other student co-op houses in Ann Arbor's Inter-Cooperative Council [see Resource listing] both by location and social interaction. In 1993 we were voted by the ICC as "Most likely to be forgotten." 1/6/95

OUR HOUSE

132 Paddock Place
Victoria, BC V9B-5G2
CANADA

(604)727-0840

One United Resource Youth Program is a project which is to be run "by and for" the youth, with a large resource of "adult supporters." The program is intercultural, intergenerational, and interfaith. Though the work is primarily community based, the results are intended to be "global." The mission is to provide a forum for exploration of issues including multicultural awareness, race relations, power in relationships, cross-cultural conflict resolution, and celebration of diversity with unity. [cc] 3/15/94

OWL FARM

P.O. Box 133
Days Creek, OR 97429
(541)679-3266

OWL Farm is 147 acres of open woman's land held by the Oregon Woman's Land Trust (see Resource listing). All wimmin and girls are welcome to visit our beautiful meadows, forests, gardens, and orchard; guidelines on boy-children vary depending on consensus of the current residents. For further information about visiting our wonderful lesbian community, please write in advance. We request that only womyn write for info (SASE requested). 9/6/92

PACIFIC FAMILY CO-OP

1730 Commercial Way
Santa Cruz, CA 95062
(408)479-7657

The site of Pacific Family Co-op was previously a travel trailer park, then a mobile home park, and now a housing cooperative. Situated near the freeway, the neighborhood is both low-income residential and a business area. In 1989 the tenants organized, with the help of the Santa Cruz Community Housing Corporation, to convert the site into a cooperative. The tenants became owners in 1991. Residents are all low income, and the membership is ethnically diverse. Please include SASE with inquiries. 9/10/94

PADANARAM SETTLEMENT

Route 1, Box 478
Williams, IN 47470
(812)388-5571

Padanaram Settlement, established in 1966, is a spiritually oriented community of individuals. It operates its own schools, kitchen, bakery, and craft shops. The economic

base is sawmilling, and compost and bark mulch companies. We are not affiliated with any one group, but seek friends among other communities. We envision the ICU, an International Communal Utopia made up of a network of smaller communities. We hold semiannual (spring and fall) conventions, and an open house yearly during mid-October. Visitors are welcome, but must write or call ahead. Those who wish to join should plan to visit first. For more information write Attn: Rachel Summerton. 7/1/92

PANSY FARM

Vancouver, BC
(COMMUNITY LISTING REMOVED)

Lost contact. 4/19/96

PANTERRA

(Forming)
8579 Hardscrabble Road
Westfeild, NY 14787
(716)326-3993

Community in the forming stage, presently two adults looking for others to help develop a conference center (moved onto the land in '92). Nonviolent, vegetarian, consensus-based, Pantheistic, working toward universal oneness of consciousness. 6/21/94

PARKER STREET CO-OP

Berkeley, CA
(510)549-0107

We have here 24 one-bedroom apartments in a couple of three-story buildings. Population is 24 adults and two children. There's no shared kitchen and dining area, but we do have monthly potluck/meetings and a modest roof deck. On the ground, traditional ivy and asphalt are slowly giving way to garden space. We're a limited equity co-op, so state law limits the selling price of a person's share when that person moves out. This keeps the housing permanently affordable.

We're self-managed, so that's mainly what our meetings are about. Half of the members, due to lack of interest, don't attend any meetings...and that doesn't cause too many problems. However, when a vacancy arises, we select for people who will get involved. 9/7/94

PARNASSUS RISING

(Forming)
P.O. Box 33681
Phoenix, AZ 85067-3681

Parnassus Rising (Reborn Commies ha ha! Acts 2:44,45; and Acts 4:32-35) projects communitarian intentional family growing into intentional community seeking alternative sexual, religious, economic, political orientation, and privacy rights with nonpolitically *Korrect* human rights, not consensus; prefer Americans who have put their lives on the line for American freedoms.

We seek people like ourselves: sexually/ politically liberated; no cowed, guilt-ridden, or white-male bashers; skilled, knowledgeable, *Communicative*, hard working, adventurous, literate, clean of STDs/HIV I & II (willing to get tests regularly); No Smoking (anything), No Dope (anything), No Boozing (abuse of any sort of alcoholic beverage), No Compulsive Gamblers; No Fascists, Left or Right; ultimately to share *True* inventions and innovations and the benefits of non-competitive businesses, and build the humanist city, *Parnassus*. If willing to relocate, send SASE with recent resumé in cursive/longhand. 12/16/94

PEACE FARM

HCR 2, Box 25
Panhandle, TX 79068
(806)335-1715

The Peace Farm is a 20-acre farm located across from the rail exit of the nuclear train at Pantex—the United States' nuclear weapons assembly plant. The Peace Farm's mission is to create an environment for peace through peaceful means, to assert that peace can exist only where there is justice, and to develop an ecological model for nonviolent social change. Subscriptions are $5/year for Peace Farm's bimonthly newsletter, *The Advocate*. SASE requested. 5/12/92

PEACEFUL GARDENS VILLAGE

(Forming)
P.O. Box 441
Sagle, ID 83860
(208)263-3240 (msg.)

[Formerly Down to Earth Living.] We are a small group of people (3 adults, 3 children) forming an intentional community. We intend to build a shop or find land with a suitable building for our ceramic business and other crafts: candle making, doll making, soap making, and space for other artists and craftsmen; plus a kitchen, library, office, and bath. We are interested in growing herbs, edible flowers, gourmet foods, and some farm animals for personal use and for profit. We'll eventually be a self-sufficient community with sustainable agriculture, striving for eventual alternative energy sources. We will investigate building aesthetically with materials such as tires, hay, stone, wood, stucco, etc.—quality homes, basically affordable, but keeping beauty in mind. We are spiritual people, believing in the invisible Life Force: Beings going through the Earthly experience. You may conceptualize God in any manner, as long as you can locate this God inwardly, believing in God through Nature.

This area is scenic, with a rural atmosphere and community spirit. Many people feel spiritually called to this area to participate in changes for a better world and return to "down-to-earth living." Idaho's northern panhandle has winters which are cold and snowy, providing winter recreation and beautiful mountain views—with lakes, rivers, and creeks all around. Sandpoint will be relatively close for some seasonal jobs with Schweitzer Mountain and a large 43-mile lake Pendereille. We have a storefront on Main Street in Sandpoint to sell products produced by our cottage industries.

The community will be multigenerational. Our vision is of a self-sustaining lifestyle built on the idea of cooperation and sharing certain aspects of daily life to cut costs—people with a common goal governed by consensus. We welcome inquiries from all interested persons. SASE required. 1/6/95

PENINGTON FRIENDS HOUSE

**215 East 15th Street
New York, NY 10003**

(212)673-1730

The Penington Friends House is a Quaker sponsored and managed living community located near Greenwich Village in New York City. We are a residential community in which a diverse group of individuals share their personal and spiritual growth while pursuing their own life goals and achievements. We are located in a brownstone on a tree-lined street, and offer private and double rooms together with shared community space — such as a beautiful double parlor, an outside courtyard, and a kitchen and dining room. Our food is prepared by professional chefs, and it reflects our ethnic diversity. The Penington is a good place for those who do not wish to be isolated in an apartment while living in New York City. 7/8/92

PERMANENT AGRICULTURE LAND TRUST

**(Forming)
5724 Fresno Avenue
Richmond, CA 94804**

(510)528-2109/528-5215

Ecology is the web and structure of life. In an effort to preserve this delicate web, we are forming a community land trust which has permaculture and holistic

resource management as its central theme. We intend to purchase sufficient land so each household has approximately 10 acres personally controlled, surrounded by as much community controlled land as possible. We hope community members will be interested in self-sufficient, independent lifestyles while cooperating on larger projects for the community.

We intend to limit community size to around 10 households (50–60 individuals); if more are interested we would start new communities. We feel strongly about limiting family size to (hopefully) 2 children per couple. We desire multigenerational and racially/ethnically diverse community.

We feel religion to be a personal, not a community, focus. We strongly encourage homeschooling and alternative educational choices for community children. Prospective members will have to read and agree to the founding bylaws of the Permanent Agriculture Land Trust, which will be legally binding. Eventually we hope to form a college with the community as our campus. We are a new group and are actively seeking new members, so feel free to contact us. SASE required. 4/9/93

PETER MAURIN FARM

41 Cemetery Road
Marlboro, NY 12542

(914)236-4774

A small Catholic Worker community (est. '33) of old and young working for a balance between prayer, work, and study; strict organic gardening; short-term emergency shelter when space available. Members handle their own finances, and share several mostly vegetarian meals each week. Ecologically oriented, with strong focus on the land. Open to visitors; please call ahead. [cc] 6/20/94

PHANTO BOLO

(Forming)
P.O. Box 594
Cripple Creek, CO 80813

(719)661-4555

Located on a beautiful 2000-acre ranch on the southwest slope of Pikes Peak, Phanto Bolo offers real community for the self-sufficient/alternative-minded. This part of Phantom Canyon was the sacred hunting ground of indigenous peoples. Phanto Bolo is structured around individual

8- to 10-acre parcels (available at $1000 to $1500 per acre from private holdings). Several families have built or are developing self-sufficient alternative housing. Individual owners are encouraged to create year-round greenhouse food production (several Earthships are now planned). Many community members already plan to share land with newcomers who will show willingness for themselves and their community, and Phanto Bolo is cooperating with other local communities to create a Pikes Peak regional alternative network of ideas and resources.

The spiritual emphasis of most members is based on neo-Native American ideals, with a community council facility erected for this purpose. Earth-loving people interested in combining maximum personal freedom with loving community spirit are welcome at Phanto Bolo. SASE requested. 10/8/93

PHILOXIA

RR1, P.O. Box 56
Marlbank, Ontario K0K-2L0
CANADA

(613)478-6070

In ancient tongue, the word "Philoxians" meant "Lovable Strangers," a name given to those few who were saved from the perils and destruction of their ancient homeland known as Mu. Today the Philoxians gather on one of the world's largest ley lines (high energy points) as a small loving family resuming their respected works and antiquated artistry. The lifestyle features resort and bed & breakfast facilities, gourmet vegetarian macrobiotic cuisine, a whole grains brick-oven bakery, a craft shop, a beeswax candle business, nature trails, and a zoo. We have also published three popular books (*From Grits to Gourmet*, *The Pheylonian Odessey*, and *Alpha, Mu, Omega*) and offer private consultations relating to health, life, disease, natural cures, diet, and preventative medicine. SASE requested. 6/17/92

PHOENIX COMMUNITY

6116 Ironton Court
Englewood, CO 80111

(303)741-2243

Phoenix is a group marriage, now two women (40 and 53) and one man (52), based on deep and intense love and our interest in healing, growth, and transformation. We hope two more men and then one more woman will join us to form a six-person gender-balanced group mar-

riage. Our vision is to work together as healers, and for that all three of us are volunteer therapists-in-training. We are especially interested in the transpersonal—in reaching causal levels of mind and reality together, and exploring their exciting phenomena, processes, and energies (such as archetypes, prana, and mind fusion). We are unabashedly committed to intense and honest lifetime relationship: bright, upscale, urban, and competent. Our work is primary...but we also play and travel.

We're non-smokers, moderately health-oriented, highly heterosexual, and fidelitous to each other. When we visualize who might join us, we see, ideally, people in their late 30s or their 40s, successful in life and in relationships, with interests like ours, and seeking (and capable of) very, very deep intimacy. To arrange a visit, please write us and tell us about yourself, your vision for relationship, and your major interests. 12/12/94

PHOENIX COMMUNITY

(Forming)
1524 E Colter Street #231
Phoenix, AZ 85250

(602)274-3130

We are in the forming stage of a cohousing community in the greater Phoenix area, and intend to develop the community around cooperation and friendships. We intend to share our human resources to create an environment for personal growth. We intend to share many physical resources so we can live lighter on the land. Our present thinking is to share a clubhouse, eating facilities, workshop, gardening, laundry facilities, etc. We would like to hear from people interested in using cooperation, not competition, to create a better way of life. Religious and political people are welcome; however, we do not intend to affiliate with any particular ideology. SASE requested. 12/19/93

PICEON FARMS

Salem, MO
(COMMUNITY LISTING REMOVED)

Lost contact. 4/6/96

PILOT MOUNTAIN ECOCOMMUNITY

Pilot Mountain, NC
(COMMUNITY LISTING REMOVED)

Community has folded. 4/15/95

PIONEER VALLEY COHOUSING

(Forming)
120 Pulpit Hill Road
Amherst, MA 01002

(413)253-4090

The Pioneer Valley Cohousing Group has created a style of housing that encourages a strong sense of community, supports our need for privacy, makes life affordable, and provides a secure and enriched setting for children and adults. We have a place where people know their neighbors in a meaningful way, a neighborhood where different traditions and values are respected, and where we can all have a sense of security and belonging.

Our group purchased a 25-acre meadow site in North Amherst where we built 32 units and a large common house, moving in June–Sept 1994. Our seven acres contain a clustered mix of single, duplex, and triplex buildings. While residents own their own homes, they also own a share of the common house for dining and other community activities. Optional dinners several nights a week, gardens, play and work spaces, hiking trails, and other shared amenities chosen by residents have social and economic advantages. The common house includes a large kitchen/dining hall, children's playrooms, guest rooms, laundry facilities, library, and recycling center.

The community is a short walk from a municipal lake, recreation park with tennis, swimming, and playing fields, a small shopping center, library, university, and public transportation. Please include a SASE with inquiries. 1/19/95

PLEASANT VIEW

Hutterian Brethren
300 Rosenthal Lane
Ulster Park, NY 12487-9799

(914)339-6680
http://www.bruderhof.org/

One of the Bruderhof communities. [See main listing for "Hutterian Brethren" in the Resources section.] 5/19/93

PONDEROSA VILLAGE

Goldendale, WA
(COMMUNITY LISTING REMOVED)

No longer wish to be listed. 4/11/96

PORT CENTAURI

(Forming)
112 Colorado Avenue
Pueblo, CO 81004-4214

(719)546-3654

Port Centauri is a settlement for pioneers ready, willing, and able to address today's challenges; we are a small group of serious, focused individuals. Our path follows Ayn Rand's objectivism: "The concept of man as a heroic being, with his own happiness as the moral purpose of his life, with productive achievement as his noblest activity, and reason as his only absolute." Port Centauri requires a commitment to personal growth, group interaction, and interfacing with the Earth. One must be self-motivated and creative, and have let go of their fears, doubts, and negativity. This is not a place to "hang out," to "escape," or to preach.

Our immediate focus is on being self-sufficient and independent of the present government, economic, health, education, and social systems. Long-term we will plant seeds for a new civilization in an environment conducive to spiritual advancement and exploration of the unknown. The Port is 2000+ acres of high plains arid ranch land in southern Colorado. Our priorities include building "Earthships," green houses, water systems, farming areas, and independent energy systems. Each settler must carry their weight and provide for personal needs. Sharing and assisting are accomplished through agreements which are mutually acknowledged and accepted as balanced exchanges of energy. SASE requested; long distance calls returned collect. 1/11/93

POSITIVE COLLEGE

(Forming)
2003 Grove Street #4
Boulder, CO 80302-6562

(303)415-0149/440-9515 Fax

MISSION STATEMENT: Our goal is not to prove the past but to endow the future...and to have fun doing it. OUR PHILOSOPHY: Truth = Trust = Love = Friendship = Happiness = Freedom.

I would like to be married to a beautiful sexy wife woman who doubles as a secretary, nurse, counselor, mother of my children, business manager, household manager, social secretary, chauffeur. It seems like I may need more than one woman. Impossible? I say no. If the vibes are right, why not? I am not advocating

that everyone do this—I'm just saying I'd like to try.

Anyone can leave at any time with a prearranged disbursements agreement —what you come with you take with you; all income is divided as follows:
  25% Self savings (take with)
  25% P/C endowment (leave)
  25% Self expenses (take with)
  25% Group costs (leave)
There are no rent or taxes to pay; the house and grounds will be privately owned. In case of a split, child support by whomever the child stays with.

Send clear picture and friendly letter and receive same in return. What have we got to lose with a promised honest, nonviolent, friendly experiment where no one is obliged unless they want to be? SASE requested. Thanx! [cc] 12/24/94

POSITIVE LIVING CENTER & COMMUNITY

(Forming)
344 Indiana Avenue
Venice, CA 90291

(310)399-0032

We are an urban, beach community inspired by the mystic Osho to create a growing community of healthy, conscious people within an existing town—Venice Beach. Our general focus is on spiritual development (though non-religion). We live in four households, and each of our 40 adult members is expected to contribute 6 hrs/mo to the community. Please include SASE with inquiries. [cc] 1/10/95

PPAALS

(Forming)
Professionals, Performers,
and Artists Living Space
309 E 108th Street #AB
New York, NY 10029

(212)996-7318/996-4333

PPAALS is the effort of one individual, Ma Amritananda, to create a supportive, creative, nonviolent, and drug-free environment in which performing artists and persons in the arts community of Manhattan may live in harmony. It is located in a building with a recital hall and 30 other apartments, owned by an artist/scientist, Gisoo Lee. She would like to build a theater here and eventually have all spaces owned by people in the arts. PPAALS occupies two of these spaces, 3400 sq. ft. total, and many artists live in the building. Each performer may have the

38x24 meditation and performing area to do a fund raiser once per month; 30% of the proceeds go to a third world child. There are two such rooms with 15-foot ceilings and track lighting, walls good for art display. We have a piano and a public address system.

There are two kitchens (one vegetarian), three baths (one with shower only), a music practice room, an artists' area, and five bedrooms. A shared space with furniture is $400 plus utilities; private room is $600. Meditation hours are 9AM and 9PM daily. Meditation classes are available at no charge.

Playground and park across street. Near bus and subway. Cats allowed. Minimal storage. Laundry 1/2 block. Visitors $150/wk when available: Fax photo ID, proof of income, letter of intention, references; Fed-Ex money order for one week's rent. We hope to create/promote MentalAid, a national mental health telethon. Call for info. Luxury quality. SASE required; phone call preferred. 5/2/94

PRAG HOUSE

747 – 16th Avenue East
Seattle, WA 98112

(206)325-9848 / 623-7035

Prag House is Seattle's oldest collective household, operating continuously since July 1972. It is one of the communities within the Evergreen Land Trust [see Resource listing]. The house is owned by ELT and cannot be sold nor can any Prag House member sell any interest in the house. All decisions made within Prag are by consensus minus one, with the exception of adding a new member. All important decisions are made at monthly house meetings. We do not have an overall religious or political philosophy other than a toleration for each other's idiosyncrasies and a humanistic orientation to our outside activities. SASE required. [cc] 12/17/94 [83]

PRAIRIE RIDGE COMMUNITY

(Forming)
6119 Steinke Road
Fall Creek, WI 54742

(715)877-2611

Prairie Ridge Community is in the early stages of forming on 200 acres in west central Wisconsin, ten minutes from Eau Claire, a city with a population of 60,000. We value a strong commitment to a close-knit extended family-style community with an emphasis on fostering ecological stewardship of the land.

We hope to develop a community based on •Strong ecological values; sharing an overall respect for life, the land, and the rhythms of nature. •A commitment to equality, tolerance, flexibility, real world cultural and age diversity, and respect for individual differences. •Interdependent care for each other while respecting each other's privacy. •A desire to work out problems with honesty and openness while developing skill and enjoyment in the art of communication, group process, and consensus. •Sharing what we learn from cooperative living with the larger community. •Nurturing a recognition of the spiritual dimension underlying all our plans, activities, and interactions. •Our vision includes development of a land trust with joint ownership, individually owned energy-efficient homes arranged in clusters, sustainable agriculture, shared evening meals, regular meetings and gatherings, and land restoration projects.

We are looking for new members to share our vision, values, and venture. Please include SASE with inquiries. 7/29/93

PRUDENCE CRANDALL HOUSE

(Re-Forming)
Oakland, CA

(510)652-7600

The Prudence Crandall House is a long-term (20+ years for two of the original three), intergenerational (ages 7 to 77) collective house of three adults, one child, and three cats. We have different fields of work, with a mutual interest in each others' activities. What we share is deep concern for peace, ecology, feminism, and justice.

We own our lovely old 1908 house and garden, and each adult has a bedroom and a separate work room; we share the common spaces. We also share three meals every week, and some childcare. So we have both privacy and communal

cooperation.

Who is Prudence Crandall? A white teacher who, before the Civil War, enrolled black students in her school. The Massachusetts legislature passed a law making her school illegal. She continued her activities elsewhere, and is a role model. 3/14/94

PUMPKIN HOLLOW FARM

Route 1, Box 135
Craryville, NY 12521
(518)325-3583 / 325-7105

Pumpkin Hollow Farm was founded in 1937 to provide a peaceful, harmonious, natural setting in which the essential spirituality of the individual could thrive and be integrated into day-by-day relationships with others. This purpose stems from the theosophical principle that the way we live is the true key to what we are, as well as what we aspire to be.

We rejoice in the small pleasures of life. The atmosphere is intimate and friendly, and newcomers find it easy to become involved. Workshops and seminars are an important ingredient in an overall program of study, meditation, discussion, work, and relaxation. Everyone of "like-minded" spirit is invited to participate fully. We offer these adventures in learning every weekend from April to October. For personal retreats, midweek or longer stays are possible.

Pumpkin Hollow is operated by the spirit and hand of volunteerism. Both long- and short-term residents contribute in the areas of vegetarian cooking, office work and registration, housekeeping, gardening and landscaping, or general maintenance. The benefits are inviting: 130 acres of natural beauty, stimulating workshops and seminars, daily meditation practice, spiritual growth through giving, deep friendship, room, board, and living expenses. Applications and inquiries are welcome. 10/4/93

PURPLE ROSE

1531 Fulton Street
San Francisco, CA 94117

Purple Rose is an active collective household. We take our collectivity seriously—but we also enjoy our playtime together, and the closeness that the whole experience brings about.

Collectively owning our old Victorian house means freedom from landlord-imposed restrictions, but also more respon-

sibility for maintenance. (Two previous housemates are on the title as a matter of form, but they do not "own" the house.)

Most evenings we share family-style dinners (primarily vegetarian). We also value being very open and direct—talking a lot with each other in a very personal way, about very personal things. Some of this happens at our weekly house meetings.

Presently we have 10 members who can only be classified politically as independents—though we lean towards working for a better life for all people, not just a favored few. We are avid recyclers, do our best to maintain the planet, and use organic products when feasible. We feel we are working for the future in the present time. Please include SASE with inquiries. [cc] 12/8/93

QUAKER HOUSE RESIDENTIAL PROGRAM

(Re-Forming)
5615 S. Woodlawn Avenue
Chicago, IL 60637
(312)288-3066

The Residential Community at Quaker House (QHRP) is made up of women and men, students and working people—with various religious heritages and differing life goals. What we share in common is a desire to commit our lives to moral, purposeful action; to grow spiritually; and to seek ways of being of service to others. Most residents do volunteer work with public school kids.

Established by and under the care of the 57th Street Meeting of Friends in Chicago, QHRP is an opportunity for 8 or 9 people to live together in community for one or two years, sharing the facilities of a large 19-room house which is also the Quaker Meeting House. Residents exchange ideas, work together, encourage one another, and enjoy each other's company. A residential director gives assistance in planning and realizing such community-building activities as outings, study groups, work projects, service projects, and many fun times together. Group decisions are made using the Quaker principles of clearness and unity, though one needn't be a Quaker to live here.

Each resident has his/her own room, or

may choose to share with another resident. Quaker House takes care of food purchasing and dinner preparations (five days a week) in order that residents can devote more time and energy to individual and group activities, spiritual growth, and service. Residents are responsible for minor household chores; a housekeeper maintains most areas of the house. [cc] 10/8/93

QUAKERLAND

PO Box 592
Ingram TX 78025

An intentional community that expresses Quaker values of simplicity, friendliness to the environment, and a loving community with business conducted according to Friends' tradition. 10 households creating community to support spiritual growth and ecological sustainability. Meeting house completed on 142 acres in central Texas hill country, 1-1/2 hours from San Antonio. Community (nonprofit) ownership of land; private ownership of dwellings. Expected 20–40 households. SASE required. 5/5/94

QUARRY HILL

**P.O. Box 301
Rochester, VT 05767-0301**

(802)767-9881 (Msg.)

Quarry Hill, Vermont's oldest and largest alternative community, was founded in 1946 as an artists' retreat—Quarry Hill has been a haven for creative and open-minded people for 45 years. During the 1960s and 70s we experienced a surge in population and became a closely knit community, though not a planned, "intentional" one. Among the few rules: *absolutely no violence toward children*. We run a small private school. Folks generally make their own expenses, though members help each other out as necessary. Families typically eat on their own, with occasional potlucks.

We are always happy to meet energetic, nondogmatic, helpful people! Unfortunately, county zoning regulations have determined that our population is maxed out—so we can only take in new members at the rate that old members move out. Visitors are welcome! We have a small dormitory. Bring tents for summer camping (the best season for visits). Please write or call before planning a visit, and ask for our brochure. Small financial contribution requested, or work exchange if broke. SASE requested. [cc] 1/12/95

QUMBYA CO-OP

**5405 S. Ridgewood Court
Chicago, IL 60615**

**(312)643-8854 Haymarket Hse.
(312)667-5100 Bowers House**

Qumbya Co-op is a student housing group in Hyde Park, Chicago. It is composed of Haymarket House (est. 1989 and named for the Haymarket affair in Chicago, 1886) and Bowers House (est. 1991 and honoring a local co-op leader, Howard Bowers). We are a member of NASCO [see Resource listing]. Over half our members are students at local universities and colleges; the others work in a variety of jobs and pursuits. Besides living and eating together, and making decisions via house meetings and our Board, we collaborate on a variety of projects. These include gardening, home improvements, workshops on issues in group living, neighborhood involvement, music, home brewing, parties, outings, and supporting each other in our political activism, education, and personal growth. SASE required. 11/8/93

RAINBOW HEARTH SANCTUARY — NEIGHBORHOOD COMMUNITY ON LAKE BUCHANAN

**(Re-Forming)
HCR-5, Box 836
Burnet, TX 78611**

**(512)327-5633 Austin#
(512)756-7878 Land**

Rainbow Hearth Sanctuary is a center for a semi-intentional neighborhood community. Our research and educational focus is eco-spiritual, based on permaculture, interspecies communication, music and arts, wilderness experience, and life skills development.

Our 30-plus-acre neighborhood of private landholders is bordered by a large lake and enormous ranches recognized as critical for water quality and wildlife habitat. Most of our members are self-employed in areas including computers and technology transfer, holistic health, entertainment, writing, landscaping, and building. We combine simple lifestyles with high-tech capabilities. Our children are wise to the ways of nature and free to roam.

Interested persons may rent available rooms and houses and/or purchase their own lot(s). Rainbow Hearth offers a few select campsites and rooms in a closer community context and has developed

Before you ride off into the sunset...

Note that all community descriptions in this book have been written by the groups themselves, and are unverified by the *Directory* staff. Please take this into account when making travel plans, or when using this book to help decide where to live for the rest of your life!

a year-long Earth-keeper internship program of particular interest to committed college-age men and women desiring to explore powerful and effective alternatives to mainstream options. Spiritual/physical regeneration retreats also available. SASE inquiries welcome. [cc] 10/19/93

RAINBOW HOUSE

**1115 Tennessee
Lawrence, KS 66044**

(913)843-3704

The Rainbow House is a cooperative consisting of 10 women and men who are interested in using creative ideas to maintain a peaceful and enjoyable living situation. We share the responsibilities of the house's operation—from housework, to decision making on house policy. There is no manager and no leader. We are a group of equals working for ourselves and for each other.

We have a great old house in Lawrence, Kansas, which has a solar greenhouse and a huge organic garden plot. Everyone at the house has his/her own room; we share a living room, dining room, kitchen, bathrooms, and laundry. Although we require group interaction to function, the house is large enough to afford each person the privacy he/she needs.

House members devote some time each week to the house's operation. This includes a weekly house meeting, some housework, and an occasional fix-up project. We feel that the time spent is well worth the benefits of living in such a fun and enjoyable place. 1/9/93

RAINBOW JUNCTION

**(Forming)
P.O. Box 291
Adin, CA 96006**

Rainbow Junction, a community in rural NE California, puts a major emphasis on our personal spiritual evolution, but despite our spiritual orientation, we are without any one religious belief. Also of importance is nurturing a peaceful, loving attitude (Rainbow Consciousness) amongst ourselves. It is also important to us that we live free of drugs, alcohol, and violence. We are Rainbow Family-oriented and recognize the current New Age awareness and its positive implications for how we perceive and relate to ourselves, each other, and our environment.

The land is an excellent site for alternative energy implementation, and we are attempting to make full-scale use of this. We are pro eco-housing which includes a major focus on bus-homes. It is our feeling that their extreme affordability may help to provide a solution to urban homelessness.

Organic gardening and cottage industries are among our other interests, and we hope to eventually become largely self-sufficient. Other future community ventures will include alternative schooling for children that they may grow and learn in an unstructured environment. We hope to someday be able to provide food for groups feeding homeless and poor people, and baked or cottage industry-crafted goods for urban alternative co-ops. Inquiries welcome. SASE requested. 4/30/92

RAINBOW VALLEY AGRICULTURAL COOPERATIVE

(Re-Forming)
Route 2, Box 28
Sanger, TX 76266
(817)458-0253

We are an alternate lifestyle/appropriate technology type of community, structured as an agricultural cooperative occupying a 224-acre valley east of Sanger, Texas. All members hold in common about 120 acres of bottom land, creeks, plains, and deep woods. The remaining 90–95 acres are divided into homesites ranging in size from 1 acre to 4 acres. There are a dozen owner-built structures on our land—a few wooden homes, but mostly earth-sheltered ferro-cement domes. We have our own well, and water is available from our own water cooperative. Telephone lines have been brought into the valley (underground) but no power lines. Our goal is to be a totally energy self-sufficient community. Our charter prohibits connections to the nuclear grid. Each member is responsible for his/her own power needs (photovoltaics, wind generators, or gasoline-powered generators).

We want to enable individual freedom, privacy, and self-determination to the greatest extent possible. At the same time we intend to create a community of cooperative work and play. We are looking for new members—not unannounced "drop-in" visitors—but serious, mature persons who want to join as equal members in our community. Mail

inquiries only, and please include SASE. 1/9/95

RAJ-YOGA MATH AND RETREAT
NEW NAME:
HOLY FIRE HERMITAGE

Deming, WA

(COMMUNITY LISTING REMOVED)

Lost contact. 4/10/96

RAPHA COMMUNITY

(Non-Residential)
c/o Julia Ketcham
1420 Salt Springs Road
Syracuse, NY 13214
(315)449-9627

Rapha (from the Hebrew word for healing) began in the late '60s as a small ecumenical house church. We are non-residential with shared volunteer rotating leadership, and make decisions by consensus. We are incorporated as a nonprofit tax-exempt service organization. We are committed to each other to be a caring extended family as we make the spiritual journey together. This sacred work has led us from our Judeo-Christian beginnings, to increasing openness to all spiritual paths, to a planetary consciousness.

We live out our vision by trying to be honest and faithful with each other, and by trying to learn healthy conflict resolution and forgiveness when we fail each other. We weep and we celebrate together. We try to evoke in each other true calling by worshiping together, by going on weekend retreats, by shared meals, recreation, service projects, and study. We meet once a month for worship and divide into small groups called cells which usually meet every two weeks. Some recent cells are a dream interpretation group, a group to enhance spirituality, a group to encourage body awareness and movement, a massage group, a women's group, a men's group, a group making a quilt to be used when any of us are sick, and a group about ecology. Please include SASE with inquiries. [cc] 10/5/93

RAVEN ROCKS

Southeastern Ohio

Raven Rocks, est. 1970, is a small rural project in the northern edge of Ohio Appalachia. It is a community of purpose, brought together and held together by

common values and goals which have found focus in the effort to pay for, restore, and set aside for permanent preservation more than 1000 acres of hill and ravine lands. The original environmental concern—to rescue the property from strip mining for coal—has grown to include a variety of member-financed projects, including several structures above and underground, that utilize a wide range of conservation techniques and solar strategies. The larger of two underground buildings was designed for public demonstration, and will incorporate seven solar strategies in one structure. Also part of this demonstration will be a biointensive garden. All agricultural projects—including our Christmas tree operation, grass-fed cattle, and gardens at all the homes—have been organic since the initial purchase. Most of our acreage has been set aside for natural restoration of the hardwood forest native to the area. The entire property, including the homes and other improvements, is designed as permanent preserve, and hence not available for sale or development.

Ten of 11 current members are from the original group of 19. Members earn their own livings, then volunteer the time required (about 7000 hours annually) to raise Christmas trees that pay for the land, and to do the work of the corporation, which was set up as legal owner.

Education—or re-education, for those of us who are adults—has been a fundamental interest of this group. Most of our efforts, therefore, have had an educational intent—whether to educate ourselves or others. We are striving to get more of our multifaceted public statement and demonstration in place, and fear that the effort could be jeopardized by too much premature publicity and traffic. Hence, for the immediate future we are withholding phone number and information about location. 4/23/94

R.E.A.C.H. COMMUNITY

(Forming)
P.O. Box 1041
Taos, NM 87571
(505)751-0462

This prototype Earthship community is perched on 55 acres of mountainside near Taos Ski Valley. All homes are completely independent of municipal power, water, and sewage—using instead photovoltaic systems, catch-water systems, and composting toilets. As described in the books

Earthship (Volumes I, II, and III) by Michael Reynolds, these are passive-solar, rammed-earth structures that can be owner-built from recycled materials.

Earthship communities allow members to build on land owned in common—for a much smaller investment than purchasing land individually. Primarily residential, the REACH community intends to share studio space, a laundromat, and meeting room. Building an Earthship stops the train of consumption; it demands nothing from the planet and cuts the owner's living expenses down to almost nothing. Here and in other Earthship communities, the members will have time to be neighbors. Currently we are builders, architects, actors, artists, musicians, and therapists age 0–70. Clients live among the service providers. [See separate listing for sister community "STAR."] 11/11/93

REBA PLACE FELLOWSHIP

727 Reba Place
Evanston, IL 60202

(847)328-6066 (8am–5pm)
(847)475-8715

Reba Place Fellowship was established in 1957 in Evanston, Illinois, just north of Chicago. Our basis for membership is that this is a Christian lay community: we support each other, and those in need, in all aspects of living a "whole" life. We are associated with both the Mennonite Church and the Church of the Brethren, although in practice we are ecumenical.

We have about 60 adult members and 35 children living in the Fellowship's 40 residences. This includes both families and singles, with some shared living households. Our diet varies from one subgroup to the next, with a majority being vegetarians. We practice total income sharing at the community level. Some members have outside careers, but their income goes into the common fund.

Ministries include shelter for the home-less, work with refugees from Cambodia and Central America, low-income housing, many types of personal counseling, a peace witness program, and others.

Anyone who embraces this lifestyle and wants to participate is welcome. Please write if you'd like more information. Written inquiries preferred. 10/13/92

RECREATION CENTER

Pahoa, HI

(COMMUNITY LISTING REMOVED)

Focus has shifted to doing business enterprises; no longer doing the community aspect. 2/27/96

RED MOUNTAIN

(Forming)
Route 1, Box 140
Crowley Lake, CA 93546

(619)935-4560/935-4590 Fax

Red Mountain is seeking members who wish to live close to wilderness and who are interested in personal and spiritual growth. We are at 7000 ft. elevation, within walking distance of the John Muir Wilderness and near hot springs and skiing. We have from time to time hosted classes on Native American spirituality and Yoga, and informal get-togethers for people interested in spirituality.

Most of the land here is owned by the Forest Service or other government agencies, and is reserved for open space. We have one acre, bounded on two sides by open space land. Accommodations include a number of one-bedroom apartments and a house with large kitchen and meeting room. Organic food is delivered monthly by Mountain People's Warehouse.

Members are responsible for their own incomes and for rent on or purchase of their living spaces. There is currently no communal business, however the community founder has business experience and is interested in supporting members in business efforts. Also, some employment is available in the nearby resort town of Mammoth Lakes. Call or write to arrange a visit. 3/21/94

REEVIS MOUNTAIN SCHOOL OF SELF-RELIANCE

HC02, Box 1534
Roosevelt, AZ 85545

(520)467-2536 (msg.)

We are a spiritually oriented, self-reliant, wholesome natural foods farm family; we grow our own fruits and vegetables. We share a common vision in the awakening of our Eternal Divinity. The awakening is learning about and bringing forth our unlimited Divine Self. We live what we love and follow a path of joy!

Our land is located in a remote high desert riparian valley at 3400 ft. elevation surrounded on three sides by the Superstition Wilderness mountains over 5000 ft. high, approximately 15 miles south of Roosevelt Lake.

In our rustic lifestyle we offer a three-month work exchange program where participants join in our daily activities such as meditation, inspirational readings, singing, organic gardening, orchard, general farm activities, herb processing, healthful food prep, learning and using healing techniques, etc. An important aspect of our being together is that we are mutually enriching to each other's lives. The work exchange rate here is $15 a day for the first 20 days. Send for an application.

We wildcraft herbs for our herbal remedies cottage industry. Send for tincture catalog.

The sanctuary of the mountain setting offers a quiet retreat. As a retreat guest, stay in one of our yurt-type dwellings for $30 a day, or bring your own tent for $20 a day (includes meals).

We operate Reevis Mt. School which offers classes in a variety of self-reliant skills such as natural healing, plant identification, meditation, fasting, stone masonry, T'ai Chi, land navigation, aboriginal skills, and wilderness emergency training. Write for brochure of class schedule. Include $1 for mailing requests. 6/7/92

REFUGIO DEL RIO GRANDE

402 E. Harrison, 2nd Floor
Harlingen, TX 78550

(210)421-3226 Voice/Fax

Refugio Del Rio Grande is a blending of different cultural, religious, and spiritual traditions. It was organized as a refugee camp to provide hospitality for the flood of Central Americans in the 1980s, using land initially intended for an agricultural cooperative based on traditional farming methods. We seek self-reliance, and hope to broaden the permanent community to incorporate younger members and families (particularly those with children) so that Refugio may extend its vision into the future while remaining grounded in the values of our ancestors, martyrs, and mentors—particularly those who have made great sacrifices in the eternal struggles for justice, and peace. 1/13/95

REINA DEL CIELO

Route 4, Box 123
Lexington, VA 24450

Reina del Cielo (Queen of Heaven), was founded in 1972 in Louisiana. Our community now numbers 15 adults, including 5 ministers, and 10 children. Reina del Cielo was established to provide a spiritual atmosphere for the study of ancient wisdom as revealed through the Una Kenya Mystery School...a continuation of the ancient wisdom as brought to Earth by the sons of God. It has continued through the ages in a direct link through its initiates who are keepers of the ark of the covenant. While the community has always been open to public view, the School itself operated under the hermetic seal of silence until 1988. Now we feel that contact with other groups is an important part of our mission, so we offer lectures and classes to the public.

Our community is a living experiment where families live, work, and pray together. We govern ourselves by a board of officers, elected from among our Church organization, serving under the guidance of our Minister and Church Board. Our whole structure is based upon "Love is the fulfilling of the Law." We study the ancient scriptures and teachings of all ages and cultures. We follow the teachings of the Christ, and work toward the day when that Love will manifest throughout the Earth. SASE requested with inquiries. [cc] 12/18/94

REJENNERATION HOUSE

(Forming)
Box 42
Jenner, CA 95450
(707)632-5458

ReJenneration is a family village cluster now forming on 5 knolltop acres in an ecologically diverse canyon on the Sonoma coast less than two hours from San Francisco. Our current plans include two or three buildings in which to live and work, and developing ample garden space. The first building has been completed so we have immediate openings for a couple of energetic and creative folks ready to further the dream. We are looking for a final total of 5–8 partners with a long-term vision of shared ownership.

Values will be clarified as the group evolves; therefore, our Chart info (page 204) roughly represents where we are going. Values now include simplicity; shared meals; Earth stewardship; respect for biological, cultural, age, and spiritual diversity; hard work; and a healthy, balanced lifestyle. We have long-term goals of becoming a sanctuary for our urban-dwelling friends, who can use our nearby variety of eco-systems to regenerate their personal spirit and connection with the planet. Please send SASE and a brief personal history. If you include a phone number, we may call. 10/18/93

REMAR

917 S. Western Avenue
Chicago, IL 60612
(312)243-3304/243-2317
(312)243-3406 Fax

Remar is an international Christian outreach ministry born in Vitoria, Spain, 12 years ago, with the purpose, given by God, to provide free help to all kinds of people in need—including drug addicts, alcoholics, homeless people, etc. We've found ways to get them off all drugs (including smoking) and into family life and cooperative businesses. Remar now has communities in 21 countries: Spain, Portugal, Germany, Switzerland, Austria, U.K., U.S.A., Brazil, Ecuador, Mexico, Guatemala, El Salvador, Nicaragua, Peru, Argentina, Costa Rica, Chile, Ivory Coast, Ghana, and Burkina Fasso. No one in Remar receives any kind of payment; all work is voluntary for God and His glory.

Remar receives no outside financial support, and is free to all people who come here for help. Our ministry is supported by our business (thrift stores), our own work, and donations. In Illinois we have three thrift stores in Chicago, and four homes with a population of 50 that includes couples, children, men, and women. We also have centers in Racine, WI, and in Laredo and Austin, TX. Our vision is to expand and develop the work throughout the U.S., giving homes to more people in need, and providing them with the opportunity to change their lives through the power of God. 1/12/95

RENAISSANCE COMMUNITY

Turners Falls, MA

No longer a community—evolved into a cooperative neighborhood and is not looking for new members. 4/19/96 [41, 53]

RIVENDELL COOPERATIVE

**731 West Genesee
Lansing, MI 48915**

(517)485-6520

Rivendell is a seven-person vegetarian cooperative in an older neighborhood of Lansing. A mixture of students and non-students of different ages, we are concerned about such issues as the environment, peace and justice, local community, etc., and attempt to provide a non-sexist, non-racist, egalitarian, and low-cost household in line with these values. Our food is purchased in bulk, providing healthy meals at a low cost. House decisions are made by consensus. We share a willingness to work out problems in the open, and to give up some privacy. Members each have about 10 hours of jobs each month. We have a variety of links

with local peace and justice and folk music communities. Openings occur randomly; current monthly charges are $215. 5/2/92

RIVER CITY HOUSING COLLECTIVE

**802 E. Washington Street
Iowa City, IA 52240**

**(319)337-4733 Anomy House
(319)337-8445 Kazan House**

Our goal is to provide quality housing for the community at a cost below the Iowa City market average. Quality housing includes good maintenance, caring landlords (ourselves), and a healthy social environment. We keep our costs low by requiring each member of the collective to do a minimum of sixteen hours of work per month (eight hours are for the overall collective which includes committee work, board meetings, and maintenance; the other eight hours are for the house in which you live). House hours include cleaning, cooking, and house meetings. Each house buys food as a unit, saving money with quality and quantity purchases. Nightly communal meals are served and each member cooks in the rotation. Members learn management, cooking, maintenance, and communication skills—as well as a sense of living in community/cooperation with a diverse group of people. Members provide the ideas, guidance, support, and energy to make the collective work. People often join the co-op for the economy, but stay for the community. [cc] 1/10/93

RIVER COMMUNITY HOMES

**1061 Hallen Drive
Arcata, CA 95521**

(707)822-7816

The River Community Homes Co-op consists of six townhouse apartments, one large community room, an office, and shared laundry facilities. Members are predominantly single moms and their children. We have a large children's playground, and a year-round children's program that includes crafts, video nights, and dance nights. Videos are also available free to members.

The co-op is near a bus stop in a rural area surrounded by farms, a freeway, and other apartments in a low-to-moderate income area. Our resources include a large composting area for member families. The co-op is self-managed ("directed management") and was built from the

ground up as a local economic development project. Please enclose SASE with inquiries. 9/13/94

RIVER FARM

**3231 Hillside Road
Deming, WA 98244**

(360)592-5222

We live in the Pacific Cascadia bioregion in the northwest corner of the United States, and are one of the five communities in the Evergreen Land Trust [see description in Resources section]. Eight adults and three young people live here, and there is some turnover.

Our community is maintaining protected wildlife areas; practicing organic, ecologically sensitive farming; and acting as an educational source for the community and each other. Our farm is a mixture of forest, gardens, and fields. We also have sensitive areas of marsh and streams, a good size river, and mountainside.

We value independence and practical homesteading. We help each other with living, and work to improve our communication skills. We are open to written correspondence, and endeavor to network with similar folks—especially those battling clearcuts near your land, as we are. Summer intern positions possible. Please, mail inquiries only. [cc] 12/17/94

RIVERSIDE COMMUNITY COOPERATIVE

**(Forming)
Route 2, Box 229-A
Colfax, WI 54730**

(612)632-2527 / 729-5001

We are a group of individuals who want to create an environment which will facilitate the growth and health of ourselves and our children while minimizing our impact on the land and the life present on that land. At present we are six adults (ages 24–45) and two children (ages 5 and 7). We are in the process of forming, and anticipate growing until we eventually reach a maximum of about 25 adult members.

Our vision includes a clustered cohousing development with small energy-efficient homes; a common house for meetings, social gatherings, community meals, childcare, guest rooms, laundry facilities, etc.; and lots of room for play and growth. We welcome visitors, but you should call first: Sarah Proechel or Rick Bensman at (715)632-2527, or Charlie Borden or Richelle Schenfeld at (612)729-5001. Please include SASE with correspondence. 7/5/93

ROCKY MOUNTAIN DHARMA CENTER

4921 County Road 68-C
Red Feather Lakes
CO 80545
(970)881-2184

Rocky Mountain Dharma Center is a contemplative center founded in 1971 by Chogyam Trungpa Rinpoche. It is a mountain retreat for the practice of Tibetan Buddhism, the secular path of Shambhala, and other contemplative traditions. RMDC hosts programs based on meditative practices year round, with large summer programs for hundreds of people. The RMDC staff lives on 500 acres all year and has a close-knit sense of community based on shared values of contemplative life.

We work regularly on group process with a vision of creating a functional enlightened society that can accommodate many more people than our current staff of 39. We are planning to begin construction of a large facility to house up to 450 people year-round, supporting programs up to 3 months long. Under the leadership of Osel Rangdrol Mukpo, RMDC is dedicated to propagating the vision of enlightened society both within RMDC and in the world at large. Inquiries are welcome. SASE required. [cc] 3/29/93

ROSY BRANCH FARM

320 Stone Mountain Road
Black Mountain, NC 28711
(704)669-4625

Rosy Branch Farm is a neo-indigenous forest community with an interest in ancient cultures and permaculture. Begun in '85, we originally came together through a meditation group with ecological and spiritual interests. We currently have 6 families living on the land (50 acres) with at least one more to come. We are not actively seeking new members, but we're into cooperation and sharing information—including labor exchange, trading visits, etc.

We're into what might be called high-tech simple living—fairly affluent, but downwardly mobile in a substantial sense. Economically each family is fairly

independent, though we're developing right livelihood at the community level. We have created a nonprofit project called Good Medicine which works to raise awareness of the large population of Mayan people in Guatemala and Mexico. We believe that indigenous values are valuable to the Earth—there's a lot for our culture to learn about living within the limits of our resources. We arrange periodic trips to their region, help the weavers sell their goods, and publish a quarterly newsletter called *Maya Time*. Community and cooperation are very helpful in pursuing this work. [cc] 8/14/93

ROWANWOOD CONSERVER SOCIETY

RR2, Oro Station
Ontario L0L-2E0
CANADA
(705)835-2674

Rowanwood is a residential cooperative community on 92 rolling acres in rural Ontario. We're here because we enjoy doing things together, and spending time in each other's company. We share a commitment to conservation, to steward our farm, to be an extended family, to care for each other, and to share our learnings in cooperative living.

Member families live in individually built houses on one-acre sites owned by the cooperative. Our membership meets twice monthly for business, making decisions by consensus, and once for a potluck supper. Other committees (e.g., finance, conserver) meet as necessary. Each member shares in the work of the community—contributing as individuals, in small teams, and at community work parties. Children are

encouraged to participate in the work as well.

Relationships are characterized by respect for individual differences, trust, clearness, and openness. We value personal and family privacy, and a sense of humor. We acknowledge and respect a variety of spiritual values and motivations, and recognize that the spiritual dimension of our community is fundamental to what we do and how we do it. If you write, a SASE would be appreciated. [cc] 9/11/92

ROWE CAMP & CONFERENCE CENTER

King's Highway Road
Rowe, MA 01367
(413)339-4954

We are a small community, founded in 1974, committed to offering weekend retreats, and a summer camp for teenagers [see Resource listing]. Members of our "intentional community" are here to do that work first (160+ hours each month)...living as a loose-knit community comes second. We are also affiliated with the Unitarian Universalist Association. Visitors are welcome, but they must pay and/or work. [cc] 4/19/93 [85]

RUDOLF STEINER FELLOWSHIP COMMUNITY

241 Hungry Hollow Road
Spring Valley, NY 10977
(914)356-8494

We are an intergenerational care community centered around the care of the elderly but taking up the care of handicapped young adults—children in need of special help and one another. Our care extends to the land, animals, and objects we are responsible for. We are very hard working, seeking to incorporate ideas from the spiritual world into our daily life rather than merely talking about them. Our impulses come from the work of Dr. Rudolf Steiner.

We live a rural type existence in an urban setting, and have a varied life. We support ourselves through social, therapeutic, and educational efforts such as our medical practice, biodynamic farming, metal shop, wood shop, candle shop, gift shop, print shop, weavery, and pottery as well as our care activities. We do most of our own small building and maintenance work. We have a child's garden for our preschoolers, and our children attend the local Waldorf School. We have a rich study and cultural life. Music and art are emphasized.

Our spiritual ideas permeate our community organization, economics, work activities, education, and cultural life. We are open to new co-workers who have at least an interest in learning more about Rudolf Steiner, want a full and varied life and who are unafraid of hard work—inner and outer—in the service of others. We welcome inquiries and prearranged work-along visits. 5/5/92

SAINT BENEDICT'S FARM

P.O. Box 366
Waelder, TX 78959
(210)540-4814

St. Benedict's Farm was founded in 1956 as a lay Christian community, based on the Rule of St. Benedict—the first word of which is "Listen." We are fervent Catholics, though not "officially" sponsored by the church. Presently we are three men and two women.

Our family is *monastic*, that is, concerned with our day-to-day living and growing together toward God. Our lifestyle includes poverty, celibacy, simplicity, obedience, prayer, study, work, and worship. We have a lot of concern for the substance of monasticism, but very little for its forms—thus it is difficult for some to see our life as really being monastic. We earn our living by running a photography business, a beef cattle breeding operation, and a recording studio. We believe strongly in self-support, and in the idea of working together as a family at whatever we do to earn a living. No special skills are required, only willingness to contribute whatever one can. Our dress is simple and uniform—made of blue denim. In our daily life we operate largely on consensus and consultation, though we have an abbot as our teacher and primary decision maker. We are open to new members who are willing to make a wholehearted dedication, without reservation. 8/8/93

SAINT FRANCIS COMMUNITY

P.O. Box 10
Orland, ME 04472
(207)469-7961

Member Emmaus International, we are from every walk of life. We work as volunteers at H.O.M.E., a producers' cooperative including stores, learning center, shelters, gardens, land trust, home building, job training, and more. We try to follow four steps: 1) help those in need; 2) teach skills so people can learn to help themselves; 3) help in ways that build community rather than individuals; 4) work to overturn systems of oppression.

We homestead on 80 acres of rocky soil, raising draft horses and teaching others how to use them. We practice sustainable development, build our houses with used material, try to live simply so others can simply live. At the height of Reagan's war on Central America, we joined the underground railroad and each month brought several refugee families from Florida, helping them relocate in Canada. Several of them stayed with us. One of our dwellings, the Inn, now has electricity and running water. Most have electricity. We meet for breakfast together and have community dinner two nights a week. On Saturdays we work together with the draft horses, harvesting our winter fuel, gardening, building. As our refugee families struggle to learn English, others of us struggle to learn Spanish. SASE requested. 6/9/93

SAINT FRANCIS & THERESE CATHOLIC WORKER HOUSE

52 Mason Street
Worcester, MA 01610
(508)753-3588

Left-wing Catholics in the tradition of the Catholic Workers, focused on peace and justice work. Presently 4 adults and 3 children sharing all income and most dinners (vegetarian). The property is owned by a community land trust. Open to visitors and more adult members, especially women. [cc] 6/20/94

SAINT HERMAN OF ALASKA MONASTERY

(Forming)
Beegum Gorge Road
Platina, CA 96076

A missionary brotherhood devoted to living and disseminating the traditional Eastern Orthodox way of life. Our monastery, located in a wooded isolated area of northern California, offers a secluded and austere life for men only. [Women who are interested in traditional Orthodox monasticism are encouraged to contact a nearby affiliate, the St. Xenia Skete, P.O. Box 200, Wildwood, CA 96076-9702.] Visitors of both sexes are welcome at our monastery, and are expected to participate in the demanding cycle of daily church services, as well as to offer their labor when needed.

We have little to offer those seeking intentional or spiritual community, and we encourage only the deadly serious to stay. Our sole restitution in this world consists in seeing lives touched and transformed as a result of the self-sacrifice attendant on the monastery's overall goal of making available in print (books, magazines, pamphlets, etc.) the centuries-old wisdom of Christian Spirituality. However, even this we do not expect, having given up houses, brethren, wife, and children for the only sure reward, "in the world to come, life everlasting." (Luke 18:30) For something totally different, pay us a visit. For transformation of life culminating in death to this world, and the abiding desire for the Kingdom to come, come to live and struggle together with us. [cc] 7/13/92

SAINT JOHN'S ORDER

(Re-Forming)
642 Myrtle Ave
San Francisco CA 94080
(415)615-9529/255-9225

St. John's Order is a religious community founded in the late 1960s by Bishop Dr. Ajari Pemchekov. He descended from the Russian Lamaist tradition and Russian Old Believers of Siberia, a unique place where various religious traditions merged and were assimilated, i.e., Christianity, Shamanism, and Buddhism.

Being a charismatic man of profound religious experience, knowledge, and vision, he sought to plant the seeds of esoteric Dharma in the West, reconciling those teachings with people's Christian background. He assimilated and synthesized teachings from Christianity with those of Tibet and Japan through his own spiritual practice. He brought religious students together to live in a community where they can study and practice the Dharma.

The Tibetan teachings are readily available here in the West, but Japanese esotericism has rarely been taught. Our community provides a unique opportunity for people to study both. Meditation, recitation of Sutras, and participation in pujas and services are open to the public.

Two sisters of the Order, longtime students of Bishop Dr. Ajari, provide community leadership and continue to hand down his teachings to others. Community members participate in maintaining the large community residence, in feeding the poor, visiting the elderly, and doing devotional service.

We welcome new members who would live in our community in order to experience and study the Dharma, sharing the joys of religious communal life. Ours is a vegetarian, non-alcoholic, drug-free community. 9/17/94

SALT SPRING CENTRE

355 Blackburn Rd
Salt Spring Island BC V8K 2B8
CANADA
(604)537-2326

Salt Spring Centre is a spiritual community based on the principles and practice of Ashtanga Yoga, the eight-limbed Yoga path. This includes the practice of ethical principles, yoga postures, breathing exercises, and meditation. We are blessed to have the guidance of a living master, Baba Hari Dass of Mt. Madonna.

In addition to our spiritual practice we have an alternative school with about 24 children, and a large garden with fruit orchard, vegetables, flowers, culinary and medicinal herbs. We also provide week and weekend programs for individuals and groups, and offer various types of healing treatments such as massage, reflexology, sauna, and herbal steambox.

Presently our community is made up of 7 adults and 4 children, as well as an "extended family" of contributors throughout the island community. All the adults who live at the community make regular work and financial contributions to the centre, and we are currently looking at expanding our cottage industry potential. Members contribute approximately 140 hours per month, and $150 per person. We are vegetarian, and try to maintain a balanced and wholesome lifestyle, living a nonviolent and simple life. We welcome visitors, guests, and potential community members...though we advise

people who might be interested in joining our community that it is based on Yoga and selfless service—and consequently requires a substantial commitment. SASE requested. 4/23/92

SANDHILL FARM

Route 1, Box 155-CD
Rutledge, MO 63563
(816)883-5543

Sandhill Farm is a small communal farm located in NE Missouri. We currently number 8 adults and 3 children. We grow most of our food on our 135 acres; the land is woods, hay ground, row crops, pasture, and land-in-recovery. We plant large organic gardens and enjoy the fruits of our orchard. We also produce organic foods for sale, including sorghum, honey, tempeh, and garlic.

We tend to work hard, especially during the growing season. We get satisfaction from practicing self-sufficiency —processing food, maintaining the farm, homeschooling, healing at home. We like to keep our lifestyle simple and healthy for ourselves and the planet.

We share meals, income, vehicles, and recreation. We try to be accepting and supportive of individual interests and needs. Equality, nonviolence, and honesty are values we share. We hold meetings several days a week to discuss issues and make decisions by consensus. We are involved in local affairs—recycling, community theater, hospice work. Sandhill is active in both the Federation of Egalitarian Communities and the Fellowship for Intentional Community.

We welcome visitors most times of the year, and appreciate extra hands during our growing season—especially our sorghum harvest (Sept-Oct). Please write to introduce yourself to us and to arrange a visit. Visitors are welcome for up to 1 week, with extension possible. 2/14/95 [73, 83, 85]

SANDY BAR RANCH

(Forming)
P.O. Box 347
Orleans, CA 95556
(916)627-3379

Once a Karuk Native American settlement, Sandy Bar Ranch is nestled in a beautiful valley carved out by the Klamath River in the heart of the Six Rivers National Forest. We are a collective enterprise using consensus decision making dedicated to stewardship of the land.

Our focus is to be another healing spot in the global network. Our vision as we learn and teach about our bioregion, is to engage in a constructive dialog with all sectors of society to develop ways of living with and on the Earth without destroying it. We have a conference and retreat center on the Klamath River, and an organic garden and fruit tree nursery. Our goal is to create a sense of community amongst all people. [cc] 9/24/94

SANTA ROSA CREEK COMMONS

887 Sonoma Avenue
Santa Rosa, CA 95404
(707)523-0626

A limited equity housing cooperative for all ages, located on 2 acres near central Santa Rosa, fifty miles north of San Francisco. We have 27 units, a community room, laundry facilities, and a wooded area on the creek. We hold three shared values: a desire to live cooperatively, environmental awareness (edible landscaping, composting, energy efficiency, recycling), and nonviolence (including conflict resolution and concern for peace and harmony in our community).

Members of the co-op decide community matters through a consensus process. Residents serve on committees, and are responsible for managing and maintaining the property. All members participate in an ongoing educational program about the principles and practices of cooperative living, and we enjoy many shared social events such as holiday celebrations, play days, monthly shared meals, book discussions, autobiography sharing, and other activities initiated by members.

Members purchase shares, based on the size of the unit occupied, at the time of occupancy. We reserve ten shares for low-income members ($800 to $2,500); unassisted shares are $8,100 to $12,000. We pro-rate the monthly carrying charges to meet expenses. Applications are being received for future occupancy. 8/2/94

SASSAFRAS RIDGE FARM

Buck Route, Box 350
Hinton, WV 25951

Sassafras Ridge Farm is a community of several households with adults in their 30s–40s, and 8 children. Households are each autonomous and privately owned.

Visitors only; no memberships open.

The farm consists of 240 acres of mountains and valleys, including 20 in hay, 40 in pasture, woods, several creeks, two ponds, and a clean, canoeable river nearby. Activities include gardening, animal care, fencing, firewood, construction.... Households and childcare are based on equal access and responsibility. We celebrate the Earth holidays, and offer religious freedom of choice. Within this community, one or two households are willing to trade accommodations and meals for a few hours of labor daily. Again: visitor prearrangements must be made in writing; no memberships open. We suggest initial visit of 2–5 days. Please include SASE. 6/10/92

SEADS OF TRUTH, INC.

(Forming)
P.O. Box 192
Harrington, ME 04643
(207)483-9763

"Solar Energy Awareness Demonstration Seminars" is a not-for-profit group establishing a "self-sufficient" alternative energy community and seminar center on 60 acres in rural Maine. We are using a community land trust model, and stress voluntary cooperation and mutual aid—working with others, using group concensus, and sharing. Families will have their own living space (bedrooms, kitchen, bath) and share "common" space, greenhouse, and independent electricity. We're still in the formative stages. Please write or call. SASE requested. 8/17/92

SEEDS OF PEACE

P.O. Box 31076
Flagstaff, AZ 86003-1076
(520)774-3645

Seeds of Peace is an activist collective, recently relocated on 40 acres outside of Flagstaff, Arizona. Since 1986, we have provided logistical and organizing support for groups of people acting on their principles to bring justice and sustainability to our world. We share income, and members participate in both our political work and our home life. Consensus process is used for decision making, and we are open to new members who share our commitment to creating the world we want to live in.

Currently we are supporting Native American land sovereignty rights efforts, as well as ongoing work with forestry,

homelessness, AIDS, first amendment, and ecological awareness activists. We are a 501(c)3 educational organization, and are using the land base to set up an ongoing educational center with permaculture and dry crop farming, sustainable energy systems, and training in cooperative social structures. On the land we are using converted buses for housing, with a commitment to build/convert more space as people come. Water catchment and our 1000-gallon trailer provide water, and solar power provides electricity. Write to arrange a one-week visit, well in advance. A message phone is answered in town. 1/27/95 [83]

SEVEN SPRINGS FARM

Route 1, Box 95-D
Mountain Grove, MO 65711

Seven Springs is an intentional community with a 20-year history. We each hold the deed to a five-acre parcel, and hold the balance of our 120 acres in common. Our community is nestled in the Missouri Ozarks Mountains approximately 80 miles from Springfield. Currently our population consists of a mixture of single and family households—with ages ranging from teenagers to 53. We support ourselves through outside employment. We are bound together by our philosophy of ecological land stewardship and our choice to live in community. We have no other underlying philosophy. We are not presently seeking new members. 4/23/92 [22]

SEVEN WAVES

(Forming)
P.O. Box 3308
Central Point, OR 97502
(503)826-2853

[Formerly listed as Seven C's Inter-Networking Cohousing Estate in Medford, Oregon] Seeking committed (people need people) relationships, honesty, compatibility, self-trusting, fidelity. Shared practical ideas; visions building values to induce a healthy life, co-expand self-skills, exchanging beneficial rich intra-family friendships. We offer our land for cultivation of the soil (stewardship of land trust/certificate to new units of one's own); the driving force of our wishes is to expand our intentional rural ranch, share, love-better family, quality of life, joy that comes from reaching out to others in equality of like-minded souls,

with efforts of persons with a serious interest in self-reliance. We have two ranches in a picturesque river valley, on 100 acres of rural green oasis, a tall forest-like dude ranch paradise. It's real, living freedom...love it.

We seek similar friendships. We neither smoke, nor drink, nor do drugs—and ideally want to find personal inter-fulfillment. Looking to share our ranch home site with stable, mature, self-sustainable single mothers, fathers, or couple(s). Age, race, no obstacle. Seeking person(s) as family who has respect for him/herself and others (habits very "important" to us!!) and who are responsible and into the pursuit of sharing dreams. Idealistic personal heterosexual growth goals; wholesomeness tuned with others (believers) of nuclear or historic intentional lifestyle welcomed. Please include photos and informed introduction, and include SASE. 1/26/93

SHANNON FARM

Route 2, Box 343
Afton, VA 22920
(804)361-1417

Shannon is currently home to over 60 adults who range in age from the 20s to the 70s, and over 20 children from infants to teens. We share 520 rural acres at the base of the Blue Ridge Mountains, 27 miles west of Charlottesville.

No belief system or common focus has defined our community since its founding in 1974. Minimalist and middle-class lifestyles coexist, and we share a belief in the inherent worth and dignity of all, regardless of gender, race, age, sexual orientation, financial resources, property, or income. While committed to our intentional group, we remain connected to the larger society through our jobs, friendships, and individual interests.

Making community decisions by consensus tends to heighten our awareness of the skills required to resolve differences. We reserve the option of deciding issues by a 60% majority vote, although we have done that only once, 18 years ago.

The land and all buildings are owned by the community, though members finance their own homes and hold long-term leases on the completed structures. So far, 27 houses for individuals or families, 3 group houses, and several small cabins have been built. We also have farm buildings, a large cabinet shop complex, and an area for small industry. Our homes are situated in clusters, one of which is exclusively solar powered. Membership does not require a capital investment. The community is financed through monthly dues: 5% of after tax income from provisional members and 7% from full members.

Over half of us commute to work. Members support themselves by woodworking, teaching, health care, computer programming and sales, counseling, food and domestic services, management, insurance, construction and home renovation, and landscaping. Agricultural pursuits include CSA and individual gardens, an orchard, a vineyard, and berry patches. A few members care for their own farm animals and manage our large hay fields.

After an initial visit, people who wish to explore Shannon further are responsible for finding their own housing and livelihood while they get to know us. Shannon does not have a common kitchen, or apprenticeship opportunities. We are not set up to provide long stays for visitors, nor do we design our on-going community work projects specifically for visitor involvement. For more information, please send a SASE to Visitor Coordinator, Shannon Farm. 1/16/96 [77(D), 82, 83]

SHARINGWOOD

**22020 East Lost Lake Road
Snohomish, WA 98290**

(206)788-5585/487-1074

Sharingwood is a cohousing community on 38 forested acres. We have built 11 houses out of 30, and have 25 adults and 10 kids. Members are economically self supporting. The first phase is a neighborhood cul-de-sac full of kids playing and people talking. We do community dinners, have a playground, small garden, campground, and are planning a common house. No political or religious ideology to subscribe to; we are mellow and easygoing, make decisions by consensus, and tend to move slowly. We have a variety of ages and situations, although income level tends to be middle-class due to development and building costs.

Phase II of the community is waiting to be planned for five acres with 13 units.

Infrastructure from phase I is ready to be extended into phase II (road, utilities, etc.). Bank loans are possible, legally organized as a condominium; group process is in place. We need your energy and vision to help us design and develop phase II. We seek members of all races, religions, sexual preferences, etc. Contact Joseph Losi (206)788-5585 or write to us. 10/21/94 [85]

SHARON SPRINGS COHOUSING

**(Forming)
372 Sharon Road
Fairview, NC 28730**

**(704)628-2468/628-0077
(704)438-4629**

The Sharon Spring Community presently has 4 households who have been working, meeting, and playing together for one year. We have 24 beautiful acres of pasture and forest in the center of Fairview Valley, 20 minutes from Asheville, NC. We decided to develop one third of the land as building sites for 12–20 families. The rest of the land will remain forest or pasture. One of our goals is to build a pond.

In both our commonly owned facilities and in our individually owned homes, we want to use environmentally sound practices. Our south-facing hillside is ideal for solar heat and power. We are planning the construction of a community house which will consist of a dining room and kitchen, as well as rooms for children and recreation. Projected land and development costs per family, including the community house, roads, and pond will be $15–20,000. That money will give members title to a building site and access to all commonly owned land. Members will be responsible for financing and constructing their own homes. We have a working membership agreement and are preparing bylaws and covenants. Surveys are planned for individual lots of 1/4 to 1/2 acre. We welcome diversity of age, race, sexual preference, and religion. Contact Kendall Hale (704)628-2468 or Susan Smith 628-0077. 8/25/93

SHENOA

**Retreat & Learning Center
P.O. Box 43
Philo, CA 95466**

**(707)895-3156 9am-5pm
(707)895-3236 Fax**

Shenoa is a Findhorn-inspired retreat and learning center located in a wooded area of Mendicino County, 2-1/2 hours north of San Francisco. Its mission is "to serve the growing planetary need for spiritual renewal, community, and reconnection with nature and all dimensions of life by operating a self-sustaining business managed with cooperation, creativity, and integrity."

We have been privileged to host Eileen Caddy and Dorothy McLean, strengthening our link to Findhorn, and have presented seminars on creating communities and centers so others could benefit from our hard-earned insights. We sponsor Elderhostel seminars and host a wide variety of programs and teachers contributing to positive personal and planetary transformation.

Shenoa has a small core staff that live on the site year-round, and a much larger seasonal staff that works from April through November during the main "season." At Shenoa, community is important but is secondary to running the retreat center. Short-term work-exchange arrangements are possible (25 hrs/wk, camping) if your skills fit with our needs at the time. There are a limited number of staff positions available during any work season. We have a one-acre organic garden, a garden intern program, and a land stewardship program.

Our rustic, supportive, and well-run retreat facility is available to individuals, and for workshops and conferences. Please write or call for more information or a calendar of events. 10/6/94 [83]

SHEPHERDSFIELD

**777 Shepherdsfield Road
Fulton, MO 65251-9473**

(573)642-1439

Shepherdsfield is a Christian fellowship which tries to live as the Early Christians did and as recorded in the Acts of the Apostles, including the "sharing of all things in common." We have accepted Jesus Christ as the Way, the Truth, and the Life. Through Him we have found answers to the many questions that arise in trying to live together, and in reaching out to others.

We presently have about 100 souls associated with our community. We are located in a farming area within driving distance of Columbia and Jefferson City, Missouri. We earn our living through an organic bakery, a wallpapering and painting company, several cottage industries, and some printing and publishing.

We have a large ministry that reaches over the world in studies of Scripture and principles of Life. We operate our own school for our children, and take seriously the task of raising children in an environment of "purity and childlikeness."

Our desire has been to show others that Christianity is not limited to the institutional forms that have so disenchanted many people and led them to reject the claims of our Master, Jesus of Nazareth. We would not want to mislead anyone by claiming our life is a Utopia that requires little or no effort for the individual. Quite the contrary, true peace and brotherhood can only be accomplished when the utmost of diligence is applied in living out and promoting the necessary qualities. That requires struggle in order for the goodness of God to be "fleshed out" in us. However, we find great joy in living for Him in the present, and seeing ourselves and others changed from day to day.

If you would like to visit us, please write or call in advance. We have varying lengths of visitation before a person may apply to become a novice, which can eventually lead to becoming a member. We request that you include a SASE with inquiries. [cc] 1/5/93

SHIBBOLETH, THE

Chino Valley, AZ

(COMMUNITY LISTING REMOVED)

4/10/96

SHILOH COMMUNITY

P.O. Box 97
Sulphur Springs, AR 72768
(501)298-3299/298-3297

The Shiloh Community, founded by E. Crosby Monroe in southwestern New York in 1942, has actively followed a communal way of life since its inception. Our underlying focus has always been spiritual growth, both as individuals and as a community, and living our lives in a way that reflects this priority. Our spiritual focus has evolved independent of any specific religious affiliation, and might be most accurately described as an Esoteric Christianity that also integrates teachings from other disciplines. Although Rev. Monroe died in 1961, the community has continued to thrive.

We have always been a self-supporting community, following a progression of occupations—from general farming, dairying, meat processing, flour milling, baking, retail, then wholesale distribution. By the mid-'60s we needed an improved setting for our family and businesses, so in 1968 we acquired a grand hotel in the beautiful Arkansas Ozarks —which now serves as our central facility (including offices, our bakery, a health food store, a community cafeteria, and a retirement center for our elders). Other community-owned businesses include a nursery and preschool, and the Shiloh Christian Retreat Center. Our Sun Rise Acres Bakery now uses only stoneground whole grain flours and natural sweeteners

and oils in the manufacturing of Shiloh Farms bread.

At this stage of our development, many of our members are "Senior Citizens"—respected elders who continue to be actively involved in our daily life to the extent they are able. However, running all these businesses is very demanding, and we'd like to attract some younger families to take on some of the responsibilities (and satisfactions). We have created a very comfortable, supportive, and safe community environment for raising a family, and hope to attract others who appreciate how our commitment to spiritual values makes this lifestyle possible.

And a word about our "conservative" nature. Newcomers often arrive with inspired visions and enthusiastic energy for implementing new ideas, then find themselves frustrated by the unwillingness of our oldtimers to jump on the bandwagon. We do value creativity and enthusiasm, but hope that it will be balanced by maturity and commitment. Essentially, it may take a while to prove yourself, moving forward one step at a time. Patience and hard work are the assets most likely to win our confidence. 1/12/93

SHINING WATERS RETREAT

(Re-Forming)
Route 3, Box 560
Fredericktown, MO 63645
(573)783-6715/726-5133

Shining Waters Retreat is located outside

Fredericktown, Missouri, less than a 2-hour drive from St. Louis, in the beautifully forested Ozarks. The grounds contain a large lake, 2 houses, 3 dormitories, a large kitchen and meeting room lodge, and seven other buildings. Residents and guests enjoy vegetarian meals; no drugs, coffee, or tobacco; and practices of yoga, meditation, and other healthful spiritual disciplines. Events abound on weekends, and groups can schedule events for 60 or fewer people, although camping is available and popular. Anyone can apply for residency, and family units are preferred. 8/16/93

SHORT MOUNTAIN SANCTUARY, INC.

Route 1, Box 84-A
Liberty, TN 37095
(615)563-4397 (msg.)

Short Mountain Sanctuary (SMS) is a not-for-profit corporation chartered in Tennessee as a land trust. SMS also provides a place for its residents and members to undertake projects in sustainable agriculture, holistic forestry, low-cost shelter, and alternative energy.

The residents of SMS are Gay men and Lesbian womyn, their families, and friends. On the land they work on self-reliance and celebrate the Earth's cycles. All major decisions are made by consensus.

SMS is a working farm with a herd of goats, organic garden, chickens, beehives, fruit trees, and herb beds. The main structures are a post-Civil War cabin with additions, a large barn, and other outbuildings. Organizational income derives from annual membership dues ($75), and registration fees for two 9-day gatherings in May and October. Residents pay a fixed amount each month for food and supplies. Visitors are welcome, but need to write in advance (please enclose SASE). Daily fees for food and land use are $7 for non-members, and $3 for members.

SMS is presently the home of *RFD: A Country Journal for Gay Men Everywhere.* RFD has been in production now for 19 years, and is a reader-written magazine [see resource listing]. 5/18/92

SICHLASSENFALLEN

1139 North 21st Street
Milwaukee, WI 53233
(414)933-2063

Sichlassenfallen is a community of 7 adults sharing a common interest in important shared values: simple living with the environment, equality, peace, and community service. These values have remained central over a quarter century, with new members adding richness to an ever-changing community. Poet, philosopher, Catholic nun, Moslem, and community volunteers are part of the present community.

We are part of a large housing co-op actively involved with area communities and various issues. Our lifestyle is consistent with our established values: decisions are by consensus, with majority rule if necessary; house expenses, chores, and responsibilities are shared; and personal freedom of thought and choice are important. Although we do not have specific community projects or goals at this time, we support individual efforts.

While we are a stable community, occasionally we seek new members; so please contact us if you are relocating in our area. Also, we enjoy contact and visitors from other communities, and we have a large 100-year-old home located near the downtown area. Please contact us in advance. 8/11/92

SIERRA HOT SPRINGS

P.O. Box 366
Sierraville, CA 96126
(916)994-3773

Sierra Hot Springs has a colorful history. Native Americans held it sacred and revered it for healing and ritual. Later, it provided the early immigrants and miners of the gold rush with the luxury of a hot bath.

The attractiveness of the hot springs has been carefully preserved. Its few buildings are unobtrusively set where nature left a place for them in the shadows of elegant pine trees on the steep Sierra slopes 5000 feet above sea level. In the springtime the alpine meadow, clad in pastel blooms, becomes a feast for the spirit. Deer, raccoon, chipmunks, squirrels, porcupines, and many species of birds drink and forage there.

Today this 600-acre, beautifully located hot springs has evolved into a clean and sober spiritual community dedicated to the protection of these magical waters while keeping them open to the public. Training is available in techniques of spiritual enlightenment and healing methods to integrate spirit, mind, and body.

Sierra Springs Community is currently seeking skilled members. The community is especially interested in people who have construction skills. A nondenominational spiritual lifestyle is supported, with an emphasis on holistic health. Please, no smoking, drugs, or alcohol. For more information, call Carol at the number listed. SASE requested with inquiries. 2/5/93

SIKH DHARMA / 3HO FOUNDATION

There are over one hundred Sikh Dharma/3HO Ashrams around the world. The ashram community consists of students, teachers, individuals, and families who wish to live and share the technologies and practices of the Sikh Dharma/3HO way of life in an environment of consciousness and purity. Sikh Dharma's mission focuses on the areas of health and healing, yogic lifestyle, education in the art and science of humanology, the experience of one's full awareness and potential—and community service.

We offer a variety of camps and intensives designed for personal transformation. Weekend Intensives, White Tantric Yoga Courses, Summer and Winter Solstice Camps, Women's Camp, and Yoga Festivals are a few samples of ongoing programs that Sikh Dharma offers each year to thousands of participants worldwide. These provide an opportunity to practice yoga and meditation, eat a healthful vegetarian diet, take many and varied classes in healing arts, and to network with people from around the world. [Additional background information listed in the Resources section.] The five major North American centers are:

- **Guru Ram Das Ashram** 1/13/95
  1620 Preuss Road
  Los Angeles, CA 90035
  (310)858-7691 / 274-8085
- **Hacienda De Guru Ram Das**
  Route 3, Box 132-D
  Espanola, NM 87532
  (505)753-9438 / 753-1999
- **Guru Ram Das Ashram**
  368 Village Street
  Millis, MA 02054
  (508)376-4525 / 376-0845
- **Guru Nanak Dwara Ashram**
  2302 North 9th Street
  Phoenix, AZ 85006
  (602)271-4480 / 256-9447
- **Guru Ram Das Ashram**
  1739 Whitewood Lane
  Herndon, VA 22170
  (703)430-8800 / 450-7767

SILVERLAKE CO-OP

1646-1/4 N. Coronado Street
Los Angeles, CA 90026

(213)413-3454

Silverlake Co-op, Inc. is a scattered-site co-op (43 units) made up of single family homes, duplexes, and triplexes covering 10 city blocks in a low-to-moderate income neighborhood that is ethnically mixed. The Board of Directors, elected by the members at an annual meeting, meets monthly—as do several Board committees. Please include SASE with inquiries. 9/13/94

SIRIUS COMMUNITY

Baker Road
Shutesbury, MA 01072

(413)259-1251
esirius@aol.com

Sirius Community, named after the star known esoterically as the source of love and wisdom for the planet, was begun in 1978 on 86 acres of land, founded by former members of the Findhorn Community in Scotland. Today we are about 20 members from many spiritual paths, and 13 children. We have many associate members across the country and the world.

Our vision is to attain the highest good in all levels of creation: field and forest, plants and animals, humans and angels, earth and stars. We strive to honor the Divine Presence in all life, in love, truth, cooperation, meditation, and service to the world. We are a group of diverse people from different backgrounds who are working to respect and appreciate our differences, yet joyfully cooperating. What we are doing can be applied globally, for the tensions between nations pose a similar challenge. In any polarity or conflict, we work to create a balance between the people and issues involved, focusing on wholeness rather than the separateness of the parts.

Our tools include a weekly meeting and open discussion by all adult members; governance by group meditation and consensus; attunement to God, to nature, and to each other. We strive to live close to the earth without being bound to it. For us "appropriate technology" is computers as well as composting toilets and woodstoves. We also strive toward right livelihood. A few of us work at Sirius or in our own businesses, but most of us are employed outside the community. We work in such fields as social and health services, domestic service, solar construction, socially responsible investment, media, publishing, and educational services. We grow some of our vegetables and build our own houses. We share equally the expenses of the land and work on community projects one day a week. Most of us participate in evening community meals and a food buying club. We host visitors from many countries, and make ourselves available to those on a spiritual quest and those in transition seeking a better life.

As a nonprofit, tax-exempt educational center, we continue to offer a variety of educational programs—from solar construction to New Age politics, from organic gardening to holistic healing. We seek to serve the world through our meditation,

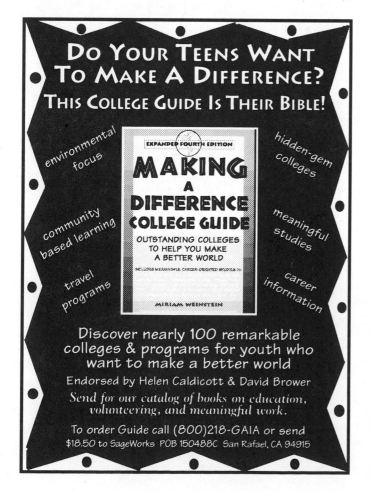

and work as a group to create positive thought-forms of peace and healing for the world—knowing that energy follows thought. Together we are building Sirius into a center of Light, a place where cooperation is a dream that works. Our vision of service is to help build a Network of Light which radiates positive energy and hope for the future throughout the world. 5/13/92 [53, 74, 85]

SISTERS OF DIVINE PROVIDENCE

(Forming)
8351 Florissant Road
St. Louis, MO 63121
(314)524-3803

As the Congregation of Divine Providence, we are united by our experience of and trust in a God who cares. That divine care is made known in us, those called to care for others and for the Earth as co-creators of a just world. Those who experience God's faithful care cannot but have hope for the future. Trusting in this God who will provide for our every need, we embrace a simple lifestyle and find support in communities of faith, prayer, and loving trust. 10/16/93

SIVANANDA ASHRAM YOGA RANCH COLONY

P.O. Box 195
Woodbourne, NY 12788
(914)434-9242

An international network of Sivananda Yoga Vedanta Centers is thriving in major cities on four continents—founded by Swami Vishnu-Devananda to spread the teaching of Swami Sivananda. The organization is staffed by volunteer "Karma Yogis," and student membership is well over 80,000.

The Yoga Ranch in the Catskills of southeastern New York was established in 1975 and is presently the home to 15 resident adults and no children. Our focus is on five basic points for radiant health and inner peace: proper exercise, proper relaxation, proper breathing, proper diet, and positive thinking and meditation. Our daily practices include yoga, meditation, chanting, and vegetarian meals. We also enjoy a sauna, pond, cross-country skiing, and beautiful nature trails. Come as a guest, a Karma Yoga volunteer, a resident, or a teacher trainee. We also have ashrams in Canada, California, India, and the

Bahamas. For more information, write for our brochure. 12/11/92

SIX DIRECTIONS FOUNDATION

(Forming)
Box 398
Monroe, UT 84754

There are various levels of involvement, from a core of four directors of the nonprofit foundation, to the tribe of members with natural leaders and circles of radiating overlap. The core idea is optimal health—individual, family, community, planetary. One focus is partnership parenting—conscious conception, freebirth, home education. Another is ecowise, affordable housing. A core group of about 7 families participate in a health food co-op, weekly yoga class and woman's circle, occasional men's group, holyday celebrations, yearly Family Vision Quest, potlucks, building projects, retreats, etc. The 6D foundation is leasing 35 acres of wilderness canyon land. There are privately owned homes and a 135-acre hot springs facility with possible homesites, greenhouse, and restaurant. A small general store used for the co-op is also a library/classroom. Plenty of agricultural land available.

Elders: Molly Willett, 72, PhD Health Ed; Rico and Jaennine Baker, founders of 6D, authors of *Conscious Conception*, workshop leaders; Randy Riis, former Stelle Community member, eco-builder, Third World activist; Lori and Mike are inventors/appropriate technology salespeople; Jill and Mike manage the hot springs, Mike raises fish, plants, and trees; Dave and Judy Grow own the hot springs and other large businesses; Steve Thomas, consultant, workshops. SASE requested with inquiries. [cc] 12/4/93

SKY RANCH

[renamed Circle Op Springs.]

SKY WOODS COSYNEGAL

P.O. Box 4176
Muskegon Heights, MI 49444

We believe the heart of our humanity is an essentially social nature whose fullest realization is one with the destiny of community. We believe that global survival depends on compassionate commitment of all our resources to create a truly advanced social and ecological awareness. We

must replace competition and aggression with mature skills of cooperation and humanization.

We are a holistic, politically conscious community that has existed for over 15 years. We seek out the wisdom of the ages and other cultures, using a lifelong learning process to evolve an ever more harmonious and accountable lifestyle. Community has given us the high privilege of real-life participation in mutual self-creation.

We think we have made credible advances over sexism, ageism, racism, and possessiveness toward material resources or others. Those advances have been based on rational self-criticism; democratic consensus/majority decision making; full disclosure relationships; ample group communication and expression; collective sharing and control of all socially significant material resources; and a firm rejection of one of the last strongholds of the competitive mentality —preferential monogamy or possessive relationships. Our exhilaration and sustaining ideal is a fully egalitarian community.

Some of us have already committed ourselves to a lifetime together. We have a few acres of beautiful wooded hill country on the shore of the inland sea, a small organic farm, a home, and several cottage industries. We produce some arts and crafts, and are deeply into alternative energy, holistic health, nutrition, organic gardening, and orcharding. We welcome visitors, but request that arrangements be made in advance. 8/31/92

SKY-JAHNNA, THE

(Forming)
P.O. Box 918
Idyllwild, CA 92349
(909)659-2740

We are a man and woman with four daughters. Our tribe-seed is re-growing extended family, branch, and tribe... soul-by-soul, based on vital, committed, and sacred relationship. We see community as a matter of human relationship. Gardens and land flow from it. We feel that what gives a simple family strength —chemistry, solid courtship, communication, commitment—is also needed in further family layers. Growing coherently from the inside out, we are courting other folks and families like us. We'll call it our first Branch (clan).

Our grandiose trips are mostly over,

and we're content to secret away a viable Culture-seed. Into meditation, bhakti, kids at home, emotions (RC, Rebirthing), simplicity, abundance, good eating, good astrology, and many songs. Husband makes living as an astrologer. Aiming for semi-remote farming self-sufficiency with our people. The link to our Promised Land abides in our real bond with each other. We'll enjoy responding to personal letters (kindly include your date of birth, city, and time if possible.) Hoping for sister sites in England, Uruguay, Nova Scotia, and Northern California. Blessings galore! —Cynthia and Ski-Jasper. 9/10/93

SKYFIRE

(Forming)
529 Chestnut Street
Lindsburg, KS 67456
(913)227-2800

We see Skyfire as a community of scholar/technicians who are living the ideas we develop and believe in, a center for the study and application of sustainable technology. We expect to work part time at the center, and part time teaching and applying sustainable technology in the local and world community.

We plan earth-sheltered housing that utilizes seasonal storage of heat, and plan to live off the electrical grid, utilizing sustainable energy as much as possible. The community will hold land as joint property; houses will be on long-term lease; most other things will be privately owned. We intend that the community

remain small enough and flexible enough to allow individual variations. We should all expect to make allowances for one another's individual needs and desires—as well as strengths, weaknesses, and gifts.

Walter is a population geneticist (plant and animal breeder). Paul is an artisan, inventor, and economic theorist (plumber, electrician, carpenter, metalworker, and writer). We are looking for people with a family orientation—people who have new ideas and new skills oriented toward sustainability, and putting them into practice—people who match and challenge us intellectually, not disciples of our ideas. SASE required. 12/3/94

SOCIETY FOR HUMAN SOLIDARITY

(Forming)
1341 S. Pinecrest
Wichita, KS 67218
(316)686-7100

[Formerly the Midwest Community/Center for Creative Interchange.] If you look upon the prevailing social, economic, and political order as being utterly destructive of a truly human existence and totally beyond reform, we would like to invite you to join with us in an agreement to act as a decision-making body—the nucleus and model of an alternative society. Our ruling concern is this: discovering and providing the best possible conditions —not only for us, but for all people— to undergo continuous transformation

through creative interchange. By "creative interchange" we mean the order of events that go on between people in a more or less limited way, including each of the following sub-events as essential and integral parts: 1) An emerging insight into and empathy with what each other is trying to communicate about his or her non-programmed thoughts and feelings; 2) An integrating of these thoughts and feelings with one's own; 3) An expanding of one's appreciable world; 4) A widening and deepening of a sense of significant relationship among those involved in the interchange. We believe that creative interchange can deliver people from destructive conflict with each other— if they make it their ruling concern—and lead them along the paths of human fulfillment as nothing else can. 12/12/94

SOCIETY OF FAMILY SOLIDARITY

(Forming)
Bountiful Lakes Chapter
30520 Rancho California
**   Road #107-130**
Temecula, CA 92591
(909)695-9586

Society of Family Solidarity is a fraternal, familial, mutual benefit society of select family-oriented individuals, affording an environment of multiple chapters in diverse districts, regions, and zones— ennobling the inalienable premise that is self-evident in accordance with natural law and the Law of Nature. PURPOSES

& GOALS: To mobilize men and women of diverse fields into interdisciplinary teams and to afford them outlets for their creative talents; to train and be trained; to strengthen techniques in which to inculcate and infuse leadership responsibility based upon the talents of the individual. ADMINISTRATION: Each chapter is administered by locally elected members who are responsible for/to the general well-being of members, following standardized guidelines in health and general well-being, continuing education, economic enhancement, cultural-social enhancement, ethics, and community and civic enhancement. GENERAL ECONOMICS: Each chapter will progressively acquire proportional interest in other organizations engaged in trade and commerce, manufacturing, mining, agriculture, warehousing, transportation, communications, engineering and construction, energy, general service industries including retail services, banking, finance, and insurance. Please respond by mail. 9/16/94

SOJOURNERS COMMUNITY

(Re-Forming)
1323 Girard Street NW
Washington, DC 20009
(202)387-7000
(202)328-8842 (S/J Mag)

Sojourners is an ecumenical, Christian-based community in inner-city Washington DC. We are rooted in the teachings of the Bible and the call of daily application of faith in our lives. The vision of community is radical discipleship that brings together evangelicalism and social justice, spirituality and politics, prayer and peacemaking. For 20 years, Sojourners has pursued a lifestyle of economic sharing, spiritual growth, peacemaking, feminism, and justice.

Sojourners is located in the inner city to demonstrate the radical call to live and work alongside the poor, to feed the hungry, to make a place for the outcasts—the call to put Christian faith into action. Our ministries include a learning center for neighborhood kids; a large food distribution program that feeds 200 families each week; *Sojourners* magazine (focusing on faith, politics, and culture); national justice organizing; and a year-long internship program. Community members also work in other service-related jobs, including nutrition services for disabled individuals, and teaching high school

math to at-risk students. We also have a social worker, and a gardener and poet. Our worship, held Sundays at 5pm, is open to the public. 7/29/93

SONG OF THE MORNING

(Forming)
9607 Sturgeon Valley Road
Vanderbuilt, MI 49795
(517)983-2147

A retreat center (ashram) with plans to develop into a planned urban community. Currently 12 staff live on the site, hosting retreats and classes, open to the public, for those who wish to learn and practice the teachings of Yoga, a science of self-realization.

Among the classes are clear light, healing, rebirthing, meditation, chanting, and Hatha Yoga. There are silent retreats, and others focused on nutrition or health. We also host children's summer camps.

The new planned urban community is accepting deposits for leases to build. We welcome requests for information. Please include SASE with inquiries. 9/10/94

SONGAIA

Residential Learning Center
22421 – 39th Avenue SE
Bothell, WA 98021-7911
(206)486-2035/486-5164
http://www.songaia.com/

Situated on an 11-acre wooded rural site just 30 minutes from Seattle, Songaia is an established intentional community choosing an earth-conscious, sustainable, "extended family" lifestyle with members ranging in age from 2 to 56. We believe community is an integral part of a healthy social environment, and understand ourselves to be involved in creating new and viable modes of living for the future—sharing our learnings with those we encounter.

We value simplicity and cooperation, and enjoy singing, celebrating, and telling stories. We have an outreach effort that keeps us connected in the Seattle area and beyond through sponsorship of seminars and hosting of events such as Earth Day, sweat lodges, and summer youth programs. Approximately 30% of our members are renters. We keep our living expenses low through shared resources and bulk purchasing, and supplement our menu with tons of fruits and vegetables from our organic gardens. In 1990 we decided to expand our numbers and

began exploring more appropriate living facilities, modeling our growth on the cohousing concept. We anticipate 12–15 households, beginning construction around spring 1994. 9/15/93

SONORAN ECO-VILLAGE

(Forming)
P.O. Box 42663
Tucson, AZ 85733

The Sonoran Eco-Village Community is purchasing 130 acres of irrigated, chemical-free, agricultural land 9 miles north of Benson, Arizona, 1 hour from Tucson, suitable for 25+ households.

We are an intentionally planned multi-locational community which will develop modes of living to emphasize cooperation, creativity, personal responsibility and growth, harmonious living, sustainability, and self-reliance. Our basic principles are inclusiveness, diversity, nonhierarchical self-governance, consensus process, solidarity, sharing, and mutual support. The community hopes to create a mutually supportive environment for projects in education, healing, spiritual growth, chemical-free agriculture, appropriate technology, and light living. We will experiment with and demonstrate technologies, building designs, and techniques which are ecological, efficient, and empowering, using indigenous materials and labor. We are committed to improving interpersonal relationships through honesty, openness, and willingness to change.

Seeking additional members. $5,000 membership fee plus monthly fee based on number of members. Shared membership possible. Contact Rod Bunney at (520)577-2719. SASE required. 3/24/94

SOUTHERN CASSADAGA SPIRITUALIST CAMP MEETING ASSOCIATION

P.O. Box 319
Cassadaga, FL 32706
(904)228-3171/228-2880

Designated as a Historic District on the National Register of Historic Places, the Southern Cassadaga Spiritualist Camp Meeting Association is a unique religious community, founded in 1894. We are located on a 55-acre tract of land, off of I-4, midway between Daytona Beach and Orlando, Florida. While members may own the homes they live in, the Association retains ownership of the land and offers lifetime leases. We also own and manage two apartment buildings.

The purpose of our community is to promote the understanding of the religion, science, and philosophy of Spiritualism, and to offer a nurturing environment for like-minded people. We have ongoing educational programs for those wishing to develop their mediumship and/or healing abilities, and we also offer ministerial courses. A number of mediums, healers, and ministers live and work on the grounds. Our unique offerings attract many visitors to our church services, Spiritual/Metaphysical Bookstore, and our counselors. Seminars and workshops are also offered frequently, and the public is invited to attend all activities. Please write for our Annual Program, enclosing $1 to cover shipping and handling. 7/29/93

SOUTHSIDE PARK COHOUSING

**438 "T" Street
Sacramento, CA 95814**

(916)444-2712

We are a cooperative group, self-managed,

and using consensus to make decisions. We have affordable home ownership options, a balance of privacy and community, and a practical but spontaneous lifestyle. Shared facilities include common house, workshop, gardens, play areas, and laundry. This is a mixed community of all ages, with many family groups— a safe supportive environment for adults and children.

Construction was completed in September of 1993, with a total of 25 households (townhouses with 1–4 bedrooms priced from $85,000 to $165,000) and peripheral covered parking. Presently all units are occupied, and we have a waiting list of prospective members who hope to join when openings become available. Call or write for info. SASE required. [cc] 2/2/93

SPARROW HAWK VILLAGE

**12 Summit Ridge Drive
Tahlequah, OK 74464**

Sparrow Hawk Village, an intentional spiritual community, was established in 1981. Currently 76 adults and 14

children are living on 430 acres in the western Ozarks.

The community is located at the end of a county road four miles off Oklahoma State Scenic Highway 10. It is nestled among gentle rolling forest filled with abundant wildlife and natural, serene beauty. Community gardens, orchards, horse pastures, and about two miles of recreational river frontage, bordered by 600 acres of primitive state forest, significantly add to our quality of life.

SHV is open to members of all faiths. While many villagers are esoteric Christian, we are blessed with members of various Western and Eastern religions, adding to the diversity of our spiritual experience. Our residents are involved in the healing arts, music, counseling, dowsing, teaching, meditating, spiritual dance, and esoteric studies. This is a place of growth. Energy vortexes here accelerate personal and interpersonal evolution.

The national headquarters of Light of Christ Community Church and Sancta Sophia Seminary are located here. This campus includes a beautiful church, esoteric library, bookstore, gift shop, and

offices. In addition to providing a full class schedule, the church and seminary sponsor well-known speakers and diverse workshops. Consequently many students, guests, and visitors are welcomed into our homes as they come to participate in these activities. Daily meditations and Sunday services are available in the LCCC sanctuary and in village homes.

Community government styles have been evolving for the last 14 years. In the early stages of development, the founders utilized the hierarchical pattern of governing. An association of property owners, the next evolutionary form, was initiated by the founders and is democratic in style. It deals with issues of property values and ownership issues, and was the first attempt to form a community government. The Sparrow Hawk Community Association was created in early '94. Available to everyone, it functions through a modified consensus format.

Sparrow Hawk Village is approximately 10 miles from Tahlequah, Oklahoma, capital of the Cherokee Nation and location of Northeastern State University. We invite you to visit, study, or live in Sparrow Hawk Village. If you are interested in visiting, guest rooms and campgrounds are available for a nominal fee. Reservations are recommended. For those interested in living here, there are homes and homesites for sale. Please include SASE when writing. 10/26/94

SPAULDING UNIT

**2319 Spaulding
Berkeley, CA 94703**

The Spaulding Unit, which began in 1978, is a diverse group of individuals who share a respect for the Earth and each other, a network of mutual support, a commitment to open communication and positive change, and who celebrate together in the joy and mystery of life. The Unit, located on a relaxed side street in Berkeley, is a large, pleasant house surrounded by big trees, a garden, and a medley of urban wildlife (squirrels, birds, butterflies, salamanders, raccoons, possums...). Currently, we are a loose-knit cooperative of five to seven adults, two dogs, cats, and several regular irregulars. Our interests range from music to mayhem. We share food, chores, meals, rent, utilities, triumphs, woes.... We maintain a permanent guest room for friends and travelers. If you are interested in learning more about us or making a visit, please

write to us and let us know something about you and your travel plans. SASE requested. 12/11/92

SPIES FOR SANITY

**(Forming)
Mike O'Neill
c/o Kent Murphy
11 River Rise Road
New City, NY 10956
(914)638-6700**

We are, and we seek, individualists who accept that life will always be chaotic, hierarchical, and short. But! it can be a hierarchy of grace: no bosses, saints, or stars; everyone equal—that is, flawed, afraid in some ways; gifted, beautiful, brave in others. When everyone is the natural leader in their best ways, chaos and death are transcended while this life lasts. After life, who knows...? Sadly, most people's fear of death and chaos gets the best of them, spellbinds them into following false elitist orders—fascist ones for traditionalists; feel-good ones for alternativists. And so brute hierarchy rules almost everywhere on Earth...and almost everyone has to defer to it to some degree: even relief workers must eat as others starve at their feet.

We publicly fight for good causes like ecology and life rights where we dare. But, first and foremost, we acknowledge —without sugar coating, rage, or guilt—our private survival compromises with elitism and consciously bear them in mind as a witness for sanity. We believe humankind's collective good-will power might some day dispel its collective ill-will only if enough of us are willing to be unflinchingly honest with ourselves. If we're not, we and our causes become elitism's silent partners. We feel that any community lucky enough to be a safe haven within the mainstream of consciousness is obliged to relentlessly treat it with good-willed candor. Our main means of doing so are through the arts, especially comedy, drama, and music. 10/9/94

SPIRAL WIMMIN'S COMMUNITY

**HC 72, Box 94-A
Monticello, KY 42633
(606)348-6597/348-7913**

Spiral Wimmin's Community (Spiraland) is 250 acres in the foothills of south-central Kentucky, in the Cumberland Valley. Covering a ridge and valley of for-

est and cleared land, Spiral includes three springs, a good barn, a log cabin, and new dwellings wimmin are building.

We recognize that the land is a sacred heritage, belonging to herself—part of the complex web of life in which we learn to play our part harmoniously with the rest of her creatures and plants. Our community is based on Permaculture principles. Our actions on the land are to enhance the diversity and abundance of life forms, to preserve and build the soil, to work with the cycles and forces of nature. We look at the land as a self-sustaining ecological system capable of fruitfulness for all time.

We are currently 7 wimmin living on the land. There are two houses, a cabin, and another house being built. We offer room and board to wimmin in exchange for help in building. Visitors welcome. Please write or call for more information (include SASE). 4/21/92

SPIRICOASIS

**(Forming)
P.O. Box 65012
Toronto, Ontario M4K-3Z2
CANADA
(416)429-2468**

The Spiricoasis (Spirit, Cooperation, Oasis) mission is to inspire personal and planetary brilliance through educational programs and supporting facilities designed to enrich an individual's spiritual, mental, emotional, and physical well-being and the relationship of the individual with self, others, and the planetary environment. We are guided by principles which include appreciation of the miracle of life; opening to the possibility of direct experience of a higher power; the innocence in each newborn human life; acknowledging the inherent wisdom in each person; supporting self-directed growth and maturation; freedom in making personal choices which do not impose on or violate any other person or another person's freedom of choice; sacredness of and harmonious coexistence with all other persons, animals, and the environment; achieving peak performance and surpassing preconceived limitations; opening to the possibility of that which is beyond all limitations; sacredness of the human body and of human sexuality; optimal physical fitness; physical nurturing and sexual expression guided by mutual respect, honor, and openness to joining. 12/28/93

SPRING VALLEY BRUDERHOF

Hutterian Brethren
RD2, Box 446
Farmington, PA 15437-9506

(412)329-1100/329-0942 Fax
http://www.bruderhof.org/

Became a Bruderhof in 1990. [See main listing for "Hutterian Brethren" in the Resources section.] 6/1/92

SPRINGTREE COMMUNITY

Route 2, Box 536
Scottsville, VA 24590-9512

(804)286-3466

We are a group of 4 mid-age adults and 1 teen living together as an extended family. Our home (est. '71) is 120 acres. We share all income, eat meals together, organize work by preference.

Living frugally is important to us. We grow much of our own food, maintaining organic gardens and orchards, chickens, and bees. We support ourselves with income from outside jobs and farming. An experimental agroforestry project—combining food trees with pasture and animals—is one of our extra activities.

We intend to remain a small, close group, with a maximum of 8 adults. As we grow older, we work to keep the community an expression of our changing needs for both stability and adventure, individual effort and group cohesiveness. We are interested in commitment and compatibility. We meet weekly to plan and discuss issues, using consensus; and twice monthly for personal concerns.

We advise a two-week initial visit for

those interested in membership. We also offer 3- to 6-month internships for those interested in organic gardening and country living skills. To arrange a visit or for more information write and tell us about yourself. SASE requested. 4/26/92 [Cmtas1, 14, 77(D)]

SRI AUROBINDO SADHANA PEETHAM

(Re-Forming)
2621 W US Hwy 12
Lodi, CA 95242

(209)339-1342, ext 5

[Formerly Atmaniketan Ashram, reincorporated in 1993.] Our community is a living laboratory for the practice of Sri Aurobindo's Collective Yoga of Integral Perfection. All seekers sincerely aspiring to become a selfless instrument in the progressive manifestation of a "Divine Life" upon Earth are welcome to collaborate. This is not a meditation retreat—but a place for those who, with their whole heart, mind, life, and body, wish to serve the Divine with dynamism and concentration. We are also developing a new center in Lodi, California. Please call or write the Pomona center for further information about activities in either location. 7/29/94

S.T.A.R. COMMUNITY

(Forming)
P.O. Box 1041
Taos, NM 87571

(505)751-0462

The second Earthship community is 15 miles west of Taos on 640 acres of rolling mesa land in the shadow of Tres Orejas Mountain [see separate listing for sister community "REACH"]. There is also a third community, STAR II, that is coming together. All homes and businesses are completely "off the grid" using photovoltaic electrical systems, catch-water cisterns, greywater planting areas, and composting toilets. Earthships, as described in the books of the same name by Michael Reynolds, are passive-solar, rammed-earth structures that can be owner-built from recycled materials.

We are actively demonstrating ways to save the planet and the creatures on it in the way we build. At STAR we will all grow some of our own food in our individual Earthships, and will open businesses to provide necessities for the community.

We currently help each other with construction, and make plans for new

projects knowing that soon we will have almost no bills to pay and can then devote our time to more creative concerns than making money. We are builders, architects, teachers, therapists, business and sales people, and scientists. We range in age from 0 to 70 and represent all types of households. 11/11/93

STARLAND HUTTERIAN BRETHREN

Route 2, Box 133
Gibbon, MN 55335

(507)834-6601

[See main listing for "Hutterian Brethren" in the Resources section.] 6/1/92

STARSEED COMMUNITY

(Forming)
672 Chapel Road
Savoy, MA 01256

(413)743-0417

We are presently one family living on 130 acres in a remote area of Massachusetts, up in the hills. Our six buildings include two houses and a cabin. We are currently developing an educational center for retreat and recovery, and aspire to maintain a safe, loving environment for healing. We hope to find other adults and families interested in supporting this kind of a center, and are seeking people to join us in the formation of a core group. SASE required. 7/14/94

STELLE COMMUNITY

127 Sun Street
Stelle, IL 60919

(815)256-2212

Stelle was founded in 1973 by the Stelle Group, a not-for-profit organization, in order to create a supportive environment where personal development would be made a foremost priority. The founding values of personal responsibility, life-long education, positive attitude, and cooperation still play a vital part in the community.

Today no single organization oversees all aspects of community life. The Stelle Group, now only one small organization among many, continues its philosophical/educational pursuits with an award-winning accredited school and publishing a quarterly journal. Governing and running the community are left to other organizations.

Stelle has its own water/sewer treatment plants and telephone mutual. Homes are owned privately, and residents support themselves individually, many as entrepreneurs. Stelle has a small pond, an orchard, a greenhouse, developed lots, and undeveloped commercial and agriculturally zoned land available. We welcome self-reliant, cooperative people who value life as an educational experience to come join us in our venture. For more information contact the Stelle Area Chamber of Commerce at the address/phone listed above. 1/15/93 [63, 66, 76]

STEPPINGWOODS

(Forming)
c/o Jemma Crae
6012 Coos Bay Wagon Road
Roseburg, OR 97470
(541)679-4655

Steppingwoods is a 120-acre wooded land in southern Oregon that is seeking Lesbian feminists in personal recovery for community sharing. We have one structure on the land as of 1992. No drugs, alcohol, or tobacco. Supportive Lesbian/Gay community in the area. SASE requested. 6/17/92

STEWART LITTLE CO-OP

211 Stewart Avenue
Ithaca, NY 14850
(607)273-1983/273-2218

An urban cooperative (est. '72) with 7 women and 7 men (age range 20s to 40s) emphasizing community living and cooperative decision making by consensus. A gay-friendly and ethnically diverse environment. We share nearly all dinners (vegetarian). Members are responsible for their own finances. Send inquiries to the House Membership Coordinator, and please include a SASE with your inquiry. [cc] 6/20/94

STILL WATER SABBATICAL

(Forming)
P.O. Box 598
Plains, MT 59859
(406)826-5934

We are an unincorporated association, legally structured on a nonprofit, religious basis. Our statement of faith and brochure are available on request. We stress a need for open, healthy, productive discussion and the avoidance of dogma.

During the past 2 years we have worked toward developing reliable funding sources; we prefer not to rely on donations, and cannot guarantee deductibility. Our temporary facility consists of our homes, a small research library, and a shop located on 40 acres. The site is operated as a homestead.

On-site members, the Board, and off-site voting members are required to commit to our statement of faith and the goals and ideals of Sabbatical. We welcome the input, visits, and support of others; our mailing list already includes people in this category.

Our library resources are available by correspondence or visitation. Due to the size of our current staff, please be patient with our response time (SASE requested). Currently, we cannot assure visitors of lodging, and therefore, must insist that we be contacted before you visit our area. 12/7/93

STONEHEDGE

(Re-Forming)
RR1, Enterprise
Ontario K0K-1Z0
CANADA
(613)358-2304

Founded as "Dandelion" in 1975, we underwent a change two years ago from a completely income- and labor-sharing communal system to what we defined as a resource-sharing cooperative. We wanted to begin within the broadest context possible and "see what happened." We consider important such things as the freedom to pursue interests outside and away from the co-op, and also the opportunity for people to form closer shared situations within that group. What has happened so far is some of each.

As a whole we share an interest in the farm operation, though the level of involvement varies. We share basic housing and utility costs; bulk food, and the farm product proportionate to labor and financial contributions. Different combinations of us practice more extensive food, domestic, space, and business sharing.

Currently we are 5 adults and 3 children. We welcome a modest number of visitors and require $5/day contribution to defray costs. If you wish to contact us we recommend the phone, as it takes us some considerable time to reply by mail. [cc] 4/15/93

STUDENT COOPERATIVE ORGANIZATION, INC.

23 Elliott Street
Athens, OH 45701
(614)592-2839

Our goal is to provide alternative housing, primarily for students, in Athens. We live just five minutes away from the Ohio University campus, but we also have a few non-students. Our housing cooperative is intended to encourage democratic self-managed living in a tolerant environment and to promote co-op economic systems and co-op values.

Members are asked to make a commitment to our community by sharing house jobs and chores, attending weekly meetings, and helping with maintenance projects. Our decisions are made using majority vote for the more complex decisions. We currently have one house with ten members, and we are active members of the North American Students of Cooperation (NASCO). NASCO Properties, in Ann Arbor, Michigan, holds the deed to our house. SASE required. 3/11/94

SUNBURST

(Forming)
2515 Suwannee Dr
Cocoa FL 32922
(407)636-1354

"Sunburst" is a community whose ideology revolves around combining alternative technology education with holistic living. Our vision is to create a perfect utopia, combining the latest technological advances in bioculture and energy efficiency.

Some of the interest and skills of current community members are solar and wind power, filtered rainwater, natural-style parenting, homeschooling, music, and worker-owned cooperative businesses. The community plans to be self-supporting, providing jobs through intense aquaculture, hydroponics, beekeeping, and recumbent bicycle making.

Sunburst is a home for those who share high ideals and who know that tomorrow is built today. We are presently in the "formative stages"; we do not yet have the land, but are building the relationships and the organizational foundations of a community. We plan to buy several large parcels of land, build a cluster of energy-efficient domes, and develop a conference/education center which demonstrates conservation of energy resources and sustainable agriculture. The land will be held in a community land trust.

Like-minded persons who are ready to develop and explore themselves in a setting of openness and trust are invited to inquire about Sunburst, either as a prospective member or as an investor in a socially responsible alternative environment. Please include a SASE with inquiries. 2/19/93

SUNFLOWER CO-OP

**1122 South 3rd Street
Austin, TX 78704**

(512)447-1268/447-1344

A small urban community cooperative practicing personal growth, vegetarianism, and conflict resolution through open communication and mediation. We operate by consensus and by shared labor and resources. 8/20/93

SUNFLOWER FARM

**12900 Parmiter Road
Amesville, OH 45711**

(614)448-6688/593-7456

Sunflower Farm, established in l975, is a community of ten families on 100 acres in southeast Ohio, near Athens. Sunflower is an alternative of independence and interdependence, and a response to dependence on costly, impersonal, large-scale institutions. There are ten five-acre private homesteads, and 50 acres owned in common. Adults' ages range from the mid 30s to mid 50s, with 2 children. We have artisans, engineers, computer specialists, social service workers, teachers, and more. We are presently full—there are no openings for new members at this time.

Athens allows us outside and in-community jobs, and has a 19,500-student university and medical school, excellent cultural and recreational resources. Cooperative activities include gardens, orchard, laundry, dining, community meetings, childcare program, woodworking, stained glass, and intermediate technology weekend workshops. We encourage new intentional community development, and offer programs and workshops in self-reliance skills. We are demonstrating that creative living and caring, cooperative environments are possible. 12/18/94

SUNFLOWER HOUSE

**1406 Tennessee
Lawrence, KS 66044**

(913)749-0871/841-0484

Sunflower House is a 30-member student housing cooperative founded in 1969. We have three major purposes: 1) to provide high-quality, low-cost, student-managed housing; 2) to provide an educational environment where members can learn practical skills (cooking, carpentry, bookkeeping, plumbing, etc.); and 3) to serve as a research site for the design of procedures that promote harmonious, cooperative, egalitarian relationships among members (the Cooperative Living Project).

Each member has his or her own bedroom, while we share a variety of common areas (6 bathrooms, 2 kitchens, living room, TV room, game room, workshop). We work 5–10 hours per week within the community. The money we contribute through monthly fees covers

our expenses, and any surplus is rebated to members at the end of the year. Major decisions are made at weekly meetings. A board of directors meets infrequently to provide direction on the overall vision of the cooperative. We follow the six cooperative principles, and we belong to NASCO (North American Students of Cooperation). Mail inquiries are preferred, and please include a SASE. 4/22/92 [80/81]

SUNNIER PALMS

**(Forming)
8800 Okeechobee Road
Fort Pierce, FL 34945**

(407)468-8512

Sunnier Palms is the culmination of Naturist individuals, couples, and families from diverse backgrounds who have loaned equal amounts of interest-free money to purchase land for their intentional community in southernmost Florida, where they maintain a rent-free lot. Our location was chosen to allow members and guests to be nude at work and play most days, all day, and enjoy the benefits of sun, air, and water to the entire body. Each individual and family is responsible for creating their personal income (which may be a private cottage industry within the community) while also contributing their time and talent where and when possible to sustain and benefit the community in a variety of ways, some of which create income for the community but never personally profit the members.

Sunnier intentions include promoting equality, peaceful relationships, respect for the environment; developing community values; providing a forum for health, nature, nutrition, small-scale farming, sound ecological practices, body acceptance, and discovering similarities in all humans. Sunnier welcomes additional Naturists to actively participate in the furtherance of our community intentions —to visit for a day, a vacation, or a lifetime. SASE requested. 8/23/92

SUNNYSIDE FARM

**(Forming)
9101 Holiness Highway
Mokane, MO 65059**

(573)676-5609

A new community Christian bible church (Acts 4:32–35) starting with one large loving family in a communal house built by a non-Christian community in the '70s. We are answering the call from the last days of God's prophet RG Stair: to leave the cities and come back together to wait for the soon return of Our Lord Jesus Christ, perfecting an end time holy remnant, a glorious church, and "Be found of Him in peace without spot and blameless" (2 Peter 3:14).

Our home is located in a secluded rural setting surrounded by 500 wooded acres (can't see smoke from neighbors' chimney, accessible only by boat during high water). Theology is mostly 7th Day Adventist, lifestyle is like conservative Mennonite (including uniform dress and biblical role of women), worship is old-time Pentecostal—how's that for a combination? The King James Bible is our rule book. No television. We practice faith healing and use herbs and natural remedies for health maintenance. We have good river-bottom garden land. Our school uses a Mennonite curriculum. Family identity is recognized within the family of God, and children are considered a blessing from the Lord.

We maintain political neutrality. Our kingdom is not of this world. We are gentle spirits, seeking the fellowship of the same. Please include a SASE with inquiries. [cc] 11/26/93

SUNRISE RANCH

(Re-Forming)
5569 N. County Road 29
Loveland, CO 80538
(970)679-4200

Sunrise Ranch is a fifty-year-old Emissary community located in Eden Valley, 10 miles west of Loveland, Colorado. The Emissaries (also known as Emissaries of Divine Light) are a worldwide spiritual organization dedicated to restoring humankind's consciousness of divine identity and co-creating a home for God on earth. Therefore, the demonstration of practical spirituality through community lifestyle is one of the Emissaries' main activities.

Sunrise Ranch currently has about 100 residents, including children, and five to twenty long-term visitors at any one time.

The community has weekly worship services, an elected governing council, weekly community meetings, organic gardens and farm, and hosts workshops and retreats for groups of 15-50. About half the residents work in their own businesses on or off the property, and the others are involved in community endeavors such as gardening, child/elder care, property maintenance and administration and providing settings for workshops and retreats.

We are classified in this directory as "Re-Forming." This is true in a certain way as many of our systems—economic, governmental, managerial—are transforming. But what is firmly in place at Sunrise Ranch is our commitment to our spiritual heritage, including a firm foundation in service to God and Life. We continue to be excited about discovering the many ways that commitment can manifest.

We welcome visitors; please call before arriving. For those wishing to stay overnight, our rates currently are $45/person per night ($35/person double occupancy)

N. American s

meals included. There is a process for becoming a community member which you can discuss with a council member after visiting. 8/31/95 [67, 71/72, 85]

SUNSET HOUSE

(Re-Forming)
2708 Sunset Avenue
Oakland, CA 94601

(510)534-9276

We are in the early stages of re-creating a family sized co-owning community consisting of 7–8 adults of varying ages, cultural backgrounds, and sexual orientation in a beautiful, unusual, and large urban home that has been shared for 15 years. There is space for 2 or 3 non-owners. We intend to share emotional warmth, openness, and honesty in our interpersonal relations and commitment to work out conflicts soon after they arise. Our goals are generally progressive environmental and other social values; working toward a world filled with partnership, democratic participation, and concern for future generations;

healthy vegetarian food purchasing and preparation; conserving of energy, water and recycling and composting; willingness to live with children and persons of varying ages, ethnic backgrounds, and sexual orientation; material goods as we are freely willing to share. If you resonate with these goals, we would love to hear from you. Please write to the above address with a SASE. We will reply soon. 5/1/93

SUNSET HOUSE

915 Sixteenth Avenue
Seattle, WA 98122

(206)323-9055

Sunset House is one of five communities in the Evergreen Land Trust network in Washington State [see Resource listing]. Members are students or working folks, and membership is fairly stable. Decisions are made by consensus and members hang out socially, but we have very little other structure. We're not presently seeking new members, and we're not equipped to host visitors. [cc] 6/30/94

SUSAN B. ANTHONY MEMORIAL UNREST HOME

(SuBAMUH)
P.O. Box 5853
Athens, OH 45701

We are a community of 4 women residents and several nonresident members, ages 40 through 68, ardently feminist, ecologically attuned, politically active. We share 150 acres 10 miles from Athens, Ohio, home of Ohio University (18,000 students) and near Hocking College (4500 students). We operate a campground for individual and groups of women (by advance reservation only). We are part of a growing women's community in southeast Ohio with monthly gatherings, coffeehouses, newsletter, and a NOW chapter.

SuBAMUH is becoming an Ohio non-profit land trust. Major decisions are made by consensus of residents with input from nonresident members. We seek a balance between individual freedom and the welfare of the community. Members are involved in feminist and lesbian activism,

OUR COMMUNITIES DON'T JUST END AT OUR PROPERTY LINES.

ON THIS MAP THEY DO.

YOU CAN SUPPORT COOPERATION, INCOME SHARING, NON-VIOLENCE, PARTICIPATORY GOVERNMENT AND ENVIRONMENTALISM BY BECOMING A **FRIEND OF THE FEDERATION OF EGALITARIAN COMMUNITIES.**

RECEIVE OUR NEWSLETTERS, CONFERENCE LISTINGS, AND "COMMUNITIES" MAGAZINE.

SEND A $40 DONATION (OR WRITE FOR MORE INFO) TO: FRIENDS OF THE FEDERATION 138 TWIN OAKS RD., LOUISA, VA 23093

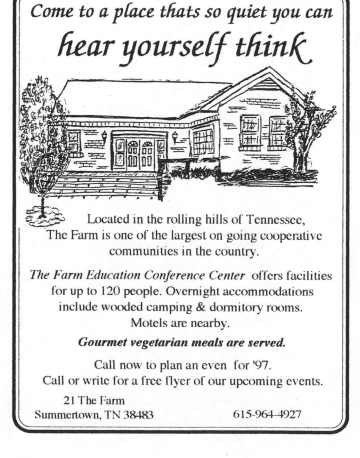

Come to a place thats so quiet you can *hear yourself think*

Located in the rolling hills of Tennessee, The Farm is one of the largest on going cooperative communities in the country.

The Farm Education Conference Center offers facilities for up to 120 people. Overnight accommodations include wooded camping & dormitory rooms. Motels are nearby.

Gourmet vegetarian meals are served.

Call now to plan an even for '97.
Call or write for a free flyer of our upcoming events.

21 The Farm
Summertown, TN 38483   615-964-4927

peace and justice issues, conservation, recreation, and above all desire safe, congenial, inexpensive living space for women. Women could build their own dwelling, bring in a mobile home, convert an outbuilding into a living unit, or share the farmhouse. The terrain is uneven with steep ridges. Accessibility is problematic.

We invite written inquiry (please enclose SASE) from feminists seeking community. Pioneering a women's community may be the most challenging and rewarding experience of a lifetime. 12/19/94

SWEETWATER COMMUNITY LAND TRUST

Route 3, Box 177
Mansfield, MO 65704

(417)741-7363

Sweetwater Community Land Trust holds 480 rural acres on the Gasconade River —60 acres farmland, the rest wooded. Our community structure is a hybrid of communal and private: All land is owned and managed by the Trust, which gives 99-year leases for 10-acre homesites. The Trust is managed by a council composed of all leaseholders; decision making is by consensus. Buildings, tools, vehicles, businesses, etc., are privately owned. Individuals and families manage their own finances.

Sweetwater operates as a "neighborhood" where members determine their own levels of involvement, cooperation, support, and sharing within the community—from totally private at one end, to cooperative housing, gardens, businesses, etc., at the other. The Land Trust is not a community government—its sole legal function is holding title and leasing land. We are "social anarchists"—we govern by developing cooperative arrangements rather than relying on a "government." Our primary focus as a community is land stewardship and environmental quality, along with optimization of human well-being and relationships. Send #10 SASE (with 2 stamps) for details about visits and membership. [cc] 1/4/93

SYNERGY HOUSE

550 San Juan Avenue
Stanford, CA 94305

sirna@xenon.stanford.edu

We are a student-run cooperative on the Stanford University campus. We cook, clean, and subvert the system together. Vegetarian/vegan cuisine, an organic

garden, and communal living provide a thrilling antidote to the sterility of our surroundings. Residence in Synergy is limited to Stanford students (both undergrad and graduate), but we love guests and nonresidents who come over regularly for dinner. Past Synergy mottoes have included: "If it moves, hug it; if it doesn't, compost it" and "Why borrow from a friend when you can steal from the establishment?" We'd love to hear from communards at other institutions of "higher learning," so get in touch! SASE requested. [cc] 9/24/94

SYNTONY

(Forming)
P.O. Box 6306
Captain Cook, HI 96704

Aloha! We are a 3-adult polyfidelitous family, together 12 years, looking to meet others interested in either expanded family or community. We are communal on a family level, and collaborative on a community level. Our politics lie on the anarchist end of Libertarianism, so we support individuality while still valuing cooperation with clear agreements for group energy. We live rurally on the Big Island of Hawaii, are vegetarians, gardeners, and live off the grid. PEP is our publishing company [see Resource listing], and we produce a quarterly magazine, *Loving More*; a book, *The Polyfidelity Primer*; and host an annual conference promoting polyfidelity and other committed group relationships. Our vision includes a 6-adult family with possible children. As a family we'd love to live clustered near other families to share larger projects and celebrations. Our spiritual perspective is very eclectic, based in love and nature. We already enjoy being part of a supportive network, and seek contact with adventurous singles, dyads, and groups to exchange energy and possibly link up. Do we have something to offer each other? Can we have an exciting win-win impact on each others' lives? SASE requested. 8/31/93

Communities magazine
Journal of Cooperative Living

▶ Supplements the *Communities Directory* with current information about communities in North America — including those now forming.

TALIESIN COMMUNITY

(Forming)
P.O. Box 494
Maybrook, NY 12543

Forming as a residential land trust community with a nonprofit educational center. Inspired by the Findhorn Community, we honor all traditions that contribute to experiencing the Earth as sacred. We are dedicated to spiritual ecology, consensus, communication skills, and conflict resolution. Write, or send $3 postage to receive Prospectus. 1/23/94

TANGUY HOMESTEADS

37 Twin Pine Way
Glen Mills, PA 19342

Est. '45 as an INTENTIONAL community, with a primary goal to develop low-cost housing that would be cooperatively owned, with no limitations on membership with respect to color, race, or creed. Families had about 2 leased acres each, with 10 acres of community land. Today most of Tanguy's houses are on deeded rather than leased land, and few could still be characterized as low-cost. Our present 38 member families vary in race, political preference, religious point of view, and job skills.

Each resident adult is asked to regularly attend monthly membership meetings (where we make community decisions), take part in work days, and serve on at least one committee—where most of our organization and program are carried out. One challenge: right now about one quarter of the members are very active, while another quarter seldom participate. Our $30 monthly assessment is used to maintain community-owned land and buildings, to pay taxes and insurance, and to support various community activities.

Celebrations, holidays, an annual camping trip, pottery classes, dances, and weekly potlucks all contribute to our spirit of community living. Prospective members need to get to know us before a house becomes available—by attending potlucks, membership meetings, other community events; and by discussing with various members the many aspects of our community. [cc] 1/12/95 [84]

TEKIAH COMMUNITY

(Re-Forming)
Route 1, Box 35
Check, VA 24072
(540)651-3412

[Formerly the Institute for Sustainable Living.] We are located in Floyd County, in the Blue Ridge Mountains. Since merging with Abundant Dawn (see also) we have been growing quickly. We currently have a small farm but expect to move to a larger property within the next two years. Meanwhile, we are getting our financial ducks in a row: refining our farmers' market methods and starting a portable sawmill business. We are also creating a 501c3 nonprofit corporation for a demonstration farm and Sustainable Lifeways Center.

We consider ourselves part of the global movement toward joyful, sustainable lifeways. We are committed to creating a largely self-sufficient community which blends all the parts of our lives—physical, spiritual, emotional, and intellectual—into an integrated nourishing whole.

We grow organic vegetables, and we eat together regularly. We handle conflict responsibly and openly. We respect spiritual diversity, and we share rituals of celebration and transition with each other.

Our concept of sustainability includes personal responsibility for ourselves, each other, and the natural world; a commitment to directing energy toward healing the ills of society; loving, respectful attitudes towards each other and our children; a focus on ecology and land stewardship; an emphasis on holistic education and childrearing, including the creation of a school within the community; a commitment to supporting personal growth and creative expression; egalitarian sharing of work responsibilities and income; and economic, architectural, and decision-making systems that support all the above. Call or write to schedule a visit. SASE requested. [cc] 10/1/95

TEN STONES

(Forming)
RR 2 Box 2120
Charlotte, VT 05445
(802)425-4525/985-9717

It is our purpose to build an intentional community on our 88 acres of rural land in Charlotte, Vermont, that embraces the interconnectedness of all life. We feel that Western Culture, and America in particular, is fragmented and individualistic, too hurried, materialistic, and damaging to the environment. The current ways are unsustainable. Our society has lost touch with the myths and dreams that have provided inspiration in the past. Our intent is to revive these passionate points and in the process create a place where we can be gentle with ourselves, our children, our land, and contribute to building a new world. SASE requested. 5/13/93

TERAMANTO INC.

10218 – 147th Street SE
Renton, WA 98059-4103
(360)255-3563

Our aims: benefit our neighbors near and far, resolve conflicts in so doing, conserve the natural environment. We accept new residents, plan to divide later to form a rural sister.

We're semi-rural, 30 minutes from Seattle—9 adults and 1 child in three houses, building a fourth, with another 1/3 acre for a fifth. We plan a community building for our pasture. We work together in our construction, organic garden/ orchard, house repairs, gathering firewood. Weekly and spontaneous are meals, meetings—business, meditating, philosophizing. Decisions are by consensus. We exclude drugs, tobacco, alcohol abuse, and are mostly vegetarian. Each gives an equal monthly share of the cash and labor outgo of one's household. Most work outside part-time. Enterprises are planned here for self-sufficiency.

Our projects: supporting the NW Preservation Trust (conserves open space and provides land for low-income housing), solar energy applications, peace demonstrations, communities' conferences, Habitat for Humanity construction. Prospective visitors are welcome to write, enclosing SASE, or phone (between 7:30–8:00AM Pacific Time is best) for appointment times. 7/30/92

THREE SPRINGS

(Forming)
P.O. Box 710
North Fork, CA 93643-0710
(209)877-7113/877-7891 Fax

We are a newly formed community located in the exact geographic center of California, in the foothills of the Sierra Nevada mountains. Our land has a beautiful year-round stream with waterfalls and swimming holes; many canyons, trees, and meadows; covering 160 acres we care to preserve. We plan to grow food on four acres, surrounded by three year-round springs and a flume. Along with growing food for sustenance, we will work with alternative forms of shelter, such as fired clay, Earthships, etc.

Socially, we plan to develop a community-owned land trust with consensus voting, also creating cottage enterprises for self-sufficiency and living lightly on the land. Our nonprofit organization "Integrated Earth" has a primary focus of giving back the wealth of information that we have, as well as what we will gather through our work and experience in developing the Three Springs Community. We will also be developing a multimedia communications facility to share our discoveries.

We are currently a core group of 9 members, bonded together by our care for humanity and the planet we live on. We are open to share our land and vision with others, and welcome new members. Feel free to call or write. SASE requested. 7/21/94

TIMEWEAVE

Boulder, CO

(COMMUNITY LISTING REMOVED)

Timeweave is now a community center, not a residential intentional community. We still act as a referral service, often helping people connect with things they seek. See also, Solstice Institute, in the Resources section. 12/17/95

TOADHOUSE

(Non-Residential)
Site: Shaver Lake, CA
Contact:
P.O. Box 16379
San Francisco, CA 94116
(415)864-1488

Toadhouse is a cooperative recreation housing community with a jointly owned cabin at Camp Sierra in the National Forest in California. We are together at our cabin annually, semi-annually, for cooperative camp, and for work weeks. We are a share corporation (ten family shares) and at present have seven member families who have bought in and pay a monthly amount to cover our overhead. Present and former Toads often maintain close friendships developed as Toad members, which keeps community continuity and extended-family relationships beyond economic choice, i.e., into the realm of intentional community. 7/16/94

TOLSTOY FARM

Rt 3 Box 72-W
Davenport, WA 99122

Tolstoy Farm (1963) is an eclectic community stewarding 240 acres of canyon land in eastern Washington, 32 miles NW of Spokane. About the only thing all have in common is organic gardening. There are two parcels (160 and 80 acres), each corporately owned, with land designated for common use and leased "homesteads." On the "160" there are 10 adults and 4 children, and most homes are solar electric. On the "80" there are 5 adults and 5 children, and most homes are "on the grid." Members earn money working outside jobs and some home businesses. Occasional openings for new members occur when a departing member sells. No profit or capital gain is allowed on lease transfers. Some households take in apprentices who wish to experience our lifestyles. Farm alumni own five adjoining parcels.

We try to respect Mother Earth, ourselves, and each other. We believe that individual freedoms and community consensus can coexist. We are tolerant, liberal, and ethical. We vary from hermits to one family interested in polyfidelity. Except for weekly potlucks, we find little need for community meetings. Those wishing "all your info" should tell us about yourself, and inspire us to find the time to write. Please enclose a SASE. [cc] 11/7/93 [84]

TORONTO TORI COMMUNITY

(Non-Residential)
43 Albany Avenue #2
Toronto, Ontario M5R-3C2
CANADA

(416)538-3108

The Toronto TORI Community gathers about eight times a year, from as far away as New York City and San Diego. TORI, an acronym for Trust, Openness, Realization, and Interdependence, was outlined by Jack Gibb in his book *Trust* and presented in workshops around the continent in the '70s. The Toronto gatherings jelled into a community, based on those four ideals, that has continued ever since. With an experimental approach to process, we "create" community anew at each gathering, and trust the inclinations of participants to provide for the needs of the group. We're family-oriented, and we're proud of what the kids who have been with us all their lives have grown up to become. The ongoing community, without organizational formalities other than a bank account, depends upon volunteers for everything from searching out meeting sites to publishing our newsletter. Important decisions are made by the group as a whole whenever possible, in community meetings that are as unstructured as is the community itself. Visitors are welcome at our gatherings, and membership consists of just choosing to be part of us. 8/8/94

TRAILS END RANCH

Box 2406
Hot Springs, AR 71914
(501)767-2431

Trails End Ranch was established in 1983

in north central Arkansas. We are a group of like-minded people interested in our emotional and physical well-being. We seek basic self-sufficiency, organic gardening, and alternate power sources. We have a modified lifestyle, family network —social equality and decision making. We strive to help those around us, and the animals of our local environment. Considering world and local conditions, we are gradually drifting toward self-sufficiency and survivalism. Purposes: improve social, economic standard of living, reduce overhead, work on ecology, increase survival preparedness. All members enjoy a great deal of travel. We are looking for sincere dedicated individuals to help build this lifestyle in our beautiful semi-mountainous region with an abundance of lakes, streams, timber, and hiking trails. The members think this is a unique community for selective individuals with a sincere desire to work and play. SASE requested. 12/2/92

TRIFORM CAMPHILL COMMUNITY

Route 4, Box 151
Hudson, NY 12534

(518)851-9320/851-2864 Fax

Triform is a small Camphill community which includes young adults with disabilities. Our task is building a vital community life that offers each person the conditions for healing and growth. We are one of 80 Camphill places worldwide based on insights given by R. Steiner through

anthroposophy, and K. Konig's work in social therapy-curative education. Administratively independent, we share Camphill's common goal of providing dignified work, a supportive social environment, and a vibrant cultural life for and with handicapped people.

Located on 81 acres of farmland in rural NY, we have 5 houses, a barn and dairy, bakery, weavery, workshop, and community center. Each household is an extended family of single or married house parents, children, and people with special needs. Land work is central; we practice biodynamic methods of gardening and farming. We work in the houses, bakery, and fabric arts workshop. We offer an education program of art, academic, and practical skills courses. All participate in plays, outings, festival celebrations. Of 45 residents, half are people with social or mental handicaps, half are coworkers. Long-term coworkers have made a commitment to community life. We also have young volunteers, many from Europe, who stay for 6 months or more and may take seminars. [cc] 10/27/93

TRIPLE CREEK

Chesaw Route, Box 74
Oroville, WA 98844

(509)485-2702/485-3816

[Formerly Antakarana Circle.] We are a twelve-year-old community of about 13 adults and 9 children, located near Chesaw, a small town in the highlands of north

central Washington. Because we live in separately owned households, have independent livelihoods, and hold meetings only when absolutely necessary, we are more like a little village than a commune. Our homes are spread out over 530 acres of land that is collectively owned and certified as organic; many of us have productive gardens, and one family runs a seed company. Everyone has either an outside job or a cottage industry of some kind. Our shared values are nonviolence, cooperation, and stewardship of the land. We believe in living peacefully and simply, and are all involved in a grassroots movement to protect the Okanogan highlands from exploitation by multinational mining companies. Our decision-making process is egalitarian: by consensus if possible, by majority vote when necessary. We are open to new members of varied spiritual, intellectual, and sexual orientations who share these Earth-centered values with us. Prospective members are subject to approval after a one-year trial period; housing is limited, and new members might have to build their own dwellings. NOTE: We will *only* respond to telephone calls. 12/1/92

TRUTH CONSCIOUSNESS

•**Sacred Mountain Ashram**
 & Community Center
 10668 Gold Hill Road
 Boulder, CO 80302-9716

(303)447-1637/459-3538

• **Desert Ashram
& Community Center
3403 W. Sweetwater Drive
Tucson, AZ 85745-9103
(520)743-0384**

Truth Consciousness was founded in 1974 by Swami Amar Jyoti as a vehicle for spiritual awakening. The primary focus is the uplifting of human consciousness into a life in tune with the Divine. The organization presently maintains ashrams and community centers in Boulder, CO, and Tucson, AZ. These centers provide a setting for devotees and disciples to grow spiritually under the direct guidance of the Master. Some devotees live residentially together, others live in mainstream community. Meditation, yoga instruction, retreats, and biweekly Satsangs (spiritual discourses) are open to all sincere seekers. Guests are welcome to visit the centers by special arrangement. While there is never a fee for any of these programs (other than retreats), donations are always welcome. 12/19/94

TWIN CITIES COHOUSING NETWORK

**(Forming Groups)
Minneapolis, MN**

An umbrella organization in the greater St. Paul/Minneapolis area. [See Resource listing.] 1/10/94

TWIN OAKS

**138-D6 Twin Oaks Road
Louisa, VA 23093**

**(540)894-5126/894-4112 Fax
TwinOaks@mcimail.com
http://www.ic.org/twinoaks/**

Twin Oaks is a community of 100 people living on 450 acres of farm and forest land in rural Virginia. Since the community's beginning in 1967, our way of life has reflected our values of equality, ecology, and nonviolence.

We are economically self-sufficient. Our hammocks and casual furniture business generates most of our income; indexing books and making tofu provide much of the rest. Still, less than half of our work goes into these income-producing activities; the balance goes into a variety of tasks that benefit our quality of life—including milking cows, gardening, cooking, and childcare. Most people prefer doing a variety of work, rather than the same job day in, day out.

A number of us choose to be politically active in issues of peace, ecology, anti-racism, and feminism. Each summer we host a women's gathering: "Women—Celebrating Our Creativity," and each fall, we host a Communities Conference where we welcome both experienced communitarians, and seekers who are new to community living.

In spring 1992 Twin Oaks reached maximum population, and instituted a waiting list for membership. Visits are arranged by letter, not over the phone; first write to us (well in advance of your proposed stay) for our visitor info, including a schedule of our upcoming visitor periods. If you visit and are accepted for provisional membership, the wait to join may be several months or longer. We completed new housing in the fall of 1995, and this has had some effect on our membership housing situation. Please write to us for more information. [Cmtas1, 1, 3, 9, 16, 21, 28, 32, 33, 35, 43, 45, 47, 61, 63, 73, 76, 82, 83, 84, 85]

TWIN PINES COOPERATIVE COMMUNITY

**835 Pomeroy Avenue
Santa Clara, CA 95051**

(408)249-8994

TPCC is a limited equity housing cooperative in a high-density urban neighborhood. We have 10 buildings spread over two city blocks, with 8 two-story townhouse units per building. Individual units are 2 or 3 bedrooms with carport, outdoor storage, and fenced patio. Common areas include a swimming pool, rec room, office, young children's playgrounds, an older children's area, and picnic tables.

Members elect a Board of Directors at an annual meeting, and active committees include Pets, Finance, Social, and Member Selection. The social committee deals with children and non-community issues, and plans children's use of the rec room, pool games, the Christmas party, movies, videos, and an Easter egg hunt. There are usually about 30 members attending Board meetings.

A 3-bedroom unit is $380 per month —extremely affordable when compared to similar units in the neighborhood which go for $900. TPCC is diverse ethnically, and houses low-to-moderate income families. The driving force is a few members who were here when TPCC was founded over 20 years ago. 9/13/94

UNION ACRES

**Route 1, Box 61-J
Union Hill Road
Whittier, NC 28789**

(704)497-4964

Union Acres is founded on spiritual, ecological, and egalitarian principles, and based on consensus, simplicity, and wholesome living. Our purpose is "to live as neighbors in peace, harmony, and ecological balance; to respect and support one another and all forms of life; to attune to and act in harmony with the universal life force which is the essence of all existence." Guidelines promoting harmony and conflict resolution are provided, but the freedom and privacy of individuals are maintained. There is no requirement to ascribe to any religious or political ideology other than attunement to the "good of the whole."

24 homesites between one and five acres lie nestled in the Great Smokey mountains, with seven acres set aside as common land. We now have two tracts available for sale to like-minded individuals or families to join us. Group decisions are made by consensus. Common property includes nature trails, creek, meadow, gardens, and a community building. Group endeavors include community organic gardens, cooperative homeschooling, a food co-op, recycling center, shared meals, and recreation. Potential cottage industries in holistic retreats, workshops, whole foods, alternative building, fiber arts, etc. SASE requested. 5/12/92

UNITED RESEARCH LIGHT CENTER

**P.O. Box 1146
2200 Highway 9, South
Black Mountain, NC 28711**

(704)669-6845

The Center was begun in 1970 with the intent to heal the Earth, and thus the individual, through Light prayer and meditation ("Light" is a quiet and powerful state which, when experienced, puts one in harmony with the universe, adding to universal harmony and personal health). Our resident staff of three live cooperatively, and hope for others to buy land here and live with us. Sacred prayer is practiced twice each day, and we offer classes in yoga, meditation, inner strength, and unconditional love; plus weekend programs and longer retreats. Our goal is to have 24-hour meditation in our dome in order to create a place of good energy. 6/28/94

UNKNOWN TRUTH FELLOWSHIP WORKERS

(Forming)
HCR 1, Box 23
Warrensburg, NY 12885

(518)623-2831

Unknown Truth Fellowship Workers believes in the true religion now as well as seeks it. Vibes come from it directing us. We are celibate as "the Kingdom is unmarried, man left wives, I am the resurrection." We ally with such communes as Yahwehists, Shakers, Serpent Handling Pentecostals, Cave Saints, Waldenses, Native Americans, Naturalists, UFOs, etc. We eat Kosher and organic. In seeking truth much is yet to be learned. Weider exercise, outdoor living, Shamanism, genetic structuring, astrology, archeology, gold mining, rock hounding, crafts, herbs, much more. We also have a writing ministry.

Yahwehists teach the name Christ Jesus comes from Greek manuscripts XEs-sex equal to 666. All, millions of close encounters say no creator and savior a charlatan. A few books we recommend are *Subliminal Seduction* by Key, *The Sacred Mushroom and the Cross* by Allegro, *Foxfire 7*, and *Gnostics*—Inner Light Publications, Box 753, New Brunswick NJ 08903.

Funds permitting, we hope to purchase land for our commune and Truth Research Center. The good old Revival Spirit will prevail. Our library of 5000 volumes is available to members. We mail out the book *Snake Handlers*, illustrated, by Carden and Pelton for $5, and also distribute other literature. All queries answered. SASE requested. 2/14/94

THE VALE

P.O. Box 207
Yellow Springs, OH 45387

(513)767-1461/767-1511

Established in 1961, we now have ten member families and three non-member families living on 40 acres of mostly wooded land near Yellow Springs, a town of about 4000 and home of Antioch College. Each family lives in its own home and earns its own living outside the Vale. We manage the land and utilities together.

We govern by consensus. Several families are Quakers. Some families are vegetarians, most families have vegetable gardens, some have chickens and goats.

We are family-oriented, and desire families who share concern for the natural environment, the wider society, and for the well-being of the family unit. Interested people must live here for at least a year before applying for membership. 3/11/94 [4]

VALLEY OF LIGHT

(Re-Forming)
Box 34
Deer, AR 72628

(501)575-0567

Valley of Light is a spiritually oriented community whose emphasis is on self-realization and self-sufficiency, located on 55 acres in a secluded valley inside 15,000 acres of a National Wilderness. Projected land use includes separate areas for community activity, residences, and cropland/pasture.

GOALS: Create a time/space where the self-realization of each member is fully supported and nurtured. Live in harmony with each other and nature. Share spiritual life together. Flow with Universal Energy so all actions are appropriate. Become self-sufficient so that conditions "outside" have little effect on the community.

NOTES: The community is Egalitarian. The structure consists of Goals, Membership Requirements, Membership Rights, and Agreements. There is a 3- to 6-month trial membership period (by consensus). The diet is basically vegetarian. Planned: homeschooling, cottage industries, separate sleeping quarters for each family; all other facilities are communal. There is a membership fee, and a permanent member may "purchase" a 99-year lease on a one-acre parcel. The Valley is a "multi-spiritual path" community, open to all people regardless of age, sex, race, or ideology, according to consensus of current members. 5/28/92

VASHON CO-HOUSING GROUP

P.O. Box 275
Vashon, WA 98070
(206)463-2945/567-4410

After three years of wrestling bureaucracy, digging utility trenches, and getting the first two houses built, we discover we've become a family in the process. Egad! This is what it's about, right? *Vashon* is a small town, rural island near Seattle. We have 12 acres near town with wetlands, trees and rain, and 18 homesites (only 5 of which are spoken for so far). *Cohousing* means a pedestrian-friendly, interactive neighborhood with private ownership of homes, joint ownership of land and common house. *Group* means those of us adventurous enough to try it. No political or religious affiliation. Our spirit shines best through shovels, toolboxes, and good cooking. We help each other. 12/1/93

VEGAN COHOUSING WORKING GROUP

(Forming)
PO Box 40684
San Francisco, CA 94140
(415)487-6335
bboyd@ccsf.cc.ca.us
http://www.cohousing.org/specific/vegan/

Creating an ecological, vegan-friendly cohousing community for eight to 25 individuals and families in an urban neighborhood, Target date: 1997±. At least all common meals will be vegan. Aiming for maximum affordability for very low-income people. No sects or gurus involved. Phone calls returned collect, or send SASE. 9/17/94

VEILED CLIFFS

(Forming)
15826 State Route 218
Scottown, OH 45678
(614)256-1400

We're a small group (4 humans, 2 mastiffs, a cat, and a puppykitty) living on 145 acres in SE Ohio. Our few cottage industries are insignificant as yet, but we hope to eliminate our debt within a few years and begin construction of our new home. Currently, we live in an old farmhouse, and we look forward to getting more space. Our land is mountainous, which adds beauty but makes home and garden sites hard to find. We want 60% or better self-sufficiency, and have goats and chickens to help reach that goal. Our purpose is to live with regard for other people, living beings, and the Earth. We share the belief that living equals growing/learning, and that honesty, openness, and compassion must be the foundation of our interactions. We are a Community-in-Dialog with the Federation of Egalitarian Communities, and members of the F.I.C. Thus, we share all income and hold all property in common, give all members equal voice (using consensus for decision making), strive for nonviolence, and work for community networking. We recycle and compost, and try to live lightly on the Earth. We welcome visitors (with notice!) and inquiries, but please include SASE. Our future looks bright, and we are looking for new members. 11/23/92

VICTOR TRADE CO-OP

Victor, CO
(COMMUNITY LISTING REMOVED)
Community has folded. 9/1/95

VINE & FIG TREE

11076 County Road 267
Lanett, AL 36863
(334)499-2380

Est. 1986, VFT is now 6 adults, 2 dogs, 1 cat, and many many Mexican bean beetles and other family members on 240 rural Alabama acres. The VFT vision: to live loving nonviolence—on and with the land, among ourselves, and with all creation. "And *everyone* 'neath the vine and fig tree, shall live in peace and unafraid; and into plowshares beat *our* swords, *we* shall learn war no more." Yes, we have grape and blackberry vines and fig trees! And the rest of it we're working on.

The VFT problem: all this land! and how best to do and be here, learning permaculture but a lot of the land still covered with cows to almost pay the taxes, a long way to consensus, and we're off on part-time jobs, and peace/justice activism, and working on the relationship, and caring for elderly parents, and there is no security (and here is no security, either).

The VFT solution: all of the above, plus such good friends old and new (Hey Mac and John and Nikki and Daniel Earl and all!) and joys of music, consensus, compost, war tax resistance, lambsquarters, working on the trailer and/or tractor, loving you, our tomatoes, muscadine jam gifting, supporting battered women and death-row friends, walking From Trident to Life, Always Coming Home, working on the relationship some more, singing just one more song, and having just one more little bite, and much, much more! SASE requested. [cc] 11/11/92

VISION FOUNDATION

Caring Rapid Healing Center
1620 Thompson Road
Coos Bay, OR 97420
(503)267-6412/269-5712 Fax
(800)545-7810
(COMMUNITY LISTING REMOVED)

The residential community has folded. Its founder, Ken Keyes Jr., moved on to start the Caring Rapid Healing Center, focusing on rapid methods for psychological healing, with a written guarantee of effectiveness (the first ever offered for work in the field of mental healing). The main emphasis is on inner child injuries that have been dysfunctionally programmed into the unconscious mind during the first few years of life. A Work/Learn program is available for volunteers. Ken passed away in early '96, and the center will likely relocate this summer to the San Francisco Bay Area. 3/27/96

VIVEKANANDA MONASTERY & RETREAT CENTER

6723 Fenn Valley Road
Fennville, MI 49408
(616)543-4545/543-4114

Situated on 108 acres of land, the Vivekananda Monastery and Retreat offers a quiet rural setting with facilities for individual and group retreats. This is a branch of the Vivekananda Vedanta Society of Chicago [see separate listing]. Our residential community is comprised of celibate adults who share a willingness to work, and acceptance of the path of others. We offer regular classes, and a schedule of conferences, concerts, and meditation workshops. Write for more information. 4/26/92

VIVEKANANDA VEDANTA SOCIETY

5423 South Hyde Park Blvd.
Chicago, IL 60615

(312)363-0027

The Vivekananda Vedanta Society of Chicago is a branch of the Ramakrishna Math and Mission which has its headquarters at Belur Math, India. The Chicago center was founded in 1930, although Swami Vivekananda participated in the Parliament of Religions held in Chicago in 1893—becoming the first Hindu monk to bring the message of Vedanta to the West.

The Society maintains a temple, monastery, and guest house in Chicago, and a monastery with retreat facilities in Michigan. Both centers maintain bookshops which are open every day, and libraries of books on eastern and western religion and culture. 4/26/92

WALKER CREEK FARM

1802-C Peter Burns Road
Mt. Vernon, WA 98273

(360)724-4402

Walker Creek Farm is a member of the Evergreen Land Trust, and is home to 8 adults and 7 children. Our purpose is to protect and develop this piece of land in a safe way. We all grow gardens, plant trees and many other plants. Ducks, chickens, and sheep live here also. Our community is a group of nuclear families that pull together to take care of the land and each other. We do things very impromptu and naturally. We value being a part of the larger community, and stay active in various ways. Folks are welcome to visit; we like to show people another example of community. We have our own water and electric systems, and can inspire folks to do the same. We are not open to growth at this time. SASE requested. 12/17/94

WE'MOON HEALING GROUND

(Re-Forming)
P.O. Box 1395
Estacada, OR 97023

(503)630-7848

We live in a circle: We'Moon healing in the sanctuary of Mother Earth. Although this has been womyn's land for twenty years now, we're still just learning how to live in peace with ourselves, each other, and the Earth in a healing way. The small group of womyn who are here now is currently (late '92, early '93) in the process of re-forming as an intentional, sustainable, egalitarian, eco-lesbian-feminist, amazonian-witchy-matriarchal, artistic, spiritual, (r)evolutionary community.

We produce *We'Moon: Gaia Rhythms for Womyn* (an astrological moon calendar and appointment book) every year. We celebrate the cycles, seasons, and ourselves in our life and work together. With our few humble structures in place, we are consciously creating We'Moon culture —a safe space for healing into wholeness, nourishing an organic garden, and maintaining (possibly expanding) land structures. We are likely seeking new members: organic gardeners, healers, builders, artists. Please respect that we are in the process of reorganizing ourselves so what we say now may have changed and evolved by the time you contact us. Please plan plenty of time for contacting us and possibly arranging a visit. Blessed be on your path. Please include SASE. [cc] 12/30/92

WELLSPRING

(Forming)
P.O. Box 72
Newburg, WI 53060-0072

(414)675-6755

Mission: "To live in harmony with self, others and the Earth."

Wellspring is a not-for-profit educational organization founded March, 1982. Public programs flow from its mission and span wellness education, ecology and gardening, the arts, and personal growth. In 1988 Wellspring moved to the country. Nestled in a tranquil valley, along the Milwaukee River, Wellspring's 31.5 acres offer nature trails, woods, meadows, and gardens for guests and residents. Its land, bordering the Kettle Moraine, is 10 miles from Lake Michigan and 35 minutes from downtown Milwaukee—an easy driving distance for program participants or those who want to

enjoy the land. Once a private estate, its cozy buildings are used year-round for conferences, meetings, or retreats for individuals and small groups.

Wellspring's organic garden program is a school for biodynamic gardening. Interns exchange room and board for 25 hours work/study. The garden program demonstrates that many people can be fed on small acreage (1 acre feeds 150). The garden season runs from March to November. Customers receive fresh garden produce weekly for 25 weeks, delivered to their urban neighborhoods. This is a form of Community Supported Agriculture.

During the 5 years on the land, 25 different people have been residents at Wellspring, never exceeding 5 residents at any one time. Most have been part-time staff. We share a common philosophy and love for the land. Aware of our mission, community happens—though we didn't set out to be an "intentional community."

Plans are under way to expand the land to 100 acres, create more garden space (orchards, grain fields, vineyards), and build a cohousing intentional neighborhood overlooking the valley. There are still openings for homeowners and renters who want to live in this ecovillage. SASE requested. [cc] 11/10/92

WELLSPRING HOUSE, INC.

(Re-Forming)
302 Essex Avenue
Gloucester, MA 01930

(508)281-3221

Our "core" community is the heart of a larger group of other staff, volunteers, board, and "friends" who together carry out our threefold mission of shelter, housing, and education—in a spirit of hospitality. We make a home and homes. We operate a shelter for homeless families, offer education and training for empowerment, do economic development, and create affordable housing. Through our second corporation, a community land trust, the "core" community members share a simple lifestyle, and share home with homeless families. We teach (locally and through lectures nationwide), garden (organically), pray, sing, and party. We are ecumenical, feminist (including men), busy, and efficient. We are united by mission, not formal commitment. We earn salaries, contributing some to the work. We are growing in scope, reputation, friends...but plan to be small enough to be friendly. Our goal is social transformation, and formerly homeless women are now part of the work. We are interested in new members and in interns who care about our mission rather than those seeking community. 6/30/92

WESLEYAN CHRISTIAN COMMUNITY

P.O. Box 668
Vashon Island, WA 98070

(206)463-9123

The Wesleyan Christian Community was formed in 1977, growing out of a Church congregation which desired the richer and more fulfilling Christian experience and life experience that community can provide. We have also organized a Retreat Center to provide a haven where people—no matter what their religion, race, or nationality— may come for help to deal with their spiritual, emotional, and relationship problems. This inner-healing ministry, developed over a period of 22 years, is accomplished through counseling, workshops, and in-residence programs. The only charge while here is for the food.

We also provide for the staff and their families (28 adults, 20 children) a warm, loving, and supportive extended family environment in which to live and work.

Each family lives in their own quarters, and handles their own money. Each member is presently making a monthly contribution to finance a major construction project, and tithes 15% to finance our inner-healing ministry.

The community is governed by the members through a weekly meeting, where a unanimous vote is required on all issues. SASE requested. 4/23/92

WESTCHESTER COHOUSING GROUP

(Forming)
P.O. Box 475
Hastings, NY 10706-0475

(914)639-4146/639-1300 Fax

We are a group that has been active in Westchester County, New York, for four years, educating ourselves and the public about the cohousing concept, investigating sites, drawing up preliminary plans, and building membership. We are looking at sites in central Westchester that are within a one-hour commute of New York City. Our community will ideally be located on a site with plenty of green space, near a town with a MetroNorth train station and good public schools.

We intend to create a cross-generational neighborhood for singles, families, and the elderly. We encourage anyone to join us, regardless of age, race, religious outlook, or sexual orientation, who desires more community in his or her life.

The Westchester Cohousing Community is aiming for an average price of $180,000 for a 2-bedroom dwelling unit. Units will range in size from 1 bedroom to possibly 4 bedrooms.

Membership in WCC requires a membership fee or deposit of $10,000, payable over six months, to be used toward the eventual cost of your unit, and $25/mo in dues for day-to-day operating expenses. Non-voting associate members may join for $250 that will apply toward the full membership fee. 1/13/95

WESTSIDE VEGETARIAN COMMUNITY

(Re-Forming)
12479 Walsh Avenue
Los Angeles, CA 90066

(310)823-7846/823-0287

The WVC is a vegetarian cooperative centered around conscious living. We recycle nearly everything, buy primarily organic

food, and share cooking responsibilities and maintenance chores. We eat no meat and very few milk products in the house.

We have a spacious home located near Marina Del Rey (one mile from the ocean) close to a bike path and shopping. There are seven bedrooms, a living room, a quiet room, four bathrooms, and off-street parking. We also have a sun deck, a vegetable and ornamental garden, a back cottage, and a storage shed. The home is owned by a partnership of tenants.

We are looking for people who want to share and create a vision of community, and have the energy to make it work. 6/17/93

WESTWOOD COHOUSING

(Forming)
P.O. Box 16116
Ashville, NC 28816

(704)252-2118
**http://www.www.automatrix
.com/~bak/westwood.html**

A cohousing community on a 4-acre site with woods, creek, and gardens in a quiet neighborhood in Asheville, NC, in the Blue Ridge mountains, close to city amenities and national forest. Our plan includes 23 energy-efficient, privately owned dwellings clustered around a central building for optional community activities, meals, and fun; pedestrian-friendly commons, with parking kept at perimeter; and several work studios for residents. For site design and landscaping we're using permaculture principles: knowledge of natural ecosystems for harmonious integration of landscape and people.

Early members are helping design the site and buildings; construction is due to start in '95. Price range $60,000–$120,000. Westwood welcomes diversity by age, family types, races, occupation, income levels, sexual orientations, religious beliefs. Common facilities and some dwellings will be wheelchair accessible. Priorities: wholesome environment for children, efficient utilization of resources, opportunities for members to learn skills that enhance community life, and service to the wider neighborhood. Please include SASE with inquiries. 6/30/94

WHEEL COMMUNITY GATHERING

(Forming)
10 Applebough Lane
Rose Valley, PA 19063

(215)565-4058
(215)642-4459 (Message)

We are a gathering of folks working to build support and maintain community. We gather at least once a month in homes to give love and support, share community events, info, concerns, interests, and news of ongoing projects. Some of us share housing. We dream of living together on a daily basis, but have not been clearly led in any direction so we stay put. Most of us homeschool and are vegetarian. We share a reverence for life and connection to all living things. Spiritual practices vary, but we all share in times of silence, prayer, and meditation. We can't do it alone; please join us. Ongoing projects: feeding homeless; music mak-

ing; bimonthly publication of essays, poems, prayers, artwork—we welcome contributions; homeschool co-oping; food co-op. Please write or call (SASE requested). 11/10/92

WHITE BUFFALO FARM

**1675-4110 Olde River Road
Paonia, CO 81428**

(970)527-3041

A 20-year-old cooperative community dedicated to realizing ourselves. Although our primary focus is participation in the realization of the Divine, we are open to many spiritual paths. Several families jointly own the property, and we share all income. Major decisions are by consensus. Our membership includes 5 women and five men, and we have no space for new members. Located in lovely mountain country. Our visitor/guest policy is loose, and depends on how people fit in. In some cases, visitors can arrange to be paid for working here. Please write ahead. 6/24/94

WHITE HOUSE

**1133 White Street
Ann Arbor, MI 48104**

(313)761-2509

We are one of many self-styled co-op houses here in town. There are currently 3 men and 3 women ages 25–40, and a funky old cat. We are mostly working people, from bakers to teachers, plus a grad student or two.

Our community changes as the people come and go, though people often stay for 2 or 3 or more years. Some of the constants are vegetarian meals together every night; emphasis on organic and whole foods; sharing of all household responsibilities; occasional meetings with informal consensus decision making; mutual respect; and a friendly, fun, relaxed atmosphere. We often hang out together, and include many people from outside the house in our gatherings and activities.

Our house has close ties to the "co-op community" here in Ann Arbor. We are very near one of the food co-ops, and usually have at least a couple people living here who work there or at one of the other co-ops/collective businesses in the area. There is a high level of political and ecological consciousness, and a lot of active involvement in world and local concerns among

household members. We value our diversity as well as our commonality. SASE required. [cc] 4/21/94

WHITEHALL CO-OP

**2500 Nueces
Austin, TX 78705**

(512)472-3329

Founded August 6, 1949, Whitehall Co-op is Texas' oldest housing cooperative. The 13-member household includes a variety of ages and occupations, and everyone contributes equally to monetary costs and household labor. Whitehall is a non-sexist, non-racist, non-competitive living environment. All decisions are made by consensus.

Our goals include obtaining intimate, meaningful tribal/familial bonds, emotional support, and spontaneous and planned creation and play. We are learning proper use of resources, non-competitiveness, and communication skills. We want to be a part of a significant, non-exploitive socio-economic movement.

The household is vegetarian, though fish meals are occasionally prepared. No smoking of any sort is allowed in Whitehall. All members have individual rooms with semi-private bathrooms. Whitehall was the first Texas recipient of funds from the National Co-op Bank (Washington, DC) in '79 for use in construction of a professional-grade kitchen. 8/11/93

WHOLE HEALTH FOUNDATION

**1760 Lake Drive #101
Cardiff, CA 92007**

(619)753-0321

Whole Health Foundation is a vegetarian whole health home, one mile from the ocean in S. California (near San Diego). We share an organic garden, jacuzzi, sauna, outdoor solar shower, laundry; kitchen distilled water system, electric wheatgrass juicer, Norwalk juicer, food dehydrator; and an indoor garden for sunflower and buckwheat greens, wheatgrass, and sprouts. A non-smoking, no drugs, and no pets home.

We conduct workshops on community, and offer management and organization consulting. We also conduct low-cost workshops ($85 for 3 days) on community building, and sell books on health and natural hygiene, water distillers, food supplements, spirulina, and intestinal

cleansing products.

New residents housing is available for $425 per month for established vegetarians and raw food people. Fasting and rejuvenation programs available for $450 per week, supervised, including books and instruction; $295 weekly, unsupervised. Monthly raw food potlucks. Visitors welcome at $25 per person per day. Contact William Polowniak at the above address. SASE required. 3/20/93

WINDWARD FOUNDATION

**55 Windward Lane
Klickitat, WA 98628**

(509)369-2000

Single parents, retirees, gifted kids (human and caprine), and dreamers from 8 to 76 are pioneering a woodsy community, seeking saner social systems, practicing nearly lost crafts, and exploring the holistic relationships involved in living close to the land in a sustainable lifestyle. Windward is a think tank, an operating farm, a school for self-reliance, and an extended family. It's an 80-acre research and development park with more than a hundred tons of tools of all kinds, including a foundry and a dairy. It's a synergy machine that empowers people by combining their life experiences, training, and insights to minimize wasted effort. It's a place to hide away in peace and beauty to write a book or focus on a project you've always wanted to tackle.

Windward is a nonprofit co-op that owns the land while members retain their own assets and organize projects to suit their interests. We emphasize cooperative and egalitarian association, and operate by the consensus process.

Our journal, *Notes From Windward*, is 20 pages that covers both the theory and practice of life at Windward (8 issues/year for $15; sample $3). Note: only established subscribers are considered for possible membership or permission to visit. 7/7/92 [80/81]

WINSLOW COHOUSING

**353 Wallace Way NE
Bainbridge Island, WA 98110**

**(206)842-2872/842-2610
http://www.cohousing.org/
specific/winslow.html**

Winslow Cohousing is located on Bainbridge Island in Puget Sound, 30 minutes west of downtown Seattle by Washington State ferry. Escorted tours are available at 10:15AM on Saturdays. Call (206) 780-1323 to confirm you are planning to come. Un-escorted tours are not available.

We are organized as a Cooperative with 30 dwelling units and a common house. Unit types range from studios to four bedrooms. All units are self-sufficient, with kitchens, dining areas, living rooms, bedrooms, and bathrooms. The group formed in 1989, started construction in 1991, and moved in early in 1992.

Cohousing started in Denmark in the early '70s. The history of cohousing development is described in detail in the book *Cohousing, A Contemporary Approach to Housing Ourselves* by Kathryn McCamant and Charles Durrett, ©1988 Ten Speed Press. We highly recommend reading it if you are interested in what we have done. It is full of plans, photos, interviews, and data about the cohousing communities in Denmark and the States. Send $3 for info package with plans. 10/13/93

WISCOY VALLEY COMMUNITY LAND CO-OP

Route 3, Box 163
Winona, MN 55987
(507)452-4990

Our 356-acre farm is located in the scenic bluff country of S.E. Minnesota. We've been here since 1976, and aspire to treat the land, and each other, with respect. Currently 24 adults (ages 33–52) and 8 children (ages 6–12) live in 14 separate households in valley and ridgetop "niches." We're individually minded folks with no common ideology although we share concerns for ecology and equality. Our differences make us a varied and interesting group. Livelihood is created by a multitude of talents providing income from both home-based businesses and outside jobs. The land also supplies us with an abundance of food for the body and soul.

Our homes are owner-built and designed with energy efficiency in mind, utilizing passive solar, wood heating, and off-grid solar/wind electric. Members own their homes, but the land is owned in common, as well as the original farmhouse and outbuildings which are the community's center for meetings, gatherings, recreation, and utilitarian functions. We are not actively seeking new residents, as we're presently at full capacity. We wish to help others find or start new communities by providing information, inspiration, or connections. SASE requested. 6/22/94

WOLF CREEK RADICAL FAERIE SANCTUARY

P.O. Box 312
Wolf Creek, OR 97497
(541)866-2678

The Wolf Creek Sanctuary is the manifestation of Nomenus' statement of purpose to "create, preserve, and manage places of cultural/spiritual sanctuary for Radical Faeries and their friends to gather in harmony with nature for renewal, growth, and shared learning." Nomenus is incorporated as a church under 501(C)3 of the Tax Code and is a resource for issues concerning the connections between gay men's sexuality and spirituality. The land is also available to outside groups as a rustic gathering/retreat center with primitive campsites and limited indoor lodging, and supports a small group of residents who are members of, and in service to, Nomenus. SASE requested. 11/14/93

WOMAN'S WORLD

(Forming)
P.O. Box 655
Madisonville, LA 70447
(504)892-0765

Woman's World—a lesbian rural group in the early stages of creating safe living space. We are flexible, adventurous risk takers interested in a secure lesbian nation. We will build houses for individual living with both private and community ownership of property, as desired (solar design preferable). We have clean air, water, and soil (great for crops!), and a woodworking shop in progress. High quality living is a major goal. Some available resources include lessons in co-counseling, carpentry, machine maintenance, conflict resolution, Wiccan, and communication. The social outlets in the area include over 100 rural lesbians who gather on a regular basis. We appeal to women who love the land and seek simple outdoor pleasures, who want to grow things and breathe free. Each woman provides her own living structure with help, trades of labor, materials, knowledge, time, money, or consultation. Our vision includes R.V. living, organic produce, house construction, barter, and tribal organization for common projects. Spiritual preferences are completely autonomous! SASE requested. 6/27/92

WOMANSHARE

P.O. Box 681
Grants Pass, OR 97527
(541)862-2807

Womanshare is a home and family of lesbians on 23 acres in southern Oregon. We hold gatherings and events for women, and welcome visitors. 1993 was our 20th anniversary. Womanshare has a visitor cabin, hiking trails, shared meals, and work projects. We ask visitors to give a donation of $10–30 per day, which includes meals. We are a family of women, and while you are here you have the opportunity to share in our daily life and work on the land. There is a main house, open to all, and individual cabins for members and visitors. We have hot water, wood heating stoves, an outdoor composting toilet, electricity, garden, and hot tub. Please call or write in advance to arrange a visit, and include a SASE. We are periodically open for new members or for extended visits. Please let us know if you are interested. 11/10/93 [85]

WOMEN'S CO-OP

20 N. Franklin Street
Madison, WI 53703

We are a community of 8 cat-affirming women. Some of us work, and some go to school. Our house is centrally located in downtown Madison in a quiet and diverse neighborhood. [It's owned by the Madison Community Co-op network—see Resource listing.] We take turns making great vegetarian meals and working in our beautiful garden. We welcome open-minded women who are interested in creating a safe and sane environment. Please include a SASE with inquiries. [cc] 12/21/94

WOODBURN HILL FARM

1150 Woodburn Hill Road
Mechanicsville, MD 20659
(301)884-5615

Woodburn Hill Farm was founded on a formerly Amish farm in 1975. After thirteen years of communal sharing of meals, work, childcare, and expenses, in 1988 we turned to a co-op model with family units more independent. A return to the previous model would be possible with the right people and energy.

The place is owned by our corporation of 31 shareholders, all connected with the Farm over the years. Decisions are made by consensus. Residents can be shareholders or not, but both types pay rent to the corporation to cover expenses. There are currently 8 adults and 3 children on 128 acres. We've one main house with common areas, three separate family houses, two trailers, assorted barns, and a wildlife refuge. Our heat is mostly woodstoves. We work locally in education, art, and the helping professions.

We try to "live lightly" here: gardening organically, recycling, composting. We tend toward vegetarian, and are loosely committed to holistic health and non-sexist working. All adult residents share in the upkeep, and responsibilities are met with monthly work days and rotating chore signups.

We are looking for creative, stable individuals who value cooperative living, ecological and social justice, spirituality, and celebrations. Those interested should contact us in advance of a visit (please enclose a SASE). 6/9/92

WOODCREST BRUDERHOF

Hutterian Brethren
P.O. Box 903
Rifton, NY 12471-0903
(914)658-8351
http://www.bruderhof.org/

Christian, rural, communal. Community manufactures Community Playthings (educational play equipment) and Rifton Equipment for the handicapped. Visitors arrange in advance. Write for information. [See main listing for "Hutterian Brethren" in the Resources section.] 6/1/92 [84]

WYGELIA

(Forming)
2919 Monocacy Bottom Road
Adamstown, MD 21710-9312
(301)831-8280

We are a group of three adults living together on 65 acres of hilly wooded land about 40 miles from Washington, DC, and six miles from Frederick, MD. We represent a broad spectrum of training and skills, including fabric crafts, upholstery, engineering, blacksmithing, foundry, woodworking, and more. We have a large and well-equipped shop space. The property is owned by one member; he wishes it wasn't. We have a large house with space for 2–4 more members, and land for one more house within present zoning rules. We have one tiny garden which sometimes grows a good crop of beans; the soil is terrible.

We have a commitment to open communication, personal growth, and not keeping resentments. We have meetings whenever one of us wants one.

We will be a haven for arts/crafts people and high-tech people who seek a secluded extended-family type of home. Income earning opportunities abound on the land and within driving distance. 9/13/94

YAHARA LINDEN CO-OP

2117 Linden Avenue
Madison, WI 53704
(608)249-4474

The Yahara Linden Gathering is comprised of six adults and one child who share a comfortable, three-story, Victorian home, garden, greenhouse, and occasional common meals. Individuals have professions and personal income within this vital Midwestern city. The co-op is political and into civil liberties and human rights. Religion, politics, and sexuality are one's personal choice. Decision making is by consensus. A non-equity co-op, Yahara Linden has existed since 1974 and as a household is involved in environmental and peace issues. This co-op is an alternative to landlord-owned rental housing in Madison. Visitors are welcome as guests of individual members; advance arrangements are necessary. 7/24/94

YASODHARA ASHRAM

Box 9, Kootenay Bay
BC V0B-1X0
CANADA
(604)227-9224/227-9225

Established by Swami Radha on the shores of Kootenay Lake in British Columbia, Canada, Yasodhara Ashram is a yoga retreat and study center now in its 30th year. We offer introductory and advanced courses in many kinds of yoga. Over the past 37 years Swami Radha has adapted and reinterpreted the ancient yogic teachings into a form readily accessible to the Western mind. All our courses are based on her work, and include a unique approach to Hatha yoga and a practical and grounded method of working with the Kundalini system. We also offer Mantra instruction as well as a self-

reliant way of interpreting dreams. The basis of Swami Radha's teachings is integrity and a groundedness in life that is reflected in the Ashram as a whole.

We live on 140 acres in our spiritual community, on the shores of a pure sparkling lake surrounded by mountains and trees. Here we give classes and workshops, and publish and edit books, tapes, and a journal called Ascent. There are opportunities for people to come as a temporary resident to live and work with us. We manage a small farm, and grow much of our produce. The Ashram is recognized as an educational institution by the Canadian government. 11/4/93

YELLOW HOUSE, THE

1404 Ruby
Kansas City, KS 66103
(913)342-5967

The Yellow House is a 110-year-old, 3-story Queen Anne in a central city neighborhood. Its residents share the rehab and maintenance of the house, and contribute their skills to the nearby Franklin Community Center which houses a co-op grocery, a coffee shop, daycare, and social services.

Core residents have a 20-year history of work with neighborhood organizing, small business management, community health care, alternative church formation, strategic planning, environmental activities, and higher education. Short-term visitors welcome—who are interested in inner-city development and health care. 12/18/94

YOGA SOCIETY OF ROCHESTER

93 Spruce Avenue
Rochester, NY 14611
(716)235-1810

The Yoga Society of Rochester is a nonprofit, multi-path community which offers classes, workshops, and a residential living experience for people of diverse backgrounds who are interested in the study, practice, and teaching of yoga, meditation, and related disciplines of spiritual growth. The YSR has two identities: first, we are an educational membership organization, offering a wide range of classes and workshops in yoga and other personal growth modalities. Second, we are a community of, presently, 7 adults and 3 children living at the YSR. As a community we emphasize personal growth and cooperation. Overall governance is in the hands of a board of directors working in conjunction with the body of residents. Decisions within the house and board, and between the two, are made using a formal consensus process. Our facility is a large city house which provides both instructional and residential space. We have a large yard used for recreation and for our gardens. We are always open to expanding our membership and educational program, and sometimes have openings for new housemates. We can accommodate small numbers for brief periods of time, and can arrange special programs for small groups. Our newsletter will be sent upon request. 6/27/94

YOGAVILLE

Satchidananda Ashram
Route 1, Box 1720
Buckingham, VA 23921
(804)969-3121

Satchidananda Ashram/Yogaville is the international headquarters for the Integral Yoga Institutes (we have many associated

urban centers). Yogaville is situated on 750 secluded acres of wooded hills and fields in rural Virginia, with a panoramic view of the James River and the Blue Ridge Mountains. Here, under the guidance of the Reverend Sri Swami Satchidananda (Gurudev), people of all faiths and backgrounds have come together to study and practice the principles of Integral Yoga to attain mental and physical health, ease, and peace. Yogaville is designed to serve as a model of how we can all live and work together in harmony while still enjoying our individual differences. Residents include both singles and families, and individuals who have chosen to make a formal commitment as monastics or as ministers. Our children's education programs include a preschool, primary school, and secondary school.

At the center of Yogaville is the Light Of Truth Universal Shrine (LOTUS), dedicated to the Light of all faiths and to world peace. It houses altars for all the major world religions, and representative altars for other known and still unknown faiths. The LOTUS is a center for silent contemplation and meditation, and embodies the message "Truth is One, Paths are Many." We also publish and/or distribute many spiritual materials including books, magazines, cassettes, and videotapes. 10/15/92

ZEN BONES
INTENTIONAL SPIRIT

(Forming)
2815 – 9th Street
Berkeley, CA 94710
(510)540-0215

We are a clean and sober community relying on 12-Step philosophy, with a goal to become self-sufficient. We believe that life has choices beyond mere survival; that we can escape the loop of financial insecurity by creating a circle of spiritual and economic unity; that we can maintain our serenity and sobriety by sharing the strength of our spirituality; and that we can develop our own products, grow our own produce, support one another in business efforts, come together in a group

effort to become self-sufficient using the labor, creativity, and diversity of the group. We seek to be part of a network of houses, communities, databases, workshops, and schools exploring the world's spiritual, artistic, and cultural heritage. We foresee developing our own insurance and venture capital. Meditation and archery are practiced. SASE required. 12/8/93

ZEN MOUNTAIN
MONASTERY

Box 197
Mt. Tremper, NY 12457
(914)688-2228

A residential center (est. '80) for male and female monastics and lay persons who are training in the tradition of Zen Buddhism. The daily training schedule includes Zen meditation, chanting services, work practice, art and body practice, and personal study with the resident Zen teacher John Daido Loori. Current membership of 12 women and 12 men is comprised mostly of people in their 20s and 30s. We share mostly all meals, and are primarily vegetarian. Members pay monthly rent, but there's also a work scholarship program. 6/20/94

ZENDIK FARM
ARTS FOUNDATION

Star Route 16C-3
Bastrop, TX 78602
(512)303-4620/303-1637
http://www.eden.com/
~zendik/

Zendik Farm is a cooperative community of artists, activists, and organic farmers committed to the survival of the human species through the practice of the Earth-saving philosophy known as Ecolibrium. Founded 23 years ago, we are a working model of a sustainable society based on honesty, cooperation, creativity, and universal responsibility. Located on 300 acres outside of Austin, Texas, we practice organic farming, dance, mechanics, music, eco-activism, carpentry, video, pottery, animal care, theater, photography and film, eco-architecture, publishing, metal work, and natural healing. We survive financially from donations brought in by our apprenticeship program, music tapes, and quarterly magazine—the largest and most widely distributed underground mag in the world. Our TV shows are run in series on Access cable stations in cities around the world. We believe that Ecology is the only true religion, Truth the only valid pursuit, and Cooperation the only workable social ideal. Zendik Farm offers long and short apprenticeships and internships for school credit. Call or write for details. Send $2 for a copy of *Zendik Farm Magazine*, and include SASE with correspondence. 6/9/92

ZEPHYR VALLEY COMMUNITY CO-OP

(Forming)
Route 1, Box 121-A
Rushford, MN 55971

Zephyr Valley Co-op is a newly formed rural community with a vision of sharing, neighborliness, and cooperation. We intend to use the land and its resources sustainably, to treat one another respectfully, and to resolve conflicts peacefully. Our 550-acre farm includes valleys, bluffs, crop land, forest, wetland, and streams. The land and buildings are owned by the co-op; individual houses will be privately owned. Members may rent co-op land and buildings for private business and or livelihood use. Current member interests include organic gardening, free-range poultry, rotational grazing of livestock, building musical instruments, folk music, wetland and woodland restoration. Deci-

sions regarding co-op concerns are made by consensus with each member having an equal say. Decisions regarding lifestyle, living standards, employment, hospitality, family life, diet, spirituality, etc., will be private matters. Not actively looking for members until 1996. SASE requested. [cc] 6/29/94

ZION'S ORDER, INC.

South Range Ranch
Route 2, Box 104-7
Mansfield, MO 65704

(417)924-3307/924-3350

Our community, located 1-1/2 miles off the nearest blacktop, is 10 miles from the nearest small town and 50 miles from Springfield, MO. Our dwellings are on a high ridge that gives us a panoramic view of the country 'round about. Our ranch consists of 1175 acres, generally hilly, covered with lots of timber, many pastures, and hay fields. We have plenty of space for hiking, picnics, and game areas. Our drinking water comes from two wells, each of which is over 300 feet deep; our water is very good.

As a group we like to "gang up" on projects as much as possible, giving us a chance to exercise our religion as Jesus

Christ taught. We have a few milk cows for milk, cheese, and butter, plus a beef herd. We raise rabbits for commercial use as well as our own meat. We send out a crew of men and women who vaccinate chickens that are being raised as "ready-to-lay hens" to be sold to commercial egg layers. We also load these hens onto large trucks for delivery. One of our brothers repairs broken TVs and resells them. We also have a few riding horses. Please enclose SASE with inquiries. 1/22/93

ZIRKLE'S BRANCH

(Re-Forming)
Route 1, Box 413
West Hamlin, WV 25571

Free-range goats, sheep, poultry, organic gardening; no electricity, no alcohol, no guns. Individual cabins one-mile walk back in a hollow. Write a letter, come visit; after two years go on the deed. We will disagree —let's fight it out (make the commitment). We welcome gays, lesbians, families, minorities, Earth and animal lovers. Vegans OK, but we butcher our animals with love. Come make a home for yourself in the woods. SASE required. 7/5/92

NEW NORTH AMERICAN LISTINGS

Agape
(Forming)
2062 Greenwich Road
Ware, MA 01082
(413)967-9369
Agape is a lay contemplative community with a nonviolent education ministry and witness. We set aside a part of each day for silence and prayer, and also invest energy in local, regional, and global concerns relating to institutional violence. In addition, we have a full life here at Francis House, the community homestead. We cut wood for heat, garden for our food, and build and maintain our own dwellings. We have a permanent caretaker family, long-term residents (3 months and up), and an active nonresident community of over 100 people. Volunteers share in all aspects of the community life: office work, homesteading, childcare, and hospitality. Internships are from two weeks to three months. 6/1/95

Earth in Clover
(Forming)
4826-B Yeager Road
Concrete, WA 98237
(360)428-9176
Seeking to create visionary community with small band of self-selected people on 21 acres on Skagit River, North Cascades. Planning permaculture, food and solar energy self- reliance, building, singing, dancing. Community decisions to be made by mem-

bers. For description of vision, contact Howard Wechsler at above address. 12/2/95

Eden Project, The
(Forming)
P.O. Box 849
Glen Ellen, CA 95442
Environmental land cooperative, on 1680 acres in Mendocino County, that will be run by a Consensus Council of all members. A common Farm, a protected forest, plus 84 homesteads (3-acres each) situated along the valley rim, each with use of 3 acres of farmland. Buy-in option: one day's work per week for those with real desire but no real money. We ask members to practice good land stewardship, and limit building on the homesteads to one passive solar main home, one small cabin, and a small barn/workshop. Interested? — send a letter about yourself and $3 for our 20-page prospectus. 7/30/95

Eden Ranch Community
(Forming)
P O Box 520
Paonia, CO 8142-0520
(970)835-8905
Ecological cluster of 10-15 dome, strawbale, or earth homes on 65-acre mesa. Primary focus on the deepest essence, respect, and honoring of all life. Seek self-supporting members desiring to work on biodynamic permaculture farm. Create your own business, or work in nearby towns. Diversity in thought and age; consensus decision-making. Common land in Community Land Trust. Commun-

ity center for shared evening meals, holistic therapies, child and elder care. Future plans for retreat/learning center. $15,000 memberships, plus cost of home and monthly assessments. Call or write for prospectus, sample newsletter. Send $3 for bylaws, $10 for home video. 10/11/95

Forming Community
2956 Trimble Street
Vancouver, BC V6R-4A1
(604)224-1070 / 224-5070
We want to create a sustainable, environmental community, and to grow organically with the guidance of the spirit of the land. We are exploring relating (monogamy), alternative education, natural building, and positive social opportunities. We are vegetarians who meditate and prefer a drug/alcohol/tobacco free culture. We have 8 children, aged newborn to 20. We live simply; grow some of our own food; and are planning private enterprises like a meditation/healing retreat, a bicyclers/backpackers campground, a home for elders, a sanctuary for battered women, and a craft product. We plan to cluster our homes and enterprises in a village, with a community hall at the hub for shared meals and gatherings. We seek others who resonate with this vision, and are ready to act on it. 12/5/95

Forming Community
c/o Paul Lauzier
RR1, Box 5140
Lubec, ME 04652
Have 100 acres to share with idealists keen on hand

New listings are published in our quarterly *Communities* magazine (see p.440). The listings above are new since the first printing.

work in spiritually oriented community seeking to promote Gandhian "villagism" primarily by practicing it. Founder is an artisan committed to local self-reliance and voluntary poverty (limiting use of resources to basics: no power machinery, electricity, or telephone; minimal earnings and spending; no government welfare or services; travel only rarely in auto-mobiles). "Villagism" emphasizes small-scale production and local self-sufficiency, especially in basic necessities, and avoids trade merely for profit. It is a non-exploitive, service-oriented, ecologically sustainable system. 8/10/95

Freakish Little Clan, A
423 Capp Street
San Francisco, CA 94110

A vegan community that has been going for one year. No additional information has been received. 9/13/95

Galilee
(Forming)
3300 Marathon Street #8
Los Angeles, CA 90026-2845

An egalitarian, non-denominational village of spiritual travelers who recognize the teachings of the world's religions as One Truth expressed as many truths. We encourage creative and artistic ways, and are an income-sharing cooperative corporation oriented toward networking with other groups for mutual economic, social, and spiritual benefits. Our earth-oriented existence includes experiments with organic farming and indoor farming. At this point we have neither land prospects nor financing. [Recently moved from Portland, OR, to Los Angeles, CA.] 2/17/95

Grandma's Place, Inc.
HC02, Box 240
St. Maries, ID 83861
(208)689-3552 / 689-9180

(Est. '93.) 12 individual households (room for five more) on 120-acre organic farm in beautiful northern Idaho, using alternative energy. The land is owned in common with shared expenses; families own their own homes. Consensus decision making. We value individual freedom, and welcome diversity of lifestyles and beliefs. We envision a multigenerational, multicultural, peace-loving community where members actively resolve their conflicts. Visitors welcome — call or write first. Prospective members need to spend time with us first, before purchasing a share or building a home. SASE requested. 1/16/96

Locust Grove Farm
(Forming)
Route 2, Box 19
Creola, OH 45622

A recently organized 501(d) income-sharing agrarian community, with traditional family values, in southeast Ohio. Organic farming, poultry, farmers' market, bakery, canning, and woodworking businesses operating; other suggestions considered. Naturalistic spirituality. Amish views of technology. Community school planned. No smoking. We presently farm with a tractor, but plan to add horse power for local trips and field work. Hard-working intentional peasant singles, families, and couples (regardless of age) send $1 for info packet. See Reach Ad for more info. 1/16/96

Manau Kendra
(Forming)
P.O. Box 105
Ben Lomand, CA 95005-0105
(408)425-3334 VoiceMail

Forming a family of refinement, clan of clarity, tribe of truth. Yes vegan, no alcohol, no drugs, no smoking, no tobacco. Let's unify and co-op to get land in Northern California, or (?), and grow organic fruit

and nut tree nurseries and groves, organic edible landscapes 'n' gardens. Children and families appreciated. Let's co-create a safety zone to raise holy kids. Call/write Brother Little Star * Thakar Sevadar at the above address. 4/27/95

Nasalam
(Forming)
Route 3, Box 332
Fair Grove, MO 65648
73527.1676@cis.com

A spiritual community forming on sacred land in the Ozark Plateau of SW Missouri. We honor all beliefs while having a foundation of our own blend of beliefs, goals, and practices. Vegetarian, substance free, primarily interested in polysexual (i.e., gay/bisexual) individuals oriented toward a polyamorous, polyfidelitous lifestyle with strong tribal overtones. Though the community is being initiated by a spiritual group, the Order of Melchizedek, one need not necessarily become a member to live here. We should be moving into our new home by the time this is in print. Please write for more information. 6/23/95

Plow Creek Fellowship
Route 2, Box 2-A
Tiskilwa, IL 61368
(815)646-4730

A Christian congregation (est. '71), from various denominations, affiliated with the Mennonite church. Members commit to Jesus as Lord, pacifism, fidelity in marriage and chastity outside of marriage, consensus decision making, and a communal economic life. We run a farm and numerous businesses; some members have outside jobs. We have Sunday morning worship, two common meals a week, weekly sharing groups, a weekly members' meeting, Saturday morning work projects, and many fun events. Our ministries include an Overground Railroad (hosting refugees), assisting dysfunctional families, and support & care for workers in other countries. Visitors welcome. 6/1/95

Potash Hill
Arts & Education Community
(Forming)
33 Potash Hill Road
Cummington, MA 01026
(413)634-0181

13 privately owned 2–4 acre lots in western Massachusetts; 60 acres of common land with buildings. Educational, dormitory, dining, business, and studio facilities available. Our intent is to establish and maintain meaningful connections with others who value a similar lifestyle, and to pursue the highest possibilities in all aspects of living: relationships, the arts, natural healing, education, business, alternative energy, gardening, celebration, and fun. We value personal autonomy. Currently we are 12 members, including 3 children. Call or write for more information. 7/27/95

Red Road Farm
(Forming)
HCR1, Box 59
Cairo, NY 12413
(518)622-8499

We're a small group of individuals who are into learning as much as we can about love and God. We see the best way to do this is by loving and helping each other, and having a strong love of Mother Earth and all other of the Great Spirits' creations. We are into gardening and being as self-sufficient as possible. Visitors and all people are welcome to get in touch with us. 10/6/95

Southwest Sufi Community
(Forming)
• Site: Silver City, NM
• Contact: c/o Ellen Fietz Hall

2223 Hooper Road
Yuba City, CA 95993
(916)671-0987
71534.3425@compuserve.com

Buying 1900 acres for community in SW New Mexico — a spiritual refuge, retreat facility, and healing center. Camps and seminars. Permaculture, extensive organic garden, some nature preserve areas. Democratic governance, with ongoing consensus building and conflict resolution processes. Envision 40–80 households with a variety of living arrangements — communal, cooperative, and neighborly. Charter memberships to Sufi movement folks: $2500 (or pledge $600/yr for 5 years). Write or call for a video of the land and details about the community and land purchase. 6/21/95

Spectra
c/o Rob Sody
73 Holly Hill Estates
Smyrna, DE 19877
(302)653-2029 Voice
(302)653-0494 BBS

Spectra (formerly the New Family Experiment/Blackbird Pagan Connection) is developing its own religion and monastic community. We are a growing, fluid community of members and friends, resident and nonresident. We hope to learn, grow, and work toward a new tribal-style family form within the context of a Pagan/Wiccan Earth-centered spirituality. We encourage positive social change through positive personal change and activism; sponsor weekly rap sessions; and do organizational development. Please write or call if you would like to visit. Ideas and input always welcome. SASE requested. 1/30/95

Vajra Community
Zangdog Palri
Red Mountain Retreat Center
Bisbee, AZ
(415)487-6339 VoiceMail
vajra@sirius.com

160 acres with powerful energy conducive to meditation, yoga, and spiritual practice. Guidance by three Tibetan Buddhist Rinpoches teaching ways to facilitate and accelerate one's psychic and spiritual evolution. Diversity of spiritual traditions encouraged, also integrating modern science. Abundant fresh water, good topsoil, organic gardens and orchards. Planning to create a healing center here, and a center for research, development, and demonstration of alternative energy technologies. Looking for new members, and for donations to support community development. 10/4/95

West Hills Cohousing
7415 SW Virginia Avenue
Portland, OR 97219-3040
(503)246-9648 / 245-6506

Our evolving mission: "To establish a community [of diverse people, of diverse ages] that fosters the spiritual connection between ourselves, with others, and with our environ-ment through simplicity, sustainability, cooperation, and service." We are conducting a feasibility study of a 4-acre site — a bit of a paradise in northwest Portland, in a natural setting with trees and brook, yet only 15 minutes to downtown, and within one mile of the new light rail. Construction of 24 dwellings scheduled to begin spring '96. We're governed by consensus. Write or call for information including a free packet of material. 8/15/95

Yew Wood Healing Centre
93640 Deadwood Creek Road
Deadwood, OR 97430
(503)964-5341

We received a postcard from this group asking to be included in the next Directory. 7/28/95

New listings are published in our quarterly *Communities* magazine (see p.440). The listings above are new since the first printing.

About the RRDDLNoR
The Renamed, Regrouped, Dead, Disbanded, Lost, & No Replies...

Jillian Downey

When we originally created our communities database, we merged every existing list that we could put our hands on—quite a challenging undertaking! The biggest problem was that mistakes were perpetuated in newer compilations that used the old lists as source material. We'd clean up our data, then the outdated info would reappear the next time we integrated a "new" list.

Another major problem was duplications. A group might go by two different names, may have changed names, may have relocated to another address (or even to another state), or may have both a street address and a P.O. Box.

We've tried to eliminate all those mistakes and duplications from our database, and include this section so that others can clean up their lists too. Hopefully you'll give us feedback if you have information more current than ours.

We actually had contact with some of these groups by letter or phone, perhaps even getting a tentative "Yes" to being listed, but couldn't get final confirmation no matter how many messages we left on their answering machines. In other cases we sent a letter and never heard anything in response. Both types of groups are indicated here by the label "**NoResp**."

If our letter was returned by the Post Office, our code is "**BadPO**" and will be followed by the "☞Return to Sender" explanation stamped on the letter. Many of the groups in both of these categories are still likely to be around and viable—our letter may have been lost, the group may have forgotten to reply or might have been too busy, or they may have preferred to remain anonymous.

We did hear from more than 150 groups who told us that "We are still a community, but don't wish to be listed at this time." Those groups are not mentioned by name anywhere in this directory, not even in this list.

A number of the groups, those in the early forming stages, did not feel ready to announce their existence through a full listing. Those which hadn't yet settled on a name are noted here as "**Forming**," and where we had a contact person's name, it has been included in parentheses.

Groups listed as "**New**" are those we were unable to contact because their referral came to our attention too late—this directory would still be in the "idea" stage if we kept trying to chase down all of the leads that we dug up. In any event, we did not send a letter to any groups with this classification.

"**Insuff**" means that we received a lead, but have insufficient address or phone information to make contact. "**Dupe**" is a duplicate; the group is (or was) known by more than one name. "**ReName**" is similar, except that the community actually changed its name. Some of these "Dupe" and "ReName" groups have current listings, and are noted as such; others are merely cross-referenced to other names in the RRDDLNoR section. "**SubNet**" means the group is a subset of a community network with a main listing; the local did not submit a separate entry.

"**NLC**" means the group reported that they are no longer a community (but may still be a loose cooperative or some other alternative form). "**Never**" means they said they have never considered themselves to be a community (though they may still look like one to us). "**Limbo**" groups are presently dormant or in transition...still around in some form or other, but not feeling that they could represent themselves as viable communities at this point. "**M/R**" means the group has been moved to the Resources section, usually at their own suggestion. Some of these are noted as possible candidates for the Resources section, but we didn't get a confirmation.

"**Defun**": Some of these communities have folded entirely, others have re-emerged as new incarnations, still others have been absorbed into other groups. We've tried to use reliable sources to verify "defunct" listings, yet we caution that one person's first-hand experience can be quite different from another's.

The communities movement is dynamic and ever-changing, providing a constant source of grist for the rumor mill. We enlist your help in our efforts to sort the kernels of truth from the misleading and unsubstantiated chaff. We've included a feedback form (one of the yellow cards at the back) which we hope makes this task easier. ⚇

ALABAMA

Name	Location	Status	Notes
Caritas	Sterrett	NoResp	
Free-Thought Religious Org.	Munford	Never	
Land of Peace	Prattville	Never	
Malbis Plantation	Daphne	NoResp	
Morningside	Birmingham	Defun	"Return to Sender"
New South Lifestyles	Wetumpka	BadPO	"Forwarding Order Expired"
Sandridge, John	Gadsden	NoResp	

ALASKA

Name	Location	Status	Notes
First Church in Community	Fairbanks	Insuff	
Kenny Lake	Copper Center	BadPO	"Return to Sender"
Kin'aii Consultants	Anchorage	NoResp	

ALBERTA

Name	Location	Status	Notes
Affordable Sustainable Community	Calgary	New	
Barnabas Christian Fellowship	Calgary	NoResp	
Common Ground Group	Olds	Defun	Group has folded
Onoway Center	Onoway	NoResp	
Native Shelter Society Society	Calgary	NoResp	

ARIZONA

Name	Location	Status	Notes
Adobeland	Tuscon	NoResp	
Arcosanti	Mayer	NoResp	
Biosphere II	Oracle	Insuff	
Capricorn Ranch	Yucca	BadPO	"Forwarding Order Expired"
Cascebel Clayworks	Benson	NoResp	
Child's Garden	Tucson	NoResp	
Children of Light	Dateland	NoResp	
Cielo en Tierra	Huachuca City	NoResp	
Concord	Snowflake	NoResp	
Forming (Amondragon-Rosh)	Phoenix	NoResp	
Forming (Raoult Bertrand)	Cave Creek	NoResp	
Four Corners Project	Flagstaff	NoResp	
Friends United Church of Kindness	Bisbee	BadPO	"Moved/NFA"
Guru Nanak Dwara Ashram (3HO)	Phoenix	SubNet	
Holy Trinity Monastery	St David	NoResp	
Inspiration Sanctuary	Sedona	NoResp	
Leela Spiritual Life Community	West Sedona	NoResp	
Making Contact	Tucson	NoResp	
Miracle Valley	Miracle Valley	Insuff	
New Earth	Bisbee	BadPO	"Addressee Unknown"
People of Joy	Scottsdale	BadPO	"Forwarding Order Expired"
Prescott CoHousing	Prescott	NoResp	
Rancho Linda Vista	Tucson	New	
Saint Francis in the Foothills	Tucson	NoResp	
Sanctuary Enterprises	Mesa	New	
SHE Land Trust	Tucson	NoResp	
Tree of Life Rejuvenation Center	Patagonia	New	
Tucson CoHousing	Tucson	New	
United Order Effort	Colorado City	New	
Whetstone Community	Benson	BadPO	"Return to Sender"
Windspirit	Winkleman	ReName: Christmas Star	

ARKANSAS

Name	Location	Status	Notes
Arco Iris	Ponca	NoResp	
Foundation of Ubiquity	Jasper	Insuff	
Ganashyam	Pelsor	NoResp	
Heartsong Farm	Nail	NoResp	
Little Portion Franciscan Hermitage	Eureka Springs	NoResp	
Living Lightly Village	Fayetteville	Never	"Return to Sender"
Lothlorien Fellowship	Harrison	BadPO	"Return to Sender"
Maud's Land	In the Ozarks	Never	Fictitious name from book
Spinsterhaven (OWLT)	Fayetteville	NoResp	
Whypperwillow Land, Inc.	Eureka Springs	BadPO	"No Such Number"

BRITISH COLUMBIA

Name	Location	Status	Notes
Bread of Life	Abbotsford	Defun	Folded
Canadian Life Colleges Assoc.	Victoria	NoResp	
Caravan Theatre Farm	Armstrong	NoResp	
Circling Dawn	Vancouver	NoResp	
Collin van Uchelen & friends	Vancouver	NoResp	
Doukhabours	Argenta	Insuff	
Essene Community	Matsqui	NoResp	
Forming (A. Hadorn)	Hagensborg	NoResp	
Gardom Lake/Twin Islands	Salmon Arm	NoResp	
Genesis Community	Lumby	NoResp	
Gestalt Community	Kuper's Island	Insuff	
Goldstream Gardens	Qualicum Beach	NoResp	
Hailos Community	Vernon	Defun	Folded in '93
Hollyhock Farm	Cortes Island	NoResp	Educational Centre.
Iskcon	Burnaby	NoResp	
Lasqueti Community	Lasqueti Island	Insuff	
Lofstedt Farm Community	Kaslo	New	
Quadra Island Community Centre	Quathiaski Cove	Never	Public community center
Stock's Meadow	Kelowna	BadPO	"Unclaimed"
Thera Community	Galliana Island (?)	Insuff	
Troopers, The	British Columbia	Insuff	
Vancouver Dilaram House	Vancouver	NoResp	
White Spruce Farm	Fernie	NoResp	

CALIFORNIA

Name	Location	Status	Notes
Abacus Planned Community	San Francisco	Defun	Folded '91
AIM House	Oakland	Insuff	
Amaranth	San Francisco	Defun	Dispersed '90
Annapolis Springs Ranch	Annapolis	NoResp	
Aquarian Minyan	Berkeley	NoResp	
Aquarian Research Group	Agoura	Never	Never was a community
Art Ranch	Sacramento	NoResp	
Ashby Ave. House	Los Angeles	NLC	
Atmaniketan Ashram	Pomona	ReName: Sri Aurobindo Sadh. Pthm.	
Avadhut Church	Santa Cruz	Never	Never was a community
Babaji Yoga Sangam	Norwalk	BadPO	"Return to Sender"
Backyard Commons	Berkeley	New	
Bartimaeus Commuity Church	Berkeley	Defun	Disbanded '84
Bayland Family	San Jose	BadPO	"Return to Sender"
Bayou 22	San Francisco	NLC	
Bee Song Honey Farms	Weed	NoResp	
Belvedere House	San Francisco	NLC	
Benicia Waterfront Cohousing	Benecia	Limbo	Land deal fell through
Berkeley Poets Commune	Berkeley	NoResp	
Beverly-Kingsley Community	Los Angeles	ReName: Hale Byodo Corazon	
Big Wheels Ranch	Montgomery	NoResp	
Bob Guzley & Friends	Santa Cruz	NoResp	
Boddhi Pacific	Los Gatos	NoResp	
Brotherhood of Holy Translators	Los Angeles	BadPO	"Forwarding Order Expired"
Buddhist Community	Salinas	New	
Camp Joy	Boulder Creek	NoResp	
Campbell Hot Springs	Chico	ReName: Consciousness Vill/Rebirth	
Casa Bonito	San Francisco	NLC	
Casa Verde	Berkeley	ReName: GreenPLAN	
Catalpa Farm	Santa Cruz	NoResp	
Catchtail Community	Santa Cruz	Limbo	Regrouping; seeking land
Catholic Worker Farm	Sheepranch	NoResp	
Cave, The	San Francisco	Defun	Folded in '90
Cedar	Camptonville	BadPO	"Addressee Unknown"
Center of the Pumpkin	Occidental	NLC	No longer a community
Christ Faith Mission	Los Angeles	NoResp	
Circle I Farm	Los Molinos	NoResp	
City of Friendship	New Cuyama	Limbo	Prob. not; see Geltaftan (R)
Cntr. Psychological Revolution	San Diego	ReName: Center for Examined Life	
Co-op Communities Project	San Francisco	Defun	Folded in '83; See Kidstown
Cohousing Community Forming	Orinda	NoResp	
Commty f/ Emotional Self-Devel.	Santa Cruz	Defun	Dissolved '80
Community Christi	San Anselmo	NoResp	
Community Evolving	North San Juan	ReName: Blackberry	
Comptche Community Farms	Comptche	Defun	Never really jelled
Cooperative Village	Ukiah	Defun	Disbanded '80
Cornerhouse	Berkeley	NoResp	
Cornucopia West	Soquel	NoResp	
Daga-Ray	San Francisco	NoResp	
Dawn Horse Communion	Middletown	NoResp	
Dennis' House	San Francisco	New	
Dhyanyoga Centers Inc.	Soquel	NoResp	
Djarma Community	Ojai	Defun	Land Sold '92
Earth First! Household	San Francisco	BadPO	"No Forwarding Address"
Earth Island Institute	San Francisco	Never	See Resources Listing
Eclectia	(Northern rural?)	Insuff	
Empty Gate Zen Center	Berkeley	NoResp	
Esoteric Fraternity	Applegate	NoResp	
Essene Mother Earth Church	Big Bend	NoResp	
Family of Unlimited Devotion	Philo	Insuff	
Farallones Rural Center	Occidental	Never	Never was a community
Figuero Arms Apartments	Los Angeles	New	
Finders West	Albany	NoResp	
Firestone Community	Los Angeles (?)	Insuff	
Fiveohone	San Francisco	New	
Forever Young	San Mateo	Defun	Folded
Forming (Bill Yenner)	Mill Valley	New	
Forming (Daniel Grobani)	San Francisco	NoResp	
Forming (Magdalena Leones)	Richmond	New	
Forming (Oriel)	San Raphael	NoResp	
Forming (Pat Patterson)	Monrovia	NoResp	
Forming (Steve Dorst)	Berkeley	New	
Forming (William Heintz)	Glendale	NoResp	
Franciscan Workers of Junipero Serra	Salinas	New	
Freeman House	Petrolia	NoResp	
Garden Community Land Trust	Covelo	Defun	Dissolved '86
Good Neighbor Co-op	Encinitas	New	
Good Times Commune	San Francisco	Defun	Disbanded '81
Greenfield Ranch	Calpella	NLC	No longer a community
Greenhouse	Goleta	NLC	No longer a community
Greenhouse	Oakland	Limbo	House may be sold in '95
Group W House	San Francisco	NLC	Very informal now
Grove St. Collective	San Francisco	BadPO	"No Forwarding Addrress"
Guru Ram Das Ashram	Los Angeles	SubNet	See Sikh Dharma/3HO
Gus Beatman & Friends	Oakland	New	
Hanuman Fellowship	Santa Cruz	NoResp	
Hardscrabble Hill Center	Berkeley	NoResp	
Harmony Farm	Fallbrook	NLC	
Harrad West	San Francisco	Defun	Lost lease '68; to "Goodlife"
Harvest Forum	San Francisco	NoResp	
Harwood House	Oakland	NLC	No longer a community
Haste Street Collective	Berkeley	Defun	Sold to Land Trust '91
Heartland	Berkeley	NoResp	
Heliopolis	Oakland	NLC	Regrouped '84; see Brigid
Heron Court	Redwood City	New	
Hidden Valley	Colfax	NoResp	

N. American

Name	Location	Status	Notes
Hog Farm	Berkeley	NoResp	
Holy Order of Mans	San Francisco	NLC	No longer a community
Home	Malibu	NoResp	
House of Love and Prayer	San Francisco	BadPO	"Moved/NFA"
Housing Co-op in Venice	Venice	New	
Human Potential Foundation	Los Olivos	NLC	Changed to business focus
Hurd's Gulch	Fort Jones	New	
ICSA Ananda	San Francisco	NoResp	
Ilarne	Crockett	BadPO	"Addressee Unknown"
Institute of Human Abilities	Oakland	Insuff	
Institute of Mentalphysics	Yucca Valley	NoResp	
Internat'l Buddhist Meditation Cntr.	Los Angeles	NoResp	
Intertribal Friendship House	Oakland	M/R	Native American (NoResp)
Johnston Center (Bekins Hall)	Redlands	NoResp	
Jungian-Senoi Institute	Berkeley	NoResp	
Juniper House	Oakland	New	
Kempton House (Current Residents)	Oakland	BadPO	"Mail Refused"
Kerensa Co-op Community	Menlo Park	NLC	Community folded c. '72
Kids-Il-eat Ivy Farm	Cool	BadPO	"Forwarding Order Expired"
Kilowana	Calistoga	Defun	Folded c. '86
La Tierra (cohousing)	Sebastapol	NoResp	
Land House	Monte Rio	NoResp	
Landlab	Pomona	NoResp	
Laughing Cat Farm	Bolinas	Defun	
Lavender Hill Womyn's Retreat	Elk	Defun	Folded
Lemurian Fellowship	Ramona	NoResp	
Limesaddle	Oroville	Defun	Folded in the '70s
Live Power Community Farm	Covelo	NoResp	
Lopez & Friends	San Francisco	Limbo	Nghbrhd getting dangerous
Lyman Family, The	Hollywood	Insuff	
Lyons Valley Co-op	Talmage	BadPO	"Addressee Unknown"
M & M	Albion	Never	Mostly living separate lives
Ma-Na-Har	Oakhurst	Insuff	
Mariposa School	Ukiah	NLC	Reorganized spring '90
Martin De Porres Catholic Worker	San Francisco	Never	
McMillan House	Santa Cruz	NoResp	
Meadowlark Healing Center	Hemet	NLC	No longer a community
Medicine Ways	Valley Ford	BadPO	"Addressee Unknown"
Meditation Mount	Ojai	Never	Never was a community
Merry Crew	San Francisco	Defun	
MLK / Marcius Garvey Co-op	San Francisco	New	
Monarchy of Christania	Santa Barbara	BadPO	"Moved, Left No Address"
Monastery of the Risen Christ	San Luis Obispo	NoResp	
Monroe-Ashbury House	San Francisco	NoResp	
Moonshadow Ranch	Ukiah	NoResp	
Morehouse / San Francisco	San Francisco	NoResp	
Morehouse	Lafayette	New	
Mount Baldy Zen Center	Mount Baldy	NoResp	
Mt. Kailasa Farm	Hopland	NoResp	
Multibear Family	San Jose	NoResp	
Murphy Street House	Grass Valley	Defun	
Murrieta Hot Springs	Murrieta	Never	
Napa Cohousing Community	Napa	BadPO	"Return to Sender."
Naturalism	Los Angeles	BadPO	"Addressee Unknown"
New Essene Community	San Diego	Defun	Site: Enchnt. Garden Cmty.
Nityananda	Sebastapol	Defun	Disbanded '86
No Name Given	Berkeley	BadPO	"Addressee Unknown"
Nonagon	Garberville	Insuff	
Oasis: Hal/Al/Rose	Salt Flats	Insuff	
Ocean Song	Occidental	NoResp	
Old Mill Farm School	Mendocino	NoResp	
Omega Fellowship	Los Gatos	NoResp	
Omega Salvage	Berkeley	NoResp	
One Life Family	Santa Monica	NoResp	
Order of Saint Benedict	Central Valley	NoResp	
OSA Rainforest Reserve Coalition	Eureka	NoResp	
Ozone House	Mountain View	BadPO	"Moved/NFA"
Pacha Mama	Susanville	BadPO	"Moved/NFA"
Paradox House	San Francisco	Never	Collective household
Peace Gardens	Oakland	NoResp	
Peace House	Pittsburgh	NoResp	
Peralta	Carmichael	NoResp	
Pier House	Santa Monica	Never	
Platypus House	San Francisco	Insuff	
Playground, The	Oakland	New	
Plenty International	Jamul	Never	See Resource Listing
Plow Creek	Calpella	Never	Never was a community
Psico	Pasedena	NoResp	
Questhaven	Escondido	Insuff	
R.E.F. California	Tiburon	NoResp	
Radiance Media Ministry	Eureka	NoResp	
Rainbow Star Community	Hornbrook	NoResp	
Ramagiri	Sonoma County	NoResp	
Ranch, The	San Francisco	NoResp	
Redwood Monastery	Whitethorn	NoResp	
Religious School Natural Hygiene	Santa Cruz	Limbo	Presently dormant
Renaissance (Brotherhd. of Man)	Oregon House	NoResp	
Revolutionary Tomato	Oakland	ReName:	Listwig Mir
Richmond House	San Diego	New	
Rio Bonito Cooperative	Sutter Creek	NoResp	
Riparia	Chico	NoResp	
Roandoak of God Christian Commune	Morro Bay	NoResp	
Round Mountain Cooperative	Ukiah	Defun	Folded Sept. '86
Russells Mill	Murphys	Defun	Folded '87
Sahm's Place	Boulder Creek	Limbo	Still in formative stage
Saint Xenia Skete	Wildwood	NoResp	
San Francisco Zen Center	San Francisco	NoResp	
San Rafael House	San Rafael	Insuff	
Sanatana Dharma Foundation	St. Helena	NoResp	
Santa Rosa Catholic Worker	Santa Rosa	BadPO	"Forwarding Order Expired"
Saugus Commune	Southern CA(?)	Defun	Folded '92
SBSHC: Student Housing Co-op	Isla Vista	New	
Self-Sufficient Community	Beverly Hills	BadPO	"Forwarding Order Expired"
Shahan	Santa Cruz	NoResp	
Simpletons	Santa Cruz	NoResp	
Sivananda Yoga Center	West Hollywood	Insuff	
So. Calif. Alliance for Survival	Los Angeles	BadPO	"Return to Sender"
Spiritual Community/NAM	Berkeley	NLC	No longer a community
Spiritual Rebel Center	Venice	ReName:	Positive Living Center
Spring Hill (Cohousing)	Petaluma	NoResp	
Starcross Monastery	Santa Rosa	NoResp	
Stardance	San Francisco	ReName:	Purple Rose Collective
Suburban Palace	San Francisco	NoResp	
Summerfield School	Santa Rosa	NoResp	
Summerland Inn	Summerland	NLC	Co-founder died; now B&B
Sun Mountain	Tollhouse	NoResp	
Sunburst	Santa Barbara	ReName:	Builders, The (UT & NV)
Sunrise House	Berkeley	NoResp	Forming summer '89
Sweetwater Community	Guerneville	Insuff	
Syntropy Institute	Palo Alto	NoResp	
Table Mountain Ranch	Albion	NoResp	
Tahl Mah Sah Zen Center	Los Angeles	NoResp	
Taorima	Ojai	NoResp	
Temple of the People	Halcyon	NoResp	
Transpersonal Institute	Stanford	Never	Possible Resource listing
Treehouse	Oakland	NLC	Community folded 5/89
Troop 69	San Francisco	NoResp	
26th Street House	San Francisco	NoResp	
UCHA: Student Co-op	Los Angeles	NoResp	
UCSA: Student Co-op	Berkeley	New	
Ukiah Research Institute	Ukiah	Defun	Dissolved mid '80s
Union House	Santa Cruz	NoResp	
Unity Center	Walnut Creek	NoResp	
Universal Life Church	Sacramento	NoResp	
University of Trees	Boulder Creek	Limbo	Not "currently" a cmty.
Urban Ecology House	Oakland	Defun	House sold '80s
Urban Stonehenge	San Francisco	Limbo	Nghbrhd getting dangerous
Vajra Bodhi Sea	San Francisco	NoResp	
Vedantic Center	Agoura	NoResp	
Villa Sarah	Altadena	Defun	House was sold '93
Village Homes	Davis	Never	Ecological neighborhood
Village Oz	Point Arena	Defun	Possibly reviving (?)
Wholistic Counseling	Berkeley	NoResp	
Wilderness Cmty Eagle Connector	Santa Rosa	NoResp	
Willow	Napa Valley	M/R	Possible Resource listing
Winterwood (Cohousing)	Nevada City	NoResp	
Y.C.C. Communities	Three Rivers	NoResp	
Yana Trails Community	Cohasset Stage	BadPO	"No Forwarding Address"
Yorkville Women's Land	San Francisco	BadPO	"Forwarding Order Expired"
Zen Center of Los Angeles	Los Angeles	NoResp	

COLORADO

Name	Location	Status	Notes
Adventure Trails Survival School	Black Hawk	NoResp	
Aurca	Gardner	NoResp	
Auroville International USA	Sacramento	M/R	See Resource listing
Blossum Family	Denver	BadPO	"Box Closed/NFA"
Blue Moon Mountain Ranch	Ft. Collins	New	
Boulder CoHousing	Boulder	New	
Center for United Endeavors	Aspen	BadPO	"Box Closed"
Circle of Friends	Boulder	BadPO	"Addressee Unknown"
Cochetopa Dome Ranch	Conifer	NoResp	
Community Durango	Durango	Defun	Disbanded before got going
Crestone Mountain Zen Center	Crestone	NoResp	
Denver CoHousing	Denver	New	
Divine Light Mission	Denver	BadPO	"No Such Number"
Dunton Hot Springs	Telluride	Defun	Land sold '94
Durango CoHousing	Durango	New	
Eden Ranch	Aurora	New	
Emissaries, The	Loveland	M/R	Network listed: Resources
Episcopal Community	Denver	NoResp	
Essenes of Kosmon	Grand Junction	Insuff	
Family, The	Evergreen	NoResp	
Gathering Place, The	Morrison	New	
Greyrock Commons CoHousing	Ft. Collins	New	
Highline Crossing CoHousing	Littleton	New	
Hooker House	Denver	NLC	Now a private residence
Jubilee Brotherhood	Colorado Springs	BadPO	"Moved/NFA"
Libre	Gardner	Insuff	
Lindisfarne Institute	Crestone	NLC	
Malachite Farm	Gardner	NoResp	
Many Sisters Mountain Cmty	Red Feather Lakes	New	
Mesa Verde Eco-Village	Boulder	Defun	Folded '94
Nairopa Institute	Boulder	Never	Never was a community
Ontological Society	Loveland	NoResp	
Paradise Valley Commuity	Saguache	NoResp	
People House	Denver	New	
Rancho Sereno	Loveland	New	
Red Rock Community	Southern	Insuff	
Shepherd's Gate	Denver	New	

(continued, first state block)

Community	Location	Status	Note
Shoshoni Yoga Retreat	Rollinsville	New	
Stillpoint	Wetmore	NoResp	
Sunset Goodearth Farm	Fort Collins	Never	Never was a community
Universal Ashram & Sanctuary	Denver	BadPO	"Forwarding Order Expired"
Victor Bolo	Victor	ReName: Victor Trade Co-op	
Weld County	Golden	Defun	Disbanded summer '94
Wilderness Ranch	Bellevue	New	
Windblown Ranch	Fort Collins	NoResp	

CONNECTICUT

Community	Location	Status	Note
Autognomics Institute	Mystic	Insuff	
Bonsilene	New Haven	NoResp	
CNVA Farm	Groton	Insuff	
Community of Saint Luke	Stamford	NLC	No longer a community
East River Community	Guilford	NLC	No longer a community
Emmaus Community	Stamford	NoResp	
New Haven Zen Center	New Haven	NoResp	
San Daimiano Community	New Britain	BadPO	"Addressee Unknown"

DELAWARE

Community	Location	Status	Note
Ardencroft & Ardentown	Wilmington	Insuff	
New Family Experimt/Blackbird Pagan	Townsend	BadPO	Moved; address update 2/95

DISTRICT OF COLUMBIA

Community	Location	Status	Note
Black Hebrew Israelites	Washington	Insuff	
Church of the Savior	Washington	NoResp	
Community of Hope	Washington	NoResp	
Devadeep Rajneesh Sannyas Ashram	Washington	NoResp	
Dunamis Vocations Church	Washington	NoResp	
Eighth Day Community	Washington	BadPO	"Moved/NFA"
Olive Branch Catholic Worker	Washington	NoResp	
Saint Francis Catholic Worker	Washington	NoResp	
Society for Human Development	Washington	NoResp	

FLORIDA

Community	Location	Status	Note
Believers Fellowship	Naples	NoResp	
Crystal Springs Wilderness Retreat	Zephyrhills	NoResp	
Dayglo	Gainesville	BadPO	"Addressee Unknown"
Earthstar's	St. Augustine	Never	Privately owned, no group
Florida Group Retreat	Leesburg	NoResp	
Forming (Art & Gwen North)	Summerland	NoResp	
Forming (Rodgers-Hendricks)	Santa Rosa Beach	NoResp	
Gaia Community	Sarasota	Insuff	
Guru Ram Das Ashram	Melrose	NoResp	
Heart Lodge	De Leon Springs	NoResp	
Heilbron Springs	Starke	NoResp	
Highland Gospel Fellowship	Sebring	NoResp	
Jungle Community	Fort Lauderdale	NoResp	
Kashi Ranch	Roseland	NoResp	
Long Leaf / Circledance	Melrose	NoResp	
Mammies Acres Organic Farm	LaCrosse	NoResp	
Monastery of the Desert Wind	Tampa	NoResp	
Mooraway Group, The	Sarasota	New	
P.A.L.M. Family	West Palm Beach	NoResp	
Peckerwood Community	Tallahassee	Never	Never were a community
Rainbow Ranch	Jupiter	Never	
River Sink Community	Tallahassee	Insuff	
Spes Nova Community	Tampa	NLC	
Sunrise Community	Tallahassee	New	
Sycamore Land Co-op	Greensboro	Never	Just a neighborhood
TORIC	Margate	NoResp	
Villa Serena	Sarasota	BadPO	"No Such Number"
Walking Wood	Miami	NLC	No longer a community
Wetumpka Farms	Quincy	NLC	Folded '84
Woodville Grapevine	Tallahassee	NoResp	

GEORGIA

Community	Location	Status	Note
Albemarle Organic Cmty. Garden	Atlanta	NoResp	
Alleluia	Augusta	NoResp	
Atlanta Community	Atlanta	NLC	No longer a community
Community of Hospitality	Decatur	NoResp	
Featherfield Farm	Albany	Defun	
Forming (William Wehunt)	Dahlonega	NoResp	
Home In America	Jefferson	BadPO	"Forwarding Order Expired"
Lake Clair Cohousing	Atlanta	NoResp	
Logos	Atlanta	Insuff	
Lovingwell Community	Atlanta	Limbo	Curently dormant
Metanoia Community	St. Marys	Limbo	Transit'n; prob. move to FL
Sevananda	Atlanta	Insuff	
Word, The	Fitzgerald	New	
Yonder's Farm / Swan's Nest	Jeffersonville	NoResp	

HAWAII

Community	Location	Status	Note
Dharma Buddhist Temple	Honolulu	NoResp	
Forming (Ben Hopkins)	Haleiwa	NLC	
Forming (John Kent)	To be determined	NoResp	
Good Karma Farm	Captain Cook	NoResp	
Hawaii Center Ecological Living	Keaau	BadPO	"Return to Sender"
Healing Village	Pahoa	NoResp	
Hui Io	Kailua	NoResp	
Maui Zendo	Haiku	BadPO	"Forwarding Order Expired"
Ohana Aloha	Waumanlo	NoResp	
Ohana Mauka	Pahala	Limbo	Planning to re-form
Organic Kauai Produce	Kapaa	ReName: Gaien	

IDAHO

Community	Location	Status	Note
Down to Earth Living	Sandpoint	ReName: Peaceful Gardens	
Forming (Alan Krivor)	Sandpoint	BadPO	"Forwarding Order Expired"
Friendship House	Boise	NoResp	
Lucark Community	Hope	BadPO	"Moved/NFA"
Sandpoint	Sagle	Defun	Never got off the ground
Two Rainbows	Boise	BadPO	"Addressee Unknown"
Viola Community	Viola	NoResp	

ILLINOIS

Community	Location	Status	Note
Aquarius	Phillips Township	Insuff	
Austin Fellowship	Chicago	NLC	No longer a community
Bonhoffer House	Chicago	Insuff	
Changes	Chicago	NoResp	
Chicago Meditation Center	Chicago	NoResp	
Children of God ("The Family")	Chicago	BadPO	"Addressee Unknown"
Covenant Community	Evanston	NLC	No longer a community
Dharmadhatu Meditation Center	Chicago	BadPO	"Forwarding Order Expired"
Hudgeons Creek Farm	Carbondale	BadPO	"Addressee Unknown"
Juneway Co-op	Chicago	New	
Kishwaukee Tribe	De Kalb	BadPO	"Forwarding Order Expired"
Medicine Wheel	Alto Pass	BadPO	"Return to Sender"
Midwest Collective / MNS	Chicago	NLC	No longer a community
Monroe Street Living Collective	Bloomington	BadPO	"No Forwarding Address"
New Earth	Oblong	Never	Never was a community
Plow Creek Fellowship	Tiskilwa	NoResp	
Salem Communal Brotherhood	Rock City	NoResp	
SWAMP (Sangamon River Cmty)	White Heath	Defun	Folded; land sold 1/94
Swedenborg Group	Glenview	NoResp	
Synergy	Carbondale	NoResp	
The Community	DeKalb	NoResp	
Unit One	Urbana	New	
Valley Cooperative School	Dundee	BadPO	"Forwarding Order Expired"
Vanguard Group	Wheeling	BadPO	"Return to Sender"

INDIANA

Community	Location	Status	Note
Brothers of the Holy Cross	Notre Dame	NoResp	
Chrysalis	Helmsburg	NLC	No longer a community
Earthworks	Plymouth	NoResp	
Elkhorn Ranch (Cygnus, Inc.)	Richmond	NoResp	
Fellowship of Hope	Elkhart	NLC	New focus; leadership probs
Freedom Farm	Freedom	NoResp	
ICA / Earthcare	Indianapolis	M/R	See Resource listing
Kneadmore Life (Plum Creek)	Nashville	Defun	Court action dissolved '89
Light of the World Mission	Evansville	Insuff	
Patchwork Central	Evansville	NoResp	
Saint Meinrad Archabbey	Saint Meinrad	NoResp	

IOWA

Community	Location	Status	Note
Amana Society	Amana	NLC	No longer a community
Arch, The	Clinton	NoResp	
Davenport Catholic Worker	Davenport	NoResp	
Kindred Community	Des Moines	Defun	Disbanded 12/89
Strangers & Guests Cath. Worker	Maloy	NoResp	
Third Place House	Mt. Vernon	ReName: Hawk Circle Cooperative	
Thoreau Center	Des Moines	NLC	

KANSAS

Community	Location	Status	Note
Children Kansas	Wichita	BadPO	"No Such Number"
Forming (Virginia Hamill)	Shawnee	New	
Kansas Zen Center	Lawrence	Never	Never was a community
Marion Mennonite Brethen	Hillsboro	BadPO	"Return to Sender"
Midwest Community	Wichita	ReName: Soc. for Human Solidarity	
New Creation Fellowship	Newton	NLC	Never was a community
Planetary Project Foundation	Newton	NoResp	
Sungreen Co-op	Wichita	NoResp	
Y.C.C. Communities	Wichita	NoResp	

KENTUCKY

Community	Location	Status	Note
Cedar Hollow Community	Milltown	BadPO	"Addressee Unknown"
Covenant Community	Lexington	NoResp	
Earthward Bound	New Haven	Defun	
Gathering	Louisville	ReName: Just Creations	
Godsland	Kettle	NoResp	
Just Creations ("The Gathering")	Louisville	NoResp	Possible Resource Group
Lexington Zen Center	Lexington	NLC	No longer a community
Longcliff Collective/Community	Sunnybrook	NoResp	
Middle of the Rainbow	Tompkinsville	NLC	No longer a community
New Covenant Fellowship	Beverly	Never	Never was a community
Passionist Religious Order	Erlanger	NoResp	
Polestar	Elkton	BadPO	"No Forwarding Address"
Quaker Action	Hindman	BadPO	"Forwarding Order Expired"
Rainbow Ridge	Richmond	NLC	See Resource Listing
Tupelo Ridge	Huff	BadPO	"Return to Sender"
Windspirit Farm & Music Cmty	Kettle	NLC	No longer a community

LOUSIANNA

Community	Location	Status	Note
Alive	New Orleans	NLC	No longer a community
Harmony Community	Lafayette	NoResp	
Jesus the King Community	New Orleans	NoResp	
Open House Community	Lake Charles	ReName: Holy City	
Suneidesis Consociation	New Orleans	NoResp	

*The Renamed, Regrouped, Dead, Disbanded, Lost, and No Replies

N. American

MAINE

Name	Location	Status	Comment
Atkins Bay Farm	Phippsburg	NLC	No longer a community
Battlebrook Farm Trust	Danforth	NLC	No longer a community
Birdsong Farm	North Berwick	BadPO	"Forwarding Order Expired"
Coventree (Womonground)	Troy	NoResp	
Downeast Community	Freedom	Defun	Defunct
Energy Systems Parameters	Thorndike	NLC	No longer a community
Fayerweather	Freeport	BadPO	"Forwarding Order Expired"
Gathering Ground	Dexter	Limbo	May be ready next time...
Home Emmaus	Belfast	Insuff	
Leavitt Hill Farm Community	New Vineyard	NLC	No longer a community
Nancy's Farm	Thorndike	NLC	No longer a community
Osprey Community	Penobscott	NLC	No longer a community
Paula & Winnie	S. China	NoResp	
Whiten Hill Farm Community	Thorndike	NoResp	
Women's Cmty (Lynnsey/Tracy)	Penobscot	NoResp	
Womland Trust	Troy	NoResp	

MANITOBA

Name	Location	Status	Comment
Common Ground	Winnipeg	NoResp	
Forming (Pat Mooney)	Brandon	Insuff	
Land Co-op	Beresford	NoResp	Several families
Matthew House Fellowship	Winnipeg	NoResp	

MARYLAND

Name	Location	Status	Comment
Arrowhead Farm	Crofton	BadPO	"Return to Sender"
Casa Caritis/ Emmanuel House	Baltimore	NoResp	
Covenant Life Christian Cmty.	Wheaton	NoResp	
Dayspring Church	Germantown	NoResp	
Deva Commuity	Burkittsville	NLC	No longer a community
Downhill Farm	Hancock	Defun	"Forwarding Order Expired"
Forming (Louise Smallen)	Gaitherburg	NoResp	
Forming Coho (Fred Wolfson)	Baltimore	NoResp	
Friends of the Retarded, Inc.	Towson	Never	Never was a community
Giza Farms	Waldorf	NoResp	
Koinonia	Stevenson	Defun	Folded
Lamb of God	Timonium	BadPO	"Return to Sender"
Metanoia House	Baltimore	NoResp	
Network of Light	Chevy Chase	NoResp	
Pilgrim Community	Annapolis	NoResp	
Red Oak Community	Adelphi	Never	Cooperative group house
Savitria	Baltimore	NLC	No longer a community
Society for Human Devel.	Cheverly	NoResp	
Unknown Name	Kensington	Insuff	
Waterfarm	Chestertown	Defun	No longer a community
Women's Community	Takoma Park	NoResp	

MASSACHUSETTS

Name	Location	Status	Comment
AAO Boston	Somerville	NoResp	
Agape Fellowship House	Jamaica Plain	BadPO	"Forwarding Order Expired"
Antrockies	Amherst	BadPO	"Forwarding Order Expired"
Battlebrook Farm	Cambridge	BadPO	"Return to Sender"
Bebop Co-op	Allston	BadPO	"Return to Sender"
Broadway House	Cambridge	NoResp	
Butterworth Farms/Octagon House	Orange	NLC	
Center of the Light	Great Barrington	NLC	No longer a community
Centerpeace	West Medford	NoResp	
Community of Jesus	Orleans	NoResp	
Cummington Cmty of the Arts	Cummington	Never	Never was a community
Dutch Mountain	Jamaica Plain	BadPO	"Addressee Unknown"
Earthdance Cooperative	Plainfield	NLC	5/92 became dance center
Ecologos	Milton	NoResp	
Fare-Thee-Well Homeless Center	Huntington	NoResp	
Farm & Wilderness Foundation	Belmont	NoResp	
Fort Hill	Roxbury	NLC	No longer a community
Friends Crossing Community	North Easton	NLC	Didn't develop as planned
Guru Ram Das Ashram (3HO)	Millis	SubNet	See Sikh Dharma/3HO
Hop Brook Commune	Amherst	BadPO	"No Forwarding Order"
Indian Line Farm	Great Barrington	Never	CSA (Resource?)
Institute for Cooperative Cmty.	Cambridge	BadPO	"Addressee Unknown"
Interface	Newton	BadPO	"Forwarding Order Expired"
Island	Belchertown	NoResp	
Joyworks Farming Collective	Mendon	NoResp	
Kindred Spirits	Allston	BadPO	"Addressee Unknown"
Maji	Jamaica Plain	BadPO	"Addressee Unknown"
Millenium Fellowship	Reading	Never	Never was a community
Millers River Educational Co-op	Phillipston	NoResp	
Old Joe Clarks	Cambridge	NoResp	
Pine Street Cohousing	Amherst	New	
Random People House	Somerville	NoResp	
Sacramento House	Cambridge	Never	
Spanish House	Brookline	BadPO	"Addressee Unknown"
Spring Hill	Ashby	M/R	Resources listing (NoResp)
Temenos Retreat Center	Shutesbury	Never	Never was a community
Top O' The Ten	Allston	NoResp	
Unadilla Farm	Gill	NLC	No longer a community
Waldo Collective	Somerville	Defun	Some to "Common Unity"
Woolman Hill	Deerfield	NLC	No longer a community

MICHIGAN

Name	Location	Status	Comment
Ahimsa House	Ann Arbor	NLC	Lost lease spring '94
Ann Arbor Cohousing	Ann Arbor	Insuff	
Ann Arbor Shim Gum Do Zen	Ann Arbor	NoResp	
Apple Farm	Three Rivers	Insuff	
Aradia Inc	Grand Rapids	BadPO	"Forwarding Order Expired"
Belanger Creek Community	Suttons Bay	Never	Never was a community
Christ's Community	Grand Rapids	NoResp	
Church of the Messiah	Detroit	NoResp	
Community Farm of Ann Arbor	Dexter	BadPO	"Return to Sender."
Detroit Peace Community	Detroit	NoResp	
Earth Community	Detroit	NoResp	
Farm, The	Allegan	NLC	No longer a community
Forming (Willy Green)	Grand Rapids	NoResp	
Goodrich Club	Albion	Insuff	
Great Lakes Rainbow	Ann Arbor	BadPO	"No Forwarding Address"
Israelite House of David	Benton Harbor	BadPO	"Return to Sender"
Israelite House of David	Benton Harbor	BadPO	"Return to Sender."
Kuntree Bumpkin/Hickory Farms	Whitmoor Lake	NoResp	
Leelawau Land Lovers	Maple City	NoResp	
Liberty Community	Vassar	BadPO	"Return to Sender"
Menominee River Fellowship	Wallace	BadPO	"Moved/NFA"
New utopian community	Buchanan Twnshp.	Insuff	
Obonaudsawin Farm	Lexington	NoResp	
Saint Agnes Community	Detroit	NoResp	
Saint Gregory's Abbey	Three Rivers	Never	Never was a community
Sherwood New Age Community	Williamstown	BadPO	"Return to Sender"
Sunshower Farm	Lawrence	Insuff	
Sylviron Center	Blanchard	Limbo	Start has been delayed
Upland Hills Eco Awareness Cntr	Oxford	NoResp	
Wellness House	Okemos	NoResp	
Word of God	Ann Arbor	NoResp	

MINNESOTA

Name	Location	Status	Comment
Agora Community	St. Paul	NoResp	
Bethany Fellowship	Bloomington	NoResp	
Common Harvest Community	Minneapolis	NoResp	
Disciples of the Lord Jesus Christ	Winona	Insuff	
Fellowship of Believers	Grand Rapids	NoResp	
Forming (Ned Rousmaniere)	Minneapolis	NoResp	
Forming (Robert Hurston)	Taylor Falls	New	
Herbert Lynch	Edwa	New	
Intentional Cmty. Workgroup	Pine City	Defun	Folded early '94
Linden Tree Community	Underwood	NLC	No longer a community
Little Dipper Farm	St. Peter	BadPO	"Return to Sender."
New Prairie Fellowship	Farwell	Limbo	Undergoing major changes
Northwoods Community	Minneapolis	Defun	Folded early '94
Plowshare Collective	Minneapolis	BadPO	"Forwarding Order Expired"
Sacred Heart Community	Duluth	BadPO	"Return to Sender"
WEB	Minneapolis	NoResp	
Windtree Farm	Motley	NoResp	

MISSISSIPPI

Name	Location	Status	Comment
Camp Sky Spirit	Ovett	New	
Internat'l Soc. Krishna Consc.	New Talavan	Insuff	
Old South Vedic Society	Washington	NoResp	
Voice of Calvary	Jackson	NoResp	

MISSOURI

Name	Location	Status	Comment
Broadway Covenant Community	Kansas City	NLC	Still exist as a church
Brookside Collective	Columbia	NoResp	
Brookside Fellowship	Kansas City	Defun	Disbanded
C.S.A./Zarephath-Horeb	Pontiac	Defun	Same as U&I (folded)
Cass Catholic Worker	St. Louis	NoResp	
Cattail Land Cooperative	Columbia	NoResp	
Christian Community Center	Troy	NoResp	
Covenant Community	Kansas City	NLC	No longer a community
Davidian 7th-Day Adventists	Exeter	NoResp	
Forming (Alice Lawler)	Marble Hills	NoResp	
Forming (Brian Latham)	Bloomfield	NoResp	
Forming (Dara Vinayaga)	Kansas City	NoResp	
Forming (Leslie Nichols)	Gainesville	NoResp	
Forming (Risa Mire)	Galena	NoResp	
Gathering	Kansas City	BadPO	"No Such Number"
Hawk Hill Land Trust	Brixey	NoResp	
Holistic Life Center	Jane	Insuff	
Ironwood	Birch Tree	BadPO	"Forwarding Order Expired"
Jesus People USA Farm	Doniphan	NoResp	
Karen Catholic Worker House	Saint Louis	NoResp	
Little Farm	Stanberry	NLC	Never came together
Meramec Watershed CLT	Jamestown	Dupe	See Moniteau Farm (below)
Moniteau Farm/The Spiral Inn	Jamestown	NoResp	
Morning Glory Community	Arnold	NLC	No longer a community
New Life Farm	Brixley	NoResp	
Sunnyside Collective	Columbia	Defun	Possibly reviving (?)
Third Avenue Co-operative	Columbia	Limbo	Widespread life changes
U & I Community	Eldridge	Defun	Folded fall '86
West Walden Farm	Anderson	NoResp	

MONTANA

Name	Location	Status	Comment
Bitterroot SP Healing Cmty.	Hamilton	BadPO	"Return to Sender"
Church Univ. & Triumphant	Corwin Springs	NoResp	
Community Covenant Church	Missoula	NLC	No longer a community
Deep Ecology Community	N.W.	Insuff	
Friends Unlimited, Inc.	St. Ignatius	BadPO	"Forwarding Order Expired"
Frontier Life	Alberton	Never	Never was a community
Madison River Conf & Ed Center	Three Forks	Defun	Folded '94
Missoula CoHousing	Missoula	Defun	Disbanded '94
Purdin, Wayne & Julie	Bozeman	NoResp	
Species Life House	Missoula	NLC	No longer a community
Turah	Bonner	NoResp	

Community	Location	Status	Notes
Universal Healing Arts	Lavina	Never	Never was a community
Wolf Creek Community	Bozeman	NoResp	

NEBRASKA

Community	Location	Status	Notes
Greensfields Resistance Cmty.	Omaha	NoResp	

NEVADA

Community	Location	Status	Notes
Eckankar	Las Vegas	Never	"Insufficient Address"
Meta Tantay	Carlin	NoResp	

NEW HAMPSHIRE

Community	Location	Status	Notes
Burch House	Littleton	New	
Forming (Charmaine Bennett)	Hancock	NoResp	
Forming (Donna San Antonio)	Wolfeboro	NoResp	
Meeting School	Rindge	NoResp	
Merriam Hill Community	Greenville	Never	Never was a community
Mettanokit Community	Greenville	NLC	Another Place Farm (NLC)
Shaker Farm	Enfield	BadPO	"Forwarding Order Expired"
Tobias Community	Wilton	NoResp	

NEW JERSEY

Community	Location	Status	Notes
Circles of Light New Age Cntr.	Bridgeton	NoResp	
Community of God's Love	Rutherford	NoResp	
Family of Friends	North Bergen	Dupe	See "Holistic Cmty." (below)
Forming (Kristina Dillman)	Lambertville	NoResp	
Forming (Susan Deckert)	Hightstown	Defun	Folded '93
Genesis Farm	Blairstown	M/R	See Resource Listing
Hermitage, The	Bridgewater	BadPO	"Addressee Unknown"
Holistic Community	Mt. Freedom	BadPO	Moved: NC; Leaders in Jail
Homeland Community	P.O. Milltown	BadPO	"Return to Sender"
Intentional Family	Stillwater	BadPO	"Addressee Unknown"
Labsum Shedrub Ling	Washington	NoResp	
Mill Hill Community Land	Trenton	Defun	
Peace Weavers	Lambertville	New	
People of Hope	Covenant Station	NoResp	
Strengthen Our Sisters	Hewitt	Never	Women/children's shelter
2-D Co-op	Princeton	NoResp	
Vineland Community	Vineland	NoResp	

NEW MEXICO

Community	Location	Status	Notes
Aggressive Christian Missions	Beronio	New	
Alamosa Farm	Monticello	NoResp	
ARF	Santa Fe	NoResp	
Buchanan Community	Silver City	BadPO	"Addressee Unknown"
CEED Ecological Village Cmty.	Santa Fe	NoResp	
Christain Tribal Community	Beronio	Dupe	"Aggres. Christns" (above)
City of the Sun	Columbus	NoResp	
Eden Community	AZ/NM Border	Insuff	
Fiesta Family	Dixon	NLC	No longer a community
Forming (Chris Wuest)	Santa Fe	NoResp	
Forming (Grace Hanson)	Albuquerque	BadPO	"Not At This Address"
Hacienda De Guru Ram Das	Espanola	SubNet	See Sikh Dharma/3HO
In God We Trust, Apache Creek	Reserve	Defun	Never got off the ground.
Jemez Bodhi Mandala	Jemez Springs	NoResp	
Jerusalem Community	Belen	NoResp	
New Age Co-op	Silver City	BadPO	"Forwarding Order Expired"
New Buffalo	Arroyo Hondo	New	
NM Women's Land Trust	Tesuque	NoResp	
Ojito	Velarde	Limbo	May regroup in the future
Osha Commune	Albuquerque	NoResp	
Pecos Community	Pecos	Insuff	
S.T.A.R. II Community	Taos	NoResp	
Santa Fe Community School	Santa Fe	NoResp	
SEEDS of Change	Gila	NoResp	
Tawapa	Placitas	Defun	Folded '93; lost the land
Theater of All Possibilities	South of Santa Fe	Insuff	
Tierra Madre, La Madera	Santa Fe	New	
Treelane Earthlove	Mora	Defun	Never got off the ground
Vallecitos Retreat	Vallecitos	NoResp	
Water Creek Co-op Village	Santa Fe	BadPO	"Addressee Unknown"
Water Creek Partnership	Tesuque	Defun	In transition toward cmty.
Willow Southwest/Galisteo Inn	Galisteo	Defun	Land sold by owner
Women's Land Trust	Santa Fe	New	

NEW YORK

Community	Location	Status	Notes
Acharya Sushil Jain Ashram	Staten Island	NoResp	
Akwenasa	Ghent	BadPO	"Forwarding Order Expired"
Albany Christian Cmty.	Glenmont	BadPO	"No Forwarding Address"
Ananda Marga	Corona	NoResp	
Arunachala Ashram	New York	BadPO	"Moved/NFA"
Barry Hollow Land Co-op	Brooktondale	NoResp	
Beachtree, The	Monticello	BadPO	"Forwarding Order Expired"
Bear Tribe	Harriman	NoResp	
Beech Hill Pond	West Danby	NoResp	
Brookside	New York	NoResp	
Catholic Liturgy Cmty.	Staten Island	NoResp	
Chogye Internat'l Zen Center	New York	BadPO	"Forwarding Order Expired"
Common Ground	Saugerties	BadPO	"Forwarding Order Expired"
Communal Arts Colony	New York	NoResp	
Community of God	South Glen Falls	NoResp	
Convent of Saint Helena	Vails Gate	NoResp	
Dandelion Hill	Newfield	NLC	No longer a community
Dawes Hill Commune	West Danby	NoResp	
Dayspring	Himrod	NLC	No longer interested
Earthfriends	Scarsdale	Limbo	Not happening yet
Everything for Everybody	New York City	Insuff	
Farm Club Collective	Geneva	NoResp	
Fish Cove Inn	Hampton Bays	NoResp	
Forming (Rob S.)	Nelson	New	
Global Walk/Liveable World	New York	NoResp	
Havagoats	Binghamton	NoResp	
Hilarian	Slatterville Springs	BadPO	"Addressee Unknown"
Household of Faith	Bronx	Defun	Folded; now regular church
Inst. Evolutionary Research	New York	NoResp	
Int'l Cntr. for Integrative Studies	New York	NoResp	
Integral Yoga Institute	New York	NoResp	
Jews for Jesus	New York	BadPO	"Box Closed/NFA"
Kairos	New York	NoResp	
Kriya Babaji Yoga Sangam	New York	BadPO	"Addressee Unknown"
Lily Dale	Lily Dale	NoResp	
Ma Yoga Shakti Int'l Mission	South Ozone Park	NoResp	
Matagiri Sri Aurobindo Center	High Falls	NLC	No longer a community
New Covenant Community	Oswego	BadPO	"Forwarding Order Expired"
Northwoods	Alpine	BadPO	"Return to Sender"
Omega Institute	Rhinebeck	Never	See Resources listing
Omviron	New York	NoResp	
Oneonta Community	Oneonta	NoResp	
Pax Christi	Bronx	BadPO	"Addressee Unknown"
Phoenicia Pathwork Center	Phoenicia	M/R	Possible Resource listing
Quarter Moon Farm	Ithaca	BadPO	"Moved/NFA"
Religious Society of Families	Frewsburg	Insuff	
SEADS of Truth, Inc.	Massapequa	SubNet	See SEADS (NY)
Seneca Women's Peace Camp	Romulus	NoResp	
Sivananda Yoga Vedanta Cntr.	New York	NoResp	
Skyview Acres	Pomona	Insuff	
St. Sebastian's Parrish Assoc.	New York	NoResp	
Sunrise Farm	Bath	BadPO	"Forwarding Order Expired"
Syda Foundation	South Fallsburg	NoResp	
Turtle Creek Farm	Spencer	NLC	Never was a community
Unison (Friends of the Mtn.)	New Paltz	M/R	Possible Resource listing
Urban Homesteaders Assoc.	New York	BadPO	"Addressee Unknown"
War Resisters League	New York	Never	Resource group
Watson Homestead	Corning	BadPO	"Return to Sender"
Weed Mine Farm	Copake	BadPO	"Addressee Unknown"
Wild Earth	Canton	BadPO	"Temporarily Away"
Women's Art Colony Farm	New York	NoResp	
Zen Community of New York	Yonkers	NoResp	
Zen Studies Society	New York	NoResp	

NORTH CAROLINA

Community	Location	Status	Notes
Aionic Talents	Chapel Hill	BadPO	"Return to Sender"
Aloe Community	Cedar Grove	Defun	Folded in '80.
Blue Mountain	Chapel Hill	BadPO	"Return to Sender"
Bonnie Haven Inn	Hendersonville	BadPO	"Return to Sender"
Center of Light	Chapel Hill	NoResp	Possible Resource group
Commune De Green Bean	Chapel Hill	NoResp	
Dance the Dream Awake	Carboro	NoResp	
Earth Center/Village	Swannanoa	M/R	Teaching village, non-res.
Forming (Brian Felstein)	Chapel Hill	NoResp	
Forming (Jim Tremblay)	Morganton	Never	
Full Circle Farm	Durham	NoResp	
Harmony Mountain Acres	Blowing Rock	ReName:	Apple Tree Acres
John C. Campbell Folk School	Brasstown	NoResp	
Light of the Mountains Cmty.	Leicester	Defun	No longer a community
Nahalat Shalom Community	Hot Springs	NoResp	
North Carolina Biodome	Waynesville	NoResp	
Ox Creek Community	Weaverville	BadPO	"Return to Sender."
Rowland, Mary	Raleigh	NoResp	
Running Water	Bakersville	BadPO	"Forwarding Order Expired"
Schola Contemplationis	Pfafftown	Defun	Disbanded '86
Shalom Community	Brown Summit	Defun	Folded '93
Singing Waters Assoc.	Purlear	NLC	No longer a community
Solar Chariot Schools, Inc	Greenville	BadPO	"Moved/NFA"
Star Farm	Star	NLC	No longer a community
Star Trek Community	Cary	NoResp	
Stillwind Community	Sugar Grove	NLC	No longer a community
Suburban Partners	Durham	BadPO	"Addressee Unknown"
Toehold	Burnsville	NLC	Plans didn't materialize
Twin Streams Educational Cntr.	Chapel Hill	NoResp	

NORTH DAKOTA

Community	Location	Status	Notes
Daystar-Gardner	Fargo	NoResp	
Forming (Sandy Parsons)	Grand Forks	NoResp	

NOVA SCOTIA

Community	Location	Status	Notes
Akala Point	Tantallon	NoResp	
Baxters Harbour Co-op	Canning	NoResp	
Cmty. in Barrington Passage	Barrington Passage	Defun	Moved to new location '93
Cmty. in Yarmouth	Yarmouth	Defun	Folded '92
Cmty. in/Myrtle Tree Farm	Waterville	Defun	Folded '92

OHIO

Community	Location	Status	Notes
A.S.	Mount Vernon	NoResp	
Athens Land Co-op	Glouster	ReName:	Edges
Casa del Pueblo	Dayton	NoResp	
Church of God & Sts. of Christ	Cleveland	NLC	Now network of churches
Entwood	Athens (vicinity)	Defun	Folded c. '81
Forming (F. Little)	Cincinnati	NoResp	
Forming (Holly Knight)	Yellow Springs	New	
Forming (L. Agriesti & J. Minor)	Columbus	NoResp	

N. American

Name	City	Status	Note
Forming (M. Winegarner)	Monroeville	BadPO	"Forwarding Order Expired"
Golgonooza	Millfield	NoResp	
Goss Fork Community	Whipple	NLC	No longer a community
Grailville	Loveland	NoResp	
Helpless Far	Amesville	ReName:	Far Valley Farm
Imago	Cincinnati	NoResp	
Laughing Buddha Farm	Amesville	Defun	Folded
Lookout , The	Cincinnati	NoResp	
Moon Ridge	Guysville	NoResp	
Mud City	Athens	Insuff	
Our Kibbutz	Ewington	NoResp	
Paideia	Athens	ReName:	Carpenter Village
Servant Community	Cincinnati	Defun	Disbanded 12/87
Sisters of Saint Joseph	Cincinnati	BadPO	"Addressee Unknown"
Son of God Community	Cleveland	Defun	Fewer people; folded
Southern Rainbow	Cincinnati	BadPO	"Moved/NFA"
Sun Circle Family	Akron	NoResp	
Tucker's Cabin	Athens	NLC	No longer a community
Way, Inc.	New Knoxville	NoResp	
Wild Turkey Hollow	Athens	Insuff	
Wolf Run	Athens	Defun	Unconfirmed

OKLAHOMA

Name	City	Status	Note
Common Ground Farm	Snow	NoResp	
Community of the Servant	Oklahoma City	NoResp	
Hummingbird Medicine Society	Stillwell	BadPO	"Forwarding Order Expired"
Walden Hill	Stillwater	NoResp	

ONTARIO

Name	City	Status	Note
Alternative Growth Institute	Ottawa	NoResp	
Alternative to Alienation	Toronto	BadPO	"Addressee Unknown"
Bakavi	Merrickville	Defun	Folded '84
Bright Community Farm	Bright	NoResp	
Chalbo	Holyrood	NoResp	
Cloud Mountain	Killaloe	NoResp	
Cobwebs	Thunder Bay	NoResp	
Community in Kingston	Kingston	Defun	Folded '92
Dandelion	Enterprise	ReName:	Stonehedge
Earth Bound	Maynooth	Never	
Family Pastimes	Perth	Never	Make co-op games (R?)
Farm, The	Lanark P.O.	NLC	No longer a community
Forming (Dean Bond)	Toronto	NoResp	
Heartwood	Willowdale	BadPO	"Return to Sender"
I Am	Madoc	BadPO	"Moved/NFA"
Ingersoll Fellowship AA	Ingersoll	NoResp	
Lanark Hills	Perth	NLC	No longer a community
Maple High Farm	Roslin	BadPO	"Addressee Unknown"
Marble Rock	Kingston	NoResp	
Morningstar Farm	Berkeley	Never	Two families
Nazareth/Bethany House	Hamilton	NoResp	
Ontario Zen Center	Toronto	Defun	Folded
S.O.I.L.	Toronto	BadPO	"Return to Sender"
Stone Soup Collective	Toronto	Defun	
Toad Hollow Cmty. Farm	Bracebridge	Defun	Interpersonal Relationships
Twin Valley School	Wardsville	Defun	"No Forwarding Address"
Wilderness Seekers	Chapleau	BadPO	"Moved/NFA"
Zen Lotus Society	Toronto	ReName:	Buddh. Soc. Comp. Wisdm.

OREGON

Name	City	Status	Note
Appletree Co-op	Cottage Grove	NLC	Sold land in '92
Barnes & Friends	Portland	NoResp	
Bee Farm	Ashland	BadPO	"Return to Sender"
Blue River	Finn Rock	Never	Never was a community
Cabbage Lane	Wolf Creek	NoResp	
Celebrations	Yamhill	NoResp	
Center for Well-Being	Creswell	NLC	No longer a community
Cherry Grove Center	Gaston	Defun	"Forwarding Order Expired"
China Gardens	Cave Junction	NoResp	
Christ Brotherhood	Eugene	Defun	Prophecy invalidated '88
Crabapple	Eugene	Defun	Defunct
Crack of Dawn	Ashland	NLC	No longer a community
End of the Road House	Cottage Grove	M/R	Resource: "Aprovecho"
Folly Farm	Grand Ronde	Defun	"Forwarding Order Expired"
Food Farm	Days Creek	BadPO	"Forwarding Order Expired"
Galilee	Portland	New	Info received 2/17/95
Goldenwimmin	Wolf Creek	Defun	Disbanded
Ham	Portland	NoResp	
Hearthwind	Umpqua	Defun	Disbanded '83
Highway Missionary Society	Wilderville	Defun	Disbanded 12/87
Human Dancing	Ashland	NoResp	
Illuminati Family	Cloverdale	Insuff	
Ithifien	Sheridan	NoResp	
Jeshua Ben Josef	Eugene	Never	Never was a community
Land House	Forest Grove	NoResp	
Land Lovers	Portland	BadPO	"Return to Sender"
Living Love Cntr. (Ken Keyes)	Coos Bay	ReName:	Vision Foundation
Living Treet	Deadwood	NLC	No longer a community.
Lorien Family Land	Eagle Point	Defun	Folded
May One Cooperative	Eugene	NoResp	
McKenzie River Co-op	Finnrock	Never	
Mist Farm	Mist	New	
Mizpah Community	Woodburn	Never	BadPO "Return to Sender"
Mountain Grove	Glendale	M/R	See Resource Listing
Om Tribe	Veneta	NoResp	
OnGoing Concerns	Portland	New	

Name	City	Status	Note
Oregon Peaceworks	Salem	NoResp	
Osho Ansu Meditation Center	Lake Oswego	NoResp	
Planet Earth Clay Works	Myrtle Point	Never	Never was a community
Portable Village	Philomath	M/R	Resource: "Dwell Portably"
Rainbow Farm	Drain	NoResp	
Rainbow House	Eugene	NLC	No longer a community
Rainbow Valley	Eugene	NoResp	
Rajneeshpuram	Antelope	Defun	"Forwarding Order Expired"
Rivendell Farm	Cave Junction	BadPO	"No Forwarding Address"
Riverland	Beaver	NoResp	
Rock Creek	Deadwood	NoResp	
Rock Foundation	Portland	NoResp	
Round Table Cath. Worker	Portland	NoResp	
Russian Old Believers/Staroveri	Woodburn	Insuff	
Sabin Community	Portland	New	
Sandra Moilanen	Clatskanie	NoResp	
Seven Springs Community	Dillard	Never	Never was a community
Shiloh Retreat & Study Center	Dexter	Defun	Lost to IRS '88; Lost Valley
Siuslaw Educational Project	Blodgett	NoResp	
Sugar Loaf Mountain Family	Myrtle Point	NoResp	
Sunny Valley/Living Arts	Grants Pass	Insuff	
Terracommun 2000	Portland	BadPO	"Box Closed/NFA"
Thunderhawk	Portland	BadPO	"No Such Number"
Two Rivers Farm	Aurora	NoResp	
Universing Center	Cottage Grove	BadPO	"No Forwarding Address"
Whitefeather Farm	Tiller	NoResp	

PENNSYLVANIA

Name	City	Status	Note
Agape Campgrounds	Mt. Union	NoResp	
Ananda Vrati	Eastern	NoResp	
Bark Mill Hollow Commune	Airville	NLC	Never was a community
Bawa Muhaiyaddeen Fellowship	Philadelphia	NoResp	
Blue Sky	Allison Park	NoResp	
Body of Christ Community	Glen Mills	NoResp	
Circle of Good Hope	Landenberg	NoResp	
Deep Run Farm	York	Defun	Sold; into SoL Loan Fund
Father Divine's Peace Mission	Gladwyne	NoResp	
Forming (Alexandra Bricklin)	Philadelphia	NoResp	
Forming (David Kennedy)	Ontanna	BadPO	"No Forwarding Address"
Forming (George Jacobs)	Macungie	NoResp	
House of Umoja	Philadelphia	New	
Int'l Church of Ageless Wisdom	Wyalusing	NoResp	
Jubilee Fellowship	Philadelphia	Defun	
Living Word	Philadelphia	NoResp	
Mount Saint Benedict Priory	Erie	NoResp	
New Village	Fayette County	Insuff	
Northeon Forest	Easton	BadPO	"Forwarding Order Expired"
Oneida Farm	Dillsburg	Never	A women's working farm
Pax Center	Erie	NoResp	
Pendle Hill	Wallingford	M/R	Possible Resource listing
Philadelphia Fellowship	Philadelphia	Never	Never was a community
Pittsburgh Friends Meeting	Pittsburgh	Insuff	
Rabbity Hill Farm	Dalton	Defun	Never jelled; land sold 7/90
Sonnewald Educat'l Homestead	Spring Grove	Never	Was model organic farm
Warren Light Center	Sharon	NoResp	

QUEBEC

Name	City	Status	Note
Colonie Chetienne	Montreal	BadPO	"Addressee Unknown"
L'Arche	Stanstead	NoResp	
La Cité Ecologique	Ham-Nord	Defun	Suspended Operations 7/91
Les Plateaux Commun-ô-Terre	Anse St. Jean	NoResp	
Terre De Vie	St-Aubert	Insuff	

RHODE ISLAND

Name	City	Status	Note
Copifawna	Foster	NoResp	
Genesis	Providence	NoResp	
New World Rising, A	Providence	NoResp	
Walden Three	Providence	Defun	"Return to Sender"

SOUTH CAROLINA

Name	City	Status	Note
Guardians of the Earth	Ruby	NLC	No longer a community

SOUTH DAKOTA

Name	City	Status	Note
Plainview Colony	Ipswich	BadPO	"Forwarding Order Expired"

TENNESSEE

Name	City	Status	Note
Ceten Ered	Rural(?)	Insuff	
EarthStar; Ecanachaca CLT	Sewanee	ReName:	Jump Off CLT
Far Away Farm	Sparta	Defun	Disbanded '84
Forming (Fran Archer)	Chattanooga	Limbo	Trying to get a house
Harmonic Edge Community	Primm Springs	Defun	12/94 Irreconcilable diffs
Nobodies Mountain	Livingston	NLC	No longer a community
Okra Ridge Farm	Luttrell	Defun	Disbanded
People of the Living God	Beersheba Springs	NoResp	
Pepperland Farm Camp	Farner	NoResp	
Pisgah Center	Pikeville	NoResp	
Sycamore Hollow Farm	Celina	BadPO	"Forwarding Order Expired"

TEXAS

Name	City	Status	Note
Blue Heron, Inc.	Austin	NoResp	
Church of the Firstborn	El Paso	NoResp	
Church of the Redeemer	Houston	Defun	Never was a community
College Houses Co-ops	Austin	NoResp	
Community of God's Delight	Dallas	NoResp	
Dallas CoHousing	Carrollton	New	

Davies Homestead	Uvalde	Never	Two families living closely
Earth Current Farm	Red Rock	NoResp	
East Side Group	Austin	BadPO	"Return to Sender"
Forming (Gary Paul Olson)	Dallas	NoResp	
Forming (Richard Moss)	W. of San Antonio	New	
Four Seasons	Call	BadPO	"Forwarding Order Expired"
Hygeiana Paradise	Lago Vista	BadPO	Original address temporary
Jonah House	Dallas	NoResp	
Love Heals Family	Del Valle	NoResp	
Metaphysical Inst. for Research	Dallas	NoResp	
Mill Fall Cooperative	Austin	NoResp	
Panhandle Permaculture	Bushland	NoResp	
Pigeon City	Fort Hancock	NoResp	
Quicksand Farm	Manor	NLC	
Rainbow Ridge Ranch	Kyle	BadPO	"No Such Number"
Regrouping in Dallas	Dallas	NoResp	
Scarlet Circle Creative Living	Austin	Defun	Never jelled; land for sale
Sheltrano	Pearsall	Defun	Folded
Shepherd's Bush Centre	Dallas	NoResp	
Sunat Community	Amarillo	Insuff	
Tabor House	San Antonio	New	
Violet Crown CoHousing	Austin	New	
Whitehawk Community	Sanger	NoResp	
Woolcroft Farm	Commerce	Limbo	Will probably sell the land

UTAH

Angel Canyon	Kanab	NoResp	
Apostolic United Brethren	Bluffsdale	NoResp	
Church Jesus Solemn Assembly	Big Water	NoResp	
Eider	Kanab	BadPO	"Forwarding Order Expired"
Eskdale Center	Murray	NoResp	
Genesis I	Salt Lake City	ReName:	See "The Builders"
Slickrock Society	Moab	ReName:	Sky Ranch

VERMONT

Catalyst Group, The	Brattleboro	NoResp	
Dimetradon	Warren	NoResp	
Earth Bridge	Putney	NoResp	
Earth People's Park	Norton	Defun	Land vacated '93
Earthwings	Orange	NoResp	
Entropy Acres	Barton	NLC	No longer a community
Frog Run Farm	East Charleston	NLC	No longer a community
Greenhope Farm	East Hardwick	Never	Two people on the land
Heifer Hill	West Brattleboro	NoResp	
Hill	Putney	NoResp	
Howl /VT Women's Land Trust	Winooski	NoResp	
Kendrick, Anne & Friends	Putney	BadPO	"Return to Sender."
Land Trust c/o Linda Sigel	Burlington	NoResp	
Maples	Putney	NoResp	
Mullein Hill Farm	West Glover	BadPO	"Forwarding Order Expired"
New Hamburger	Plainfield	NoResp	
Packers Corner Farm	Guilford	Insuff	
School House	Shelbourne	BadPO	"Forwarding Order Expired"
Sunray Meditation Society	Bristol	NLC	No longer a community

VIRGINIA

Akwenasa	Howardsville	Insuff	
Baker Branch	Louisa	NLC	
Blackwater Homesteads	Boston	Defun	Trying to sell land
Broad Street Mennonite	Harrisonburg	NoResp	
Carmel-in-the-Valley	New Market	NoResp	
Charlottesville CoHousing	Charlottesville	New	
Chrysalis	Mt. Sidney	Never	Discussion/Social Group
Community of the Servant	Richmond	BadPO	"Return to Sender"
Fellowship of the Inner Light	Virginia Beach	NoResp	
Guru Ram Das Ashram	Herndon	SubNet	
High Meadows	Clifton Forge	New	
Holler View Farm	Alexandria	New	
Institute for Sustainable Living	Check	ReName:	Tekiah
Jordan Hollow Farm Inn	Stanley	Never	Possible Resource group
Jordan River Farm	Huntley	NoResp	
Keshavashram Int' Meditation	Warrentown	Never	Never was a community
Monacan Ridge	Faber	ReName:	Deer Rock
Mulberry Group, Inc.	Richmond	Defun	Folded
Partners	Virginia Beach	Limbo	Moving: location unclear
Seekers Faith Community	Mclean	NoResp	
Sevenoaks Pathwork Center	Madison	M/R	Possible Resource listing
Society of Saint Andrew	Big Island	NoResp	
Stoneyfoot Farm	Rockbridge Baths	NoResp	
The Nethers Community	Sperryville	Insuff	
Travianna Farm	Check	NoResp	
Turtle Land for Wimmin	Arlington	NoResp	
Winged Heart Homestead	Alum Ridge	Defun	Defunct: Land sold '92
Zephyr	Floyd	NoResp	

WASHINGTON

Abrupt Edge	Ione	Dupe	See Sarrodaya (below)
Aliya	Bellingham	BadPO	"Addressee Unknown"
Alom Community	Sumner	NoResp	
Antakarana Circle	Oroville	ReName:	Triple Creek
Asponola Colony	Reardon	ReName:	Hutterian Breth./Spokane
Aushet	Tonasket	NLC	No longer a community
Black Walnut Association	Olympia	NoResp	
Brandywine Forest	Olympia	NLC	No longer a community
Can-Do Farm	White Salmon	BadPO	"Forwarding Order Expired"

Center Family	La Center	BadPO	"Return to Sender"
Chrysalis Farm	Davenport	New	
Common Ground Farm	Olympia	NoResp	
Coyote Clan	Kettle Falls	NoResp	
Crystal Seed	Seattle	ReName:	Blue House, The
Delphi	Olympia	Defun	Land deal fell through
Doe Bay Village	Olga	NoResp	
Earth Child	Davenport	BadPO	"Addressee Unknown"
Earth in Clover	Seattle	New	
Earth Vision: Bear Tribe	Spokane	NoResp	
Forming (John Burnell)	Olympia	NoResp	
Forming (Tara/Diana Cushing)	Olympia	NoResp	
Forming (Terri Spencer)	Arlington	New	
Forming (Wilson)	Indianola	NoResp	
Goodearth Family	Olympia	BadPO	"No Such Number"
Green Dragon	Olympia	NoResp	
Ground Zero	Bangor	Defun	Folded in early '92
Harmony Farm	Olympia	NoResp	
Holden Village	Chelan	NoResp	
Home Front CLT	Seattle	ReName:	Homestead CLT (below)
Homestead CLT	Seattle	NoResp	
Lanka	Republic	Never	Never was a community
Light	Port Angeles	NoResp	
May Valley	Renton	Insuff	
Mill Creek Goat Farm Family	Colville	NoResp	
Misty Mountain Farm	Curlew	NoResp	
New Cohousing	Seattle Area	New	
Nolla Journal	Bainbridge Island	NLC	See In Context (Resources)
Old McCauley Farm	Lopez Island	NoResp	
Olympia Cohousing	Olympia	New	
Olympia Community	Olympia	New	
Pala	Coupeville	NoResp	
Puget Ridge Cohousing	Seattle	New	
PWA Community	Seattle	Limbo	Hasn't come together yet
Rainbow Ridge Cohousing	Montesano	NoResp	
Rosewind Cohousing	Port Townsend	New	
Saint Clare's Hermitage	Deming	BadPO	"Temporarily Away"
Sarrodaya Community	Ione	Never	Never was a community
Sarvodaya Comu'tarian Society	Oroville	NoResp	
Seattle Dharma Center	Seattle	BadPO	"Moved/NFA"
Second Mile Community	Eatonville	Defun	Disbanded c. '85
Seeseelichel	Bellingham	NoResp	
SkySong	Issaquah	BadPO	Moved to Montana
Society of Love Alchemists	Lake Stevens	BadPO	"Return to Sender."
Sun at Midday	Olalla	NLC	No longer a community
Sun Meadow	Tonasket	NoResp	
Sunbow	Auburn	Defun	Disbanded '88
Sunday Evening Cohousing	West Seattle	New	
Sunshine Family/Frosty Meadows	Tonasket	NoResp	
Svaha Community	Near La Conner	Insuff	
Swinomish Tribal Community	La Conner	NoResp	
Turnip Town Team	Seattle	NoResp	
Uppity Womyn & Friends	Seattle	NoResp	
Waukon Inst. Co-Creative Art	Waukon	ReName:	Earth Cycle Farm
Wilderness Family	Tonasket	NoResp	
World Mission Dept.	Seattle	NoResp	

WEST VIRGINIA

Bhaktiras	Moundsville	NoResp	
Catholic Worker Farm	West Hamlin	Defun	Disbanded
Claymont Court	Charles Town	NoResp	
Community Lead	Coon Creek	Insuff	
Community of Saint Martin	Moyers	BadPO	"Moved/NFA"
Don't Have a Name Yet	Unger	NoResp	
Forming (WV)	Pullman	NoResp	
Iris Mountain (Stillpoint Council)	Berkeley Springs	NLC	Folded '80 (Still Resource?)
John Filligar Cath. Worker Farm	Alderson	NoResp	
Misty Bottoms Farm	Jumping Branch	BadPO	"Forwarding Order Expired"
Mountain Land	Weston	BadPO	"Return to Sender"
Mountain Laurel	Berkeley Springs,	NoResp	

WISCONSIN

Active Acres	Dodgeville	NoResp	
Bounty	New Auburn	NoResp	
Coldfoot Creek	Pembine	NLC	'88 now "Outdoors" school
Delphos Wilderness Society	La Crosse	NoResp	
Foggy Bottoms	Gays Mills	New	
Folklore Village Farm	Dodgeville	New	
Forming (Mark Ludwig)	Madison	Limbo	Not off the ground yet
Hickory Draw Eco Co-op	Gays Mills	New	
Hoot Owl Ranch/Sweet Earth	Gays Mills	New	
Institute of What Have You	Gays Mills	BadPO	"No Forwarding Address"
Luna Circle Farm	Soldiers Grove	NoResp	
Melting Snow	Madison	Defun	Folded; sold house '92
Philadelphia Cmty. Farm	Osceola	NoResp	
Rainbow Nation	Madison	M/R	See "Rainbow Guide"
Rock Ridge Community	Dodgeville	NoResp	
Shiloh Community	Lone Rock	BadPO	"Addressee Unknown"
Taliesen	Spring Green	Never	Never was a community
Wilderness Way	Wascott	NoResp	
Willow Gold	Spring Green	NoResp	
Wilmont Center	Wilmont	NoResp	
Wooden Bridge Community	Monroe	NoResp	

• Plus 153 Communities that requested we not list them in this directory.

Save at least 10% (maybe more!) on your long distance calls ...and help FIC at the same time!

The Fellowship for Intentional Community (a nonprofit organization) has entered into a cooperative relationship with Affinity (a unique long distance telephone carrier) to offer you a guaranteed 10% savings over your current long distance service.

In addition to the savings you'll experience, Affinity will automatically contribute 5% of your reduced long distance phone bill to the Fellowship. By using Affinity's services, you'll help fund FIC's efforts to make the world a better place.

FIC is convinced that Affinity offers reliable telephone service and demonstrates a sustainable way of doing business—one that moves away from advertising-driven consumerism and toward a more efficient, community-based delivery of services.

How does Affinity work?

Since 1989, Affinity has been purchasing large blocks of phone service from the major carriers—brokering connect time to the public while providing its own customer support and billing services. Because it uses the same hardware as America's foremost telecommunications providers, Affinity can ensure reliable, top-quality service that equals or exceeds anything else available. As an Affinity customer you'll have access to the latest in technology, calling card privileges, operator assistance, and easy long distance direct dialing (1-Area Code-Number). There are no service reductions or hidden charges involved in making the switch from your current carrier.

And remember, Affinity guarantees they'll save you at least 10% (5–20% for businesses) off your current phone plan—regardless of the deal you now have—or they'll double your money back.

How can Affinity offer savings like this?

First, Affinity does not advertise. That cuts expenses tremendously—and the savings are passed on to the customers and cooperating organizations. Affinity depends solely on word of mouth and customer satisfaction to promote its services.

Second, Affinity buys phone service in huge quantities that qualify for deep discounts—and more savings.

Third, Affinity bills in *tenths* of a minute. While most phone companies round *up* to the next whole minute, Affinity charges for only the actual number of six-second increments you use.

How can I join?

Switching to Affinity is easy—you don't even have to be a Fellowship member. Just fill out the blue response card bound inside the back cover of this book, or copy the form below and mail it to us. We'll do the rest. Or you can sign up right now by calling Affinity direct at 800-670-0008. Be sure to enroll as an FIC supporter, and give them our ID number: 971061-000/200-020081.

Although there is usually a small fee (generally $5 or less) for switching your service, Affinity will send you a certificate in that amount to use as a credit on your first bill. If you have any questions, call us 9–5 Pacific Time at 360-221-3064.

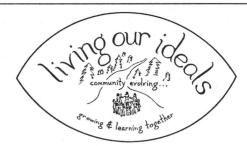

(ADVERTISEMENT)

About the International Listings

Archives: Hundred Mile Lodge

*T*his section features communities in countries other than Canada, Mexico, and the United States. Because our research efforts were focused primarily on North America, this sampling represents only a fraction of what exists on other continents. For more extensive international referrals, see "Community Directories," "Community Networks," and "Community Referrals" in the Index.

This section is in three parts: (1) a cross-reference Chart, arranged alphabetically; (2) an index of the communities, sorted alphabetically by country; and (3) a list of 70 international communities, including addresses and phone numbers where available.

A community's listing is where you're most likely to get a sense of how the group sees itself—that's where each group was given room to tell its own story...to share its vision, its history, its daily life. Hopefully these descriptions will give you a feeling for the community, beyond the facts and figures. However, there's a lot of information in the Chart that doesn't appear in the Listings, so use both for the best overview of each community. The codes used in the Chart are identical to those used in the North American Listings (see key on page 189).

Some abbreviations used frequently in the listings:
SASE – Enclose a self-addressed stamped envelope.
[cc] – The group cannot commit to responding promptly to letters.
2/1/95 – The date (at the end of a listing) that the entry was submitted, or that the group confirmed the accuracy of the information.
[2, 9] – Numbers in brackets at the end of some listings refer to back issues of *Communities* magazine that feature information on that group. A summary of back issues begins on page 434.

The information in the Chart is based mostly on community responses to questionnaires that we sent out. An "**N/Q**" in the "Survey Date" column indicates a group that did not submit a questionnaire; in these cases, we have tried to fill in some of the blanks based on other information (such as the group's descriptive listing, or our own personal knowledge). In a few cases we've reprinted Chart data from the previous *Directory*, indicated by a "**PrevDir**" entry in that column.

A few general disclaimers: As in most questionnaire-based research, different communities may have interpreted the same questions in different ways. It was sometimes impossible for us to tell if groups (including our own research team) had applied the same standards and definitions to each question that appears on this Chart. Furthermore, it is impossible to do justice to the vast variety of communities and community experiences by attempting to quantify them in a yes/no or multiple-choice format.

We can't guarantee that the information in the Charts and Listings is accurate—each community decided what to say about itself, and changes may have happened since the information was submitted. We edited only for length and clarity, and caution each reader to verify all information before deciding to get involved with any of the groups listed.

While we don't pursue leads to international groups with the same vigor that we apply to those on this continent, we do plan to continue expanding our international database. If you have any leads or new information about community groups living beyond the shores of North America, please drop us a line (use the blue Corrections & Additions card bound inside the back cover).

Clearly, the communities movement is a broad-based and dynamic reality—with valuable experiences and insights to share among its members and with those "other" realities. We hope this directory will help us discover our common concerns, and provide opportunities for sharing that wisdom. (▲▲)

	Forming, Reforming / Non-Residential	Year Established	Rural, Urban or Both	Open to More Adults?	Open to More Children?	Total Population	# Adults	# Children (<19yrs)	Percentage Women	Identified Leader	Leadership Core Group	How are Major Decisions Made?	Join Fee	Income	Who Owns Land	Acres of Land	Survey Date
Aequanimitas Assoc Inc	F	90	R	Y	y				50%	N	Y	O	Y	both			1/93
Atlantis Commune		73	R	Y	y	15	10	5	58%	Y	Y		N	shared	cmty	350	4/92
Atmasantulana Village		83	R	Y	y	42	42	0	71%	Y	Y	L G	Y	indep	mix	14	9/92
Auroville																	
Backyard Tech	F	77	R	Y	y	3	3	0	67%	Y	N	L	Y		indiv	.5	1/93
Barn		86	R	Y	n	9	9	0	67%	Y	Y	C	N	indep	other	7	1/93
Beech Hill Community	RF	83	R	Y	y	25	17	8	53%	N	Y	C		indep	clt	6	8/94
Billen Cliffs		82	R	Y	y	187	125	62	46%	N	N	C M	Y	indep	mix	1000	3/93
Black Horse Creek		83	R	Y	y	34	23	11	30%	N	N	C M	Y	indep	cmty	960	10/93
Braziers Park Schoo		50	R	Y	m	14	13	1	33%	N	Y	C	N	indep	cmty	50	2/93
Bundagen Co-operative Ltd		82	R	Y					45%	N	N	C M	Y	indep	cmty	600	12/92
Center for Harmonious Living	F	84	B	Y	y	20	16	4	56%	Y	Y	M	N		mix	24	5/93
Centrepoint Community		78	R	Y	y	120			50%	Y	Y	C		shared	clt	92	6/92
Christiania		71	U	M	m	1000	800	200	50%	N	?	C M	N	indep	mix	80	2/93
Christians		82	U	Y		28	22	6	39%	Y		C	N	shared	indiv		4/92
Communauté de Chambrelien		78	R	Y		30			50%	N	Y	C	N	shared		40	1/93
Communauté de Sus		83	R	Y	y	150				Y	Y	C L G O	N	shared	other		12/95
Communidade de Londrina		92	B	Y	y	50			48%	Y	Y	C L G O	N	shared	other		12/95
Community in Sydney	F	95	U	Y	y	35				Y	Y	C L G O	N	shared	other		12/95
Crescent Road		78	U	N	n	25	20	5	56%	N	Y	C M	N		other		4/92
Darvell Bruderhof		20	R	Y	y	266	134	132					N		cmty		PrevDir
Dolphin Tribe																	
Ecolonie		89	R	Y	y	40				N	Y	M	Y	indep	n profit	17	10/93
Ecoville	F	93	B	Y	y	20				Y	Y				other	410	10/93
Findhorn Foundation		62	B	Y	n	140	118	22	63%	N	Y	C	Y		cmty		8/92
For the Earth, For Life		82		Y	y	300											12/94
Fusion Arts Colony																	NQ
Kibbutzim Federation		10	R	Y	y	lots!								shared	cmty		8/92
L'Arche (La Borie Noble)		58	R	Y	y	44	27	17	57%	Y	N	C	N	shared	mix	1112	12/92
L'Arche International		64	R	Y	y					Y	Y		N		cmty		4/94
La Atlantida	RF	78	R	Y	y	7	5	2		Y	N	L	N	shared	other	200	5/92
La Vigne	RF	86	R	Y	y	26	21	5	62%	Y	Y	C G	Y		mix	10	12/92
Landelijke Vereniging Centraal Wonen			B	Y	y									indep			2/93
Laurieston Hall		72	R	Y	y	33	24	9	46%	N	N	C	N	indep	co-op	135	4/92
Le Jardin Sauvage	F	90	B	Y	y	41	41	0	49%	Y		L	Y	indep	mix	14	1/93
Lower Shaw Farm		75	U	N		13	6	7	50%	N	N	C	N	indep	other	3	4/92
Mandala	RF	75	R	M	m	30	22	8	48%	N	Y	C M	Y	indep	cmty	280	6/92
Michaelshof																	
Mickleton Emissary Community		80	B	Y	y	48	41	7	57%	Y	Y	C L G	N	indep	cmty		4/92
Mitraniketan		56	R							Y	Y	M	N	both	cmty		3/93
Montclaire	F	95	R	Y	y						Y	C	Y	shared	clt	250	12/94
Mt Murrindal Community		83	R	N	n	9	7	2	43%	N	N	C	Y	indep	other	125	12/92
Neve Shalom, Wahat Al-Salam		78	R	Y	n	46	46	0	50%	Y	Y			indep	ldlord		8/93
New Creation Christian Community		74	B	Y	y	900	650	250	50%	Y	Y	C G		shared	clt		7/92
Niederkaufungen		86	B	Y	s	53	41	12	46%	N	N	C		shared	cmty	14	9/92
Ontos		80	R	N	n	10	5	5	40%	N	Y	C	N	shared	indiv	700	1/93
Osho Commune Int'l		60s		Y	y	700				Y				both	cmty		3/93
Owa Hutterian Brethren				M	m								N	shared	cmty		PrevDir
Plum Village		82	R	Y	y	32	30	2	67%	Y	Y	L G	N		n profit	75	1/95
Rainbow Valley Community		74	R	Y	y	25	13	12	54%	N	N	C	Y	indep	cmty	250	4/93
Redfield		78	R	Y	y	29	21	8	45%	N	N	C	N		cmty	17	5/92
Riverside Community		41	R	Y	y	75	41	34	60%	N	N	C	N	shared	cmty		3/93
Shrubb Family	RF	71		Y	y	10	4	6	75%	N	N	C	N		cmty	1	4/92
Sonnenhof	F	87	B	Y	m	8	6	2	50%	Y		C	N	indep	cmty	20	1/93
Spiritual Family Community Group																	NQ

KEY *Open to More…:* M = Maybe. *Decisions:* C = Consensus, M = Majority, L = Leader, G = Group of leaders or elders, O = Other. *Who Owns Land:* CLT = Community Land Trust, Cmty = Community, Indiv = Individual, Ldlord = Landlord, Mix = Combination of more than one, N Profit = Non Profit Organization, Subgrp = Subgroup of members. *Income:* Shared = Members Share Income, Indep = Handle Own Finances. *Survey Date:* PrevDir = Previous Directory, NQ = No Questionnaire. Date is when survey questionnaire was completed or last updated by community.

Map / Index Name	Eat Together How Frequently?	What % of Own Food Is Grown?	Organic Food in Diet	Diet	Caffeine in Diet	Alcohol in Diet	Tobacco in Diet	# Children (<19yrs)	% Home Schooled	% Cmty Schooled	% Private Schooled	% Public Schooled	Spiritual Path	Primary Purpose and/or Focus
Aequanim	nearly all meals	>50%		vgn	none	none	none		50	50	0	0		total health and natural harmony
Atlantis	nearly all meals	>50%		veg	yes!	yes!	none	5						bio-energy and self-sufficiency!
Atmasant	nearly all meals	6–20%	often	veg	none	none	none	0					Eastern	holistic healing community
Auroville														
BakyrdTech	nearly all meals	>50%		omni	none	some	none	0						redesign life support systems
BarnThe	nearly all meals	6–20%	yes!	veg	often	some	ok	0					Buddhist	insight and realization
BeechHill	2–5 times/wk	21–50%						8	0	0	0	100		ecological
Billen	1–3 times/mo	6–20%		omni	some	some	often	62	0	0	2	98		billen cliffs solar village
BlackHorse	1–3 times/mo	21–50%		omni	often	some	some	11	0	0	0	100		land sharing permaculture
BrazierPk	nearly all meals	21–50%						1						psycho-social evolution by group consciousness
Bundagen	1–3 times/mo	6–20%		omni	often	often	often	5	0		10	85		alternative living by the sea
CenHarLiv		21–50%		veg	ok	ok	none	4	0	0	0	100		spiritual education service love
Centrept	nearly all meals	6–20%				some	none		0	0	0	100		grow clear and loving people!
Christiania	1–3 times/mo	1–5%			ok	ok	ok	200	0	0	100	0		learning to be real anarchy
Christians	nearly all meals	1–5%	some	omni	often	some	ok	6					Other	to work for love and not for money
ComDeChamb		21–50%							0	0	0	100		???? and service
ComDeSus	nearly all meals	21–50%	yes!	omni	some	none	none		100	0	0	0	NSOM	new social order in messiah
ComDeLondr	nearly all meals	21–50%	yes!	omni	some	none	none		100	0	0	0	NSOM	new social order in messiah
CmtyInSydney	nearly all meals	21–50%	yes!	omni	some	none	none		100	0	0	0	NSOM	new social order in messiah
CrescentRd	nearly all dinners	1–5%						5	0	0	0	100		extended family living
Darvell								132	0	100	0	0	HB	hutterian brethren
Dolphin														
Ecolonie	nearly all meals	21–50%		veg									Other	ecology center; simple living
Ecoville				veg										sustainablity, democracy
Findhorn	nearly all dinners	6–20%	yes!	no red	often	some	some	22	0	50	0	50	Other	education demonstration spirit
ForTheEarth													NAm	native support; green politics
FusionArts														christians developing visual arts
Kibbutzim		>50%							0	100	0	0	Jewish	jewish settlement; cooperation
LArcheBorie	nearly all dinners	>50%		veg	some	some	none	17	40	0	0	60		gandhian non-violence
LArcheTros	nearly all meals												Ecu,Chr	integrating the disabled
LaAtlan	nearly all meals		yes!	veg				2	0	0	0	100	RomanCath	christian living, self-sufficiency, perfection
LaVigne	nearly all meals	6–20%	often	omni	some	ok	ok	5	0	0	0	100	EDL	simplicity and personal growth
Landelijke	2–5 times/wk	6–20%												cohousing network
Lauriestn		>50%		omni	ok	ok	ok	9	0	0	0	100		cooperation, personal growth
LeJardin	2–5 times/wk	>50%	yes!	veg	ok	ok	ok	0					Buddhist	living skills center
LowrShaw	nearly all dinners	6–20%		omni	some	often		7	0	0	0	100		connect explore be responsible
Mandala	rarely	6–20%		omni	often	some	some	8	0	0	0	100		making community: conservation
Michaelshof														
Mickleton	nearly all meals	1–5%	yes!	omni	often	ok	ok	7	0	0	20	80	EDL	learning to trust life
Mitranik	nearly all meals	6–20%		no red	ok	none	none		0	100	0	0		personal development of indiv thru community
Montclaire	2–5 times/wk	>50%		veg					0	100	0	0	Qk,O	independent/interdependent model
MtMurrin	rarely	6–20%		veg	ok	ok	ok	2						living together peacefully
NeveShal	rarely	None						0	0	0	0	100	Ecu,O	peace and coexistence
NewCreatn	rarely	1–5%	some	omni				250	0	0	0	100	Prot	charismatic/evangelical church
Niederkauf	nearly all meals	21–50%		omni	often	often	often	12	0	58	0	42		common cash, consensus
Ontos	2–5 times/wk	21–50%	yes!	veg	none	none	none	5	0	0	0	100	Ecu,O	ecumenical health retreat
OshoIntl													Ecl,E	rajneesh teachings
OwaHutter													HB	hutterian brethren
PlumVillage	nearly all meals	21–50%		veg				2	0	0	0	100	Buddhist	mindfulness in daily life
RainbVal-NZ	1 time/wk	6–20%		omni	often	often	ok	12	0	0	0	100		cooperation—land stewardship
Redfield	nearly all dinners	21–50%		omni	some	ok	ok	8	0	0	0	100		sustainability
Riverside								34						pacifism, simple living
ShrubbFam	nearly all meals	1–5%		veg	often	ok	ok	6	50	0	50	0		permaculture care children fun
Sonnenhof	nearly all meals	21–50%		veg	often	ok	ok	2	0	0	0	100		openness and love
SpiritFam														no info submitted

KEY *Food codes:* omni = includes red meat, no red = no red meat—includes fish or poultry and dairy, veg = vegetarian—no meat—includes dairy, vgn = vegan—no meat or dairy. *Spiritual path:* B = Buddhist, Chr = Christian, E = Eastern, Ecl = Eclectic, Ecu = Ecumenical, EDL = Emissaries of Divine Light, HB = Hutterian Brethren, NAm = N.American Indian, NSOM = New Social Order in Messiah, O = Other, P = Pagan, Prot = Protestant, Qk = Quaker, RC = Roman Catholic, UU = Unitarian Universalist.

	Forming, Reforming Non-Residential	State/Prov. or Country	Year Established	Rural, Urban or Both	Open to More Adults?	Open to More Children?	Total Population	# Adults	# Children (<19yrs)	Percentage Women	Identified Leader	Leadership Core Group	How are Major Decisions Made?	Join Fee	Income	Who Owns Land	Acres of Land	Survey Date
Stichting de Natuurlyhe Weg	RF		85	R	M	m	43	32	11	53%			O		shared			1/94
Svanholm			78	R	Y	y	135	75	60				C		shared	cmty	1033	PrevDir
Taena			41	R	N		24			50%	N	N			indep			12/92
Timatanga Community			72	R	Y	y	23	13	10	46%	N	N	C	N	indep	cmty	4.5	8/93
Tui Land Trust			84	R	Y	y	48	25	23		N				indep	clt	145	10/93
Universal Life																		NQ
Utopiaggia			75	R			35	20	15						shared	cmty	250	8/93
Villaggio Verde	RF		82	R	N	n	28	19	9		N	Y	G		indep	cmty	9	1/93
Waldos	F		92	B	Y	y	11	9	2	40%	N	Y	C	N	indep			7/92
Wattle Hills Station	F		89	R	Y	y	28	14	14	29%	N	Y	M	Y	indep	other	89,000	2/92
West End Catholic Worker			82	R	Y	y	7	6	1	50%	N	N	C	N	shared	indiv		1/92
Yamagishism Life			58	B	Y	y					N	N	C	N		other	8649	10/92
Yurt Farm Living and Learning Centre	RF		81	R	Y	y	12	8	4	38%	Y	Y	C L	N	both	indiv	1000	10/93
ZEGG			83	R	Y	y	108	96	12	60%	N	Y	C	N		cmty	40	3/94
Zeven Rivieren			90	R	Y	y	16	12	4	58%	Y	Y	C M L G	N	indep	other	80	11/92

KEY *Open to More…:* M = Maybe. *Decisions:* C = Consensus, M = Majority, L = Leader, G = Group of leaders or elders, O = Other. *Who Owns Land:* CLT = Community Land Trust, Cmty = Community, Indiv = Individual, Ldlord = Landlord, Mix = Combination of more than one, N Profit = Non Profit Organization, Subgrp = Subgroup of members. *Income:* Shared = Members Share Income, Indep = Handle Own Finances. *Survey Date:* PrevDir = Previous Directory, NQ = No Questionnaire. Date is when survey questionnaire was completed or last updated by community.

International Communities List (by Country)

AUSTRALIA
Aeqaunimitas Assoc Inc (Aeqaunim)
Backyard Tech (BakyrdTech)
Billen Cliffs (Billen)
Black Horse Creek (BlackHorse)
Bundagen Co-operative Ltd (Bundagen)
Christians (Christians)
Fusion Arts Colony (FusionArts)
Mandala (Mandala)
Mt Murrindal Community (MtMurrin)
Ontos (Ontos)
Wattle Hills Station (WattleHill)
West End Catholic Worker (WestEnd)
Yurt Farm Living and Learning Centre (YurtFarm)

AUSTRIA
For the Earth, For Life (ForTheEarth)
Sonnenhof (Sonnenhof)

BRAZIL
Communidade de Londrina (ComDeLondr)

COLOMBIA
Atlantis Commune (Atlantis)
La Atlantida (LaAtlan)

COSTA RICA
Dolphin Tribe (Dolphin)

DENMARK
Christiania (Christiania)
Svanholm (Svanholm)

ECUADOR
Waldos (Waldos)

FRANCE
Communauté de Sus (ComDeSus)

Ecolonie (Ecolonie)
L'Arche (La Borie Noble) (LArcheBorie)
L'Arche International (LArcheTros)
La Vigne (LaVigne)
Le Jardin Sauvage (LeJardin)
Plum Village (PlumVillage)

GERMANY
Michaelshof (Michaelshof)
Niederkaufungen (Niederkauf)
Universal Life (UnivLife)
ZEGG (ZEGG)

GREECE
Center for Harmonious Living (CenHarLiv)

INDIA
Atmasantulana Village (Atmasant)
Auroville (Auroville)
Mitraniketan (Mitranik)
Osho Commune Int'l (OshoIntl)

ISRAEL
Kibbutzim Federation (Kibbutzim)
Neve Shalom, Wahat Al-Salam (NeveShal)

ITALY
Utopiaggia (Utopiaggia)
Villaggio Verde (Villaggio)

JAPAN
Owa Hutterian Brethren (OwaHutter)
Yamagishism Life (YamaLife)

NETHERLANDS
Landeliijke Vereniging Centraal Wonen (Landelijke)
Stichting de Natuurlijke Weg (Stichting)

NEW ZEALAND
Centrepoint Community (Centrept)
Community in Auckland (CmtyInAuk)
Rainbow Valley Community (RainbVal-NZ)
Riverside Community (Riverside)
Timatanga Community (Timatang)
Tui Land Trust (TuiTrust)

RUSSIA
Ecoville (Ecoville)

SCOTLAND
Findhorn Foundation (Findhorn)

SOUTH AFRICA
Zeven Rivieren (ZevenRiv)

SWITZERLAND
Communauté de Chambrelien (ComDeChamb)

UNITED KINGDOM
Barn (BarnThe)
Beech Hill Community (BeechHill)
Braziers Park School (BrazierPk)
Crescent Road (CrescentRd)
Darvell Bruderhof (Darvell)
Laurieston Hall (Lauriestn)
Lower Shaw Farm (LowrShaw)
Mickleton Emissary Community (Mickleton)
New Creation Christian Community (NewCreatn)
Redfield (Redfield)
Shrubb Family (ShrubbFam)
Spiritual Family Community Group (SpiritFam)
Taena (Taena)

ZIMBABWE
Montclaire (Montclaire)

Map / Index Name	Eat Together How Frequently?	What % of Own Food Is Grown?	Organic Food in Diet	Diet	Caffeine in Diet	Alcohol in Diet	Tobacco in Diet	# Children (<19yrs)	% Home Schooled	% Cmty Schooled	% Private Schooled	% Public Schooled	Spiritual Path	Primary Purpose and/or Focus
Stichting	nearly all meals	21–50%		no red	none	none	none	11	0	0	0	100		universal love
Svanholm								60						whole lives
Taena	1 time/wk	6–20%							0	0	0	100		traditional village
Timatang	rarely	21–50%						10	0	100	0	0		school and garden
TuiTrust	nearly all dinners	21–50%						23	0	100	0	0		human potential & communication
UnivLife														no info submitted
Utopiaggia		6–20%						15						communitarian ideals
Villaggio	nearly all meals	6–20%						9	0	0	0	100		to live for to be and not for to have
Waldos	nearly all meals	None		omni	often	ok	ok	2						healthcare services
WattleHill	rarely	21–50%		omni	often	some	some	14	100	0	0	0		grow trees and simply live
WestEnd	nearly all meals	21–50%	often	veg	some	none	none	1					RomanCath	hospitality, resistance, self-management
YamaLife	nearly all meals	>50%							0	50	0	50		i prosper with all men and nature
YurtFarm	nearly all meals	6–20%		omni	often	some	ok	4						learning to live with less
ZEGG	nearly all meals	21–50%						12	0	0	0	100		living without fear or violence
ZevenRiv	nearly all meals	6–20%	some	omni	often	often	ok	4	0	0	0	100	EDL	attunement with life

KEY *Food codes:* omni = includes red meat, no red = no red meat—includes fish or poultry and dairy, veg = vegetarian—no meat—includes dairy, vgn = vegan—no meat or dairy. *Spiritual path:* B = Buddhist, Chr = Christian, E = Eastern, Ecl = Eclectic, Ecu = Ecumenical, EDL = Emissaries of Divine Light, HB = Hutterian Brethren, NAm = N.American Indian, NSOM = New Social Order in Messiah, O = Other, P = Pagan, Prot = Protestant, Qk = Quaker, RC = Roman Catholic, UU = Unitarian Universalist.

AEQUANIMITAS ASSOCIATION, INC.

(Forming)
Box 341
Spring Hill, QLD
4001 AUSTRALIA
(073)930-360

The Aequanimitas Association (formerly Equanimity) has been formed to establish sanctuary/retreat centers for those wishing to live for periods of time with supportive friends in pursuit of total health and harmony with nature. Aequanimitas homelands will have fresh pure air, first water from pure mountain springs, and fertile soil away from all forms of pollution. Members will live free from the effects of technological and personal pollutants, enjoying times of togetherness, eating healthy foods, experiencing personal growth activities, swimming, singing, dancing, playing music, and developing social skills (caring, sharing, and loving kindness) in an atmosphere of compassion for each other and nature. Personal memberships are available at $500 each. We expect to develop the first of many sanctuaries in the first months of 1993. Memberships provide access to any of the future Aequanimitas homelands purchased. In its holistic approach, Aequanimitas Association fosters low-impact living and the expression of creativity in all natural forms. 1/21/93

AREA CODE
911
ALERT!

If you're having trouble getting through on the phone to some of the groups listed in this directory, double check the Area Code! A number of the codes are brand new—and some branches of the phone company are not keeping pace with the new developments. If so, try the old area code (if the new one's not working), and ask your local phone company to make the new connections....

ATLANTIS

Icononzo
Tolima
COLOMBIA, South America
Books Information & Orders:
Atlantis Embassy
21 Harringay Park
London N8 UNITED KINGDOM

[NOTE: Atlantis' Ireland branch sold all its property in '92 and has joined the branch in Colombia.] Atlantis is a lively close-knit farming community living in a Colombian mountain jungle with a warm but not sweaty climate. We're vegetarian, non-religious, and into sex, psychic phenomena, noisy self-expression, self-sufficiency, and fun. Our origins lie back in 1970 in the primal therapy movement. We lived for 15 years on a wild windy Irish island free of electricity and "civilization." We moved here to get further away from authoritarian interference.

We're extremely radical, straight-talking, and very hardworking. No drugs, no smoking, no machines; loads of kids and animals. You will like us if you hate hypocrisy, compromise, and the shallowness of the modern world; if you're not scared of your body, its strength and its moods; and if you've got a great sense of humor and a desire for self-knowledge. You will feel uncomfortable here if you prefer intellectualizing to physical activity; if you are rigidly homosexual; if you think tolerance more commendable than passion, or if you adhere to any untouchable belief-system. Visitors welcome without announcement; no money needed; plenty of bedding and food. Bring seeds and kids' clothes, tools, musical instruments, energy. There are 7 books about us available through our London Embassy. 5/21/92

ATMASANTULANA VILLAGE

Near MTDC Holiday Resort
Karla 410405
Maharashtra, INDIA
0091-21147-Karla 82 and 83

Atmasantulana Village is a holistic living, healing, and learning community—an ancient university for modern times founded and inspired by Shri Balaji Tambe, an Ayurvedic doctor. This community was created by and for members all over the world, those who could visualize the need for it and accept a simple life with the principle of "service above self." Atmasantulana Village is a space in nature surrounded by mountains, close to a beautiful river, about 110 km from Bombay, offering facilities for cultural and educational activities. Ayurveda is practiced here—an ancient holistic healing system, including preventive medicine and alternative therapies for purification of body, mind, and soul. The healing work done in the Village is an opportunity for the residents to offer their services. Nature, fresh air, healing, music, devotion, pure food, and natural medicine are yielding miraculous results. Courses are offered in Art of Living, Yoga, Meditation, Massage, and Ayurveda. The Aum Temple, unique in the world and open to people of all religions and beliefs, is the nucleus of the community. The Village is a model; we hope that such communities will develop all over the world as they are the answer to the disintegration of modern life. SASE requested. 9/25/92

AUROVILLE

- **Attn: Secretariat**
  605-101 Tamil Nadu
  INDIA
  011-91-41386-2170
  011-91-41386-2274 Fax

USA Contact:

- **Auroville International USA**
  P.O. Box 162489
  Sacramento, CA 95816
  (916)452-4013

Auroville is a "universal township" of over 800 people living and working on 2000 acres near Pondicherry, India. Auroville was created in 1968 to realize the ideal of Sri Aurobindo who taught the Karma Yoga—Auroville is for those who want to do the yoga of work. It is designed to bring about harmony among different cultures, and for understanding environmental needs of man's spiritual growth. Services, made up of the persons actually involved or interested in a particular work, do the necessary administration and coordinating in specific areas. There is no institutionalized authority as such, and major policy decisions are referred to the general meeting where all members of Auroville are free to participate.

Auroville is in a rural setting, and conditions are simple in most of the 40 different settlements. The electrical supply, telephone service, and water supply are subject to breakdown. Health services of various kinds (including dental) are available. Food in the common kitchens is basic, and mostly vegetarian. For purposes of external communication, we publish the *Auroville Review* and various newsletters. [See Resource listing for Auroville International, USA.] 7/25/94 [33]

BACKYARD TECH

(Forming)
Attn: Dr. Pat Howden
Cone Street
Macleay Island, QLD
4184 AUSTRALIA
(074)095-100

We're developing and promoting all practical aspects of simple, stimulating, and micro-budget lifestyles including life support systems for all those seeking "The Great Escape," even in an apartment or suburban garden.

We prove that your crises in housing, health, energy, education, pollution, financial, transport, and food are a myth. Our means: open house, grand tour, alternative library, workshops, publications, and inventions. Our aim: live for free. Any day is good for sharing and caring about nature and neighbors on this bay island with an adjacent rainforest, only a $2 barge to the mainland and 20 miles to Brisbane.

Accommodations are very basic in this gorgeous setting; neighbors nearby. Ideal folk will be scientifically interested in *all* aspects of self reliance. Please enclose $2 for postage and handling —thanks. 1/21/93

BARN, THE

Lower Sharpham Barton
Ashprington, nr. Totnes
Devon TQ9 7DX
UNITED KINGDOM
0803-732661

The Barn is a working retreat center, a place where people come to retreat temporarily from the world at large and also to work practically on the land. They observe both these disciplines as well as the discipline of community life.

Throughout the day we seek to sustain a contemplative atmosphere. We meet three times daily and meditate quietly

together. We are based in the Buddhist tradition but are nondenominational and do not require people to follow any prescribed method of practice. However, a commitment to meditation practice is necessary, and previous experience of guided meditation retreats is expected. People are expected to be fully involved in the daily and weekly schedule of activities. We eat together twice a day and take turns preparing vegetarian meals. Domestic responsibilities are also shared. We devote one evening a week to a community meeting where we discuss personal matters as well as broader issues pertaining to life at The Barn. Accommodation is in seven single rooms.

We have an organic vegetable garden and are responsible for an area of woodland. One afternoon a week is devoted to creative expression. SASE requested. 1/19/93

BEECH HILL COMMUNITY

(Re-Forming)
Morchard Bishop
Crediton
Devon, EX17-6RF
UNITED KINGDOM
0363-877228

Beech Hill is a spacious country house with converted outbuildings located in rural Devon. We have 6 acres of grounds and gardens. All cultivation is organic, and we farm vegetables, fruit, and ornamental plants. Providing accommodation and facilities for groups at our educational center is a major source of income. Some of us earn a living outside, and some work within the cooperative. To live here happily and effectively people need good will, personal initiative, tolerance, and stability. Dogmatism and preaching are definitely not wanted.

The cooperative's aims are summed up as follows: 1) To achieve maximum flexibility for individuals within collective policies. 2) To try to find an optimum balance between private and collective ownership. 3) To enable people to use and develop skills. 4) To provide a meeting place where people can share ideas, information, and experience. 5) To create structures and opportunities which maximize possibilities within the current social and economic climate. 6) To be aware of the impact of our work and lives on the environment and to develop projects accordingly. We welcome visitors and ask

that they write about themselves before coming. We will them send them more detailed information about Beech Hill and suggest visiting dates. 8/29/94

BILLEN CLIFFS PROPRIETARY LTD.

265 Martin Road
Larnook, NSW
2480 AUSTRALIA
(066)337-147

Billen Village is set in a fertile valley in subtropical northern New South Wales, Australia. Its eastern view is of the Billen Cliffs, "billen" meaning flat top in the Bungelung language of the Australian Aborigines. Our land has been in the process of regeneration for the last ten years. Community members are conscious of land care and the preservation of wildlife—and with nature's help, large areas of bare cattle grazing land are now returning to forest.

The community has just entered its second decade of existence with vitality. There are now 70 households living in Billen Village, of which 98% use alternative energy (mainly solar power). The community is in the process of building its own arts and crafts work space, community hall, and children's playground. With the aim of becoming self-employed, members are pooling their knowledge and resources to establish cooperatives in the production of arts and crafts, music, organic farming, eco-tourism, natural therapies, and much more. In order to establish and integrate these projects, much discussion and planning have taken place and are still in motion. This process has created and enhanced solidarity and friendship among the members of Billen Cliffs. 3/16/93

BLACK HORSE CREEK

Eden Creek Road
via Kyogle, NSW
2474 AUSTRALIA
(066)333-133

We are 19 adults and 11 children living on 967 acres—a Proprietary Limited Company with 25 shares and several for sale. Some primary aims of the community include alternative technology, wildlife sanctuary, food production, and economic viability. Visitors should be willing, community-minded people. 10/1/93

BRAZIERS PARK

**School of Integrative
Social Research
Ipsden, Wallingford
Oxon, OX10 6AN
UNITED KINGDOM**

**0491-680221 (office)
0491-680481 (residents)**

Braziers is a resident community and a nonresident network of interested members and associates. Its main aims are to carry out group research into positive health and holistic living, and to seek new ways of working and thinking together which could offer hope of renewed human progress. At the same time it is open to the public as a residential adult education college which offers weekend seminars and summer schools. All tutors for courses are volunteers who come as guests of the community. A number of British and overseas student volunteers are welcomed in the community (subject to prior application and acceptance) which has built up an international reputation. Various publications are available on sale from Braziers, including "Implications of the Gregarious Habit in Man," £2.50, post free. 2/5/93

BUNDAGEN CO-OPERATIVE LTD.

**P.O. Repton
Bellingen, NSW
2454 AUSTRALIA
(066)534-529**

We are a diverse community of 100 adults and 60 children living on 600 acres of rural land by the sea. Some of our concerns and aims include permaculture, the environment, low cost/impact living, alternative housing/technology, personal growth, creative leisure, and (of course) surfing. Please write for additional information. SASE requested. 12/23/92

CENTER FOR HARMONIOUS LIVING

**(Forming)
Griva 23
Halandri
Athens, 15233
GREECE**

**01-68-18220
02-99-23316**

Our community is comprised of two parts, one in the city (Athens, Greece) and the other in the countryside about forty minutes by car. The city group runs a spiritual center which offers lectures, seminars, classes, and workshops offering concepts and techniques for creating and maintaining physical, emotional, mental, social, and spiritual harmony. About 7 members run this center (which serves about 2000 people) as well as a health food store adjacent to the center.

The second group of about 13 persons lives in our country retreat center which emphasizes biological and biodynamic vegetable and fruit farming (for sale at our health food store). We follow a program of exercise, chanting, and meditation morning and evening. People come for intensive seminars or personal attention in their self healing process.

We all work without pay, taking only our room and board. Each is free to relate to God in his own way, although all are asked to attend two years of weekly seminars offered at the city center, enabling us to have a common language. Our goals are spiritual growth, restoration of the environment, and healing of individuals and groups through teachings and service to them. [cc] 11/1/93

CENTREPOINT COMMUNITY

**P.O. Box 35
Albany, Auckland
NEW ZEALAND**

9-415-9468/415-8471 Fax

Centrepoint is a rural community with a dozen agricultural and craft-based businesses located in a lush, green, secluded valley just north of Auckland. About 130 people (half of them children)

live, play, and work here in an intensely cooperative and communal lifestyle. Visitors are welcome on Sat. afternoons at 1:30, or by arrangement—NZ$25/day AP per person; longer term visits NZ$170 per week—negotiable.

Adults who become full members commit themselves to live together intimately, openly, and cooperatively, putting all their assets and earnings into the Trust. At present adults take $10/week pocket money, and the community provides for all their basic needs. Community decisions are made by consensus at weekly business meetings. Our fundamental "raison d'être" is to encourage and provide the environment for the development of authentic, loving, and response-able individuals: men and women who want to discover more of their essential traits and capacities, and thus learn to take responsibility for themselves, their community, and their world. We run 2-day, 3-day, and 7-day residential workshops (brochure on request). Send NZ$10/yr for our newsletter, or NZ$5 for our book *Inside Centrepoint* (236 pp). Please include at least US$2 with correspondence to cover overseas postage. 7/10/92 [76]

CHRISTIANIA

**Badsmanstrœde 43
Copenhagen 1407 K
DENMARK**

45-31-577195

Begun in 1971 in response to a visionary essay published in an alternative paper, Christiania is a small independent city occupying an abandoned military base. Probably the biggest squat in Europe, it has a permanent population of some thousand people, rising to over twice that number in the summer. The shared vision is that of an ecological city based on low economy and vast self-government. It is a melting pot out of which many initiatives elsewhere in Denmark develop.

At a collective level residents provide all their own services—from street cleaning and rubbish collection, to keeping out violence and the abuse of hard drugs. Residents have organized themselves into various councils: the Common Meeting (the ultimate ruling body), Treasurer Group, "Busy-ness" Council, and a Cooperative Workers Meeting. Decisions are by consensus, and all Christianites have access and the right to speak at all meetings. Most expenses are covered by the Collective Fund which gets its income from residential fees, from payments by workshops and businesses, and from various fund-raisers.

The city of Copenhagen is sometimes actively disruptive and occasionally supportive—but never quite sure whether or not to accept Christiania as a part of the city. Meanwhile, Christiania has put forward its Green Plan by means of an exhibition and a publication which articulates its vision for the future development of a green city area in balance with nature. [cc] 8/31/93 [34]

CHRISTIANS

Box 353
Geelong, VIC
3220 AUSTRALIA

We are 23 adults, 5 kids, trying to practice the teachings of Christ. All possessions and money are shared; all work is done for love, not money, and we find that we still have enough to live on and be happy. We aim to demonstrate this idea to the world through publicity, and engage in nonviolent protest against materialism, trying to draw attention to the imbalance between rich and poor—especially in the 3rd World. We also emphasize quality relationships between commune members.

Members often travel widely to distribute our literature, educate the public, and attract new members. Adult members are encouraged to increase skills and develop leadership, and we wish to educate our own children. Group projects vary depending on which aspect of social life we decide to address. Our literature is available free to anyone on request. Visitors are welcome for one week, and we require participation in work and discussion. Please write first. We also welcome discussion with others who share our ideals—whether or not they consider themselves Christian. We are not concerned with self-sufficiency, but rather are actively confronting society to bring a change in attitudes and values. Our favorite slogan —Greed Breeds Mean Deeds! 4/19/92

COMMUNAUTÉ DE CHAMBRELIEN

CH-2202 Chambrelien NE
SWITZERLAND
038-45-15-26/45-13-19

Our community, created by two couples who've shared a flat since 1973, is on an old farm about 10 km from Neuchatel. Our core group has grown to include

three other families who live in two other former farms in the village of Chambrelien. (Much work had to be done to renew these buildings.) Our vision is influenced by the L'Arche Communities of Lanza del Vasto (disciple of Gandhi in France), sensitivity to ecological issues, North-South relationships, nonviolence, and the work of Rene Macair—a French philosopher who theorized the emergence of the "Reseaux Esperance" (hope nets) in Western Europe.

Macair's values are the basis of the Rule of our community: 1) Spirituality: we are a Christian ecumenical community. 2) Ecology: we keep an organic garden and breed cattle on 10 hectares; we heat our houses with wood, etc. 3) Self-reliance: we try to be partially self-sufficient, work only part-time outside our community, and have a consensual decision-making policy. 4) Nonviolence: in personal relationships and political actions. 5) Taking care of the destitute: children with parental problems, or people with psychological difficulties. Some people live with us short-term as well. 6) Simplicity (coherent with the other values): living with our numerous children, the sharing is not easy—our income must support the members of all the families (we are about 30 people altogether). Write in French, if possible. SASE requested. 11/1/93

COMMUNAUTÉ DE SUS

New Social Order in Messiah
Tabitha's Place
64190 Sus
Navarrenx, FRANCE
011-33-59-66-1428

Communauté de Sus began in 1983 after migrating from southern Germany. We live together in the foothills of the Pyrenees Mountains in southern France. Our people are made up of mostly French, German, and Spanish brothers and sisters, but there are people here from almost every country in Europe. We have come out of the old social orders here in Europe, with their histories of hatred and division, and have come into a new social order in Yahshua.[See network listing for the "Community In" Associa-tion in the Resources section.] 12/26/95

COMMUNIDADE DE LONDRINA

New Social Order in Messiah
Raposo Tavares 711
E.P. 86010 Centro Londrina
Parana, BRAZIL
011-55-43-221-5714

Communidade de Londrina began in 1992 after a handful of faithful disciples moved here from Fortaleza, many miles to the north. We are about 60 in number, and work with our hands as we operate a small café and bakery. We also make and sell futon furniture. We have a common life here where all our needs are met, and there are no needy among us. The greed that is seen by the division between rich and poor in this country is being exposed here for what it is. [See network listing for the "Community In" Association in the Resources section.] 12/26/95

COMMUNITY IN SYDNEY

New Social Order in Messiah
12-14 Albyn Road, Strathfield
Sydney, NSW2135, AUSTRALIA
011-61-2-642-6816

This community began when all 35 of us moved from Auckland, N.Z. in 1995. We are striving with all our heart to live a life of pure devotion to our God. We are learning from the mistakes of the early church as we live and work together and offer hope to the disillusioned who come to Australia to find the promised land. If you are looking for a radical life of covenant love, come and visit. We welcome you at any time. [See network listing for the "Community In" Association in the Resources section.] 12/26/95

CRESCENT ROAD COMMUNITY

4, 6 & 8 Crescent Road
Kingston Hill
Surrey, KT2 7QR
UNITED KINGDOM

Formed in 1978, the Crescent Road Community includes twenty-five members, including children, living as an extended family. Our three houses are owned by our housing association. Our concerns are diverse, predominantly parochial, yet we share resources and decision making just enough to function and remain moderately hospitable. Please include SASE with correspondence. [cc] 4/2/93

DARVELL BRUDERHOF

Hutterian Brethren
Robertsbridge
East Sussex TN32 5DR
UNITED KINGDOM
0580-880-626

Membership requires a lifetime commitment. Our first call is to Christ and this cannot be separated from the brothers and sisters to whom we are pledged. We do not feel that any one pattern for daily life is the answer, but we do believe in a life of Christian brotherhood that comes from an inner change of heart, following Jesus completely in every aspect of life.

Our children are educated up to high school age by members in our own schools. Our principal livelihood is derived from the manufacture of nursery play equipment and equipment for the handicapped.

Inquiries are welcomed. Visits can be arranged, but please write in advance so as to ensure accommodation. Guests are asked to share in the work and life in an open and seeking way. [See main listing for "Hutterian Brethren" in the Resources section.] 6/18/92

DOLPHIN TRIBE, THE

(Forming)
COSTA RICA

(COMMUNITY LISTING REMOVED)

[Formerly The Dolphin Society.] Lost Contact. Letters Returned. 1/11/96

ECOLONIE

Centre Ecologique
International
1 Thietry, Hennezel
88260 FRANCE

029-07-00-27 Office
029-07-01-12 Visitors

We are a growing international community which includes persons of all ages and nationalities. The organization Ecolonie, founded in 1989, currently includes 30 members and 10 residents. We want to live in friendship with the earth, and see ourselves as embodied in the living web of the cosmos. We strive for a respectful relationship with one another, the Earth, and all living beings. We are seeking a simple lifestyle without waste of natural resources and energy, and without unnecessary consumption. Our aim is self-sufficiency in agriculture and energy production. We want to establish a community of common respect, and spiritual tolerance and support.

Through seminars we want to establish a basis for demonstrating and sharing our ideas. We don't, however, believe in absolute "global guidelines" or truths. A seminar/guest house and a natural campground have been established. Agricultural work is developing, and we have acquired several animals. Projects for alternative energy are in the planning/making. The second weekend of each month we offer introductory sessions. Advance notice required for all visits! Any support or voluntary help with our work is greatly appreciated. To become a member or supporter of the Ecolonie, please write for more information (and include an international reply coupon). See you soon! 10/10/93

ECOVILLE IN SAINT PETERSBURG

(Forming)
RUSSIA

- **E-mail via EcoNet:**
  alyona@sovamsu.sovusacom
  vshestak@sovamsu.sovusacom
  7(812)310-9186/113-5896

US Coordinator:

- **Diane Gilman**
  Context Institute
  P.O. Box 11470
  Bainbridge Island, WA 98110

  (206)842-0216/842-5208 Fax
  EcoNet: incontext

Ecoville, begun in March '92, is a project designed to facilitate the development of democratic and ecologically sustainable communities in Russia. Its development strategies include: 1) a center for information, expertise, training, and demonstration of ecologically sustainable community living; 2) training programs in St. Petersburg and other parts of Russia; 3) facilitation of educational interning for Russians in the West; 4) publication of materials supportive of sustainable community development; 5) construction of a rural demonstration sustainable community; 6) ecologically and socially beneficial businesses in St. Petersburg and the community.

Three of the core members have completed farming certification, and a village site has been secured in the Novgorod region where a team of 17 people from the project began reconstruction of two houses and food growing during the summer of '93. A translating and publishing business has been started, and ecological businesses have been researched. 10/12/93

NOTE: Mail cannot be used to reach Ecoville; phone calls are more dependable, though they take a while to arrange; e-mail is very prompt and reliable.

FINDHORN FOUNDATION

The Park
Forres, IV36 OTZ
SCOTLAND

0309-690311/673113 Fax
reception@findhorn.org

The Findhorn Foundation was founded in 1962 on the principles that God, or the source of life, is accessible to each of us at all times, and that nature, including the planet, has intelligence and is part of a much larger plan. While we have no formal doctrine or creed, we believe an evolutionary expansion of consciousness is taking place in the world, creating a human culture infused with spiritual values. The Foundation, a charitable trust, is a center of education and demonstration. It now includes approximately 150 resident members of varying ages and nationalities living in several sites in the area.

A wider community is growing around the Foundation as people with shared values and vision are coming to live alongside us. This wider population helps to enable an arts center, conferences, a holistic health department, the Moray Steiner School, *One Earth* magazine, and various independent businesses. The Foundation's business division includes a natural foods and book store, Findhorn Press, and a company that makes solar panels. The Development Wing has begun to replace original temporary buildings with new structures that are ecologically sound.

Please write for information on books, tapes, and guest programs. Prospective visitors are requested to write well in advance to the Accommodations Secretary. 8/11/92 [22, 28, 74, 83, 84]

FOR THE EARTH, FOR LIFE— WORKING CIRCLE HOPI

Obersdorf 35
Bad Mitterndorf
A-8983 AUSTRIA

The nonprofit association "For the Earth, for Life—Working Circle Hopi—Austria" has existed since 1982. We support traditional Indian issues, e.g., anti-uranium mining, religious rights, protection of sacred places, etc. We support by donations, letter campaigns, and by publishing the issues in alternative and spiritual magazines. We cooperate with Thomas Banyacya, Sr., Janet McCloud, and other traditional Indian leaders. We work for green spiritual politics in Europe, too. We have over 300 members and supporters in Austria, Germany, Switzerland, Italy, etc.

The core group, which runs the association together with other people, considers itself a community, which encourages people to build up small communities or circles of friends. Because of a lot of work and a lot of children and a lack of time we request you to understand that we are not open to visitors. Irregular meetings for members and friends are organized by the association. 5/11/92

FUSION ARTS COLONY

P.O. Box 293
Mornington, Victoria
3931 AUSTRALIA

A community of Christians concerned with developing skills and understanding in the visual arts. We have 15 adults and 5 children living on 2 rural acres. Other concerns and aims of the community include craftwork, philosophy, healing, therapy, and personal growth. Visitors should plan to share the cost of board. 2/20/93

KIBBUTZIM (ISRAELI)

There are 269 Kibbutzim in Israel. [See network listing in Resources section.] 8/6/92

L'ARCHE, COMMUNAUTÉ DE

La Borie Noble
Roqueredonde 34650
FRANCE
067-44-09-89

The community is made up of men and women, married or single, who commit themselves by a vow to the service of others, following the philosophy of Gandhian nonviolence. This involves manual work, simple rustic living with a minimum of mechanical tools, a search for inner knowledge, and nonviolent commitment to the cause of peace and justice.

Community members hold all resources in common. Each person contributes what they can and receives according to their needs. We consciously limit these needs to avoid consumerism and exploitation of the Third World. All major community decisions are made by consensus. We are vegetarian, living on 120 acres of arable land, producing most of our own food: wheat, vegetables, eggs, butter, and cheese.

The Ark is independent from all religious and political affiliation, and it respects each person's outlook and fidelity to their own tradition. Only fanaticism and sectarianism (whether religious or anti-religious) are unacceptable. We try to live a coherent, unified life under the guidance of the spirit of truth which animates our prayers and all aspects of our life.

We hold courses in French, English, and German for those who want to know more about community life. Please include a SASE with correspondence. 12/12/92 [29]

L'ARCHE (INTERNATIONAL)

BP 35
Trosly-Breuil
60350 Cuise-la-Motte
FRANCE
44-85-61-02

L'Arche, started in 1964 by a Canadian, Jean Vanier, is an international family of communities for people with developmental disabilities and those who wish to share life with them. L'Arche is not just an attempt to provide homes for people, it is an attempt to live out the gospel and put forth an alternative lifestyle. Today there are 100 L'Arche communities around the world, including 40 in Canada and the US. The charter which unites them all states: "We believe that each person whether handicapped or not, has a unique and mysterious value. The handicapped person is a complete human being and as such has the right to life, to care, to education, and to work. We also believe that a person who is wounded in his capacity for autonomy and in his mind is capable of great love which the Spirit of God can call forth, and we believe that God loves him in a special way because of his poverty."

Assistants and persons with a disability live in the same home, sharing the daily tasks of life: preparing meals, house chores, helping with personal hygiene if needed. Sharing life in this daily way invites the assistant to develop bonds of friendship and trust that are mutually growthful and life-giving. Assistants initially come to serve, and slowly they discover they are receiving more than they are giving. [See N. American listings for L'Arche Homefires, L'Arche Daybreak, L'Arche Mobile, and L'Arche Syracuse.] 4/30/94

LA ATLANTIDA

(Re-Forming)
Apartado 7566
Carrera 58 #2A-143
Cali, COLOMBIA
57-923-517309

[Previously listed as: Comunidad Rural "La Atlantida."] Our rural community is located five minutes from Cajibio, a two-hour drive from Cali, Cauca, Colombia. We have 200 acres, mostly plain, part forest; cows, horses, fruit; 80 beds in 20 bungalows; a recreational room, billiards and pool table, basketball court, and other sports. A small river crosses the farm; electricity with our own 25-KV transformer, TV

3 channels; 18 bathrooms; 2000 meters above sea level in an Andes valley; year-round spring and summer; Spanish language. Members must grow their own food and provide for their personal belongings; sleeping facilities are free. The zone is totally secure—no violence, no guerrillas, no bad people; it is a harmonious and beautiful place.

Our intention to consolidate a Christian community based in the command of Jesus to love God and all forms of creation, preparing for His second return within the next future. Prefer couples with or without children; singles only if an equal number of males and females. Members must be very Christian with respect for other members, responsibility, and cooperation; no drugs, no free love. Our main objective is to achieve perfection, in harmony within ourselves and with all creation forms, in order to find internal peace and the seven colors in the aura, and to develop each member's sense of serving without expecting anything in exchange. 5/15/92

LA VIGNE (CENTRE INTERNATIONAL)

(Re-Forming)
La Sauge
38620 Velanne
FRANCE
076-07-60-40/07-17-76
076-07-19-95 Fax

Set in the foothills of the French Alps, La Vigne is a place of simplicity and well-being, providing a safe environment for deep personal change. It is the home of about 25 individuals from different backgrounds—a working example of the emergent "common European home." We speak English, French, Italian, German, Hungarian, Dutch and Danish...but you are likely to hear Russian, Hebrew, Spanish, Uzbek, and even Hindi and Zulu spoken at the dinner table. Our many visitors come for seminars, workshops, and classes offered by resident and visiting facilitators on a variety of subjects—from

---

ʞɔɒqpɘɘℲ•Feedback

If you're like us, you know this book forward and backward. Please take a few minutes to fill out the Directory Evaluation Survey on pages 411–412, and let us know what you think—how did we do?

"The Art of Living" to "Co-counseling" to "Reflexology," etc., etc.

Come and visit us. You may stay at our nearby inn, L'auberge du Val D'Ainan (250FF/night), in local B&Bs (220FF/night), or in our camping site (150FF/night). Prices include full board and lodging. Visit La Vigne for meals, or join our daily work activities or our workshops and healing programs. Enjoy the gentle beauty of the countryside.

We also offer a fully equipped conference facility for up to 100 people, including simultaneous translation equipment for your workshops. For further information contact Marco Menato at the address/fax listed above. [See main listing for the Emissaries network in the Resources section.] SASE requested. 12/14/92

LANDELIJKE VERENIGING CENTRAAL WONEN

Grenadadreef 1-J
3563 HE Utrecht
NETHERLANDS
030-612585

Network of cohousing projects in the Netherlands. [See Resource listing.] 2/12/93

LAURIESTON HALL

Castle Douglas
Kirkcudbrightshire, S.W.
DG7 2NB SCOTLAND

We are a group of 26 adults and 8 children living in and around a spacious old mansion in the heart of the Galloway countryside. Founded in 1972, we own about 130 acres of land, live quite independent lives, and manage our collective affairs by consensus government at a weekly meeting. We place a high value on cooperation toward personal growth. Each adult is expected to contribute both financially and by working roughly half of the week, usually within one of our work committees. We produce a large amount of our food and dairy products; gather wood weekly from local forests; and generate enough electricity for lighting and hot water.

Between March and October we host conferences, with about 1500 paying visitors each year. We have our own lake, sauna, and conservation areas. If you want to get to know us, come for an event or during one of our maintenance weeks held three times a year. We have no fixed ideology or leader. People live either

singly, in nuclear families, or small communal groups. All visitors must write to make advance arrangements. 4/6/92

LE JARDIN SAUVAGE

(Forming)
Echourgnac
24410 Sainte Aulaye
Dordogne, FRANCE

Living Skills Centre created to: •Offer people the chance to sample and enjoy living without causing pollution or suffering to others anywhere in the world. •Receive guests of any nationality who want to live in harmony with nature and make international friendships. •Show how desertification can be reversed, famines avoided, and natural habitats reestablished, by food forest gardens. Courses: •Holistic healing and health-building. •Physiological, biological, psychological, and ecological factors in building immunity to disease and creating optimal health. •Animal psychology. How to understand behaviors, reactions, communications, needs, and illnesses. •Herb craft. How to use common wild plants, know their medicinal and nutritional values, which are available when we need to find plants to fulfill our requirements. Daily nature walks. Practice making all sorts of herbal products for house, skin, and health, and tooth powders, insect repellents, perfume articles, etc.

The price of any of the above holidays is 1500FF per week, per person. Checks payable to Michelle Compton in French Francs. All meals are vegetarian. Do you prefer to attend to your own food or to share food preparation, etc.? SASE required. 1/9/93

LOWER SHAW FARM

Old Shaw Lane
Shaw, Swindon
Wiltshire SN5 9PJ
UNITED KINGDOM
0793-771080

An ex-dairy farm, now a green 3-acre oasis in an area of 1980s development. Home to a community of 6 adults and 7 children, swelling to 3 or 4 times that number during events. We operate as a meeting place for weekend and week-long "alternative" courses, conferences, and learning holidays. (For full current program write with SASE.)

Our farm has substantial organic fruit, vegetables, and an herb garden—plus an assortment of animals (including goats, poultry, peacocks, and bees). The community has no collectively stated religious or party political base, but we do try to forge individual diversity into a core of common aims and values that include providing a meeting place for the exchange of ideas, information, experience, and skills; encouraging ecological resourcefulness and due consideration for both our immediate and global environment; increasing our individual sense of social responsibility; and learning to live and work well together.

Visits and short-term residency are possible, but only by prior arrangement. Please write. 8/6/92

MANDALA
(Re-Forming)
M.S. 394
Warwick, QLD
4370 AUSTRALIA

We are 30 or so individuals living in family groups on 280 acres set among mountain country 85 miles SW of Brisbane. Some of the finest bush scenery in Australia is on our doorstep. Mandala was started in 1975; many founding members remain. Our goal is to form and constantly reform an intentional community which makes a virtue of our diverse membership and is fully integrated with the wider world.

We patiently practice consensus; encourage leadership in all our members; try, in the absence of a leader or a single strong religious, philosophical, or behavioral base, to develop trust and acceptance. In so doing, we've had lots of heartaches but lots of laughter down the years. Most of us spend most of our working time on our own careers or projects. However, work is steadily going ahead on improving/conserving our shared land: tree planting, building, etc. We are currently working on a project to possibly expand our land holdings and then, in cooperation with others, expand and intensify our activities. We feel that community is needed in this world as never before. Visitors welcome, but we like to hear from them first. SASE requested. 6/15/92

MICHAELSHOF
Hutterian Brethren
Birnbach 5231, GERMANY

(COMMUNITY LISTING REMOVED)

Michaelshof was abandoned in '94 due to neo-Nazi activity around it. Members relocated to Darvell Bruderhof and several of the US Bruderhofs. 11/12/95

MICKLETON EMISSARY COMMUNITY
Mickleton House, Mickleton
Gloucestershire GL55 6RY
UNITED KINGDOM
0386-438251/438727

We are 12 years old and comparatively large. We experience a degree of harmony which most visitors find remarkable. Yet nobody joins us because they're looking for a good community. (On that basis, they would probably be disappointed.) People find themselves living here because they have been attracted by something intangible about the central attitude to life of those who live here. They also come because they have a strong urge to change and to add their own personal contributions.

The community works without rules or belief system because of a basic agreement about our job on earth. We are part of a worldwide network of people, both in and out of communities, loosely known as Emissaries, and aim to "magnify the finest qualities of character in every field of human endeavor."

We live in communal and family homes in the neighborhood, and work at a wide variety of jobs, both in and out of the village. In the central building, Mickleton House, we have meetings—each of them accompanied by a meal for all of us and our visitors. For those interested, we offer an educational program including seminars on "The Art of Living." [See main listing for the Emissaries network in the Resources section.] 4/1/92

MITRANIKETAN COMMUNITY
Mitraniketan P.O.
Vellanad 695-543
Kerala, INDIA
047288-2045/2015

Mitraniketan is a rural educational community (est. '56) to encourage people to "think globally and act locally," to

develop the whole individual, and to offer a replicable model for Third World countries. It is a non-political, non-sectarian, non-commercial registered charity promoting grassroots development, training, and education.

Our 70 acres of lush hilly land are home for about 100 adults and 300 children and adolescents. Residents operate a farm, a weaving cooperative, a handicrafts cooperative, various shop facilities, a publishing unit, several schools, an arts and sports unit, a library, three hostels, a home for the aged, and a commercial garden. We host numerous conferences and seminars on development, education, nature preservation, and allied themes.

Mitraniketan helps 100 villages operate adult education centers, 10 nurseries with 30–60 children each (with medical checkups and mothers' meetings for health and nutrition classes), and 20 youth clubs for environment protection. We also organize local farming efforts, construct local sanitation facilities, provide family counseling, and have built 20 low-cost houses.

We invite world servers from all over to come share their skills, time, talents, and funds. Mitraniketan provides food, accommodations, training, and a hearty welcome. If interested, please write about yourself and ask for our brochure. A voluntary contribution is appreciated from those who can afford it. 3/15/93

MONTCLAIRE COMMUNITY
(Forming)
Protem Address in Zimbabwe:
• **c/o Dell Smith**
  24 Hopely Avenue
  P.O.Greendale
  Harare, ZIMBABWE
USA Contact Address:
• **Attn: June Lang**
  238 W. Chestnut Street
  Lancaster, PA 17603-3547
  (717)394-6971 Fax (Attn: Linda)
  (717)394-6466

Envisioned: A working farm, demonstrating Community Values as family and global values; independent and INTER-dependent; inclusive of generational age groups and needs. Developing sustainable systems to achieve and ensure basic human needs. Desiring to be at-one with nature, having reverence for all beings. Being a positive contribution to the neighborhood, committed to working for balance—within the Montclair community, the larger community, Marondera, Zimbabwe, the

International

Globe, the Universe! Grassroots activity with aspirations to be an international node for sharing skills, information, to support and revitalize the working principle of the connectedness of everything; working for world peace. Recognizing that inner work and service to humanity are pivotal in creating a better world for all.

Nonhierarchical systems; consensual decision making; prepatriarchal cooperative models with a commitment to personal and spiritual growth; and creating a warm, gentle, compassionate, supportive atmosphere for the full development of each member. A demonstration of the advantages of separating the ownership of land from the ownership of one's home (the CLT model). Quaker religious base, inclusive of other spiritual paths including Anthroposophy. Vegetarian and macrobiotic diet encouraged as a principle for social change and health. A nonsmoking and drug-free environment with holistic approaches to health, education, housing, agriculture, and economics. Aiming to be self-sustaining and self-sufficient whenever practical. 12/18/94

MT. MURRINDAL COOPERATIVE

**W. Tree Via Buchan
Victoria
3885 AUSTRALIA
(051)550-218**

We are a registered Community Settlement Cooperative located in East Gippsland, Australia. We have 50 hectares of land, half cleared, half bush. Cleared paddocks are grazed by local farmers' cattle in return for fence maintenance, etc. Our current population is seven adults and two children.

Each family is responsible for its own economic well-being; there is no sharing of income. We have orchards, chickens, and a large vegetable garden which are communally worked. We have no over-riding philosophy other than cooperation with each other and with our neighbors, and the avoidance of chemicals in our gardening and farming practices. We would be happy to respond to any inquiries. 12/15/92

NEVE SHALOM WAHAT AL-SALAM

- **Oasis of Peace
  D.N. Shimshon
  99761 ISRAEL**

  011 972 2912 222

US Address:

- **121 Sixth Avenue #502
  New York, NY 10013-1505**

  (212)226-9246

A rural community of 23 women and 23 men, established in the mid-'70s with an ecumenical spiritual basis, and a primary focus on peace and coexistence. We live a cooperative lifestyle with elected leaders, and make our decisions using consensus. We live mostly in single family residences, and families have independent finances. 8/31/93

NEW CREATION CHRISTIAN COMMUNITY

**Nether Heyford
Northampton
NN7-3LB   UNITED KINGDOM
44-(0)1327-349991/349997
(fax)**

The NCCC is a major part of the Jesus Fellowship Church which is reformed, evangelical, and charismatic. The community exists as around 60 "households" spread across much of England. The community attempts to recapture the zeal and inspiration of the first Christians who had "everything in common," combined with an up-to-date appeal as a living church with a radical vision. The church is growing and spreading through its high-profile "Jesus Army" gospel outreach, including work among the homeless, drug abusers, prisoners, and ex-prisoners —many of whom have found new hope and new life in Christian community. Visitors are always welcome, but please try to contact us first before traveling from the USA! 2/20/96

NIEDERKAUFUNGEN (KOMMUNE)

**Kirchweg 1
34260 Kaufungen
GERMANY
0049-5605/3015**

Kommune Niederkaufungen was founded in 1986. The original group consisted of 15 people, and by now we are about 40 adults (22 men, 18 women) and 12 children; the planned size is 100. We live in a village 10 km away from the city of Kassel (pop. 200,000) in central Germany, so we are rather semi-urban. We understand ourselves as a political but undogmatic group. We don't orient along a specific community tradition or in spirituality.

Our main principles are shared income, decision making by consensus, reduction of nuclear-family structures, reduction of gender-typical hierarchy, Left understanding of politics, collective work structures, ecologically and socially sound products.

Our areas of work are carpentry, vegetable growing, seminar work, animals, playschool, architecture/planning, kitchen, construction, leather and clothing, metalwork, administration, external jobs (15%).

Newcomers go through a 3–6 month trial period, and we expect new members to bring in what they have. We frequently have weekends and weeks for interested people. Visitors have to check with us in advance. SASE requested. 1/25/93

ONTOS

**Gelantipy Road
Buchan Post Office
Victoria
3885 AUSTRALIA
(051)550-275/550-223**

Ontos is a small residential community on 700 acres in the foothills of the Snowy Mountains. There are 5 basic guidelines: being self-supporting, being a place of service, spiritual attunement, environmental sensitivity, and being a healthy/relaxed residential center of light. We put a great deal of our time and energy into running healthy lifestyle retreats for people seeking a peaceful health holiday— featuring vegetarian meals, yoga, stress management, bushwalking, talks, organic garden and farm tours, meditation, and alternative lifestyles. When we are closed to the general public we still accept visitors for the Willing Workers on Organic Farms program (where people experience and assist our farm, orchards, gardens, hothouses, and retreat center in exchange for room and board). In addition to running health holiday programs, the farm is also used for promoting organics, and we have hosted both permaculture and "grow organic" retreats (the most recent attracted over 250 people for 3-day residential program). Because we have motel units, camping, cabins, and a dormitory/conference center, our community is often used for a variety of events in spirituality, creative arts, and personal development. Visitors are welcome, but must write ahead. SASE requested. 1/13/93

OSHO COMMUNE ITERNATIONAL

- **17 Koregaon Park
Poona 411-001
INDIA
(011-91-212)660-963
(011-91-212)664-1812 Fax**

USA Info/Booking:

- **(714)633-5232
M-F 4:30-6:30pm PST**

Osho was a spiritual master, also known as Bhagwan Shree Rajneesh, who passed away in 1990. There are still about 500 Osho Centers around the world, with the main ashram located in Poona, India. In the US there are about 50 centers. [See resource listing for additional information.] 3/1/93

OWA, NEW HUTTERIAN CHURCH OF

**1807 Owa, Kurobane
Tochigi Pref. 324-02
JAPAN**

[See main listing for "Hutterian Brethren" in the Resources section.] 6/1/92

PLUM VILLAGE

- **Meyrac
Loubès-Bernac
47120 FRANCE
33-53-94-75-40/75-90 Fax**

US Contact Info:

- **Community of Mindful Living
P.O. Box 7355
Berkeley, CA 94707**

  **(510)527-3751/525-7129 Fax
parapress@aol.com**

Plum Village is a community practicing mindfulness under the guidance of Vietnamese Zen master Thich Nhat Hanh. Since 1983, many Vietnamese and Westerners have visited Plum Village and have created a life of mindfulness woven into all daily life activities. This enables us to meditate throughout the day—while eating, walking, working, and enjoying a cup of tea together. All visitors help in the preparation of the meditation halls for sitting and celebrations, preparation for meals, cleaning the bathrooms, emptying garbage, watering plants, washing dishes, cleaning the kitchen, etc., as part of the daily practice of engaging mindfulness continuously. Residents and visitors participate in all scheduled activities and observe the Five Wonderful Precepts which are the very foundation of our being together as a sangha. Every week we recite the Precepts together to help strengthen that foundation. We refrain from smoking, drinking, and sexual practice during retreats in order to focus our energy toward deepening our mindfulness practice in the community.

Accommodations are very simple, either in dorms or 4-person rooms; there are a limited number of rooms available for married couples. During Summer Retreat we receive children of any age; at other times children must be 12 or older. Please write for additional information about schedules, programs, and fees. Advance reservations are required for all our retreats. 1/19/95

RAINBOW VALLEY

P.O. Box 108
Takaka, Golden Bay
NEW ZEALAND
03-525-8209

A community of individuals. Our 100 hectares are an open valley between forest-covered hills. The Anatoki River leads up to wilderness and down to the wider community of Golden Bay. Community is first and foremost about people, not land. The people cooperate and share in different ways and at different levels. Differences are respected. Communication is recognized as vital. We want the community to be an environment which encourages cooperative work in all its forms, self expression, and self exploration.

We aim to follow the path of nonviolence (physical and emotional) in conflict resolution. Affairs pertaining to the whole community are resolved through meetings, with consensus always the aim. A company structure represents us legally,

in which all members are entitled to equal shares. Children play an important part in our community, helping us achieve a sense of extended family. Our Community House has a vital role as the heart-place, channeling communication, social life, and community spirit. The farming/gardening/conserving of communal land is a strong focus, while various arts and crafts manifest another dimension. All residents are responsible for their own income. Produce is sold for agreed purposes or is shared. Visitors are welcome when there is space. SASE requested. [cc] 4/2/93

REDFIELD COMMUNITY

Buckingham Road
Winslow
Buckinghamshire
MK18-3LZ UNITED KINGDOM
044-296-713661
redfield@gn.apc.org

Founded in 1978, Redfield was conceived as largely a land-based project with an associated educational center. The organic growing, animal care, and estate management aspects have been developed over the years and have now been taken further with the use of Permaculture design techniques. The educational aspect of the Community, however, is only just coming to fruition. We have recently set up an educational charity and now operate the Redfield Centre—a residential facility where courses can be run. There are several craft workshops; a gallery in a converted hay loft puts on contemporary art exhibitions; an artists' co-op is proposed; a training group is in the making; and event organization and publishing are skills which are also being developed.

There are usually about 23 adults and their children living here—all in one very large Victorian house with 17 acres of grounds. We share a lot of our lives with each other on an informal basis (cooking, child rearing, sitting around chatting, cleaning, etc.) but we do not income share. In the past most people have earned a living outside, and this has often led to a feeling of diffusion; we are now looking at more opportunities for people to work on site. Sometimes it's very busy here, and sometimes you can hear a pin drop! Please write for information about membership and visiting, and enclose SASE with International Reply Coupon. 5/1/92

RIVERSIDE COMMUNITY

Route 2, Upper Moutere
Nelson, South Island, LMO-805
NEW ZEALAND

Riverside Community was formed in 1941 by Christian pacifists, and many of the men spent the war years in prison as conscientious objectors. Members now follow whatever religious path they wish. There are about 75 people, half of them children.

We have no leader, and decisions are made by consensus at our weekly meetings. We meet 3 times a week for shared meals in the dining hall; other meals are eaten at home. Most people work in the community, and each adult receives the same weekly cash allowance regardless of what work they do. The aim is to live simply without the conflicts that arise when some are rich and powerful and many are not. We wish to behave toward all other human beings with love and not violence. Sometimes we fail this.

All houses and vehicles are owned by the community. Members own their own furniture and personal belongings. Income is from the dairy farm and apple orchards which are run conventionally. Organically grown vegetables, apples, and berries are being produced in increasing volumes, and we hope one day to be completely organic in our farming and horticulture. Recently we built two refugee units for use by people who need to spend time in a safe environment. 2/3/93

SHRUBB FAMILY

(Re-Forming)
Shrubb Farm Cottages
Larling, Norwich
Norfolk NR16 2QT CT
UNITED KINGDOM
0953-717844

Shrubb Family is housed in three 17th-century cottages. We are a close-knit, extended family. Decisions tend to get made organically "on the hoof." Kids outnumber adults 2:1 so caring for them is a major element of our day. Laughter is a powerful force in our lives; we love music, parties, are prepared to row and kiss and make up, are broadly tolerant of individual beliefs and ideals, and have no special religious or political stance.

The community is in the midst of big changes. Longer established members have left, and newer members share a strong commitment to the development of an eco-friendly lifestyle—two are permaculture graduates who want to promote perma-culture from Shrubb Community.

Our dream is to expand the amount of accommodation by building eco-friendly housing in East Anglia. We welcome visitors—especially those concerned with the well-being of the planet and with skills in gardening, building, architecture, music, and art. Please include a SASE with inquiries. 6/4/92

SONNENHOF

(Forming)
Ritterkamp 7
Rappottenstein, A-3911
AUSTRIA
(01143)02828-264
(01143)02822-52266 Fax

We are creating a safe environment for exploring group consciousness, and at the same time we use this group energy to serve others. Sonnenhof is a place of healing, and a living example of an ecologically oriented cooperative lifestyle that is able to fit the needs and challenges of our time. We regularly practice fasting for physical and emotional cleansing, regeneration, and expansion of awareness.

We are open to long-term guests who would like to spend some time here learning with us in daily life. Our immediate goal is the formation of a nucleus of 8–10 adults who explore life together as a group of equal partners, developing methods that are helpful to promote a holistic communal existence.

Our vision includes the development of future-oriented buildings that are designed to suit the landscape, using high-end experimental technology in the fields of alternative energy and advanced communication systems. Sonnenhof is a nonprofit oriented foundation, and is not bound by any fixed philosophy of life in any particular spiritual or religious direction. We are seeking to find synthesis. 1/25/93

SPIRITUAL FAMILY COMMUNITY GROUP

26 Third Avenue
Northville
Bristol BS7-ORT
UNITED KINGDOM

This group returned an update coupon from the 1992 edition of the Communities Directory, but no further information has been received. 9/14/93

STICHTING DE NATUURLIJKE WEG

Aengwirderweg 385
8458 CJ Tjalleberd
NETHERLANDS
05 131-9769

The Foundation for the Natural Way is a nonprofit dedicated to the advancement of natural health care for animals. Facilities include stables and land for 100+ horses, and an arena to train horses for show, jumping, and work. This arena has been the site of several symposiums, attracting hundreds of people interested in improving the health, living conditions, and performance of their animals. Treatments begin with a natural, organic diet including herbs and vitamins, much social contact, frequent interactions with caregivers, unique exercise, and homeopathic/herbal cures. All treatments are individualized based on the specific needs of each animal and the capabilities and desires of the owner. Long-term, chronic diseases and dysfunctions such as cancer and infertility have been treated with success. Injuries, bone and muscle problems, metabolic weaknesses, and behavioral problems can also be alleviated or cured. The Center also distributes the horse and dog products of Dr. Schaette—an anthropological herb company. Full advice and follow-up are offered with these products.

The Center is the collective effort of 45 persons including 12 children. This community is egalitarian and spiritually based. Visitors are welcome; advance contact is preferred to allow adequate time to arrange accommodations and an orientation. 2/14/94

SVANHOLM

Svanholm Gods
4050 Skibby DENMARK
42-32-16-70

The Svanholm Collective consists of about 75 adults and 60 children ranging in age from zero to 76 years (most of us are around forty). We also have a number of agricultural trainees, and usually quite a few visitors on fairly long-term stays. We own an estate with 625 acres of farm land and 408 acres of park and woodlands. When we bought the property in 1978 we wanted to live in a production collective based on shared work, shared economy, and shared decision making. We wanted WHOLE lives, with influence on our work and daily living, and a place where our children would thrive with animals and fresh air. We live in "house-groups" in various buildings in and around the estate, and these are the centers of the daily social life.

Most of us work at home, although about 30 people have outside jobs. Our main production is ecological farming (700 tons of organic produce last year). We operate a mill and a shop where we sell grain, flour, and fodder. We pool all income into a common fund, and we each receive a monthly allowance for clothes, amusements, and pocket money. Our decision-making authority is the communal meeting, which is held once a week. We do not vote, but discuss our way to agreement. Please call or write for more information. 3/15/93

TAENA

Whitley Court
Upton St. Leonards
Gloucester GL4 8EB
UNITED KINGDOM
0452-68346

Six family houses on a 135-acre dairy farm are living as an intentional village. We began during WWII as a pacifist commune in Cornwall. After a few years we came under the influence of C.G. Jung, and this led to an interest in Yoga, meditation, and Eastern religions generally. Through this we were drawn to the Roman Catholic Church and, one by one, during the late forties, were received into the Church. In 1952 we moved to our present home which adjoins Prinknash Benedictine Abbey.

In 1961 we changed to a village basis,

and since then each family has been functionally separate and has developed varying interests and occupations. Though there are many living here who are not members of any church, our central act as a community is the weekly celebration of Mass in our chapel, offered by one of the monks from the Abbey. Occupations include farming, painting, silversmithing, stone and wood carving, calligraphy, pottery, counseling, and teaching T'ai Chi Ch'uan. Visitors are welcome, but please contact us first by letter. 1/2/93 [77(D)]

TIMATANGA

9 Mamari Road
Whenuapai
c/o Bose 47114 Ponsonly
Auckland, NEW ZEALAND
64-09-416-4329/376-2086

Semi-rural, 20 minutes from a city of 500,000. Own your own dwelling, share other amenities. 13 adults, 10 kids. We operate an A.S. Neil/John Holt type of school that is now twenty years old. 8/2/93

TUI LAND TRUST

Wainui Inlet
RD 1, Takaka
Aotearoa, NEW ZEALAND
03-525-9654

Tui Land Trust was formed in '84 to create an international Community Village for Holistic Living. We are seeking wholeness through fulfilling relationships with ourselves, others, and the planet. Our projects: a healing retreat, sanctuary, and educational center; a place for holistic children's education; a craft workshop and farming cooperative (which may eventually offer training in "employment" and life skills). The craft workshop and a visitors' lodge are operational; our healing center is nearly completed.

We are presently 25 adults and 23 children, ages 0–72, with members from eight nations. A primary objective is to live close to the land and to create an environment supportive of children and personal growth. Our group has had long-term involvement with human potential and communication development. We have no specific common religious or political creed or spiritual leader. Our teachers are all around and within us. Children are regarded as communal as well as parental responsibility. We each contribute to community expenses, and are responsible for earning an income.

We come together for our daily lunch; our weekly business meetings; and for such events as meditations, sharings (for creative expression, healing, and personal growth), celebrations, work bees, and "Tukis" (a way of deep and open communication adopted and adapted from the Maori culture). We welcome visitors who are genuine in their interest to participate in community life and work. Please write or phone in advance to arrange your visit. Stays of more than two weeks require special agreement by the whole community. 10/29/93

UNIVERSAL LIFE

Postfach 5643
Würzburg 97006
GERMANY
011-49-931-39030

A new community in Germany which returned an update coupon from the 1992 edition of the Communities Directory. No further information was received. 8/1/93

UTOPIAGGIA

Villa Piaggia
1-05010 Montegabbione
ITALY
39-763-87020

Utopiaggia is an intentional community of twenty adults and fifteen kids aged 2–17. Apart from one Italian person we are all German, living on 250 acres in three houses in the hills of Umbria. Four members have full-time jobs on the land (sheep, cows, and the production of cheese), and the others have different jobs on the outside. We haven't given up our ideas about communitarian living that we started with in 1975, but we've certainly mellowed down to an enlightened group living with some basic values in common and lots of private space for everybody. We ask visitors to schedule visits at least a week in advance, and to contribute to our household expenses with something like $20/day per person. 8/1/93

VILLAGGIO VERDE

(Re-Forming)
Località San Germano
28010 Cavallirio (NO)
ITALY
0163-80-260/80-451

An experimental center of the New Aquarian, theosophical way of life. Residents should know how to live the teachings of the Gospel, in which it is taught not to judge, but to understand and love others as ourselves. Our primary aim is the development of self-consciousness, and endeavoring to overcome ignorance, fear, anxiety, and selfishness—to experiment with a new way of life, happy and free, without exploitation, without anxiety and meanness. In addition to the Gospel, our basic books are *I Am* by the Count of the Saint Germain, the *International Guide of the Age of Aquarius*, and the magazine *L'Età dell'Acquario*. People who would like to join the Villaggio Verde should clearly understand the meaning of these words: "God, give me the serenity to accept the things that I cannot change, the courage to change the things that I can, and the wisdom to know the difference." 1/21/93

WALDOS

(Forming)
Apdo. 1702-5370
Quito, ECUADOR
South America
5932-627757 (voice/fax)

Waldos is a community begun in 1992, formed by a group of health care professionals who, after reading *Walden Two*, have come to identify with many of the concepts presented, especially shared resources and group action. "Dos" comes from two in Spanish, hence the name Waldos. Our economic base is a small community hospital we have founded in a semi-rural valley outside of Quito, the capital of Ecuador (South America). The hospital began operation in July 1992, and has been very well received by the larger community. It serves primarily poor patients, and we are basically self-financed except for the medical equipment which is mostly donated from the United States. If a single description of our group were solicited it would be that we all share a similar concept of humanitarian (socially oriented) medicine.

Our original group consists of 9 adults and 2 children (five nuclear families). We are 5 physicians, two lab techs, a nurse, and a dentist (but growing). The group is all of Ecuadorian nationality except for one American citizen. Ages range from 20 to 43, and the gender mix is equal. Our challenge is to get the "community" aspect of Waldos off the ground, and we have a keen desire to begin living as a community in the very near future. (We are lacking of any experience of how to make that happen—wisdom of that kind shared through correspondence or even possibly a visit here would be very helpful.) 9/1/93

WATTLE HILLS STATION

(Forming)
PMB 51 Mail Centre
Cairns, QLD
4871 AUSTRALIA
(070)603-275

We are a conservation and organic oriented community establishing fruit, nut, and timber tree orchards and plantations in the poor soils of an 89,000-acre property in the remote wilderness of Cape York Peninsula in the tropical north of Queensland. Several families share the property. We have river access to the sea and Great Barrier Reef, 4WD road access during dry season (May–Nov), and air access to our airstrip most times. Nearest store is 1/2 day's drive or boat trip. Schooling is by correspondence and radio. Modern conveniences are supplied by ourselves as we are not linked into any of the wider community's services, so we appreciate conserving resources and what it means to have to provide our own power, water, rubbish disposal, etc. Freight expenses are high, and goods require a lot of personal handling (i.e., like loading a huge barrel of fuel onto the back of a truck by hand). Help needed in planting trees, building, gardening in exchange for food and basic accommodation. If you plan to visit, we need advance notice, and leave your drugs, drink, and smokes (if any) behind! Bring

your ideas, enthusiasm and a strong back! SASE required. 2/2/93

WEST END CATHOLIC WORKER

269 Boundary Street
West End, Brisbane, QLD
4101 AUSTRALIA
(078)441-369

A small Christian community attempting to live out the basic Christian principles. Our three primary values are hospitality, resistance, and common purse or self-management. We earn our money from bread, soap, and odd jobs. One of our members is a relief youth worker. We share all our money, and take personal responsibility when using it. Our resistance is non-violent, and we refuse to pay fines after acts of civil disobedience. We resist the makers of war wherever and whenever. East Timor is a grave concern as it is so close and we are so responsible. Hospitality is given to those who need a bed for a short while. We often have people staying a lot longer. We pray together through the week, hold liturgies every week, and have regular scripture study. We try to live simply and responsibly. People are welcome to stay with us for experience, but we must have advance notice so that we can organize space. 12/22/92

YAMAGISHISM LIFE TOYOSATO JIKKENCHI

International Department
5010 Takanoo-cho, Tsu-city
Mie-Pref. 514-22
JAPAN
0592-30-8028
0592-30-8029

A network of about 40 communities in 7 countries, all working as one body, one family, with the aim of happiness for all people on this earth. The largest community has about 1600 members; the smallest about 20. Activities: large-scale agriculture, food processing and distribution, construction, planning, software production and distribution, medical care, boarding school, seminars for adults, children's parodies weeks,

international exchange. Non-religious, non-political. 10/4/92

- **Yamagishism**
  Henderson Drive M.S. 216
  Innisfail
  4860 AUSTRALIA
  (067)70-644-177
- **Jikkenti Campinas de Vida de**
  Yamagishi-smo Agropecuaria, Ltd.
  Rod. SP-340 km 138 - C.P. 29
  13 820 - Jaguariuna -SP
  BRAZIL
  55-0192-97-1173
  55-0192-97-3034 (Fax)
- **Yamagishism Agrar GurbH.**
  Gartenweg 179
  D-0 4731 Gorsleben
  GERMANY
  0049-0161-223-6659
- **Yamagishi-kai**
  555 Kawahigashi Iga-cho, Ayama-gun
  Mie-Pref. 519-14
  JAPAN
  05954-5-4594
  05954-5-3329 (Fax)
- **Keong-gi-do Hyang-nam Sii Hyeon Ji**
  Keong-gi-do Wha-Seong-gun
  Hyang-nam-myeon Gu-mun 3
  Cheon-ri-San 141-1
  KOREA
  82-0339-2-3920
  82-0339-52-0104 (Fax)
- **Landw. Genossenschaft**
  f. Yamagisism Leben
  Seelmatten
  8361 Neubrunn
  SWITZERLAND
  41-052-45-37-77
  41-052-45-37-12 (Fax)
- **Yamagisism Life Thai**
  Jikkenchi Co, Ltd.
  1/2MU 8th Bangsomboon Road
  Tumbon Ongkharak Amphur Ongkharak
  Nakornnayok 26120
  THAILAND
  66-02-235-2414-2421

YURT FARM, THE

Living & Learning Centre
(Re-Forming)
Graben Gullen Road
Goulburn, NSW
2580 AUSTRALIA
(048)292-114/(024)511-128

Learning to live with less. The Yurt Farm near Goulburn, a historical city in NSW Australia, welcomes international visitors to help run the farm and children's camp in exchange for room and board—or to join the cooperative group and escape the consumer lifestyle, living and working on our beautiful but basic 100-year-old farm set in rolling hills amid gum trees with kangaroos and kookaburras. We value creativity more than distraction or money. 100 farm and bush survival activities are led by the irrepressibly enthusiastic Mike Shepherd, Australia's Yurt Man and Pied Piper, in his village of 18 yurts (wooden round houses) with wind and solar power. Artistic, agricultural, and people skills are highly valued; innovation is encouraged. Outgoing, enthusiastic Americans are always welcomed with open arms! 10/3/93

ZEGG

Rosa Luxemburg Str. 39
D-14806 Belzig
GERMANY
033841-59530

ZEGG is a community of 100 adults and 12 children located fifty miles southeast of Berlin, Germany. It is part of a larger project called MEIGA 3000, which was started in 1978 by Dr. Dieter Duhm, best-selling author and well-known leader of the German student movement in the 1960s and '70s.

ZEGG focuses on the issues of personal growth, free sexuality, and the development of new ways of living in community. But their research also extends to the areas of energy physics, resonance technology, and healing. ZEGG designed its own non-polluting heating system, a water treatment facility using marsh plants instead of chemicals, and its own organic garden. In 1993, ZEGG launched a whale and dolphin research ship called the Kairos, which sails off the west coast of Africa communicating with the cetaceans through music and sound.

But ZEGG's greatest achievement has been to learn to love freely, without jealousy or competition in their relationships. Their goal is to establish a world without fear, without violence, and without sexual repression.
[See North American listing for the Network for a New Culture, a sister community forming in Philomath, OR.] 3/7/94

ZEVEN RIVIEREN

P.O. Box 611
Stellenbosch 7599,
SOUTH AFRICA
27-2231-91324/91278 Fax

[Formerly the Hohenort, at a different location.] Zeven Rivieren is a large 300-year-old farm in the beautiful Banhofer Valley, near the town of Stellenbosch. In 1990 this Emissary community succeeded the Hohenort as the headquarters community for the Emissaries in southern Africa. Those who live at Zeven Rivieren, as well as the many who, in various ways, support its operation, are aware of the important part a community of this nature can play in what is emerging in southern Africa. Although still a relatively new community, Zeven Rivieren is already playing a significant role as a reference point of "home" for an increasing number of people. [See main listing for the Emissaries network in the Resources section.] 11/18/92

NEW INTERNATIONAL LISTINGS

Please see the Yellow Cards on the last page for information on obtaining the *Directory* Updates. The descriptions of these communities are condensed to fit.

COMMUNITY IN PENNIGBUTTEL

New Social Order in Messiah
Unter den Linden 15
27711 Osterholz-Shambeck,
GERMANY
011-49-47-918-9657

This community in northern Germany began in 1995 with several German families from the Communaute de Sus. [See network listing for the "Community In" Association in the Resources.] 12/26/95

COMMUNIDAD DE SAN SEBASTIAN

New Social Order in Messiah
Paseo de Ulia, 375
Casa "Cuatro Vientos"
San Sebastian 20013, SPAIN
011-34-43-58-00-29

This small community began in 1994 with several Spanish families who moved here from Communaute de Sus. [See network listing for the "Community In" Association in the Resources.] 12/26/95

COMMUNITY IN NOTTINGHAM

New Social Order in Messiah
7 Mount Hooton Road
Nottingham NG7 4AY
UNITED KINGDOM
011-44-115-970-8380

This community is a small, warm household that began in early 1995. [See network listing for the "Community In" Association in the Resources.] 12/26/95

ENERGY WORLD WILD GOOSE COMPANY

87360 Verneuil
Moustiers, FRANCE
0033-15568-2530

Received a reply card asking to be included in the next Directory. No additional information has been received. 8/17/95

LEBENSGARTEN STEYERBERG & ECOVILLAGE INSTITUTE

Ginsterweg 3
D-37595 Steyerberg
GERMANY
http://www.gaia.org/
05764-2754

80 members. The buildings and land are held in common. Open to more members. Offers advice for seeking and initiating of communities. 6/19/95

UFA-FABRIK

Internationales Kulture
Centrum
Viktoriastraße 13
D-12105 Berlin, GERMANY
030-755-030

In the summer of `79, over 100 people took over the desolate grounds of the former UFA Film studios, creating a comprehensive work and living project for innovative social, cultural, and ecological lifestyles. 6/25/95

GANAS
a fifteen year old, New York City intentional community
IS EXPANDING INTO THE COUNTRY
and we need good new people to help in both places

WE'RE BUYING 75 BEAUTIFUL ACRES of woods, fields, streams, a pond, a pool *and a 65 room (and bath) country hotel in upstate New York's Catskill Mountains.*

THE PLAN IS TO BUILD A LEARNING CENTER, A SMALL HOTEL & A COUNTRY COMMUNITY to add to our New York City facility. We expect to grow from 75 adults to over 100 in the process.

OUR GOALS (in the city and in the country) are truthful inter-personal communication; better cooperative problem solving; responsible autonomy; and more loving relationships. All this boils down to happier, more meaningful lives in a reasonably sane cooperative society.

WE'RE STARTING THE CENTER SO WE CAN LEARN NEW THINGS and teach what we've learned. We need exposure to a far bigger range of people and learning experiences than our city life alone can offer. The idea is to create programs of many kinds that can help us become better functioning individuals, while achieving our common goals as a community. More varied work choices are also important to us.

But mostly the point is to have easy access to both country & city living with good possibilities for enjoying the best of both worlds.

WE PLAN TO OFFER THE PUBLIC (& OURSELVES) 3 KINDS OF PROGRAMS

1. FITNESS ACTIVITIES PROGRAMS will include breathing and relaxation exercises, meditation, yoga, visualization/imagery, tai-chi, aerobics, calisthenics, weights, muscle toning and strengthening. Biofeedback, massage, and a range of bodywork programs will also be available.
Feedback learning methods will be adapted to use with all of the above activities.

Exercise rooms will be equipped with large TV screens, video cameras, mirrors on the walls and ceilings, and a whole range of work-out equipment.

2. CULTURAL LEARNING PROGRAMS. Unusual theater and music workshops for professionals and others will focus on increasing skills, and decreasing problems that interfere with freely letting go into performance.

Public performances in our cabaret or outdoor stage might include concerts, musicals and improvisations, and we might also have jazz clinics, festivals, and many other entertainments.

Other workshops, possibly for Singers, Dancers, Magicians, Comedians, Mimes, Clowns, Jugglers; or for poets, playwrights, painters, sculptors, photographers, and for craftspeople of all kinds; and eventually art exhibits, craft shows, poetry readings and original plays. These are all part of the plan.

3. PERSONAL GROWTH PROGRAMS include bodywork such as Feldenkrais, Trager, Bioenergetics, and Alexander Method, Psychodrama, Gestalt, feedback learning groups, all kinds of awareness workshops, as well as Music, Dance, Art and Poetry as means of emotional communication, conflict resolution, and more.

All fees to the public will be as low as we can make them.
Workshop scholarships will be available to all of the working staff, both in Ganas (NYC) and in the country.

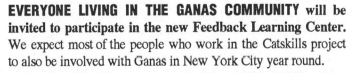

FACILITIES AT THE CENTER will include attractive rooms for 150 people and campgrounds that accommodate another 200; exercise equipment, a pool, a sauna, sports facilities and many games, rowing and fishing equipment, indoor and outdoor stages.

Food will be served in 4 buffets that include:
1. a normal meat and potatoes diet with good salads.
2. a range of vegetarian dishes available to everyone.
3. fat-free, sugar-free, low calorie foods with lots of desserts.
4. special diets for participants in health education programs.

Leisure activities for guests (and us) will include live theater, music, dancing, swimming, hikes, picnics, etc. Instructional videos will teach control of weight & smoking; care of skin, hair & nails; facial firming; and many kinds of folk and ball room dancing.

EVERYONE LIVING IN THE GANAS COMMUNITY will be invited to participate in the new Feedback Learning Center. We expect most of the people who work in the Catskills project to also be involved with Ganas in New York City year round.

If you would like to live, work and play in close community with interesting and interested people (in the city, in the country, or both); if you care about communication and if you believe in reasonable problem solving based on truth (and want to learn how to do it better); if you think that cooperatives can help to create saner societies; if you believe that recycling is a pretty good way to earn a living; and if you really enjoy working productively (or want to learn how to); *if such things feel true for you right now ... please call us.*

YOU ARE INVITED TO VISIT and PERHAPS BECOME PART OF OUR EXCITING NEW BEGINNINGS.

357

GANAS

a residential facility of the Foundation for Feedback Learning (FFFL), a non-profit corp. committed to exploring new applications of performance feedback to creative learning.

IS AN ONGOING LIVING EXPERIMENT IN OPEN COMMUNICATION dedicated to developing responsible autonomy and caring relationships based on problem solving dialogue that joins reason with emotion in daily interaction.

WE GIVE TOP PRIORITY TO LEARNING TO PAY ATTENTION, HEAR & RESPOND TO EACH OTHER so we can think together well, decide together wisely and live together happily, whenever possible. We believe that learning to let go and listen is prerequisite to love and to productive work, a good life, and a better world.

OUR GOAL IS TO ENJOY LIFE EVERY DAY while creating our world together the way we want it

PREPARATIONS (*here in NYC*) ARE STARTING NOW for work in the country project beginning next spring. We expect to start renovation and program preparation in May of 1996. The hotel will start accepting guests and workshop programs will begin in the summer of 1997.

RIGHT NOW WE NEED HELP getting ready for the new venture. Because we will need people for both places, it's important for us to train more sales people, managers and merchandise processors, and people who can (or want to learn to) repair and refinish furniture, sew, or create toys and other products out of scrap wood for the Ganas stores. We also need an auto mechanic and an electrical repair person. Once we get started in the country, we'll need people who want to raise and/or prepare food, help with the hotel and with all the work that goes into creating a smooth running rural community, and also painters, carpenters, gardeners, and handymen/women.

WE'RE ALSO LOOKING FOR GOOD WORKSHOP IDEAS AND GOOD PEOPLE to implement them. The Center will need workshop leaders who are capable of taking full responsibility for developing, managing, and conducting their own programs. What's wanted are people who have interesting things to teach and the necessary skills to make the whole thing work — and who will live at Ganas some of the time if possible. We will help, but essentially they will be responsible for their own programs.

EVERYONE IN GANAS WILL BE INVITED TO WORK IN THE COUNTRY CENTER either part time or full time (in and/or out of season). Hopefully, many people who work in the Catskill programs will opt to live and work at Ganas in NYC during the winters.

GANAS BACKGROUND INFORMATION STARTS IN THE 70'S: The Foundation for Feedback Learning began in Arizona in 1973. In 1976 we moved to San Francisco.

In 1980 six of us moved to NYC and founded the community, which is now called Ganas. We've been very lucky. All of us are still here. In fact, very few of the people who really got involved over the years have left. Most of us have learned to understand each other very well and care very much. By now we are truly a closely bonded, large extended family.

In 1994 we began the work of the Feedback Learning Institute for Intelligent, Interactive Problem Solving — (F.L.I.P.S.).

In the spring of 1996, the Feedback Learning Center will continue the Institute's (F.L.I.P.S.) work in the Catskill Mountains.

LIVING & WORKING FACILITIES in the city community are good. For the better part of 15 years, we focused on creating the secure, comfortable, rewarding environment we thought necessary for living out our feedback learning experiments and for making a good life together. Now we finally feel ready to put our attention more fully into our central purposes.

We've grown from 6 to over 75 people and share 8 large residences. Most of us work in our 4 commercial buildings nearby. We renovated our buildings to suit our needs and our pleasure — and they really do.

The community is located in a racially mixed, lower middle class, suburban neighborhood, a half-hour 50¢ ferry ride from Manhattan.

The houses are connected by picturesque walkways, surrounded by flower and vegetable gardens, many trees (some fruit bearing), lots of berry bushes, a small swimming pool, a large deck, outdoor fireplaces and eating space, and many pretty spots for hanging out. It all feels very rural, although we have views of NY Harbor and the Manhattan skyline.

Living space is comfortable, attractive and very well maintained. The food is plentiful, excellent, and varied enough to suit most people, including some vegetarians. Dinner is at 7, but people can prepare meals for themselves whenever they like, in one of 3 fully stocked, well-equipped community kitchens.

Cable TVs; VCRs; extensive video, music, audio-tape and book libraries; an equipped exercise room, a ping-pong and a pool table; 5 laundries; 4 stocked kitchens and dining rooms; ESL programs; and feedback learning materials are available to everyone.

Biofeedback equipment, computers and software, good sound systems, slide shows and projection equipment, copy facilities, and a carpentry workshop can be accessed by special arrangement.

FUN AT GANAS consists of parties, outings and trips in small or large groups, singing, making music, play readings, extensive birthday celebrations, jokes, and often just hanging out and enjoying each other.

AGE, LIKE EVERYTHING ELSE ABOUT GANAS PEOPLE, IS DIVERSE.
The majority are between 30 and 50. A few children have lived here, but never very many. We have no organized child care programs. Most of us live in couples, some married, some open, some not. A few are polyfidelitous. The rest engage in the usual social practices.

Ganas has the international quality of the city. People of many races, nationalities, religions, professions, educational backgrounds, personalities, and life views live together in surprising harmony.

A RATHER UNUSUAL SOCIAL AND POLITICAL STRUCTURE HAS EVOLVED,
probably because of our desire to create as many life style options as possible. We have several very different but quite complementary kinds of population at Ganas. The first, called the core group, consists of ten people, five men and five women, who serve as the community's Board of Directors. Core group members pool all their time and talents, as well as their material things. They're also committed to exchange thoughts, feelings and feedback. This group is open to, but not seeking new members. The demands made on them are such that few people opt to join.

The second is an extended core group of about 30 people interested in some aspect of the Ganas philosophy. They do not share resources, are not necessarily committed to join any particular activity, or to exchange feedback, expose their own emotional reality, or accept anyone else's. However, many of them do opt to participate in these things. They share in almost all decision making, and several have invested money in specific projects.

The third population consists of 35 to 40 people who generally stay from about 3 months to 3 years. Some work in the community. Most are employed elsewhere. A few are students. They tend to form close social sub-groups, many of whom hold very different but surprisingly compatible philosophies. They are not much involved with Ganas' goals and activities, but almost all of them enjoy the Ganas experience. Many have reported on its extraordinary value to them years after leaving.

DECISION MAKING PROCEDURES AT GANAS
arc not fixcd. Matters that require major resources or policy issues are usually made by consensus of the extended core group after dialogue with everyone available. Occasionally, group interaction leads to a majority decision. Area coordinators and department managers have authority to decide, but only after distributing information and getting input. Almost anyone can have an area of work or administrative function to coordinate if they are willing to take responsibility for it.

RULES AND AGREEMENTS:
Because we deal with problems daily, we are able to limit ourselves to only 4 rules:

1) Non-violence to people or things; 2) No free rides (everybody is required to work productively or pay their expenses); 3) No illegality (including illegal drugs). 4) a new rule, requires that people bring their complaints about the community or people in it to the group, where the problems can be discussed and resolved with the people involved.

People breaking one of these rules will be asked to leave.

We make agreements easily and change them often. Anyone can bring up any issue any time, and almost anything can be changed or modified, if that's what it takes to meet people's needs or requests.

None of this consistently goes according to plan, but we work on it.

THE GANAS VISION
is of a small world in which autonomous individuals solve problems together easily, govern themselves cooperatively, and thoroughly enjoy the process. We dream of developing open minds with which to know each other better. We want to learn how to give up self-conscious, competitive power plays and status seeking aggressions, so we can welcome anyone who wants to join us — with pleasure.

Hopefully, if we succeed, what we create will be replicable.

GOOD COMMUNICATION IS OUR MOST CENTRAL VALUE.
Of course, we include emotional and other nonverbal exchanges in our definition. We've found performance feedback to be the most important and the hardest kind of information to give and to accept. All the years of trying have demonstrated one thing for sure. People would rather be right than wise. Hardly anybody really *wants* criticism of what they think or what they do. Most of us get irritated, offended, feel controlled or possibly attacked, even by simple disagreement. Often, it is *most* difficult to listen to the things we *most* need to hear. Still, nobody can deny that it's probably necessary to identify mistakes before trying to correct them — to know what's missing before we decide what to learn. We agree on these principles, so most of our time is spent trying to give feedback the welcome it deserves, regardless of *how* it's delivered. We've opted to increase our receptivity to intake rather than try to control the output of others. The idea is to disclose what's *really* happening and then work out what's wanted; instead of masking reality, hiding unpopular thoughts and feelings, and living in a haze of unknowns and deceptions. We created an environment in which we really *are* safe to do this — but we don't always *feel* safe. Much too often, most of us still hide our truth and recoil from others when they present theirs. It's a full time job learning to do better. Progress is slow but it's happening.

We have used many methods, including relaxation, visualization, meditation and other mind quieting procedures; many forms of behavioral recordkeeping including problem and mood tracking; and study groups that define terms needed to discuss both theories of behavior and currently troublesome interactions. The approach we rely on mainly is direct feedback in dialogue. Therefore, group involvement is a daily event at Ganas. From 7:30 to about 10 every morning (later on weekends) we get together for breakfast, and that's when most of the work of feedback learning really happens. We discuss our business as well as personal problems. This is the time for exploring hidden agendas and defenses, and for thinking about how we communicate (or don't) about whatever is going on.

At dinner, and for a few hours after dinner most evenings, a number of us remain in the dining room to talk about the day or about things that didn't get resolved that morning, or to get to know visitors, read plays, or do what any family does when they hang out together in the evening. We often spend Sunday that way, too.

Nobody who lives at Ganas is required, or knowingly pressured to engage in any of these conversations or activities. However, everybody is invited to participate to whatever extent they are willing.

Since at least 25 or 30 people are somewhat committed to try to express feelings and thoughts freely, and a fairly large number of them usually opts to be present for our group events, many people find these situations difficult — even frightening — at first. But the process seems to be valuable enough for most to find the rewards worth the effort, and participation keeps growing.

359

WHAT GANAS OFFERS AND DOES NOT OFFER is not always clear. *We are not a therapeutic community* and we don't give feedback to everyone. People have to be willing (and thought to be *able*) to make good use of direct feedback before we do. Personal issues do come up spontaneously and sometimes quite publicly, but they are only discussed in depth with consent and clear cooperation.

We feel that our group discussions are simply on-going, truth seeking, problem solving dialogues. But because we are involved with new behavior change methods, and confront rather than avoid conflicts, Ganas groups are often mistakenly thought of as personal therapy. In fact, we rarely offer the kind of "support" that many people seem to expect of therapeutic intervention — at least we don't usually do what seems to be wanted.

Those not familiar with interaction as direct as ours often find the process too cerebral or too emotional, too invasive or too controlling, and the whole thing can be experienced as cold or even unkind. People who fear or dislike exposure of anger or strong feelings are not usually comfortable here. People with serious emotional problems seeking help aren't likely to find it here. Those who want to learn how to think, love, and bring expressions of reason and emotion together in dialogue will probably enjoy Ganas very much. People who want to understand and contribute to others might find a treasure house of value for themselves here.

Some Ganas concepts have been simplified down to cliches that are possibly convenient enough to be worth repeating. Here are a few examples: "Love is selfish. It is the source of all pleasure and strength." "It's possible to find something to love (or at least like) in almost anyone." "If you don't see, hear, feel and *know* the beloved, who or what are you loving?" "Truth must be delivered and heard with all the feeling involved or it's not the truth." "Truth (or what you can find of it) is almost always a gift, never an insult." "Ignorance is dangerous, and what you don't know hurts you very much." "We rarely control events, but we totally shape our responses to them." "The do-er is not the deed, but the creator and change agent." "Feeling follows thought; action decisions follow feelings; when thought and feeling are not in awareness, rationalization and defenses follow action. These are not thought but *do* pass for it."

ECONOMICS: Recycling is the community's business. Most of our work happens in 4 retail stores called Every Thing Goes. One refinishes and sells furniture; the second sells clothing. The third is a gallery. The original store sells everything else. The businesses are all near the residences. They are well organized, efficiently run, attractive and profitable.

Approximately 35 people work in the businesses. Another 15 people work at home. Full time work is minimally 40 hours a week and often more. That covers all expenses plus $200 per month. Workers have always received a share of the profits as well. This year, we are offering shares in the new Catskills property instead.

Most of Ganas shares a very strong work ethic that involves learning to enjoy whatever you do and doing it as well as you possibly can. Creating models of profitable, ecologically sound cooperatives that recycle is an important social goal to us. Our long term economic plan is to provide substantial personal income. As resources grow, Ganas plans to support many new ventures proposed by members. The Catskills Center is one of these.

VISITORS, GUESTS, AND PEOPLE WHO MIGHT LIKE TO LIVE AND/OR WORK AT GANAS should call to make arrangements. If we have space, you will be welcome.

When you get here, feel free to participate in our discussions if they interest you. You will be encouraged to ask questions about anything, say whatever you want — even if it's personal — and express whatever you feel. But then you will be expected to hear responses. Most of our group discussions are facilitated because they are related to our feedback learning work, or may be if the conversation goes that way. Therefore, if the facilitator or anyone else in the group feels that your input is inappropriate, ill informed, or an interference with what's happening at a particular time, they'll tell you so and explain why. Someone will be available to discuss information about people, or the background of specific conversations, or to update you when necessary or to discuss community agreements, feedback learning theory and practice, or anything else you'd like to know. However, all that may have to wait until a more appropriate time if whatever is happening cannot be interrupted just then.

If you come for a day, we'll try to make time to show you around and talk with you. If you stay for the evening, there is no cost for dinner (except perhaps helping with the dishes). That's usually the best time to meet a lot of the people, ask questions, and tell them about yourself. If you happen to come on an evening when an important conversation is going on, you will get to witness our process.

People staying for a night to a week are asked to pay $25 a day and help out some. Visitors coming for longer stays usually pay expenses at the rate of $150 a week if they don't work here. If you decide to try living at Ganas for a while, all your expenses can be met with one fee of $450-600 a month. That covers space, food, toiletries, laundry supplies — everything except telephone. If you want to work in the community, we'll discuss our needs and your skills when you get here. Please bring expense money with you in case it doesn't work out. Whether you work here or pay expenses, you will be asked to help out in some way for at least a few hours a week.

For more information, or to arrange for a visit, call 718-720-5378, fax 448-6842, or write to Ganas, at 135 Corson Avenue, Staten Island, NY 10301-2933.

About the Resources

Magic, Inc.

*I*n this section we list organizations whose work could be helpful to those seeking, or already involved in, "cooperative alternatives." We also include publications that cover subjects relevant to shared living and shared work (such as personal growth), or topics that frequently come up as a focus for various communities (such as environmental advocacy). We cover areas as diverse as community organizing and networking, health care, economics, work, law, food, housing, communication and facilitation, relationships and family life, energy and environment, politics, education, decision making, self and spirit, and culture.

Our Listings were solicited from people both in and out of community, and comprise a representative (but by no means exhaustive) overview of groups making significant contributions in the development of a more peaceful, just, cooperative, and ecologically harmonious world. Each of these groups was judged by at least one person we know to be worthy of inclusion; time and space limitations have undoubtedly meant that some other groups, equally worthy, have not been included.

We generally avoided listing groups that are specifically local in scope, preferring to emphasize networks and umbrella organizations. Our rationale is that regional or national groups will likely be good sources of information and/or referrals—regardless of the locale of the person making the inquiry. For example, we've not included many of the food co-ops, alternative schools, or health clinics referred to us. We made two notable exceptions to this policy: we've included local groups that (1) are projects or businesses organized/operated by one of the communities listed in the *Directory*, or (2) have such a unique focus or style of operation that a listing might serve as an important model for replication.

We hope that the resources described in this section will provide you with access to the wide range of groups working for a better future. If you don't find specifically what you are looking for, we hope that by starting with the groups that *are* listed, you will find a referral to the group or resource you seek. If you're lucky, it will be no more than a SASE or two away.

The feedback we've requested regarding the Community Listings applies to Resource groups as well—if you know of any groups that you think should be seriously considered for the Resources section of future *Directories*, please let us hear about them. To make your part easier, the bottom response card on the last page will prompt you for the information we need from you. Thanks for your help! ⚇

ABUNDANT LIFE SEED FOUNDATION

P.O. Box 772
Port Townsend, WA 98368

(360)385-5660

Abundant Life Seed Foundation is a nonprofit organization whose purposes are 1) to acquire, propagate, and preserve the plants and seeds of the native and naturalized flora of the North Pacific Rim, with particular emphasis on those species not commercially available—including rare and endangered species; 2) to provide information on plant and seed propagation; and 3) to aid in the preservation of native and naturalized plants through cultivation. The Foundation sponsors the World Seed Fund, which provides seeds to those who most need and can least afford them. For each $100 donated, we send 400 packets of fresh, open-pollinated seed, appropriately selected, postpaid for distribution through any agency in any country that is working to end hunger (donors may opt to specify a country). Members of Abundant Life Seed Foundation pay $8–$25/year (sliding scale) and receive the annual seed and book catalog as well as periodic newsletters. 5/12/92

ABUNDANT LOVE INSTITUTE

• P.O. Box 4322-C
San Rafael, CA 94913-4322

(415)507-1739
pad@well.sf.ca.us

—or—

• P.O. Box 6306
Ocean View, HI 96737

(808)929-9691/929-9831 Fax

After working separately for over ten years to launch the Polyamory Movement, PEP's Ryam Nearing and IntiNet's Deborah Anapol have joined forces in producing *Loving More Magazine* and in hosting regional polyamory conferences and workshops covering every aspect of expanded, loving relationships. In addition to their quarterly magazine, they offer two books on polyamory basics: *Love Without Limits* and *The Polyfidelity Primer*,

personal ads and referrals to local support groups, a lending library (including Rimmer's out-of-print classics), on-line computer conferencing and referrals, and more. Send $6 for a sample copy of *Loving More Magazine*, or a SASE for information about membership, benefits, and events. 12/21/94

ACRES, U.S.A.

P.O. Box 8800
Metairie, LA 70011-8800

(504)889-2100
(504)889-2777 Fax

Acres U.S.A. believes that in order to be economical, agriculture must be ecological. We publish a monthly newspaper featuring a wide range of articles on eco-farming and human health, operate a bookstore, and host an annual conference on sustainable agriculture. We offer information on soil dynamics, cultivation methods, organic soil amendments, and radical analyses of the American farm position vis-a-vis agribusiness, "Big Government," multinationals, etc. Subscription rates: U.S. $20 per year; international $23 (U.S. funds only). Samples: $2.50. Write for our free book catalog. 6/1/95

ACTION LINKAGE

P.O. Box 684
Bangor, ME 04401

(207)945-4330

We are a network of independent individuals who communicate with each other in an interactive dialog style on a variety of issues related to personal and social transformation. Our monthly newsletter ($50/year) includes sections on learning, economics, community, computers and society, cooperatives, libraries, and religious values. Please write for more information. 3/15/94

AERO

417 Roslyn Road
Roslyn Heights, NY 11577

(516)621-2195
(516)625-3257 Fax

The Alternative Education Resource Organization, founded and directed by Jerry Mintz, is sponsored by the School of Living. AERO helps people who want to change education to a more empowering and holistic form. It helps individuals and groups of people who want to start

new community schools (public and private), or change existing schools. It also provides information to people interested in homeschooling their children, or finding private or public alternative schools. It publishes a newsletter, *Aero-Gramme* ($15/yr), which offers networking news from many different realms of alternative and holistic education. It also has a national directory of alternative schools and homeschool resources, videos, speaking and consulting services; and compiled *The Handbook of Alternative Education* (500 pages, 7300 entries) available for $75 in hardcover (paperback won't be out for a year). 6/27/94

AFS

American Field Service
Intercultural Programs
220 East 42nd Street, 3rd Fl.
New York, NY 10017

(212)949-4242/(800)AFS-INFO

AFS is an international, nonprofit, non-governmental organization that promotes intercultural learning through worldwide exchange programs for students, teachers, adults, and families. Since its founding, AFS has been a people-to-people movement that transcends national, social, political, and religious barriers. We have a long-held commitment to socioeconomic diversity and are the only major citizen exchange organization in the U.S. which actively recruits minority, handicapped, and underprivileged teenagers, often with no expense to these participants. In 1993 *Money Magazine* listed AFS as the number one most efficient education charity in the U.S. Participants in AFS programs gain a more profound cultural understanding of other societies—which is essential to the achievement of social justice and lasting peace in a world of diversity. 8/3/93

ALLIANCE, THE

P.O. Box 143
Yonkers, NY 10710

(RESOURCE MAY BE DEFUNCT—LOST CONTACT 4/96)

We are a community pen-pal service for people who love community, and who look forward to receiving mail that shares their joy in expressing those feelings. We are most interested in hearing from other communities as well—so that intentional community can grow here in New York City. 1/14/94

ALTERNATIVE PRESS INDEX

P.O. Box 33109
Baltimore, MD 21218

(410)243-2471

The Alternative Press Index has been publishing since 1969. It is the most complete index available for periodicals that chronicle social change in the United States and around the world. Published quarterly, the API is a comprehensive guide to over 200 alternative, progressive, and radical newspapers, journals, and magazines. Articles are indexed by subjects in a format similar to the *Reader's Guide to Periodical Literature*. Over 10,000 citations appear in each issue, including over 400 book and film reviews. Institutional subscriptions are $125/year; individuals or movement groups $30. We also publish a *Directory of Alternate & Radical Publications* which is available for $4. 6/11/92

ALTERNATIVES CENTER

1740 Walnut Street
Berkeley, CA 94709

(510)540-5387

[Formerly Urban Alternatives.] "Planning and Facilitating: Democratic Meetings" (video), "The Mondragon Cooperatives" (video and several publications), "A Vision for Cooperatives," "Cooperative Democracy," "Converting Multi-Unit Housing into Limited Equity Cooperatives" are examples of our more than a dozen publications. We also offer education and consulting services in our region to cooperatives and communal groups. 1/11/93

AMERICAN YOUTH HOSTELS (AYH)

P.O. Box 37613
Washington, DC 20013-7613

(202)783-6161

Hostelling International/American Youth Hostels, a nonprofit organization, promotes international understanding through its network of hostels and educational and recreational travel programs. Hostels are inexpensive, dormitory-style accommodations for travelers of all ages. The AYH network includes over 200 hostels nationwide in major cities and beautiful natural settings. Most hostels have rooms available for couples, families, and large groups. AYH is the U.S. affiliate of the International Youth Hostel Federation which maintains 6000 hostels in 70 countries. 9/9/92

ANIMAL TOWN

P.O. Box 485
Healdsburg, CA 95448-0485

(800)445-8642

Cooperative games have been played in many cultures for centuries, but very few games today are designed so that all players strive toward one common goal. Most competitive games cause players to feel isolated or left out. Cooperative and noncompetitive games encourage children and adults to feel good about each other during the game process... they like making joint decisions, sharing, and helping one another. A good game has excitement, fair play, harmony, and a good challenge. We are a mail-order company that invents and manufactures cooperative board games for children and adults. Please write for one of our free catalogs. 1/5/95

APPROPRIATE TECHNOLOGY PROJECT

Volunteers in Asia
P.O. Box 4543
Stanford, CA 94309

(800)648-8043
(415)326-8581/326-3475 Fax

The primary function of the A.T. project is the production and sale of the Appropriate Technology Microfiche Library, updated in 1992 to contain the complete text on microfiche of over 1000 of the most useful appropriate tech books from around the world. We also sell the Appropriate Technology Sourcebook, which has been the standard reference for people working in village technology and small-scale development for over fifteen years. The sourcebook, also updated and revised in 1992, contains complete price and ordering information for over 1200 appropriate tech books, and serves as an index for the microfiche library. Call toll-free to place orders or for more information. 5/28/92

APROVECHO RESEARCH CENTER

80574 Hazelton Road
Cottage Grove, OR 97424

(541)942-8198
(541)942-0110 Fax Service

Aprovecho Institute is a nonprofit international membership organization devoted to research and education in ecologically sustainable and culturally appropriate technologies and lifestyles. Our 40-acre Research Center houses resident staff, interns, our main office, our garden and forest, and most of our research facilities. Three-month internships include practical experience and instruction in organic gardening, permaculture, appropriate technology, ecoforestry, and community living. These cost $500/mo and start March 1, June 1, and Sept. 1 each year. Some interns participate in affiliated programs in Mexico, Tanzania, and elsewhere. We also hold shorter courses and workshops, do consultations, publish educational materials, and produce a quarterly newsletter. Memberships are $30/yr. While our fuel-efficient wood cookstove designs are internationally known, we are increasingly involved in various solar technologies, agroforestry, bioregional self-reliant food growing, cross-cultural exchange, and community building. Send SASE for more information. 1/17/95

AQUARIAN RESEARCH FOUNDATION

5620 Morton Street
Philadelphia, PA 19144-1330

(215)849-1259/849-3237
(800)641-6545 Community Info
arosenblum@mcimail.com

Aquarian offers better phone deals! We can provide the lowest cost long-distance service with free personal accounting codes, 800 numbers, no surcharge phone cards. We can reduce your lowest present rate at least 10% or give you day/night interstate calls for 13.5–14.5 cents per min. Aquarian is using this service and whatever revenue it provides to help build national and worldwide cooperative movements.

Earth will have two *billion* youth, mostly unemployed, between the ages of 10 and 21 by the year 2000. How? Infant mortality has dropped far more than birth rates. Neither Capitalism nor Communism can support such numbers ...so it is urgent to spread the message of cooperative alternatives across America and the planet. We use our 4-place Cessna to fly folks on communal visits we can arrange. Write for a sample of the *Aquarian Alternatives Newsletter*; small donation or 55¢ SASE helps. [See separate listing in the Communities section.] 1/10/95

ARTHUR MORGAN SCHOOL

**1901 Hannah Branch Road
Burnsville, NC 28714**

(704)675-4262

A coeducational boarding/day school for 24 students in 7th–9th grades. Students are involved in working, studying, hiking, caring, coping, learning, and living in a small intentional community in the Black Mountains of North Carolina. [See separate listing for Celo Community.] 1/3/94

AUDUBON EXPEDITION INSTITUTE

**P.O. Box 365
Belfast, ME 04915**

(207)338-5859

Graduate and undergraduate students participate in a consensus-run, community-based environmental education program which travels throughout the U.S. and Canada. Students observe and study societal patterns of behavior and their impact on our fragile ecosystems. Students become active participants in a community and an educational process which emphasizes total involvement in the conservation and preservation of the planet Earth.

Leadership, conflict resolution, and creative problem-solving skills are emphasized in conjunction with progressive teaching techniques and a deep ecological perspective. Environmental issues are explored by meeting directly with the people involved in them—political leaders, corporate executives, environmental activists, loggers, miners, nuclear industry representatives, and many others. 7/30/93

AUNT LINDA

**P.O. Box 85
Rainbow Lake, NY 12976**

(518)327-3222

[Formerly "Hugs for the Heart."] Want to teach your children at home? Share your life philosophy with them 24 hours a day! Comprehensive new resource list includes all the information you need to get started—books, magazines, organizations, curriculum providers, catalogs, and Aunt Linda's "Down to Earth" Q&A sheet. All resources are coded secular/non-secular so you don't waste your valuable time and money—or precious trees and paper!

Discover a joyful, holistic, family learning experience that allows you the freedom to live your ideals. Send $4 to Linda Dobson at address above. Happy Learning! 5/22/92

AUROVILLE INTERNATIONAL USA

**P.O. Box 162489
Sacramento, CA 95816**

(916)452-4013

Auroville International has its main offices in Holland and its secretariat in Paris. It has members in most parts of the world and centers in Holland, France, USA, Canada, Sweden, Italy, Germany, Switzerland, and the United Kingdom. These centers are bases of support for and information about Auroville—providing videos for purchase or rental, some books, overviews, project brochures, postcards, and a calendar. The centers are nonprofit organizations, and can receive and channel donations to the community in India. 7/25/94

BEHAVIOR ANALYSIS & CULTURAL DESIGN

**Center for
the Study of
Social Work Practice
622 W. 113th Street
New York, NY 10025**

(212)854-8600

Behavior Analysis & Cultural Design is a special interest group of the Association for Behavior Analysis. The goals of BACD are to share information about cultural design, and to actively encourage and support the growth and development of experimental communities. Through annual meetings and our newsletter, we share data on community behavioral experiments and we organize symposia, panels, and workshops on relevant topics. Our members are interested in the design and analysis of variables that impact individuals at the cultural level, as well as the interface between the behavior analysis of culture and related fields such as anthropology, sociology, economics, and political science. 1/19/93

BIO-DYNAMIC FARMING & GARDENING ASSOC.

**P.O. Box 550
Kimberton, PA 19442**

**(215)935-7797 / 983-3196 Fax
(800)516-7797**

The Bio-Dynamic Farming and Gardening Association (founded in 1938) provides technical assistance, education, research, training, conferences, human support, biodynamic compost preparations, books, magazines, and videos. It serves the USA, Canada, and Central America...and is connected with other biodynamic groups worldwide. Membership dues are $20/yr. and include the quarterly magazine *Biodynamics* and a bimonthly newsletter. Consumers nationwide can call toll-free to request information about Biodynamic and Community Supported Agriculture (CSA) farms and gardens in their area, and may also request a free copy of the brochure, "Introduction to Community Supported Farms/Farm Supported Communities." The association also offers a free resource catalog featuring publications and audio/video tapes about CSAs, highlighting grower and consumer success stories. 6/30/93

BIOREGIONAL PROJECT

**P.O. Box 3
Brixley, MO 65618**

(417)679-4773

The Bioregional Project was created in 1982 to aid in the development of the Bioregional movement in North America. In the long term we work for the reformation and redesign of human societies according to ecological laws and principles, toward the time when human population can live in mutually beneficial cooperation with—and within—the planet's naturally occurring ecosystems.

Our work takes the following forms: 1) We can answer your general questions and put you in touch with people active in your area. 2) We write and publish booklets, pamphlets, and general information on bioregionalism. 3) We can come to your area to give lectures and other educational presentations. 4) We can help you organize bioregional events, conferences, or congresses.

The focus of bioregionalists includes sustainable economics and business, appropriate technology, organic agriculture/permaculture, renewable resource development, forest husbandry, water quality, land stewardship, peace, "all-species" rights, conservation and environment protection, holistic health and education, media and communications. 1/4/93

BOOK PUBLISHING CO.

P.O. Box 99
Summertown, TN 38483

(800)695-2241

The Book Publishing Co. is owned and operated by members of The Farm, an intentional community founded in 1971 in rural Tennessee. We publish a number of books on topics as varied as midwifery, vegetarian cooking (notably tofu and tempeh cookbooks), and community lifestyles. [See ad for *Builders of the Dawn* on page 252.]

BOUND TOGETHER BOOKS

1369 Haight Street
San Francisco, CA 94117

(415)431-8355

We are an all-volunteer, collectively operated anarchist bookshop...now 18 years old. We carry a range of alternative political and cultural titles, both historical and contemporary, with a special emphasis on anti-authoritarian materials (although many gay, women's, and magic titles grace our shelves as well). We also carry magazines and a large array of pamphlets.

Our intent is to provide a cultural/political perspective to the public—something beyond the "fast food" mentality that prevails in book publishing—and to help sustain the small presses that put out alternative political/cultural materials. We also do a Prisoners Literature Project, and put out a mail-order catalog, regularly updated (available for two 25¢ stamps, for return postage). 8/23/94

BRIARPATCH NETWORK

San Francisco, CA

Established in 1974, our primary purpose is to promote Right Livelihood (figuring out what creative socially responsible things you want to accomplish in life, then finding a way to support yourself by doing it), mutual support, and socializing through a very loose "personal" network. Network membership includes over 400 alternative business organizations ranging from benevolent dictatorships to worker-owned businesses. The success rate for member businesses is 80% (a phenomenal accomplishment when contrasted to

the 20% success rate of small businesses in the US). The network regularly sponsors workshops and networking socials, and has a team of roving consultants who visit member businesses every Wednesday (scheduled in advance, by request only). Membership is open, and dues are voluntary—but to get involved you need to be introduced by a friend or acquaintance who is already a member (we have a "no publicity" policy). 8/15/94

BROWN, STEPHAN

Consultant
303 Hardister
Cloverdale, CA 95425

(707)894-9466

Stephan Brown, founder of Shenoa Retreat and Learning Center, offers consulting and workshops on the practical realities of developing communities and centers for retreats, conferences, and workshops. Areas covered include ownership, management, legal, financial, and real estate.

BUSINESS ETHICS MAGAZINE

52 S. 10th Street #110
Minneapolis, MN 55403

(612)962-4700

The only national magazine of socially responsible business, offering practical advice and thoughtful views on new styles of management. It covers progressive personnel management, environmental marketing, social investing, ethical case studies, employee ownership, and more. Includes interviews with enlightened corporate leaders, company news, trend analysis. Encourages perspective on life and work through "Musings" and "The Pursuit of Happiness." 6 issues/year for $25. 9/2/93

CANBRIDGE

c/o Laird Schaub
Route 1, Box 155-D
Rutledge, MO 63563

(816)883-5545 Voice/Fax

CANBRIDGE (Consensus And Network Building to Resolve Impasse and Develop

Group Effectiveness) is a consulting team of experienced communitarians who help groups make their meetings more productive and enjoyable—while getting through and beyond the "tough" issues. We offer training in consensus and meeting facilitation, and are available to facilitate any size group or boulder-strewn agenda where skilled, outside support is particularly valuable. We work constructively with both rational and emotional input, and emphasize teaching the skills that we demonstrate—so that next time your group will be better prepared to negotiate those rocky moments without relying on outside navigators. Write or call us if you're interested in enhancing your group's vitality, cohesion, and effectiveness. 2/14/95

CANTERBURY SHAKER VILLAGE

288 Shaker Road
Canterbury, NH 03224

(603)783-9511

Canterbury Shaker Village is a historic site museum—created to rediscover, preserve, interpret, and celebrate the purposeful way of life led by the Shakers from the 1780s to the present. Serenely sited on 694 acres on a rolling hilltop, Canterbury Shaker Village guides the public through a world of beautiful images preserved through the ongoing stewardship of manuscripts, photographs, artifacts, and 24 original buildings. Respectful interpretation of the Shaker traditions and demonstrations of their timeless crafts offer insights into the values lived by a utopian religious community. A restaurant offering Shaker-inspired food, and a gift shop featuring Shaker reproductions are on site. 11/23/92

CARETAKER GAZETTE

1845 NW Deanne-K
Pullman WA 99163-3509

(509)332-0806

The *Caretaker Gazette* is a unique newsletter containing job openings, shared living arrangements, advice and information for property caretakers, housesitters, and landowners. Property caretakers can enjoy rent-free living by bartering their skills. Published since 1983, the *Caretaker Gazette* includes letters, caretaker profiles, and classified ads. We provide a free advertising service for folks looking to promote cooperative living on their land; many intentional cooperative communities have had great success in finding members by placing free ads in the *Gazette*! Each issue contains over 50 job opportunities, partnerships, apprenticeships, and cooperative living arrangements throughout the world. A bimonthly publication, subscriptions are only $15/half year (3 issues), $24/year (6 issues), or $44/two years (12 issues). All new subscribers will also receive a complimentary copy of the Gazette's "Report on Caretaking" which contains an in-depth look at caretaking issues. 1/18/95

CATALYST
P.O. Box 1308
Montpelier, VT 05601
(802)223-7943
(RESOURCE MAY BE DEFUNCT—LOST CONTACT 4/96)
Catalyst is a grassroots organization that connects economics, ecology, and human rights. We offer resources on economic alternatives and corporate (lack of) accountability. Current projects include bioregional organizing, economic alternatives discussion series, corporate research, and focusing on jobs and empowerment in Vermont to create a sustainable economy. We publish a quarterly (more or less) journal, included with membership, $25/yr. 1/5/93

CAUSE
Creative Alternatives
Using Sustainable Energy
P.O. Box 479
Sequim, WA 98382
(360)683-1437
(RESOURCE MAY BE DEFUNCT—LOST CONTACT 6/95)
Our purpose is to educate the public on renewable energy and alternative transportation resources via their practical application. 8/31/93

CENTER FOR COMMUNAL STUDIES
8600 University Boulevard
Univ. of Southern Indiana
Evansville, IN 47712
(812)464-1727/464-1960 Fax
Center for Communal Studies serves as an international clearinghouse for community information. CCS is a research facility with a communal database and an archival collection of manuscripts,

photographs, recordings, publications, and artifacts from 130 historic and nearly 550 contemporary intentional communities. CCS sponsors conferences, seminars, classes, speakers, publications, small research grants, and related educational projects. We welcome inquiries, program suggestions, and materials for the Center archives. 6/28/94

CENTER FOR CONFLICT RESOLUTION
731 State Street
Madison, WI 53703
(608)255-0479
A nonprofit educational collective offering workshops, consultations, intervention, and a resource center providing information on conflict, group process, and problem solving. We have also sponsored several conferences on peace-related issues and social concerns, and have provided training for nonviolent action.

We have compiled *A Manual for Group Facilitators* and *Building United Judgment: A Handbook for Consensus Decision Making*, available for $14.95 each (plus shipping and handling). Workshop topics include conflict resolution, decision making, meeting skills, facilitation, communication skills, program planning, and community organizing. Fees are on a sliding scale, and workshops are individually tailored to meet the needs of specific groups. Please write for more information. 1/5/95

CENTER FOR COOPERATIVES
University of California
Davis, CA 95616
(916)752-2408/752-5451 Fax
The Center for Cooperatives is an outreach unit of the University of California which supports cooperative development through communication about and support for cooperatives. The Center serves housing, agricultural, consumer, childcare, credit, and other cooperatives—drawing its teaching and research resources from both academia and the broader cooperative community. The center 1) offers member and director education programs to those involved in cooperatives, and develops resource materials for all levels of interest; 2) conducts research on economic, social, and technical developments; and 3) seeks to inform the public on cooperatives and their significance in the economy. Write for our free catalog

of publications including the new *Cooperative Housing Compendium* ($14.95 + $3.00 shipping). 2/11/94

CENTER FOR INTEGRAL COMMUNITY
P.O. Box 1777
Big Fork, MT 59911
The Center for Integral Community provides group facilitation services to help any group build community in whatever way suits them. You can benefit from our workshops if you are an existing or forming intentional community group, a spiritual group, a work group, etc. We believe that true community is the next phase of global evolution, the primary cure for human physical and spiritual suffering, and the primary source of our true joy. Our services are free.

We also maintain the Integral Community Network for those interested in cooperatively designing an integral community-building model and associated group processes. We publish a book describing the integral model called *Building Integral Community* (suggested donation: $10 to $20 per copy). Our integral community-building model includes these dimensions: inner (soul), outer (institutional), inclusion (from individual to planetary and universal), depth, and duration. We seek to maximize community on all these dimensions. 4/15/94

CENTER FOR POPULAR ECONOMICS
P.O. Box 785
Amherst, MA 01004
(413)545-0743
The Center for Popular Economics holds workshops and institutes on economics for activists and educators with critical perspective of US capitalism and international profiteering. Call or write for more information. 12/7/92

CENTER FOR SACRED SCIENCES
1430 Willamette #164
Eugene, OR 97401-4049
(541)345-0102
The Center for Sacred Sciences is a nonprofit tax-exempt organization dedicated to the creation and dissemination of a new Worldview based on the wisdom of humanity's great spiritual teachers, but presented in forms appropriate to our

present scientific culture. To this end we offer weekly Sunday talks given by our Spiritual Director (Joel), meditation instructions, videos, and workshops. We also maintain a library of books and tapes including mystical classics, new physics, mythology, psychology, and women's spirituality. Write to the address above to receive more information and our free newsletter. Call for the times and locations of events. 12/7/92

CENTRAL ROCKY MOUNTAIN PERMACULTURE INST.

P.O. Box 631
Basalt, CO 81621

(970)927-4158

CRMPI, a nonprofit organization, offers permaculture design consulting for the creation of integrated food production systems for farms and communities. Week-end sustainable agriculture workshops can be given on-site at your community. CRMPI hosts many educational programs, including a five-week certified permaculture design and self-reliance internship,

Special Outreach 2-for-1 Offer

Help us get the word out about intentional communities...and we'll help you get the word out about whatever you'd like to advertise in our quarterly, *Communities* magazine.

Here's the deal: for every copy of this directory you buy for a library, we'll ship the book with your compliments and give you dollar-for-dollar credit toward *Communities* advertising. What's to lose? See the display ad on page 351 for details about this fantastic 2-for-1 offer.

on its 8-acre forest garden demonstration farm (with outdoor terraced beds for organic gardening; high altitude orchard; and a 2300 square foot greenhouse with an integrated heating system incorporating solar energy, compost, and chickens as a source of heat for year-round production). In Nicaragua, CRMPI has established an organic garden classroom at an elementary school in Teotecacinte as part of a sister city project, and is developing a permaculture demonstration farm there to help provide information on sustainable agriculture. 1/18/93

CHILDREN OF THE GREEN EARTH

P.O. Box 31087
Seattle, WA 98103

(206)523-6279

Children of the Green Earth is a nonprofit educational organization committed to creating a global network of children who, by planting and caring for trees, experience themselves as stewards of the Earth and as part of one human family. Members receive newsletters containing articles on tree planting projects being done worldwide, folk tales of tree planters, contacts for international partnerships, and a list of resources for teachers. Please write or phone for more information. 5/25/92

CHURCH OF ALL WORLDS GREEN EGG MAGAZINE

P.O. Box 1542
Ukiah, CA 95482

(707)485-0481

CAW (est. '62) is an organization of individuals who regard the Earth and life on it as sacred. Living in harmony and understanding with life's myriad forms is a religious act. In 1968 CAW was the first of the Neo-Pagan Earth Religions to obtain full Federal recognition.

While we prescribe no particular dogma or creed, our commonality lies in our reverence and connection with Nature and with Mother Earth, seeing her as a conscious, living entity. We embrace philosophical concepts of immanent divinity and emergent evolution, and are essentially "Neo-Pagan" (an eclectic reconstruction of ancient Nature religions, combining archetypes of many cultures with other mystic and spiritual disciplines).

CAW has chartered a number of subsidiary branch congregations known as

"nests" through which we practice and teach our religion [see community listing for Crow's Nest]. The Church publishes a quarterly, *Green Egg* magazine, which features interviews, essays, fiction, comics, environmental action, columns, and an extensive reader forum. One-year subscriptions are $18 US, $25 Canada, $31 overseas air; back issues are $5 US postpaid. 9/20/94

CIRCLE NETWORK

P.O. Box 219
Mt. Horeb, WI 53572

(608)924-2216/M–F 1–4pm

Circle Network is an international referral and information exchange network of Wiccan, Pagan, Goddess Spirituality, Shamanic, and other Nature Spirituality practitioners, groups, communities, and centers. Circle Network is linked through a variety of networking periodicals including resource directories and a quarterly news journal. The network's annual gathering is a week-long Summer Solstice festival. Within Circle Network there are several specialty networks: the Pagan Spirit Alliance encourages friendship and support among Pagans; the Lady Liberty League focuses on Pagan religious freedom issues and actions; the Pagan Academic Network facilitates communication among professors, scholars, and students engaged in Pagan-related research and academic publishing. Circle Network, founded in 1977 by Selena Fox, is a service of Circle Sanctuary, a Wiccan church and Pagan resource center [see community listing]. Free literature with more details is available upon request. 12/15/94

CIRCLE OF SONG

Full Circle Press
P.O. Box 428
Amherst, MA 01004

(413)256-1186
(800)275-2606

A ceremonial resource book, ideal for community celebrations and rituals. Features over 300 songs and chants for all ages with music and lyrics from many global sources, 40 dances, 34 guided meditations, 60 illustrations, and an extensive index and resource guide. This impressive, inspiring collection is organized by thematic divisions for easy use, divided into categories such as sacred space, the elements, honoring our relations, love and healing, etc. Includes a large contemporary Neo-Pagan section as well as chants drawn from the

Native American tradition, the women's and men's movement, and the world's major religions. $17.95 Postpaid. 2/17/94

CIRCLE PINES CENTER

8650 Mullen Road
Delton, MI 49046

(616)623-5555

Circle Pines Center is a nonprofit educational and recreational cooperative located on 360 acres of meadows, forests, and a lake in southwestern Michigan. We operate a summer camp for families and children—featuring noncompetitive games, cooperative work projects, peace education, group-building activities, canoeing and swimming, nature studies, and creative arts. Our work with peace education is based on the premise that the caring relationships we develop and model with each other will further efforts down the line in supporting each other in group actions. We are open year-round, hosting a Winter Weekends cross-country skiing and natural healing program, and providing conference and seminar space in the spring and the fall. 12/10/94

CMHA

California Mutual
Housing Association
2500 Wilshire PH#B
Los Angeles, CA 90057

(213)385-5365

The California Mutual Housing Association (CMHA) is a statewide organization that provides training and support services to resident-controlled housing, including existing limited-equity housing cooperatives and tenant associations aspiring to ownership. Participants in these programs include public housing residents, subsidized housing residents, and other very low-income, low-income, and moderate-income residents living in other forms of affordable housing. 9/7/94

CO-OP AMERICA

1612 K St NW #600
Washington, DC 20006

(202)872-5307

Co-op America is a nonprofit member-controlled, worker-managed organization dedicated to building a more cooperative, peaceful, and just economy...and a healthy, safe environment. We strive to stop corporate irresponsibility, to create green businesses and green jobs, to unleash the power of a real green consumer movement, and to build sustainable communities. By teaching people how to vote with their dollars, we are changing the way America does business. Co-op America puts members in touch with an alternative marketplace of businesses, co-ops, "green" producers, alternative trading organizations, and other groups that put their values into their business. Member benefits include a quarterly magazine; *Boycott Action News*; a catalog of environmentally and socially responsible products; a *Socially Responsible Financial Planning Handbook*; the *National Green Pages*, a directory of responsible businesses; and access to an investment service, travel service, health insurance program, VISA card through a socially responsible institution, and long-distance phone service in conjunction with Working Assets. Membership is $25 for individuals, and $60 for organizations. (Organizations receive different benefits, including listing in the *National Green Pages*, reduced advertising, access to our mailing lists, and more.) 6/11/92

CO-OP CAMP SIERRA / CAZADERO

1442-A Walnut Street #415
Berkeley, CA 94709

(510)595-0873

Co-op camp celebrated its 55th season in 1995. Camp is for families, single-parent families, and singles. Cooperators from all over California (and elsewhere) come to relax in the beautiful Sierra Mountains in July, and at the Russian River in August, enjoying outings and recreation, socializing, and discussions about issues related to worker, housing, and consumer cooperatives. Attendees are members of all types of cooperatives, and many get involved in planning and implementing camp activities.

A morning discussion series—facilitated by key resource people from the cooperative movement—is at the core of the education program. To make it easier for adults to attend, there is a supervised

children's program at this time. Afternoons are open for relaxing or for outings and adventures, and evenings are packed with optional slide shows, sing-alongs, carnivals, volleyball, and the like. There is also quite a teen scene.

The camps have a full array of facilities, and rates vary according to choice of accommodations—ranging from private cabins to tent camping. Traditionally camp has been held the first two weeks in July at Camp Sierra (the 2nd week now includes the annual Twin Pines Cooperative Housing Institute), and we've added a 3rd week held at Cazadero in August. There is also an annual winter trip during ski season. Write for information packet. 9/1/95

CO-OP RESOURCE CENTER

1442-A Walnut Street #415
Berkeley, CA 94709
(510)538-0454

The Co-op Resource Center, established in 1980, has 17 cooperative member organizations. We publish a free catalog of resource materials available by mail. The 1994 catalog holds some 400 items ranging from books, to reprints, to T-shirts, and audio/visuals for cooperatives of all kinds. We also act as a clearing house for the sharing of information and technical resources among cooperatives and like-minded organizations. 7/27/94

COHOUSING CENTER

103 Morse Street
Watertown, MA 02172
(617)923-1300/923-4987 Fax

The Cohousing Center, founded by Marc Daigle, John Adelberg, and Mino Sullivan, is a development management and architectural design firm specializing in creating cohousing communities. The Center provides a way for people to come together to envision and create cohousing neighborhoods. Through public outreach and education, the use of an extensive database, introductory meetings, and technical workshops, the Center helps each group build a strong membership.

The firm's approach is to enable groups to focus on the essential aspects of creating their communities while removing the burdens of the technical details of the development process. Our services include group facilitation, public relations, project management, site search and acquisition, feasibility studies, land planning and architecture, financing, and construction

management. The Center is currently assisting three greater Boston cohousing groups as well as groups in Peterborough, NH, and Providence, RI. 7/18/94

COHOUSING COMPANY, THE

1250 Addison Street #113
Berkeley, CA 94702
(510)549-9980

The CoHousing Company is an architectural design and development firm formed to facilitate the creation of cohousing communities. Its principals, Kathryn McCamant and Charles Durrett, authored the book *CoHousing: A Contemporary Approach to Housing Ourselves*, available from us for $24.45, which introduced the concept to this country. Since then we have completed several communities on the West Coast and consulted with many others nationwide. We guide resident groups through the entire development process, including group formation and facilitation, site search and acquisition, group process, participatory design, architectural services, finance, and management. We act as a nationwide clearinghouse of cohousing activities, and offer workshops and slide presentations across the country. 3/8/93

COHOUSING NETWORK

P.O. Box 2584
Berkeley, CA 94702
(510)526-6124

The CoHousing Network is the publisher of *CoHousing*, the quarterly journal of the

COHOUSING COMMUNITIES

...combine the autonomy of private dwellings with the advantages of community living. Residents participate in the planning and design of the community so that it directly responds to their needs. Each household has a private residence, but also shares extensive common facilities with the larger group (such as a dining hall, children's playrooms, workshops, guest rooms, and laundry facilities). Although individual dwellings are designed to be self-sufficient and each has its own kitchen, the common facilities (and in particular the common dinners) are an important aspect of community life for both social and practical reasons.

— SEE THE INDEX —

cohousing movement. The journal includes news about cohousing projects under development throughout the U.S. and Canada, reports on life in cohousing communities, educational features about critical issues in development/management of communities, interviews with key figures in the cohousing movement, and resource listings. Members of cohousing groups and communities in every part of the U.S. and Canada participate on the editorial team of the journal, which has been published since 1987. Subscription rates: $25 per year or $5 for a sample copy. 2/7/94

COLUMBIANA MAGAZINE

Chesaw Route, Box 83-F
Oroville, WA 98844
(509)485-3844

A bioregional journal of/for the Intermountain Northwest, published by a nonprofit group, which offers space for the writers and artists of the region. All materials published are relevant to that particular bioregion, and include articles on environmentally sensitive visions, lifestyles, and political choices; self-help health care and nutrition; home-based businesses; family concerns; alternative technology; sustainable agriculture/permaculture; urban and rural feminism; natural and regional history; international concerns; reviews of relevant books, magazines, and music; regional fiction and poetry. Subscriptions $15/year for 6 issues. 3/15/94

COMMITTEE FOR UNIVERSAL SECURITY

Zero Tolerance Toxic Campaign
1095-A Smith Grade Rd.
Santa Cruz, CA 95060
(408)429-9623

The Committee for Universal Security disseminates information concerning the threat of toxic synthetic petrochemicals. We are calling for a security movement to prevent chemical annihilation from the massive amounts of bio assault chemical compounds which are produced worldwide.

We mandate a halt to all usage of petroleum, uranium, chlorine, and coal —as these four raw materials are the basic toxic components of synthetic engineering which is poisoning the world to death. We urge that the environmental movement be upgraded to a security movement, and that all human efforts be put to the task of securing the planet from imminent chemical catastrophe. We offer support to people who have been chemically injured, and recognize that the growing number of chemically injured people is indicative of the problem that toxic technologies is causing. It is clear to us that the natural biological chemistry of the life design is under assault and being altered by invasive chemical compounds. 1/1/93

COMMUNES NETWORK

c/o Redfield Community
Buckingham Road
Winslow
Buckinghamshire
MK18-3LZ ENGLAND

44 226296 713661
e-mail: redfield@gn

Communes Network is a loose, British-based collection of people who are involved or interested in communal living in all its shapes and sizes. Our magazine, also called *Communes Network*, is our open channel for communicating with each other—to exchange information, news, opinions, and our experiences of collective living. It comes out about four times a year and features a regular column devoted to People needing Places needing People. Traditionally, editorship of the magazine has moved from group to group, but we are now looking into the possibility of concentrating production but having an editorial group drawn from a number of communities. *Diggers and Dreamers*—the biennial directory of British communities, has blossomed from *Communes Network* and is now produced as a parallel publication designed to reach a wider audience. Communes Network gatherings are also held from time to time and have

---

---

proved to be a useful forum for exchanging ideas. A subscription covering 8 issues of the magazine costs £7.50 in the UK; £9.50 for worldwide surface mail; and £13.50 for airmail to North America (cheques to "Communes Network," sterling only please). 5/10/92

COMMUNITIES CONNEXION

P.O. Box 8608
Portland, OR 97207

(503)284-0573

Networking process for all intentional-spiritual communities in the Cascadia Bioregion. Weekly Monday evening meeting held in Portland, Oregon, with potluck, introductions and networking, community bulletin board, resource center, and guest speakers on a wide range of topics related to creating intentional, multicultural, sustainable, spiritual community. $3 donation requested to help cover costs. Write or phone for additional information. 12/10/93

COMMUNITIES, JOURNAL OF COOPERATIVE LIVING

Editorial Office:
• Route 1, Box 155-D
Rutledge, MO 63563

(816)883-5545

Subscriptions:
• 138-D6 Twin Oaks Road
Louisa, VA 23093

(540)894-5126

Since 1972, *Communities* magazine has reported on the development of intentional communities—from people building together in urban neighborhoods, to rural farm communities—with articles on community politics and group dynamics, family life and relationships, health and well-being, work and food cooperatives, and other areas of innovation and expertise developed by or applicable to community living. Each quarterly issue includes articles on a featured theme, numerous columns by movement veterans, book reviews, "Reach" ads (for people looking and groups with openings), a calendar of community events, and a "Directory Update" section (with address changes plus any new listings that have been received). *Communities* is published by FIC, also the publisher of this directory. One-year subscriptions are $18 ($22 foreign). [See ad on inside front cover.] 2/14/95

COMMUNITY BOOKSHELF

East Wind Community
Tecumseh, MO 65760

(417)679-4682

Community Bookshelf is a mail-order book selling business which is communally run by East Wind, a rural industrial commune in south central Missouri. We pride ourselves on our fast personal service. Write for our free catalog of books on community, co-ops, and other aspects of alternative living and politics. [See ad on inside back cover.] 6/19/92

COMMUNITY CATALYST PROJECT

Geoph Kozeny
1531 Fulton Street
San Francisco, CA 94117-1334

CCP provides research, networking, and support for intentional communities and cooperatives. Our ambitious staff (presently one full-time volunteer) has to date visited nearly 300 communities. These field visits include research about each group's history, philosophy, and approaches to work, family, and daily life. This information is then shared with each subsequent group visited (and with the public) through slide shows and informal discussions.

CCP also provides referrals for people wanting to join a community (Geoph coordinated the Listings section of this directory) and for communities in need of particular information or skills. Expertise includes planning, design, and construction; publications and flyers (desktop publishing); photos and slide shows; facilitation and focalizing. Due to heavy project loads and mail forwarding delays, answering detailed correspondence is

---

impractical; phone calls work best—if you send in requests or questions, include times and phone number where you can be called collect. Most CCP work is funded by donations. [cc] 2/14/95

COMMUNITY CENTER FOR GAY/BI SPIRITUALITY, HEALING, AND THE ARTS

c/o Bemis Erectus Community
36 Bemis
San Francisco, CA 94131-3020

(415)334-6550 Gay
(415)587-5939 Bi
(415)861-0371 Fax
fcook@igc.apc.org

Gay Spirit is a group of men who do drumming, chanting, dance and expressive movement, shamanic journey work, healing, celebratory ritual. Sometimes we do these things outdoors, especially on equinoxes and solstices, to be closer to the earth. Our focus is earth-centered spiritual ways of knowing and acting in the world.

Men Meeting Men parties provide a wholesome, heartful alternative to the bar and bathhouse scenes. The parties include communication and sensitivity workshops, camaraderie, and a chance to meet diverse brothers in a safe sex, love, and intimacy-positive environment.

Dreambody Cinema Project is a group of movie buffs, screenwriters, and process workers who gather monthly to look at videos and sift out what can be useful in bringing transformation and paradigm shifts toward partnership culture. If Cinema is a collective dream of our society, how can we dream up a brighter future? Hosting such leading-edge groups at Bemis Erectus is our pride and joy [see community listing]. 1/2/95

COMMUNITY DIALTONE

1442-A Walnut St #151
Berkeley, CA 94709

(510)644-8085

Imagine you could create a telephone company specifically to serve the needs of intentional community—that's Community Dialtone. Community Dialtone gives you the kind of autonomy and self-reliance in your communications infrastructure that solar and wind power give you in your energy systems. We can provide design and installation of complete systems for any size community...including switching equipment, outside cable, inside wiring, telephones, voicemail, computer

networks, and more. Community Dialtone includes a range of features to make phone service more friendly and useful. Fully digital (ISDN) service is available. Systems can be configured to operate from alternative power sources. In many cases, the cost is significantly less than your local Bell company's service. Phone us to find out more; free initial consultation. 9/24/93

"COMMUNITY IN" ASSOCIATION

New Social Order in Messiah

"The Community In" Association:
[See individual community listings]
• Community in Island Pond
• Community in Boston
• Communauté de Sus [Int'l.]
• Community in Rutland
• Community in Sydney [Int'l.]
• Community in Bridgeport
• Community in Basin Farm
• Community in Buffalo
• Community in St. Joseph
• Community in Providence
• Comunidade de Londrina [Int'l.]
• Community in Winnipeg

Isn't there a tree where birds of every feather can flock together and find a nest, a place to belong, a home? Is living together close enough to really care for one another just an elusive dream? Will every attempt of diverse groups of people to love in unity of heart, mind, and purpose always be destined for miserable failure?

There is one network of communities here in the U.S. and elsewhere around the world where living together in peace and unity is real, and is growing as a whole new social order. Social means living together in communities. Order means a group of people united in an organized fashion. So this new social order is made up of a group of people who live together in actual communities, having the spiritual power to relate to one another in a new and living way, sharing an eternal companionship that is unattainable by mere human effort.

The life of this new social order is being expressed through a tribal people who follow Yahshua, the Messiah spoken of in the Bible. As this people, we have been steadily growing for twenty years. We are in New England, the Midwest, southern France, Brazil, Canada, and New Zealand —becoming spiritual Israel. We all work together to support ourselves, raise our children, teach them at home, and share a common life like

the disciples of Yahshua did in the first century (Acts 2:42–47; 4:32–37).

We are not held together by our own self effort, striving to perfect our human nature so that we can attain the perfect intentional community. Living in community by self effort doesn't bear good fruit. It ultimately fails, leaving damaged people in its wake, with a bad taste in their mouths.

What sets us apart from intentional communities is that we do not ask people to give up their lives in this present age, their dreams, desires, ambitions, agendas, and possessions just to live in one of our intentional communities. To do so would be like inviting you into a loving death or hell on earth as the old saying goes.

Instead our Master, Yahshua, called us to give up our lives in order to save us from eternal death and to give us eternal life. We couldn't get this life by self effort, but only by absolute surrender of our sovereignty to Him. In return, He gave us His life which is eternal life. Now, by the energizing power of His life within us, we have begun to experience this eternal life in advance of the new age to come as a witness, a signal, a sign, and standard of what it will be like then. So, when the new age comes as a result of our lives together, we too will share in it with our Master, Yahshua, when He returns (Rev, 11:15).

These tribal communities are becoming a nation that bears the fruit of what eternal life produces—love being perfected in unity. We have come together from many nations and backgrounds, both religious and nonreligious, to be a living demonstration of this unity that can only come about in Yahshua. It is possible now, in this life, but only because our Master has forgiven us of our sins and poured His love out in our heart by His Spirit, which enables us to live this new life now in this age, together.

Men were meant to love as our Master loved when He was on earth. This is how we become friends. And if this friendship is rooted and founded upon true faith in our Creator and divine love for one another, it will endure. As foretold by the prophet Ezekiel, birds of many different feathers from all races and all nations will flock together to find shelter in God's mighty tree (Ezekiel 17:23; Rev. 5:9,10).

This life is coming into existence because God is doing something extraordinary in these most difficult and confusing days. It is happening because His love is compelling men and women to give up their causes, their agendas, their possessions, and all their ambitions to follow Yahshua, the Messiah, in obedience to his word. To gain this life on earth now, it costs you everything. Our Master offers eternal life which always brings a person into a common life, true fellowship with birds of every feather who will never leave you or forsake you.

Eternal life is a totally new life, and to get this new life here and now, you must terminate your present independent life, come to Messiah's habitation, and surrender. In doing so, you will be immersed into a life together with others where you must be ready to be taught by God, through His people, a whole new way of living, thinking, and being. If you want to save any portion of your life in this present social order, you will lose it—that is, you will go to eternal death. But if you are ready to lose your life, utterly abandon it, for the sake of Messiah and the good news we proclaim, you will save it—which means that you will inherit eternal life (Mark 8:35).

Yahshua is the Son of God who died in our place for our sins. He suffered the death that we all deserve for the times we ignored our consciences. He knew the selfish center of man's heart that is the root cause of the massive problems plaguing the earth. He knew His people would sense their own personal guilt, their part in this destruction we see all around us. He knew they would want a way out, a way to be forgiven, a way to have a whole new existence. He knew they could be drawn to his love that was demonstrated for them when He died on the cross That's why anyone who actually believes that He died for their sins, will actually no longer live for themselves, but for Him who died and rose again on

their behalf (2 Corinthians 5:14,15). They will give all their possessions and all their energy to see His people gathered together as one nation (Acts 4:32–27).

This, in a nutshell, is what we're all about. If after reading this you're still looking for intentional community, life in the twelve communities listed below is not for you. But if you are looking for actual community, if the life we have talked about here stirs your heart and challenges your spirit, come and see. "Whoever has the Son, has the life." (1 John, 5:12). 6/15/93

COMMUNITY SERVICE, INC.

**P.O. Box 243
Yellow Springs, OH 45387**

**(513)767-2161
(513)767-1461**

Community Service, Inc. is a nonprofit organization started 50 years ago to help small communities become better places to live. Its purpose is to promote the small community as a basic social institution involving organic units of economic, social, and spiritual development.

The work of CSI is carried on through our bimonthly newsletter, mail-order book service, correspondence, and annual conference. Membership is the means of supporting and sharing in the work of Community Service. The basic $25 annual contribution includes a subscription to our bimonthly newsletter. Write or phone for a free sample of our newsletter and book list. 12/10/92

COMMUNITY-SEEKERS' NETWORK OF NEW ENGLAND

**c/o 15 Marcus Rd
Sharon MA 02067**

(617)784-4297

We are a regional network for joining and starting Intentional Communities, and for learning about issues that are relevant to the Communities movement, as a whole. We have established/are creating: meetings, dinner, group trips to established communities, a Newsletter with a "Many-to-Many/Open Letters Forum, and a Catalogue of Vision Statements by individuals, Core Groups, and Communities that are reforming. We welcome inquiries from outside our region. 2/15/96

COMPOST PATCH, INC.

**306 Coleridge Avenue
Altoona, PA 16602**

(814)946-9291

The Compost Patch, Inc. is a nonprofit educational and networking center. We cover a broad spectrum of alternative ideas and movements. Our newsletter writes about those innovative and imaginative individuals, groups, and communities that are moving beyond the industrial values that no longer work. We are a clearinghouse for materials on the issues described above, as well as information about the waste crisis. Write for sample issue of our newsletter. 1/2/93

COUNCIL ON ECONOMIC PRIORITIES

**30 Irving Place
New York, NY 10003-2386**

(212)420-1133

CEP is an independent, public interest organization that researches corporate social responsibility, environmental issues, and conversion to a peace economy. Since 1969, CEP has published more than 1000 studies, books, and reports on such issues as child care, pollution, and the politics of defense contracting. Recent publications include: *Students Shopping for a Better World* (CEP & Ballantine Books), a guide that rates the policies of 166 companies on the environment, women's and minority advancement, and disclosure of information; *Shopping for a Better World* (CEP & Ballantine Books), a guide to socially responsible supermarket shopping; and *The Better World Investment Guide* (Prentice Hall), which profiles major ethical funds and evaluates 100 large and small publicly held companies. CEP members receive a free copy of our shopping guide, a free subscription to our monthly *Research Reports*, and a 20% discount on all CEP publications and products. 12/11/92

CRSP

**Co-op Resources
& Services Project
3551 White House Place
Los Angeles, CA 90004**

**(213)738-1254
e-mail: crsp@igc.org**

CRSP is a 14-year-old nonprofit tax-exempt organization committed to small ecological cooperative communities. We are a membership organization with an extensive lending library of books, publications, audio and video materials. We have a publications list, provide a start-up package for Local Exchange Trading Systems, provide frequent opportunities for discussion on a broad range of related topics, publish an occasional newsletter, and provide some technical assistance for urban neighborhood groups which want to retrofit for sustainability. Two books, coedited by our staff, include *Sustainable Cities: Concepts and Strategies for Eco-City Development* ($22) and *Cooperative Housing Compendium: Resources for Collaborative Living* ($17). Membership is $25/yr. for individuals and $50/yr. for organizations and includes free use of library materials, discounts on publications, use of hotline, and occasional newsletter. We also provide coordination and technical assistance for the Los Angeles Eco-Village Demonstration [see article on page 109]. 5/10/94

COMMUNAL STUDIES ASSOCIATION

P.O. Box 122
Amana, IA 52203

http://www.ic.org/csa/

The Communal Studies Association was founded in 1975 as the National Historic Communal Societies Association, and changed its name in 1990 to reflect its expanded emphasis upon current as well as historic intentional communities.

The CSA and its Pacific Coast Chapter each sponsor an annual conference at a historic or current community. CSA meetings are scheduled for Estero, FL (Oct. 12–14, '95) and the Amana Colonies site near Cedar Rapids, IA (Oct. '96).

Communitarians and anyone studying movements and groups organized in community are invited to submit proposals for sessions, presentations, formal papers, panels, and performances from their experience and research. For program consideration, please submit to CSA headquarters, at least six months before meetings, a brief presentation summary and personal qualifications.

We publish both a newsletter and a scholarly journal, *Communal Societies*. Newsletter items should go to Richard Kathmann, Oneida Mansion House, 170 Kenwood Ave., Oneida, NY 13421. Journal manuscripts are submitted in duplicate to Michael Barkun, Dept. of Political Science, Syracuse NY 13244-1090.

Individual memberships are $25; Institutional $50; Journal subscriptions alone are $15. We can also be found on the World Wide Web.

We welcome inquiries, conference presentations, and materials for the Center archives (which have already grown to include material on 130 historic and 550 contemporary communities. [See separate listing for CCS). 5/1/94

DANCE NEW ENGLAND

P.O. Box 426
Brookline, MA 02146

(617)661-7138

Dance New England is made up of city dances held in New England and New York—cooperativly run, "alcohol-free, smoke-free, barefoot" dances happening on a regular basis (usually weekly). We hold 3 weekend events in different cities throughout the year, and a 16-day event during August in Maine.

Dance and movement forms that we teach and practice include: contact improv, African, various martial arts, voice and movement, drumming, theater, mime, yoga, jazz dance, sleaze dance, etc. Dancing, working, and living together as a cooperative community raise challenges beyond learning choreography. Community meetings at every DNE event address such disparate issues as equity and volunteerism, dance and sexuality, sexism and racism, and parenting within the community. DNE wants to make dance and community available and accessible to any and everyone. Our membership directory, including a list of all our dances, is available for $5. 10/1/93

DATACENTER

464 – 19th Street
Oakland, CA 94612

(510)835-4692/835-3017 Fax

The DataCenter is a nonprofit library and research center serving the social change community—here and abroad—as a storehouse of organized, accessible information. Our data bank includes reports, on-line databases, and a vast file system updated daily with articles from nearly

500 periodicals and newspapers from the mainstream to alternative presses. Issues documented in our collection include human rights, the Third World, corporate social responsibility, labor, environment, censorship, new right movements, U.S. government and foreign policy, and many more. Our collection also includes 3000 books and references and about 350 serial publications. People may access this information by visiting the library, purchasing DataCenter publications, or contracting for customized research or clipping services. Please call before visiting. Our services are fee-based. We offer pro-bono support to qualifying patrons. 11/3/92

DEEP DISH TV NETWORK

339 Lafayette Street
New York, NY 10012

(212)473-8933/420-8223 Fax

A national grassroots/public access satellite network linking community producers, programmers, activists, and viewers. Deep Dish is devoted to decentralizing media by providing a national forum—in addition to our own productions, we have a distribution cooperative for programs made independently around the world and/or locally. Deep Dish thrives on diversity and encourages creative programming that educates and activates the viewer. We seek out programs by and about people rarely seen on television: people of color, women, working people, people of different ages and from many regions. We're available on over 200 cable systems around the country, as well as selected public television stations. Call your local cable system for information. Anyone with a home dish can receive Deep Dish unscrambled on commercial "C" band satellite transponders. Check a satellite television guide, or contact our New York office. 1/5/95

DIGGERS & DREAMERS

c/o Redfield Community
Buckingham Road
Winslow
Buckinghamshire
MK18-3LZ ENGLAND

44296 712161
redfield@gn.igc.org

Diggers and Dreamers is an up-to-date directory, listing more than 80 British communities—both existing and embryonic. The aim of the book is to provide a public face for the communal and cooperative living movement in Britain and thus to increase public awareness. We hope that it will also help people join or set up new communities, help existing communities find new members, and provide material for educational use and research. The 92/93 edition (our second) also features articles on the history of communalism in Britain (both recently and in the 19th century), change and growth, and sustainable communities of the future. The Directory devotes a page to each community, and includes a map and overview chart. The Resources section features articles on aspects of setting up a community, a glossary, lists of useful addresses, a bibliography, and an international section listing hundreds of overseas communities. 216 pages on 100% recycled paper; £9.00 (cheques to "Diggers & Dreamers," sterling only please) surface mail worldwide. Our aim is to produce a new version of the book every two years so a '95 edition should be available by mid year, and the price will probably then change. 5/10/92

DIGGERS & DREAMERS IS ALSO AVAILABLE IN THE UNITED STATES THROUGH COMMUNITY BOOKSHELF (SEE SEPARATE LISTING).

DORMANT BRAIN RESEARCH

P.O. Box 10
Black Hawk, CO 80422

(RESOURCE MAY BE DEFUNCT—LOST CONTACT 6/95)

Cooperative living most often is destroyed by ego. The human brain is 90% dormant; this dormancy causes ego. Ego is retrogression, like driving a 10-cylindered personality jeep firing only one piston and trying to get over the Rockies of interpersonal trust and neurosis.

Science has discovered a systematic, step-by-step method to self-circuit progressively into the numb central nervous system. This first triggers the "nirvana" transcendence implosion. IQ and creativity then increase dramatically. That neurological foundation suggests the basis for perfect love community; the biological mechanism for warless Earth.

Intentional communities are invited to become brain teaching centers. Research reports describe how. Send SASE (business sized) and a donation. 7/10/92

DWELLING PORTABLY

P.O. Box 190-CD
Philomath, OR 97370

[Formerly: The Message Post.] Information

about living in tents, tipis, vans, trailers, domes, small cabins, etc. How to build shelters and furnishings that are comfortable, simple, low-cost and earth-friendly. Many tips. Candid feedback. Sample $1. 4/15/92

E.F. SCHUMACHER SOCIETY

Route 3, Box 76-A
Great Barrington, MA 01230
(413)528-1737

The E.F. Schumacher Society promotes a holistic approach to economics, emphasizing self-reliance...using local resources and serving local needs. They've done a lot of pioneering work on community financing: decentralized financial institutions and mechanisms for small-scale farming, cottage industries, and cooperatively structured small businesses. They have a SHARE program which works with alternative economics, and an alternative currency project called "Berkshares." They also offer workshops and much information about land trusts and low-cost housing. 10/23/93

EAGLE CONNECTION

PO Box 10287
San Rafael CA 94912,
(415)454-2294

The Eagle Connection serves an international network of innovative organizations working for personal, communal, and global transformation through an open cross-cultural and spiritual exploration. It disseminates information on individuals and groups developing imaginative holistic solutions to critical social, economic, educational, health, and environmental problems. It assists foundations, corporations, and individual philanthropists in the effective targeting of funding to transformative projects. Membership is open by subscription to organizations and individuals. Members receive a newsletter, *The Eagle Connector*, every two months. Members may request, free of charge, an *Eagle Connector* entry to spotlight a special event, job opening, organizational innovation, special need, etc. *The Eagle Connection* offers assistance to individuals and

groups in finding resources, allies, and skills. Annual fee $20 (N. Am.); $25 (overseas). 6/5/94

EARTH BASE ONE PROJEX

P.O. Box 1328
Bloomington, IN 47402-1328
(812)336-5334

Earth Base Projex—terrestrial analog to proposed Marsbase, biospheric research and development, energy alternatives, high tech fused with total recycling, educational focus. Send SASE for basic information or $1 for more details. Not your ordinary organization. Write to find out—specialists in total energy linkage. 12/5/92

EARTH CARE PAPER CO.

PO Box 8507
Ukiah CA 95482
(800)347-0070

Earth Care strives to be an environmentally and socially responsible business. Our emphasis is to offer customers environmentally sound recycled paper products as well as educational information about recycling and other environmental issues.

Our catalog offers an attractive range of quality recycled paper products ranging from notecards to computer paper. Several artists are featured in the catalog, and are commissioned on items sold. Earth Care helps organizations raise funds through promotion of recycled paper, and also donates 10% of its profits to organizations who are working to solve environmental and social problems. Please write us for a free catalog of recycled paper products. 6/1/92

EARTH ISLAND INSTITUTE

300 Broadway #28
San Francisco, CA 94133
(415)788-3666 / 788-7324 Fax
earthisland@igc.apc.org

Earth Island is a nonprofit organization working for environmental preservation and hence, political reform. We publish a quarterly, the *Earth Island Journal*, which covers such topics as rainforest preservation, saving the dolphins, the Climate Protection Institute, dealing with nuclear and toxic waste, and information on bioregional and Greens groups. We sponsor over 20 diverse projects working on these issues (including cooperative efforts with Central American and Soviet environmentalists), and have more than two dozen affiliated Earth Island Centers in the U.S. (and one each in Italy, Thailand, and Russia). Annual membership is $25. 1/5/95

EASTERN COOPERATIVE RECREATION SCHOOL

480 Valley Road #C-7
Montclair, NJ 07043

(201)509-0756

Established in 1940, ECRS is a nonprofit organization of people dedicated to creating humanistic leadership in recreation, and working to bring people together through games, dancing, folk dancing, crafts, and dramatics. The nature of the work is to help the participants develop their creativity while having fun and creating a sense of connectedness. Summer School, Winter Workshop, and several weekend retreats are held throughout the year. Members have a voice in policies and programs, elect the board of directors, and cooperatively run all activities. ECRS is financed and governed by its members. 5/10/94

ECO-HOME

4344 Russell Avenue
Los Angeles, CA 90027

(213)662-5207

Eco-Home is a demonstration home and community resource center for ecological living in the city. It demonstrates physical systems needed to sustain concentrated human habitation nontoxically, such as solar technology, water conserving organic gardens, recycling, and composting. Recognizing that 50% of the water used in Southern California residences gets poured on lawns and gardens, Eco-Home's front yard has been turned into a "Xeriscape"—a drought-tolerant landscape of plants that can survive on natural rainfall once they are established. Tours are conducted several days each week.

The Eco-Home Network is a membership organization and support group of people who are practicing or are interested in moving toward a more ecological life. Memberships are $15/year ($20 for a household) and include a subscription to the quarterly *Ecolution*; discounts on events, books, and other items; and access to the Eco-Home Library. 5/29/92

ECONET / PEACENET

Institute for
Global Communications
18 DeBoom Street
San Francisco, CA 94107

(415)442-0220/546-1794 Fax
support@igc.apc.org

EcoNet, PeaceNet, LaborNet and Conflict-Net are computer-based communication systems dedicated to helping the world environmental/peace/worker/mediation movements communicate more effectively. All are accessible, usually through a local phone call, in the U.S. and in 70 foreign countries. EcoNet offers more than 200 public "conferences" in which users can read valuable information on a wide variety of topics—including news on Nicaragua, citizen diplomacy, offshore drilling, rainforest preservation efforts, toxic wastes, environmental legislation pending, the Greenpeace and Sierra Club newsletters, nuclear free zones, etc. Peace-Net has a similar index more oriented toward peace and justice issues. In most public conferences, users can also contribute information in response to others, or as new topics. Private conferences can also be set up to permit a selected group of users to conduct such activities as planning an event or writing a joint publication. There is a $15 joining fee, a $12.50 monthly subscriber fee, and some usage fees based on location. They now have a spiffy Graphic User Interface that offers full Internet access and World Wide Web. 1/13/95

ECOVILLAGE NETWORK OF NORTH AMERICA

c/o The Farm, P.O. Box 90
Summertown, TN 38483-0090

(615)964-4324
(800)692-6329 USA Fax
(615)964-2200 Int'l Fax
2745871@mcimail.com

An ecovillage is a human-scale full-featured settlement which harmlessly integrates human activities into the natural world, is supportive of healthy human development, and can be successfully continued into the indefinite future.

The Ecovillage Network of North America is an independent, nonprofit, research and educational organization which serves as a catalyst and clearinghouse for sustainable redevelopment. ENNA surveys, catalogs, coordinates, and assists ecovillages and intentional communities throughout North America. Working with the Global Ecovillage Network, the Farm Ecovillage Training Center, and others, ENNA provides services and educational resource assistance in key areas such as leadership; communication of values; ownership and economics; architectural design; energy, waste, and water; agriculture and animal husbandry; recreation, the arts, celebration, and consciousness. 1/10/95

ECOVILLAGE TRAINING CENTER

The Farm, P.O. Box 90
Summertown, TN 38483-0090

(615)964-4324
(800)692-6329 USA Fax
(615)964-2200 Int'l Fax
natlaw@igc.apc.org

In 1993 and 1994, we developed the capability to provide live-in training in appropriate technologies for interested persons in former Soviet bloc countries, the developing world, and those closer to home. Among our regular courses are short (weekend) and long (8–10 day) workshops in such subjects as strawbale construction, soya technologies, forest mushrooms, Permaculture design, alternate energy, waste treatment, organic gardening, midwifery, and many other subjects. Please write or call to get on our mailing list for course announcements, or come to one of our open events like the Annual Harvest Festival and Energy Fair. 12/2/94

ELFIN PERMACULTURE

P.O. Box 672
Dahlonega, GA 30533-0672

Elfin Permaculture provides lectures, workshops, and design courses on a free-lance basis. All Elfin PC events are initiated and organized by local hosts. We teach worldwide, and can arrange special terms for groups in poor countries. Upon request we can produce workshops and design courses geared to specific communities. Though we prefer to teach people to produce their own permaculture designs, we also provide consulting and design services.

We offer Advanced Permaculture Training (APT) programs in which each APT student designs (with guidance) his/her own program of permaculture research, outreach, design, and implementation. The APT course requires a minimum of one year, and a maximum of four. We are presently seeking a location to establish a teaching/learning center. Please write for details and rates. For a list of Permaculture publications, send SASE to our sister enterprise, Yankee Permaculture, at this address [see separate listing]. 1/27/95

EMISSARIES, THE
(International Network)

The "Emissaries" are an association of individuals in many countries [formerly known as Emissaries of Divine Light] who share the premise that the same spirit that creates and sustains life is also a source of wisdom and direction for those who find attunement with it. Self-discovery is only possible in the context of a greater whole, and is known through giving whatever is practical, helpful, and balanced in any situation.

Over a dozen Stewardship Communities, situated around the globe, comprise the backbone of the network. While there is no official organization to join, an ongoing context is provided for shared creative work. All of these centers have literature available; most offer seminars, regular weekly meetings, and spiritual leadership classes.

Emissary communities listed in this directory: Glen Ivy, Green Pastures, Hundred Mile Lodge, King View, La Vigne, Mickleton, Sunrise Ranch, and Zeven Rivieren [formerly Hohenort]. 10/19/94

EMPLOYEE-OWNED BUSINESS INSTITUTE

**7500 W. Mississippi Ave #E-126
Lakewood, CO 80226**

(303)369-1617

The Employee-Owned Business Institute is a Denver-based organization dedicated to the creation and growth of 100% employee-owned businesses called worker cooperatives. In worker co-ops, each employee/owner has one equal vote and shares in the business' profits and/or losses.

With the current changes in economic and labor situations in America and around the world, we recognize the importance of educating, empowering, and supporting people in being employee-owners. We do this through public speaking, newsletters, video presentations, and seminars. Beginning in January '95 we are offering a one-year curriculum detailing

the elements necessary for creating a successful worker co-op.

We are creating cooperative schools around the country based on the 37-year-old worker cooperative system developed in Mondragon, Spain. Incorporated in our work are the teachings of Will Schutz, W. Edwards Deming, Stephen Covey, Peter Senge, Joe Dominguez, and Vicki Robin. Write or call for more information. 12/21/94

ENERGIE UND UMWELTZENTRUM

(Energy and Environmental Center)
**am Deister
3257 Springe/Eldagsen
GERMANY**

05044380/1880

The Energie und Umweltzentrum (Energy and Environmental Center) is a self-organized association working for more than ten years in the following areas: renewable energies, energy saving, ecological building, and environmental conservation. The Center was bought in 1981 and altered to be able to function as a model. As a result of energy upgrading (alterations in the building and the heating system, as well as the installation of 2 solar panels) fuel consumption was reduced by 70%. Water-saving technology (the use of well water, and a rain-water collecting system) reduced main water consumption by 50%. Also on the grounds are a reed-bed sewage system, an organic garden, and an orchard. Now the 30 members of permanent staff earn their living by working in further education, organizing expositions, and by consultation. We consider ourselves to be a self-managed, nonprofit project where everyone has the same vote and the same hourly wage. 1/21/93

ENVIRONMENTAL ILLNESS RESOURCES

Communities Directory has been getting an ever-increasing number of inquiries seeking communities that are appropriate for people with environmental illness (EI), also known as multiple chemical sensitivity (MCS). While there are a few such communities in our database [see index], more are needed. One of our readers has put together the following list of related resources: 6/7/94

- **HOME GROWN GREEN**
  Rich Kimball
  **105 Franklin Street
  Roseville, CA 95678-3308**
  (916)773-5751

  Resource directory of products, services, information, support groups.

- **NEW REACTOR, THE**
  **Environmental Health Network
  P.O. Box 1155
  Larkspur, CA 94977**

  Has housing ads for EI/MCS, numerous related articles, alternative products, etc.

- **OUR TOXIC TIMES**
  **Chemical Injury
  Information Network**

  **Cynthia Wilson
  P.O. Box 301
  White Sulfur Springs
  MT 59645**

  Publication, and co-coordinates national EI/MCS housing network and village in Montana.

- **WARY CANARY, THE
  —and— ENVIRON**
  **Zee & Ed Randegger
  P.O. Box 2204
  Ft. Collins, CO 80522**
  (970)224-0083

  W.C. explores suitable locations for EI/MCS housing; *Environ* focuses on sites and less toxic building materials.

EVERGREEN LAND TRUST

**747 Sixteenth Avenue East
Seattle, WA 98112**

web@halcyon.com

Evergreen Land Trust is a collection of 5 communities. ELT is a nonprofit that owns

the land that each of the communities occupy, however, each community is totally independent to manage itself and select its members as long as it operates within the spirit and bylaws of ELT, which reflect environmental and cultural concerns. We meet twice a year as an ELT board, with 2 reps from each property. None of the properties can be sold, nor can any occupant sell any interest in a community's property. 12/17/94

EXPERIMENTAL LIVING PROJECT

**Department of
Human Development
University of Kansas
Lawrence, KS 66045**

(913)864-4840

The Experimental Living Project is a research project in the Department of Human Development and Family Life at the University of Kansas. Established in 1969, its purpose is to investigate the application of the principles of behavioral psychology to the design of procedures that promote cooperative relations among individuals—especially those living collectively in a single household. The project is currently staffed by two faculty members and two students. Eight master's theses and six doctoral dissertations have been completed on a variety of areas (e.g., egalitarian work sharing, participatory decision making, new member education, officer accountability). Students spend at least two years living and working as members of the student housing cooperative that serves as the research setting for the project [see community listing for Sunflower House]. Work with the project leads to a PhD in applied behavior analysis. 5/13/92

FACTSHEET FIVE

**P.O. Box 170099
San Francisco, CA 94117-0099**

A bimonthly review of alternative/ underground 'zines (small-circulation magazines of the fanatic, or devoted, depending on your view of the subject matter). Self-described as "the 'Zine of crosscurrents and cross-pollination," each issue includes hundreds of short, helpful, funny reviews covering 'zines of a confounding variety—anarchistic, evangelical, xerox- and mail-art, bioregional, libertarian, animal rights, music...and many more. Subscriptions are $2 per issue ($2.75 first class); six issues for $11 ($15 first class). 3/15/94

FAIR TRADE FOUNDATION

**65 Landing Road
Higganum, CT 06441**

(860)345-3374/347-2043 Fax

When we buy clothing, crafts, or household goods we may notice the label "Made in India...Mexico...Indonesia...." But it's hard to know how often that means women working in crowded factories, where the heat is stifling and light insufficient...their profit and pay at the mercy of sweatshop owners and greedy middlemen.

The goal of the Fair Trade Foundation is to establish direct and fair trading links between community producers in the Third World and consumers in the U.S., and insure that the products are of high quality and reasonable cost. Our program seeks to increase market opportunities which consider environmental impact, healthy working conditions, and fair distribution of income—rewarding the producers with sustainable business. We are working with groups around the world to develop a label to verify that products meet these criteria, and have produced a 25-minute video about fair trading which you can show to your friends, business, church, or discussion group. $25 membership includes subscription to our quarterly newsletter and discounts on selected products; $50 memberships are eligible to receive the video at no extra cost. 3/15/94

FEDERATION OF EGALITARIAN COMMUNITIES

**c/o East Wind Community
Box DC-5
Tecumseh, MO 65760**

(417)679-4682

The Federation of Egalitarian Communities (est. '76) is a network of North American intentional communities. Each FEC community holds its land, labor, and other resources in common, and is committed to equality, ecology, cooperation, participatory government, and nonviolence. There are six member communities and three communities-in-dialog, ranging in size from homesteads to small villages. Three have been in existence for at least 20 years, two others for 15 years.

We encourage social and labor exchanges among member communities, the pooling of resources, and support of community-owned and community-operated industries. We value cooperation above competition, and the creation of a healthy, supportive environment above materialistic gain...how we do things is as important as what we do. Delegates from each community meet at least once a year in open meetings to discuss issues and make decisions about intercommunity programs.

Federation communities offer a clear alternative to traditional lifestyles: men and women share the nurturing of children, making decisions, constructing buildings, preparing meals, and operating businesses. All of our communities are seeking growth and generally welcome the opportunity to share their lives with others. Write for a copy of our brochure ($2 donation requested), or send for a free index of our "Systems & Structures Packet" (a collection of bylaws, membership agreements, labor and governance systems, visitor policies, etc., available for a little more than the cost of copying and postage). 12/6/93

FEDERATION OF HOUSING COLLECTIVES RESOURCE UNIT

**P.O. Box 8437
Stirling Street
Perth, 6849
WESTERN AUSTRALIA**

(09)227 6685

The Federation of Housing Collectives Resource Unit provides advice, advocacy, and training to each of the twenty (at least) developed or developing rental housing cooperatives in Western Australia. Write for more information. 5/21/92

FELLOWSHIP FOR INTENTIONAL COMMUNITY

Route 1, Box 155-CD
Rutledge, MO 63563

(816)883-5545 Voice and Fax
5012004@mcimail.com

The Fellowship (publisher of this Directory) is a network that provides alliance building, support services, and referrals for intentional communities, community networks, individuals seeking community, and other interested organizations. Our major purposes include: 1) to facilitate the exchange of information, skills, and economic support among existing and developing communities, and to encourage social interaction between them; 2) to demonstrate and facilitate applications of intentional community and cooperative experiences to the larger society—through forums, talks, demonstration projects, and workshops; 3) to build trust among communities and acceptance by others through a variety of celebrations and other activities; 4) to increase global awareness that intentional communities are modeling ecological alternatives, opportunities for personal and community development, and methods for peaceful social transformation; and 5) to support resource centers and academic institutions in the development of archives and programs relating to the study of intentional communities.

The FIC also publishes *Communities* magazine, maintains a Speakers Bureau, and is developing a revolving community loan fund. 2/14/95

FOUNDATION FOR COMMUNITY ENCOURAGEMENT

109 Danbury Road #8
Ridgefield, CT 06877

(203)431-9484

FCE offers opportunities for people to experience community and discover new ways of being together. Building and maintaining ongoing community require: 1) communicating with authenticity; 2) dealing with difficult issues; 3) bridging differences with integrity; 4) relating with love and respect. FCE's program includes workshops, speakers, seminars, conferences, and consulting. These focus on

teaching groups how to achieve and maintain community, identify common purpose, and accomplish agreed upon goals. FCE's work encourages tolerance of ambiguity, the joy of discovery, and the tension between holding on and letting go. FCE began as an outgrowth of the writings of Dr. M. Scott Peck, author of *The Road Less Traveled* and *The Different Drum*, and his perception of the great need for community throughout the USA, Canada, and the world. 10/15/92

FOURTH WORLD SERVICES

P.O. Box 1666
Denver, CO 80201-1666

(303)371-0815

Fourth World Services provides resource materials useful in education for intentional community. Currently, three booklets are available: "Introduction to Intentional Community: The Concept, Value & History of Intentional Cultural Design"—includes a poster titled: "Timeline of Communitarianism: Movements & Literature" ($4); "Classifications of Communitarianism: Sharing, Privacy, and the Ownership and Control of Wealth" ($3); and "Community, Inc.: Legal Incorporation for Intentional Community" ($5).

These monographs on communitarianism are researched, written, and published by A. Allen Butcher after 14 years' experience working with various movement organizations and living in various collective houses and communal societies. Each booklet includes a glossary of terms and resource listings. Add $1 postage and handling per booklet, or all three for $14 postage paid. Bulk orders of over 20 booklets get a 40% discount. 7/30/93

FSC/LAF

Federation of Southern
Cooperatives/ Land
Assistance Fund
100 Edgewood Ave, NE #1228
Atlanta, GA 30303

(205)652-9676 (Alabama#)

Since 1967 the Federation of Southern Cooperatives (FSC) has been the primary focal point for the rural cooperative movement among southern black and poor white farmers and rural residents. The Land Assistance Fund (LAF) was formed in 1971 to help black landowners across the South purchase "primary agriculture" land, and to retain property

threatened by creditors, tax collectors, and unscrupulous land dealers. The FSC/LAF represents the merged program and shared history of both groups.

Building on the work of the Civil Rights Movement, the Federation has organized a community based cooperative economic development movement among 30,000 low-income families working in over 100 rural communities in eleven southern states. It provides services, resources, technical assistance, and advocacy to its membership of cooperatives and credit unions and their individual member families. Individual memberships are $100 per year and can be paid in installments; family memberships are also available. 7/21/93

GAP MEDIA PROJECT, THE

142 W South College
Yellow Springs, OH 45387

(513)767-2224/767-1888 Fax

Recognizing that the mainstream media seldom report news of peace and social justice issues, the Gap Media Project is dedicated to filling that gap through increasing the circulation of the alternative press. We see the alternative press as a general news source, a resource for developing community through increasing accessibility.

UNDERLYING BELIEFS—The Gap Media Project asserts that millions of Americans are ready to accept an alternative to a competitive materialistic way of life, but are isolated from examples of communities which are living successfully in cooperation and peace. That the news and opinions of an American population wishing to live in an economically sustainable fashion based on cooperation and peace are available but not readily accessible to millions of people in the general public. That people who are now deprived of alternative news sources will gain the strength of empowerment through gaining access to the news and views of a cooperative society. That mainstream newspapers, magazines, television, and radio have stopped serving the public in favor of serving government and corporate interests.

Our goal for 1993 is to set up a national network to distribute periodicals from the alternative press—free to the public, but with payment to publishers to cover costs. Editors, publishers, and anyone else wishing to join this grassroots effort to develop community are invited to join in. Write or call Paul O'Keefe. 8/27/93

GARBAGE

**Practical Journal for
the Environment
P.O. Box 55197
Boulder, CO 80322-6519**

**(508)283-3200 Editorial
(800)234-3797 Subs**

Garbage follows many environmental issues, keeping a close eye on critical areas (recycling; composting; pollution; etc.). A good source of leads for paper companies that produce high quality, low-priced recycled products. $21/year (6 issues). 3/15/94

GELTAFTAN FOUNDATION

**Cal-Earth
10225 Baldy Lane
Hesperia, CA 92345**

(714)625-4383

"Anybody in this world should be able to build a shelter for his or her family with the simplest of elements—earth, water, air, and fire...every man and woman is a doctor and a builder, to heal and shelter themselves" (*Ceramic Houses & Earth Architecture*, by Nader Khalili). The Geltaftan Foundation is the focus for several thousand people who build, live in, or are interested in earth/ceramic houses. Founded in 1985 by architect Nader Khalili, AIA (whose innovation it was to fire adobe buildings after construction, fusing them into ceramics), Geltaftan sponsors the California Earth Art and Architecture Institute (Cal-Earth) where Khalili and his apprentices build and research timeless architecture built of the four universal elements; natural principles of wind, sun, gravity, shade; the principle of the arch for construction; synectics; the poetry of the Persian mystic, Rumi; and building anywhere in the world,

including the moon and Mars, with the available on-site materials. 3/21/94

GENESIS FARM

**41-A Silver Lake Road
Blairstown, NJ 07825**

Genesis Farm is an Ecological Learning Center and Community Supported Garden. While we are not a residential intentional community, we welcome students for our programs. We offer courses in The New Cosmology and experiential workshops in natural foods cooking, sustainable agriculture, art, and ritual. We offer summer programs for children, and teacher training in earth studies. We have a strong commitment to preserving small family farms and developing land trusts. Genesis Farm, in cooperation with St. Thomas University in Miama, FL, offers a master's program in Earth Literacy. Local interest is developing in planning for a cohousing community; for further information call Driscoll-Kellys at (908)362-8164. If you would like a calendar of events and to be added to our mailing list, please send $5. 5/18/93

GEO

**Gaia Education
Outreach Institute
Derbyshire Farm
Temple, NH 03084**

(603)654-6705

Gaia Education Outreach Institute (GEO) is a nonprofit organization working for an education that promotes sustainable, creative, compassionate living. Our goal is to educate for the love of life. Key learning tools include a sense of place, ecological literacy, sustainable community, the universe story, mindful living, and life celebration. Programs include: 1) Geocommons College Year, a residential-travel-service term at exemplary, sustainable small communities in Europe, India, and the USA, with credit through the University of New Hampshire; 2) a service-learning network of sustainable enterprises (schools, farms, businesses, etc.) for people of all ages to volunteer and apprentice; 3) Monadnock Geocommons Village, an educational ecovillage [see

communitiy listing] in the early design stage; 4) Monadnock Life Education Center for bioregional courses, resources, businesses, celebrations, and renewal. We also publish the quarterly *GEOLetter*. 11/26/94

GEO NEWSLETTER

**P.O. Box 5065
New Haven, CT 06525**

(203)389-6194

The Grassroots Economic Organizing Newsletter is a bimonthly publication that focuses on cooperatives, collectives, self-management, social justice, and building coalitions of labor/community/ environmental activists. Each issue includes a column on "Finding Funding," and news from around the world on workplace democracy, labor, community and citizen initiatives, the environment, and a calendar of related events. GEO relies heavily on volunteer labor and tax-deductible donations. Individual subscriptions are $15/year; library and organization rate is $24 (includes option of extra copies). 3/15/94

GLOBAL VILLAGE ACTION NETWORK

**Falls Brook Centre
RR#2, Knowlesville
Glassville, NB
E0J-1L0 CANADA**

Publishes *A Guide to Community-based Sustainable Groups and Centres* (1991, 135 pages; includes descriptions and contact information for over 100 self-help and resource groups in 37 countries). Copies of the guide are $25 to individuals and NGOs, $45 to institutions and governments. Price includes postage and handling. 10/12/93

GLOBAL VILLAGE INSTITUTE FOR APPROPRIATE TECHNOLOGY

**c/o Ecovillage Training Center
P.O. Box 90, The Farm
Summertown, TN 38483-0090**

**(615)964-3992
(800)692-6329 USA Fax
(615)964-2200 Int'l Fax
2745871@mcimail.com**

A nonprofit (est. '80) that researches promising new technologies that could benefit humanity in environmentally friendly ways. Our philosophy: emerging technologies linking the world together are not ethically neutral, but often have long-term implications for viability of natural systems, human rights, and our common future. Programs have included research into food and energy sciences to improve food security and reduce climate-altering dependence upon fossil fuels; using new communications media for demonstrations of alternative economic and social experiments; and multidisciplinary research into ways to narrow the gap between the developed and developing world without undue negative cultural and environmental impacts. We do not maintain an active mailing list and do not welcome interns or offers to assist. Information inquiries welcome.

Global Village Video, a project of the Institute, produces several hours of instructional programing each year which airs on local cable systems, and is available on videotape. For a catalog of publications contact Total Video at P.O. Box 259; Mushroompeople at P.O. Box 220; or send a fax to our toll-free number. 1/10/95

GLOBE-LIB

1150 Woods Road
Southampton, PA 18966
(215)357-3977

Retribalize! Those practicing decentralization, dispute resolution, group process, gentleness, and honesty should inspire others to feature such values in the transformation of the institutional matrix. Globe-Lib and its subsidiary Galaxia promote decentralized world federal government through a new project, Home Rule Globally, which hopes to write a decentralist world federal constitution. Individuals who at any time were elected to a local government office but have never been national bureaucrats can pay $5 to become candidates for delegates to the Home Rule Globally convention. Individuals, tribes, and communities can join Globe-Lib. 5/31/92

GREENER PASTURES INSTITUTE

P.O. Box 2190
Pahrump, NV 89041-2190
(702)382-4847

[Formerly: Relocation Research.] GPI is a national clearinghouse which assists individuals in planning a move from large urban centers to smaller cities and towns in rural areas of the U.S. (some foreign locales). Our newsletter regularly profiles new or expanding intentional communities (being committed to all types of rural alternatives) but is primarily an information source for real estate, job/business opportunities, comparative statistical data on states/counties/towns, health/medical facilities, etc. We're an excellent springboard to more extensive research and travel. If you write for free information, a SASE would be appreciated.

NOTE: We're in the process of moving to Ponderosa Village in Goldendale, WA. The Pahrump, NV, address and phone will be good through the end of '96. 10/10/94

GREENHOUSE EXPERIMENT

305 Middle Brook Road
Greer, SC 29650-3306
(864)268-2635

"Greenhouse Experiment"—a 23-page illustrated proposal for an alternative community school to build awareness of and modify our behavior, and to develop community-building skills in response to the L.A. riots of April '92 and our life experiences. We use architecture as context to show eight elements of learning. Community Culture: a pivotal element to identify beliefs that prompt us to act, and myths that lead to truth and deep understanding. Also, integrated elements for skill development: Community Building, Performance, Reconciliation, the Art of Making Shelter, Gardening and Conservation, Livelihood at Home, and Community Assembly: a place to interact, show and practice our skills. Our objective is to build networks of people interested in dialog and sharing information. We also try to locate people doing similar work. To order one copy of "Greenhouse Experiment" send $2.50 check to Don Cuddihee, architect, at the above address. 1/22/93

GREENMONEY JOURNAL

West 608 Glass Avenue
Spokane, WA 99205
(509)328-1741

A socially responsible investing and green consumer resource newsletter. *GMJ* is bimonthly. Subscriptions are available at $25 a year for businesses and corporations, $20 a year for individuals and nonprofits.

Each issue of *GMJ* highlights resources and investments available in the area of SRI. We also review green publications, list SRI information organizations, and write about green consumer resources. We also sponsor information seminars in Spokane, WA. Please write or call for FREE sample copy or more information. 12/16/92

GROODY, HOEWING & ASSOCIATES

3712 Keowee Avenue #C
Knoxville, TN 37919
(423)525-7376

Every year Ed Groody & Ann Hoewing (trained by M. Scott Peck, the originator of the Community Building process) provide a limited number of no cost/low cost Community Building Workshops for existing and newly forming intentional communities. This process helps communities move out of conflict and chaos, and to experience new ways of being together that are authentic, empowering, compassionate, and respectful. 8/7/94

GROUNDWORK

P.O. Box 14141
San Francisco, CA 94114
(415)255-7623

GroundWork [formerly *Green Letter*] is a national grassroots magazine covering community organizing and direct action. We cover environmental issues, peace and anti-nuclear organizing, women's news, Native American issues, social justice, gay-lesbian-bisexual news, alternative and intentional communities, art and resistance, and more.

GroundWork encourages our readers to send photos and articles on their activities. We are a volunteer collective, and welcome input. Every issue features over 50 photos of events around the country and around the world—images you won't see in the mainstream media.

GroundWork operates on a very tight budget, and we count on contributions from our readers to publish. Subscriptions are $10–$100! Call for a free sample issue. 6/14/93

GROWING COMMUNITY ASSOCIATES

**P.O. Box 5415-D
Berkeley, CA 94705
(510)869-4878**

We help communities, nonprofits, businesses, and groups of all kinds clarify or renew their vision and mission, develop strategies and skills for healthy group functioning, and weather the conflicts and challenges that inevitably arise as a group moves from one phase of development to another. We also help clients identify their current phase of development and assess their readiness to move to the next level. We explore the changes in values and attitudes that groups and organizations need to embrace if creating community is to be more than an empty slogan or an unattainable ideal. In our consultations, workshops, and trainings, we respond to the particular needs and circumstances of each client rather than impose a model of how community and cooperation should operate. The skills and processes we teach include healthy and effective communication, group decision making, meeting facilitation, and conflict mediation. We, the founding partners—Carolyn Shaffer, M.A., coauthor of *Creating Community Anywhere*, and Sandra Lewis, PhD, clinical psychologist and group facilitator—include among our associates a rich network of experienced resource people. 8/30/94

GROWING COMMUNITY NEWSLETTER

**Back Issues
PO Box 169
Masonville, CO 80541-0169**

Growing Community newsletter, published in 1993–1994 (now a 6-page column in *Communities* magazine), offers practical advice from experienced communitarians about forming new intentional communities in the 90s—what works and what doesn't work—so YOU don't have to reinvent the wheel. Decision-making processes (including consensus), legal options, finance and land development, zoning, children in community, alternative buildings and structures, food and gardening for community, living "off the grid." Profiles of successful and newly forming communities; what community founders would have done differently; and abundant resource listings—books, periodicals, videos, audiotapes, conferences, and consultants on creating new communities

nowadays. $5 per issue, $38 for the set of 8. Send for description of subjects covered in each back issue. 8/11/95

GROWING WITHOUT SCHOOLING

**Holt Associates
2269 Massachusetts Avenue
Cambridge, MA 02140
(617)864-3100**

We continue the work of educational critic John Holt by publishing *Growing Without Schooling* magazine and running a book and music store catalog. Our purpose is to show that people of all ages can learn, make friends, and find work without going to school. Some common GWS stories: innovative ways to learn reading, math, science, history; finding volunteer work and apprenticeships; how single parents, parents who work outside the home, people of color homeschool. Also included: interviews, book reviews, resources, directory of families and groups. Our mail-order catalog sells hundreds of books about education, family life, math, writing, history, science, and more. We have published book sets about learning disabilities, homeschooling in the news, kids earning money. Send for a free catalog and sample issue of *GWS*. Subscriptions are $25/6 issues. 8/3/93

HABITAT FOR HUMANITY

**121 Habitat Street
Americus, GA 31709
(912)924-6935/924-6541 Fax**

Habitat For Humanity is an ecumenical, grassroots Christian ministry with the goal of eliminating poverty housing. There are over 1100 affiliated projects in the U.S., and 164 projects in 35 other countries, primarily in developing countries. Funding comes from individuals, churches, corporations, foundations, and other organizations which are moved by concern and compassion to help those in need. Mortgage payments are put into a local "Fund for Humanity" and recycled to build new houses. No government funds are used for construction, though

grants are accepted for land acquisition and infrastructure costs. Habitat operates with a core group of paid clerical and support staff, but relies primarily on volunteer labor. Each affiliated project is run by a local board. 1/5/95

HANSON, CHRIS

**Cohousing Resources
174 Bushby Street
Victoria, BC V8S-1B6
(604)480-4815 Voice and Fax**

Consultant specializing in cohousing projects. Services include feasibility studies, ownership options, land acquisition, design, planning, legal hoops, budgets, schedules, and group process. 5/15/95

HIGH TRUST ASSOCIATES

**4023 – 14th Ave S. #A2
Minneapolis, MN 55407
(612)823-5235**

High Trust Associates is an educational organization providing the general public with low-cost workshops emphasizing community. Our evolving mission is to be a collaborative, joyful, learning community that joins with other individuals, organizations, and nations to discover, create, and live an evolving, unifying theory, grounded in daily life, that is relevant to all forms of matter, life, and spirit. The High Trust Community aims to give each of us a chance to create a loving and trusting community, one which will nurture the process of each member growing in a way that he or she chooses. We learn to become more proactive, trusting the organic flow, the person, and the process. We discover and search together, collaborate together, celebrate and honor each other, and tune into the cosmic vision. Call or write for information about HTA meetings open to everyone. 12/14/94

HIGH WIND ASSOCIATION

**W7136 County Rd. U
Plymouth, WI 53073
(414)528-8488 Outreach
(414)528-7212 Bookings**

"To walk gently on the earth, to know the spirit within, to hear our fellow beings, to invoke the light of wisdom—and to build the future now."

This vision has attracted thousands to High Wind's experimental exploration of ways for people to live more harmoniously with nature and each other. An ecological village, High Wind is located 55 miles north of Milwaukee on a 128-acre farm with rolling meadows, woods and springs. Innovative education around values for sustainable futures has been a central activity in this residential community since 1981, combined with interests in shelter-building and renewable energy. Many seminars are held in conjunction with the University of Wisconsin. Some of the 17 residents are engaged on-site in guest/learning programs, networking, subscription farming, furniture making, and desktop publishing. *Windwatch*, High Wind's semiannual journal, details its activities, evolution toward a sustainable village, and the relationship between alternative models and mainstream culture. High Wind also operates a major alternative bookstore in Milwaukee.

A newly forming team of technical designers and avant garde scientists will join hands with futurist thinkers and educators, along with business entrepreneurs, to deepen a demonstration for sustainable development that can respond to existing urban challenges around the country. 10/8/93

HOME EDUCATION PRESS

P.O. Box 1083
Tonasket, WA 98855
(509)486-1351

Home Education Press is the largest publisher of homeschooling books and publications in the US. We publish the 64-page *Home Education* magazine, over a dozen helpful booklets, and several books, including *Alternatives in Education*, a book detailing the options available to families outside the public school system, including Waldorf and Montessori, community and alternative schools, and learning resource centers. We believe that learning should begin in the home, and that education of a child should be directed by the learner himself. Write for our free 16-page informative catalog detailing homeschooling questions, listing support groups nationwide, and including excellent resources from a variety of sources. 5/12/92

HOME POWER MAGAZINE

P.O. Box 520
Ashland, OR 97520
(541)475-3179

If you want to make your own electricity, heat your home, or drive a car without using fossil fuels—*Home Power* can help

you. Understandable technical information about using renewable energy in your home or business. Photovoltaics, wind power, home-sized hydroelectric, batteries, inverters, efficient appliances, methane and hydrogen production, solar cooking, water pumping, solar heating and architecture, electric vehicles, home-brew projects, product reviews, and more. Written by people who live and work with renewable energy. Published bimonthly since 1987 using only solar and wind produced electricity. A one-year subscription (6 issues) is $15.00. Each 116+ page issue is printed on 30% post-consumer, non-chlorine recycled, coated paper using soybean based ink. 9/1/92

HORTIDEAS

460 Black Lick Road
Gravel Switch, KY 40328
(606)332-7606

A monthly which features abstracts and reports on the latest research, methods, tools, plants, books, etc., for vegetable, fruit, and flower gardeners—gathered from hundreds of popular and technical sources worldwide. Readers are encouraged to contribute ideas, clippings, and reviews. Annual subscriptions are $15 for second class US; $17.50 for first class US, Canada, and Mexico; Overseas $20 surface, $30 air mail. 5/23/92

HOSPITALITY EXCHANGE

1338 Foothill Drive #199
Salt Lake City, UT 84108-2321

HE is a cooperative network/directory of friendly, travel-oriented people who have agreed to offer each other the gift of hospitality when traveling. Only people listed in the directory may use the information. The entire household is involved in a membership because all will be affected by a visitor's presence. So the fee of $15 for the calendar year covers any member of the household when traveling—whether it's an apartment or a large communal group. As of May '93 we have 325 member households in 28 countries and 35 states. 60% of our members are in North America. Europe is also well represented, and a few members live in Australia, New Zealand, Japan, Asia, Africa, and Latin America.

Members are sent the Spring directory, plus Summer and Fall updates. When planning trips, members call or write others they'd like to visit, asking for one or two nights' lodging. If the timing is wrong, one may decline to host at all. When

contacted about a visit, a member can look up the person's listing in the directory. 12/8/94

HUTTERIAN BRETHREN

Riverview Directory
RR6, Box 21, Site 600
Saskatoon, SK
S7K 3J9 CANADA

In 1528 a group of Anabaptists decided to pool their goods and unite in Christian brotherhood. The church was persecuted all over Europe, and Jakob Hutter, who became their leader in 1533, was burned at the stake. There have been Hutterite colonies in North America since the 1870s, though most were forced to migrate to Canada during WWI (they refuse to do military service or use violence, hold public office, or swear oaths). Today there are over 40,000 members living in 360 Hutterian settlements and Bruderhofs in Canada, the USA, Europe, and Asia.

Hutterites believe in the Apostles' Creed, baptism of adult believers, the Lord's Supper as a Meal of Remembrance, community of goods, leadership in the Church, Church discipline, and lifelong faithfulness in marriage. Family life is important, with father at the head of the family, and mother at his right hand. Single members are included in family households. Divorce and remarriage are not allowed. Unmarried visiting couples may not share overnight accommodations. They educate their children in their own schools and day nurseries. Each colony has common work and a common purse. Hutterite groups manufacture Community Playthings (educational play equipment) and Rifton Equipment for the handicapped. Hutterian Anabaptists, mostly in the West, farm on a large scale. For more information send for their Plough Publishing House catalog and a free issue of their periodical, *The Plough*, which discusses current issues and is a platform for keeping in touch with fellow Christians and interacting with other movements.

See individual community listings for: Catskill Bruderhof* (NY), Crystal Spring* (MB), Darvell* (England), Deer Spring* (CT), Fan Lake Brethren† (WA), HB/Spokane† (WA), Michaelshof* (Germany), New Meadow Run* (PA), Owa* (Japan), Pleasant View* (NY), Spring Valley* (PA), Starland* (MN), Woodcrest* (NY). A complete and

*Bruderhof groups †Hutterite groups

up-to-date Directory of all Hutterite colonies is available for $7 ($6 US) from Riverview Colony at the address noted above. 2/22/95

ICA/EARTHCARE

3038 Fall Creek Parkway
Indianapolis, IN 46205
(317)925-9297
(317)925-9298 Fax

The "Indianapolis House" on Fall Creek Parkway is provided to the Institute of Cultural Affairs (ICA) by the Indianapolis Foundation. It is an office center by day, and a home for the four residential staff families by night. All staff earn their living in human-service type jobs, and volunteer their time to maintain the ICA Program Center and coordinate its diversified program ventures. One of our programs, The Ishmael Center for Personal & Community Refocusing, will empower individuals and organizations that are making a difference in urban transition. In promoting long-range, inclusive, ecological, and spirit-filled models for a healthy urban lifestyle of the future, we envision a city that works in all of its parts for and by all of its people. [See also: Institute for Cultural Affairs in the Resources section.] 1/6/95

ICSA

International Communal
Studies Association
Yad Tabenkin Institute
Ramat Efal 52960
ISRAEL

The ICSA was formed during an international conference held at Yad Tabenkin, in Israel, in 1985. The purposes are to provide an international clearinghouse for research; to maintain and distribute lists of communal organizations and scholars; to conduct conferences; and to issue a journal, a bulletin, bibliographies, and conference proceedings. International conferences are held every three years; the next will be in late May 1995, in Israel. Individual memberships are $15; Institutional $30. 11/8/94

IICD: INSTITUTE FOR INTERNATIONAL COOPERATION & DEVELOPMENT

P.O. Box 103
Williamstown, MA 01267
(413)458-9828

A nonprofit organization founded in 1986. IICD is dedicated to promoting global understanding and international solidarity. We are a cooperative, and the people on staff all have longtime commitments and have initially been students on one of our programs (this is the best introduction to the work of the institute).

IICD organizes travel, study, and solidarity courses to Africa and Latin America. In Mozambique IICD volunteers work on a tree-planting project; in Zimbabwe, on a project with street children; and in Nicaragua and Brazil, the projects are community construction work. The programs are 6–12 months including preparation and follow-up periods in the U.S. You are welcome to contact us...please write or call. 8/18/93

IN CONTEXT

P.O. Box 11470
Bainbridge Island, WA 98110
(206)842-0216

In Context is a quarterly which explores and clarifies just what is involved in a humane, sustainable culture, and articulates practical steps and useful insights to help us get there. Acclaimed for the best coverage of emerging issues in 1991 by *Utne Reader*, it explores personal, cultural, and planetary change through in-depth articles and authoritative interviews. Sample topics: living together, sustainable communities, politics, population, play and humor, gender, business, sustainable development...and many more.

Context Institute, publisher of *In Context*, also provides consulting, lectures, innovation diffusion game, and occasional special reports. *In Context* is $24.00/year, sample issue $6.00. Sustainer subscription is $35, including an in-house newsletter twice a year plus *In Context*. 10/12/93

IN THESE TIMES

**Institute for Public Affairs
2040 N. Milwaukee Ave, 2nd Fl.
Chicago, IL 60647-4002**

(312)772-0100

In These Times believes that to guarantee our life, liberty, and pursuit of happiness, Americans must take greater control over our nation's basic economic and foreign policy decisions. We believe in a socialism that fulfills rather than subverts the promise of American democracy, where social needs and rationality (not corporate profit and greed) are the operative principles. Our pages are open to a wide range of views, socialist and non-socialist, liberal and conservative. We welcome comments and opinion pieces. Published 26 times a year. Subscriptions are $34.95 ($59 for Institutions, $47.95 for outside the US and its possessions). 3/15/94

INFINITE LIGHT FELLOWSHIP, INC.

**3320-B Thompson Avenue
Muskegon, MI 49441**

(616)755-6676

The Infinite Light Fellowship, Inc., is a central organization to set up a global network of affiliates for spiritual, educational, charitable, and healing purposes. It is nonprofit and tax-exempt under Section 501(c)(3) of the IRS Code.

The Fellowship develops and publishes literature for personal home practice or for study groups, including meditation, spiritual growth, spiritual healing, dreamwork, well-being, and self-mastery of our angelic nature. The Fellowship syndicates the Caiman Connection, a column for monthly or quarterly periodicals, featuring readers' experiences and focusing on dreamwork and alternate realities.

The Fellowship offers nonprofit, tax-exempt status for persons who are developing: 1) local learning and healing centers; 2) communes for retreats, conferences; 3) long-term healing communities; and 4) other tax-exempt purposes. 3/29/93

INNOVATIVE HOUSING

**2169 E. Francisco Blvd. #E
San Rafael, CA 94901**

(415)457-4593/457-0549 Fax

Innovative Housing, a nonprofit organization, has organized several hundred shared households on the West Coast— heavily concentrated in the San Francisco Bay Area, but also strong in the Pacific Northwest and in Southern California. We offer workshops which introduce people to group living, then help them form compatible groups by clarifying needs and desires, and by teaching shared living skills. Usually, I/H holds "master leases" on rental properties, acting as go-between for conservative landlords and the more liberal householders. With a heavy ratio of low-income participants, almost half are single parents or elderly. Innovative Housing has worked closely with the CoHousing Company, and publishes a monthly newsletter. 1/6/95

INSTITUTE FOR COMMUNITY ECONOMICS

**57 School Street
Springfield, MA 01105-1331**

(413)746-8660

The Institute for Community Economics (ICE) is a national nonprofit organization which provides technical assistance and financing to community land trusts (CLTs) and other community-based organizations working to produce and preserve affordable housing, land, and other economic resources in communities where they are most needed. ICE's mission is to help communities develop the tools and local institutions needed to assert control over their land, housing, and capital in order to ensure their appropriate use and just allocation.

ICE coordinates a national network of over 90 CLTs operating in 23 states in the US. ICE's nationwide revolving loan fund accepts loans from socially concerned individuals and makes low-cost loans available to nonprofit housing groups. Write for free information and ICE's list of publications. 7/1/92

INSTITUTE FOR CULTURAL AFFAIRS

Information Services

The Institute of Cultural Affairs, an international organization founded as the Ecumenical Institute in Chicago in 1954, is today active in some 29 countries. Our network has a spiritual focus which is inclusive of all faiths, and which places a high value on diversity, participation, and globality. Each center is staffed by a group of volunteers. The following are North American residential centers for the ICA, which may also be known as the Global Order, or as Order Ecumenical: 7/29/94

- **ICA/Chicago**
  4750 N. Sheridan Road
  Chicago, IL 60640
  (312)769-6363
  [Direct general inquiries here, addressed to "Information Services."]
- **ICA Earthcare/Indianapolis**
  [see listing, p. 383]
  3038 Fall Creek Parkway
  Indianapolis, IN 46205
  (317)925-9297
- **ICA/Mexico City**
  Instituto de Asuntos Culturales
  Oriente 158 No. 232
  Colonia Moctezuma
  15500 Mexico D.F., MEXICO
  (52)5-571-4135
- **ICA/New York**
  629 East 5th Street
  New York, NY 10009-9998
  (212)673-5984
- **ICA/Phoenix**
  [see listing, p. 261]
  4220 North 25th Street #4
  Phoenix, AZ 85016
  (602)468-0605
- **ICA/Seattle**
  1504 – 25th Avenue
  Seattle, WA 98122
  (206)323-2100/322-6266
- **ICA/Toronto**
  577 Kingston Road, Suite 1
  Toronto, Ontario
  M4E-1R3 CANADA
  (416)691-2316
- **ICA/Washington**
  1301 Longfellow Street, N.W.
  Washington, DC 20011
  (202)882-6284
- **Songaia**
  [see listing, p. 305]
  22421 – 39th Avenue SE
  Bothell, WA 98021-7911
  (206)486-5164

There are also ICA residential centers in these cities on other continents. Write ICA/Chicago or ICA/Phoenix for additional information.

- Bombay, India
- Brussels, Belgium
- Guatemala City, Guatemala C.A.
- Hong Kong
- Kuala Lumpur, Malaysia
- Nairobi, Kenya
- Rio de Janeiro, Brazil
- Sydney, Australia
- Taipei, Republic of China
- Tokyo, Japan

INSTITUTE FOR DEEP ECOLOGY EDUCATION

**P.O. Box 2290
Boulder, CO 80302**

(303)939-8398 Phone/Fax

A nonprofit project, evolved from the work of Joanna Macy, John Seed, and Bill Devall, that expands on their trainings in deep ecology theory and practice. IDDE sponsors regional trainings and an annual Summer School, plus does consultations with other institutions to help develop deep ecology curriculum and programs. IDDE also works to build coalitions among educators, activists, and other organizations involved in this work; to develop deep ecology as a field; and to bring the deep ecology perspective to the environmental debates of our time. 8/14/93

INSTITUTE FOR LOCAL SELF-RELIANCE

**2425 – 18th Street, NW
Washington, DC 20009**

(202)232-4108

The Institute for Local Self-Reliance is a nonprofit research organization which promotes the development of healthy local economies through proper utilization of local resources and the use of environmentally sound technologies. We work with local governments, community groups, and businesses to achieve locally managed, sustainable economic development. Our research currently focuses on innovative and affordable alternatives to petroleum-based plastics, state-of-the-art scrap-based manufacturing operations, and the best recycling programs and technologies. We offer technical assistance in both rural and urban regions throughout the U.S. Write to us for a list of publications. 5/21/92

INSTITUTE FOR SOCIAL ECOLOGY

**P.O. Box 89
Plainfield, VT 05667**

(802)454-8493

The Institute for Social Ecology, established in 1974, became independent in 1981. We strive to create educational experiences that enhance people's relationship to the natural world and to each other. The purpose of our programs is the preparation of well-rounded students who can work effectively as constructive participants in the process of ecological reconstruction. Programs are conducted in an intimate educational community of shared learning in the hills of rural Vermont. Learning modes include lectures, seminars, tutorials, study groups, field trips, and hands-on projects. The social ecology approach to education is non-authoritarian and student centered. Students work on projects that combine theoretical learning with hands-on experience and practice. We integrate study, critique, and creative work into a holistic process that fosters self-understanding, cultural knowledge, and a deeper sense of people's relation to the natural world. Programs include Ecology and Community, Design for Sustainable Communities, Women and Ecology, an M.A. in Social Ecology through Goddard College, and a Study Tour to Kerala, India. College credit is available. Call or write (to Dept. C) for a program catalog. 12/28/92

INTEGRITY INTERNATIONAL PUBLISHING

**Box 9
100 Mile House, BC
V0K-2E0 CANADA**

As the tides of change keep rising in our world, *Integrity International* (the journal of Emissary Foundation International) plays an increasingly vital role—providing a balanced, penetrating perspective of what is happening, and highlighting creative endeavor wherever it occurs. Each issue covers a broad spectrum and introduces you to men and women all over the world whose concern is also for common sense and integrity in living.

We offer readers of this directory a special opportunity to subscribe to our journal at the introductory rate of $18 for one year (six issues, regularly $22 US). 8/10/92

INTER-COOPERATIVE COUNCIL

**Room 4002, Michigan Union
Ann Arbor, MI 48109-1349**

(313)662-4414

ICC was formed in 1937 by the housing co-ops on the University of Michigan campus—in order to gain greater efficiency and economy in certain functions such as recruitment of new members, paying the taxes and mortgages, and overseeing large maintenance projects. In addition, ICC helps train new members and officers so that houses run more smoothly.

Our housing co-ops are owned and managed by the students who live in them. There are 16 group and 2 apartment houses located on both Central and North campus. The number of members in each house ranges from 13 to 150, with the average being about 33. The buildings range from wood frame to brick, from historic to modern. We have non-smoking houses, coed houses, an all-women's house, and houses that serve vegetarian meals. Most houses serve dinner daily, while breakfast and lunch are do-it-yourself.

Houses are run democratically, each member having an equal voice. At house meetings, students decide how much to spend on food, when quiet hours will be, what newspapers to subscribe to, what to do about a problem member, what work needs to be done, and so on. We rely on members to do all the work needed to run the houses (cooking, cleaning, planning, bookkeeping, etc.) Each member puts in 4–6 hours of work per week.

Eating and working with housemates, participating in group decision making, and sharing good times help our members develop close bonds. This strong sense of community combined with the knowledge of shared ownership is what turns co-op houses into homes. 6/28/93

INTER-COOPERATIVE COUNCIL

**510 West 23rd
Austin, TX 78705**

(512)476-1957

Inter-Cooperative Council co-op houses offer affordable, convenient learning environments and supportive communities for university and community college students. For 50 years, ICC members have maintained and improved our houses for future generations of students seeking democratic control of their living situations. Currently there are 7 ICC houses near the U.T. Austin. Ranging in size from 11 to 33 members, all of our 60-(plus)-year-old houses are homey and intimate. Group meals, parties, sports teams, and volunteer groups add to the community atmosphere. We are preserving smaller family-sized housing in an increasingly densely packed, high-rise dominated area. We are also promoting self-reliant, culturally and environmentally responsible living. Our nonrestrictive membership policies introduce students from many backgrounds. Two houses are vegetarian and two are graduate/upper division houses. Non-student members are also accepted. 12/14/92

INTERFAITH CENTER ON CORPORATE RESPONSIBILITY

475 Riverside Drive
New York, NY 10115

(212)870-2295/870-2023 Fax

ICCR vigorously challenges corporations to make peace and social justice concerns part of the decision-making formula in business. Churches in America are stewards of billions of dollars of stocks and bonds in pensions and endowments. Members of the ICCR (churches, dioceses, and religious communities) accept the unique challenge of addressing issues of corporate responsibility with our resources, particularly our investments. Our covenant is to work ecumenically for justice in and through economic structures, and for stewardship of the earth and its resources. We publish *The Corporate Examiner* ten times yearly —reviewing publications and media, presenting opinions and ideas, and examining U.S. church and corporate policies and actions on nuclear weapons, environment, foreign investment, minorities and women, health, hunger, energy, human rights, and alternative investments. Please write for membership and subscription information. 1/5/95

INTINET RESOURCE CENTER

P.O. Box 4322-C
San Rafael, CA 94913-4322

(415)507-1739
pad@well.com

Merged. [See Resource listing for Abundant Love Institute.] 12/21/94

KEN KEYES CENTER

Renamed: Caring Rapid Healing Center
1620 Thompson Road
Coos Bay, OR 97420

(541)267-6412/269-2388 Fax

In 1972 Ken Keyes wrote his most famous book, the *Handbook to Higher Consciousness*. Today the center in Coos Bay focuses on rapid methods for psychological haling,

with a written guarantee of effectiveness (the first ever offered for work in the field of mental healing). The focus on inner child injuries that have been dysfunctionally programmed into the unconscious mind during the first few years of life. A Work/Learn program is available for volunteers. They will be moving to California. 9/21/95

KERR ENTERPRISES, INC.

P.O. Box 27417
Tempe, AZ 85285

(602)968-3068

The originator of the solar box cooker [see listings for Solar Box Cookers], Kerr Enterprises distributes plans, kits, and fully assembled cookers. Write for price list. 4/15/92

KIBBUTZIM FEDERATION

ICD (International Commune Desk)
P.O. Ramat Efal
52 960 ISRAEL

There are 269 Kibbutzim, and they come in all shapes and sizes—from a few dozen souls, to 1500. The first Kibbutz, Degania, was founded in 1910. Today, four generations live side by side in the older communities. Except for three urban Kibbutzim, all have a mixed agricultural and industrial economic base. All are fully communal, both in production and consumption. Living in a small, closely knit community generates a high quality of life, both ecologically and socially. At one time the Kibbutz movement's main purpose was turning the Jews (coming to the state of Israel from 160-odd countries) into workers, farmers, and other productive members. Today a special project is absorbing newcomers from the Diaspora, and helping them adjust to Israeli life. Many Kibbutzim welcome volunteers, both Jewish and non-Jewish. Please write for more information —an International Reply Coupon will be most welcome! 8/6/92

KIDS TO THE COUNTRY

The Farm School
51 The Farm
Summertown, TN 38483

(615)964-2534

The Farm School provides inner city kids who are homeless refugees or otherwise

disadvantaged with a chance for a country experience of horse riding, swimming, canoeing, crafts, computer, and conflict resolution. The children are sponsored by businesses, churches, and individuals who recognize that meaningful experience gives the kids a richer point of view. Direct inquiries to Mary Ellen Bowen, Director. 10/1/93

KOKOO

Huset, Rådhusstræde 13
DK-1466 Copenhagen K.
DENMARK

3315-52-53

Kokoo is the Danish Communes Association—established in 1969 with offices in Copenhagen and Aarhus. The office has one staff person for a 7-month duty cycle; wages are paid by City Hall because we run a very efficient youth housing service. We run a matching service for communes looking for people and vice versa, and a free legal aid service staffed by experts on housing legislation. A small band of Kokoo activists produces a magazine, various folders on legal issues, communal cookbooks, etc. A larger, more amorphous group of supporters are occasionally called upon to write articles, raise money, run campaigns, give talks at schools, etc. 3/15/93

KRAUS, MARY

Architect
67 North Pleasant Street
Amherst, MA 01002

(413)253-4090

Mary Kraus is an architect specializing in cohousing and sustainable communities, with an emphasis on affordable, healthful, environmentally sound design. Taking the approach of a facilitator, she uses guided visualization and participatory design workshops to create an environment in which people can discover and develop their own ideas and inspirations. She helps groups to find common ground while celebrating their diverse design preferences. Her approach involves attentive listening and a deep respect for each community's individual needs and character. The goal of this participatory process is that the design be a direct reflection and integration of the group's ideas.

Mary is a registered architect with a strong background in energy-efficient design and environmentally sustainable materials and systems. She has been researching healthful indoor environments for over ten years, and has designed healthful interiors in low-budget situations. Her technical expertise combined with her ability to facilitate group process enables her to work effectively to bring a community's dreams into form.

Mary is a resident of the Pioneer Valley CoHousing community in Amherst, Massachusetts. 1/19/95

LAND INSTITUTE, THE

**2440 E. Water Well Road
Salina, KS 67401**

(913)823-5376

The mission of the Land Institute is to help transform agriculture to protect the long-term ability of the earth to support a variety of life and culture. We are dedicated to good stewardship of the earth, and the development of a sustainable agriculture—one that halts the damaging exploitation of the agricultural resource base and allows people to continue growing food. The Land Institute is engaged in a range of interdependent activities including agricultural research, education, public policy work, and programs to conserve agricultural resources. 8/3/93

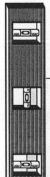

LAND TRUST ASSOCIATION

**14 Western Road
Henley on Thames
Oxon RG9 1JL
ENGLAND**

44-491-579065

The objects of the Land Trust Association are to facilitate the dedication of farm land and estates to the public benefit by means of charitable land trusts, and in this manner ensure their preservation, use, and development for the continuing long-term benefit of rural communities and the public in general. 4/28/92

LANDELIJKE VERENIGING CENTRAAL WONEN

**Grenadadreef 1-J
3563 HE Utrecht
THE NETHERLANDS**

030-612585

National association of cohousing projects in Holland. Each household has its own house or apartment and one share in the common facilities, which typically include a fully equipped kitchen, play areas, and meeting rooms. Residents share cooking, cleaning, and gardening on a rotating basis. By working together and combining their resources, collaborative housing residents can have the advantages of a private home and the convenience of shared services and amenities. 2/12/93

LEFT BANK DISTRIBUTION

**4142 Brooklyn NE
Seattle, WA 98105**

(206)632-5870

Left Bank Distribution, a project spawned by Left Bank Books (our collectively owned store in its 19th year in Seattle's Pike Place public Market), sells books, pamphlets, and periodicals wholesale, retail, and as an international mail-order supplier. While we are "anti-state, anti-capitalist, and anti-authoritarian," we are by no means anti-people. In our diversity as a collective, our common belief is in people's ability to be autonomous and cooperative with one another as long as they aren't constrained by governments, parties, religions, or economic systems. We carry a lot of books that reflect this attitude, as well as a wide selection of "progressive" materials. We have also published a dozen books and pamphlets. We carry over 50 other radical presses,

including over 1000 titles. We recently released the International Blacklist, which features over 5000 listings of anarchist and independent groups and projects from all over the world. Contact us for catalogs and info. 6/3/92

LINKWAY CENTRE

**87 Wordsworth Road
Lombardy East
Johannesburg
2090 SOUTH AFRICA**

011-882-4299

The Centre encourages work in the humanities and sciences that promotes human values and potentials. Our activities consist of training, research, work-study programs, individual consultations and treatments, and various projects and conferences. We specialize in stress management, whole health, new lifestyles, personal empowerment, Psychosynthesis, community projects, training and treatment in physical therapy, and creative initiatives—as well as alternative education and the promotion of multicultural understanding. 12/4/92

LIVING VILLAGE DESIGN

**P.O. Box 1734
Boulder, CO 80306**

(303)449-4264

Living Village Design uses a whole-systems approach to designing intentional communities. Our planning team provides a broad range of professional skills including architecture, Earth-friendly building techniques, landscape design, and group process. We ground our designs in the timeless qualities of architecture, in a permacultural approach to site development, and in the village or intentional community as a social model.

By observing and imitating natural systems, we create a symbiosis of the natural and built environments. Through the integration of humans, animals, plants, structures, and landscapes, we can help find sustainable solutions for your community's material and non-material needs.

We express today's emerging ecological values in the context of community, demonstrating how people can live on the planet in a balanced, graceful, and healthy way. We offer expertise and assistance in all aspects of the community development process. 11/30/94

MACROCOSM USA

P.O. Box 185
Cambria, CA 93428-0185
(805)927-8030/927-1987 Fax

A nonprofit clearinghouse of information for progressive social change. We compile and edit material into utilitarian formats such as handbooks, databases, newsletters, and reports. Currently we offer a directory/handbook, *Macrocosm USA: Possibilities for a New Progressive Era* for $24.95. It contains 14 chapters compiled from excerpts and original material submitted by the alternative press and organizations. Directory section contains over 5000 organizations, periodicals, media sources, publishers, businesses, and reference directories and guides. Communities included. Foreword by Marilyn Ferguson. 8-1/2x11, 432pp. Handbook and our quarterly newsletter, *Possibilities*, are free with membership: $30 students; $45 individuals; $60 nonprofits; $90 businesses. Specialized reports and database also available. In 1993 we launched an affordable computer bulletin board ($12/year with free connect time) that provides access to conferences, files, e-mail services, and our huge interactive database of progressive organizations and resources described above. 8/19/93

Have Computer Will Travel?

If you're interested in community and want to be connected with others electronically, there are an ever-expanding number of choices available to you. For entry points onto the information highway, see the World Wide Web ad on page 416, and the e-mail addresses on page 438.

MADISON COMMUNITY COOPERATIVES

306 North Brooks
Madison, WI 53715
(608)251-2667

MCC, established in 1970, owns 9 cooperative houses in Madison, WI, home of the University of Wisconsin. The combined population of these houses is 180–190 members, mostly students and university employees; all members own part of the company and part of the house they live in. Network decisions are made by a board comprised of MCC staff and representatives of each house. Individual houses are self-governing, working out the cooking and chore schedules by consensus; one house is all women, seven have vegetarian meals. 6/20/94

MEDIA NETWORK

39 West 14th Street #403
New York, NY 10011
(212)929-2663/929-2732 Fax

Media Network is the nation's premier broker of information on films and videos which foster social equality, cultural democracy, peace, and conservation of the environment. We operate an information center that compiles and disseminates information on available social-issue media including: 1) acclaimed media guides which evaluate new films and videos, 2) a quarterly magazine, and 3) fiscal sponsorship for independent producers. Our resources are used by schools, libraries, community groups, issue activists, media specialists, and concerned individuals seeking alternatives to Hollywood and mainstream television. We host an ongoing series of conferences and community workshops on broadening the use of independent film and video, and offer intensive training seminars that teach health care providers how to better serve their constituencies by using media to educate and facilitate discussion. Membership: Individuals $25–$100; Organizations/Institutions $50–$250. 8/6/93

METAPHYSICAL COMPUTER B.B.S.

P.O. Box 614
Vanbrunt Station
Brooklyn, NY 11215

BaphoNet is a free metaphysical computer bulletin board with 65 separate message areas. Over 60 megabytes of free files to download, many of which can't be found anywhere else. Our Chat Line numbers are:
- (718)499-9277 at 1200 baud
- (718)499-0513 at 9600 baud
- Netmail address is: 1:278/666.0

7/14/92

MORNINGSTAR ADVENTURES

9789 – 13 Mile Road
Leroy, MI 49655
(616)768-4368

Morningstar Adventures, Inc., is a nonprofit organization and spiritual life center formed to provide primarily women opportunities to develop their personal identity and to discover their uniqueness through the recognition of what God intends. We provide safe, rustic retreat and play shop space for 1–12 persons. Presently, two women live in community at the center. Our lifestyle is a commitment to devotion, simplicity, wholeness, and creativity as a foundation to the spiritual midwifery of others. We practice eco-spirituality. Write for more information or call. 5/18/92

MOTHER JONES

731 Market St #600
San Francisco, CA 94103
(415)665-6637/665-6696 Fax

Mother Jones delivers a unique blend of tough investigative reporting, spirited writing on everything from politics to the arts, as well as humor and award-winning graphics. *Mother Jones* is published by the Foundation for National Progress, a nonprofit tax-exempt organization which researches the controversial issues that lead to social change. Subscriptions are $18 per year (six issues), foreign $28. 3/15/94

MOUNTAIN GROVE

Center for New Education
P.O. Box 818
Glendale, OR 97442

The Mountain Grove Center for New Education is a nonprofit educational foundation governed by a Board of Directors whose positions are held by both resident and nonresident members. We continue to explore MGC's purpose, which is, in brief, to serve humanity through the channel of education and community, and to pursue these as a lifetime experiential process.

MGC is in the process of developing services and projects that align with our philosophies and commitments, and we welcome others who have developed similar projects and/or services. Participation requires a strong commitment to honesty, integrity, and autonomy, as well as financial stability and compatibility with others on the land. If you feel yourself compatible with our commitments and goals, and have a project and/or service to offer that will align with our purpose and goals, we welcome hearing from you. Please include a SASE with your letter. 5/1/94

NALSAS

P.O. Box 2823
Santa Fe, NM 87504
(505)471-6928/474-3220 Fax

The National Assoc. for Legal Support of Alternative Schools (NALSAS) is a national information and legal service center designed to research, coordinate, and support legal actions involving non-public educational alternatives. We challenge compulsory attendance laws—as violative of First Amendment rights and state provisions for non-compulsory learning arrangements (such as home schooling). NALSAS helps interested organizations and individuals locate, evaluate, and create viable alternatives to traditional schooling approaches. We also accredit NALSAS members. Dues are $30. 1/5/95

NASCO

North American
Students of Cooperation
P.O. Box 7715
Ann Arbor, MI 48107

(313)663-0889/663-5072 Fax

NASCO works toward a socially responsible, fiscally stable, North American student co-op movement. Supported financially by student cooperatives, we are their trade organization, providing operational assistance and consulting, encouraging the development of new student co-ops, and serving as an advocate for student co-ops in the US and Canada. Services include *Co-op Voices*, a student co-op newsletter; the NASCO Cooperative Education & Training Institute, a weekend of courses, discussions, films, and networking for those involved with student co-ops; cooperative publications sales; the NASCO Internship Network; and much more. Student co-op development work is done by related corporations: NASCO Properties and Campus Cooperative Development Corporation. 8/10/93

NATIONAL ACCESS TELEVISION

419 Park Ave. South, 4th Fl.
New York, NY 10016

(212)925-7553

National Access Television, on the air since 3/1/94, broadcasts a wide variety of new channel ideas as well as public and leased access-type programs. Programing is in the clear to satellite dish viewers, and many cable companies across the country cherry-pick shows for their local access channels. NATV features a broad range of programs including Christian inspiration, rap and jazz performances and interviews, show biz news, home video-making tips, comedy, gay/lesbian, Eckankar, environmental coverage, and "Weird TV." 6/29/94

NATIONAL ASSOCIATION OF HOUSING COOPERATIVES (NAHC)

1614 King Street
Alexandria, VA 22314

(703)549-5201

NAHC is a nonprofit national federation of housing co-ops, professionals, organizations, and individuals promoting the interests of co-op housing communities. NAHC formed the Center for Cooperative

Housing to provide technical assistance in developing co-op housing and linkage between local sponsors, the co-op network, and federal programs. We provide technical assistance and training to housing co-op boards and members to help them improve the operation of their co-op. Membership includes the "Cooperative Housing Bulletin"; the *Cooperative Housing Journal*; and discounts on publications, conference registrations, and other items and services. 12/8/92

NATIONAL COOPERATIVE BANK

1401 Eye Street NW #700
Washington, DC 20005

(202)336-7700/336-7622 Fax
(202)336-7663 Free booklets

NCB is a private, cooperatively owned financial institution which provides commercial, investment, and development banking services to cooperative businesses nationwide. We offer a variety of financial services, including short- and long-term loans at commercial rates of interest. Our affiliate NCB Development Corporation provides business planning and risk capital to start-up cooperatives.

NCB publishes a free booklet on affordable housing called "Report on Low-Income Lending," and another on "How to Organize a Cooperative" (includes effective use of advisors and committees, keeping members informed and involved, maintaining proper board/manager relations, following sound business practices, conducting businesslike meetings, and forging links with other cooperatives). For free booklets write Attn: Nancy Spilsburg. 1/5/95

NATIONAL FEDERATION OF COMMUNITY BROADCASTERS

666 – 11th Street NW #805
Washington, DC 20001

(202)393-2355
nfcd@aol.com

NFCB is a membership organization that was formed to facilitate information, expertise, and program sharing between community-oriented public radio stations; to help groups start such stations; and to lobby for those stations with national funders, public radio entities, and Congress. Each year NFCB hosts a 3–4 day conference with workshops covering topics important to community broadcasters.

(Continued...)

Community stations usually encourage local people to learn how to host and engineer programs, to be news reporters, or to get involved in other ways. The programming on community stations is often quite diverse, often featuring alternate points of view and music not often played on other stations.

NFCB has 102 participating member stations and 125 associates in all parts of the U.S., and also has close ties with the worldwide radio association AMARC. To find out if there is a community station near you, or for help in starting a station, please write. 1/5/95

NATIONAL HOMESCHOOL ASSOCIATION

PO Box 157290
Cincinnati OH 45215
(513)772-9580

The National Homeschool Association (NHA) exists to advocate individual choice and freedom in education, to serve families who choose to homeschool, and to inform the general public about home education. We have a quarterly publication, and an annual conference held in the late summer/early fall. NHA is committed to emphasizing the diversity of homeschoolers while encouraging the acceptance of homeschooling as an individualized approach to education. Annual membership (includes publication) is $15, resource information packet $3. 8/10/93

NATIONAL WAR TAX RE-SISTANCE COORDINATING COMMITTEE (NWTRCC)

P.O. Box 774
Monroe, ME 04951-0774
(207)525-7774

The National War Tax Resistance Coordinating Committee (NWTRCC) is a coalition of local, regional, and national groups that support conscientious objection to military taxation through protest, war tax refusal (WTR), and redirection of war taxes to peaceful purposes. NWTRCC maintains a national network of affiliate groups, contacts, alternative funds, and counselors who provide information on WTR. We publish a bimonthly newsletter, produce and disseminate WTR literature, provide technical assistance on WTR organizing, coordinate tax day actions, and organize semiannual national meetings. For many people, WTR and alternative

economics, including community living, go hand-in-hand. Basic packets of WTR information are free on request. 1/4/93

NATIVE SEEDS/SEARCH

2509 N. Campbell Ave. #325
Tucson, AZ 85719
(520)327-9123

Native Seeds/SEARCH is a nonprofit, seed conservation organization involved in collection, distribution, research, and education. We focus our activities on the traditional native crops (and their wild relatives) of the U.S. Southwest and northwest Mexico. The food crops of this region are delicious, nutritious, and better adapted to the harsh environments of the low hot deserts and dry rocky uplands than are most modern vegetables. In addition, the native peoples and long-term residents of the Greater Southwest have a rich folk science associated with these fiber, dye, medicinal, ceremonial, and food plants.

Members receive a quarterly newsletter, and 10% discounts. All proceeds go toward our continuing efforts to preserve these plants in their native habitats and in seed banks, and to study their seemingly boundless benefits for humanity. Annual memberships are $18, our catalog is $1. 5/14/92

NATURAL HYGIENE, INC.

P.O. Box 2132
Huntington, CT 06484
(203)929-1557

We publish the bimonthly *Journal of Natural Hygiene.* We have a research department that provides information on 700 subjects related to symptomology. We host two conferences annually and are a source for books, audiotapes, and videotapes. We produce two regular radio programs featuring health topics on WPKN (out of Bridgeport, CT) and Pacifica Radio WBAI (out of NY). Our president, Jo Willard, has hosted the WPKN radio program for the past 21 years, and WBAI for 2-1/2 years. 12/18/92

NATURAL RIGHTS CENTER

The Farm, P.O. Box 90
Summertown, TN 38483
(615)964-2334/964-3992

The Natural Rights Center is a nonprofit, public interest law project of Plenty USA [see separate listing], and is associated

with the United Nations Department of Public Information. Philosophically we don't equate security with firepower, technology, or property. We hope to create real security by making the world a healthier, safer, and fairer place to live.

Our projects are directed toward averting future suffering. We fight industries that poison future peoples or squander their vital resources. We challenge agencies that discount future lives in order to gratify society's present desires. We work to improve the process of justice, and to enlighten the democratic discussion.

Current projects include toxic waste dumping, atomic veterans and radiation victims, protection of natural areas and wildlife, human rights and voting rights, nuclear power and nuclear waste, nuclear weapons testing and deployment. The natural rights we're defending reach beyond the rights of the two-leggeds. They include the needs of the four-leggeds, those with fins, and wings, and roots in the ground. 12/2/94

NCACS

National Coalition
of Alternative
Community Schools
P.O. Box 15036
Santa Fe, NM 87506
(505)474-4312

National Coalition of Alternative Community Schools (NCACS) is an organization of individuals, families, groups, and private schools who are united in their desire to create a new structure for education. We are committed to a process that 1) empowers people to actively and collectively direct their lives, 2) requires active control of education by all involved, and 3) develops tools and skills for social change. We publish a quarterly newsletter, and the largest directory of alternative schools and resources—with over 400 listings in 47 states and 18 countries. We also hold a national conference each spring, and various regional conferences. 1/4/95

NEIGHBORHOOD WORKS, THE

**Center for Neighbor-
hood Technology
2125 W. North Avenue
Chicago, IL 60647**

(312)278-4800 / 278-3840 Fax

The Neighborhood Works is a bimonthly, nonprofit news magazine. We write about what low-and middle-income communities are doing to address issues of housing, energy, environment, economic development, and transit. We share with you the resources for making your neighborhood work. Subscriptions are $30/year. 12/12/92

NEW AGE JOURNAL

**P.O. Box 53275
Boulder, CO 80321-3275**

(617)787-2005 / (800)234-4556

The *New Age Journal* is a bimonthly magazine that focuses on living a more natural and holistic lifestyle. We publish an annual directory of resources which features Holistic Health & Natural Living, Personal Growth & Exploration, Social Change, and includes everything from self-help options, to ecologically conscious household products, to socially responsible investing. Subscriptions in the U.S. are $24/year. 3/15/94

NEW CATALYST, THE

**P.O. Box 189
Gabriola Island, BC
V0R-1X0 CANADA**

(604)247-9737

After five years of publishing a 36-page quarterly tabloid covering the environmental, bioregional, peace, feminist, and community movements in the west, *The New Catalyst* has now divided its publications in two: the tabloid still exists in a free 16-page version oriented mostly to local and regional issues, and the more enduring "feature" material of continent-wide relevance is now packaged twice yearly in book form as our Bioregional Series. An $18 subscription gives you *The New Catalyst* magazine plus two books from the Bioregional Series. 3/8/91

NEW ENVIRONMENT ASSOCIATION, THE

**270 Fernway Drive
Syracuse, NY 13224**

(315)446-8009

The Association, begun in 1974, provides a framework and process for cooperative efforts that can contribute to the creation of an alternative future—a "New Environment"—as well as for mutual support and personal change. Our long-range goal is new communities that are humanly and environmentally sound and incorporate various New Environment principles. A wide range of topics get addressed at our general meetings and study groups, from organic gardening and holistic health, to new economics and alternative education. Activities vary and depend on member interest. Currently, priorities are to establish an NEA house in Syracuse that will be owned by our land trust, and to develop a small nature study and retreat center north of Utica. Members gather periodically for weekend retreats, and pursue specific projects in small working groups. Our monthly newsletter reaches readers across the US and in several other countries. A sample copy is sent upon request. 1/22/93

NEW MILLENIUM PUBLISHING

**P.O. Box 3065
Portland, OR 97208**

(503)297-7321 / 297-0436 Fax

New Millennium [formerly Centaur Press] publishes *Transformative Adventures, Vacations & Retreat*, an international directory of 300+ host organizations. The first edtion was released in early 1994—a 304-page book profiling 305 organizations that each year host more than 3000 opportunities for transformative experience, ranging from weekend getaways to multi-month community sojourns.

The directory includes personal growth centers; meditation and prayer retreats; holistic health family camps and vacation spas; emotional and physical recovery centers; healing journeys and pilgrimages; plus wilderness programs such as vision quests. 235 of the organizations operate exclusively in North America. 46 operate in the British Isles and continental Europe. The rest are in places like the Caribbean, Mexico, India, and Australia. All provide lodging and meals (over 95% are vegetarian or offer vegetarian options) and conduct

their programs in English. The book retails for $14.95 (U.S. Dollars) and can be purchased by mail with a check for $18 (or the U.S. Dollar equivalent in most foreign currencies). Discounts are available for purchases of 10 or more books. Wholesale and distributorship inquiries are welcome. 12/17/93

NEW ROAD MAP FOUNDATION

**P.O. Box 15981
Seattle, WA 98115**

The New Road Map Foundation, an all-volunteer nonprofit organization, has focused for many years on helping people shift to low-consumption, high-fulfillment lifestyles. They have created a number of tools for sustainability: the best-selling book *Your Money Or Your Life* by Joe Dominguez and Vicki Robin ($11); "All-Consuming Passion: Waking Up from the American Dream" ($1), a collection of fascinating statistics woven together to tell a story about our patterns of consumption and how they affect both our personal lives and the planet; and "How Earth Friendly Are You?—A Lifestyle Self-Assessment Questionnaire" ($2). These can be ordered from QTS, P.O. Box 15352, Seattle, WA 98115 (make checks payable to "QTS"). *Transforming Your Relationship with Money and Achieving Financial Independence* (the audiocassette/workbook course on which *Your Money or Your Life* is based) is available for $60 from New Road Map at P.O. Box 15981, Seattle, WA 98115. 10/2/94

NEW SOCIETY PUBLISHERS

• **Attn: Pat Hoyt
4527 Springfield Avenue
Philadelphia, PA 19143**

**(215)382-6543
(800)333-9093 Orders M–F 10–5
M/C, AmEx, & Visa only**

Canadian Office:

• **P.O. Box 189
Gabriola Island
BC V0R-1X0**

(604)247-9737

New Society Publishers is a not-for-profit, worker-controlled publishing house committed to fundamental social change through nonviolent action. We are connected to a growing worldwide network of peace, feminist, environmental, and human rights activists, and we strive to meet their (your!) needs. We are proud to publish books by and for activists—books in which we try to see the world in new ways; to find new connections and repair old ones; to build a more just, peaceful, and joyful world. And we are proud of our efforts to practice what we preach in our organization and in the way we conduct business. For more information please give us a call. 6/29/94

NICA

Northwest Intentional Communities Association
22020 East Lost Lake Road
Snohomish, WA 98290

The Northwest Intentional Communities Association serves as a hub for communication, organization, and cooperation between local, regional, and national residential community organizations. Our quarterly newsletter features community profiles, announcements, and informative articles.

Potential future projects include creating a skills exchange network, publishing a directory, and helping new communities get started. Membership is open to anyone interested in communities, seeking information, or wanting opportunities to network. Send $5 to become a member and receive the newsletter for one year. To get a sample copy of the newsletter send a stamped, self-addressed envelope. 10/16/94

Where in the world will you find us next?

Twice a year, the Fellowship holds three-day board meetings, and *you're* invited! FIC board meetings are open to all—and there's no better way to find out what's happening in the movement, or to explore ways you can lend a hand in the exciting work of building a cooperative network. For info on upcoming meetings, see the Calendar section of *Communities* magazine, or write FIC, Route 1, Box 155-CD, Rutledge, MO 63563.

NOLO PRESS

950 Parker Street
Berkeley, CA 94710
(510)549-1976/548-5902 Fax

Nolo Press is the nation's leading and most highly respected publisher of self-help law books. Nolo was founded in 1971 with the idea of making the law more accessible to ordinary people. Our books have helped demystify the legal system, including consumer issues, small business, wills and estate planning, family law, taxes, zoning, and more. We publish a quarterly, *Nolo News*, to keep readers up to date on law changes that affect Nolo books and to provide practical legal information to our readers. 3/15/94

NOMENUS

• **P.O. Box 170358**
San Francisco, CA 94117

(541)866-2678 (OR#)

Radical Faerie Gatherings info:

• **Wolf Creek Sanctuary**
P.O. Box 312
Wolf Creek, OR 97497

Nomenus is a nonprofit corporation which was founded in 1985 to locate and purchase land trusts for faerie sanctuary space. Since that time Nomenus has broadened its base—we have hosted three large West Coast gatherings of the Radical Faeries, and produce the *Faerie Home Companion*. Our promotion of radical awareness includes participation in bookstores, the California Men's Gathering, fundraisers, etc. We publish *Nomenews* to inform members of gatherings, projects, fund-raisers, land reports, and land developments.

We also maintain a computerized Faerie Database (fey dish). 1/8/95

NORTHCOUNTRY COOPERATIVE DEVELOPMENT FUND

400 – 19th Ave. S, 2nd floor
Minneapolis, MN 55454
(612)339-1553

Northcountry Cooperative Development Fund is a community development loan fund serving cooperatives throughout the upper Midwest. Founded in 1979 by a handful of Twin Cities' food co-ops, NCDF has grown and prospered, making over 220 loans to a wide variety of consumer, housing, worker, and small agricultural co-ops

in nine Midwestern states. A cooperative itself, NCDF is owned and managed by its member cooperatives. For information about joining or investing in NCDF, please contact our office. 8/3/93

NORTHLAND POSTER COLLECTIVE

P.O. Box 7096
Minneapolis, MN 55407
(612)721-2273/721-2160 Fax
(800)627-3082

Northland Poster Collective is a 15-year-old producer of art that celebrates justice, sisterhood, cooperation, ecology, diversity, and grassroots organizing. We distribute posters, T-shirts, buttons, cards, bumper stickers, and other items for end use or fund raising. We also custom print all of these items on a nationwide basis.

We create social history posters for schools, and provide training on the use of art in labor organizing. The collective offers various levels of paid memberships—including generous discounts—to those who support our work. We welcome submission of artwork and ideas. Our catalog is available on request. 12/26/93

NORTHWEST COHOUSING QUARTERLY

711 West 11th
Eugene, OR 97402
(541)343-5739

We provide information about cohousing projects in the Northwest, including several projects in the Seattle-Puget Sound area. Cohousing is forming community in an age-diverse setting, with people owning their private homes but sharing a common dining facility. Our publication reports the progress of existing projects and has book reviews, letters, and articles about finance, organizational structure, development, decision-making styles, solar design, participatory design, and management. 12/23/93

NSS SEMINARS, INC.

P.O. Box 620123
Woodside, CA 94062
(415)851-4751/851-1265 Fax

National Sexuality Symposium Seminars, Inc., promotes a positive view of sexuality. Services include a quarterly magazine titled the *Not Naughty News* which contains interesting and informative articles and columns on sexuality and relationships.

We also sponsor an annual national conference and exposition with 40 speakers on sexuality and relationship topics, plus a huge exhibit area and many social events. Call or write for additional information. The conference is held in the San Francisco Bay area in September. 1/4/93

NUCLEAR FREE AMERICA

325 East 25th Street
Baltimore, MD 21218

(301)235-3575/462-1039 Fax
PeaceNet: "nfa"

Nuclear Free America is a nonprofit educational resource center and clearinghouse for the nuclear free zone movement. NFA works closely with existing nuclear free zones and campaigns—providing them with a variety of legal, educational, and organizing resources. NFA also promotes socially responsible investing and purchasing (encouraging individuals, organizations, and communities not to do business with nuclear weapons contractors) and maintains a detailed database of nuclear weapons contractors.

Contact NFA for information about nuclear-free consumer products and on how to declare your home, property, or community a nuclear free zone. 5/14/92

OMEGA INSTITUTE

260 Lake Drive
Rhinebeck, NY 12572

(914)266-4444/266-4828 Fax
(800)944-1001 Reservations

Omega Institute for Holistic Studies, founded in 1977, is the largest nonprofit vacation/learning center on the East Coast. Over 10,000 people participate in 250 weekend and week-long workshops during the 5-month summer season. We have an 80-acre lakefront campus located in the rolling hills two hours north of New York City. Workshops at Omega explore new ideas in the arts, psychology, health, fitness, business, global thinking, spirituality, and preventive medicine. Our faculty are the leaders and innovators in their fields. We also sponsor educational and wilderness trips throughout the world, 6-week

winter programs on St. John's Island (in the US Virgin Islands), and winter courses at other sites in the Northeast. Write or call for more information and a free descriptive catalog. 1/5/95

OMEGA NEW AGE DIRECTORY

6418 S. 39th Avenue
Phoenix, AZ 85041

(602)237-3213
(800)888-OMEGA

Since 1972, the *Omega New Age Directory* has been providing New Age news... important information and insightful articles about UFOs, holistic health, Earth changes, ESP, women's rights, astrology, and spiritual practices. A real newspaper, the *Directory* covers local, national, and international news of interest to New Agers. We also have a comprehensive directory of all the New Age churches and study groups in Arizona; a directory service for psychic readers and counselors; and another directory for healing practitioners. Every religion is part of the New Age. 5/16/92

ONE BY ONE

c/o Wilson
3920 East 17th
Eugene, OR 97403

One by One is a support network for people who have bonded themselves together through a common vow of nonviolence, and a commitment to not cooperate with a system/world view that is oppressing all life on earth. Although this vow is not tied to any one spiritual path, we relate to the Biblical term "Babylon" as a description of the self-destructive society we live in today. The Babylon system continues only because of our individual participation in its violence (both directly and indirectly), and its end will only come when enough of us, one by one, refuse that participation. We have found that taking this vow with others is a profoundly empowering and liberating experience; we are given new courage to see the ways in which our lives are supporting Babylon, and the strength to sever that support. Much of our inspiration has come from the Community of the Ark in France. Our goal is to eventually form an Ark-like community in the U.S., and to seed the creation of others. Send SASE for more complete info. 6/28/94

ONE EARTH MAGAZINE

The Park, Findhorn
Forres, IV36-OTZ
SCOTLAND

(+44-1309) 691128
http://www.mcn.org/
findhorn/home.html

One Earth: the quarterly magazine of the Findhorn Foundation and the spiritually oriented open community which is growing up around the original spiritually guided community at Findhorn, Scotland. Published since 1975, it addresses issues arising out of experience and concerns of this intentional community and its past members and friends worldwide. Articles by and interviews with renowned progressive thinkers and practitioners, as well as quality submissions from the general public. Main focus is on spiritual community, personal growth, social development, environmental stewardship, interpersonal relationship, gender relationships, spiritual paths and religion, arts and crafts, music, reviews, therapies, courses, and retreats. Editorial and visual submissions welcome. Subscriptions at US$20 (surface), US$26 (airmail) for four issues. US$ checks and Mastercard, Visa welcome. 11/17/92

ONE WORLD FAMILY TRAVEL NETWORK

81868 Lost Valley Lane
Dexter, OR 97431

(541)937-3351

The One World Family Travel Network, created to educate individuals about the alternatives to mass tourism, emphasizes programs designed around the themes of socially and environmentally responsible travel. Dianne Brause, its founder, emphasizes that travel which promotes cultural understanding and good will among people, and tours which teach appreciation, protection, and restoration of the natural environment, can contribute to a more peaceful world. Examples include educational and scientific expeditions, citizen diplomacy, environmental restoration, volunteering and work camps, retreats and cross-cultural sharing (including learning from indigenous peoples), among others. A directory listing over 250 of these resources is available for $8.50 postpaid. Make checks out to Dianne Brause. 5/23/92

OPEN FORUM NETWORK

**5567 Multnomah Blvd
Portland OR 97219**

(503)246-5143

The Open Forum Network is an independent organization that provides information about the Cerro Gordo community near Cottage Grove, Oregon. It is intended for current and future residents of the community, investors, and others who are inspired by the Cerro Gordo dream. Our intention is to maintain an ongoing dialog between all interested parties on any and all subjects related to Cerro Gordo. Call or write for more information. 12/31/94

OREGON WOMAN'S LAND TRUST

**P.O. Box 1692
Roseburg, OR 97429**

(541)679-3266

The Oregon Woman's Land Trust (OWLT), founded in 1975 by Northwest Lesbian Feminists, is a nonprofit, tax-exempt

corporation. We are an umbrella organization for OWL Farm [see community listing] and are dedicated to accessibility of land to lesbians and other wimmin who might not otherwise have access. We are also committed to preserving and protecting Mother Earth. OWLT hopes to include other lesbian lands in our organization sometime in the future. Write for more information. 9/6/92

OSCA

**Oberlin Student
Cooperative Association
Wilder, Box 86
Oberlin, OH 44074**

(216)775-8108

OSCA, est. 1950, is a unique co-op in that it houses and feeds 174 student owners and feeds an additional 440 student owners in dining facilities. Individual houses are self-managed, and decisions for the association are made democratically, with representation from all of the individual units. Some decisions are by simple majority; most are by consensus. OSCA buys food from local farms as much as possible; special provisions are made for members with vegetarian and kosher dietary preferences. The co-op owns some of its facilities, and leases most from the University. 11/15/93

OSHO CENTERS

in North America

There are about 500 Osho (Rajneesh) Meditation Centers around the world, with the main ashram located in Poona, India [see International listings]. In the US there are about 50 centers, some fairly communal, some quite decentralized:

- **Osho America**
  Santa Ana, CA (714)771-8475
- **Osho Bindu**
  Encinitas, CA (619)632-8872
- **Osho Padme**
  New York, NY (212)675-6529
- **Osho Payonidhi**
  New York, NY (212)725-6337
- **Osho Rachana**
  Redmond, WA (206)233-8526
- **Osho Viha**
  Mill Valley, CA (415)381-9861

OTHER OSHO RESOURCES:

- **Chidvilas**
  P.O. Box 3849
  Sedona, AZ 86340

(800)777-7743
Credit card orders only.
Their catalog features thousands of Osho books & tapes.
- **Osho Times Newspaper**
  P.O. Box 318
  Mill Valley, CA 94942
  Subscriptions $60/year
- **Osho Cable Network** 10/22/93
  P.O. Box 148
  Ojai, CA 93024
  (805)646-0773
  Schedules, newsletter, videos for sale.

OUT ON BALE, UNLTD.

**1037 E. Linden Avenue
Tucson, AZ 85719**

(520)624-1673

Out-On-Bale, Unlimited, is the central source for the best and latest information. Their newsletter, *The Last Straw* explains everything you'd ever want to know about strawbale technology. They also have some dandy videos available describing the technology, and host periodic demonstrations and workshops in the Southwest. 4/14/94

OZARK REGIONAL LAND TRUST

**427 South Main Street
Carthage, MO 64836**

(417)358-4484

Ozark Regional Land Trust (ORLT) is a nonprofit organization operating in the Ozark hills of Missouri and Arkansas. ORLT designs community and conservation land trusts which permanently protect the ecology of the land. The use of community land trusts (CLT) provides a lifetime residential stewardship opportunity within a setting of community cooperation. ORLT provides assistance to newly forming CLTs. CLTs can also become legal affiliates of ORLT. Currently ORLT has two CLT affiliates protecting a total of 750 acres. ORLT supports the formation of community associations which are ecologically based, democratic, non-speculative, and providing access to the landless. ORLT allows each CLT to make its policies, manage its land, and take care of day-to-day operation; this arrangement makes each CLT a unique community experiment, and builds leadership skill. The experience of each CLT is shared with other CLTs through ORLT. Residential opportunities are still available. 12/24/92

OZARKS RESOURCE CENTER

P.O. Box 3
Brixey, MO 65618
(417)679-4773

The Ozarks Resource Center is an educational institute dedicated to providing research, education, technical assistance, and dissemination of information on various subjects including appropriate technology, environmentally responsible practices, community economic development, sustainable agriculture, and self-reliance for the family, community, and bioregion. 7/15/92

PARENTS LEADERSHIP INSTITUTE

P.O. Box 50492
Palo Alto, CA 94303

The Parents Leadership Institute offers classes and resource groups for parents who want to learn from each other as they build close relationships with their children and good lives for themselves as parents. PLI publishes a series of useful pamphlets on parental listening skills—dealing with children's crying, tantrums, fears, and anger, for example. Please write for more information. 5/20/92

PEOPLE FRIENDLY BUSINESS

5294 Franklin Street
Hilliard, OH 43026

**(RESOURCE MAY BE DEFUNCT—
LOST CONTACT 1/96)**

People Friendly Business (PFB), is a work-from-home group that encourages businesses to place the needs of people before greed, money, and status. We educate people on creative, inexpensive ways to work from home—such as worker-owned co-ops, manufacturing from home, etc. We focus on marketing and advertising your goods and services via support groups, networking, referrals, and a mail order catalog that lists products and services of PFB supporters. The catalog gives you a market for your goods; prices are wholesale or retail, and we encourage our members to buy from each other. To learn more, send $25.00 with a 9x13 SASE plus $3.00 postage. We will send you a book called *At Home, At Work: How to Make Money with People Friendly Business* and place you on our mailing list. You may also work from home for PFB as a sub-contractor, or learn how to start a support group in your community and earn money for doing it. 12/4/92

PEP

P.O. Box 6306
Ocean View, HI 96737
(808)929-9691/929-9831 Fax

Merged with Abundant Love Institute [see separate listing]. 12/21/94

PEREGRINE FOUNDATION

KIT Newsletter
P.O. Box 460141
San Francisco, CA 94146-0141
(415)821-2090

The Peregrine Foundation is a charitable, educational public foundation created to assist families and individuals living in or exiting from experimental social groups. Its first project started in 1989 as the *Keep In Touch* newsletter for the approximately 1000 ex-members of the Bruderhof communities (Hutterian Brethren). New projects include the *MOST Newsletter* (for alums of the Morning Star and Wheeler's Ranch "open land" communities) and Carrier Pigeon Press, which will publish 4 to 6 titles a year. Its first publication, *The Community That Failed* by Roger Allain, is a memoir by one of the leaders of the now-defunct South American Bruderhof communities. Subscriptions: *KIT* Bruderhof newsletter is $20 annually; the *MOST Newsletter* is $12. Write for a brochure or a free issue. 10/14/92

PERMACULTURE ACTIVIST, THE

P.O. Box 1209
Black Mountain, NC 28711

"I believe we can design our way out of the present ecological crisis. Four years ago thinking shifted from denying that we had environmental problems, to the awareness we have today. Now we're working for a shift from people knowing that there are problems, to knowing that there are already solutions." —Lea Harrison, permaculture teacher.

The *Permaculture Activist* reports the work of grassroots landscape designers and social change artists from across the continent and around the world. Join the conversation. 4 issues/$16 (International $20). Also books, charts, videos, design resources, workshops, referrals, and connections for agroforestry, village settlement, pattern literacy, specialty crops, biological architecture, and much, much more. 1/26/95

PERMACULTURE DRYLANDS INSTITUTE

P.O. Box 133
Pearce, AZ 85625
(520)824-3465/824-3542 Fax

Trainings and resources for design of sustainable dryland homes and communities. Membership: $15–25 per year. Members receive the *Permaculture Drylands Journal*. Call or write for course and publications listing. 1/22/93

PLANET DRUM FOUNDATION

P.O. Box 31251
San Francisco, CA 94131
Shasta Bioregion

Planet Drum Foundation's primary focus is bioregionalism, a grassroots approach to ecology that emphasizes sustainability, community self-determination, and regional self-reliance. The Green City Project brings a bioregional approach to sustainable urban living. Planet Drum has published an international directory that lists over 150 different bioregional organizations and contact people. The directory is included in issue #15 of *Raise The Stakes*, a regular Planet Drum publication, and updated in issue #18/19. Annual membership (including two issues of *Raise The Stakes*) is $20/year, $25 outside North America. 6/17/92

PLENTY USA

P.O. Box 394
Summertown, TN 38483-0394
(615)964-4864
plentyusa@mclmall.com

In 1974 The Farm in Tennessee [see community listing] started an outreach program called Plenty. In its first ten years, Plenty established a clinic in Bangladesh, a tree nursery in Lesotho, and a wind-powered electric lighting system in a Carib Indian school in Dominica. It provided disaster relief in Third World countries and free ambulance service to the South

Bronx. It went to sea with Greenpeace and gave the Rainbow Warrior its radiation monitoring equipment. Plenty put Native American FM stations on the air, and pioneered amateur-band television and radio to keep its remote outposts of volunteers connected. In 1978, Plenty formed a scientific research team and litigation project to work on environmental issues and human rights. It founded the Natural Rights Center [see separate listing], the Environmental Resource Center in Portland, OR, and has been helping build a model ecovillage in Russia. By operating a retail store (The DeColores Fair Trade Center in Davis, CA) which sells arts and crafts from many of the projects, Plenty has empowered more than 120 women's co-ops with economic independence in Chiapas, Mexico, and in Guatemala. The *Plenty Bulletin* is mailed quarterly to all donors. 1/10/95

PUEBLO TO PEOPLE

P.O. Box 2545
Houston, TX 77252-2545

(713)956-1172/956-8443 Fax
(800)843-5257

Pueblo to People is a nonprofit organization founded in 1979. We work at the grassroots, supporting organizations of the poor themselves. Selling their products through PTP not only provides them with badly needed income, but gives them a chance to learn organizational skills and democratic methods many of us take for granted. With these skills other community problems are addressed; without these skills, many of the issues are never raised. Write for a free catalog of products from Central and South American Cooperatives. 1/5/95

QUARTERLY ALTERNATIVE REVIEW

P.O. Box 946
Mountain View, AR 72560

The *Quarterly Alternative Review* magazine is a grassroots tabloid that reviews material which is of interest to the alternative and back-to-the-land community of the Ozark bioregion. Each issue includes news and community announcements. Distributed free in alternative businesses

and co-ops across the Ozarks. Subscriptions $8.00 for 4 issues. We barter for ads. 6/23/94

RADICAL ROUTES

24 South Road
Hockley, Birmingham B-18
ENGLAND

02-551-1679

Radical Routes is a federation/network of radical housing co-ops and workers co-ops set up by mostly young unemployed and homeless people in Britain. We are mainly based in the cities, but have land in the countryside too. Controlled by member co-ops on a "one co-op, one vote" basis, we provide personal, technical, and financial help to members. We also serve as an ethical investment agency, attracting investments from supporters and reinvesting it in member co-ops at low interest rates, and helping set up new co-ops with such loans and coordinated help on legal, economic, and group process issues. All member co-ops agree to do work for the organization, attend gatherings, and fulfill various cooperative and ethical criteria in their activities. We're organizing sustainable complexes of cooperatives spread around the country, and welcome both short-term and long-term visitors. 10/6/92

RAIN MAGAZINE

Center for Urban Education
P.O. Box 30097
Eugene, OR 97403-1097

Alternative political, social, and economic organizational strategies and practices to encourage the development of self-reliant, directly democratic, and ecologically viable communities. Quarterly, $20/year. 3/15/94

RAINBOW GUIDE, THE

P.O. Box 3213
Madison, WI 53704

An annual directory listing people involved with Rainbow ideals and happenings—as well as Rainbow community listings. The '93 edition listed well over

2000 names. The Rainbow Family of Living light is an open-membership tribe that gathers every year at the World Peace Gathering (commonly known as the "Rainbow Gathering") held the first week of July each year. The 1995 Gathering was held in the Gila National Wilderness in SW New Mexico. Please include SASE with inquiries. Donations welcome. 1/2/93

RAINBOW LANDS PROJECT

P.O. Box 276
Charleston, SC 29402

[Formerly the Land-Link Network.] We are putting out a guide that includes information on forming or formed intentional communities. We also list other publications or groups that are resources for alternative energy options or sources for community listings, especially Rainbow-oriented communities and literature. Updated listings will be made available, when possible, at land councils, regional and national Rainbow Gatherings. Hopefully this guide will share a wide range of resources and ideas from communities that will help accomplish the wider vision of self-sufficiency for all of us. For an update send SASE, with donation if possible, to the above address. Please also send us any corrections or verifiable information on available Rainbow-oriented lands. 1/5/93

RAINBOW RIDGE

Richmond, KY 40475

(RESOURCE LISTING PULLED)
11/1/95

REAL GOODS

966 Mazzoni Street
Ukiah, CA 95482-3471
(800)762-7325 (CA)

(707)468-9292/468-0301 Fax
(707)744-2101 Tech Assistance

http://www.well.com/
www/realgood/

Real Goods is in business to provide knowledge and products to redirect the world toward a sustainable future where all living things are recognized as interconnected. Our merchandise provides tools that facilitate independent living and energy self-sufficiency and that are free of exploitation and environmental abuse throughout their lifecycles. We offer the world's largest and most thorough selection of alternative energy products, and publish an annual *Solar Living Sourcebook* which contains nearly 700 pages of products, charts, graphs, sizing, and design instructions...for photovoltaic, wind, and hydro power systems; super-efficient refrigerators; composting toilets; instantaneous and solar hot water heaters; compact fluorescent lighting; water conservation; books, maps, toys, and gifts. Write or call for a free catalog. 10/1/94

RECLAIMING

P.O. Box 14404
San Francisco, CA 94114

Reclaiming is a collective of San Francisco Bay Area women and men working to unify spirit and politics. Our vision is rooted in the religion and magic of the Goddess—the Immanent Life Force. We see our work as teaching and making magic—the art of empowering ourselves and each other. In our classes, workshops, and public rituals we train our voices, bodies, energy, intuition, and minds. We use the skills we learn to deepen our strength (both as individuals and as community), to voice our concerns about the world in which we live, and to bring to birth a vision of a new culture. We also publish a newsletter. 11/30/92

RENEW AMERICA

1400 – 16th Street NW, #710
Washington, DC 20036
(202)232-2252

Renew America is the nation's only environmental educational group specializing in broad-based environmental programs identifying, verifying, and promoting positive community-based models for change. We promote solutions to environmental problems by facilitating the replication of successful environmental initiatives that have been endorsed by local community and state leaders. Through these models we demonstrate that it is possible and practical to prevent pollution and to restore damaged environments. We also publish the *Environmental Success Index*, a directory of more than 1600 community-based environmental solutions, available for $25 ($15 for nonprofit organizations). 2/2/93

REVISION

The Journal of
Consciousness and Change
Heldref Publications
1319 – 18th Street NW
Washington, DC 20036-1802
(202)296-6267/296-5149 Fax

ReVision is a dense quarterly journal of consciousness and change. Each issue rigorously covers a theme with contributions from popular scientists, mystics, scholars, and others. *ReVision* has been described as "the academic journal of the New Age." Annual subscriptions are $50 for institutions, $30 for individuals. 3/15/94

RFD

P.O. Box 68
Liberty, TN 37095
(615)536-5176

RFD, A Country Journal for Gay Men Everywhere is now in its 19th year of publication. A reader-written journal, the topics, stories, reviews, poetry, art, and opinions are as diverse as its eclectic readership. *RFD* is published by the Short Mountain Community, also listed in this directory. Sample latest issue $5.00; $18.00 one year second class; $25 first class. 11/27/92

ROBERT K. GREENLEAF CENTER FOR SERVANT-LEADERSHIP

921 E 86th St #200
Indianapolis IN 46240
(317)259-1241

"The servant-leader is servant first... [taking care] to make sure that other people's highest priority needs are being served.... The best test, and most difficult to administer, is: do those served grow as persons; do they, while being served, become healthier, wiser, freer, more autonomous, more likely themselves to become servants? And what is the effect on the least privileged in society; will they benefit or, at least, not be further deprived?" —RKG (d. 1990)

The Robert K. Greenleaf Center for Servant-Leadership works to publish and promote ideas about servant-leadership and to connect colleagues in a network of learning and dialog. The Center publishes Robert Greenleaf's seminal series of books and essays about servant-leadership; conducts workshops and seminars; assists organizations seeking to implement servant-leadership in their operational philosophy; and offers books, videos, and audiotapes on related themes. Contact the Center to receive a resource catalog and further information on programs. 4/12/94

ROCKY MOUNTAIN COHOUSING ASSOCIATION

1705 – 14th Street #160
Boulder, CO 80302
(970)584-3237

RMCA is a volunteer-staffed nonprofit educational corporation established in 1991 to promote the understanding, appreciation, and development of cohousing in the Rocky Mountain region (including MT, WY, CO, UT, NM, AZ, and TX). We serve primarily as an information hub, collecting and disseminating information within the region via a phone network and a quarterly publication. We also provide a regional update insert for the quarterly *CoHousing* journal.

RMCA connects potential cohousing residents with new and existing projects, and links cohousing groups with information and resources. We sponsor roundtable discussions for developing groups, schedule quarterly introductory slide presentations on cohousing, and maintain an evolving list of professionals who are familiar with the cohousing process. RMCA is also working to familiarize local political, legal, and professional bodies with the concept of cohousing.

RMCA has organized annual regional conferences since 1991, and hosted the First North American CoHousing Conference in 1994. Individual memberships are $35 per year, and include a subscription to *CoHousing* with the RMCA insert, book discounts, special rates for conference participants, and professional and community referrals. Memberships are also available to cohousing groups at all stages of development ($200/year). 10/29/94

ROCKY MOUNTAIN INSTITUTE

1739 Snowmass Creek Road
Snowmass, CO 81654-9199
(303)927-3851/927-4178 Fax

Rocky Mountain Institute is a research and education foundation whose goal is to foster efficient and sustainable use of resources as a path to global security. Membership includes a subscription to our bimonthly newsletter. 1/5/95

RODALE PRESS

**33 E. Minor Street
Emmaus, PA 18049-4113**

Rodale Press is the leading publisher of periodicals related to ecological alternatives and self-sufficiency, including *Organic Gardening*; *New Shelter*; *New Farm*; *Organic Gardening*; and *Prevention* magazines. 3/21/94

ROWE CAMP & CONFERENCE CENTER

**Kings Highway Road
Rowe, MA 01367**

**(413)339-4216
(413)339-4468**

Rowe Camp & Conference Center, in the beautiful Berkshires 3 miles from Vermont, is an antidote to TV. Since 1924 we have run a small, intelligent, and creative summer camp for teenagers. Since 1974 we have run weekends and week long retreats for adults and families on a wide variety of religious, political, psychological, and health issues. Are you a parent who wishes your children could get in touch with their innate idealism? Have you longed for a place to spend a weekend where people drop their masks but not their integrity, a place to meet a variety of different people, a place you could afford and still touch the beauty of the natural world? Write or call for a free copy of our beautiful flyer [see listing in Communities section]. 4/19/93

RSVP

**Rural Southern
Voice for Peace
1898 Hannah Branch Road
Burnsville, NC 28714**

(704)675-9590

RSVP provides organizing assistance, networking, and training in the work for justice, peace, and a healthy environment. We seek to affirm our common humanity and protect our environment by creatively resolving conflict, promoting positive alternatives, and affirming the wisdom of grassroots people as they work for nonviolent social change. We work primarily in the rural communities and small cities of the southeast, but also nationally and internationally. We publish *Voices,* a journal of grassroots community organizing. Our Listening Project is a unique community organizing tool we have developed. 9/29/93

SCHOOL OF LIVING

**Route 1, Box 185-A
Cochranville, PA 19330**

Founded in 1934, the School of Living explores options for decentralization, cooperative living, and land reform. SoL offers training conferences, financing for Community Land Trust (CLT) development, permaculture demonstrations, monetary and economic reform activities. It administers a regional CLT alliance for intentional communities, homesteaders, and other residential users wishing to place land in trust. It sponsors AERO (Alternative Education Resource Organization), promotes Geonomics (collection of earth user-fees and their distribution as a citizens' heritage dividend), and publishes a quarterly journal: *Green Revolution.* 12/23/93

SEAC

**Student Environmental
Action Coalition
P.O. Box 1168
Chapel Hill, NC 27514**

(919)967-4600

SEAC is a nonprofit student-run network of over 2000 campus and high school environmental groups across the country. The SEAC national office provides training, information, and support for young environmental activists. SEAC is actively working to broaden the environmental movement, tackling the issues of social justice, racism, sexism, and inequality. 12/15/93

SEED SAVERS EXCHANGE

**Route 3, Box 239
Decorah, IA 52101**

The Seed Savers Exchange is a network of mostly small-scale growers and gardeners dedicated to preserving our heritage of open-pollinated heirloom vegetables, fruits, and nuts. The network's underlying purpose is to protect the genetic diversity of our food crops. The SSE's yearbook, published each January, lists varieties that have been saved...then members exchange and grow each other's seeds.

Three other valuable references works produced by SSE are Garden Seed Inventory (a complete list of all commercially available non-hybrid vegetable seeds); Fruit, Berry, and Nut Inventory; and Seed to Seed (detailing seed-saving techniques for the vegetable gardener). Write to receive a four-page color brochure detailing SSE's projects and publications, enclosing $1 with your request. 7/1/92

SHARED LIVING RESOURCE CENTER

**2375 Shattuck Avenue
Berkeley, CA 94704**

(510)548-6608

SLRC is committed to creating Shared Living Communities that integrate cooperative living, affordability, and ecological housing design. Services include slide-talk presentations; profile-consultation sessions; workshops; and community location, site, and building design studies. Our emphasis is on the new extended family, energy and resource self-reliance, co-ownership and democratic management, reducing car dependency, etc. The primary concepts we use are the Village Cluster/Cohousing model, the Urban Cooperative Block, and the Octagonal Cluster group house. Call or write for more information about our services or our new book—*Rebuilding Community in America: Housing for Ecological Living, Personal Empowerment, and the New Extended Family.* 3/1/94

SHEARWATER GROUP, THE

Seattle, WA 98103

(RESOURCE LISTING PULLED)
Address & Phone Bad 12/17/95)

SHIMER COLLEGE

P.O. Box A-500
Waukegan, IL 60079
(847)623-8400

Shimer College is a 4-year, accredited, degree-granting institution. Students graduate and leave so we are not an intentional community according to any usual definition. We do, however, have some similarities.

The college is governed by the Assembly in which all students, faculty, and staff have an equal vote. The college's operations are determined by a collection of committees on which all community members are represented. Faculty and administration are a single group. All classes are discussion with 12 students or fewer.

Our dedication to dialog spills over into the whole community. We see dialog as the ideal vehicle for conflict resolution, personal growth, academic progress—for the college's existence and growth. We like to think that we provide an education for life, not training for a specific career. Those interested in intentional communities, homeschooling, alternative lifestyles, and independent thinking often find Shimer appealing. 8/4/93

SIERRA CLUB

730 Polk Street
San Francisco, CA 94109
(415)776-2211

For over 100 years the Sierra Club has been fighting to protect the earth's fragile systems. We've successfully lobbied for laws to limit air and water pollution, and to regulate poisonous toxic chemicals. We've won protection for swamps and meadows, rivers and mountains, deserts and prairies...those natural places which permit the earth to heal and renew itself. We have consistently been an effective voice for a world healthful for all its inhabitants. The unique power of the Sierra Club springs from our active grass-roots membership...volunteers who give freely of their time and expertise. Please write if you'd like to become a supporting member, or if you want to participate in our work. 5/28/92

SIKH DHARMA / 3HO FOUNDATION

International Secretariat
P.O. Box 351149
Los Angeles, CA 90035
(310)552-3416 / 557-8414

Sikh Dharma began over 500 years ago with a simple message of truthful living and the fundamental unity of humanity, all created by One Creator, all of us citizens of one community. It reaches out to people of all faiths and cultural backgrounds, encouraging us to see beyond our differences and to work together for world peace and harmony.

The Healthy, Happy, Holy Organization (3HO), founded in 1969 by Yogi Bhajan, is a nonprofit educational and scientific foundation dedicated to the upliftment of humanity. 3HO brings to the public the science of Kundalini Yoga, and offers complete lifestyle guidelines on nutrition and health, interpersonal relations, child rearing, and human behavior. It embraces vegetarianism, Ayurvedic formulas, abstinence from drugs, yoga, and meditation. You do not need to be a Sikh to practice or teach the 3HO lifestyle.

3HO hosts three worldwide yoga festivals each year, as well as a camp for women held in New Mexico—where women break from their routines to experience their individual identities as women and their lives as a seeker of truth. The network also operates several preschools that combine Montessori and Waldorf techniques with the Sikh Dharma teachings, and sponsors youth camps in New Mexico and in upstate New York. Call for more information on these gatherings, or to contact the center nearest you. [The five major 3HO centers in North America are listed in the Communities section.] 1/13/95

SING OUT

P.O. Box 5253
Bethlehem, PA 18015-0253
(610)865-5366 / 865-5129 Fax

Sing Out is a nonprofit tax-exempt corporation dedicated to the preservation of the cultural diversity and heritage of traditional folk music; to support creators of new folk music from all countries and cultures; to expand the definition of folk music to include ethnic music; and to encourage the practice of folk music as a living phenomenon. An $18 annual membership includes a subscription to our folk-song magazine, *Sing Out!*, which has come out quarterly since May of 1950. We also nationally syndicate a weekly one-hour folk music program available to all National Public Radio stations, and maintain a resource center—a multimedia library containing thousands of recordings, books, periodicals, photographs, video-tapes, and ephemera. This is a free resource for members! We also publish *Rise Up Singing*, a 288-page folk-song sourcebook with words, guitar chords, and sources to 119 songs of all sorts: traditional, political, folk, rock, Motown, children's, and more —$17.95 for one copy; $8 plus postage on full cartons (30 copies). 11/12/94

SIRIUS EDUCATIONAL RESOURCES

P.O. Box 1101
Greenbelt, MD 20768
(301)441-3809

Books and lecture tapes by Corinne McLaughlin & Gordon Davidson, cofounders of the Sirius Community in Shutesbury, Massachusetts. Our latest book, *Spiritual Politics*, is available for $14.95 (postpaid). Write for a free brochure. 12/4/94

SKIPPING STONES

P.O. Box 3939
Eugene, OR 97403
(541)342-4956

Skipping Stones is a nonprofit children's magazine that encourages cooperation, creativity, and a celebration of cultural, environmental, and linguistic richness. It offers itself as a playful forum for communication among children from different lands and backgrounds. *Skipping Stones* is an international quarterly journal that is recognized as a leading resource in multicultural education. We accept art and original writings in every language and from all ages. Special theme issues include Native American Societies, Rainforests and Indigenous People, In Praise of Our Planet, Spanish-English bilingual, Soviet Republics, Women of Many Ages and Places. Regular features include pen pals, bookshelf, Rhymes and Riddles, Noteworthy News, creative activities, Dear Hanna.... Subscriptions: $15 ($20 institutions), single copy $5 each. Low-income discount: 50%. Complete set: $60. 11/2/93

SOCIETY AND NATURE

Aigis Publications
P.O. Box 637
Littleton, CO 80160

Society and Nature is the only international journal of social and political ecology which provides a comprehensive forum on contemporary social and ecological concerns. Through an open dialog

between social ecologists, eco-socialists, radical greens, feminists, and activists in the land-based and indigenous movements, the journal strives to foster a new liberatory project toward a free and ecological society. Each issue is organized around a central theme and features many leading radical thinkers of our time— including Andre Gunder Frank, John Clark, Janet Biehl, Ward Churchill, Murray Bookchin, Chaia Heller, Daniel Chodorkoff, L. Susan Brown, Cornelius Castoriadis, Marta Fuentes, and others. Among the themes explored are Feminism and Ecology, Ethnonationalism and the New World Order, Socialism and Ecology, Science and Technology, Green Economics, etc. One year $20 USA; $25 International. 3/4/93

SOCIETY FOR UTOPIAN STUDIES

Attn: Lawrence Hough
Poli-Sci ECU
Greenville, NC 27858

Founded in 1975, the Society of Utopian Studies is an international, interdisciplinary association devoted to the study of both literary and experimental utopias. We have active members from a wide variety of disciplines—including Classics, Economics, Engineering, History, Literature, Philosophy, Political Science, Psychology, Sociology, Foreign Languages, and the Arts. Membership is open to all persons with utopian interests, and our ranks include architects, futurists, urban planners, and environmentalists. Membership includes announcements of meetings and our newsletter, *Utopis Discovered*, which contains information about upcoming conferences, workshops, and publications in the field. Dues are $25 per year ($15 for students, unemployed, and retired). 7/8/92

SOLAR BOX COOKERS NORTHWEST

7036 – 18th Avenue NE
Seattle, WA 98115
(206)525-1418 Voice/Fax
tsponheim@accessone.com
sbcn@igc.apc.org

An offshoot of SCI [see following listing], this group publishes a newsletter called *Solar Box Journal*, available with a 1-year membership for $25. SBCN works to promote solar cooking both in this country and abroad, emphasizing local as well as international action, and invites par-

ticipation in all forms. Becoming a voting member requires 12 hours of volunteer labor or $50. 1/13/95

SOLAR COOKERS INTERNATIONAL

1724 Eleventh Street
Sacramento, CA 95814
(916)444-6616/444-5379 Fax
sbci@igc.apc.org

Solar Cookers International (SCI) is a nonprofit educational organization that promotes the spread of solar cooking to help people and environments worldwide. SCI supports information exchange among solar cooking advocates and experts worldwide, helps organizations to adapt solar cooking to local needs, and develops educational materials on solar cooking. In January 1995, SCI began a pilot project to teach solar cooking to refugees at a camp in northwestern Kenya. SCI's work is supported by donations and by the sale of educational materials within the U.S. and Canada. Popular materials include a foldable, portable solar cooker and an instruction booklet called "How to Make and Use a Solar Box Cooker." 1/17/95

SOLSTICE INSTITUTE

P.O. Box 348
Boulder, CO 80306-0348
(303)447-2681
(303)939-8463

AtSolstice@aol.com

The Solstice Institute promotes:
• A more sustainable lifestyle;
• Cooperation and personal growth;
• Practice of non-violence;
• Respect for diversity; and,
• The pursuit of joy;
It is our intention to:
• Create intentional community using consensus processes and sustainable building methods as models for joyous and purpose-filled living; and,
• Network with people and organizations, and develop cooperative relationships. We are a regional resource for community-scale endeavors, and welcome new friends, collaborators and contacts. We attempt to live the models we promote. Current projects include supporting the formation of a network of cooperative households in Boulder, creating a live-in demonstration of a more sustainable urban lifestyle, and building small worker-owned businesses. We also use artistic expression as an opportunity to

explore personal growth and build community. The core group makes decisions by consensus.

SOUTHERN OREGON WOMEN'S NETWORK

2000 King Mountain Trail
Sunny Valley, OR 97497

An organic extended community, loosely referred to as the Southern Oregon Women's Network, with roots in the "back to the land" movement and the Women's Liberation Movement of the '60s and '70s. By 1980, one could find small and large collectives of women living on land in this area, and there were growing women's communities in three major cities: Ashland, Eugene, and Portland.

Most but not all of us are white, ranging in age from 7–70. We come from different class, religious, and educational backgrounds. We differ in our sexual and political identities, yet in all this diversity there exists a common ground: our shared commitment to expressing our creativity, living on the land, and healing ourselves.

We create safe physical and psychic space to enhance women's personal growth—recovery from childhood sexual abuse, incest, drug and alcohol abuse, and dysfunctional family dynamics have become priorities in women's lives. We share resources and skills, and define ourselves to varying degrees as feminists, lesbians, and separatists. We practice new ways of relating to each other, and explore new forms of family, clan, tribe, and community. Please send SASE with $1 for further information. 9/25/94

SPIES FOR SANITY

487 Mountain Road
Lyman, NH 03585
(603)838-6358

A free network for individualists whose code of ethics transcends the traditionally and alternatively correct. [For a more complete description, see listing in the Communities section.] 10/9/94

SUN, THE: A MAGAZINE OF IDEAS

107 North Roberson Street
Chapel Hill, NC 27516
(919)942-5282

The Sun is a self-described "magazine of ideas." Since 1974 they have explored the words of Ram Dass, Wavy Gravy, Patricia Sun, David Spangler, and other luminaries through stories, essays, interviews, and poems. They also have a lively reader-submission policy. Every issue exudes a kind of warmth, integrity, and spirit of human discovery sorely missing from most publications (alternative or otherwise). Subscriptions are $32/year. 6/18/92

SUSTAINABLE COMMUNITY HOUSING SOCIETY

c/o the Arusha Centre
233 – 10th Street NW
Calgary, Alberta
T2N-1V5 CANADA
(403)270-3201

The Sustainable Community Housing Society promotes and demonstrates participatory communities: those which actively involve residents-to-be in building their homes and neighborhoods, through a process known as co-design. SCHS promotes the concepts of environmental, economic, and social sustainability in

communities; developing urban communities which conserve more while polluting and consuming less. The Society is currently working to create a resource centre for information on sustainable communities. It is also working with the Affordable Sustainable Community project team of the Faculty of Environmental Design at the University of Calgary, collaborating to eventually build a demonstration project in Calgary. Become a member or become more informed by contacting Tamara Lee at (403)283-6985; Tim Nourse at (403)246-8787; or by writing to us c/o the Arusha Centre noted above. 8/17/93

TIES CANADA

Turtle Island Earth Stewards
Box 3308
Salmon Arm, BC
V1E-4S1 CANADA
(604)832-0153 / 833-4676 Fax

Since 1975 TIES has acted as a resource group for intentional communities to place their land in trust, to establish land stewardship plans with particular focus on alternative forestry, agriculture, and permaculture. TIES also assists in all aspects of the formation, management, and execution of trust agreements. We provide information, expertise and consulting services for anyone interested in the promotion of ecologically integrated community development. Our work brings together people and land in a symbiotic harmonious relationship. 10/20/94

TIES USA

Turtle Island Earth Stewards
615 First Street #3
Langley, WA 98260
(360)221-5186

TIES USA works with intentional communities, providing expertise, consulting, and resources for a variety of critical areas. Specialty areas include group visionings, process work, consensus decision making, and meeting facilitation. 1/3/95

TOOLS FOR CHANGE

P.O. Box 14141-C
San Francisco, CA 94114
(415)861-6838

Tools for Change is an adult education institute founded by Margo Adair (author of *Working Inside Out*) and Sharon Howell. It is dedicated to transforming domination of one another and nature, to living in harmony where diversity is a source of strength and the sanctity of all life is honored. It offers facilitation, mediation, training, and consultation services, along with a variety of publications.

Ever wonder why we hear so much about diversity from communities and organizations which remain so homogeneous? Or how come, despite our best intentions, we keep finding ourselves in relationships that reflect our society's patterns of domination and submission? Our two pamphlets: "The Subjective Side of Politics" and "Breaking Old Patterns, Weaving New Ties: Alliance Building" are on the cutting edge of untangling what gets in the way of building effective alliances across the lines of race, class, gender, age, sexual orientation....

These booklets expose the invisible barriers that block our ability to work cooperatively together. They are full of concrete strategies for creating a context that welcomes everyone's contribution. They can be purchased by sending $9 to Tools for Change at the above address.

Trainings available include Transforming Relations of Domination; Ecology, Feminism & Power; Communication & Conflict Resolution; Healing Alienation & Building Community; Effective Leadership & Facilitation Skills; Strategies for Movement Building & Community Organizing; Intuitive Problem Solving; Spirituality & Politics. Tools for Change is committed to financial accessibility; call for further information. 9/14/92

TRANET

P.O. Box 567
Rangeley, ME 04970
(207)864-2252

TraNet is a transnational network of, by, and for people in all parts of the world who are changing the world by changing their own lifestyles—are helping one another toward local self-reliance—are adopting appropriate technologies (AT). TraNet holds that people themselves can and should be responsible for their own development and for the well-being of one another. Cooperative personal and community actions can replace reliance on the governments of nation-states which are inherently competitive and war mongering. Solidarity among people at the grassroots can bring peace and equity. TraNet has a primary goal of linking people with one another to raise the level of dialog and practice of alternative and innovative ideas which will transform the whole Earth. Global problems of peace, pollution, and population must be solved by local actions. Members of TraNet are assisted in contacting other members and in establishing programs of mutual aid. 12/15/93

TURTLE ISLAND OFFICE

Cress Spring Farm
4035 Ryan Road
Blue Mounds, WI 53517
(608)767-3931

Turtle Island is a Native American Indian word used to describe North America. The Turtle Island Office (TIO) is an information center for both the general public and the internal network of the bioregional movement. The office was created at the third North American Bioregional Congress held August '88 in Squamish, British Columbia, in Canada. Current projects of the office include a bioregional registry and archive, skills exchange, grant funding research, and the North American Bioregional Congress.

We do not have a national office. The function of the clearinghouse is to connect people and give background information. This structure was consciously chosen to embody decentralization. Every two years representatives from Turtle Island gather at the North American Bioregional Congress [see Calendar]. We have two bioregional bookstores [see listings for *The New Catalyst* and for Planet Drum]. 12/3/94

20/20 VISION

1828 Jefferson Place
Washington, DC 20036
(202)833-2020

20 minutes a month to help save the earth—a small commitment that makes a world of difference.

Our goal is to influence policymakers to protect the earth by reducing militarism and preserving the environment. *20/20 Vision* cuts the big issues down to size, making citizen advocacy convenient, sustainable, and effective.

Every month you'll receive clear information on the issues you care about—protecting the environment and preserving peace. We'll find you the best 20-minute action you can take at home to lobby your legislators or other policymakers—based on information tailored specifically for where you live. You'll know whom to contact, when to call or write, and what to say. Your voice, in concert with others working on the same issues, can really make an impact. *20/20 Vision* makes sure the time you are willing to spend is time well spent. 7/29/93

TWIN CITIES COHOUSING NETWORK

P.O. Box 7304
Minneapolis, MN 55407-0304
(612)930-7580

We are an umbrella organization for several cohousing core groups that are developing sites in the greater St. Paul/Minneapolis area. One site has begun operation with eight units and has plans to build 16 to 18 additional townhouses in 1994. The network provides information on cohousing via forums, meetings, and a regular newsletter. 1/10/94

UNDERCURRENT

P.O. Box 323
Victor, CO 80860

(719)685-1495

The Undercurrent is developing a fluid network/trade route for all communities. Developing alternatives and giving them back freely to all who want them is what "UC" is all about. We are planning to implement this project in three stages: 1) create a communications network that will consist of a central database of alternative resources and communication links between people and communities that will enable us to... 2) form a fluid trade route that will incorporate the talents of people who love the labor of travel along with community "busbarns," public access PCs, and a cooperative bus line we call "The 100th Monkey." This will form a level of cooperation necessary for... 3) network projects, where communities join powers to synergize their efforts in areas such as environmental and political networked assaults. Work includes light retrofit of existing communities, regreening of environmentally damaged areas, developing regional healing facilities and everything else that the combined efforts of our communities can grow. 1/18/95

UNION OF CONCERNED SCIENTISTS

26 Church Street
Cambridge, MA 02238

(617)547-5552

The Union of Concerned Scientists is a nonprofit organization sponsored by donations from some 100,000 individuals, including many thousands of scientists. UCS produces both printed and video educational materials on a variety of issues, including global warming, nuclear power, and renewable energy. They have been at the forefront of the movement to increase

public awareness of the dangers of nuclear power and to promote safe, renewable energy alternatives. You may become a UCS sponsor and receive the quarterly publication, *Nucleus*, by making a tax-deductible contribution of any reasonable amount. 5/18/92

URBAN ECOLOGY

405 – 14th Street #701
Oakland, CA 94612

(510)251-6330

We are a nonprofit, primarily volunteer organization with worldwide membership that works on rebuilding cities in balance with nature. We believe that all parts of the city are interrelated—transportation, land use, economics, community, energy, buildings, recycling, natural and agricultural systems—and all can contribute to a city that is socially just and ecologically sustainable. We strive to create mixed-use communities near transit nodes; revise transportation priorities to favor non-auto transit; restore damaged urban environments; create affordable and racially and economically mixed housing; nurture social justice; support local agriculture; and work with businesses to support ecologically sound economic activity while discouraging pollution.

Among our various accomplishments: we developed a "Sustainable City Plan" for Berkeley, and organized the first International Ecological City Conference in 1990. Members receive the *Urban Ecologist*, "a spirited newsletter brimming with practical ideas for making North America's cities greener and more livable" (*Utne Reader*, May/June 1992), as well as up-to-date information about projects, conferences, and legal initiatives. 5/17/94

USCA / UNIVERSITY STUDENTS COOPERATIVE ASSOCIATION

2424 Ridge Road
Berkeley, CA 94709

(510)848-1936/848-2114 Fax

The USCA is the largest student housing cooperative in North America, housing over 1200 people. Although a private nonprofit corporation, the USCA works in cooperation with the University of California to provide housing for its students.

About 900 of the USCA's members live in room-and-board houses scattered around the Berkeley campus, including 15 large houses each of which functions

as a separate cooperative household with elected managers for room assignment, work organization (housekeeping, food service, etc.), and maintenance. A central support staff of about 25 non-members provides technical information to members as well as oversees day-to-day administration (such as housekeeping applications and organizational financing). We also provide warehousing and support services to individual house food programs. 1/5/95

UTNE READER

- **1624 Harmon Place**
  Minneapolis, MN 55403
  (612)338-5040

Subscriptions:

- **P.O. Box 1974**
  Marion, OH 43305
  (800)736-UTNE

The *Utne Reader* offers "the best of the alternative press" six times a year, drawing articles from a wide range of alternative publications. Its aims are to "enlighten, incite, and encourage independent thinking." Through its "Off the Newsstand" section, it offers access to valuable and interesting periodicals that readers might not otherwise discover. New subscriptions are $24 for one year. 3/15/94

VETERANS FOR PEACE

P.O. Box 3881
Portland, ME 04104

(207)773-1431/773-0804 Fax

An organization of military veterans engaged in educational and humanitarian activities. Open to veterans of all eras; the extensive military background of our members gives credibility to our stance as peace activists. We are working to provide a legacy of real security for future generations. Independent chapters take on diverse projects ranging from the Abolish War Campaign, to the Children's Rescue Project evacuating wounded children from areas of conflict. Veterans for Peace is officially recognized as an NGO by the United Nations. 7/28/93

Resources

WALDEN FELLOWSHIP, INC.

P.O. Box 250164
New York, NY 10025-1532

(212)316-3456

Walden Fellowship is a nonresidential community that exists to encourage the development of cultural practices which maximize long-term reinforcement and minimize coercion for all persons, in a manner consistent with the survival of all species. Grounded in the work of B.F. Skinner and adapted based on continuing experimentation, the Fellowship was formed to provide a model of interlocking contingencies resulting in a high level of reciprocal reinforcement among its members (mutual support) and a locus from which such practices may be extended into the larger society (service). The Fellowship organizes monthly gatherings which prompt and reinforce self-management and effective cultural practices among members; designs, tests, and implements behaviorally oriented service programs and activities in the community; and provides workshops and individual and family consultation to assist clients in constructing more reinforcing and less coercive lives. 1/20/94

WALDEN TWO INTERNATIONAL ASSOCIATION

c/o Los Horcones
Apdo 372
Hermosillo, Sonora
83000 MEXICO

This association was founded by Los Horcones for the purpose of sharing information about our developments and findings with those persons who would not live here but want to participate in some way in the development of a Walden Two community. We also disseminate information about the basic characteristics of a Walden Two and its social contributions—and to increase the degree in which we receive technical, economic, or any other kind of help. Members receive our newsletter, arti-cles published by and about Los Horcones, and invitations to seminars and other activ-ities. Memberships are $17/year. 12/14/88

WAR RESISTERS LEAGUE

339 Lafayette Street
New York, NY 10012

(212)228-0450

Our work is to resist war in all its forms, by providing the public with information, materials, and workshops. To support our work we sell books that make a difference, plus T-shirts, posters, buttons, cards, pins, calendars, etc. Donations are always appreciated. Write if you'd like to know how to get more involved in your area. 6/20/94

WATER CENTER, THE

P.O. Box 264
Eureka Springs, AR 72632

(501)253-9431

The Water Center is a nonprofit water advocacy organization. Through our two publications we try to provide a new water paradigm. *We All Live Downstream: A Guide to Waste Treatment That Stops Water Pollution* ($10 postpaid) is a catalog of compost toilet and water conservation information, with poetry and lots of illustrations. *Aqua-terra Water Concepts* for the Ecological Society (one issue, $6 postpaid) is a periodic journal featuring metaphysical water concepts. 12/28/92

WELL, THE

Whole Earth 'Lectronic Link
27 Gate Five Road
Sausalito, CA 94965

(415)332-8410 BBS 9600+up
(415)332-6106 BBS 2400+below
(415)332-4335 A Live Person
postmaster@well.com

Central to the WELL's early growth, deliberate community-building remains an important part of its development. If you have a computer and modem you can be part of this unique community of people that meet on-line. The WELL is divided into conferences that discuss just about anything you can think of—mind, work, sexuality, Grateful Dead, and parenting are just a few. The well is an on-line computer network spawned by the *Whole Earth Review* [see separate listing]. Rates are $15/month plus $2/hour for on-line time. 3/21/94

WHOLE EARTH REVIEW

27 Gate Five Road
Sausalito, CA 94965

(415)332-1716
(415)332-3110 Fax

An "alternatives" general interest quarterly of "unorthodox cultural and technical news" which is primarily reader-supported (minimal advertising) and reader-driven (about half of the material in each issue is reader-suggested, or reader-written). The articles report on new products, promising books, art, cartoons, excerpts from hard-to-find books, and anything else that might qualify as conceptual news. The editors pride themselves in the incubation of half-baked ideas, a few of which survive. [See separate listing for The WELL.] Subscriptions $27/year. 3/15/94

Hiding your light under a bushel?

Been around for awhile but aren't listed in the *Directory*—are you a shy community? We encourage you to illuminate others with your story. Even if you aren't looking for new members, it can be valuable for others to know what you've been through, or even that you exist. We invite you to contact us about being listed in our publications—even if you prefer to keep your phone or address unpublished.

Communities Directory • Rt 1, Box 155-D
Rutledge MO 65363 • 816-883-5545

WILLIAMS, JOE

**Bookseller
174 Santa Clara Avenue
Oakland, CA 94610**

(510)428-9268

Book dealer specializing in out-of-print, rare, and hard-to-find books on the 1960s including countercultural, alternative, radical, and revolutionary materials of 20th-century America. Subject areas include, but are not limited to, the following: communes, collectives, co-ops, sexual freedom, gay & lesbian liberation, New Left politics, Weathermen, anarchism, Black Panthers, hippies, drugs, women's movement, etc. Catalogs issued. Search service offered. Write or call for details. 1/8/95

WOMAN OF POWER

**P.O. Box 2785
Orleans, MA 02653-1999**

(617)240-7877

Woman of Power is a magazine of feminism, spirituality, and politics—a quarterly with exceptional literary and artistic works. Each issue explores a major theme: Leadership, Relationships, Diversity, etc. "If we are to survive as a species, it is necessary for women to come into power and for feminist principles to rebuild the foundations of world cultures." Subscriptions: $30/year (4 issues); sample: $7. 3/15/94

WONDERTREE

**Box 38083
Vancouver, BC
V5Z-4L9 CANADA**

(604)876-5006 / 876-5004 Fax

A new educational model, based on natural learning, representing a philosophical shift in paradigms and incorporating the latest in learning technology—using workshops, written materials, video, and computer information to enhance human understanding and learning technology. WonderNet, a telecommunications network for learners and mentors, is a leading edge example of grassroots learner-based curriculum development. 8/23/93

WORLD FUTURE SOCIETY

**7910 Woodmont Ave. #450
Bethesda, MD 20814-5089**

(301)656-8274

The World Future Society is an association of people interested in how social and technological developments are shaping the future. The Society was founded in 1966, and is chartered as a nonprofit educational and scientific organization. We strive to serve as a neutral clearinghouse for ideas about the future—including forecasts, recommendations, and alternative scenarios.

Membership is open to anyone who would like to know more about what the future will hold. We presently have 30,000 members in more than 80 countries, and over 100 local chapters worldwide. Annual dues, which include a subscription to our bimonthly magazine, are $30 in U.S. currency or its equivalent. 5/22/92

WORLDWATCH INSTITUTE

**1776 Massachusetts Ave. NW
Washington, DC 20036**

**(202)452-1999
(202)296-7365 Fax
wwpub@igc.apc.org**

The Worldwatch Institute was founded in 1975 to inform policymakers and the general public about the interdependence of the world economy and its environmental support systems. Our staff analyzes issues from a global perspective and within an integrated, interdisciplinary framework. We are an independent, nonprofit research organization based in Washington, DC.

Worldwatch's reports are designed to bridge the gap left by more traditional, specialized analyses. Our papers and magazines are distributed worldwide, responding to a strong demand for comprehensive public policy research. A $30 subscription includes all Worldwatch Papers released during the calendar year, plus a paperback edition of our annual *State of the World.* 1/5/95

YAD TABENKIN INSTITUTE

**P.O. Box Ramat Efal
52960 ISRAEL**

03712221-4 / 344367

Yad Tabenkin is the Research and Documentation Center for the United Kibbutz Movement. It offers a scholarship fund for research, publishes a yearbook and selected works (including some by kibbutz members as well as papers from the labor movement and from the academic world). Yad Tabenkin also organizes Study Days and Symposia relating to both historical subjects and issues of vital immediate concern, and collaborates with different universities and institutes in the development of many projects.

We have begun taping interviews with veterans of kibbutz and the labor movement—to preserve their stories of the early days. Current study circles are discussing specific problems including economic questions; Arab-Jewish relations, security, and peace; political issues; kibbutz ideology; current kibbutz research; Israeli socialism and cooperation. 8/6/92

YANKEE PERMACULTURE

**P.O. Box 672
Dahlonega, GA 30533-0672**

Yankee Permaculture publishes the largest collection of permaculture titles worldwide, including *The International Permaculture Solutions Journal* and a series of 15 Permaculture Design Pamphlets and 30 Permaculture Papers (placed in the public domain for free reproduction by all). We also publish a series of permaculture design slide/scripts; distribute titles by important authors in the field; and make available a catalog of papers on special applications. 1/27/95

Z (ZETA) MAGAZINE

**Institute for
Social & Cultural
Communication
116 Saint Botolph Street
Boston, MA 02115-9979**

(617)787-4531

Z (Zeta) magazine is an independent monthly that gathers into one place in-depth news, opinion, and vision about the world and the Left, and was deemed the best magazine of its class by *Utne Reader.* We see the racial, sexual, class, and political dimensions of personal life as fundamental to understanding and improving contemporary circumstances—and our aim is to assist activist efforts to attain a better future. Subscriptions (12 issues) are $26 per year for individuals, or $35 per year for institutions. 3/15/94

WOOD BURNING
Central Heating

The Most Efficient Multi-Fuel Boiler Ever Designed

The HS Tarm Excel Burns Wood With Oil or Gas Backup.

Years of research and development have resulted in the creation of the HS Tarm Excel multi-fuel boilers. These boilers burn wood at over 80% efficiency and oil or gas at 85% efficiency. During multi-fuel operation, the boiler will automatically switch from wood to oil/gas whenever the wood fire dies down. This means that your home is always maintained at a comfortable temperature. Two separate burning chambers assure maximum performance from all fuels.

Hot Water Heats Best.

Experts agree, hot water (hydronic) heating is the most comfortable way to heat your home. An added bonus is the Excel's domestic hot water coil which provides plenty of hot tap water.

Excel 2000

New Technology Brings Wood Burning into the Future!

A new process known as "Wood Gasification" makes this system the most efficient wood burner ever made.* The HS Tarm Excel "bakes" the load of wood in the firebox then uses a whisper quiet fan to drive the combustible wood gas (smoke) down through the firebed into a high-temperature ceramic combustion tunnel. This super hot (2000°F) chamber ignites these gases and burns them completely, leaving no tars or vapors (creosote) to condense in the chimney.

During wood burning the advanced control system of the Excel is capable of turning off and on much like an oil or gas boiler. It can actually "idle" for hours at a time then, spring to life when more heat is needed. A single firebox load can therefore last for up to 24 hours. Operation of the HS Tarm Excel is straightforward and simple, setting new standards for user-friendliness in wood-burning equipment.

Call for further details and independent test results.

──────── **Also Available:** ────────

Tarm 2002—Wood Gasification Add-on Boiler
Tarm 500—Multi-fuel Boiler: Wood; Coal; Gas; Oil; Electric
Rockland Furnace—Warm Air Multi-fuel
Tarm AD-24—Wood Add-on Boiler

For more information on the HS Tarm Multi-fuel Boilers, send in the coupon below or call toll-free:

1-800-STAY-WARM
(1-800-782-9927)
Tarm USA
5 Main Street, Lyme NH 03768

The HS Tarm Excel Features:

A. Low Wattage Draft Fan

B. Primary Combustion Air

C. Pre-Heated Secondary Air Injection

D. High-Temp. Ceramic Combustion Tunnel

E. 2000°+ Flame for Complete Combustion

F. Heat Exchange Tubes—Wood

G. Heat Exchange Tubes—Oil/Gas

H. Rear or Side Venting

I. Tankless Hot Water Coil

J. Cast Iron Doors & Frames

K. 2" Thick Full Insulation

L. Water (64 gal.) surrounds fireboxes and heat exchangers for max. heat transfer

M. High Efficiency Oil or Gas Burner

—*Dealer Inquiries Welcome*—

(ADVERTISEMENT)

About the Appendix

Becky Steider

Working on a directory of this scope, we found that there are lots of small but vital bits of information that don't seem to belong to any one particular section. So, that's what the Appendix is for—we gathered all the orphans into a section of their own. Following is a quick summary of what's here.

Feedback
Ways We Can Help You Further...and Ways You Can Help Us

Creating this directory was a collaborative effort, and the interactive process doesn't stop with your getting this book. You may need information you haven't found in the *Directory*, or you may have news about communities or resources that we don't. Either way, we want to be in touch with you, to strengthen everyone's knowledge. Feedback can be a two-way street and we welcome traffic in both directions.

As hard as we've tried to be comprehensive, we know our information won't answer every question; we know our Charts won't direct everyone to the community of their dreams; and we know some listings will be outdated by the time they're used.

This page is meant to give you ideas about where to go for additional information, once you've gotten all you can from the *Directory*. Naturally, we recommend that you first consider going to the communities themselves. We realize though, that you may not have figured out yet which groups to approach, or you may have inquiries that cannot be answered by the communities directly. Below are responses to the questions we expect will most commonly come up.

If you have a question not included here, we invite you to send it to us along with a self-addressed stamped envelope, and we'll do the best we can with it.

Following this section is a list of suggested ways you can help us—by passing along your news and views about communities and this directory. Regardless of the nature of your feedback, please send it to us at the address at the bottom of the next page. Thanks!

How We Can Help You

What if the contact information is incorrect?
If, for instance, a listed phone number is disconnected (don't overlook the possibility that the area code has been changed!), or letters to a listed address are returned as undeliverable, please get in touch with us. We may have new information, or know where to get it.

What if you don't find what you're looking for?
Our first suggestion is to revisit "How to Use This Directory" on page 5, to see if you've tried every avenue available to you in this book. If you still can't find what you want, you can send us your specific request. Maybe you're looking for a community with characteristics not covered in the Chart or Index. Maybe you want to know if there are additional communities or resources fitting your interests that haven't been listed. We'll do what we can. There may be a charge for this service, depending on the nature of the request, and whether or not we can help. If there is a charge, we'll discuss this with you up front, before proceeding.

What if you want additional background information about a listed community?
The Fellowship keeps extensive files and may be able to help in two ways. First, we may be able to tell you some of the community's history in the movement, and the kind of people who have made it their home. To get what we have in this regard, give us a call, or send a self-addressed stamped envelope with your written request.

Second, we maintain a **Feedback File** about every community for which we receive complaints that don't get amicably resolved. For the cost of $1 per community we will tell you if there is anything in the file on that community, and, if there is, we'll send you a summary of all complaints and community responses. Payment for this service must accompany each request. (See the next page for details about how **Feedback Files** will be created and maintained.)

How You Can Help Us

Use the Additions & Corrections Card (bound just inside the back cover) to inform us of incorrect listing information, or any information about unlisted communities and resources you think belong in this book. If the form is missing, send your news to the address at the bottom of the page.

Check the Renamed, Regrouped, Dead, Disbanded, Lost, & No Replies List on page 327. These are communities we tried to contact for inclusion in this directory, but couldn't list because they didn't respond to our invitations. If you know *any* information about communities not in the Listings—even if it's a community no longer functioning—please look over our RRDDLNoRs to see if we know what you do. If you have something we don't, please use the Additions & Corrections Card to let us know the status or current contact information of these groups.

Fill out the Directory Evaluation Survey on page 411. Please take a few moments to let us know how useful the *Directory* has been for you, and your ideas about how it could be improved. We're always trying to make it better, and we need your input to do the best possible job.

Let us know if you have complaints about a listed group. If through direct contact you discover a significant difference between a community's or resource's self-description and reality, we want to know about it. Please notify us at the address below. First, we may be able to offer an innocent explanation for the discrepancy. Second, we may be able to facilitate an agreeable resolution to any dispute or complaint. Third, we will maintain a **Feedback File** on any community about which there are unresolved difficulties.

Here's how it will work. If you send us a complaint, we'll first contact you to make sure we understand all the details, and the history of what you've done to inform the community and resolve any differences directly. Possibly we can explain things in a way that will satisfy some of your concerns. However, where this doesn't satisfy, we'll contact the community and get their input on the matter. To the extent that differences are settled to the satisfaction of all, great. Where disagreement persists, we'll open a **Feedback File** on the community, which includes the comments of all concerned.

We will not publicize that we have a file on any specific community, only that we maintain files in general. For a fee of $1 per community, we will let people know whether there is a file on that group, and, if there is, provide a summary of the comments from all parties. We will *not* supply the names and addresses of people registering complaints unless they give express permission to do so. To request **Feedback File** summaries for listed communities, send a list of the groups you want to know about—plus a dollar for each name on the list—to the address at the bottom of the page. We'll send you what we have.

The Fellowship has thought long and hard on the best way to handle critical feedback about intentional communities, and we are announcing the **Feedback File**—and the above process for its creation and use—as our current best thinking on how to engage in this thorny area. On the one hand, we are concerned with seekers getting access to full information about communities. On the other, we are concerned with protecting community reputations from rash attacks. Honest misunderstandings can explain a lot, and we are reluctant to record criticisms and pass them along until we are satisfied they are substantial and unresolvable. For more detail on our thinking about the **Feedback File**, please see pages 14-15. Not the least of what we are asking for on this page is your feedback on the **Feedback File**. Let us hear how well this meets your needs!

Directory Feedback
Rt 1, Box 155-D
Rutledge, MO 63563
Phone: 816-883-5545

A Look at the Directory Editorial Team

ON THE THEORY that readers might be interested in thumbnail sketches of the lives of the people behind the scenes, here they are, ordered randomly. The full list of contributors would go on for pages, and we've included here only bios of the fanatics—those who tended to forget, for a time, that they ever led other lives.

Dan Questenberry was managing editor for the Feature Articles in this directory and also the 1990 edition. Since 1986 he has served as a board member of the Fellowship for Intentional Community, which provides management and vision for the *Directory* and other movement projects. Beginning with the 1974 Twin Oaks Communities Conference, Dan has delighted in sharing with community seekers and visiting communities which emphasize land trusts, cooperative economic systems, or spiritual awareness. He joined Shannon Farm in 1976, added a dual membership with Deer Rock in 1993, and frequently participates in movement gatherings, Communal Studies Association conferences, and working visits to other intentional communities. Dan also shares an active family life, and operates his own insurance agency.

Jillian Downey lived in Ann Arbor student co-ops for several years, and then started a group house with other community-minded folks. She became involved with the FIC first by joining the *Directory* staff in the spring of 1994. Now that it's done she plans to help with other Fellowship endeavors, such as the FIC Internet project. In between her editing job and freelance desktop publishing work, Jillian is an avid birdwatcher, loves to read, take roadtrips, garden, and shoot and print black and white photographs.

Elph Morgan began living cooperatively in 1987 and has been involved with the FIC and CSA since 1991. He keeps busy publishing a quarterly literary rag (which occasionally falls behind due to intervening tasks such as the *Directory*), working as a computer consultant with the pathetic belief that his student loans will eventually be paid off, serving on the board of the FIC, managing the FIC database, and recently helping with the FIC Internet project to provide information about community living through the World Wide Web (see page 416). Elph occasionally finds time for practicing massage, reading for pleasure, and traveling.

Laird Schaub is a founding member of Sandhill Farm, and has lived there since 1974. He's been a delegate with the Federation of Egalitarian Communities since 1980, and involved with the Fellowship for Intentional Community since its revitalization in 1986. He is currently the Fellowship Secretary and is surviving his second—and last—tour of duty as *Directory* Managing Editor. Father of two, he juggles the opportunities of parenting with his network responsibilities, the demands of organic farming, and his passion for group process.

Geoph Kozeny has lived in intentional communities for over 20 years. In pursuit of a dream, he cofounded the Stardance Community in 1978 in San Francisco, and lived there 10 years before launching the Community Catalyst Project, which takes him across the continent on visits to communities of all stripes. He gets involved in the daily routine of each group, asks about their visions and realities, takes photos and slides, and gives slide shows about the diversity and viability of the communities movement. He loves to entertain with his guitar and silly songs, and amuses himself with nonstop puns—an annoying or endearing quality, depending on your mood. This is his second stint as the *Directory* Listings coordinator.

Jenny Upton lives, loves and works at Shannon Farm Community in central Virginia. After 13 years at Heartwood Design, Shannon's woodworking shop, she still looks forward to going to work in the morning—driving out of the woods into a panoramic view of the Blue Ridge Mountains on her way to work with people who care about each other, what they produce, and how they produce it is a constant inspiration. She also finds inspiration in the ebb and flow of life in the same community for almost 20 years. Jenny has thoroughly enjoyed contributing to this edition of the *Communities Directory* and to the Fellowship organization in general. She also continues to be mother to her 19-year-old son, Conrad.

Directory Evaluation Survey

As HARD AS WE'VE TRIED to make this Directory perfect...we know it isn't. We invite you to take a few minutes to fill out and send in this two-page survey, telling us your thoughts on what worked well for you and how it can be improved. Feel free to skip questions that are awkward or inappropriate—this is not a test! The use of circles and numbers is convenient for us but if you find that doesn't work for you, please, answer as you feel comfortable. (Cut this page out or photocopy and mail it to the address on the other side.)

About You (put an "X", or something, in, around, or thru the appropriate circles)

1. AGE   ○ under 20 ○ 20-24 ○ 25-29 ○ 30-39 ○ 40-49 ○ 50-59 ○ 60-69 ○ 70+

2. NET INCOME for the last year $_____ (approximately)
   THIS FIGURE IS FOR...
   ○ individual, ○ family (# members? _____), or ○ communal income (# members?_____)

3. CHILDREN (pick one)
   I have NO children and ○ don't plan to   ○ expect to have some in the future.
   I DO have children and ○ single parent them   ○ parent them with a partner or others
                            ○ they don't live with me

4. GROUP LIVING (pick another one)
   ○ I've never lived in a group situation.
   ○ I've lived in a group house, but not in an intentional community.
   ○ I used to live in an intentional community, but don't now.
   ○ I live in an intentional community.

5. CURRENT INTEREST LEVEL (pick one that best describes your situation)
   ○ I'm just curious about community.
   ○ I'm well versed in "community" and am just looking for ideas and contacts.
   ○ I'm actively looking for a new home in community.
   ○ I'm motivated to become more involved in the communities movement.

6. I HEARD ABOUT THE DIRECTORY through... (pick some)
   ○ friend   ○ internet   ○ magazine article ○ bookstore   ○ networking event
   ○ radio   ○ television   ○ magazine ad   ○ videotape   ○ divine message
   ○ flyer   ○ book   ○ newspaper   ○ graffiti   ○ bumper sticker
   ○ speaker   ○ community   ○ telemarketer   ○ other_____

Evaluating the Directory (circle your best choices)

		IMPORTANCE TO YOU	EASE OF USE
		None / Little / Some / Important / Crucial	Terrible / Weak / Adequate / Good / Excellent
7.	Articles	N L S I C	0 1 2 3 4
8.	Maps	N L S I C	0 1 2 · 3 4
9.	Cross-Reference Chart	N L S I C	0 1 2 3 4
10.	N. American Listings	N L S I C	0 1 2 3 4
11.	International Listings	N L S I C	0 1 2 3 4
12.	Resource Listings	N L S I C	0 1 2 3 4
13.	Index	N L S I C	0 1 2 3 4

In the following section we would like to hear your suggestions for improving the various parts of the *Directory*. The space may not be adequate, so don't be shy about attaching extra sheets. For each numbered question below, please circle your best choice.

Feature Articles

14.	Breadth of topics covered	TERRIBLE	WEAK	ADEQUATE	GOOD	EXCELLENT
15.	Relevance of articles to your interests	TERRIBLE	WEAK	ADEQUATE	GOOD	EXCELLENT

Suggestions for improving: Missing topics you would have liked covered:

Community Listings—Suggestions for improving:

Resource Listings

Suggestions for improving: Missing resources you would have liked covered:

Maps—Suggestions for improving layout and presentation:

Cross-Reference Charts

16.	Relevance of categories to your interests	TERRIBLE	WEAK	ADEQUATE	GOOD	EXCELLENT

Suggestions for improving: Categories to add, drop, or do differently:

Index

17.	Breadth of index subject categories	TERRIBLE	WEAK	ADEQUATE	GOOD	EXCELLENT

Suggestions for improving:

Miscellaneous

18.	Overall layout of the *Directory*	TERRIBLE	WEAK	ADEQUATE	GOOD	EXCELLENT
19.	Operating instructions	TERRIBLE	WEAK	ADEQUATE	GOOD	EXCELLENT
20.	Value for price paid	TERRIBLE	WEAK	ADEQUATE	GOOD	EXCELLENT
21.	Usefulness of display ads	TERRIBLE	WEAK	ADEQUATE	GOOD	EXCELLENT
22.	Usefulness of Classified ads	TERRIBLE	WEAK	ADEQUATE	GOOD	EXCELLENT
23.	Usefulness of Reach ads	TERRIBLE	WEAK	ADEQUATE	GOOD	EXCELLENT

Other suggestions:

☞ please mail to Directory Evaluation, Rt 1 Box 155-D, Rutledge, MO 63563.

Calendar of Events

ONE OF THE BEST ways to explore options and make connections is to attend community events. These take many forms, all the way from spur-of-the-moment open houses to international conferences planned years in advance. We cannot begin to catalog all these opportunities in a directory that will last for several years, so we've chosen to limit the entries here to major events that are held regularly. For details about *this* year's events, you will need to contact the host group directly, or refer to the Calendar section of *Communities* magazine, our companion publication, which comes out quarterly.

It's important to keep in mind that there are many valuable events not listed here, either because we didn't know about them when we went to press, because they do not occur regularly, or because they are smaller in scope (trainings, workshops, demonstrations, seminars, lectures, etc.). Many of these will be noted in the Calendar section of *Communities*. See page 440 for magazine order form.

Fellowship for Intentional Community hosts open three-day board meetings in the spring and fall, with site rotated around North America. Contact: FIC, Route 1, Box 155-CD, Rutledge, MO 63563; 816-883-5545.

Federation of Egalitarian Communities holds an annual assembly, usually for four days in November, at one of the member communities. Open to the public. Contact: FEC Desk, Tecumseh, MO 65760; 417-679-4682.

Communal Studies Association holds a three-day conference each October at a historic communal site. Location of the site is known years in advance and rotates all around the United States. Open to the general public, the conference offers presentations by curators, historians, and contemporary communitarians. Contact: CSA, PO Box 122, Amana, IA 52203; WWW: http://www.ic.org/csa/

North American Cohousing Conference is a three-day event held each year in summer or fall. Contact: Rocky Mountain CoHousing Assoc., 1705 14th St. #317, Boulder, CO 80302; 303-494-8458.

Community Service hosts a weekend conference each October at the headquarters in Ohio. Theme varies each year. Contact: CSI, PO Box 243, Yellow Springs, OH 45387; 513-767-2161.

Society for Utopian Studies puts on an annual conference each October, focusing on Utopian thought and action, both factual and fictional. Contact: Lyman Tower Sargent, Dept. of Political Science, UMSL, St. Louis, MO 63121.

International Communal Studies Association hosts a worldwide gathering of people interested in community, every three years. For the next event contact: ICSA, Yad Tabenkin, Ramat Efal 52960 ISRAEL.

Padanaram Settlement hosts open conventions twice a year, usually in early June and mid-October. These straddle a weekend and are open to representatives from other communities and the general public. Contact: Rachel Summerton, Rt. 1, Box 478, Williams, IN 47470; 812-388-5571.

Twin Oaks Communities Conference held each Labor Day weekend, open to everyone from the seasoned networker to the casually curious. Contact: Communities Conference, 138-D6 Twin Oaks Road, Louisa, VA 23093; 540-894-5126.

Twin Oaks Women's Gathering held the last weekend in August. Contact: Women's Gathering, 138-D6 Twin Oaks Road, Louisa, VA 23093; 540-894-5126.

Rainbow Gathering is held July 1–7 each year, at a National Forest site rotated around the United States. For details about the current year's event, contact: 503-284-6600.

Ecovillage/Ecocity Movement hosts periodic conferences around the globe, including: October 7–13, 1995 at Findhorn in Scotland (contact: Accommodations Secretary, Findhorn, Cluny Hill College, Forres IV36 0RD SCOTLAND); and January 3–10, 1996 at Yoff, Senegal (contact: EcoVillage at Ithaca, Anabel Taylor Hall, Cornell University, Ithaca, NY 14853; 607-255-8276).

Communities Calendar appears in *Communities* Magazine and is also carried on our World Wide Web page located at:
http://www.ic.org/events/

Tell *Communities* Magazine about Your Community Events!

Send your event information (name, date, description of event, sponsor or host name, address, and phone) at least six months in advance to:

Communities Events Calendar
PO Box 169, Masonville CO 80541
Phone: 970-593-5615.

Classified Ads

BOOKS, MAGAZINES, VIDEOS

Circle of Song—Songs, Chants and Dances for Ritual and Celebration compiled by Kate Marks. Features over 300 songs and chants from many cultures with music and lyrics, 40 dances, 36 meditations, extensive resourse guide. "This is the finest collection of songs and chants for ritual ever published," Margot Adler, Author/Ritualist. $17.95 postpaid. 304 pp., 60 illustrations. Full Circle Press, PO Box 428, Amherst, MA 01004; 413-256-1186.

"Building Green Communities" VHS (26 minutes). Send $12.00/tape (plus $2.50 mailing) or write FFI to Greta Gaard, Dept. of English, Univ. of Minnesota, Duluth, MN 55812.

Ralph Borsodi: Reshaping Modern Culture, by Mildred Loomis. The story of the School of Living, its founder, and his ground-breaking work in cultural transformation. $17.50 post pd.; School of Living, RD1 Box 185A, Cochranville, PA 19330.

New Age Books, Etc. For price list send SASE to: Apple Tree Acres, PO Box 887, Blowing Rock, NC 28605.

Community Tools: The information tools we need to build community are often hard to find. Either they are scattered through many different books and periodicals, or they are in the minds of experts who may be hard to reach. Community Tools is a project to gather this information, edit, and disseminate it in the form of revisable booklets or expandable notebooks. Topics may include: Options for Legal Incorporation, Child Care in Community, Process and Facilitation, New-Community Development Manual, Labor Systems and Property Codes, Utopian Studies Syllabi and Reading Lists, Community Theory/Values/History/Definitions/Classifications. For a list of resources currently available, or if you would like to contribute to the production or revision of these or other materials, please contact: Allen Butcher, PO Box 1666, Denver, CO 80201; 303-355-4501.

COMMUNITY HOUSING AVAILABLE

Santa Fe CoHousing Community house for sale. We're sad to leave this wonderful place. It's supportive, beautiful, and minutes from town. The house is 2,200 sq. ft. with a greenhouse. Lease options available. Contact: 505-471-5130.

PERSONALS

S.W.M. 59 lives in intentional community. Healthy, many interests. Wants relationship with woman 40–60. For information call 509-725-0390, write Jim, Rt. 3, Box 72Y, Davenport, WA 99122.

Mature woman with property seeks able adults as partners. Abigail. 1315 Edgecliff, Fort Worth, TX 76134-1209.

SERVICES

Forming A Community?—Need Legal Help? Lawyer with many years experience forming and advising common ownership groups, land trusts, cooperatives and nonprofits available as consultant. The paperwork is important! Will travel anywhere or consult by phone/fax. Glen Spain, Attorney at Law, PO Box 11170, Eugene, OR 97440-3370; 503-689-2000.

Aquarian Research Helps People and Communities Communicate with best phone deals, 800 numbers, no surcharge travel cards. 215-849-1259. See Resources, page 363, or Listings, page 216, for toll-free number.

Book Layout? Freelance layout artist with book design and pre-press/printing experience. Jillian Downey, 313-930-0627 or 201-825-0484.

HELP WANTED

The Magic Tortoise is planning building projects spanning the next few years. We are looking for construction crews willing to camp out and share community life. See listing.

Builders/fixers needed, as partners in environmentally sound enterprises. Or run your own business here, after seventeen hours community work/week. Adirondack Herbs, 518-883-3453.

PRODUCTS

Discover Your Best Locations on Earth for community fulfillment or other life goals. These esoteric principles apply to All. Send SASE for free info: ReaLog, PO Box 918, Idyllwild, CA 92549.

We'Moon: Gaia Rhythms for Womyn: Celebrate the cycles with an international astrological moon calendar produced on womyn's land. $15 ppd. Mother Tongue Ink, PO Box 1395, Estacada, OR 97023.

Free Catalogue—100% recycled paper products for home and office. Highest post-consumer content. Unbleached. Fast delivery. Lowest prices and widest selection in the U.S. Call us right now: 800-323-2811. Atlantic Recycled Paper Company, Box 39179, Baltimore, MD 21212.

Organic Foods, nitrogen packed in cans. For price list send SASE to: Apple Tree Acres, PO Box 887, Blowing Rock, NC 28605.

Wool products for creative crafts from Triform Camphill Community: Flat sheets of felt, bags of dyed fleece, felt balls, fleece picture kits. All products are hand processed, and custom dyed in beautiful colors. Write for full description and price list: Susannah White, Triform, RD4 Box 151, Hudson, NY 12534.

Reach Ads

Reach is a classified section devoted exclusively to people looking for communities and communities looking for people.

COMMUNITIES WITH OPENINGS

New: Community Seekers' Network of New England, c/o 15 Marcus Road, Sharon MA 02067, (617)784-4297 (See listing in Resources section.)

Organic-farm-based land trust community in northern Vermont has 54 acres, main house, four separate house sites, open land and sugar bush. Contact Robert Houriet, Goodrich Farm Co-operative, RD 1, Box 934, Hardwick, VT 05843, 802-472-6352.

Namasté—Intentionally green, dedicated to integrity, permaculture and polyfidelitous extended family or "enhancing life from the heart." Seeks partners, coparticipants, networks, global transformation, hemp ecology, soil regeneration, biodiversity, social justice, *full time*. Rt 2 Box 578, Barnstead, NH 03225, 603-776-7776.

COMMUNITIES FORMING

Boston area: A couple of us within Common Unity (see listing) want to form a household based on long-term commitment, daily spiritual time, support for social change, and eventual sharing of all resources. Common Threads c/o Common Unity, Box 441713, Somerville, MA 02144-0014.

Self-sufficient/peace activist community, with alternative energy seminar center, since 1980, in down east rural Maine. Family homesteads on 50 acres on river. Many cooperative businesses and educational opportunities. S.E.A.D.S., PO Box 192, Harrington, ME 04643.

New rural lesbian community. Separate quarters intended. R.V. living possible initially. Ground floor women wanted. PO Box 655, Madisonville, LA 70447.

We are a stable couple of 22 years, warm and loving, looking for women with or without children, to form a larger family through mutual lifetime marriage commitments. He is a kind, considerate man who is affectionate, both physically and verbally. She is a warm, friendly woman who loves children and animals, and is looking for the sisters she never had. We consider companionship, talking to one another, and sharing interests the most important factors in our relationship. Also mutual respect and relating honestly to others is vital for a successful relationship. We enjoy mostly vegetarian dishes, a little wine occasionally; do not smoke or take drugs. We like our home and family related activities, and we own a small business. Philosophically, we are Christian and libertarian. Our plans are to move to Wyoming, relocate our business and build a home for all of us. Our vision is that all family members will be lifetime best friends. If you are interested in family, having a nice home, and personally raising your children instead of building an outside career, maybe our family is right for you. Drop us a note and we'll send you a letter about our family. TSF, PO Box 1854, Minden, NV 89423.

PEOPLE LOOKING

EI/MCS advocates seek: (1) existing rural and urban communities willing to learn about and share non-toxic lifestyles with chemically hyper-sensitive individuals/families; (2) others committed to forming/assisting with any/all phases of environmentally responsible, less toxic community housing projects and farms. Sandra Moilanen, 15490 River Front Rd, Clatskanie, OR 97016; 503-728-3379. Lee Grover, 121 W 3rd Ave, Ajo, AZ 85321; 602-387-6255. AGES (Advocacy Group for the Environmentally Sensitive) Ontario Office, Marie Laurin, 1887 Chaine Ct, Orleans, ON K1C 2W6; 613-830-5722. AGES National Office, Eileen Krysak, 102-453 Pendygrasse, Saskatoon, SK S7M 5H3; 306-978-0780.

Seeking community wanting collective childrearing, eating, working. Christine Douglas, PO Box 60, Occidental, CA 95465; 707-874-2462.

Index of Advertisements

About the Index

Jillian Downey

*T*he keyword Index, though by no means exhaustive, is a vital tool for rooting out some of the information packed between the covers of this book. To get the most out of your *Directory*, use this Index in conjunction with the Maps beginning on page 177 (a geographic index) and the Chart beginning on page 189 (an index of values and practices).

Our indexing is based on the listing each group provided about itself. If a community is not indexed under a particular keyword, that does not necessarily mean that the group does not practice or pursue that particular value—it may mean only that they neglected to mention that aspect in their description.

We tried to index the groups based on resources they might offer our readers, and on those recurring questions which we hear frequently from people searching for their "ideal community."

We chose not to index many of the values or daily practices of community life that got covered in the Chart. For example, if you wish to know if a group shares all its income and assets, look in the Chart and not here. Other values, such as "nonviolence" and "voluntary simplicity," are not covered in the Chart, yet were frequently mentioned in community descriptions—so we tried to cover those in the Index.

If a keyword is followed by an asterisk (*), then that issue or value was addressed in some fashion in our questionnaire, and there is a corresponding column in the Chart that indicates how the group responded.

Realizing that vocational considerations often play a major role in community searches, we also indexed many common community businesses. To the extent possible, we indexed such endeavors as restaurants, woodworking shops, food producers, etc. For the same reason, we've also indexed certain spiritual paths—such as Catholic Workers, Zen Buddhists, the Hutterian Brethren, Quakers, etc. In general, it wasn't practical to index such broad categories as Eastern Spirituality, though that classification is covered in the Chart.

Some communities included in the Listings do not appear in the keyword Index even once. Most of those submitted very brief, very sketchy descriptions that did not mention any of the specific practices or resources that we indexed.

Many of the Index categories have master listings and sub-listings (for example: Solar Energy is a subset of Alternative Energy; Workshop Centers is a subset of Conference Centers, and usually indicates a smaller capacity). We've attempted to list a group only once in a particular area—so make use of the cross-references.

The names used in the keyword Index may look strange at first glance. In the interest of enhancing readability and conserving space, we have used shortened index names. This could be the first word of a group's full name, or the entire name if it's not more than about a dozen letters long. More often it's a shorthand blending of words and abbreviations—each is unique and (hopefully) easily identifiable.

If the group's name is followed by an [F], it's tagged as a "forming" community in the Listings; an [RF] group is one that is "re-forming;" an [I] suffix indicates an entry in the International section. Within the text following each keyword, the information is bunched into three groups: first the communities, then the resource groups, then the cross-references—with a "•" separating the three parts from each other.

We hope you find this directory comprehensive and easy to use, and we need your feedback to make future editions even better. Send us your comments, ideas, and (especially) leads to groups you think should be included—use the blue response card bound inside the back cover. May your search be fruitful.... ⚲

ACADEMIC PROGRAMS
OjaiFndtn ►RESOURCES: Audubon, CenComStu, CSA, ExperLiving, GaiaEd, ICSA, InstSocEcol, ShimerColl, SocUtopStud, YadTabenk ►SEE ALSO: Study Programs, Work Study.

ACTIVISM
AbunDawn(F), Arcoiris(RF), BeaconHill, BlueMoon, BrightMrnStr(RF), Brigid, ChesterCrk, ComnPlace-MA, Currents, EarthFamFarm(RF), Fillmore, Greenhous-OH, HaleByodo(F), Heathcote(RF), HeiWaHouse, LifeCenter, ListwigMir, Orcom(F), Qumbya, Sunset-WA, SusBAnthony, Vine&FigTree, WhiteHouse, YaharaLindn, Zendik ►RESOURCES: MediaNet, New-Society ►SEE ALSO: Anti-Military, Civil Rights, Environmental, Grassroots Organizing, Homelessness, Indigenous Peoples.

ADDICTION ISSUES
SEE: Recovery.

AFFORDABLE HOUSING
CasaGrande, EastWest, Folkcorps(F), Koinonia, LifeCenter, Niche(F), NinthStreet, RiverCity, ShortMtn, SixDirectns(F), SouthsidePrk, Teramanto, Wellsprg-MA(RF) ►RESOURCES: DwellPort, Habitat, InstComEcon, SharedLivng, SustComHsg, UrbEcology ►SEE ALSO: Low-Income Housing.

AFRICA
KingdomOyo, MaatDompim(F), Zegg(I) ►RESOURCES: HospitltyEx, IICD ►SEE ALSO: South Africa.

AGRICULTURAL INSTRUCTION
Birdsfoot, Goodwater(F), Mitranik(I) ►RESOURCES: ElfinPC, HortIdeas

AGRICULTURE
SEE: Bio-Dynamics, Bioregionalism, Food-Producers, Organic Farming & Gardening, Permaculture, Seeds, Sustainable Agriculture.

ALLIANCE BUILDING
FelIntCmty, Sch-Living, ToolsChange

ALTERNATIVE ENERGY
SEE: Appropriate Technology, Conservation, Energy Alternatives, Permaculture, Solar Cooking, Solar Energy.

ALTERNATIVE LIFESTYLES
Arcoiris(RF), EarthFamFarm(RF), Ontos(I), Parnassus(F) ►RESOURCES: CmtyMag, Link-wayCntr, ShimerColl ►SEE ALSO: Relationships.

ALTERNATIVE TECHNOLOGY
SEE: Appropriate Technology.

ALTERNATIVE TRANSIT
SEE: Transportation Alternatives.

ANABAPTIST
SEE: Bruderhof, Hutterian, Mennonite.

ANARCHISM
Dragonfly, EllisIsland, FreeLandSqat, HeiWaHouse, IDA(F), Sweetwater ►RESOURCES: BndTogether, Factsheet5, LeftBank, Williams ►SEE ALSO: Self-Management.

ANCIENT WISDOM
CamelotWood, Geneva(F), HimalayaInst, ReinaDCielo, SaintHerman(F), Yasodhara ►RESOURCES: ChurAllWlds ►SEE ALSO: Spiritual Education.

ANIMAL HUSBANDRY
CEEDS, DanceWater, EastWind, GaiaPerm(F), Hawkwind(F), Headlands(RF), LaAtlan(IRF), LeJardin(IF), LosHorcones, LowrShaw(I), MardenFarm(F), NorCottonwd(F), RavenRocks, ShortMtn, Stichting(IRF), ZephyrVall(F), ZionsOrder, Zirkle(RF) ►RESOURCES: EcovilleNet ►SEE ALSO: Food–Producers.

ANIMAL RIGHTS
Adirondack(RF) ►RESOURCES: BioregProj, Factsheet5, NatRights ►SEE ALSO: Bioregionalism, Endangered Species, Vegan.

ANTHROPOSOPHY
Camphill-MN, Camphill-PA, Camphill-Sol, Camphill-Spc, Camphill-USA, Montclaire(IF), Triform ►SEE ALSO: Biodynamics, Steiner.

ANTI-AUTHORITARIAN
SEE: Decentralization, Self-Management.

ANTI-CONSUMERISM
Christians(I), LArchBorie(I), NorWoodVegan(F), YurtFarm(IRF) ►RESOURCES: Aprovecho, NewRoad-Map ►SEE ALSO: Voluntary Simplicity.

ANTI-MILITARY
BlackCat, EllisIsland, HeiWaHouse, Riverside(I), SeedsPeace, WestEnd(I) ►RESOURCES: CounEconPri, GlobeLib, GroundWork, HutterBreth, LeftBank, VetsPeace, WarResist ►SEE ALSO: Nonviolence, War Tax Resistance.

ANTI-NUCLEAR
SEE: Nuclear Disarmament, Nuclear Power Opposition.

APPRENTICE PROGRAMS
Access(F), Birdsfoot, Camphill-PA, CEEDS, DapalaFarm(F), DuckMtn(F), EarthCycle(RF), Ecoville(IF), LandStewCen(F), Shibboleth(F), Svanholm(I), Tolstoy, Zendik ►RESOURCES: Caretaker, GaiaEd, Geltaftan, Gro-w/oSch ►SEE ALSO: Internships, Karma Yoga, Residencies, Work Study.

APPROPRIATE TECHNOLOGY
AbunDawn(F), Arcoiris(RF), Black-Horse(I), Caerduir(F), NetworkNewC(F), CmtyAltsCoop, DanceRabbit(F), DapalaFarm(F), EarthCycle(RF),

Earthseed(F), EFE(F), Flatrock(RF), GaiaPerm(F), HOME(F), JubileeHouse, LongBranch, LostValley, Maharishi, MikecoRehtl(F), Niche(F), NorSunFarm, RainbVal-TX(RF), Sirius, SixDirectns(F), Skyfire(F), Sunburst(F), Sunflower-OH ►RESOURCES: AcresUSA, AppTechProj, Aprovecho, BioregProj, Columbiana, EcoHome, GlobVilInst, InstLocSelf, OzarkResCen, TraNet, WholeEarth, WrldFutSoc ►SEE ALSO: Building Technology, Energy Alternatives, Permaculture, Solar Cooking, Solar Energy, Sustainable Agriculture.

AQUACULTURE
Adirondack(RF), DragonBelly(F), GaiaPerm(F), Krutsio, Sunburst(F)

ARCHITECTURE
Alcyone(F), Cloudburst, ComnAlameda, Niederkauf(I) ►RESOURCES: CmtyCatlyst, CohoCntr, CoHousingCo, EcovilleNet, EnergieUm, Geltaftan, GreenhsExp, GreenhsExp, Kraus, LivgVillage, PC-Activist, SharedLivng, Shearwater ►SEE ALSO: Building Technology.

ARGENTINA
Remar

ART
ArtColony(F), ChristmsStr, Compound-i, DeerRock(F), Dreamtime(F), DuMá, Fillmore, FullCircle(F), Gesundheit, HighFlowing, Lothlor-IN, Moonshadow(F), OneThouSmPhm, OneWorldFam, QuarryHill, RainbHearth(RF), Redfield(I), RudfSteinFel, ShrubbFam(IRF), SparrowHawk, Triform, WeMoon-Heal(RF), WoodburnHill, Zendik, ZenMtn ►RESOURCES: CirclePines, GenesisFarm, Northland, OmegaInst, SoOregWomen ►SEE ALSO: Culture, Performing Arts.

ARTS, THE
BemisErec, Findhorn(I), Heartwood, Huehuecoyotl, LightColor(F), Mitranik(I), OjaiFndtn, PPAALS(F), SpiesSanity(F), Wellsprg-WI(F)

ARTS & CRAFTS
Arden, Billen(I), Camphill-Sol, Dapala-Farm(F), Downeast(RF), EarthCycle(RF), FusionArts(I), Hawkwind(F), IDA(F), MagicTortis(RF), RainbVal-NZ(I), SkyWoods, Wygelia(F) ►RESOURCES: OneEarth ►SEE ALSO: Crafts.

ASHRAMS
AnandaAshrm, ArshaVidy, Kripalu, OshoIntl(I), SikhDharma, Sivananda, SriAurobindo(RF), TruthConsc, Yasodhara, Yogaville ►SEE ALSO: Monasteries.

ASIA
RESOURCES: HospitltyEx, HutterBrethren.

ASTROLOGY
DuMá, Kailash(F), SkyJahnna(F), UnknownTruth(F), WeMoonHeal(RF) ►RESOURCES: OmegaNewAge

AUDIO/VIDEO
AquarResrch(RF), ComnGrnd-VA, Lichen, MuirCommons, OneWorldFam, ReCreation, SaintBenedct, ThreeSprgs(F), Yogaville, Zendik ▶Resources: AltsCntr, AquarReFdtn, Aurovil-USA, CmtyCntrGay, CoopResCntr, CRSP, DeepDish, GlobVilInst, MediaNet, NatAccTV, OshoCntrs, Wondertree

AUSTRALIA
YamaLife(I) ▶Resources: FedHousing, HospitltyEx, InstCulAffr, NewMilleni ▶See also: "Index by Country" that precedes the International listings.

AUSTRIA
ForTheEarth(I), Remar ▶See also: "Index by Country" that precedes the International listings.

AYURVEDA
Atmasant(I), Kailash(F) ▶Resources: SikhDharma

BAHAMAS
Sivananda

BAKERIES
Camphill-MN, Camphill-PA, CmtyAltsCoop, ComDeLondr(I), Downeast(RF), Innisfree, Padanaram, Philoxia, Sheprdsfld, Shiloh, Triform, WestEnd(I)

BANDS
See: Music Concerts.

BANKS & CREDIT UNIONS
SocFamSolidr(F) ▶Resources: FedSoCoops, NatCoopBank

BARTER
Anaami(F), CEEDS, DapalaFarm(F), Dunmire, Hawkwind(F), Womans-World(F) ▶Resources: CRSP, Undercurr ▶See also: Skills Exchange.

BED & BREAKFAST
DragonBelly(F), FourWinds(F), Philoxia, ReCreation, VictorTrade(F)

BEEKEEPING
Adirondack(RF), CEEDS, DuckMtn(F), LowrShaw(I), ShortMtn, Springtree, Sunburst(F)

BEHAVIORAL PSYCHOLOGY
HorconesTwo, LosHorcones ▶Resources: BehavrAnal, ExperLiving, WaldenFlshp ▶See also: WaldenTwo.

BELGIUM
Resources: InstCulAffr

BENEDICTINE
Benedictine, Taena(I)

BICYCLES
AshbyTree, CerroGordo, Sunburst(F)

BIODYNAMICS
AtlantisRis, CenHarLiv(IF), FarmHome(F), JulianWoods(RF), RavenRocks, RudfSteinFel, Wellsprg-WI(F) ▶Resources: BioDynFarm ▶See also: Anthroposophy, Steiner.

BIOFEEDBACK
HimalayaInst

BIOREGIONALISM
AtlantisRis ▶Resources: BioregProj, Catalyst, Columbiana, EarthIsland, Factsheet5, GaiaEd, NewCatalyst, PlanetDrum, TurtleIsl ▶See also: Decentralization, Environment, Permaculture.

BIRTHING
See: Home Birthing.

BISEXUALITY
Haven(F), IntlPuppydog(F)

BLACKSMITHING
See: Metal Shops.

BODYWORK
Haven(F), Kripalu, MagicTortis(RF), Rapha(N), SaltSpring ▶See also: Massage.

BOOKS—MAILORDER
EsseneSkoola(F), Koinonia ▶Resources: AcresUSA, AltsCntr, AppTechProj, BndTogether, BookPublCo, CmtyBkshlf, CmtyService, CoopResCntr, ForthWorld, Gro-w/oSch, LeftBank, NASCO, NatlHygiene, NewSociety

BOOKS—RARE (AND SEARCHES)
Resources: Williams

BOOKSTORES
Alpha, Findhorn(I), MtMadonna, SouthCasSpir, SparrowHawk, Vivekan-IL ▶Resources: HighWind

BOYCOTT INFORMATION
Resources: CoopAmer

BRAIN HEMISPHERE SYNCH
NewLand

BRAZIL
Remar, YamaLife(I) ▶Resources: IICD, InstCulAffr ▶See also: "Index by Country" that precedes the International listings.

BROADCASTING
Zendik ▶Resources: DeepDish, NatAccTV, NatFedBroad, NatlHygiene, OshoCntrs, PlentyUSA, SingOut

BRUDERHOF
CatskillBrd, CrystSpr-Man, Darvell(I), DeerSpring, Michaelshof(I), NewMeadwRun, OwaHutter(I), PleasantView, SpringVall, Starland, Woodcrest ▶Resources: Peregrine ▶See also: Hutterian Brethren.

BUDDHISM
BarnThe(I), ChagdudGonpa, KarmeChol, RockyMtnDhar, SaintJohns(RF) ▶See also: Zen.

BUILDING CONSTRUCTION
ArtColony(F), CmtyInBurl, EarthCycle(RF), EarthVillage(F), Namasté(F), Padanaram, Shannon, Sheprdsfld, SocFamSolidr(F), Teramanto, WomansWorld(F), YamaLife(I) ▶Resources: CmtyCatalyst

BUILDING TECHNOLOGY
AbunDawn(F), MikecoRehtl(F), NewJahRuslm(RF), PeacefulGrdn(F), Sirius, Sonnenhof(IF), SonorEco-Vill(F) ▶Resources: Rodale, Shearwater ▶See also: Architecture, Earthships, Ferrocement, Fired Clay Shelters, Passive Solar, Portable Dwellings, Straw Bale, Underground Buildings.

BUSINESS
OjaiFndtn, YellowHouse ▶Resources: BusEthics, CenCoops, Empl-Owned, InContext, NatCoopBank, OmegaInst ▶See also: Small Business.

BUSINESS CONSULTING
Finders, WholeHealth ▶Resources: Brown, GroComAssoc, RadRoutes

CAFES
See: Restaurants.

CAMBODIA
RebaPlace

CAMPGROUNDS
AquarRanch(RF), ComnPlace-NY, CrowCircle(RF), Dragonfly, EarthFamFarm(RF), Ecolonie(I), EsseneSkoola(F), FourWinds(F), FriendsLake, Hawkwind(F), KingdomOyo, LaVigne(IRF), Lothlor-IN, MothrEarthOp(RF), MtMadonna, Ontos(I), Ponderosa, QuarryHill, RainbHearth(RF), ReevisMtn, Sharingwood, ShiningWater(RF), SparrowHawk, SusBAnthony, WolfCreek

CAMPHILL
See: Anthroposophy, Biodynamics.

CAMPS—FAMILY
CenPeaceLif(RF), Dragonfly, ToadHouse(N) ▶Resources: CirclePines, CoopCamp

CAMPS—KIDS
BlackOak, LosHorcones, RoweCamp, SongOfMorng(F), YurtFarm(IRF) ▶Resources: Aprovecho, RoweCamp

CAMPS—WOMEN
Resources: SikhDharma

CANADA
Sivananda ▶Resources: Audubon, Aurovil-USA, HutterBreth, InstCulAffr, NASCO, Wondertree

CANDLES
LArchHomefi(F), PeacefulGrdn(F), Philoxia, RudfSteinFel

CAREER OPTIONS
Heartwood ▶RESOURCES: Caretaker, Catalyst, GreenerPast ▶SEE ALSO: Right Livelihood.

CARIBBEAN
RESOURCES: NewMilleni

CATALOG
SEE: Directories, Sourcebooks.

CATHOLIC
AgapeLayAp, HolyCity(F), Jesuit-JVC, SaintBenedct ▶SEE ALSO: Benedictine, Franciscan.

CATHOLIC WORKER
CasaMaria, CathWork-OH, CathWork-TX(RF), DenvCathWkr, HaleyHouse, HearthLArche, Noonday, PeteMaurFarm, SaintFranThr, WestEnd(I)

CELEBRATIONS
SEE: Gatherings, Rituals.

CENSORSHIP
RESOURCES: DataCenter

CENTRAL AMERICA
DanceWater, JubileeHouse, NewJerusalm(N), RebaPlace, RefugioRioGr, SaintFran-ME ▶RESOURCES: EarthIsland, HospitltyEx, IICD, PuebloPeopl ▶SEE ALSO: International.

CERAMICS
SEE: Pottery.

CHANNELING
AquarConcpt(F), Methow, OneWorldFam

CHEMICAL SENSITIVITY
Bamberton(F), Brigid, ChesterCrk, EcoVill-Ith(F), HighHorizons(F), Kidstown(RF), MultChemSens(F) ▶RESOURCES: EnvironIll

CHILDCARE
Arcoiris(RF), CathWork-TX(RF), EastWind, FreeLandSqat, GlenIvy, Homestead(F), LosHorcones, NylandCoho, PrudCrandall(RF), RainbVal-NZ(I), Riverside-WI(F), Sassafras, Sunflower-OH, TwinOaks, YellowHouse

CHILDREN-FOCUSED COMMUNITIES
Blackberry(RF), EarthCycle(RF), ElderWood(F), IonExchange(F), Lamborn, ListwigMir, RiverCmtyHm, Tekiah(RF) ▶SEE ALSO: Camps, Parenting, Play, Schools.

CHILDREN'S PROGRAMS
RESOURCES: ChilGrEarth, GenesisFarm, SkipStones

CHILE
Remar

CHINA
RESOURCES: InstCulAffr

CHRISTIAN
RESOURCES: Habitat, NatAccTV ▶SEE ALSO: Bruderhof, Catholic, Catholic Worker, Episcopal, Essene, Esoteric Christianity, Evangelical, Faithist, Hutterian, Jewish, Mennonites, Pietist, Quakers, Russian Orthodox, Shakers, Unitarian Universalist.

CIVIL DISOBEDIENCE
SEE: Anti-Military.

CIVIL RIGHTS
SEE: Equality, Human Rights, Native American.

CLEARINGHOUSE
RESOURCES: CenComStu, CoHousingCo, FellIntCmty, ICSA ▶SEE ALSO: specific topics.

CLINICS
SEE: Healing Centers.

CLOWNING
BlackOak, Gesundheit

CLTS*
Commonterra, Heathcote(RF), JumpOff(F), Meramec(RF), Montclaire(IF), PermntAgri(F), SaintFranThr, Sweetwater, ThreeSprgs(F), Wellsprg-MA(RF) ▶RESOURCES: InstComEcon, Nomenus, OregWom-LT, Ozark-RLT, Sch-Living ▶SEE ALSO: Land Trusts.

CO-COUNSELING
SEE: Peer Counseling.

CO-CREATION
ArtColony(F), Clearview(F), Earthseed(F), Gaien(F), LightMorn, Namasté(F),SistrDivProv(F)

COHOUSING
AugustGreen(F), BurlingCoho(F), CantineIsl(F), Cardiff(F), ComnAlameda, ComnGrnd-CO, DeerRock(F), DoyleStreet, EarthVillage(F), EcoVill-Ith(F), EugeneCoho(F), Geneva(F), HarmonyVill(F), LostValley, ManhattCoho(F), MikecoRehtl(F), Monadnock(F), MuirCommons, N-Street, Namasté(F), NoNameCoho(F), NylandCoho, Phoenix-AZ(F), PioneerVall(F), Riverside-WI(F), Sharingwood, SharonSprgs(F), Songaia, SouthsidePrk, TenStones (F), VashonCoho, VeganCoho(F), Wellsprg-WI(F), Westchester(F), WestwdCoho(F), WinslowCoho ▶RESOURCES: CohoCntr, CoHousingCo, CoHousngNet, GenesisFarm, Hanson, InnovHousg, Kraus, Landelijke, NWCoHoQrtr, RockyMtCoHo, TwinCities

COLLECTIVE LIVING
BlueMoon ▶RESOURCES: CommuneNet

COLLECTIVES
Christiania(I), Fillmore, Niederkauf(I), Svanholm(I), WhiteHouse ▶RESOURCES: AltsCntr, CmtyBkshlf, FedHousing, GEO-News ▶SEE ALSO: Self-Management, Worker Ownership.

COLOMBIA
SEE: "Index by Country" that precedes the International listings.

COMMUNICATION—ELECTRONIC
AquarRanch(RF), Sonnenhof(IF) ▶RESOURCES: CmtyDialtone, GlobVillInst ▶SEE ALSO: Computers, Electronics, Telephone.

COMMUNICATION—INTERPERSONAL
Acorn, Earthseed(F), Fairview, Flatrock(RF), IntlPuppydog(F), Kripalu, MothrEarthOp(RF), PrairieRidge(F), PurpleRose, RainbVal-NZ(I), SkyWoods, SocHumSolidr(F), Spaulding, StillWater(F), Taliesin(F), TuiTrust(I), Wygelia(F) ▶RESOURCES: CenConflict, CmtyCntrGay, FdtnCmtyEnc, ParentLeadr ▶SEE ALSO: Personal Growth, Relationships.

COMMUNITY BUILDING
CenPeaceLif(RF), OjaiFndtn, SaintFran-ME, TorontoTori(N), WholeHealth ▶RESOURCES: CenIntegral, CmtyBkshlf, CmtyCatlyst, CmtyMag, FdtnCmtyEnc, FedEgalCmty, FellIntCmty, GreenhsExp, GroComAssoc, GroComNews, GroodyAssoc, HighTrust, InnovHousg, SiriusEdu, ToolsChange

COMMUNITY DEVELOPMENT
AnandaMarga, Ecoville(IF), Koinonia, Sunflower-OH ▶RESOURCES: EvergreenLT, GapMedia, InContext, InfinLight, LivgVillage, NorthCntry, TIES/Canada

COMMUNITY DIRECTORIES
RESOURCES: CmtyMag, CommuneNet, Dig&Dream, FellIntCmty, HutterBreth, Macrocosm, NICA, SiriusEdu

COMMUNITY LIVING
RESOURCES: BookPublCo, CmtyBkshlf, CmtyMag, GaiaEd, NewCatalyst

COMMUNITY NETWORKS (INTERNAT'L)
AnandaVill, CmtyInIslPd, FamilyThe, Findhorn(I), ForTheEarth(I), HighFlowing, IskconFarm, LArchTros(I), Maharishi, Noonday, Remar, Sivananda, Vivekan-IL, YamaLife(I), Yogaville ▶RESOURCES: CommuneNet, CmtyInAssoc, Emissaries, HutterBreth, InstCulAffr, Kokoo, Landelijke, OshoCntrs, SikhDharma, YadTabenk

COMMUNITY NETWORKS (N. AMER.)
BuddhistSoc(RF), Builders, CmtyAltsCoop, ConscVill, CooperSt, CrowsNest(N), DOE-Farm, Jesuit-JVC, Kripalu, LifeCenter, OneWorldFam, TruthConsc ▶RESOURCES: EvergreenLT, FedEgalCmty, FellIntCmty, InterCoopMI, InterCoopTX, MadisonCC, NICA, OneEarth, OSCA, TwinCities

KEY TO ABBREVIATIONS: (F) FORMING, (RF) REFORMING, (I) INTERNATIONAL, (N) NONRESIDENTIAL, (*)SEE CHARTS

Communities Directory

CSAs
CEEDS, DapalaFarm(F), JulianWoods(RF), Wellsprg-WI(F) ▶RESOURCES: BioDynFarm, GenesisFarm

CULTURE
ChristineCn(F), CrowCircle(RF), Dreamtime(F), Earthaven(F), Earthseed(F), Goodenough(N), Sojourners(RF), Timeweave(RF), WeMoonHeal(RF) ▶RESOURCES: BehavrAnal, BndTogether, ChurAllWlds, CmtyCntrGay, Columbiana, Dance/NE, GreenhsExp, InContext, LandInst, OneWrldFam, Reclaiming, SingOut, WholeEarth, WomPower, ZetaMag

DAIRIES
Riverside(I), Taena(I), Triform, Utopiaggia(I), Windward

DANCE
Aeqaunim(IF), ChristmsStr, DanceHawaii(RF), EarthCycle(RF), EarthFamFarm(RF), FullCircle(F), HighFlowing, Lothlor-IN, Morninglory, RiverCmtyHm, SparrowHawk, Zendik ▶RESOURCES: CircleSong, CmtyCntrGay, Dance/NE, ECoopRecSch

DEATH ROW
SEE: Prisoners.

DECENTRALIZATION
RESOURCES: EFSchumach, GlobeLib, TurtleIsl ▶SEE ALSO: Greens, Local Self-Reliance, Self-Management.

DECISION MAKING*
SEE: Consensus, Facilitation, Group Process.

DENMARK
RESOURCES: Kokoo ▶SEE ALSO: "Index by Country" that precedes the International listings.

DESERTIFICATION
SEE: Restoration (Environment).

DESKTOP PUBLISHING
RESOURCES: CmtyCatlyst, HighWind

DIET
SEE: Nutrition & Diet

DIRECT ACTION
SEE: Anti-Military, Grassroots Organizing.

DIRECTORIES
RESOURCES: AERO, AltPressIdx, CoopAmer, GlobVilActn, NCACS, NewAgeJour, NewMilleni, OmegaNewAge, PlanetDrum, RainbGuide, RenewAmer ▶SEE ALSO: Communities Directories, Sourcebooks, and specific topics.

DISABILITIES
Camphill-MN, Camphill-PA, Camphill-Sol, Camphill-Spc, Camphill-USA, CenExamLife, CmtyAltsCoop, ComDeChamb(I), EFE(F), HearthLArche, Heathcote(RF), Innisfree, JubileePrtnr, LArchDaybrk, LArchHomefi(F), LArch-Mobile, LArchSyracu, LArchTros(I), RudfSteinFel, Sojourners(RF), Triform ▶RESOURCES: AFS, Gro-w/oSch ▶SEE ALSO: Wheelchair Accessible.

DISABLED EQUIPMENT
Darvell(I), Michaelshof(I), Woodcrest

DISARMAMENT
SEE: Anti-Military, Nuclear Disarmament.

DISASTER RELIEF
AnandaMarga, FarmThe(RF) ▶RESOURCES: PlentyUSA

DIVERSITY
Acorn, Earthseed(F), Flatrock(RF), Glenridge, HawkCircle, HealingGrace(F), Heartwinds(F), Heathcote(RF), HeiWaHouse, Hillegass, HimalayaInst, Homestead(F), Huehuecoyotl, Interntl-Coop, JubileeHouse, ListwigMir, LosAnEcoVill(F), LostValley, Lothlor-IN, LowrShaw(I), Mandala(IRF), Manhatt-Coho(F), Marathon, Meramec(RF), Monadnock(F), N-Street, Niche(F), NinthStreet, Orcom(F), OURHouse, PermntAgri(F), PilotMtn(F), PrairieRidge(F), Sharingwood, Sirius, SonorEcoVill(F), Sunset-CA(RF), TwinPines, ValleyLight(RF), Westchester(F), WestwdCoho(F), White-House, Zirkle(RF) ▶RESOURCES: InstCulAffr, Northland, ToolsChange ▶SEE ALSO: Multicultural, Multigenerational.

DOWSING
SparrowHawk

DRAFT HORSES
AtlantisRis, CEEDS, EarthCycle(RF), GreenPastur, LaAtlan(IRF), SaintFran-ME, Stichting(IRF)

DRAFT RESISTANCE
SEE: Anti-Military, Peace & Justice.

DREAMWORK
HighFlowing, Rapha(N), Yasodhara

DRUG ABUSE
SEE: Recovery.

EARTH CHANGES
FourWinds(F), Lothlor-IN, Methow, Shib-boleth(F) ▶RESOURCES: OmegaNewAge

EARTH RELIGIONS
CamelotWood, Earthseed(F), Hawkwind(F) ▶SEE ALSO: Native American, Pagan, Shamanism, Wicca.

EARTHSHIPS
DanceRabbit(F), PhantoBolo(F), PortCentauri (F), Reach(F), Star(F), ThreeSprgs(F)

EASTERN ORTHODOX
SaintHerman(F)

EASTERN SPIRITUALITY
SEE: Buddhism, Hare Krishna, Sikh, Sufi, Vedanta, Yoga, Zen.

ECOLOGY
CEEDS, ComDeChamb(I), Downeast(RF), DuMá, Hearthaven, Huehuecoyotl, KehillatMish(N), Kootenay, LosHorcones, LostValley, MaatDompim(F), Marden-Farm(F), Meramec(RF), Moonshadow(F), NewRoots(RF), PermntAgri(F), PeteMaurFarm, PrairieRidge(F), PrudCrandall(RF), RefugioRioGr, Shrubb-Fam(IRF), SpiesSanity(F), Taliesin(F), Timeweave(RF), TrailsEnd, UnionAcres, WhiteHouse, WiscoyVall, WoodburnHill, Zendik ▶RESOURCES: Audubon, EcoHome, GenesisFarm, GreenhsExp, GroundWork, InstDeepEco, InstSocEcol, Ozark-RLT, PlanetDrum, Soc&Nature, ToolsChange ▶SEE ALSO: Environment, Ecovillages.

ECONOMIC CONVERSION
MikecoRehtl(F) ▶RESOURCES: CounEconPri

ECONOMIC DEVELOPMENT
CEEDS, RiverCmtyHm, Wellsprg-MA(RF) ▶RESOURCES: FedSoCoops, InstLocSelf, NeighbrWrks, OzarkResCen

ECONOMICS
RESOURCES: AcresUSA, ActionLink, Catalyst, DataCenter, EagleConnec, EcovilleNet, EFSchumach, GroCom-News, NewEnviron, Worldwatch ▶SEE ALSO: Sustainable Economics.

ECO-TOURISM
Bamberton(F), Billen(I), EFE(F)

ECOVILLAGES
Bamberton(F), CerroGordo, Christiania(I), EcoVill-Ith(F), Ecoville(IF), Gaien(F), HighWind, LosAnEcoVill(F), Maharishi, MardenFarm(F), Monadnock(F), Namasté(F), SonorEcoVill(F), Wellsprg-WI(F) ▶RESOURCES: CRSP, EcovilleNet, EcovilTrain, GaiaEd, HighWind, PlentyUSA ▶SEE ALSO: Planned Neighborhoods, Sustainability.

ECUADOR
Remar ▶SEE ALSO: "Index by Country" that precedes the International listings.

EDITING
Arcoiris(RF), Lichen, Yasodhara

EDUCATION
Camphill-Spc, CrowsNest(N), Goodwater(F), Heartlight, Huehuecoyotl, LightColor(F), LongBranch, MagicInc, Maharishi, Mickleton(I), MikecoRehtl(F), Moonshadow(F), RavenRocks, Sirius, Spiricoasis(F), Stelle, Timeweave(RF), WoodburnHill, YellowHouse ▶RESOURCES: AERO, AuntLinda, EagleConnec, LinkwayCent, MtnGrove, NCACS, Wondertree ▶SEE ALSO: Academic Programs, Homeschooling, Schools, or specific topics.

Index

FINANCE & FUND RAISING (Cont'd.)
►RESOURCES: Brown, CoHousingCo, CoopAmer, EagleConnec, EarthCare, GroComNews, InstComEcon, NatCoopBank, Northland, NWCoHoQrtr ►SEE ALSO: Socially Responsible Investing.

FINDHORN-INSPIRED COMMUNITIES
LightColor(F), OneEarth, Shenoa, Sirius, Taliesin(F) ►SEE ALSO: Light Centers.

FIRED CLAY SHELTERS
ThreeSprgs(F) ►RESOURCES: Geltaftan

FOOD—INFORMATION
FarmThe(RF) ►RESOURCES: GlobVilInst ►SEE ALSO: Nutrition & Diet.

FOOD—PRODUCERS
Adirondack(RF), AquarRanch(RF), Birdsfoot, BlackHorse(I), CEEDS, Centrept(I), Chrysallis(F), CmtyAltsCoop, CmtyInBasin, DanceHawaii(RF), DeerRock(F), Dragonfly, EarthCycle(RF), EastWind, ElderWood(F), FarmThe(RF), Gaien(F), Goodrich(F), Headlands(RF), HundredMile, HutBrethSpok, K&K-Organic(F), KingView(RF), Koinonia, LArchHomefi(F), LosHorcones, Mitranik(I), NewCovent(RF), PeacefulGrdn(F), Riverside(I), RudfSteinFel, SaintBenedct, Sandhill, SandyBar(F), Shiloh, Springtree, SunriseRanch(RF), Svanholm(I), Taena(I), TuiTrust(I), Utopiaggia(I), YamaLife(I), ZionsOrder ►RESOURCES: HutterBreth ►SEE ALSO: Aquaculture, Beekeeping, CSAs, Dairies, Herbs, Hydroponics, Maple Sugaring, Mushrooms, Nutbutters, Orchards, Organic Farming & Gardening, Soy Products

FOOD—STORES
Adirondack(RF), AppleTree, Builders, Camphill-PA, Camphill-USA, CenHarLiv(IF), Findhorn(I), GriffinGorge, Hearthstone(N), SaintFran-ME, Shiloh, SixDirectns(F), Svanholm(I), UnionAcres, VictorTrade(F)

FOOD—SUPPLEMENTS
WholeHealth

FORESTRY
CerroGordo, EarthCycle(RF), Goodrich(F), RavenRocks, ShortMtn, Springtree, WattleHill(IF) ►RESOURCES: Aprovecho, PC-Activist

FOUNDRIES
SEE: Metal Shops.

FRANCE
RESOURCES: Aurovil-USA ►SEE ALSO: "Index by Country" that precedes the International listings.

FRANCISCAN
NewJerusalm(N)

FUND RAISING
SEE: Finance & Fund Raising

FUNDS, GRANTS, & ENDOWMENTS
MikecoRehtl(F), NewJerusalm(N), ZenBones(F) ►RESOURCES: CenComStu, CounEconPri, EagleConnec, FedSoCoops, FelIntCmty, GEO-News, MediaNet, NatWarTax, NorthCntry, RadRoutes, TurtleIsl, YadTabenk ►SEE ALSO: Finance, Socially Responsible Investing.

FURNITURE
CmtyInBello, CmtyInBost, ComDeLondr(I), Ganas, Wygelia(F)

FUTURE
RESOURCES: AquarReFdtn, ReVision, WrldFutSoc ►SEE ALSO: Utopian.

GAMES
Finders, Kerista(RF) ►RESOURCES: AnimalTown, CirclePines, ECoopRecSch ►SEE ALSO: Play.

GARDENING
SEE: Agriculture, Organic Gardening.

GATHERINGS—MEN
RESOURCES: Nomenus

GATHERINGS—PUBLIC
CircleSanct(N), ComnPlace-NY, CrowsNest(N), Hawkwind(F), IDA(F), IslandGroup(F), JesusPeopUSA, JumpOff(F), K&K-Organic(F), Lothlor-IN, LowrShaw(I), Moonshadow(F), New-Vrndab, OakGrove(F), Padanaram, ShortMtn, Songaia, Taena(I), Timeweave(RF), TorontoTori(N), TwinOaks, WolfCreek ►RESOURCES: CircleNet, CommuneNet, EcovilTrain, FelIntCmty, RainbGuide, SikhDharma ►SEE ALSO: Calendar on pg. 413.

GATHERINGS—WOMEN
SusBAnthony, Womanshare

GAY
BemisErec, HeiWaHouse, IDA(F), IntlPuppydog(F), PansyFarm(F), ShortMtn, WolfCreek ►RESOURCES: BndTogether, CmtyCntrGay, GroundWork, NatAccTV, Nomenus, RFD, Williams ►SEE ALSO: Human Rights, Men.

GEOMANCY
Lothlor-IN, OakGrove(F), SparrowHawk

GEORGIST
Arden

GERMANY
ForTheEarth(I), Remar, YamaLife(I) ►RESOURCES: Aurovil-USA ►SEE ALSO: "Index by Country" that precedes the International listings.

GHANA
Remar

GIBB, JACK
TorontoTori(N)

GRANTS
SEE: Funds.

GRASSROOTS ORGANIZING
Downeast(RF), HeiWaHouse, Mitranik(I), Montclaire(IF), Sojourners(RF), TripleCreek, YellowHouse ►RESOURCES: 20/20Vision, BioregProj, CenConflict, DataCenter, DeepDish, GapMedia, GroundWork, Habitat, PlanetDrum, RSVP, SEAC, TraNet ►SEE ALSO: Activism, Neighborhood Organizing, Peace & Justice.

GREAT BRITAIN
RESOURCES: Dig&Dream, NewMilleni, RadRoutes ►SEE ALSO: "Index by Country" that precedes the International listings.

GREECE
SEE: "Index by Country" that precedes the International listings.

GREEN POLITICS
DanceWater, ForTheEarth(I), Namasté(F) ►RESOURCES: BioregProj, CoopAmer, EarthIsland, EcoNet, GreenMoney, GroundWork, Soc&Nature ►SEE ALSO: Decentralization, Neighborhood Organizing, Sustainable Economics.

GREY WATER
SEE: Water Treatment.

GROUP MARRIAGE
SEE: Polyamory, Polyfidelity.

GROUP PROCESS*
EarthCycle(RF), Ganas, Goodenough(N), ICA-Phoenix(RF) ►RESOURCES: Canbridge, GroComNews, Hanson, LivgVillage, RadRoutes ►SEE ALSO: Consensus, Council Process, Facilitation, Leadership.

GROWERS
SEE: Food—Producers.

GUATEMALA
FarmThe(RF), Remar, RosyBranch ►RESOURCES: InstCulAffr

GURDJIEFF
ChangingWtr(F), InstHarDevel(F)

HAMMOCKS
Acorn, DeerRock(F), EastWind, TwinOaks

HANDICAPPED
SEE: Disabilities.

HARE KRISHNA
GitaNagari(RF), IskconFarm, NewVrndab

HAZARDOUS WASTE
RESOURCES: CmteeUnivSec, EarthIsland, NatRights

HEALING CENTERS
Gesundheit, OpenDoor, OpenDoor, Waldos(IF), YamaLife(I) ►RESOURCES: PlentyUSA, Undercurr, VetsPeace

KEY TO ABBREVIATIONS: (F) FORMING, (RF) REFORMING, (I) INTERNATIONAL, (N) NONRESIDENTIAL, (*)SEE CHARTS

HEALTH & HEALING
Aeqaunim(IF), Alcyone(F), AnandaMarga, AppleTree, AquarConcpt(F), Atmasant(I), BemisErec, BrazierPk(I), NetworkNewC(F), CmtyHouse, DuckMtn(F), EarthCycle(RF), EarthFamFarm(RF), EnchantGardn(RF), Findhorn(I), Hawkwind(F), Heartwood, Heathcote(RF), HimalayaInst, InstHarDevel(F), K&K-Organic(F), Kripalu, LaVigne(IRF), LeJardin(IF), MardenFarm(F), MtMadonna, Ontos(I), Philoxia, ReevisMtn, SaltSpring, Shibboleth(F), SierraHotSpg, Sirius, SixDirectns(F), SonorEcoVill(F), Tekiah(RF), Triform, TuiTrust(I), Wellsprg-WI(F), WholeHealth, YellowHouse, Zegg(I) ▶RESOURCES: AcresUSA, EagleConnec, InfinLight, KenKeyes, LinkwayCent, NatlHygiene, NewEnviron, OmegaInst, OmegaNewAge, Rodale, SikhDharma ▶SEE ALSO: Healing Centers, H.I.V., Homeopathic Remedies, New Age, Nutrition, Therapy.

HENRY GEORGE
SEE: Georgist.

HERBALISM
Avalon(F), JulianWoods(RF), Kailash(F), LeJardin(IF), Moonshadow(F), NorWoodVegan(F), ReevisMtn, SaltSpring, Stichting(IRF), Sunnyside(F), Unknown-Truth(F) ▶RESOURCES: NativeSeeds

HERBS
Adirondack(RF), Birdsfoot, Gaien(F), PeacefulGrdn(F)

HISTORIC SITES
Christnsbrn(RF), Fillmore, Four-Winds(F), SouthCasSpir, VisionFdtn(F) ▶RESOURCES: CantShaker

HISTORY
Folkhaven(F) ▶RESOURCES: BndTogether, CenComStu, Columbiana, CSA, Dig&Dream, ForthWorld, Gro-w/oSch, Northland, SocUtopStud, YadTabenk

H.I.V. ACTIVISM
BemisErec, HeiWaHouse

HOLLAND
RESOURCES: Aurovil-USA, Landelijke ▶SEE ALSO: "Index by Country" that precedes the International listings.

HOME BIRTHING
Anasazi(F), ComnPlace-NY, DuckMtn(F), Goodwater(F), Morninglory

HOMELESSNESS
Agahpay(RF), AgapeLayAp, AquarResrch(RF), Bijou, CCNV, CEEDS, CmtyInStJo, CmtyOfCelebr, ComDe-Chamb(I), CoventHouse, EFE(F), JesusPeopUSA, JubileeHouse, New-Covent(RF), NewCreatn(I), OpenDoor, RainbJunctn(F), RebaPlace, Remar, SaintFran-ME, SaintJohns(RF), Sojourners(RF), Wellsprg-MA(RF), WheelCmtyGth(F)

▶RESOURCES: KidsToCntry, RadRoutes, VetsPeace, KidsToCntry, RadRoutes, VetsPeace ▶SEE ALSO: Catholic Worker.

HOMEOPATHIC REMEDIES
BearCreek(F), Stichting(IRF)

HOMESCHOOLING*
Anasazi(F), CmtyInIslPd, ComnGrnd-VA, ComnPlace-NY, DuckMtn(F), Eloin, Greenwood(RF), Heathcote(RF), Niche(F), PermntAgri(F), Ponderosa, Sandhill, Sunburst(F), UnionAcres, ValleyLight(RF), WheelCmtyGth(F) ▶RESOURCES: AERO, AuntLinda, Gro-w/oSch, HomeEdPress, NALSAS, NatHomeSchl, ShimerColl

HOMESTEADING
AtlantisRis, DanceWater, EarthReLeaf(RF), Goodwater(F), HighHorizons(F), RiverFarm, SaintFran-ME, StillWater(F)

HONG KONG
RESOURCES: InstCulAffr

HORSES
SEE: Draft Horses.

HORTICULTURE
EFE(F), Riverside(I) ▶RESOURCES: HortIdeas

HOSPITALITY
BemisErec, Celo, CmtyInHyan, Cranberry-Crk, CrescentRd(I), DenvCathWkr, Dragonfly, GlenIvy, HaleByodo(F), Hearthaven, HundredMile, Koinonia, LaVigne(IRF), LeJardin(IF), LifeCenter, LostValley, Maxworks, Mickleton(I), Montebello, NewMoon, Noonday, OneWorldFam, Ontos(I), PPAALS(F), QuarryHill, ReevisMtn, Sichlassen, Sirius, Sonnenhof(IF), SparrowHawk, Spaulding, Stonehedge(RF), TuiTrust(I), Vivekan-IL, WestEnd(I), Womanshare, ZevenRiv(I) ▶RESOURCES: CirclePines, HospitltyEx, NewMilleni ▶SEE ALSO: Bed & Breakfast, Campgrounds, Hostels.

HOSPITALS
SEE: Healing Centers.

HOSTELS
MikecoRehtl(F), Mitranik(I) ▶RESOURCES: AmYouthHstl

HOT SPRINGS
Breitenbush, ConscVill, GlenIvy, Harbin, SierraHotSpg, SixDirectns(F)

HOUSING
CmtyAltsCoop, Mitranik(I), NewJeru-salm(N), OpenDoor, Tanguy ▶RESOURCES: AltsCntr, CoopCamp, CRSP, EFSchumach, FedHousing, Kokoo, NatAssoHsng, USCA ▶SEE ALSO: Affordable Housing, Cohousing, Employee Housing, Low Income Housing.

HUMAN POTENTIAL
Abode, HimalayaInst, MariposaGrp, TuiTrust(I) ▶SEE ALSO: Personal Growth, Self-Realization.

HUMAN RIGHTS
Goodwater(F), Parnassus(F), YaharaLindn ▶RESOURCES: Catalyst, CounEconPri, DataCenter, FedSoCoops, GlobVilInst, Interfaith, NatRights, NewSociety PlentyUSA ▶SEE ALSO: Civil Rights, Elderly, Gay, Homelessness, Lesbian, Multicultural, Native American, Peace & Justice.

HUTTERIAN BRETHREN
FanLake, HutBrethSpok ▶RESOURCES: HutterBreth ▶SEE ALSO: Bruderhof.

HYDROPONICS
KingView(RF), NewJahRuslm(RF), Sunburst(F) ▶SEE ALSO: Aquaculture.

INDEXES
RESOURCES: AltPressIdx, AppTechProj, DataCenter, EcoNet, Factsheet5, FedEgalCmty, RenewAmer, UtneReader

INDEXING
TwinOaks

INDIA
MtMadonna, Sivananda, Vivekan-IL ▶RESOURCES: GaiaEd, InstCulAffr, InstSocEcol, NewMilleni ▶SEE ALSO: "Index by Country" that precedes the International listings.

INDIGENOUS PEOPLES
RESOURCES: GroundWork, OneWrldFam, SkipStones, Soc&Nature ▶SEE ALSO: Native Americans, Third World.

INDIVIDUALISM
AshbyTree, Claritas(F), Downeast(RF), Dragonfly, HundredMile, SpiesSanity(F), Syntony(F) ▶RESOURCES: SpiesSanity

INFORMATION
SEE: Clearinghouses, Community Referrals, Computers, Networking, and specific topics.

INSURANCE
Shannon, SocFamSolidr(F), ZenBones(F) ▶RESOURCES: CoopAmer

INTERNATIONAL COMMUNITIES
SEE: Index by Country on pg. 342

INTERNATIONAL COMPOSITION
AquarConcpt(F), Auroville(I), CmtyInBost, ComDeSus(I), Ecolonie(I), HimalayaInst, Huehuecoyotl, InterntlCoop, KarmeChol, LaVigne(IRF), LeJardin(IF), OshoIntl(I), PlumVillage, Sirius, TuiTrust(I), YurtFarm(IRF), Zegg(I), ZevenRiv(I) ▶RESOURCES: Aurovil-USA

INTERNATIONAL NETWORKS
RESOURCES: AmYouthHstl, AppTechProj, GlobVilActn, HospitltyEx, ICSA, NewMilleni, SkipStones, SocUtopStud

INTERNATIONAL OUTREACH
Ecoville(IF), Jesuit-JVC ▶RESOURCES: EagleConnec, GaiaEd, IICD

Communities Directory

INTERNSHIPS
Earthlands(RF), LongBranch, LosAnEco-Vill(F), MaatDompim(F), MothrEarthOp(RF), RainbHearth(RF), Sojourners(RF), Spring-tree, Wellsprg-MA(RF), Wellsprg-WI(F) ►RESOURCES: Aprovecho, CentRockyMt, NASCO ►SEE ALSO: Apprentice Programs, Residencies, Work Study.

INTERSPECIES COMMUNICATION
Dolphin(IF), RainbHearth(RF), Zegg(I)

INTESTINAL CLEANSING
WholeHealth

INVESTMENTS, RESPONSIBLE
SEE: Socially Responsible Investing.

ISRAEL
RESOURCES: Kibbutzim
►SEE ALSO: "Index by Country" that precedes the International listings.

ITALY
ForTheEarth(I) ►RESOURCES: Aurovil-USA, EarthIsland ►SEE ALSO: "Index by Country" that precedes the International listings.

IVORY COAST
Remar

JAPAN
SaintJohns(RF), YamaLife(I)
►RESOURCES: HospitltyEx, InstCul-Affr ►SEE ALSO: "Index by Country" that precedes the International listings.

JEWISH
KehillatMish(N), Rapha(N) ►RESOURCES: Kibbutzim ►SEE ALSO: Kibbutzim.

JOBS
SEE: Career Options.

JOURNALS
SEE: Magazines, Publications.

JUDAISM
SEE: Jewish.

JUNGIAN THERAPY
Taena(I)

JUSTICE
SEE: Human Rights, Legal, Peace & Justice.

KARMA YOGA
Auroville(I), Sivananda

KENYA
RESOURCES: InstCulAffr, SolCookIntl

KIBBUTZIM
RESOURCES: Kibbutzim, YadTabenk

KOREA
BuddhistSoc(RF), YamaLife(I)

KOSHER
UnknownTruth(F)

LABOR
Bamberton(F) ►RESOURCES: DataCenter, EcoNet, GEO-News, Northland

LAND CO-OPS
AppleTree, BlueMoon, BrynGweled, Bundagen(I), CarpentrVil(F), Celo, ComnGrnd-AL, ComnGrnd-VA, ComnPlace-NY, DanceWater, DeepWoods, DeerRock(F), Desiderata, DOE-Farm, DuckMtn(F), Dunmire, EarthReLeaf(RF), Edges(F), FarValley, FriendsSW, Folkcorps(F), Goodrich(F), Grassroots, Greenbriar, GreeningLife, Greenwood(RF), HawkCircle, Head-lands(RF), Heartwinds(F), Homestead(F), JupiterHoll, Kootenay, Lothlor-Ont, Miccosukee, MonansRill, Mothr-EarthOp(RF), MtMurrin(I), NewLand, NewLeaf(F), NewRoots(RF), NorMountain, NorSunFarm, PermntAgri(F), Phanto-Bolo(F), Quakerland(F), QuarryHill, RainbVal-TX(RF), Reach(F), Redfield(I), ReinaDCielo, Rejenneratn(F), Renais-sance(RF), RosyBranch, Rowanwood, Sassafras, SevenSprgs, Shannon, Sky-Ranch(F), Starseed(F), Sunflower-OH, Sunset-WA, Tanguy, Timatang(I), TripleCreek, UnionAcres, Windward, WiscoyVall, WoodburnHill, ZephyrVall(F)

LAND TRUSTS*
RESOURCES: EFSchumach, EvergreenLT, FedHousing, GenesisFarm, GreenhsExp, LandTrust, NewEnviron, TIES/Canada ►SEE ALSO: CLTs.

LANDSCAPING
MothrEarthOp(RF), RainbHearth(RF), SantaRosaCrk, Shannon ►RESOURCES: LivgVillage, PC-Activist

LANGUAGE
Ecoville(IF), LaVigne(IRF) ►SEE ALSO: Español, Esperanto.

LEADERSHIP
AnandaMarga, CmtyOfCelebr, GreenPastur, Mandala(IRF), SocFamSolidr(F) ►RESOURCES: Audubon, CenCoops, ECoopRecSch, EcovilleNet, Emissaries, ExperLiving, NASCO, NatAssoHsng, Ozark-RLT, RobtGreenlf, ToolsChange, WomPower

LEFT POLITICS
Niederkauf(I) ►RESOURCES: LeftBank, Williams

LEGAL SERVICES & RESOURCES
ComnAlameda, FarmThe(RF), Goodwater(F) ►RESOURCES: Brown, ForthWorld, Hanson, Kokoo, NALSAS, NatRights, NatWarTax, Nolo, PlentyUSA, RadRoutes

LESBIAN
ChesterCrk, DOE-Farm, Heathcote(RF), OwlFarm, ShortMtn, SpiralWimm, Steppingwood(F), SusBAnthony, WeMoonHeal(RF), Womanshare, WomansWorld(F) ►RESOURCES: NatAccTV, OregWom-LT, SoOregWomen, Williams ►SEE ALSO: Human Rights, Women.

LEY LINES
SEE: Geomancy.

LIBERTARIANISM
Arcoiris(RF), Huehuecoyotl, Syntony(F) ►RESOURCES: Factsheet5, GlobeLib, LeftBank

LIBRARY
Adirondack(RF), BakydTech(IF), ChristineCn(F), Dreamtime(F), EnchantGardn(RF), Finders, Peaceful-Grdn(F), SixDirectns(F), StillWater(F), UnknownTruth(F), Vivekan-IL ►RESOURCES: ActionLink, CenComStu, CRSP, DataCenter, TraNet

LIGHT CENTERS
Alcyone(F), Findhorn(I), GreenOaks(F), Heartlight, LightColor(F), Methow, Ontos(I), Sirius, UniteReLight ►SEE ALSO: Findhorn Inspired, New Age.

LIMITED EQUITY CO-OPS
FourStreets, Glenridge, Marathon, NearyLagoon, NinthStreet, ParkerSt, SantaRosaCrk, TwinPines ►RESOURCES: AltsCntr, CMHA

LOBBYING
RESOURCES: NatFedBroad, Sierra-Club, 20/20Vision

LOCAL SELF-RELIANCE
CarpentrVil(F), LosAnEcoVill(F), YellowHouse ►RESOURCES: InstLocSelf, UrbEcology ►SEE ALSO: Bioregionalism, Decentralization, Self-Management, Sustainable Economics.

LOW-INCOME HOUSING
EFE(F), LosAnEcoVill(F), NinthStreet, PacFamily, RebaPlace, RiverCmtyHm, SantaRosaCrk, Silverlake, TwinPines, VeganCoho(F) ►RESOURCES: CMHA, FedSoCoops, InnovHousg, NatCoopBank, NeighbrWrks ►SEE ALSO: Affordable Housing.

MACROBIOTICS
Montclaire(IF), Philoxia

MAGAZINES
Agape-TN(F), BuddhistSoc(RF), Find-horn(I), GitaNagari(RF), JesusPeopUSA, MadreGrande, Orcom(F), ShortMtn, Stelle, Syntony(F), Windward, Yasodhara, Yogaville, Zendik ►RESOURCES: AbunLove, BusEthics, Catalyst, ChurAllWlds, CmtyMag, CoHousngNet, Columbiana, HighWind, HomeEdPress, HomePower, HortIdeas, InContext, Integrity, Interfaith, InTheseTime, Kokoo, MediaNet, MotherJones, NatAssoHsng, NatlHygiene, NeighbrWrks, NewAgeJour, OneEarth,

KEY TO ABBREVIATIONS: (F) Forming, (RF) Reforming, (I) International, (N) Nonresidential, (*)See Charts

PC-Drylands, PlanetDrum, QrtAltRview, RainMag, ReVision, RFD, SingOut, Skip-Stones, Soc&Nature, Sun/The, UtneReader, WholeEarth, WomPower, ZetaMag

MAGIC
CrowsNest(N), IDA(F), Lothlor-IN ▶Resources: BndTogether, Reclaiming

MAIL-ORDER PRODUCTS
LightColor(F) ▶Resources: AuntLinda, EarthCare, PuebloPeopl ▶See also: Books-Mailorder, Sourcebooks.

MALAYSIA
Resources: InstCulAffr

MANAGEMENT
See: Business, Leadership, Planning Skills, Property Management, Self-Management.

MAPLE SUGARING
BlueMoon, Goodrich(F), Morninglory

MARITIME
CmtyInWinn

MARKETPLACE ALTERNATIVES
CoopAmer, FairTrade, PeoplFriend, PlentyUSA, Undercurr

MASSAGE
Atmasant(I), EarthFamFarm(RF), Haven(F), LongBranch, Orcom(F) ▶See also: Bodywork.

MAYAN
HighFlowing, RosyBranch

MEDIA
Dreamtime(F), Sirius ▶Resources: AltPressIdx, BioregProj, CounEconPri, DataCenter, DeepDish, Factsheet5, GapMedia, InContext, Macrocosm, MediaNet, NatFedBroad

MEDIATION
See: Conflict Management.

MEDITATION
AnandaMarga, AnandaVill, Anasazi(F), ArshaVidya, Atmasant(I), Builders, CenHarLiv(IF), Communia(N), Earth-haven(F), Heathcote(RF), HimalayaInst, InstHarDevel(F), Lama, Maharishi, MtMadonna, OakGrove(F), Ontos(I), Orcom(F), OshoIntl(I), PPAALS(F), PumpkinHoll, ReevisMtn, RosyBranch, SaintJohns(RF), SaltSpring, Shining-Water(RF), Sirius, Sivananda, SkyWoods, SongOfMorng(F), SparrowHawk, Taena(I), TruthConsc, TuiTrust(I), UniteReLight, Vivekan-MI, WheelCmtyGth(F), YogaSoctyRoc, Yogaville, ZenBones(F) ▶Resources: InfinLight, NewMilleni, OshoCntrs, SikhDharma ▶See also: Buddhism, T'ai Chi, Zen.

MEN
Heathcote(RF), Rapha(N), SixDirectns(F), WolfCreek ▶Resources: CircleSong ▶See also: Gay.

MENNONITE
RebaPlace, Sunnyside(F)

MENTAL DISABILITIES
See: Disabilities.

METAL SHOPS
Maxworks, Niederkauf(I), RudfSteinFel, Skyfire(F), Windward, Wygelia(F), Zendik

METAPHYSICS
Arcoiris(RF), ChristmsStr, Orcom(F), ReevisMtn, SouthCasSpir ▶Resources: MetaphysBBS ▶See also: Consciousness, Paranormal, Spirituality.

MEXICO
Remar, RosyBranch ▶Resources: Aprovecho, InstCulAffr, NativeSeeds, NewMilleni ▶See also: Español.

MIDWIFERY
FarmThe(RF), Goodwater(F) ▶Resources: BookPublCo, EcovilTrain ▶See also: Home Birthing, Water Birthing.

MILITARY RESISTANCE
See: Anti-Military, Nuclear Disarmament, Peace & Justice, War Tax Resistance.

MINORITIES
See: Human Rights, Multicultural.

MONASTERIES
BuddhistSoc(RF), MadreGrande, SaintBenedct, SaintHerman(F), Vivekan-IL, Vivekan-MI, Yogaville, ZenMtn

MONDRAGON
Resources: AltsCntr, Empl-Owned

MONTESSORI SCHOOLS
ReCreation ▶Resources: HomeEdPress, SikhDharma

MOZAMBIQUE
Resources: IICD

MULTICULTURAL
Acorn, Anasazi(F), CoventCmty, GaiaPerm(F), HarvestHills, HOME(F), Huehuecoyotl, Koinonia, MaatDompim(F), Montebello, NearyLagoon, PacFamily, Remar, RosyBranch, Silverlake ▶Resources: AFS, Aurovil-USA, GroundWork, ICA/Earth, InContext, LinkwayCent, SkipStones ▶See also: Human Rights.

MULTIGENERATIONAL
CoventCmty, Haven(F), Kidstown(RF), ListwigMir, Montclaire(IF), PeacefulGrdn(F), PrudCrandall(RF), RudfSteinFel, Windward

MUSEUMS
See: Historic Sites.

MUSHROOMS
Resources: EcovilTrain

MUSIC
AbunDawn(F), Aequanim(IF), AquarConcpt(F), ArtColony(F), Atmasant(I), Billen(I), BlueMoon, BrightMrnStr(RF), ChristmsStr, DanceHawaii(RF), DanceWater, DeerRock(F), Dreamtime(F), DuMá, EarthFamFarm(RF), Fillmore, FriendsLake, FullCircle(F), GaiaPerm(F), GorillaChoir, HaleByodo(F), HighFlowing, Lothlor-IN, MagicInc, Morninglory, MtMadonna, NewJahRuslm(RF), NewMoon, OneWorldFam, Qumbya, RainbHearth(RF), ReCreation, Rivendell, RudfSteinFel, ShrubbFam(IRF), SkyJahnna(F), Songaia, SparrowHawk, SpiesSanity(F), Sunburst(F), Vine&FigTree, WheelCmtyGth(F), Zegg(I), Zendik, ZephyrVall(F) ▶Resources: CircleSong, Dance/NE, Gro-w/oSch, SingOut

MUSIC CONCERTS
BlackCat, Compound-i, FreeLandSqat, JesusPeopUSA, PPAALS(F), ReCreation, Vivekan-MI

MYSTICISM
ChristHills(RF), ChristineCn(F), PosLivCen(F) ▶Resources: CenSacrdSci, ChurAllWlds, ReVision

NATIVE AMERICAN
Anasazi(F), CEEDS, ForTheEarth(I), FourWinds(F), Hawkwind(F), HOME(F), PhantoBolo(F), RedMtn(F) ▶Resources: CircleSong, NativeSeeds PlentyUSA ▶See also: Earth Religions, Human Rights, Indigenous Peoples, Shamanism, Sweat Lodges.

NATURE PRESERVES
Aequanim(IF), BlackHorse(I), CircleSanct(N), FriendsLake, Greenbriar, HealingGrace(F), LandStewCen(F), Lauriestn(I), Lichen, LongBranch, Lothlor-IN, Miccosukee, RavenRocks, RiverFarm, SharonSprgs(F), Teramanto, WoodburnHill ▶Resources: CircleNet, SierraClub ▶See also: Wetlands.

NATURIST
AquarRanch(RF), Harbin, SunnierPalms(F)

NEIGHBORHOOD ORGANIZING
Resources: CRSP, GreenhsExp, Ground-Work, NeighbrWrks, SustComHsg

NEIGHBORHOOD OUTREACH
Ark, AugustGreen(F), BemisErec, CoventCmty, DeepWoods, Fairview, Headlands(RF), Hearthstone(N), Heathcote(RF), HouseLavendr, LakeVillage, LosAnEcoVill(F), Lothlor-Ont, Montclaire(IF), Morninglory, Qumbya, Sandhill, WhiteHouse, YellowHouse

NEIL, A.S. (SUMMERHILL)
Timatang(I)

NETWORKING
See: Clearinghouses, Community Building, Community Referrals, Community Networking.

NETWORKS
RESOURCES: EcovilleNet, EnvironIll, OpenForum, SoOregWomen ►SEE ALSO: Community Networks.

NEW AGE
ArtColony(F), CamelotWood, NetworkNewC(F), Dolphin(IF), Dragonfly, Findhorn(I), FourWinds(F), FullCircle(F), Harbin, Huehuecoyotl, MadreGrande, Maharishi, RainbJunctn(F), Sirius, Villaggio(IRF) ►RESOURCES: Omega-NewAge, OneEarth, ReVision, Sun/The ►SEE ALSO: Health & Healing, Light Centers, Paranormal, Spirituality.

NEW ZEALAND
RESOURCES: HospitltyEx ►SEE ALSO: "Index by Country" that precedes the International listings.

NEWSLETTERS (ABOUT COMMUNITIES)
Agape-TN(F), AquarResrch(RF), Auro-ville(I), CathWork-TX(RF), NetworkNewC(F), Centrept(I), CranberryCrk, Dreamtime(F), EarthReLeaf(RF), Headlands(RF), IslandGroup(F), Kerista(RF), LosHorcones, OpenDoor, PeaceFarm, RosyBranch, SusBAnthony, Syntony(F), TorontoTori(N), WheelCmtyGth(F), YogaSoctyRoc ►RESOURCES: NICA

NEWSPAPERS
CathWork-OH, Hearthstone(N) ►RESOURCES: AcresUSA

NICARAGUA
JubileeHouse, JubileePrtnr, Noonday, Remar ►RESOURCES: CentRockyMt, EcoNet, IICD

NONHIERARCHICAL GOVERNMENT
DOE-Farm, Montclaire(IF), Orcom(F), SonorEcoVill(F) ►SEE ALSO: Anti-Military, Peace & Justice.

NONRESIDENTIAL COMMUNITIES
CircleSanct(N), Communia(N), CrowsNest(N), Goodenough(N), Hearthstone(N), KehillatMish(N), LambOfGod(N), NewJerusalm(N), Rapha(N), ToadHouse(N), TorontoTori(N)

NONVIOLENCE
ComDeChamb(I), Currents, EdenSanct(F), OpenDoor, Panterra(F), PilotMtn(F), RainbVal-NZ(I), Hearthaven, LArchBorie(I), NewCovent(RF), PeaceFarm, SaltSpring, Sandhill, SantaRosaCrk, SeedsPeace, TripleCreek, VeiledCliff(F), Vine&FigTree, WestEnd(I) ►RESOURCES: CenConflict, CmtyBkshlf, FedEgalCmty, GroundWork, NewSociety, OneByOne ►SEE ALSO: Anti-Military, Catholic Worker, Civil Disobedience, Conscientious Objectors, Peace & Justice.

NUCLEAR DISARMAMENT
PeaceFarm, SeedsPeace ►RESOURCES: GroundWork, NatRights, NucFreeAmer, VetsPeace ►SEE ALSO: Peace & Justice, Anti-Military.

NUCLEAR POWER OPPOSITION
RainbVal-TX(RF) ►RESOURCES: Audubon, EcoNet, Interfaith, NatRights, NucFreeAmer, UnionConcrn ►SEE ALSO: Energy Alternatives, Environment.

NUTBUTTERS
EastWind

NUTRITION & DIET*
AnandaMarga, Atmasant(I), HimalayaInst, InstHarDevel(F), LeJardin(IF), LongBranch, Mitranik(I), Moonshadow(F), Philoxia, ReevisMtn, Sojourners(RF), SongOfMorng(F), SunnierPalms(F) ►RESOURCES: KenKeyes ►SEE ALSO: Fasting, Food–Supplements, Intestinal Cleansing, Kosher, Macrobiotic, Raw Foods, Vegan.

OAHSPE
EsseneSkoola(F), FourWinds(F)

ORCHARDS
AtlantisRis, BearCreek(F), BeechHill(IRF), Camphill-PA, Camphill-Sol, ChristineCn(F), DanceWater, DeerRock(F), Dorea, DragonBelly(F), Dunmire, EcoVill-Ith(F), Folkhaven(F), GlenIvy, GreeningLife, JumpOff(F), Koinonia, Lamborn, LaurelHill(RF), LosHorcones, MonansRill, Morninglory, MothrEarthOp(RF), MtMurrin(I), MultChemSens(F), NorCottonwd(F), Ontos(I), OwlFarm, EnergieUm, ReevisMtn, Renaissance(RF), Riverside(I), SaltSpring, SkyWoods, SparrowHawk, Springtree, Stelle, Sunflower-OH, Teramanto, WattleHill(IF)

ORGANIC FARMING
Anaami(F), CEEDS, EarthCycle(RF), ElderWood(F), Gaien(F), K&K-Organic(F), LowrShaw(I), Ontos(I), Svanholm(I), Zendik ►RESOURCES: AcresUSA, Rodale

ORGANIC GARDENING
Alcyone(F), BeechHill(IRF), DapalaFarm(F), DuckMtn(F), EnchantGardn(RF), Findhorn(I), LongBranch, LostValley, MothrEarthOp(RF), ReevisMtn, Sirius, Springtree, Zegg(I) ►RESOURCES: AcresUSA, CentRockyMt, EcoHome, EnergieUm, GreenhsExp, NewEnviron, Rodale ►SEE ALSO: Biodynamics, Permaculture, Seeds.

OVERPOPULATION
RESOURCES: InContext, TraNet

PACIFISM
SEE: Peace & Justice, Anti-Military, Nonviolence.

PAGAN
Avalon(F), Brigid, CircleSanct(N), CrowsNest(N), Dragonfly, Glendower(F), IDA(F), Lothlor-IN ►RESOURCES: ChurAllWlds, CircleNet, CircleSong, Reclaiming ►SEE ALSO: Earth Religions, Shamanism, Wicca.

PARANORMAL PHENOMENA
SEE: Astrology, Channeling, Dowsing, Earth Changes, Faith Healing, Geomancy, Metaphysics, Mysticism, UFOs.

PARENTING SKILLS
ComnPlace-NY, OpenDoor, SixDirectns(F), Sunburst(F) ►RESOURCES: CmtyBkshlf, Dance/NE, ParentLeadr, WELL/The ►SEE ALSO: Single Parents.

PASSIVE SOLAR BUILDINGS
Alcyone(F), AtlantisRis, ComnPlace-NY, EcoVill-Ith(F), Eloin, NorCottonwd(F), OakGrove(F), Reach(F), Sirius, WiscoyVall ►RESOURCES: HomePower ►SEE ALSO: Building Technology, Earthships, Underground Buildings.

PEACE
RESOURCES: NewCatalyst, RainbRidge

PEACE & JUSTICE
BeaconHill, Bijou, ChesterCrk, CoventCmty, ComnPlace-MA, Dorea, Hearthaven, Jesuit-JVC, LArchBorie(I), ListwigMir, LostValley, MarthasCoop, Moonshadow(F), NeveShal(I), NewCovent(RF), NewJah-Ruslm(RF), OpenDoor, PeaceFarm, PrudCrandall(RF), RebaPlace, Rivendell, SeedsPeace, Sichlassen, Sojourners(RF), SusBAnthony, Vine&FigTree, Woodburn-Hill, YaharaLindn ►RESOURCES: AFS, EcoNet, GapMedia, GlobeLib, Ground-Work, Interfaith, NatWarTax, NewSociety, RSVP, SEAC, WELL/The ►SEE ALSO: Activism, Catholic Worker, Economic Conversion, Grassroots Organizing, Human Rights, Prisoners, Refugees, Social Transformation, Socialism, Third World, War Tax Resist.

PEER COUNSELING
BemisErec, DuMá, Haven(F), Heathcote(RF), LaVigne(IRF), SkyWoods, WomansWorld(F)

PEN PALS
RESOURCES: Alliance, SkipStones

PENTECOSTAL
Sunnyside(F). UnknownTruth(F)

PERFORMING ARTS
SEE: Dance, Music, Music Concerts, Storytelling, Theater.

PERMACULTURE
Acorn, AtlantisRis, Bundagen(I), DanceWater, Dreamtime(F), Earthaven(F), EarthCycle(RF), Edges(F), GaiaPerm(F), HighHorizons(F), JumpOff(F), LongBranch, Namasté(F), Niche(F), OjaiFndtn, Ontos(I), PermntAgri(F), RainbHearth(RF), Redfield(I), RosyBranch, ShrubbFam(IRF), SpiralWimm, Vine&FigTree ►RESOURCES: Aprovecho, BioregProj, CentRockyMt, Columbiana, EcovilTrain, ElfinPC, LivgVillage, Ozark-RLT, PC-Activist, PC-Drylands, Sch-Living, TIES/Canada, YankeePC ►SEE ALSO: Sustainable Agriculture.

REFERRALS
SEE: Clearinghouses, Community Networks, Community Referrals, Networking.

REFLEXOLOGY
LaVigne(IRF), SaltSpring

REFUGEES
JubileePrtnr, NewJerusalm(N), RebaPlace, RefugioRioGr, Riverside(I), SaintFran-ME ▶RESOURCES: SolCookIntl

RELATIONSHIP SKILLS
Aeqaunim(IF), AquarResrch(RF), Atlantis(I), NetworkNewC(F), ChangingWtr(F), Ganas, Goodenough(N), LosHorcones, MariposaGrp, Montebello, OjaiFndtn, SonorEcoVill(F), Spiricoas(F), Wesleyan, Zegg(I) ▶RESOURCES: AbunLove, NSS-Sems, OneEarth

RELATIONSHIPS
SEE: Alt. Lifestyles, Communication–Interpers, Polyamory, Polyfidelity, Sexuality.

RELIGIOUS ORIENTATION
SEE: Spiritual Orientation.

RESIDENCY PROGRAMS
Avalon(F), DanceHawaii(RF), Kripalu, LowrShaw(I), RockyMtnDhar, Wesleyan, Yasodhara ▶SEE ALSO: Apprentice Programs, Internships, Work Study.

RESOURCE CONSERVATION
SEE: Conservation.

RESTAURANTS
Alpha, Builders, Camphill-PA, CmtyAlts-Coop, CmtyInBost, ComDeLondr(I), DapalaFarm(F), GriffinGorge, Philoxia, Shiloh, SixDirectns(F), VictorTrade(F) ▶RESOURCES: CantShaker

RESTORATION (ENVIRONMENT)
LandStewCen(F), LeJardin(IF), LostValley, MagicInc, PrairieRidge(F), RavenRocks ▶RESOURCES: InstSocEcol, RenewAmer, Undercurr, UrbEcology

RETAIL STORES
CmtyInBello, CmtyInBurl, CmtyInHyan, CmtyInLancas, Ganas, PeacefulGrdn(F), Shiloh, SocFam-Solidr(F) ▶RESOURCES: PlentyUSA

RETIREMENT
SEE: Elderly.

RETREAT CENTERS
Abode, Aeqaunim(IF), AnandaVill, Barn-The(I), Benedictine, Breitenbush, CenHa-Liv(IF), CenPeaceLif(RF), ChristineCn(F), Clearview(F), CmtyOfCelebr, Communia(N), CranberryCrk, DragonBelly(F), Earthaven(F), EarthFamFarm(RF), Earthlands(RF), Farm-Home(F), FourWinds(F), Harbin, Heartwood, Kailash(F), KingView(RF), Lama, Maat-Dompin(F), MadreGrande, MikecoRehtl(F), Monadnock(F), MothrEarthOp(RF), MtMa-donna, NewVrndab, OjaiFndtn, Ontos(I), PumpkinHoll, ReevisMtn, Rejenneratn(F), RoweCamp, SaltSpring, SandyBar(F),

Shenoa, Shiloh, Shining-Water(RF), SongOfMorng(F), Starseed(F), TruthConsc, TuiTrust(I), UnionAcres, UniteReLight, Vivekan-MI, Wellsprg-WI(F), Wesleyan, WolfCreek ▶RESOURCES: MornStar-MI, NewEnviron, OneWrldFam, RoweCamp

RETROFIT
EFE(F), LosAnEcoVill(F) ▶RESOURCES: CRSP, Undercurr, UrbEcology

RIGHT LIVELIHOOD
Goodwater(F), LostValley, Rosy-Branch, Sirius ▶RESOURCES: Briarpatch ▶SEE ALSO: Career Options.

RITES OF PASSAGE
OjaiFndtn, Tekiah(RF)

RITUALS
Acorn, Birdsfoot, Blackberry(RF), Bright-MrnStar(RF), CircleSanct(N), Clearview(F), ComnPlace-MA, EnchantGardn(RF), Fillmore, FriendsLake, HealingGrace(F), Heathcote(RF), Lothlor-IN, PlumVillage, SantaRosaCrk, SixDirectns(F), Syntony(F), Tanguy, Triform, TuiTrust(I), WoodburnHill ▶RESOURCES: CircleSong, CmtyCntrGay, CmtySeekNet, GenesisFarm, Reclaiming, SoOregWomen ▶SEE ALSO: Gatherings, Rites of Passage.

RLDS CHURCH
HarvestHills

ROPES COURSES
OjaiFndtn

RURAL LIVING SKILLS
Access(F), BeechHill(IRF), Birdsfoot, Bundagen(I), Dunmire, Earthlands(RF), Ecoville(IF), Huehuecoyotl, Ponderosa, SeadsTruth(F) ▶RESOURCES: CentRockyMt, HomePower, QrtAltRview ▶SEE ALSO: Survival Skills.

RURAL/URBAN SISTER COMMUNITIES
AshbyTree, Caerduir(F), CenHarLiv(IF), CmtyAltsCoop, ComnUnity(F), CooperSt, Finders, Gesundheit, Meramec(RF), Vivekan-IL, Yogavill ▶RESOURCES: Emissaries

RUSSIA
RESOURCES: EarthIsland, EcovilTrain ▶SEE ALSO: "Index by Country" that precedes the International listings.

RUSSIAN ORTHODOX
Agape-TN(F), ChristHills(RF), SaintJohns(RF)

SANCTUARIES, ENVIRONMENTAL
SEE: Nature Preserves.

SANCTUARY MOVEMENT
SEE: Human Rights, Refugees.

SANITATION
SEE: Water Treatment.

SAWMILLING
Dragonfly, Padanaram

SCHOOLS—ADULT EDUCATION
BrazierPk(I), HighWind, Mitranik(I) ▶RESOURCES: LinkwayCent

SCHOOLS—CHILDREN*
AnandaVill, FarmThe(RF), Findhorn(I), GitaNagari(RF), Greenbriar, HutBrethSpok, KehillatMish(N), KingdomOyo, Koinonia, Mitranik(I), Morninglory, MtMadonna, NewVrndab, OjaiFndtn, Padanaram, QuarryHill, RainbJunctn(F), RudfSteinFel, SaltSpring, Sheprdsfld, Sojourners(RF), Stelle, Svanholm(I), Tekiah(RF), TuiTrust(I), Yogaville ▶RESOURCES: AERO, ArtMorgSch, GreenhsExp, HomeEd-Press, KidsToCntry, NALSAS, NCACS, Wondertree ▶SEE ALSO: Homeschooling, Montessori, Neil, Preschools, Waldorf.

SCIENCE
Adirondack(RF), Folkhaven(F), Horcones-Two, LosHorcones, MagicInc, SouthCasSpir, Timeweave(RF), Zegg(I) ▶RESOURCES: CenSacrdSci, DormantBrain, EarthBaseOne, Gro-w/oSch, LinkwayCent, OneWrldFam, PlentyUSA, ReVision, SikhDharma, Soc&Nature, UnionConcrn, WrldFutSoc

SCOTLAND
SEE: "Index by Country" that precedes the International listings, ▶SEE ALSO: Great Britain.

SEEDS/SEEDLINGS
IonExchange(F), ReCreation, Triple-Creek ▶RESOURCES: AbunLife, LandInst, NativeSeeds, SeedSavers

SELF-MANAGEMENT
Christiania(I), StudtCoopOrg, WestEnd(I) ▶RESOURCES: BndTogether, GEO-News, GlobeLib, LeftBank, Ozark-RLT, School-Living, TraNet, WaldenFlshp ▶SEE ALSO: Anarchism, Collectives, Cooperatives, Decentralization, Local Self-Reliance, Nonhierarchic Gov't, Worker Ownership.

SELF-REALIZATION
ArshaVidya, ArtColony(F), GitaNagari(RF), GreenOaks(F), Heartwood, InstHarDevel(F), LaAtlan(IRF), Phoenix-CO, SongOfMorng(F), ValleyLight(RF), WhiteBuffalo ▶SEE ALSO: Human Potential, Personal Growth.

SELF-SUFFICIENCY
BakydTech(IF), Christnsbrn(RF), Claritas(F), ComDeChamb(I), ComnPlace-NY, DapalaFarm(F), DOE-Farm, Earth-ReLeaf(RF), Ecolonie(I), ElderWood(F), FarValley, FullCircle(F), HighHorizons(F), Innisfree, JulianWoods(RF), LaAtlan(IRF), LongBranch, LosHorcones, Montclaire(IF), Moonshadow(F), NewVrndab, NorSun-Farm, NorWoodVegan(F), PeacefulGrdn(F), PermntAgri(F), PhantoBolo(F), Ponderosa, PortCentauri (F), RainbJunctn(F), Rainb-Val-TX(RF), RajYogaMath, ReevisMtn, SeadsTruth(F), SevenWaves(F), Shibboleth(F), ShortMtn, SkyWoods, SonorEcoVill(F), Sunburst(F), Sunflower-OH, Tekiah(RF), Teramanto, ThreeSprgs(F), ValleyLight(RF), VeiledCliff(F), VictorTrade(F), ZenBones(F)

STEWARDSHIP
Anaami(F), Blackberry(RF), BlueMoon, ComnPlace-NY, CranberryCrk, CrowCircle(RF), CrowsNest(N), Currents, FarmHome(F), FarValley, Folkhaven(F), GoodRedRoad(F), Greenwood(RF), JulianWoods(RF), JumpOff(F), LandStewCen(F), Lothlor-IN, MikecoRehtl(F), MonansRill, Morninglory, NewLeaf(F), PrairieRidge(F), Rejenneratn(F), Rowanwood, SandyBar(F), SevenWaves(F), SevenSprgs, Shenoa, SunriseRanch(RF), Sweetwater, Tekiah(RF), Tolstoy, TripleCreek, WalkerCrk ▶RESOURCES: ChilGrEarth, Emissaries, EvergreenLT, LandInst, OneEarth, Ozark-RLT, TIES/Canada ▶SEE ALSO: Land Trusts, Sustainability, Nature Preserves.

STORYTELLING
OjaiFndtn, Songaia

STRAW BALE BUILDINGS
AbunDawn(F), Cloudburst(F), Niche(F) ▶RESOURCES: EcovilTrain, OutOnBale

STRESS MANAGEMENT
HimalayaInst, Ontos(I) ▶RESOURCES: LinkwayCent ▶SEE ALSO: Biofeedback.

STUDENT CO-OPS
Greenhous-OH, InterntlCoop, MarthasCoop, Osterweil, Qumbya, StudtCoopOrg, Sunflower-KS, Synergy ▶RESOURCES: ExperLiving, InterCoopMI, InterCoopTX, MadisonCC, NASCO, OSCA, SEAC, USCA

STUDY PROGAMS
RESOURCES: GenesisFarm, InstDeepEco

SUBSTANCE ABUSE
SEE: Recovery.

SUFI
Abode, Anaami(F)

SUMMERHILL
SEE: Neil, A.S..

SURVIVAL SKILLS
Lothlor-IN, Reevis, TrailsEnd, YurtFarm(IRF)

SUSTAINABILITY
Access(F), Cloudburst(F), DanceRabbit(F), DapalaFarm(F), Downeast(RF), Earthaven(F), EarthCycle(RF), Earthlands(RF), Earthseed(F), Edges(F), Folkhaven(F), GaiaPerm(F), Gaien(F), GreenPlan(F), HealingGrace(F), HighWind, Homestead(F), HorconesTwo, JubileeHouse, K&K-Organic(F), LakeVillage, LostValley, LoveIsrael, MikecoRehtl(F), Montclaire(IF), PilotMtn(F), Quakerland(F), SaintFran-ME, Skyfire(F), CircleOpSpgs(F), Songaia, SpiralWimm, Tekiah(RF), TenStones (F), Timeweave(RF), WeMoonHeal(RF), Windward, Zendik, ZephyrVall(F) ▶RESOURCES: Aprovecho, CRSP, Dig&Dream, GaiaEd, GlobVilActn, HighWind, InContext, InstSocEcol,
NewRoadMap, PlanetDrum, PC-Drylands, Shearwater, SustComHsg, UrbEcology ▶SEE ALSO: EcoVillages.

SUSTAINABLE AGRICULTURE
AbunDawn(F), FarmHome(F), LongBranch, NorCottonwd(F), PeacefulGrdn(F), PrairieRidge(F), ShortMtn, Sunburst(F) ▶RESOURCES: AcresUSA, EcovilleNet, GenesisFarm, LandInst, OzarkResCen, Rodale ▶SEE ALSO: Agriculture, Biodynamics, Bioregionalism, Food–Producers, Greens, Organic Farming & Gardening, Permaculture.

SUSTAINABLE ECONOMICS
CEEDS ▶RESOURCES: BioregProj, CenPopEcon, CoopAmer, FairTrade, GlobVilInst, InContext, InstComEcon, InTheseTime, ZetaMag ▶SEE ALSO: Anti-Consumerism, Bioregionalism, Cooperation, Economic Conversion.

SWEAT LODGES
Anaami(F), Cloudburst(F), OjaiFndtn, Songaia

SWEDEN
RESOURCES: Aurovil-USA

SWITCHBOARDS
SEE: Clearinghouses.

SWITZERLAND
ForTheEarth(I), Remar, YamaLife(I) ▶RESOURCES: Aurovil-USA ▶SEE ALSO: "Index by Country" that precedes the International listings.

T'AI CHI
ReevisMtn, Taena(I)

TANZANIA
RESOURCES: Aprovecho

TECHNOLOGY
SEE: Alternative Technology, Science.

TELEPHONE SYSTEMS
RESOURCES: AquarReFdtn, CmtyDialtone

TELEVISION
SEE: Broadcasting.

THAILAND
YamaLife(I) ▶RESOURCES: EarthIsland

THEATER
ComnPlace-NY, FreeLandSqat, Kerista(RF), Lothlor-IN, MtMadonna, PPAALS(F), Sandhill, SpiesSanity(F), Zendik ▶RESOURCES: Dance/NE, ECoopRecSch

THEOSOPHY
PumpkinHoll, Villaggio(IRF)

THERAPY
AquarConcpt(F), Atlantis(I), Camphill-USA, CenExamLife, NetworkNewC(F), FusionArts(I), Phoenix-CO, RudfSteinFel, Triform ▶SEE ALSO: Biofeedback, Bodywork, Disabilities, Dreamwork, Family Counseling, Gibb, Human Potential, Jungian, Massage, Peer Counseling, Personal Growth, Physical Therapy, Rebirthing, Recovery, Reflexology.

THIRD WORLD
Christians(I), FarmThe(RF), JubileeHouse, LosAnEcoVill(F), Mitranik(I), PPAALS(F), SixDirectns(F) ▶RESOURCES: Aprovecho, DataCenter, ElfinPC, FairTrade, GlobVilInst, PlentyUSA, PuebloPeopl

TIBETAN BUDDHISM
SEE: Buddhism.

TOYS
Ganas, Maxworks ▶RESOURCES: RealGoods ▶SEE ALSO: Play.

TRANSFORMATION
SEE: Light Centers, New Age, Self-Realization, Social Transformation.

TRANSLATING SERVICE
SEE: Language.

TRANSPORTATION ALTERNATIVES
Adirondack(RF), AshbyTree, Bamberton(F), GreenPlan(F), Maharishi, MikecoRehtl(F) ▶RESOURCES: CAUSE, NeighbrWrks, Undercurr, UrbEcology ▶SEE ALSO: Bicycles.

TRAVEL
RosyBranch ▶RESOURCES: AmYouthHstl, Audubon, CoopAmer, DwellPort, GreenerPast, HospitltyEx, IICD, NewMilleni, OneWrldFam, Undercurr ▶SEE ALSO: Hospitality.

TREES
EarthReLeaf(RF), MagicInc ▶RESOURCES: ChilGrEarth, PlentyUSA ▶SEE ALSO: Forestry.

TWELVE-STEP PROGRAMS
SEE: Recovery.

UFOS
Lothlor-IN, Methow, UnknownTruth(F) ▶RESOURCES: OmegaNewAge

UNDERGROUND BUILDINGS
DapalaFarm(F), RainbVal-TX(RF), RavenRocks ▶SEE ALSO: Passive Solar Buildings.

UNITARIAN UNIVERSALIST
RESOURCES: RoweCamp

UNITED KINGDOM
Remar ▶RESOURCES: Aurovil-USA ▶SEE ALSO: "Index by Country" that precedes the International listings.

URBAN CO-OPS
Arcoiris(RF), AshbyTree, BlackCat, BlueHouse, BrightMrnStr(RF), Brigid, CasaGrande, CentralPage, ChesterCrk, CmtyAltsCoop, ComnPlace-MA, Compound-i, DenverSpace, DuMá, EastWest, EFE(F), EllisIsland, EnchantGardn(RF), Fairview, Fillmore,

FreeLandSqat, GorillaChoir, Green-Plan(F), HarmonHouse, HeiWaHouse, Hillegass, HouseLavendr, LifeCenter, ListwigMir, Maxworks, MollyHare, NewMoon, OneThouSmPhm, PacFamily, PragHouse, PrudCrandall(RF), Purple-Rose, QuakerHouse(RF), Qumbya, RainbHouse, Rivendell, RiverCity, Sichlassen, Silverlake, Spaulding, StewLittle, Sunflower-TX, Sunset-CA(RF), WestsideVeg(RF), Whitehall, White-House, WomansCoop, YaharaLindn, YellowHouse ▶Resources: InnovHousg, InterCoopMI, InterCoopTX ▶See also: Limited Equity Co-ops.

URBAN LIVING SKILLS
BakydTech(IF), LosAnEcoVill(F) ▶Resources: EcoHome, ICA/Earth, PlanetDrum

UTOPIAN
AquarResrch(RF), EsseneSkoola(F), IslandGroup(F), Kerista(RF), Padanaram, Sunburst(F) ▶Resources: CSA, LeftBank, SocUtopStud ▶See also: Future, Social Transformation.

VEDANTA
ArshaVidya, RajYogaMath, Sivananda, Vivekan-IL, Vivekan-MI

VEGAN*
Compound-i, NorWoodVegan(F), OneThouSmPhm, Synergy, VeganCoho(F)

VEGETARIAN*
DapalaFarm(F) ▶Resources: BookPublCo, SikhDharma ▶See also: Nutrition.

VIDEO
See: Audio/Video.

VIETNAM
PlumVillage

VISION QUESTS
OjaiFndtn, SixDirectns(F) ▶Resources: NewMilleni

VOLUNTARY SIMPLICITY
ComnPlace-NY, HealingGrace(F), Monda-nock(F), SaintBenedct ▶See also: Catholic Worker, Right Livelihood, Simple Living.

VOLUNTEERS PROGRAMS
Camphill (all), CCNV, CoventHouse, Folkcorps(F), Gesundheit, Goodwater(F), ICA-Phoenix(RF), Innisfree, Jesuit-JVC, JubileePrtnr, Koinonia, Maxworks, PumpkinHoll, RefugioRioGr, SaintFran-ME, Sivananda, Triform, Wellsprg-MA(RF) ▶Resources: Habitat, IICD, Kibbutzim, OneWrldFam

VOUDON
KingdomOyo

WALDEN TWO
HorconesTwo, LosHorcones, Waldos(IF), WaldenTwo ▶See also: Behavioral Psych.

WALDORF SCHOOLS
Resources: HomeEdPress, SikhDharma

WAR TAX RESISTANCE
Vine&FigTree ▶Resources: NatWarTax ▶See also: Anti-Military.

WASTE MANAGEMENT
Resources: CompostPatch, EcovilleNet

WATER BIRTHING
ReCreation ▶See also: Home Birthing, Midwifery.

WATER TREATMENT
DanceRab(F), Earthseed(F), EcoVill-Ith(F), JulianWood(RF), Namasté(F), Reach(F), Stelle, WalkerCrk, WholeHealth, Zegg(I) ▶Resources: EcovilleNet, EcovilTrain, EnergieUm, WaterCntr

WEAVING
Camphill-Sol, DanceWater, Innisfree, LightColor(F), Mitranik(I), Triform

WETLANDS
DragonBelly(F), Dreamtime(F), EcoVill-Ith(F), Hilltop, IonExchange(F), LakeVillage, VashonCoho, ZephyrVall(F)

WHEELCHAIR ACCESSIBLE
WestwdCoho(F)

WICCA
BlackCat, CircleSanct(N), EarthCycle(RF), WomansWorld(F) ▶Resources: CircleNet ▶See also: Earth Religions.

WILDCRAFTING
Avalon(F), EarthFamFarm(RF), LeJardin(IF), ReevisMtn

WILDLIFE
See: Endangered Species, Nature Preserves.

WOMEN
ChesterCrk, Flatrock(RF), Heath-cote(RF), HeiWaHouse, MaatDompim(F), MollyHare, Rapha(N), SixDirectns(F), SusBAnthony, WomansCoop ▶Resources: BndTogether, CenSacrdSci, CircleSong, CounEconPri, GroundWork, InstSocEcol, MadisonCC, MornStar-MI, OmegaNewAge, OregWom-LT, PlentyUSA, SoOreg-Women, WomPower ▶See also: Feminism, Lesbian, Shelters–Women.

WOODWORKING (BUSINESSES)
Camphill-MN, Dunmire, GriffinGorge, Innisfree, NewJahRuslm(RF), RudfSteinFel, Shannon, Sunflower-OH, Wygelia(F)

WORK EXCHANGE PROGRAMS
AnandaVill, AquarRanch(RF), CenExamLife, Christians(I), Ganas, Heartwood, Ontos(I), QuarryHill, ReevisMtn, RosyBranch, RoweCamp, Shenoa, SpiralWimm, WattleHill(IF), WhiteBuffalo, YurtFarm(IRF), ZenMtn

WORK STUDY PROGRAMS
ArshaVidya, ChristineCn(F), Koinonia ▶Resources: KenKeyes, LinkwayCent

WORKER OWNERSHIP
CarpentrVil(F), CmtyAltsCoop, ComnPlaceNY, Shibboleth(F), Sunburst(F) ▶Resources: AltsCntr, BusEthics, Empl-Owned, GEO-News, PeoplFriend ▶See also: Collectives, Self-Management, Small Business.

WORKSHOP CENTERS
Acorn, Adirondack(RF), BeechHill(IRF), CenHarLiv(IF), Centrept(I), Communia(N), CrowsNest(N), Earthaven(F), GlenIvy, GriffinGorge, Hawkwind(F), Heartwood, HimalayaInst, IDA(F), KarmeChol, LightColor(F), LongBranch, MagicTortis(RF), Mickleton(I), Monadnock(F), Moonshadow(F), MothrEarthOp(RF), Niche(F), Niederkauf(I), OakGrove(F), PumpkinHoll, Redfield(I), SeadsTruth(F), SixDirectns(F), Songaia, SouthCasSpir, SparrowHawk, Sunflower-OH, TuiTrust(I), VisionFdtn(F), Wesleyan, WholeHealth, YamaLife(I), Yasodhara, YogaSoctyRoc ▶Resources: Brown, KenKeyes, OmegaInst, RainbRidge ▶See also: Conference Centers.

WRITING
Arcoiris(RF), ArtColony(F), DanceWater, JupiterHoll, MagicInc, MikecoRehtl(F), RainbHearth(RF), Skyfire(F), Unknown-Truth(F) ▶Resources: Gro-w/oSch

YOGA
AnandaMarga, Arcoiris(RF), ArshaVidya, Atmasant(I), GitaNagari(RF), HimalayaInst, InstHarDevel(F), Kripalu, MtMadonna, Ontos(I), RajYogaMath, RedMtn(F), SaltSpring, ShiningWater(RF), SikhDharma, Sivananda, SixDirectns(F), SongOfMorng(F), SriAurobindo(RF), Taena(I), TruthConsc, UniteReLight, Yasodhara, YogaSoctyRoc, Yogaville ▶Resources: Aurovil-USA, SikhDharma

YOUTH
AnandaMarga, Anasazi(F), Camphill-Spc, CmtyAltsCoop, CoventHouse, CrossesCrk, EFE(F), FamilyThe, FarmThe(RF), Kidstown(RF), Koinonia, Mitranik(I), OjaiFndtn, OURHouse, QuakerHouse(RF), RoweCamp, RudfSteinFel, Songaia, Svanholm(I), Triform ▶Resources: AFS, AmYouthHstl, Kokoo, RoweCamp, SikhDharma ▶See also: Rites of Passage.

ZEN
BuddhSoc(RF), CambrZen, PlumVill, ZenMtn

ZIMBABWE
Resources: IICD ▶See also: "Index by Country" that precedes the International listings.

ZONING
Resources: Nolo

ZOOS
Philoxia

Back Issues are $5 each, except where noted.
♦ *Indicates issues available only as photocopies.*

Communitas #1*: a new community journal; Virginia communities; Philadelphia Life Center; Alpha Farm. (Jul '72)

Communitas #2*: country life; conferences; Meadowlark therapeutic community; School of Living; Mulberry Farm; Arthur Morgan. (Sep '72)

#1 Directory '72: membership selection, Camphill Village; Twin Oaks; women & communal societies. (Dec '72) ♦

#2 Law, Communes, Land Trusts: rural poverty; Open Gate; Papaya; Changes Therapeutic Community. (Feb '73) ♦

#3 Community Market Development: Ananda; economic clearinghouse. (Spr '73) ♦

#4 Schools and Community: The Vale School; The Farm; community heritage. (Sum '73) ♦

#5 Personal Change/Social Change: community culture; Boston co-op houses; group relationships. (Oct '73) ♦

#6 Overseas Community: May Valley Co-op; Christian communes; back-to-the-land. (Jan '74) ♦

#7 Directory '74: women in community; prisoners' struggles; people of color and community. (Mar '74)

#8 Individuality & Intimacy: jealousy, open relationships, couples, singles; Christian homesteading. (May '74)

#9 Children in Community: Iris Mountain; Twin Oaks; Ananda; children's lit. (Jul '74) ♦

#10 Work: labor credit systems; Times Change process. (Nov '74) ♦

#11 Land Reform: ownership & use; planning; living on the land; Paolo Soleri; energy. (Dec '74) ♦

#12 Directory '75: Karum; networking; building a new society. (Jan '75) ♦

#13 Spiritual Life in Community: Christian, ashrams, secular, atheist, ritual; composting. (Mar '75) ♦

#14 Therapy: encounter groups; spiritual therapy; overcoming jealousy; The Farm. (May '75) ♦

#15 Research & Education in Community: survival schools; martial arts; Paolo Soleri interview. (Jul '75) ♦

#16 Planning: ecology and economics; short- and long-range contingencies; why plan? land use; alternative energy. (Sep '75) ♦

#17 Family, Sex, & Marriage: gay relationships; gender roles; childrearing; spiritual marriage; German communes. (Nov '75) ♦

#18 Government: Twin Oaks; Project Artaud; East Wind; Directory '76. (Jan '76) ♦

#19 Urban Communities: New Haven; Twin Cities; Philadelphia Life Center; taking back the night; structure & decision making. (Mar '76) ♦

#20 Middle Class Communes: how to start; interpersonal skills; teenagers in communes; sharing housework. (May '76) ♦

#21 Kibbutzim: local relations; Ananda Co-op Village; social planning; food co-ops. (Jul '76) ♦

#22 Networking in the Ozarks: kibbutz family; norms vs. rules; community market; Findhorn. (Sep '76) ♦

#23 Women & Work in the Kibbutz: Rainbow Family; leaving community; Project America. (Nov '76) ♦

#24 Building Community: physical design; culture; decentralized politics; Directory '77; Another Place Farm. (Jan '77) ♦

#25 Don't Start a Commune in 1977 ... join an existing one: Neighborhood Planning Council in DC; first assembly of the Federation of Egalitarian Communities; international communities. (Mar '77) ♦

#26 Rebuilding the City: urban co-ops: Austin, NY, DC, Greenbriar Cmty. (May '77)

#27 Movement for a New Society: social class; long-range planning; older women; Plowshare Community. (Jul '77) ♦

#28 Seabrook: a political community; middle-aged men in community; ex-Twin Oakers; Tucson Peoples Yellow Pages. (Sep '77)

#29 Democratic Management: consensus; leadership; group consciousness; The Ark. (Nov '77) ♦

#30 Directory '78: School of Living & Deep Run Farm; financing; Roger Ulrich interview. (Jan '78) ♦

#31 Learning in Community: learning for all ages; spiritual abortion. (Mar '78)

#32 Future of Community: Federation of Egalitarian Communities; Cerro Gordo; Karass; The Community Soap Factory. (May '78)

#33 A Woman's Issue: mothers & daughters; Virginia Blaisdell interview; feminism in MNS; non-traditional work. (Jul '78) ♦

#34 West Coast Communal Movement: Hoedads; Alpha Farm; co-op grocery; salvage business; other activities in California and Oregon. (Sep '78)

#35 Consumer Co-op Bank: income & resource sharing; Utopian heritage. (Nov '78)

#36 Kerista: British Columbia; Circle of Gold. (Jan '79) ♦

#37/38 Guide to Cooperative Alternatives: double issue on community participation, social change, well-being, appropriate technology, networking; *Directory of Intentional Communities*; extensive resource listings. 184 pgs. (Sum '79) ♦ (counts as three issues) $15

#39 Federation Women: the Hutterites; travel ashram community; Healing Waters; Industrial Co-op Assoc. (Aug '79)

#40 Worker-Owned Businesses: community development; urban ecology; feminist credit union; trusteeship. (Oct '79) ♦

#41 Relationships: friendships, family, sexuality; Renaissance Community. (Dec '79)

#42 Regionalism: The Southeast; Another Place; co-op anti-nuke; community resources. (Feb '80) ♦

#43 Health and Well-Being: massage; setting up a tofu kitchen; feminist retreat; radical psychiatry; community health clinic. (Apr '80)

#44 Consumer Cooperative Alliance: housing; food; arts; health; energy. (June '80) ♦

#45 Art Collectives: Freestate anti-nuke; Rainbow Family; women in Oregon communities. (Oct '80) ♦

#46 Directory '81: culture; pregnancy; economics; potlatch. (Dec '80) ♦

#47 Stories: community organizing; economics and work; culture. (Feb '81) ♦

#48 Communities Around the World: Cuba, China, Israel, India, Spain, El Salvador, England. (Apr '81)

#49 Tempeh Production: overcoming masculine oppression; social change; Consumer Cooperative Alliance; housing; credit unions; energy; insurance. (Jun '81)

#50 Dying: hospice; grieving; death in community; rituals; practical guide to home death. (Oct '81)

#51 Political Paradigms for the '80s. (Dec '81)

#52 Barter Network: Santa Cruz Women's Health Collective; worker-owned businesses. (Feb '82)

#53 Spiritual Communities: Lama, Sirius, The Farm, Renaissance, Abode of the Message, Shambhala. (Apr '82)

#54 Peace: Bright Morning Star interview; social activism; community land trust; Meg Christian; kibbutz. (Jun '82)

#55 Building Economic Democracy: Co-op Bank; legal network; Workers Trust; worker buyout; unions. (Oct '82)

#56 10th Anniversary Issue & Directory '83: best of *Communities*. (Dec '82) ♦

* *Communitas* was a predecessor to *Communities* that only ran two issues.

#57 Women in Business:
feminist therapy; Audubon expedition; Women's Resource Distribution Company; science fiction; peace movement. (Feb '83)

#58 Co-op America Debut:
catalog; Sisterfire; Consumer Co-op Bank. (Apr '83)

#59 Computers;
cooperative Arab/Jewish settlement; volunteer service; holistic living; growing pains. (Jul '83) ◆

#60 Gatherings '83:
Michigan public schools; Solidarity. (Oct '83)

#61 Parenting, Childcare, & Education:
co-op housing; Syracuse Cultural Workers; planning. (Win '84) ◆

#62 Progressive Economics & Politics:
co-op housing; new ideas for your community; kibbutz society. (Spr '84)

#63 Living in Community:
Stelle, Twin Oaks, Emissaries of Divine Light; peace efforts in Nicaragua; women's peace camp; democratic management. (Sum '84) ◆

#64 Social Notes:
the Great Alternative Life Group; old folks in a future world; case against consensus; kibbutz & education. (Fall '84) ◆

#65 Greenham Women's Peace Camp:
The Farm; education for cooperation; justice in India; spiritual fraud; Jubilee Partners. (Win '84) ◆

#66 Directory '85/'86: *Builders of the Dawn;* Stelle; Rainbow Gathering. (Spr '85)

#67 Technology in Community:
Sunrise Ranch, Ponderosa Village, Windstar, High Wind, 100 Mile Lodge, Stelle. (Sum '85)

#68 Historic Communal Societies:
the Shakers; Harmony; Zoar; Amana; Mormons; Icarians; Fourierists; Llano. (Win '85) ◆

#69 South Africa:
appropriate technology for developing countries; community homes for the mentally disabled; New Zealand; Windstar Foundation. (Win '86)

#70 San Francisco Bay Area: co-ops; clinics; housing; Cheese-board Collective. (Spr '86)

#71/72 Model Communities:
past, present, future; historic future cities; Kerista: polyfidelity. (Sum/Fall '86) (counts as two) $10

#73 FEC—10 years: social, gender, political, organizational issues. (Win '87) ◆

#74 Urban Middle-Class Communes:
Sirius; Clairemont Project; Ozark Regional Land Trust; Aprovecho & End of the Road; alternative special education; Findhorn. (Sum '87) ◆

#75 Planetization: Gaian politics; faith for the planetary age; Green movement; eco-feminism; deep ecology; Christian stewardship. (Sum '88)

#76 Education in Community: Twin Oaks childcare program; cooperative alternative education; Stelle children and education; Mt. Madonna School; Centrepoint Community; Camphill Villages; The Farm School. (Spr '90)

#77/78 *1990/91 Directory of Intentional Communities:* all feature articles in first edition of *Directory.* 129 pgs. (Nov '90) ◆ (counts as two) $10

#79 We're Back(!):
FIC highlights; Directory Update. (Fall '92)

#80/81 Vision & Leadership:
Four-Fold Way; Buddhist community; what happened to Kerista?; Goodenough; the URI split-up; Sunflower House; Co-op America; collaborative decision making; servant leadership; bullies & egos; paradigms of control & harmony; ropes course. (Spr/Sum '93) (counts as two) $10

#82 Women in Community:
women at Twin Oaks, The Farm, Shannon Farm; women in Bruderhof, Hutterite, Shaker, Oneidan, Mormon, Owenite communities; Maggie Kuhn interview. (Spr '94)

#83 Celebration of Community:
highlights of the Aug '93 gathering: Olympia, WA: plenaries—Dorothy Maclean/Findhorn, Kirkpatrick Sale/bioregionalism, Corinne McLaughlin/leadership, Gordon Davidson/spiritual economics, Noel Brown/environment; founders panels. (Sum '94)

#84 Growing Up in Community:
Idyllic, nurturing, humorous, confusing, and frightening aspects of community childhood— in commune, kibbutz, The Farm, charismatic Christian, Bruderhof, political activist, and secular egalitarian communities. (Fall '94)

#85 What We Have Learned:
transition at King View Farm, Co-op Wars; a closer look into "Cults." (Win '94)

#86 Nurturing Our Potential:
"We Have to Keep Growing?;" toward gender harmony; challenge of conflict, Aikido, Gestalt practice; multiple parenting. (Spr '95)

Back issues may go out of print at any time and be available only as photocopies. All prices include shipping.

Set of In-Print Back Issue
Approximately 40 issues. $80

Out-of-Print Back Issue Photocopies
These are not included in the set described above, and must be ordered separately. These are noted with a ◆ in the listing. Sorry, no discounts on multiple copies; price is already as low as possible.

Complete Set: Magazines and Photocopies
Includes both in-print and photocopied back issues. $300

Multiple Copy Discounts
1 issue — $5; 2–4, $4 each; 5–9, $3.50 each; 10–19, $3 each; 20 or more, $2.50 each. For in-print back issues only (photocopies are $5 each, regardless of quantity).

❑ **In-Print Back Issues**

Please send me issue #s_____

For a total of _____ magazines.   Cost (see Multiple Copy Discounts) — $ _____

❑ **Photocopied Back Issues**

Please send me issue #s_____

For a total of _____ photocopies.   Cost at $5 each — $ _____

❑ **Set of In-Print Back Issues** — (approx. 40) $80 $ _____

❑ **Complete Set** — All in-print and photocopied back issues — $300 $ _____

Total Amount Enclosed (payable in US funds to *Communities*) — $ _____
(foreign orders add 10% for additonal postage)

Name of individual or contact person   Phone Day/Evenings

Street

City/Town   State/Province   Zip/Postal Code

Please clip or photocopy and mail to: Communities Back Issues, c/o Alpha Farm, Deadwood OR 97430

Advertising Order Form

Display Ads (Mechanical Requirements for Camera-Ready Copy)

		Horizontal	Vertical		Covers
☐ Full Page	$250		7 1/4"w - 9 3/4"h		☐ Inside Front $400
☐ 2/3 Page	185	7 1/4"w - 6 3/8"h			☐ Inside Back $350
☐ 1/2 Page	145	7 1/4"w - 4 3/4"h	3 1/2"w - 9 3/4"h		
☐ 1/3 Page	102	7 1/4"w - 3 1/8"h	2 1/4"w - 9 3/4"h		Can we help you create your ad?
☐ 1/4 Page	78	7 1/4"w - 2 1/4"h	3 1/2"w - 4 3/4"h		$20 per hour for typesetting, design,
☐ 1/6 Page	58	3 1/2"w - 3 1/8"h	2 1/4"w - 4 3/4"h		layout, photography, & camera work.
☐ 1/12 Page	30	2 1/4"w - 2 1/4"h			

Classified Ads

Announcements, Books/Magazines/Videos, Support Organizations,
Services, Products, Personals. $.50 a word, minimum $10. Word count: ___ words at $.50 = $_____

Reach Listings

Communities with Openings, Communities Forming, Cohousing,
People Looking, Internships/Work Study, Resources.
Word count (up to 100 words) ___ at $.25 = $_____
Number of words over 100 ___ at $.50 = $_____
Reach Total $_____

All ads must include address and phone number. Abbreviations and phone numbers count as one word. PO Boxes count as two words. Zip codes are free.

Copy for (check one): ☐ **Reach Listing** ☐ **Classified Ad** (Please type or print clearly)

_____

_____

_____

_____

Discounts: Ad agencies: 15% discount when accompanied by prepayment. FIC members: 5% discount. Call or write for multiple insertion discounts.

Terms: Established agencies: net 30 days. All others: payment must accompany the advertisement. Make check or money order payable in US funds to *Communities* magazine.

Name _____ Phone Day/Evenings _____

Street _____

City/Town _____ State/Province _____ Zip/Postal Code _____

Payment Enclosed:
Display Ad _____
Classified Ad _____
Reach Listing _____
Discount _____
Total $ _____

Please photocopy and mail with payment to:

Communities Advertising, PO Box 169, Masonville CO 80541. Phone & Fax: 970-593-5615

Communities accepts advertising only for goods and services that we feel will be of value to our readers. We reserve the right to refuse or cancel any advertising for any reason at any time. All advertising claims are solely the responsibility of the advertiser. Ads being repeated will be rerun from the latest inserted advertisement unless otherwise specified. Ad copy will not be returned to advertiser unless prior arrangements are made at advertiser's expense. Ad rates are subject to change without notice, except when previously contracted. Advertisers will be presumed to have read this information and agreed to its conditions.

If you were there, you remember how inspiring the presentations were, and here's a chance to recapture that particular session that moved you. If you couldn't attend, here's your chance to hear for yourself what you missed.

Please circle the tapes you want, put a ☆ by every sixth tape (which is free), and fill out the form below. We have reduced the tape cost to $8.50 (postage included). *Note: A few of the tapes have areas with poor audio quality.*

PLENARIES

Caroline Estes: Challenges Facing the Communities Movement; **Kirkpatrick Sale:** Bioregionalism, Community, & the Future (C93-2)

Debra Lynn Dadd-Redalia: Sustainability & Sustenance; **Dorothy Maclean:** The Spiritual Dimensions of Community (C93-23)

Patch Adams: Prescription for Happiness—Love, Friendship, Community; **Corinne McLaughlin:** The Future of Communities (C93-78)

Gordon Davidson: What Communities Have Learned about Economics; **Noel Brown:** The Transition to Global Sustainability (C93-77)

Catherine Burton: Visions, Values, & the Future (C93-101)

PANELS

Founders 1: Small, Rural Communities (C93-4)
Founders 2: Urban Communities (C93-14)
Founders 3: Large, Spiritual Cmties (C93-26)
Founders 4: Large, Rural Communities (C93-40)
Health & Community (C93-01)
Polyfidelity (C93-25)
Realities of the Future (C93-52)
Economic Sustainability for Communities (C93-66)
Cohousing (C93-82)
FIC Board: Future Directions & Programs (C93-95)

WORKSHOPS

Adams, Patch: Humor & Health [Note: poor fidelity in several sections] (C93-43)

Adams, Patch: Community as Context for Medical Practices 1 (C93-54a)

Adams, Patch: Community as Context for Medical Practices 2 (C93-54b)

Alexander, William: Community—Survival Necessity for the 21st Century (C93-86)

Almayrac, Christian: Be Happy (C93-44)

Anapol, Deborah & Paul Glassco: Multi-Adult Intimacy: Polylove Styles & Community (C93-69)

Arkin, Lois: Urban Ecovillage Processes: Retrofitting for Sustainability (C93-17)

Bates, Albert: History of The Farm (C93-7)

Bhaerman, Steve: Transformational Power of Humor (C93-107)

Bookstein, Jonah: Kibbutz in the 1990s (C93-88)

Brown, Stephan: Shenoa—Alternative Ways to Hold Land (C93-36)

Brown, Stephan: Everything You Wanted to Know about Starting Community (C93-55)

Butcher, Allen: Dispelling the Confusion—Definition of Intentional Community (C93-12)

Cameron, Brent: Wonder-Tree Concept: a New Educational Model Based on Natural Learning (C93-68)

Canfield, Chris: Slide Show on Ecovillage Community Development (C93-11)

Childers, Laurie: Justice & Mercy in Conflict Resolution (C93-58)

Craig, Dorothy: Building Community in the Larger Community (Part 1) [Part 2 not taped] (C93-62)

Dadd-Redalia, Debra Lynn: Sustainability & Sustenance (C93-62)

Davenport-Moore, Susan: Children Who Grew Up in Community [adult discussion] (C93-21)

Erlandson, Gaya: Developing Individual Authenticity & Collective Vitality: a New Paradigm (C93-87)

Estes, Caroline: Cmty & Consensus Pt 1 (C93-29a)

Estes, Caroline: Cmty & Consensus Pt 2 (C93-29b)

Feigenbaum, Cliff: Socially Responsible Business, Investing, & Consumer Resources (C93-27)

Forsey, Helen: Circles of Strength: Community Alternatives to Alienation (C93-22)

Giglio, Nick: Cmty—A Spiritual Discipline (C93-63)

Gilman, Diane: Winslow Cohousing (C93-103)

Grace, Syndee: Activism (C93-106)

Goodenough Community: Deepening Intimacy in Community Life (C93-34)

Goodenough Community: Playing Good Games— the Way of Life at Goodenough (C93-59)

Greco, Thomas: Economic Survival in '90s (C93-30)

Greenberg, Daniel: Children in Community & Their Education (C93-15)

Haenke, David: Bioregionalism and Cmty— an Ecological Definition/Context for Cmty Life (C93-96)

Hancock, Allen & Dawn Lamp: Class Issues & Community Living (C93-57)

Hansen, Tony: Green Dollars: Setting Up & Running a Local Trade/Barter System (C93-97)

Hertzman, Ellen: Cohousing (C93-61)

Hertzman, Ellen: Cohousing (repeated session) (C93-72)

Higdon, Frank: Communitarian Movement: Politics of Community (C93-91)

Hill, Melissa: Traditional Chinese Medicine— an Introduction (C93-10)

Hill, Melissa: How to Access Chinese Medical Research, for Day-to-Day Health Care (C93-38)

Hillendahl, Lou: Conflict Prevention (C93-37)

Hillendahl, Lou: Basic Ingredients before Starting a Community (C93-42)

Ingber, Beth: Culture of Consciousness: Developing a Universal Intentional Community (C93-41)

Kenny, Robert: Decision-Making Tools (C93-47)

Kenny, Robert: Group Consciousness & Individual Spiritual Development (C93-92)

Kozeny, Geoph: Leadership, Democracy, & Accountability (C93-93)

Ladas-Gaskin, Carol: Progoff Intensive Journal (C93-5)

Lam, Diana: Relationship Skills: Facilitating, Conflict Resolution, & Dialogue (C93-50)

Licata, Nick: Prag House—10 Easy Steps for Keeping a Commune Going With No Guru or Bible (C93-56)

Linney, Joan: Conflict Resolution—Process Committee as Model and Tool (C93-49)

Maclean, Dorothy: Attuning to Nature—Attunement Within & Without (C93-51)

Metcalf, William: Alternative Lifestyles in Australia & New Zealand (C93-9)

Miller, Tim: Roots & Development of Communities of the Mid-1960s (C93-8)

Mulligan, Diego: A New Model: Choice, Diversity, & Basic Values for Sustainable Community (C93-48)

Nearing, Ryam: How to Love More Successfully: Polyfidelity (C93-46)

Nowland, Will: Credit Unions—History, How to Start, & Finding Help (C93-6)

Peterson, Joe: The Post-Community Experience: Life after the Dream (C93-20)

Pietzner, Cornelius: Festivals as a Community-Building Element (C93-71)

Questenberry, Dan: Land Trust for Cmty (C93-35)

Reed, Rico: Tolstoy Farm (C93-18)

Reed, Rico: Earth Stewards—Will We Recognize Utopia When We Find It? (C93-99)

Santoyo, Larry & Simon Henderson: Designing the Home Ecosystem & Cmty Self-Reliance (C93-100)

Schaub, Laird: Introduction to Consensus (C93-31)

Schaub, Laird: Introduction to Facilitation (C93-45)

Schaub, Laird: Community Health Insurance: Alternatives to Commercial Policies (C93-74)

Schaub, Laird & Betty Didcoct: Problems & Issues in Consensus Facilitation (C93-89)

Schechter, Lawrence: Ecovillage Housing Design (C93-75)

Shaffer, Carolyn & Sandra Lewis: Moving from Being Nice to Getting Real—Phases of Cmty Life (C93-70)

Sower, David: Economic Equality—a Worldwide Issue (C93-94)

Talbott, John: The Findhorn Community—an Eco-Village Model for Sustainability (C93-80)

van Uchelen, Collin & Jain Peruniak: Power and Control in Collective Settings (C93-98)

Wells, Marie Spicer: Transitioning to a Consensual/Team-Based Group (C93-33)

Yemelin, Valentin & Diane Gilman: EcoVille, A Russian Sustainable Community (C93-16)

Please send me the tapes circled above (put a ☆ by every sixth one free). ____ # of tapes at $8.50 for a total of $_____ ; ____ # of free (☆) tapes. Please photocopy this form and return with check in US dollars to: FIC, Box 814-D, Langley WA 98260.

Name _____ Phone Day/Evenings _____

Street _____ City/Town _____ State/Province _____ Zip/Postal Code _____

Fellowship for Intentional Community Products & Services

This book is full of offerings from the Fellowship, and we provide this page as a guide to help you find your way along this hard-copy information highway. If there is a cost for a given product or service, it's listed here. All prices include shipping and are payable in US dollars. Costs to foreign addresses, when different, are shown in parentheses.

FIC Publications

▶ Copies of the *Communities Directory*
$20 ($22) each; quantity discounts available.
See order form on page 440.

▶ *Communities* magazine
$18 ($22) one-year subscription—4 issues; $5 ($6) sample issue.
See order form on page 440.

▶ Special Offer: *Communities* advertising credit for buying institutional copies
of the *Directory*, at $30 each, for your local library or resource center.
See ad on page 351, or contact *Communities* at this address for more information.

▶ *Directory Update*—annual supplements of *Directory* additions and changes
One copy free with card return; $5 ($8) one-time fee for every *Update* published for this edition.
See order form on the blue card at the back of this book.
Note: listing updates are summarized quarterly in *Communities* magazine.

Where to Send

Communities
138-D6 Twin Oaks Road
Louisa VA 23093
540-894-5126

Updates • Referrals • Feedback

▶ Your Additions & Corrections to the *Communities Directory*
We welcome your input about inaccuracies or late-breaking news.
See blue card at the back of this book.

▶ *Directory* Evaluation Survey
Let us know what worked for you and what could be improved.
See pages 411-412.

▶ Feedback Files on listed communities
If we've received any unresolved critical feedback, we'll hold it in a file along with that community's response. For $1/community we'll send a summary of what we have.
See page 409 for details.

▶ *Directory* database searches for communities meeting special criteria
Cost varies; contact us for more information.

Directory
Rt 1, Box 155-D
Rutledge MO 63563
816-883-5545

Advertising

▶ *Communities* magazine advertising rates
See page 436.

Communities Advertising
Rt 1, Box 155-D
Rutledge MO 63563
816-883-5545

Back Issues

▶ *Communities* magazine back issue index and order form
See pages 434-435.

Communities Back Issues
Box D
Deadwood OR 97430

Electronic Information Access

▶ FIC e-mail: fic@ic.org
▶ Usenet: alt.community.intentional
▶ Web site: http://www.ic.org/

NOTE: it is sometimes more economical for us to send out printed materials rather than responding by e-mail, so please include your "hard copy" mailing address with e-mail inquiries (or phone number where we can call you collect). Thanks.

FIC Membership—and everything else

▶ Fellowship for Intentional Community—membership and information
Introductory information is free; membership fees vary.
See article on page 100; membership form on page 440.

▶ Audio tapes of the 1993 Celebration of Community
$8.50/tape; quantity discounts available.
See index and order form on page 437.

▶ Everything else related to the Fellowship

FIC
Rt 1, Box 155-D
Rutledge MO 63563
816-883-5545

Communities Directory Order Form

Number of *Directory* copies ordered _____

Total amount enclosed $_____ Check payable to *Communities* in US dollars

_____
Name   Phone Day/Evenings

_____
Street   City/Town   State/Province   Zip/Postal Code

❏ **Please send ___ copy(ies) to:** (attach additional names & addresses as needed)

_____
Name

_____
Street   City/Town   State/Province   Zip/Postal Code

(2.2)

Help us get the word out about communities—buy additional copies of *Directory* for yourself or your friends!
Price per copy: $20 for individuals; $30 for institutions.
Quantity Discounts (normal shipping charges apply; see rates below)

3-4 copies	20% off
5-9 copies	30% off
10-49 copies	40% off
50+ copies	write or call for quote

Postage & Handling
First book to each address: $3 ($5 foreign)
Each additional book to same address: $1 (
▶ Please mail w/payment to: *Communities*, 138-D6 Twin Oaks Road, Louisa VA 23(
Phone: 540-894-5126

Communities Magazine—Subscribe Today!

Communities Magazine Subscription

❏ 8 issues $33 ($40 foreign price)   ❏ 4 issues $18 ($22)   ❏ Sample issue $5 ($6)

Back Issues - $5 ($6)

❏ #80/81 *Vision/Leadership* [double issue $8 ($10)]   ❏ #82 *Women*   ❏ #83 *Celebration*

❏ #84 *Growing Up in Community*   ❏ #85 *Passages*   ❏ #86 *Nurturing Our Potential*

Total amount enclosed $_____ Check payable to *Communities* in US dollars

_____
Name   Phone Day/Evening

_____
Street   City/Town   State/Province   Zip/Postal Code

Please mail w/payment to: *Communities*, 138-D6 Twin Oaks Road, Louisa VA 23093. Prices include shipping.

(2.2)

Your source for the latest information, issues, and ideas about intentional communities and cooperative living toda

Supplements the *Directory* with current information about communities in North America—including those now forming. Ea issue presents a new theme, such as *Growin Up in Community*; *Vision and Leadership*; *Women in Community*; *Passages: What We'v Learned*; *Nurturing Our Potential*.

Regular columns appear in each issue of t quarterly, written by community founders a activists such as Corinne McLaughlin, Kat Kinkade, Lois Arkin, Geoph Kozeny, and many others.

Reach listings—communities looking for people, people looking for communities, an new groups forming now.

▶ Please mail subscriptions with payment t *Communities* at the Louisa VA address (above).

Fellowship for Intentional Community Membership

Yes, I wish to join the Fellowship!

❏ New member   ❏ Renewal

❏ Individual, $15-35 (sliding scale)

❏ Community ❏ $20 for under 10 members; ❏ $35 for 10-50 members; ❏ $50 for over 50

❏ Organization, $25-50 (sliding scale)

❏ Donor ❏ Supporting, $100 & up; ❏ Sustaining, $250 & up; ❏ Sponsoring, $500 & up

❏ Newsletter only (nonmember), $10

_____
Name of individual or contact person   Phone Day/Evenings

_____
Group name or affiliation (if appropriate)   E-mail Address

_____
Street   City/Town   State/Province   Zip/Postal Code

(2.2)

Fellowship for Intentional Community
We have a reputation for frugality—and have stretched miniscule budgets into enormous projects, such as this *Directory*, *Communities* magazine, and the August 1993 Celebration of Community. Your financial support will help us continue to compile and publish literature about cooperative living; host gatherings; foster alliances between communities; build bridges between the movement and the wider culture; and serve as a clearinghouse o community information for both seekers and media. Donations are tax deductable.
▶ Please mail w/payment to: FIC, Rt 1, Box 155-D, Rutledge MO 63563; Phone: 816-883-5545